SOCWORK 4D06

TABLE OF CONTENTS & ACKNOWLEDGEMENTS

PAGE

Service Users' Knowledges and Social Work Theory: Conflict or Collaboration? 661

Beresford, P.

British Journal of Social Work, 30.4

McMaster University School of Social Work
SW 4D06 General Social Work II
Course Outline C01/C02/C03

September 6 – April 6, 2016-2017, Mondays, 2 30 –5 20 p m
C01 Instructor Jennifer Crowson
Office KTH # 302
Office hours by appointment
Email jencrowson2@gmail com
Phone 905-525-9140 ext #23785

September 6 – April 6, 2016-2017, Mondays, 2 30 –5 20 p m
C02 Instructor Mirna Carranza
Office KTH # 309B
Office hours by appointment
Email carranz@mcmaster ca
Phone 905-525-9140 ext #23789

September 6 – April 6, 2016-2017, Mondays, 7 00 –10 00 p m
C03 Instructor Marlene Traficante
Office KTH # 302
Office hours by appointment
Email traficmm@mcmaster ca
Phone 905-525-9140 ext #23785

Table of Contents

Course **Overview**

Course Description

This class is a series of seminars aimed to deepen understanding and further develop student practice skills The course runs parallel and in conjunction with field placements in which students spend the equivalent of two days per week in social agencies, or with other organizations, in supervised practice

Course Objectives

The course is taught from a theoretical perspective compatible with the school's philosophical statement as follows

> *As social workers, we operate in a society characterized by power imbalances that affect us all These power imbalances are based on age, class, ethnicity, gender identity, geographic location, health, ability, race, sexual identity and income We see personal troubles as inextricably linked to oppressive structures We believe that social workers must be actively involved in the understanding and transformation of injustices in social institutions and in the struggles of people to maximize control over their own lives*

The course aims to help students to integrate their academic work and their practice experiences, and to think critically about social work, as they prepare for graduation into professional practice

Required Texts

The following text is required and is available through the university bookstore

- $ SW 4D06 Concurrent Custom Courseware available in the Campus Store

The following also comprise readings for this course

- $ CASW (2005) Code of Ethics and Guidebook Ottawa Canadian Association of Social Workers
- $ Lee, B , (2001) *Case Advocacy A Principles and Practice Guide for Social Workers and Other Communities* – On Reserve
- $ Solomon, R and L Visser, (2005) A Legal Guide for Social Workers Toronto OASW – On Reserve

Additional Suggested Readings

In addition to the above, assignment 6 requires each student to select and distribute to the class at least two articles (one must be an academic article and the second can be a newspaper/magazine articles, news clip, YouTube video, or other media source) on a topic they wish to discuss These articles form a major part of the class readings

As well, it is anticipated that additional readings will be sought out and suggested by students and instructor as the course proceeds In this class students are expected to be proactive learners who actively research and seek out material for use by the class in response to the placement practice issues that arise as the course proceeds (the ability of students to do this is directly related to the course objectives)

Course Requirements/Assignments

Requirements Overview and Deadlines

1	Attendance	Pass/Fail	Ongoing
2	Participation	10%	Ongoing
3	WSIB Forms	No grade	September 19/16
4	Learning Contract	No grade	September 26/16
5	Assessment	25%	November 14/16
6	Group Reading Assignment #1	5% (3 x for 15%)	November 7 /16
	Group Reading Assignment #2	5%	November 21 /16
	Group Reading Assignment #3	5%	December 5 /16
	Group Reading Assignment #4	5%	January 23 /17
	Group Reading Assignment #5	5%	February 6/17
7	Personal Reflection #1	5%	By November 28 /16
	Personal Reflection #2	5%	By April 3 /17
8	Group Supervision	20%	TBA
9	Process Recording OR Community Development Skills	20%	March 27/17

***Grading will be undertaken in accordance with the School of Social Work grading scheme**

Requirement/Assignment Details

1 **Attendance (ongoing assessment)**

Given the importance of integrating learning in the school and placement contexts, attendance at this class is compulsory Students attending less than 80% of classes will receive an automatic F grade In circumstances where attendance below 80% is entirely due to medical or other reasons approved by the Associate Dean's office, efforts will be made to arrange ways to make up the missed learning, or where that is not possible to consider allowing the student to repeat the course and placement

2 **Participation (ongoing assessment 10%)**

Students are expected to participate in a way that promotes non-competitive, cooperative and collaborative learning Students are expected to support each other through listening, encouragement and constructively challenging each other as the entire seminar group makes progress in integrating theory and practice **Please note that this 10% participation grade is not automatic** In this process the following will be graded

- $ Completing assigned readings prior to class and actively participating in the seminar in such a way that demonstrates critical engagement with the assigned readings
- $ Contributing to a seminar environment that promotes learning and growth (similar to the contribution professional social workers demonstrate in order to be constructive team members in the field)
- $ Offering and accepting constructive peer support (reading about, exploring and listening to other students and helping them develop and refine their ideas and practice)
- $ Particular attention will be given to students' participation – including their use of related readings – in discussions connected to the group supervision assignment

3 **Workplace safety form, ungraded (due September 19, 2016)**

- $ This form, distributed in the first class or available in the school's office **must be fully completed, signed, and returned to the school office by September 19 for you to continue in your placement** The completed form is necessary should you be injured while on placement

4 <u>**Learning contract, ungraded (due September 26, 2016)**</u>

- $ Learning contracts are negotiated with the student's field instructor They will take into consideration course objectives, student learning needs and interests, and the needs of the placement setting Contracts spell out the initial agreement between students and field instructors, they will change and evolve over the year They will be used to focus, monitor, and evaluate student field placements Contracts are not graded The outline for contracts can be found in the Field Instruction Manual The learning contracts must be typed and signed by your field instructor

5 <u>**Assessment** (25%) **(due November 14, 2016 in class)**</u>

- $ (10 pages plus references)
- $ Students will complete an assessment based on a clinical case from placement or prepare a report based on a policy/research or community project relevant to their placement Students should ensure that cases, names or real individuals are fictionalized to **ensure confidentiality** The purpose of this assignment is to give you the opportunity to complete a comprehensive assessment In this assignment, imagine you are writing the assessment to be reviewed by a casework team or a judge If you are reporting on a policy or community project imagine it is going to be reviewed by a government minister, regional council, or by an agency board of directors The point of this imagining is to produce a report that is accurate, robust and defendable—the kind of report or assessment that you might be expected to complete if you were in full-time employment as a social worker
  - o A part of this assignment is to explore and decide on the best format and headings to use in your assessment or report These will differ depending on the nature of the assessment you are doing and the focus of your analysis Your assessment or report, however, should contain the following
  - o A brief description of the context/situation or practice/policy
  - o An analysis of the problem(s) or issue(s) your work is addressing Describe what you understand the problem or issue to be, and why you have that understanding What areas or concepts did you consider in your assessment? How do the different actors involved in this matter view the problem or issue?
  - o A description of what you identify as both the immediate and the longer-term goals or objectives in relation to these problems or issues
  - o An articulation of what you understand to be the barriers to achieving these goals and the ways you would navigate these barriers
  - o A description of the ways your work on this case/policy will/would attempt to address these issues and an explanation of why you are approaching the work in this particular manner
  - o A description of a future plan for the case or policy—where will/could you be going with this work from here?
  - o An evaluation of the extent to which this case's/policy's goals will be or are likely

to be met if your recommended interventions, future plans, or policies are followed

- Describe and address any ethical tensions that you identify in this case/situation
- In completing the above be sure to identify a body of theory that helped guide your understanding of "the problem" and also a social worker's/client's/community's choice of remedy Note that "theory" does not necessarily have to refer to a formal theoretical framework It can also refer to any readings in the literature that you feel are pertinent to the situation
- The above assessment should comprise about 75% of your paper In the remaining 25% reflect on your work in this case and in undertaking the assessment What did you personally find enabling or constraining in your work and in the ways you conceptualized the work? How did your own social locations influence your work and understanding? What about the social locations of the clients affected by the issue/policy—do you think that that did/could have any impact on the process and outcomes? Finally, discuss how might you approach a similar type of assessment in the future in a different and perhaps more innovative way? Is there an alternate program, strategy, policy initiative, or alternative course of action that might address the situation? How might you view the situation differently? What might you do? What literature might you consult? How might it be organized?

6 <u>Group Reading Assignments</u> (5% each - total 15%)

$ Students will break into four pre-assigned groups (two under A and two under B) Each group is assigned specific dates to prepare for the discussion of assigned readings and will present on 3 dates (see schedule groups 1 & 2 on A dates, groups 3 & 4 on B dates) All students are expected to complete the readings

- November 7 Group A & B AOP, Advocacy, Empowerment
- November 21 Group A Community Development
- December 5 Group B Immigration
- January 23 Group A Mental Health
- February 6 Group B Sexual Diversity

$ The instructor will assign 1-2 questions and/or an activity pertaining to the assigned reading for that class Students will prepare a presentation in light of these questions and then facilitate a discussion with the rest of the class Each group will be graded on their critical reading of the articles, critical engagement with the questions provided by the course instructor, presentation of their ideas and questions developed for class discussion, and on their engagement of the larger class in a discussion and/or activity

7 <u>Personal Reflection Papers</u> (5% each/ total 10%) **<u>Due December 5 & April 3, 2017 – in class</u>**

$ (3 pages plus references)

$ One personal reflection paper is to be submitted each semester The reflection paper can be handed in at any time during the semester, but the first is due no later than November /16 and the second March /17

- $ Personal journals facilitate the integration of theory and practice Students often find recording their reactions at intellectual, emotional and/or spiritual levels helpful in their development as social workers These reactions may be about placement, learning goals, class, readings, specific cases, policies, and/or life experiences The intent is that, through writing, students can reflect on their experience and meaning-making processes hence uncovering emerging themes in their practice This includes reflections on how sensitivities and specific issues related to upbringing may influence their work In this assignment students need to submit a summary of the most significant theme that has emerged for them thus far The reflection must be supported by references to the social work literature and address the following
  - o Why the emergent theme(s) is important for you
  - o The implications of this theme for your work
  - o How you intend to manage this theme and its implications for your professional career
  - o How social work or other literature has informed the way you conceptualize and address the theme(s) or related issues

8 **Group Supervision Assignment** (20%)

- $ Presentation times as scheduled by instructor In pairs or groups of 3-5 people based on common placements or common ethical/policy/case issues
- $ Present to the class **a common type of case, policy, ethical dilemma, OR a community development initiative** you are working on at your placement The presentation should be 45 minutes in total, allowing for 30 minutes to share material and 15 minutes of class discussion Presentation to include the following
  - o A clear problem statement (What is the issue or problem you are addressing in your work? Whose problem is it and why? Why this conceptualization of the problem and not another?)
  - o A statement about your assessment (What are the focus and methods of your work? What are you doing in this case, how you are trying to do it, and why?)
  - o A statement about the dynamics of intervention (What is occurring in the casework relationship or in the relationship with the community or in the policy development process?)
  - o Two or three questions for the class about the case that are designed to assist you in delivering service or in developing a deeper or more critical analysis of the case or interventions being used
  - o In all of the above ensure you address what the literature says about the type of issues you are addressing and the intervention you are undertaking You are expected to have a broad understanding of what you are doing and why
- $ **One week before your presentation**, distribute to the class two sources of information (approved by your instructor) that inform your thinking and practice in this case The two sources must include at least one peer-reviewed article Examples of alternative sources include policy papers, print media, and audio or video clips The presenting student is responsible for distributing these articles to the class, along with incurring any copying and copyright costs **Immediately following the presentation**, students need to submit their presentation outline and reference list to the course instructor

- $ There will be three main areas of focus for group supervision – students will select one of these as their main focus, however each presentation should incorporate all three elements to some degree
  - o Ethical dilemma (See Appendix A for further instructions)
  - o Theory application
  - o Practice/Policy Development
- $ **The interactive nature of your presentation and full class discussion is a key component of this assignment** Following your presentation (30 minute maximum) the class will support your work by addressing your questions and the articles you distributed This discussion will be a critical and respectful exchange similar to the group supervision experience as a social work in the field The purpose of such supervision is to ensure your case analysis and intervention methods are sound, to help you better achieve your intervention goals, and **to help you problem solve any issues** that are arising in the process
- $ You will be graded on a-e above and on your ability to constructively engage in and constructively utilize the group supervision process Other members of the class are expected to read the articles you distribute, and contribute to the group supervision process by providing respectful feedback that contributes to the class learning environment Their ability to do so will form a substantial part of their participation grades
- $ Students should ensure that when presenting cases, names or real individuals are fictionalized and that no details are shared outside the classroom As well, although this exercise is viewed as "group supervision," it is not intended to give case direction, which responsibility remains with the field instructor who will have a more comprehensive view of the case than the class develops Students may, of course, share details of the class discussion with the field instructor for information purposes As well, the class instructor may share information with the field instructor, placement agency or other faculty members for student evaluation or placement management purposes

9 Selection A - <u>Process recording</u> (20%) <u>due March 27, 2017 – in class</u>

- $ This paper is to be completed by students who do therapeutic or research-based interviews in their placement setting
- $ (10 pages plus references)
- $ Students are to prepare a 10-page process recording plus references based on an interview from their placement setting The purpose of this assignment is to demonstrate and enhance your skills in working with individual clients, families, or research projects by examining, in-depth, a part of the process that occurred in that work Approximately 25% of the process recording content should be a transcription of what you regard as key and defining conversations that took place in the interview or meeting Where possible audio or video record an interview or meeting where you are a key participant Listen to the recorded interview or meeting excerpt in its entirety, and transcribe what you regard as the defining sections regarding your own learning Where it is not possible to obtain a recording you must work with the course instructor to come up with acceptable options for generating material for the process recording assignment

- $ **Process recording format**
  - o Social Worker
    - ▪ Report Social worker's words
    - ▪ Detail your own thoughts, feelings and emotional reactions Describe what evoked these for you Explain how you might have responded
    - ▪ Identify the social work/research interview skill used (if any)
    - ▪ Identify the theory, theoretical framework or knowledge base that informed the social worker
  - o Client/research participant
    - ▪ Report client/research participant words
    - ▪ Describe what you think the client/research participant was thinking and/or feeling and why you think this
    - ▪ Identify the theory, theoretical framework that shaped your analysis of the client/research participant presentation
- $ Alongside the verbatim transcription or report, briefly describe what you and the think the client/participant was feeling and why you think this Describe what evoked these reactions for you, and explain how you responded In addition, describe in detail, your assessment of what was occurring in the interview and the reasoning behind your responses In other words, describe what you were doing and why, as well as how and why the client responded in a particular way Document the skills you used, as well as the theoretical framework or knowledge base that informed your engagement with the client/participant
- $ In the narrative (75% of the paper) following the transcription be sure to address, and demonstrate by referencing your transcription, the following
  - o The extent to which you and the client/participant developed a shared understanding of the issues being addressed
  - o What you were trying to achieve and why
  - o How your words, actions and responses were designed to achieve these objectives
  - o The way theory guided your understanding of what was occurring Be sure to cite the literature in this section
  - o The future goals and direction that emerged from this interview
  - o Your view of whether this interview was a "success" and why Be sure to address "success" from the perspective of all involved, for your view, the agency view, and the client/participant view
  - o What you would do, say, ask or structure differently in future
- $ In all of the above, be sure to draw on and cite literature It is not enough to simply describe the process and what you were trying to achieve You must articulate your analysis of this process with reference to social work theory and literature You must show how your work, and your critique of the process, was purposeful and driven by social work knowledge

9 **Selection B - <u>Community Development Skills</u>** (20%) **<u>due March 27, 2017 – in class</u>**

- $ This paper is to be completed by students who do not do therapeutic or research-based interviews in their placement setting
- $ (10 pages plus references)

- $ Students will prepare a 10-page paper plus references based on the skills they have developed and have identified that they need to develop in doing future community development work The student will use their placement setting to contextualize their analysis
- $ The student will analyze the skills needed to do strong community development practice The student will complete this skills analysis in two ways First, will be an exploration of the skills honed in the placement context Students will examine which community development skills they have learned and practiced while working through their placement Second, will be an exploration of the enhanced skills they identify as necessary to doing effective community development work – these are skills they may have witnessed within their field instructor or skills that were absent but would have been beneficial
- $ All of the analysis around skills will be contextualized through their field experience and through a diversity of academic literature/theoretical perspectives on social work with communities

ASSIGNMENT & COURSE REQUIREMENTS

Assignment Submission and Grading

Form and Style

Written assignments must be typed and double-spaced and submitted with a front page containing the title, student's name, student number, and the date **Number all pages** (except title page) Assignments should be stapled together Paper format must be in accordance with the current edition of the American Psychological Association Publication Manual with particular attention paid to font size (Times-Roman 12), spacing (double spaced) and margins (minimum of 1 inch at the top, bottom, left and right of each page) Papers not meeting these requirements will not be accepted for grading In completing assignments students are expected to make use of and cite (following APA) appropriate professional and social science literature and other bodies of knowledge When submitting, students should keep a spare copy of assignments When completing assignments please do not exceed the maximum space allowed (by going over the page limit, reducing font size or line spacing) Papers will only be graded on the content that falls within the assignment space parameters

Submitting Assignments & Grading

- $ Students must obtain a grade of C+ in SW4D06 and a pass in 4DD6 to graduate or remain in the program
- $ Assignments are due at the beginning of class on the date specified Late assignments will be penalized 5% of the grade for that assignment for each day or part thereof for which they are late (weekends count as one day) All assignments must be submitted before a final course grade will be issued
- $ Do not use report covers or binders for assignments (such papers will not be accepted for grading because these covers create bulk that is difficult to manage)

Privacy Protection
In accordance with regulations set out by the Freedom of Information and Privacy Protection Act, the University will not allow return of graded materials by placing them in boxes in departmental offices or classrooms so that students may retrieve their papers themselves, tests and assignments must be returned directly to the student Similarly, grades for assignments for courses may only be posted using the last 5 digits of the student number as the identifying data The following possibilities exist for return of graded materials

1 Direct return of materials to students in class,
2 Return of materials to students during office hours,
3 Students attach a stamped, self-addressed envelope with assignments for return by mail,
4 Submit/grade/return papers electronically

Arrangements for the return of assignments from the options above will be finalized during the first class

Course Modification Policy
The instructor and university reserve the right to modify elements of the course during the term The university may changes the dates and deadlines for any or all courses in extreme circumstances If either type of medication becomes necessary, reasonable notice and communication with the students will be given with explanation and the opportunity to comment on changes It is the responsibility of the student to check his/her McMaster email and course websites weekly during the term and to note any changes

Student Responsibilities and University Policies

Student Responsibilities

- Students are expected to contribute to the creation of a respectful and constructive learning environment Students should read material in preparation for class, attend class on time and remain for the full duration of the class A formal break will be provided in the middle of each class, students are to return from the break on time
- In the past, student and faculty have found that non-course related use of laptop computers and hand-held electronic devices during class to be distracting and at times disruptive Consequently, during class students are expected to only use such devices for taking notes and other activities directly related to the lecture or class activity taking place
- Audio or video recording in the classroom without permission of the instructor is strictly prohibited

Attendance
Given the importance of integrating learning in the school and placement contexts, attendance at this class is compulsory Students attending less than 80% of classes will receive an automatic F grade In circumstances where attendance below 80% is entirely due to medical or other reasons approved by the Associate Dean's office, efforts will be made to arrange ways to make

up the missed learning, or where that is not possible to consider allowing the student to repeat the course and placement

Academic Integrity

You are expected to exhibit honesty and use ethical behaviour in all aspects of the learning process Academic credentials you earn are rooted in principles of honesty and academic integrity Academic dishonesty is to knowingly act or fail to act in a way that result or could result in unearned academic credit or advantage This behaviour can result in serious consequences, e g the grade of zero on an assignment, loss of credit with a notation on the transcript (notation reads "Grade of F assigned for academic dishonesty"), and/or 6 suspension or expulsion from the university It is the student's responsibility to understand what constitutes academic dishonesty For information on the various kinds of academic dishonesty please refer to the Academic Integrity Policy, specifically Appendix 3 at http //www mcmaster ca/academicintegrity The following illustrates only three forms of academic dishonesty

a) Plagiarism, e g the submission of work that is not one's own or for which other credit has been obtained,
b) Improper collaboration in group work, or
c) Copying or using unauthorized aids in tests and examinations

Academic dishonesty also entails a student having someone sign in for them on a weekly course attendance sheet when they are absent from class and/or a student signing someone in who is known to be absent

In this course the instructor reserves the right to use a software package designed to reveal plagiarism Students may be asked to submit their work electronically and in hard copy so that it can be checked for academic dishonesty In addition, the instructor reserves the right to request a student undertake a viva examination of a paper in circumstances where the paper appears to be written by someone other than the student themselves (i e papers written by essay writing services)

Academic Accommodation of Students with Disabilities

Students who require academic accommodation must contact Student Accessibility Services (SAS) to make arrangements with a Program Coordinator Academic accommodations must be arranged for each term of study Student Accessibility Services can be contacted by phone 905-525-9140 ext 28652 or e-mail sas@mcmaster ca For further information, consult McMaster University's Policy for Academic Accommodation of Students with Disabilities http //www mcmaster ca/policy/Students-AcademicStudies/AcademicAccommodation-StudentsWithDisabilities pdf

E-mail Communication Policy

Effective September 1, 2010, it is the policy of the Faculty of Social Sciences that all e-mail communication sent from students to instructors (including TAs), and from students to staff, must originate from the student's own McMaster University e-mail account This policy protects confidentiality and confirms the identity of the student It is the student's responsibility to ensure that communication is sent to the university from a McMaster account If an instructor becomes aware that a communication has come from an alternate address, the instructor may not reply at his or her discretion Email Forwarding in MUGSI http //www mcmaster ca/uts/support/email/emailforward html

*Forwarding will take effect 24-hours after students complete the process at the above link (Approved at the Faculty of Social Sciences meeting on Tues May 25, 2010)

Course Weekly Topics and Readings

Week 1 September 12

Topics

- Introduction to course
  - Class outline, assignments & expectations, Placements, Safety, Sexual harassment, Anti-oppression, Supervision, Confidentiality, Professional behaviour

Readings

- Course Outline
- Field Placement Manual
- Due diligence checklist
- CASW Code of Ethics
- Confidentiality Agreement
- Course readings are in the 4D06 Concurrent course pack through the bookstore

Week 2 September 19

Topics

- Integration of Theory and Practice, Ethical Social Work Practice
- Return Due Diligence Checklist and WSIB forms

Readings

- **Bogo, M , & Vayda, E (1998)** Chapter 1 – The Integration of Theory and Practice The ITP Loop *The practice of field instruction in social work theory and process* Toronto University of Toronto Press
- **Hardina, D (2004)** Guidelines for ethical practice in community organization *Social Work 49(4)* 595-604
- **Weinberg, M (2010)** The social construction of social work ethics Politicizing and broadening the lens *Journal of Progressive Human Services, 21(1)* 32-44

Week 3 September 26

Topics

- Supervision & Professional Social Work Practice
  - In addition to readings review website
  - Learning contract due
  - Supervision to support your learning goals

Readings

- OCSWSSW http //www ocswssw org
- **Adamson, C (2011)** Supervision is not politically innocent *Australian Social Work,* 1-12

- $ **Davys, M D & Beddoe, L (2009)** The reflective learning model Supervision of social work students *Social Work Education, 28(8)* 919–933
- $ **Sakamoto, I , & Pitner, R O , (2005)** Use of critical consciousness in anti-oppressive social work practice Disentangling power dynamics at personal and structural levels *British Journal of Social Work, 35* 435-452

Week 4 October 3

Topics

$ Mindfulness, Social Worker Stress and Self-care
  - o In addition to readings review websites

Readings

- $ Compassion Fatigue
  http //www compassionfatigue ca
- $ Self care starter kit
  http //socialwork buffalo edu/resources/self-care-starter-kit html
- $ **Wong, Y R , (2004)** Knowing through discomfort A mindfulness-based critical social work pedagogy *Critical Social Work, 5(1)*
- $ **Neff, K D (2012)** The science of self-compassion In C Germer & R Siegel (Eds), *Compassion and Wisdom in Psychotherapy* (pp 79-92) New York Guilford Press
- $ **Barlow, C & Hall, B L (2007)** 'What about feelings?' A study of emotion and tension in social work field education *Social Work Education, 26 (4)* 399–413

October 10 – Reading Week

Week 5 October 17

Topics

$ Social Work and Disability
  - o Review of video "Sound and Fury"

Readings

- $ Fudge Schormans, A (2010) Epilogues and prefaces Research and social work and people with intellectual disabilities *Australian Social Work, 63(1)* 51-66
- $ French Gilson, S , & DePoy, E (2002) Theoretical approaches to disability content in social work education *Journal of Social Work Education, 38(1)* 153-165
- $ Bach, M (2002) Social Inclusion as Solidarity Rethinking the Child Rights *Agenda, Working Papers Series Perspectives on Social Inclusion*, Toronto Laidlaw Foundation

Week 6 October 24

Topics

$ The Social Work Assessment
  - o What is it, How is it done?
  - o Students are expected to come to class with information about, and a readiness to discuss, the approach(s) to assessment taken at their placement

Readings

- $ Dean, R G , & Poorvu, N L (2008) Assessment and formulation A contemporary social work perspective *Families in Society, 89(4)*, 596-604
- $ Havighurst, S , & Downey, L (2009) Clinical reasoning for child and adolescent mental health practitioners The mindful formulation *Clinical Child Psychology and Psychiatry, 14(2)* 251-271
- $ Sharpe, P A , Greaney, M L , Lee, P R , & Royce, S W (2000) Assets-Oriented Community Assessment *Public Health Reports Focus on Healthy Communities, 115* 205-211

Week 7 October 31

Topics

- $ Social Work Assessment - continued
    - o In class role-play and group completion of an assessment following the assignment format

Readings

- $ **Saleebey, D (2001)** The Diagnostic Strengths Manual Social Work, 45(1) 183-187
- $ **Witkin, S L , & Harrison, W D (2001)** Whose evidence and for what purpose? Social Work, 46(4), 293–297

Week 8 November 7

Topics

- $ AOP, Advocacy, and Empowerment
    - o Application in the field – role plays
    - o Group reading assignment #1 (A & B)

Readings

- $ **Hernandez, P Carranza, M & Almeida, R (2010)** Mental health professionals' adaptive responses to racial microaggressions An exploratory study *Professional Psychology Research and Practice 41(3)* 202–209
- $ **Poole, J M (2010)** Progressive until graduation? Helping BSW students hold onto anti-oppressive and critical social work practices *Critical Social Work, 11(2)*
- $ **Larson, G (2008)** Anti-oppressive practice in mental health *Journal of Progressive Human Services, 19(1)* 30-48
- $ **Fines, M & Teram, E (2013)** Overt and Covert Ways of responding to Moral Injustices in Social Work Practice Heroes and Mild-Mannered social work Bipeds *British Journal of Social Work, 43(7) 1312-1329*

Supplemental (not mandatory) Reading

- $ Lee, B (2001) *Case Advocacy* (Available in Campus Bookstore)
- Green, D (2007) Risk and social work

Week 9 November 14

Topics

- $ Skill review I
    - o Application to placement with role plays
    - o In addition to readings review video https //vimeo com/129321035

- o Assessment Assignment Due

Readings

- $ **O'Hare, T (2009)** Chapter 5 – Supportive Skills Essential skills of social work practice Assessment, intervention and evaluation Chicago Lyceum Books
- $ **Seebohm, P Gilchrist, A & Morris, D (2012)** Bold but balanced how community development contributes to mental health and inclusion *Community Development Journal, 47(4)* 473-490

Supplemental (not mandatory) reading

- $ **McKee Sellick, M , Delaney, R , & Brownlee, K (2002)** The deconstruction of professional knowledge Accountability without authority *Families in Society The Journal of Contemporary Human Services, 83(5/6)* 493-498
- $ **Choules, K (2012)** The shifting sands of social justice discourse From situating the problem with "them," to situating it with "us" *Review of Education, Pedagogy, and Cultural Studies, 29(5)* 461-481

Week 10 November 21

Topics

- $ Community Social Work
  - o Small Group Reading Assignment # 2 (A)

Readings

- $ **van den Berk-Clark, C & Pyles, L (2012)** Deconstructing Neoliberal Community Development Approaches and a Case for the Solidarity Economy *Journal of Progressive Human Services*, 23(1) 1-17
- $ **Beck, D (2012)** A Community of Strangers Supporting Drug Recovery Through Community Development and Freirean Pedagogy *Journal of Progressive Human Services*, 23(2) 110-126
- $ **Forde, C & Lynch, D (2013)** Critical Practice for Challenging Times Social Workers' Engagement with Community Work *British Journal of Social Work,* 44(8) 2078-2094

Week 11 November 28

Topics

- $ Group Supervision Topics
  - o Personal Reflection # 1 is due

Readings

- $ Readings assigned by student

Week 12 December 5

Topics

- $ Social Work & Immigration
  - o Small Group Reading Assignment #3 (B)

Readings

- $ **Healy, L (2004)** Strengthening the link Social work with Immigrants and refugees and international social work *Journal of Immigrant & Refugee Services, 2(1/2)* 49-67

- $ **Humphries, B (2004)** An unacceptable role for social work Implementing immigration policy *British Journal of Social Work, 34* 93-107
- $ **Yee, J Y (2005)** Critical anti-racism praxis The concept of whiteness implicated In S Hicks, J Fook & R Puzzoto (Eds,) *Social Work A Critical Turn* (pp 87-103) Toronto Thompson Educational Publishing
- $ **Carranza, M E (2008)** Salvadorian women speak Coping in Canada with past trauma and loss *Canadian Social Work Review, 25(1)* 23-36

Supplemental (not mandatory) Reading

- $ **Allen, R I (2004)** Whiteness and critical pedagogy *Educational Philosophy and Theory, 36(2)* 21-137
- $ **Dick, I , & Tigar McLaren, A (2004)** Telling it like it is? Constructing accounts of settlement with immigrant and refugee women in Canada *Gender, Place and Culture, 11(4)* 513-534
- $ **Sakamoto, I (2007)** A critical examination of immigrant acculturation Toward an anti-oppressive social work model with immigrant adults in a pluralistic society *British Journal of Social Work, 37* 515-535

Week 13 January 9

Topics

- $ Skill Review II – Validation and responding to Affect
  - o In class role plays

Readings

- $ **Koerner, K (2012)** Chapter 4 - Validation Principles and Strategies *Doing dialectical behaviour therapy A practical guide* New York Guilford Press
- $ **Ruch, G (2005)** Relationship-based practice and reflective practice holistic approaches to contemporary child care social work *Child and Family Social Work, 10* 111-123

Week 14 January 16

Topics

- $ Group Supervision Topics

Readings

- $ Readings to be provided by students

Week 15 January 23

Topics

- $ Topic 1 Social Work and Mental Health
  - o Small Group Reading Assignment # 4 (A)

Readings

- $ **Koehne, K , Hamilton, B , Sands, N & Humphreys, C (2013)** Working around a contested diagnosis Borderline personality disorder in adolescence *Health, 17(37)* 37-56
- $ **Gharabaghi, K & Stuart, C (2010)** Voices from the periphery Prospects and challenges for the homeless youth service sector *Children and Youth Services Review, 32(12)* 1683-1689

- $ **Wolframe, P (2013)** The madwoman in the academy, or revealing the invisible straightjacket Theorizing and teaching saneism and sane privilege *Disability Studies Quarterly, 33 (1)*

Supplementary (not mandatory) Reading

- $ **Freud, S (1999)** The social construction of normality *Families in Society, 80* 333-339
- $ **Costa, L , Voronka, J , Landry, D , Reid, J , McFarlane, B , Reville, D & Church, K (2012)** "Recovering our stories" A small act of resistance *Studies in Social Justice, 6(1)* 85-101
- $ **Poole, J , Jivraj, T , Arslanian, A , Bellows, K , Chiasson, S , Hakimy, H , Pasini, J , & Reid, J (2012)** Sanism, 'mental health', and social work/education A review and call to action *Intersectionalities A Global Journal of Social Work Analysis, Research, Polity, and Practice,* 1 20- 36
- $ **Kirmayer, L C , Tait, C , & Simpson, C (2009)** The mental health of Aboriginal Peoples in Canada Transformations of identity and community In L J Kirmayer & G G Valaskakis (Eds), *Healing traditions of Aboriginal Peoples in Canada* (pp 3- 35) Vancouver UBC Press
- $ **Kranke, D Floersch, J , Townsend, L , & Munson, M (2010)** Stigma experience among adolescents taking psychiatric medication *Children and Youth Service Review, 32* 496-505

Week 16 January 30

Topics

- $ Group supervision Topics

Readings

- $ Readings to be provided by students

Week 17 February 6

Topics

- $ Social Work and Sexual Diversity
    - o Small Group Reading Assignment # 5 (B)
    - o Review of video Trans+sport produced by 519 Church

Readings

- $ **Markham, E R (2011)** Gender identity disorder, the gender binary, and transgender oppression implications for ethical social work *Smith College Studies in Social Work, 81* 314–327
- $ **Hayman, B , Wilkesm L , Jackson, D & Halcom, E (2013)** De novo lesbian families Legitimizing the other mother *Journal of GLBT Studies, 9* 273 – 287
- $ **Norwood, K (2013)** Meaning matters Framing trans identity in the context of family relations *Journal of GLBT Studies, 9* 152-178

February 13 – Reading Week

Week 18 February 20

Topics

- Group Supervision Topics

Readings

- Readings to be provided by students

Week 19 February 27

Topics

- Group Supervision Topics

Readings

- Readings to be provided by students

Week 20 March 6

Topics

- Social Work from Various Lenses

Readings

- **Brydon, K (2011)** Promoting diversity or confirming hegemony? In search for new insight for social work *International Social Work, 55(2)* 155-167
- **Bennett, B & Zubrycki, J (2003)** Hearing the stories of Australian aboriginal and Torres Strait islander social workers Challenging and educating the system *Australian Social Work, 56(1)* 61-70
- **McCormick, R (2009)** Aboriginal approaches to counselling In L J Kirmayer & G G Valaskakis (Eds), *Healing traditions of Aboriginal Peoples in Canada* (pp 337-354) Vancouver UBC Press
- **Beresford, P (2000)** Service users' knowledges and social work theory conflict or collaboration? *British Journal of Social Work, 30* 489-503

Supplementary (not mandatory) Readings

- **Razack, S H (2001)** Introduction - *Looking White in the Eye Gender, Race, and Culture in Courtrooms and Classrooms* Toronto University of Toronto Press
- **Chau, R C, Yu, S, & Tran, C (2011)** The diversity based approach to culturally sensitive practices *International Social Work, 54(1)* 21-33

Week 21 March 13

Topics

- Group Supervision Topics

Readings

- Readings to be provided by students

Week 22 March 20

Topics

- Make up week for outstanding
    - Group Supervision Topics
      or
    - Small Group Reading Assignment

Readings

- Readings to be provided by students

Week 23 March 27

Topics

- Special Topic – to be decided
  - General job search strategies (informational interviewing, networking, hidden job market)
  - Guest speaker from McMaster Student Success Centre
  - Process recording due

Readings

- Readings to be assigned depending on topic

Week 24 April 3

Topics

- Finishing Up
  - Personal Reflection #2 due
  - Final Class – Course review and Celebration

Appendix A – Ethical Dilemma

Ethical dilemmas are an inevitable part of social work practice, policy-making, community development work, and research As one option for the group supervision assignment, working with an ethical dilemma is designed to help you and your classmates address, in depth, a complex ethical issue and to help you develop a framework for professional decision-making

- To prepare for your group supervision presentation you will need to do the following
  - Select an ethical dilemma that has developed or come to light in your practicum
  - Describe the dilemma and the context as you see them (if helpful, identify your personal reactions to the dilemma and the struggle that you experienced)
  - Develop an outline to guide your decision-making In so doing, consult at least two sources to help you develop a decision-making framework You might use
    - **Lowenberg & Dolgoff (1992)** Ethical Decisions for Social Work Practice Illinois Peacock, chapter 3
    - **Litke, R (1982)** "Clarifying ethical conflicts through decision-making " In S Yelaja (ed), Ethical Issues in Social Work, Thomas, pp 35-53
    - **Manning, S S (1997)** The Social Worker as Moral Citizen Ethics in Action Social Work, 42(3), 223-230
- Steps
  - Apply the framework to your dilemma and outline the steps you took and the points you considered while examining the dilemma
  - In outline form, summarize the analytic process, including readings, discussions with others, and your thinking
  - Consult the CASW Code of Ethics and seek out literature regarding the specific ethical dilemma you confront, also consult with your field instructor and/or other social workers
  - Write a statement about your decision What decision did you make? How did you decide to resolve the dilemma? What would you do if you were confronted with the same situation again?
- As per the requirements of the group supervision assignment, for your presentation you will need to prepare two or three questions for the class about the ethical dilemma that are designed to assist you in resolving the dilemma or in developing a deeper or more critical analysis of it In addition, make sure that in your presentation you address what the literature says about the type of issues you are addressing and the resolution/intervention you are undertaking (you are expected to have a broad understanding of what you are doing and why) Also, distribute to the class, one week before your presentation, two peer reviewed articles that inform your thinking and practice in this case

1

The Integration of Theory and Practice: The ITP Loop Model

The Integration of Theory and Social Work Practice

Practitioners and educators in social work have always characterized the business of the practicum as the place where theory is integrated with practice. All too frequently this statement stands without further definition Integration of theory and practice (ITP), without examination, may be a kind of magical incantation through which educators, like alchemists, hope to transform a social work student into a professional social worker. Recognizing the limits of magic, even for social workers, this chapter will engage field instructors in the work of demystifying ITP and giving it operational meaning

Practitioners, to become educators, must be able to examine their own practice and articulate the thoughts, attitudes, values, and feelings that affect the actions they take. Practitioners feel that many of these actions have become 'second nature,' so that plans and behaviours may appear, to the observer, to evolve naturally. In fact, professional behaviour is based on implicit ideas and beliefs that social workers have developed through their own educational and practice experiences. This 'integrated knowledge' has to be identified so that the field educator can communicate it to the student (Bogo and Vayda 1987, 1991) In order to illustrate how to unravel 'integrated knowledge,' we will follow two case examples, one a practice situation with an individual and one involving community practice and service planning

The worker in both examples might imagine a looping process Since social work activity is both cumulative and ongoing, looping is a useful image. Each practice encounter must incorporate past experience, new knowledge, and future speculation and planning This is demonstrated in figure 1.

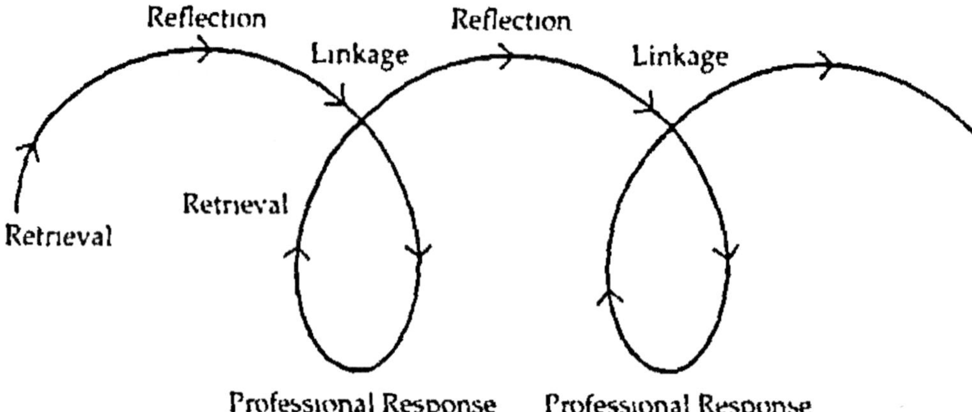

Figure 1

Retrieval

The starting point of the loop is information gathering, which we call retrieval. Retrieval is the recall of information about a specific practice situation and would include preparatory thinking as well as the contact itself. To put it another way, we mean the facts that distinguish and define any situation at the beginning of involvement.

Retrieved information from any social work situation can be divided into psycho-social, interactive, contextual, and organizational factors (Vayda and Bogo 1991) The worker and client focus on the most pressing factors, which may change with time. As new information is retrieved, the worker moves through the loop again and again until the situation is resolved.

Psycho-social factors are familiar concepts to social workers and refer to specific information about individuals, families, groups, and communities. Included are observations about behaviour, affect, and cognition, and information about formal and informal support systems. Psycho-social factors direct attention to the client system. Interactive factors refer to the creation of a new system composed of social worker and client exchanges The quality of the interaction plays a key role in the disclosure of information and facilitates elaboration. In demonstrating the loop, we have been deliberately selective and reductive. We will focus on psycho-social and interactive factors first, and add contextual and organizational factors later.

RETRIEVAL: INDIVIDUAL PRACTICE: EXAMPLE 1

The social worker is employed in a shelter for battered women. The client, a woman, aged thirty-four years, has three children, ages six, eight, and ten years, and is physically abused repeatedly by her husband. Although the police have been involved, no charges have been laid. The woman has sought refuge in the shelter several times in the past, but has always made a decision to return home. Her family has counselled her to return to her husband. She has never held a paying job and has a grade 10 education.

RETRIEVAL: COMMUNITY PRACTICE: EXAMPLE 2

In a large metropolitan city, a South Asian feminist women's group approaches the local planning council for help in establishing a service for battered women in their community. Increasing awareness has developed that wife abuse is considered a criminal offence in the wider society but is tolerated by some in the community. Males and elders in the community are feeling threatened by the militancy of some of the younger women in the community who have publicized, in the mainstream media, the fact of wife abuse in their community.

This information is illustrative of retrieval. In actual practice, more information would have been retrieved and reflected upon at this point

Reflection

Social workers are trained to subject the information they have gathered to a reflective process, which we have identified as the next step in the loop. Reflection contains elements of the rubric of 'self-awareness,' which has been a standard principle of social work practice. Reflection, as it is used in the loop, is an exploration of the social worker's personal associations with respect to the practice situation. Personal associations may arise from personality style, idiosyncratic reactions to similar life experiences, or internalized cultural values. The purpose of reflection is to gain self-knowledge of each of these processes.

Personal subjective reactions can be recalled through reflection and examined regarding their potential effect on the work to be done. It is equally important to examine assumptions and beliefs that may be perceived as truth but are cultural constructs belonging to a personal world-view shaped by one's ethnicity, race, culture, and gender. By acknowledging the validity of other assumptions and beliefs, an open dialogue can begin between worker and client. Personal experience must also be acknowledged when it is relevant to the situation of the client. While similar experiences can aid joining and understanding, it is important to acknowledge that each individual has a unique response to the same life event.

In addition, as the situation progresses and the loop repeats itself, the worker reflects on the effectiveness of interventions undertaken to bring about change. In this way, reflection begins to build an ongoing evaluation of the work accomplished.

REFLECTION: INDIVIDUAL PRACTICE: EXAMPLE 1

The worker is a strong feminist who herself had left an abusive relationship and subsequently earned a graduate degree while supporting herself through part-time employment. Through reflection she confronts her impatience with the client's pattern of returning to her abusive husband. She becomes aware that she must separate her experience from that of her client She recalls her immediate labelling of the client as helpless and dependent, unable or unwilling to make decisions and act upon them The worker knows that she can be judgmental and that this attitude could undermine her capacity for empathy and joining.

REFLECTION: COMMUNITY PRACTICE: EXAMPLE 2

The worker is a middle-aged Hispanic male with a strong sense of the importance of family preservation and the value of shared beliefs and cultural solidarity. Upon reflection, he becomes aware that he has a tendency to identify with the males and elders in the community. He becomes aware that he must find a way to join with the needs of the younger women, without losing his sense of the value the community places on family stability.

Linkage

Less familiar to social workers is the conscious application of theory to practice. This step is what we have labelled as linkage. Linkage is that part of the loop that uses cognitive associations to retrieved information and to the associations elicited through reflection, and links them with knowledge learned from reading, research studies, lectures, and general experience. The purpose is to identify and label knowledge that will help explain the practice data and the subjective reactions that have been evoked, and ultimately to use that knowledge in planning professional responses Linkage requires that facts and attitudes about the situation be abstracted or generalized to identify common elements that relate to a knowledge base. A social worker's practice is likely to be based on a well-integrated knowledge and value base consisting of practice wisdom, concepts from various theories, and empirically validated findings. Additionally, approaches or therapies that may be characteristic of a specific setting provide the theoretical linkage. These 'pieces' of knowledge become part of the practitioner's art and are used in a seemingly intuitive fashion in interacting with a practice situation (Schon 1987, 1995). Specialized practice models such as task-centred, family systems, group, and community development approaches interpret human behaviour and interpersonal adaptation, and provide social workers with specific techniques to involve clients in intervention approaches to bring about desired change.

LINKAGE: INDIVIDUAL PRACTICE: EXAMPLE 1

Psycho-social knowledge may involve recognizing the impact of the client's cultural expectations about traditional female behaviour in a marriage on her self-identity, self-esteem, and her fears about permanently leaving the relationship. Knowledge of family dynamics are also relevant, such as the emotional impact on the children and the reactivation of the woman's experience of violence in her family of origin. Knowledge of specific practice models for intervention may focus attention on eliciting support and safety planning from informal support networks such as a local single mothers' group and her family of origin. Formal support networks might include financial maintenance, subsidized housing, vocational training and education, and provisions for day care.

LINKAGE: COMMUNITY PRACTICE. EXAMPLE 2

Linking to 'pieces of knowledge' about immigration and relocation, such as an understanding of cultural beliefs brought from the country of origin, and the effect of a different set of societal expectations in the new country on identity, may inform the worker's approach to this situation. The worker asks himself, 'What do I need to think about to better understand this situation, and what do I need to know to intervene effectively?' The worker uses the practice principle of involving participants in all aspects of the process to acknowledge the group's concerns and enlists them in developing a strategy to identify and engage key persons in the community who play formal and informal roles

Professional Response

To practice social work means to take some action. This step is what we have labelled as professional response to a given set of facts at a particular point in time Each situation requires the worker and client to select the issues of highest priority for immediate focus. Using this part of the loop, the social worker grounds the ideas, knowledge, and insights just uncovered to develop specific plans and behaviours for dealing with the situation. Professional response is the selection and implementation of a plan that will inform the next encounter. Consideration of all parts of the loop conveys the dynamic interrelationship between concepts and action.

PROFESSIONAL RESPONSE: INDIVIDUAL PRACTICE: EXAMPLE 1

The worker might choose to open a discussion with the client about what choices the client feels are immediately necessary and possible for her at the time, specifically encouraging her to plan for the safety of herself and her children, through contacts with appropriate informal and formal systems, such as neighbours, extended family, and police. Later, the worker might discuss with the client her family's attitudes, experiences, and expectations.

PROFESSIONAL RESPONSE: COMMUNITY PRACTICE: EXAMPLE 2

The social worker begins to work with the women's group to help them identify all the stakeholders in the community who need to be involved from the beginning in planning a response to this community issue. The next step is to work out a detailed plan of how to involve these various potential participants and to begin implementation of the plan.

We have thus far focused on retrieval of psycho-social and interactive factors in going through the loop. However, two other important factors, contextual and organizational, influence all social work situations and need to be acknowledged. Contextual factors refer to the economic and political structures embedded in society that affect individuals and disempower certain groups through discrimination based on gender, race, ethnicity, age, and disability. In addition, societal attitudes may erect boundaries that exclude specific groups; for example, a suburban community may seem a hostile environment to visible minority persons. A particular community group may have fixed beliefs about homosexuals or lesbians, homeless persons, persons who have committed criminal offences, or persons who are either mentally or physically disabled. Social workers are committed to connect these issues to their ongoing practice responses and work toward shifts in empowerment for their clients.

CONTEXTUAL FACTORS. INDIVIDUAL PRACTICE. EXAMPLE 1

In a period of budgetary constraints, the community is less sympathetic to providing adequate resources for battered women. The re-emergence of beliefs in the sanctity and primacy of the family have created a hostile climate for women who may need protection from their partners. The attitudes of the police and the justice system toward family violence often keep women at risk. In addition, there are negative economic consequences for single women living alone with children.

Integrating this perspective expands the worker's previous professional response to include advocacy. The worker might join with others to plan a strategy for presenting the needs of battered women to the media and to various levels of government

CONTEXTUAL FACTORS' COMMUNITY PRACTICE: EXAMPLE 2

In a period of financial constraint, the government is unlikely to fund services aimed at a specific ethnic group Many people in the community have experienced discrimination which they believe is based on racial difference.

Taking this into account, the worker's professional response might be to help the women identify funding sources in their own community as well as publicizing the information from the needs assessment in the wider community.

Organizational factors refer to bureaucratic systems and to how their ideology and assumptions, rules, and procedures affect program delivery and service provision. These factors include an organization's mandate, its climate, roles and procedures, including decision-making procedures, its structure and funding, board composition, and its relationships with a network of other community agencies. Social workers use knowledge of organizational dynamics to develop interventions to make organizations more effective.

ORGANIZATIONAL FACTORS: INDIVIDUAL PRACTICE: EXAMPLE 1

The shelter's board of directors has placed a three-week limit on the length of time any woman may remain in the shelter. The worker feels this is insufficient time for adequate planning to take place and may be a reason why some clients return home to a dangerous situation before an alternative plan is in place.

The worker may seek the support of other workers, clients, and the director in making a request to meet with the board to present her concerns.

ORGANIZATIONAL FACTORS: COMMUNITY PRACTICE: EXAMPLE 2

The planning council has just published a study which some local community leaders have branded as unfair because they feel it focuses on racial divisions and criminal activity in their community. The director of the council is very sensitive to this criticism and has asked the staff to avoid any activity which could jeopardize the council.

The worker knows that survival of the council is dependent on public funding. However, he recognizes an ethical dilemma between responsibility to protect the council and responsibility to respond to community needs. The worker may inform the director that he understands the director's concern, but that he cannot let it interfere with his responsibility to provide assistance to community groups. He may agree to keep the director informed about any action which would be potentially significant to the council.

These case examples and discussion provide an introduction to how the ITP Loop Model as a process can be applied to the content of social work practice. It is a model that is generic and comprehensive, and provides a unifying structure for both practice and field instruction. Figure 2 illustrates how this framework unifies content and process

THE ITP LOOP MODEL APPLIED TO SOCIAL WORK PRACTICE: PROCESS AND CONTENT				
PROCESS	Retrieval	Reflection	Linkage	Professional Response
CONTENT	Psycho-social Factors			
	Interactive Factors			
	Contextual Factors			
	Organizational Factors			

Figure 2

Content

We have diagrammed the looping process, and we will return to a discussion of each step in this process. More complicated and complex are the factors we have labelled as content. These factors coincide with an ecological metaphor which has been widely adopted in social work practice theory to capture the profession's commitment to the transactional bonds between the person and his or her social and physical context (Hartman 1994) We have described all social work situations as involving psycho-social, interactive, societal or contextual, and organizational factors. In actual practice, however, instructors and students must consciously choose to consider only those factors which are meaningful to the specific practice situation at any point in time. This requires scanning the whole to focus attention on the most relevant factors, which, in turn, may change with time, thus requiring the selection of still other factors. Though this process sounds complex, scanning to facilitate focus is a common mental activity.

Understanding the ITP Loop Model of Field Instruction

Implicit in preparing students for service in the field is a process whereby the information, knowledge, and critical analytic base acquired by students in the academic part of professional education is translated into an ability to relate to persons seeking help and to arrive at professional decisions in a service context. Each social work school or program has developed a unique philosophy of education, specific curriculum objectives, and specific practicum regulations and procedures. However, field instruction is more than a structural arrangement between academy and agency in which actors follow a set of procedures; and field instruction requires more than providing an example for a student to observe and emulate, as a master teacher would do for an apprentice, or establishing a facilitative relationship between student and field instructor. The ITP Loop Model should assist field instructors in examining their own practice and that of their students, as well as the interaction between student and field instructor. The organizing principle is the belief that field instruction is a branch of social work practice that possesses a distinctive blend of knowledge, values, and skills that can be articulated and learned. The ITP Loop Model is applicable to all levels of practice, whether with individuals, families, groups, or communities, or in administration, policy development, or planning. It can be used in well-established or developing settings, urban or rural settings, and with undergraduate and graduate students

To review, we use the image of a looping process to depict the cumulative and ongoing nature of both practice and field instruction. For purposes of presentation, we will discuss each phase of the ITP Loop Model sequentially. However, practice and field instruction are fluid, dynamic, and integrated, and cannot be so neatly organized. In using the loop at a given time, any part will be joined with other parts as the process of retrieval, reflection, linkage, and professional response occurs. Having described a model that integrates social work theory and practice, we are ready to focus on how the practitioner, now functioning as a field educator, can use the model with students in practicum settings.

Retrieval

Since the distinctive feature of the practicum is the primacy of practice, field instruction starts with and always returns to a practice event. The entry point in the loop for the process of field instruction is the retrieval or recall of information, namely, the facts describing the given practice experience. It involves use of the observing ego, a 'mind's eye' phenomenon wherein the field instructor or student recalls a professional situation as both an observer and a participant. We have already said that social work situations include psycho-social, interactive, organizational, and contextual factors. These are reviewed as the field instructor and the student move through the loop again and again until the situation is resolved. Retrieval may involve consideration of the known facts of a situation in order to prepare for the first contact, or it may involve reactions flowing from a professional response that evolved from the preceding practice activity. Practice activities in which students are involved include individual, family, or group interviews, team or committee meetings, presentations, and reading and writing reports. Field instructors may retrieve student practice data through such methods as verbal reports, process and summary recordings, audio or video tapes, live supervision, or co-working experiences.

Students new to social work are likely to retrieve and report practice observations that are personally meaningful to them but that may not be focused The bridge between the familiar role of social persona and purposeful intervenor is difficult to negotiate. Workers know that it is the context of the encounter or the agency's service mandate that empowers the worker to investigate any situation. Students, wanting to be accepted and liked by the person they are seeing, find it difficult to ask for information which they feel might insult, embarrass, alienate, or anger the other person. For example, the student at a child protection agency sent to investigate a complaint of potential child abuse talks with the mother for nearly an hour. She reports to her field instructor that the mother was friendly, seemed very nice, and denied ever hitting or spanking her child. In response to a question from the field instructor, she said she did not ask how the mother might discipline the child or if the child ever made her angry. Rather, they mainly discussed the mother's concerns about the recent decrease in her welfare support.

The task of the field instructor is to present a structure which will frame students' random observations and affect their selection and definition of what constitutes relevant data In the above case, the field instructor and student talked about the agency's charge to ensure that children are protected and what the student, as the instrument of that charge, needs to ask the mother, who may be ambivalent about her parenting role. The field instructor also acknowledged that governmental changes in the level of support available to single mothers were affecting many of the clients of the agency In this example, the field instructor and the student have identified relevant psycho-social, interactive, organizational, and contextual content

Reflection

Reflection is a familiar concept in social work education It refers to the worker's thoughtful consideration of the practice activity and, as it is used in the loop, focuses on two elements: subjective meanings and objective effects. Reflection on subjective meanings entails an exploration of the personal associations that the student or the field instructor might have with respect to the practice situation. It involves the identification of the values, beliefs, assumptions, and attitudes which we attach to observed facts in order to make them understandable within a personal context and in accordance with our internalized notions of what is 'right.'

Social work practice has long recognized that the 'self' of the practitioner exerts a powerful influence on interpretations of and reactions to professional situations. Approaches to field instruction have given more or less attention to the student's personality dynamics, and to past or current issues in the student's life which affect his or her ability to offer effective service (George 1982) Models which used a therapeutic approach tended to interpret students' subjective reactions negatively, seeing them as interfering and hence in need of being controlled. Too often this resulted in a quasi-therapeutic supervisory model which blurred the boundaries between education and personal growth (Siporin 1981), with the result that this approach became problematic and fell into disfavour. We recognize that in their practice social workers are often confronted with extremely challenging situations, such as those of people who have been victimized in violent intimate relationships, refugees who have suffered trauma and torture, people who are dying of AIDS, and children who have been sexually abused. It is normal that these situations will elicit strong personal reactions from social workers and students. As Grossman, Levine-Jordano, and Shearer (1990) have observed, social work education has often abdicated its role of helping students learn to deal with their emotional reactions to practice. Through the phase of reflection in the loop model, the field instructor can include this focus and work with the student to identify subjective responses These can be used to advance both self-understanding and understanding of the client, and to formulate professional responses that will be helpful.

In some instances, the student will have had personal experiences similar to those of the practice situation. While these experiences can aid joining and understanding, it is important to acknowledge different reactions and unique responses to the same life event. The intent of identification of similar experiences is not to intrude into the personal life of the student; rather, when students and educators feel that their own experiences are relevant to the practice situation, the aim is to acknowledge and consciously use them. It is the practice situation that stimulates and guides the search for personal experience that will promote or retard students' ability to empathize.

Reflection is a process that has taken on a new urgency as people from many different races and cultures are struggling to find an identity and to survive in North America. Trying to meet the needs of such a diverse population is straining established practice repertoires and traditional attitudes. In addition, gender roles are shifting, conventional attitudes toward sexual preferences are being challenged, and cherished concepts of family and social support are in great need of redefinition (Hartman 1990a). Through reflection, social workers can gain self-knowledge and become aware of the influence of assumptions and beliefs that may be perceived as truth but are actually cultural constructs belonging to a personal world-view.

In summary, reflection aims to help the student gain access to personal subjective reactions to practice phenomena with which the student is engaged. These reactions can reflect internalized cultural values, idiosyncratic reactions to similar life experiences, or personality styles Through reflection, the student's feelings, beliefs, values, and assumptions are made explicit and subjected to critical thinking about their impact on interactions with the clients or participants in the practice situation, on assessments and judgments being made, and on the effectiveness of plans and interventions. Students are helped to recognize the challenges and changes that are occurring, or that need to occur, as long-held beliefs and reactions are confronted by new knowledge and experience.

In reflecting on personal associations to practice, four sets of factors must be considered: psycho-social, interactive, contextual, and organizational. Psycho-social factors might include subjective reactions to characteristics of people in the situation; to certain social problems (e g., substance abuse or the homeless populations); and to systemic or structural factors (e g., race, unemployment, or incarceration) Interactive factors might include reactions based on transference or countertransference phenomena; and idiosyncratic reactions to specific areas of comfort and enthusiasm or discomfort and anxiety.

Contextual factors may also direct student and field instructor to recall life experiences relevant to the practice situation that have produced their belief systems, social class assumptions, and cultural, ethnic, and gender-based assumptions. For example, life transition experiences such as adolescence, marriage, parenthood, aging, separation and loss, crisis reactions, and the effects of isolation all form the basis for empathy. These universal experiences, however, are filtered by poverty, social class, culture, race, and gender. The commonalities and the differences need to be reviewed and applied to the practice situation.

Organizational factors might include reactions to specific agency policies and procedures, to a climate of openness or rigidity, or to an institutionalized approach to problems based on regulations Large bureaucratic structures may be hierarchical and authoritarian, or they may permit democratic participation; and small services may be egalitarian, or they may be charged with factionalism and tension. These factors influence the interactions between social worker and client, and between student and teacher.

Table 1 outlines the factors that can be scanned by the field instructor and student in order to select those elements that may be personally relevant to the practice situation.

TABLE 1
Reflection. Personal associations to the encounter

Psycho-social factors
Reaction to characteristics of people in the situation.
Reaction to social problems (e g , homelessness)

Interactive factors.
Awareness of areas of comfort and enthusiasm, and of discomfort and anxiety, in contact situations
Awareness of the effects of transferring subjective meanings, feelings, and reactions on the part of both workers and other persons

Contextual factors·
Relevant life experiences.
Relevant belief systems: social class assumptions, culture, ethnicity, and race, and gender-based assumptions.
Awareness of the influence of specific systemic and structural factors

Organizational factors·
Reaction to the agency's approach to clients and social problems
Reaction to the agency's approach to suggestions for innovation

The following example illustrates how the process and content of reflection inform the work of the field instructor. The student is placed at a community neighbourhood centre in a working-class area that provides various drop-in programs, a legal clinic, and advocacy assistance and planning for groups responding to changing community needs and concerns. The municipality has purchased a large old home and, after making extensive renovations, announced publicly its plans for an AIDS hospice and a counselling centre for gays and lesbians. The neighbourhood is already the site of various group homes and shelters and a large mental health hospital. Many residents feel stressed and angry that this facility is being foisted upon them. They have circulated petitions demanding that it be located somewhere else. The placement agency's board and the executive director believe that the proposed facility will meet a long-standing need, but they also anticipated a negative reaction in the community.

A public meeting is organized and publicized by the centre to discuss the issue, and the student and another worker are assigned to be facilitators. Following the first meeting, the student reports to the field instructor that he lost control when people began talking and shouting at once and he was unable to impose order. He said that he lost his temper and called them a bunch of bigots. He apologized quickly, but he feels he seriously damaged his chances to work with this group in a constructive way.

The field instructor said she could appreciate the student's pain and embarrassment at what happened, but all was probably not lost. The student then said that he might have handled the shouting, but what really upset him was the homophobia he felt as he faced the group. He said his brother was gay, and he knew the prejudice his brother faced even from their own family. He just felt overwhelmed by the belief that nothing would ever change, even though the city was now ready to offer services and support.

Using reflection, the field instructor and student talked about attitudinal change as a long and often difficult process Reflective field instruction begins with a discussion of the student's own reaction based on his experience and then has to move from this interior space to connect to the professional situation by helping him to reflect on the experience and beliefs of those persons in the community who were so opposed to the hospice and centre. Together, the field instructor and the student speculated about what made these persons fearful and angry. Homophobia was a factor, but social class also played a role in their belief that more powerful people did not want social services for troubled and troublesome people located in their own communities but always seemed to choose this community. The field instructor pointed out that the centre had worked hard to be seen as one that was willing to hear out the thoughts of persons living in that community and to consider their needs and wishes. They planned how the student could use these insights to try to begin a real dialogue at the next planned meeting. This example suggests how all factors, psycho-social, interactive, contextual, and organizational, were useful and necessary to expand the student's reflective process.

Reflection must also provide for the opportunity to consider the effectiveness of an interaction or professional response that is retrieved as the situation reloops back to retrieval and reflection. For example, the student in the child protection agency, working with the potential abuse situation already described, had begun to work with the mother, seeing her twice a week. After six weeks, both the student and field instructor felt that the mother was ready to be referred to a group of other young single mothers who met weekly for companionship, relaxation, and general discussion of topics of their choice Regular contacts with the student were discontinued All went well for several months, and then the group facilitator reported that the mother had not attended for three weeks. The agency also received a phone call from a neighbour saying that she heard the child crying for hours at a time. The student called on the mother and reported that she had found her withdrawn and depressed.

On reflection, the student and field instructor agreed that the student's contact with the mother might have ended too abruptly and prematurely. Possibly the mother found the group support insufficient for her to gain the strength needed to cope more competently.

For the purpose of demonstrating how the ITP Loop Model looks when uncoiled, we can see that each of the content components is operant, although in teaching from this model, each component does not always have to be specifically labelled by field instructor and student. We can see, however, that psycho-social and interactive factors reviewed reflectively were linked with the knowledge that the relationship between client and worker cannot be too quickly or lightly dismissed even when the organizational demand on the agency for service creates pressure for very short-term service. Contextual factors influencing the current crisis in the mother's situation, such as the recent decrease in welfare support, need consideration by the student at this point as well. In addition there is a possibility that new events have occurred, such as the loss of a significant person or the threat of eviction, which might explain her current depression. The loop begins again as the student and field instructor retrieve the information necessary to understand this new development, reflect, link, and move to a new professional response.

Thus far we have focused our discussion of reflection on helping the student identify personal associations to a professional encounter. Obviously the field instructor will also have subjective reactions which reflect personality style, life experiences, or cultural values Reflection poses a dilemma for the interactive process between field instructor and student. To what extent is it useful to share personal feelings, associations, and experiences with the student? The test is the relevance of the experience either to the practice situation or to the field instructor-student dyad.

When the field instructor feels that the student is unable to empathize with or understand a practice situation either because of lack of personal experience or unwillingness to relate to personal experience, it may be necessary for the field instructor to use her or his own experience to help the student make a connection. Whenever personal disclosure is sought or given in field instruction, it is the discloser who must always remain in control by selecting what and how much it feels comfortable to reveal. For example, disclosing personal feelings and behaviour in reaction to a loss or separation may stimulate the student to think empathetically and respond in a productive way. Students may have a range of reactions to hearing about their field instructors' subjective experiences related to a practice situation. In some instances, the student will find the experience very powerful, and this might facilitate understanding or increase empathy with the practice situation. The student might feel flattered or special that the field instructor has chosen to share personal experiences, and this might further solidify the field instructor–student dyad. On the other hand, some students may feel burdened by hearing the 'story' of the field instructor, uncertain about what reaction is expected, and uncomfortable with personal disclosure. Obviously students' reactions to field instructors' subjective experiences vary according to personality and level of development The field instructor should be sensitive to how disclosure might be received.

Linkage

This step moves to a search for the professional knowledge base that makes it possible to choose a specific response to a situation from among a variety of competing responses. Linkage is that part of the loop that uses cognitive associations of both student and field instructor to the retrieved data and the associations elicited through reflection. The purpose is to identify and label knowledge that will help explain the practice data and the subjective reactions that have been evoked, and ultimately to use that knowledge in planning professional responses. Linkage addresses the way in which a knowledge base finds expression in practice, and is reconstructed as a result of practice. It encourages the student to select, from competing concepts, what is needed to construct a cognitive system of understanding that fits what has been retrieved and subjected to reflection. It is the degree to which a working hypothesis fits the situation that both student and field instructor must agree upon.

Linkage requires that facts and attitudes about the situation be abstracted or generalized to identify common elements that relate to a knowledge base. It is a process of moving back and forth between the general and the specific. In this phase, field educators conceptualize practice so that it can be clearly communicated in terms of applicable generalizations (Kadushin 1991), and they link these generalizations to the understanding of and response to a specific situation. This process is analytical. It is a search for concepts, learned by the student or practised by the field instructor, that derive from theoretical bases such as ecological systems, structural analysis, empowerment theory, feminist theory, psycho-dynamic theory, communication theory, or developmental theory. This list is not exhaustive.

The field instructor's task is not only to draw the student's attention to theoretical and empirical knowledge but also to help the student apply that knowledge in relation to a specific practice situation What is stated in general practice principles must be made situation specific. For example, how can 'start where the client is' be related to the specific student assignment? We are not suggesting that the field instructor must teach theory which may already have been taught by the school. Students carry an overload of theoretical content from the classroom which they have difficulty transferring to practice. It is the concrete situation which makes it possible for the field instructor to help the student link knowledge in order to understand the phenomena of practice.

In working with field instructors, we have found that linkage seems the most difficult component to comprehend and the most controversial. The field instructor's practice is likely to be based on a well-integrated knowledge and value base consisting of practice wisdom, concepts from various theories, and empirically validated findings. These 'pieces' of knowledge become part of the practitioner's art and are used in a seemingly intuitive fashion in interacting with a practice situation (Schon 1987, 1995). In addition, the agency may structure service in accordance with a particular therapeutic or service model. As an educator, the practitioner must search for the underlying ideas that constitute his or her cognitive system of understanding, communicate that knowledge to the student, and assist the student in developing his or her own cognitive system.

In a book aptly titled *Social Work as Art*, England (1986) states that the integration of theory and practice is a unique and intuitive process, but the social worker must be articulate about the problems and about her or his own thinking, citing the specific and selecting from the general. He argues that the worker uses theoretical knowledge, not to apply formulae, but to construct coherence from immediate complexity

For example, in identifying isolation as a concern for an individual who seems to have no supportive network, we are connecting to a knowledge and value base affirming that human isolation is an unhealthy state. In identifying an individual's sense of powerlessness to alter noxious conditions of living, we link to a theoretical base that teaches that one can effect change through understanding the institutionalization of oppression as an external force that otherwise may be perceived as personal deficiency. This understanding might suggest empowering collective action to exert pressure for change on those institutions. In identifying a struggle between adolescent and parent, we link to a theoretical base that examines appropriate developmental stages and behaviours for individuals and family members and the effect of recurring dysfunctional transactions within the family that could maintain a paralysing power struggle. Faced with a hospital team headed by an administrator who wants beds immediately, even if it means sending a patient to an inappropriate facility, we link to the knowledge that a client problem can be created by the very system charged with the resolution of problems. In working with family caregivers of the chronically ill, we link to the knowledge that counselling without some attention to the provision of concrete relief for the caregivers will be of little benefit. These are examples of practice wisdom, but they are at the same time examples of applied theory.

In field education, the student and field instructor review all knowledge relevant to a situation. This may mean exploring a variety of frames or theoretical stances to determine the best guide for understanding and acting in the current situation. This provides an opportunity for the student to use knowledge from the classroom in examining practice data Both faculty and field educators may long for a simpler time when there was a greater uniformity of thought between faculty and agency. The issue of fit between class and field has a long and tortured history in North American social work education. Each school of social work has the responsibility to communicate to the field instructors its philosophical and theoretical approaches and the content of courses, and to decide the degree to which it hopes to achieve congruence between what is taught in the school and what philosophical and theoretical approaches inform the practice of social work in the field

Controversy exists in social work regarding what theories and approaches contemporary practitioners need to know (Reamer 1994). There seems to be a belief that practice is either radical or traditional – an old social work battle-cry that refuses to be silenced. Currently some argue for teaching primarily empirically validated intervention approaches, while others champion postmodernism and the deconstruction of positivistic methodologies as a requisite for knowledge-building We believe that linkage encourages students to bring to the practicum knowledge from the classroom, or a specific perspective for assessment

TABLE 2
Linkage Cognitive associations of both student and field instructor to retrieved data and reflective awareness

Psycho-social knowledge Explanatory knowledge, model, or theory for understanding affective, cognitive, and behavioural observations of clients or groups
Interactive knowledge Explanatory knowledge, model, or theory for understanding transactions.
Contextual knowledge. Explanatory knowledge, model, or theory for understanding structural and environmental factors.
Organizational knowledge. Explanatory knowledge, model, or theory for understanding organizational behaviour and how to influence change

of a situation. In some instances there will be a good fit between the philosophical, theoretical, and empirical approaches taught and the practice experience. In others, the lack of congruence will help the student learn that no single approach or formulation applies to a specific situation without considerable custom tailoring. The student can be encouraged to apply new ideas to the current experiences in the practicum.

Assessment, and therefore intervention, must consider not only the client's psycho-social issues, but the helping system itself, as well as societal and organizational biases and blockages. Strategies flow from a full consideration of explanatory theories and remain tentative and uncertain. The ability to tolerate uncertainty resulting from the tentative quality of current theories is a quality required of all social workers Retrieval, reflection, linkage, and a professional response which is then subjected to the relooping process help workers maintain a cautious scepticism. This can lead to rethinking and research that yields new knowledge.

Table 2 outlines the bodies of knowledge that can be scanned by the field instructor and student in order to select those concepts which may be relevant to the practice situation.

Professional Response

Professional response is the selection of a plan that will inform the next encounter with the specific situation. This plan must derive from the preceding process. It is an exercise in 'if this ... then that.' Each situation requires the worker and client to select the issues of highest priority for immediate focus. As the process of relooping occurs, there will be opportunity to respond to other aspects of the information retrieved initially, as well as to re-evaluated and emerging information.

The field instructor, using this part of the loop, grounds the ideas, knowledge, and insights just uncovered through reflection and linkage to develop specific plans and behaviours for dealing with the situation. The field instructor should not move too quickly to case management and response without moving through the previous phases. It may be that several possible theoretical frames have been identified through linkage, each having its unique appropriate intervention. Specialized practice models, such as task-centred, family systems, group, and community development approaches, interpret human behaviour and interpersonal adaptation, and provide social workers with specific techniques to use in professional response.

Through discussion of a variety of perspectives, the student has an opportunity to make comparisons and to anticipate the possible effects of a specific intervention. A response or action is selected, and its effect then becomes the focus of the same process. The use of the ITP Loop Model should facilitate the student's conceptual understanding of the situation, and hence make possible a more informed response to the practice situation as the contact continues If field instructors use the loop after each encounter, the student should feel a growing sense of control over the uncertain elements of practice.

Consideration of all factors inherent in any social work situation conveys to the student the dynamic interrelationship between concepts and action. Integration demands that professional actions be informed by selection of preferred outcomes based on understanding probable consequences on the systems and actors involved. This implies that the student is encouraged to examine possible responses at psycho-social, interactive, contextual, and organizational levels, and to consider the relative effects of actions directed at one, several, or all systems. No single theory or construct is likely to provide a sufficient frame of reference. Selection of knowledge is eclectic and based on developing a preferred outcome, which is then negotiated with the systems involved Because the process is applied to complex human events, it remains tentative and is subject to revision, modification, or even abandonment on the basis of subsequent work. The looping process then returns to retrieval of the effect of the plan or action on the situation, new data are gathered, and the process begins again.

TABLE 3

Professional response: Selection of a plan that will inform the next encounter the student has with this specific situation

---

Psycho-social response:
A plan or action that will respond to the concerns or behaviours identified

Interactive response
A plan or action that will respond to interactive factors identified

Contextual response
A plan or action that will respond to the environmental or structural aspects of the situation. This plan may be for immediate action or part of a long-range strategy

Organizational response:
A plan or action that will respond to the identified organizational issues. This plan may be for immediate action or part of a long-range strategy.

Table 3 outlines the factors that can be scanned by the field instructor and student in order to select a plan which may be relevant to the practice situation.

It is probably practice wisdom that leads social workers to use the ITP loop intuitively, but in many cases with omissions. The steps of retrieval and professional action, for example, are undoubtedly always operative, but we believe that either reflection or linkage may be omitted as practice competence becomes more routine. Since students need to think through their practice responses, they must be encouraged to go through the entire cycle. Both field instructor and student need to take the time to engage in reflection and linkage.

Field instruction can teach an analytic process that begins with a practice act and moves through the loop. The ITP Loop Model provides a structure for the integration of cognitive and affective processes that we believe form the core of social work practice. It permits these two processes to be unhooked and hooked again through a conscious, analytic process. In addition, it will succeed whether one chooses to focus widely on a global problem or concern, or narrowly on a specific episode of student-client communication. For example, it can be used to focus on a single interchange in a family therapy interview; or the focus can be widened to examine a case management problem, or to consider a neighbourhood analysis of significant actors in order to develop an effective strategy for community development.

The loop can be used to teach social work practice at any level of intervention with a variety of populations, purposes, and settings. It can be microscopic or macroscopic, depending on what facts are retrieved. The choice of ends and the degree of magnification depend on the practice activity and the specific intent of the field instructor.

The ITP Loop Model and Your Practice

As we stated earlier, when social workers assume the role of field instructor, they make a transition from practitioner to educator. Social workers ask themselves, 'What do I do? Why do I practice this way? What do I know? What do I believe is important to teach?' The beginning field instructor is a competent practitioner, so that understanding the basis of your own competency is essential to achieving the skill to guide the student through the necessary steps of analytical thinking and practice interventions. Practitioners in all professions recognize that ongoing education is a lifelong process. In fact, many social workers choose to become field instructors as a way to reconnect with the university and learn new social work knowledge. As a field instructor, you may find it helpful to begin by reflecting on your own comfort as a competent practitioner, recognizing areas where you feel uncomfortable and where you feel you have more to learn. The ITP Loop Model can provide a tool to help you identify the assumptions, values, thoughts, and beliefs that underpin the actions you take in professional situations.

Using the ITP loop, retrieve a recent practice experience of yours such as working with a client, supervising staff, or conducting a community activity or a policy and planning activity. Recall your thoughts, feelings, and responses, and subject these elements to critical self-analysis using the loop. Reflect on your subjective beliefs and attitudes that were operating in your actions What aspects of your personality, life experiences, cultural values, and personal world-view were evident in the judgments you made and in your responses? You may find it helpful to scan table 1 and select those elements that are personally relevant to you in thinking about this particular situation. These elements may be universally present in your practice, or they may be stimulated by unique features in your retrieved example. This exercise may confirm what you already know about yourself and the link between your personal self and your professional self, or the exercise may provide new insights. Reflection also focuses on the effectiveness of an interaction and provides the opportunity for you to critically analyse the impact of your professional response.

The next step is linkage, in which you will identify and label the knowledge you use. Articulate for yourself what was done and why it was done. What informed your choice of approach, direction, or response? Did you think about using a specific approach and then reject it for another? What ideas were operating in this decision? In this way, you will begin to articulate the cognitive system of understanding which underpins your practice. Again, scanning table 2 may help you to elucidate the concepts you use in your thinking.

The aim of linkage is not necessarily to discover global or large-scale theory. Rather, the purpose is to uncover the ideas that inform your interventions with the specific situation at hand. The use of knowledge is complex since, as practice situations unfold, social workers find themselves using multiple concepts for understanding and intervening. For example, a wife has requested help with a difficult marriage but says that her husband refuses to accompany her for counselling. You have agreed to see her to focus on how she might engage with her husband about attending joint sessions This is an initial limited goal based on research findings that individual counselling for marital distress is more likely to result in separation or divorce than is couple counselling from the outset. While this is a valid use of general empirically based knowledge, as the work progresses, you and your client realize that her husband will not participate. This is the point at which human complexity demands flexibility and openness in helping the wife set goals and work through the ambivalence that must accompany them. Theoretical knowledge about the dynamics of bonding and separation supports this later shift in intervention.

At this point, you might want to recall a specific intervention from your own work and try to relate it to knowledge that would support that intervention, using the example just presented as a guide. You may recall how your cognitive system has changed over time and remember the influences on the development of your current views of social work. You may recollect the practice assignments, supervisors, workshops, lectures, and readings that you drew upon in the construction of your knowledge base for your practice.

Finally, think about your professional response and examine how systematic you were in integrating the insights uncovered in reflection and linkage. In retrospect, would you describe your actions as 'intuitive'? Through using the looping process, you may have arrived at new insights and ideas that you can use in planning your next encounter with this practice situation.

Reviewing your own practice experience using the loop gives you familiarity with its applicability and flexibility. As a field instructor, you will be better able to teach the loop to the student by engaging in the process of retrieval, reflection, linkage, and professional response with respect to the student's practice. Your new role of educator will involve you in helping the student build and reinforce a level of practice capability that will meet professional standards.

Guidelines for Ethical Practice in Community Organization

Donna Hardina

Community organizers often encounter ethical dilemmas in practice. Most organizers engage on a regular basis with community residents, constituency groups, local institutions, and government decision makers. Consequently, most practice activities occur outside traditional agency settings and are not directly addressed in the Code of Ethics of the National Association of Social Workers. *Although community practice principles such as self-determination, informed consent, and protection of confidentiality are identified in the* Code, *situational factors make their application different than in direct practice. This article identifies the values inherent in community practice, describes ethical issues encountered by organizers, and examines tools available to organizers for resolving common ethical dilemmas.*

Key words: *community organization; macro practice; social change; social work ethics; values*

Social work is built around an ethical code that makes it distinct from other professions. The *Code of Ethics of the National Association of Social Workers* (2000) primarily focuses on the context of clinical practice with individuals. The *Code* does not cover many of the practice situations a typical community organizer can encounter (Reisch & Lowe, 2000). For example, social action organizing often involves confrontation tactics. Picketing, demonstrations, strikes, and boycotts can be potentially harmful to members of the target group, causing humiliation, social ostracism, or loss of employment (Fisher, 1994).

Little discussion has taken place in schools of social work about the ethics of using such tactics. There are no specific provisions in the NASW *Code* that help the organizer sort out these "means versus ends" dilemmas (Reisch & Lowe, 2000). Consequently, efforts to resolve ethical dilemmas are made on a case-by-case basis (Hardcastle, Wenocur, & Powers, 1997). This can cause confusion for entry-level social workers in community practice.

In this article I explore ethical issues inherent in community organization practice and identify the values inherent in the ethical dilemmas faced by social workers who engage in community practice. Concepts such as "informed consent" and "conflict of interest" as they apply to community work are discussed. In addition, I discuss the ethical implications of using confrontation tactics. Ethical frameworks that can be used in community practice and resources available to help social workers resolve ethical dilemmas that occur in community practice are described.

Basic Community Organization Values

Lowenberg and Dolgoff (1996) distinguished between values and ethics (Hardina, 2002). *Values* are statements of an ideal that we try to achieve, whereas *ethics* offer us directives for action derived from the desired outcomes. The

CCC Code: 0037-8046/04 $3.00 © 2004 National Association of Social Workers, Inc.

NASW *Code of Ethics* identifies a number of values, such as self-determination, protection of confidentiality, equal distribution of resources, and promotion of cultural diversity in service provision that social workers must uphold. Ethical practices, most often activities that pertain to clinical work with individuals, are also identified in the *Code*. However, community organization can be viewed as a unique field of practice requiring an ethical code and a theoretical framework that commits the organizer to the struggle for social justice (Reamer, 1999). Such a commitment requires that an organizer fight to improve economic conditions and civil rights for members of marginalized groups (Rivera & Erlich, 1998). Although the NASW *Code of Ethics* is explicit about the responsibility of social workers to promote social justice (NASW, 2000, Standards 6.01 and 6.03), it does not specify actions that social workers must take to achieve it (Bull, 1989).

The NASW *Code of Ethics* (2000) primarily focuses on the context of working in or managing a social services agency. The chief limitation of the NASW *Code* for organizers is that most of their work takes place in a context outside of the agency in collaboration or conflict with individuals, small groups, and organizations. Although the *Code*'s ethical principles should be followed by all social workers, it does not begin to cover many of the practice situations a typical organizer may encounter (Hardina, 2002). Ethical practice in community work differs from clinical practice in that

- social transformation is the primary goal of the intervention.
- "clients" are primarily constituency group members, residents of target communities, and members of marginalized populations. In many instances, organizers do not have direct contact with all members of the client group. It should be noted that organizers often reject the use of the term "client," believing that it implies dependence on the social worker (Cohen, 1998).
- both the social worker and the program constituents must develop a critical consciousness about social and economic conditions that contribute to the marginalization of oppressed groups (Freire, 1970; Gutierrez & Alvarez, 2000). Although the empowerment model, the structural approach, and feminist practice incorporate principles associated with social transformation, most interventions with individuals, families, and groups do not require that participants critically examine economic and social factors that are associated with individual problems (Gutierrez, Parsons, & Cox, 1998).
- most interventions take place in partnership with constituency group members. In some situations, the group serves as the organizer's employer (Rivera & Erlich, 1998). Constituent self-determination is one of the primary objectives of community practice. Consequently, it is expected that constituents and organizers engage in mutual learning and dialogue to determine the best method of intervention (Freire, 1970; Gutierrez & Alvarez, 2000).
- the organizer may be a member of the community in which he or she is working. The organizer may be a resident of a geographic community or political district in which he or she is assigned. In other situations, the organizer may identify with or be a member of a specific demographic group (for example, an ethnic group or people with disabilities) that serves as the constituency base for the organizing effort (Delgado, 1997).
- ethical conduct is often viewed as situational, requiring that the organizer assess the seriousness of the issue, the accessibility of the decision makers, and possible risks before deciding on the use of tactics (Netting, Kettner, & McMurty, 1993; Warren, 1971).

Community Organization and Ethical Practices

The types of interventions used by the organizer, the client groups involved, the targets of the social change efforts, and the urgency of the issues involved create a number of situations that are not adequately covered by the NASW *Code of Ethics* (Warren, 1971). The *Code* is inadequate to address ethical concerns for organizers involving conflicts of interest associated with financial transactions and dual relationships with community residents. Additional areas of concern include the choice of tactics used by the organizer, situations in which the organizer's values conflict with the preferences of constituents or employers, and the concept of informed consent.

Conflict of Interest

Organizers are likely to experience a number of conflicts of interest. Many of these conflicts may occur in a slightly different context than those identified in the *Code of Ethics*. Conflicts in community practice can occur because of the nature of the interpersonal dynamics involved in organizing (often focusing on exchange of information and goods and services) and the need to mobilize and recruit participants. Problems also occur because an organizer must find appropriate mechanisms to gather information about the community and its culture. Situations in which the organizer is a member of the community he or she serves are also problematic.

Membership in the Target Community. One of the more difficult issues in community organization practice among social workers is that many organizers are members of the community they seek to organize. In many instances, advocacy organizations hire organizers who are of the same culture, gender, or gender orientation as the geographic or demographic group the organization serves. The preference for organizers who personally identify with the target community is based on the premise that an organizer must be culturally competent and have a personal understanding of the political oppression experienced in marginalized communities (Delgado, 1997). Rivera and Erlich (1998) argued that only organizers who are of the same ethnicity as constituents should attempt to organize in communities of color. Much of the practice literature, however, is premised on the belief that cultural competence can be acquired by organizers who incorporate many of the principles articulated by Freire (1970) in the organizing process: partnership with constituents, ongoing dialogue, and mutual learning (Gutierrez & Alvarez, 2000).

Membership or identification with the target community may have disadvantages as well as advantages. For example, an organizer who lives in the target geographic community may find that intervention strategies can adversely affect friends, relatives, and neighbors. An organizer charged with coordinating a boycott of neighborhood business could experience difficulty if a cousin's store was to be included in the boycott. In addition, an organizer who is part of the same marginalized population as his or her constituents may not be able to remain neutral during discussions of appropriate strategies and tactics. For example, an organizer who is a member of the lesbian, gay, bisexual, and transgender community may support a recommendation to "out" a gay politician, because of his or her own experience of oppression rather than examine the ethical implications of such an action. Consequently, organizers working within their own culture or demographic group may need to carefully weigh their personal goals and values with ethical considerations when examining appropriate tactical options.

Financial Conflict of Interest. Bringing constituents and institutions together often requires the development of social networks and the exchange of information, goods, and services. Consequently, organizers may patronize neighborhood businesses to acquire information about the community or to recruit volunteers. Delgado (1996) has written extensively about how small businesses such as grocery stores and beauty parlors play key roles in providing assistance and emotional support to residents of low-income communities. Conceivably, patronizing some businesses over others may generate conflicts of interest and make it difficult for the organizer to bring additional businesses or groups into the organizing process. Organizers may also encounter ethical dilemmas when they invest money in community businesses. Tactical decisions may be required that can help or hinder the organizer's investments (Reamer, 2003). Although most community organization work does not involve fees for services, organizers working as consultants to community groups or paid staff on political campaigns may find that certain recommendations made to employers may generate financial benefits for the consultant while putting the organization at financial risk. In such circumstances, the organizer must weigh personal interests with potential positive and negative outcomes for the organization.

Friendships with Constituents. Friendships with members of the constituency group often are essential to the organizing effort, especially when the organizer needs to acquire knowledge about the culture and lifestyle of community members (Congress, 1996; Hardina, 2002; Rivera & Erlich, 1998). Going to birthday parties, weddings, and block parties is an essential part of the organizer's role. Establishing trusting relationships with volunteers is of utmost importance. The organizer should use a combination of practice experience, guidance from peers and supervisors, and knowledge of the *Code of Ethics* to establish appropriate boundaries with constituents.

Sexual Relationships. One of the most problematic issues for an organizer is determining appropriate personal boundaries about sexual relationships. If the community is one's client, is the organizer prohibited from engaging in an intimate relationship with all community members? Obviously, such a prohibition is unfeasible (Hardina, 2002). Yet, where should organizers draw appropriate boundaries for friendships and dating situations?

The *Code of Ethics* makes it very clear that relationships with current clients, workplace subordinates, and students are prohibited (Reamer, 1999). However, organizers should add board members, employers, and targets (that is, individual decision makers and their associates) to this list (Hardina, 2002). Conflicts of interest are involved that interfere with performance evaluations and the success of organizing efforts. Most volunteers and constituents involved in organizing campaigns are also off-limits. Robinson and Reeser (2000) argued that it is the practitioner's responsibility to establish clear boundaries with constituents. It is especially important because the organizer, when recruiting participants, is generally the individual who has power in the relationship by virtue of professional status, knowledge, and possession of sensitive information. Often an organizer who works with members of marginalized groups also has power by virtue of his or her socioeconomic status, ethnicity, or gender (Rivera & Erlich, 1998). In addition, establishing intimate relationships with some constituents can lead to charges of exploitation or harassment (NASW, 2000, Sect. 1.09, 1.10, 1.11, 2.07, and 2.08). This is particularly of concern when the volunteer does not genuinely support the cause or when organizing activities may place the volunteer at risk (such as arrest or losing a job).

Choice of Tactics

Tactical methods are short-term actions used to carry out strategic interventions (Mondros & Wilson, 1994). Because of the urgency of the issue or time constraints, some tactical methods may violate social norms or put constituents and members of opposition groups at risk (Warren, 1971). Consequently, organizers must carefully weigh tactical outcomes in terms of costs and benefits as well as the unintended consequences of these methods. Two types of activities that are especially problematic for organizers involve the use of confrontational tactics and potentially sacrificing short-term benefits for more substantive changes in social policies or legislation.

Use of Confrontation Tactics. Alinsky (1971) argued that the "ends justify the means." He believed that any tactic is appropriate if it allows organizers to be successful in fighting for a cause (Hardina, 2002). For example, on a number of occasions, Alinksy brought African American volunteers into white communities and institutions to confront and frighten members of elite groups engaged in harmful or exclusionary practices (Fisher, 1994). Tactics such as these may cause humiliation, social ostracism, or loss of employment and income for the targets of the social change activity as well as participants in the action.

One of the primary ethical dilemmas faced by organizers is whether the ends of intended outcomes always justify the means or tactics used to achieve them (Reisch & Lowe, 2000). Hardina (2000) surveyed community organization instructors in schools of social work and asked them to identify tactics they felt were unethical. Respondents identified the following unethical tactics "violence, deceit, and causing personal degradation or harm" (p. 13). Other unethical tactics identified included lying or putting people at risk without adequately informing them of the consequences (Hardina, 2002).

In community organization, unintended violence can occur in relation to social change–related actions (for example, strikes, boycotts, and demonstrations). In addition, some organizers believe that the seriousness of the issue—risk of death or injury to innocent populations—could require the escalation of confrontation tactics or civil disobedience (Hardina, 2002). For example, one respondent in Hardina's (2000) study of tactical decision making described the situation in which he found the following tactics unethical:

> Violence, terrorism, destruction of property, lying, stealing (although I would have used any and all of these against the Nazis). I would have no problem with militant direct action, which is nonviolent, but against the law. (p. 13)

Long-Term versus Short-Term Gains. Organizers also confront situations in which short-term help for individuals is sacrificed for long-term goals (Bailey & Brake, 1975). For example, we may decline to help a number of individuals replace stolen food stamp benefits for the preceding month rather than asking them to participate in a class action suit that challenges the way food stamps are allocated and delivered to participants. In such cases, the immediate well-being of the individual is sacrificed for the greater good. The principle of self-determination identified in the NASW *Code* requires that constituents be fully informed and involved in making such decisions (Hardina, 2002). Helping constituents acquire resources from other service providers can soften short-term sacrifices.

Value Conflict

An issue specific to organizing has to do with whether the organizer engages in social action at odds with his or her own values (Hardina, 2002). If we are to promote self-determination and empowerment, should not the organizer follow all directives given by constituency group members? Fisher (1994), in *Let the People Decide*, described Alinsky's efforts to organize cross-culturally in the "back of the yards" neighborhood in Chicago. Recruitment of traditional community leaders and institutions to head the organizing process resulted in the adoption of conservative politics (and a failure to support integration efforts) by the organization. A similar dilemma might occur for an organizer in situations where residents decide to organize against the location of a group home or halfway house in their neighborhood. Organizers need to weigh specific ethical values (such as self-determination and social justice) and assess personal risks and benefits before taking action to resolve such conflicts. For example, is the loss of one's job the potential price for challenging one's employer? Can or should the organizer live with the ethical dilemma involved in following through with employer or constituent demands for actions that conflict with his or her own professional values?

Informed Consent

Informed consent in clinical practice often requires that clients sign written statements that list the benefits and risks associated with specific interventions. Organizers generally dispense with written consent forms. It is assumed that they will be explicit with constituents about the consequences of participation in organizing efforts. However, without written notices there are limited ways to ensure that consent has been obtained (Lowenberg & Dolgoff, 1996). We may assume that lack of a verbal response to a request for action implies consent, when in fact this is not the case (Hardina, 2002). People can decide to withdraw consent in risky situations simply by failing to act or attend certain events. One procedure used by organizers to obtain consent involves a meeting in which all members debate risks and benefits of the proposed action and attempt to reach a consensus on the tactics to be used (Lee, 1986). This procedure is probably the best method of establishing that the majority of participants support the proposed action. However, this process is also time consuming; it may not always be possible to achieve a consensus or to consult with all potential participants before the action takes place. In any case, constituents should be fully informed about the consequences of their actions, especially when personal sacrifices (such as job loss, arrest, or social stigma) are great.

Tools for Making Ethical Decisions in Practice

Although some of the principles in the NASW *Code* can be modified for use in community organization, social workers need a process for resolving ethical dilemmas encountered in practice. According to Hardcastle and colleagues (1997), ethical dilemmas occur when "ethical guidelines do not give clear directions or indicate clearly which ethical imperative to follow" (p. 22). Dilemmas must be linked to specific outcomes that the organizer hopes to achieve (Rothman, 1998). The organizer can use prevailing theories to sort out ethical dilemmas and establish appropriate goals (Hardina, 2002). Theories may be deontological, involving "good" or "right" motives or teleological, involving good or right outcomes to be achieved by the social change effort in question (Rothman).

Adherents of the deontological perspective believe that certain actions must always be taken as a matter of principle (Reamer, 1998). For example, a deontologist would maintain that the principle of self-determination must always be followed, even when time, resources, and limited access to information do not permit full consultation with constituents. Adherence to such a principle may have important implications. If an organizer maintains that all constituents must be consulted before a government grant is accepted, the organization may lose a source of funds critical for the immediate fiscal stability of the organization (Hardina, 2002).

Alternatively, a teleological perspective requires that the action produce the greatest good for individuals or society as a whole. One teleological approach, utilitarianism, mandates that all ethical decisions produce the greatest good for the greatest number (Lowenberg & Dolgoff, 1996). A teleologist could conceivably argue that "mudslinging" in a political campaign is appropriate if it results in the election of a public official who supports progressive or social work–related causes (Hardina, 2002).

Selecting one overall approach to ethical decision making when dealing with complex situations may prove confusing for community practitioners. Several tools or frameworks help organizers choose between these two approaches. These tools include

- using a decision-making framework derived from the NASW *Code of Ethics*.
- using a decision-making framework developed for the use of community practitioners in social work.

The NASW *Code of Ethics*

Some ethical dilemmas faced by social workers in community practice can be addressed directly using the principles in the NASW *Code of Ethics* (Hardina, 2002). Lowenberg and Dolgoff (1996) developed an Ethical Rules Screen. Lowenberg and Dolgoff advise the social worker to determine whether principles in the *Code* apply to the ethical dilemma examined. If the situation is not identified in the *Code* or if two or more ethical principles conflict, the Ethical Rules Screen should be applied. The principles in the Screen are to be applied in descending order:

Principle No. 1 Protection of Life
Principle No. 2 Equality and Inequality
Principle No. 3 Autonomy and Freedom
Principle No. 4 Least Harm
Principle No. 5 Quality of Life
Principle No. 6 Privacy and Confidentiality
Principle No. 7 Truthfulness and Full Disclosure (p. 63).

In addition to these principles, Lowenberg and Dolgoff (1996) recommended that the worker examine the impact of the decision on the recipient of the action and assess whether she or he can explain the rationale behind the decision to others (Hardina, 2002). The organizer must determine who is the primary recipient of his or her actions. Is the constituent or client an individual, a group of people, or society in general? Also problematic are situations in which the organizer's actions may benefit members of one marginalized group while putting another oppressed group at risk. For example, locating a homeless shelter in an area with a large transient population may seem to be a good solution to a difficult social problem. However, if the site is adjacent to an elementary school (and parents have reason to be concerned about substance abuse and prostitution-related activities), the proposed solution may put small children at risk.

The chief advantage of Lowenberg and Dolgoff's (1996) Ethical Rule Screen is that it helps social workers use a problem-solving approach to ethical decision making and provides a values framework, explicitly from the *Code of Ethics*. In situations in which ethical values may conflict with one another, social workers need to identify their own values and assess the importance of those values vis-à-vis others. Other ethical decision-making frameworks developed for social workers include Reamer's (1999), Robinson and Reeser's (2000), and Parsons' (2001).

An Ethical Decision-Making Framework for Organizers

Reisch and Lowe (2000) developed a series of steps to help community organizers who are social workers resolve ethical dilemmas:

- Identify the ethical principles that apply to the situation at hand.
- Collect additional information necessary to examine the ethical dilemma in question.
- Identify the relevant ethical values and/or rules that apply to the ethical problem.
- Identify any potential conflicts of interest and the people who are likely to benefit from such conflict.
- Identify appropriate ethical rules and rank order them in terms of importance.
- Determine the consequences of applying different ethical rules or ranking these rules differently (p. 26).

Because this decision-making model allows the organizer flexibility in choosing and prioritizing ethical rules, different organizers achieve different outcomes (Hardina, 2002). Reisch and Lowe (2000) also noted that some situations that appear to contain ethical dilemmas for the organizer are actually problems that should be addressed by others (for example, constituency group members or targets). Consequently, before confronting the dilemma in question, the organizer must determine whether he or she is responsible for handling the problem.

Constructing Your Own Ethics Model

One of the advantages of the Reisch and Lowe (2000) problem-solving approach is that it allows the organizer to sort out the implications of actions for the various parties involved, including implications for the organizer. The other advantage of this model is that it can be used in conjunction with basic principles derived from the *Code of Ethics* as identified in the Lowenberg and Dolgoff (1996) Ethical Rule Screen. Organizers can add other principles (such as mutual learning and empowerment) to develop a personal ethical framework that can be used effectively in community practice. Ethical principles may be chosen that reflect the organizer's own values, the seriousness of the issue addressed, and the preferences and culture of the participants. For example, an organizer fighting the location of a toxic waste dump in a Southeast Asian community may be faced with an ethical dilemma when clan leaders have decided to support the facility because it will provide jobs for community residents. Principles of importance to the community such as respect for one's elders should be incorporated into the organizer's decision-making framework

The model can also be configured to include additional safeguards that can enhance the decision-making process (see Figure 1). One of the first steps an organizer should take in addressing an ethical dilemma is to determine whether he or she should address the issue alone or whether the issue needs to be handled through dialogue with constituents or addressed by other individuals

Figure 1

Steps for Resolving Ethical Dilemmas

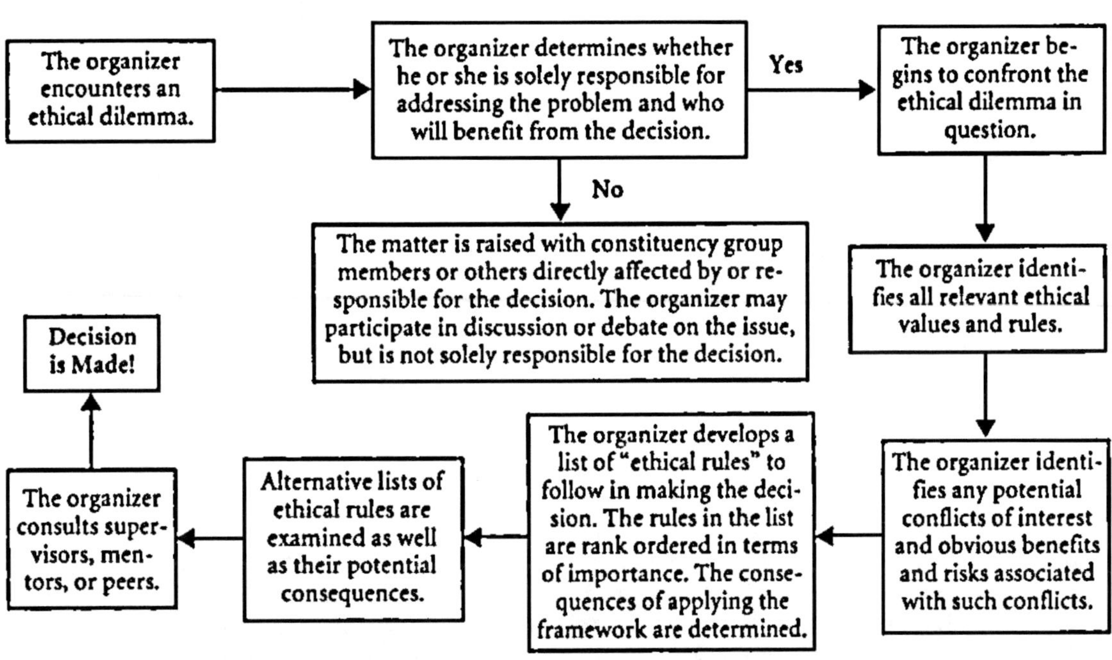

NOTE: Adapted from Reisch, M., & Lowe, J. I. (2000). "Of means and ends" revisited: Teaching ethical community organizing in an unethical society. *Journal of Community Practice, 7*(1), 19–38.

involved in the organizing process. If the organizer is responsible for addressing the issue, he or she can begin to identify the ethical dilemma in question, the ethical rules that may apply, and possible conflicts of interests he or she may encounter. The organizer should then construct a list of ethical principles to be followed in the decision-making process and rank them in order of importance. The consequences of applying this framework to the ethical dilemma should also be examined. As an additional safeguard, the organizer should examine the consequences of applying a different set of principles or rank ordering the principles differently when making a final decision.

A problem-solving approach for ethical decision making should include consultation. An organizer should not try to resolve ethical dilemmas alone in situations that involve constituents or employers (especially when the action could place constituents at risk). In addition to constituency group members, appropriate people to consult in ethical decision making include peers, supervisory staff, and organization board members. Working organizers have the experience and vision to analyze the potential impact of ethical decisions. Members of the organizer's employing organization can give insight into the potential legal implications and political consequences associated with some decisions (Tropman, 1997). Many practicing organizers find mentors (often staff from other agencies or community activists) who help them obtain the skills necessary to become social change agents (Kaminski, Kaufman, Graubarth, & Robins, 2000). NASW can provide resources for organizers involved in organizing for better working conditions or to provide better services for clients or constituents. Other professional organizations include the Association for Community Organization and Social Administration and the (non–social work-related) National Organizer's Alliance. COMM-ORG, an online organization, also provides information and support for organizers.

This model can be easily applied to situations that are likely to be encountered during community organization practice. For example, an organizer has a paid position as a field coordinator for a candidate for state governor. Recent polls have revealed that the candidate is losing 53 percent to 47 percent. The candidate's opponent has pledged to drastically cut welfare benefits for most welfare recipients. The organizer is worried that this legislation could cause substantial harm, increasing homelessness, hunger, and risk of serious health problems for many low-income families. Both candidates have pledged to refrain from negative campaign advertising. The organizer receives information about the opposition candidate from a source that has asked that his confidentiality be protected. He has given the organizer detailed proof that the candidate's opponent has purchased cocaine recently from street dealers. Releasing the information to the public may pose a serious risk for the health and well-being of the source. What does the organizer do with this information? Does he or she

- inform the candidate and the campaign manager? Argue that the release of this information to the press would ensure a victory for the candidate?
- inform the candidate and the campaign manager? Argue that this information should be turned over to the opposition candidate?
- design an "ad" campaign that uses this information to discredit the opponent? Convince the candidate that such ads are critical to the success of his campaign?
- do nothing? Put the documentation through the office shredder?

An ethical framework for this practice situation might include the following principles:

- protection of life
- privacy and confidentiality
- promoting civil discourse or refraining from mudslinging in the campaign.

If the organizer takes a teleological approach, seeking to achieve the greatest good for the greatest number, he or she might argue that protection of the lives of low-income families should be the principle given highest priority. Of less importance would be the principles associated with the candidates' pledge to refrain from negative campaigning or protecting the confidentiality of the individual who provided the information.

Alternatively, the organizer using a deontological approach would argue that certain actions are either right or wrong. In this instance, the principles associated with the candidates' pledge to refrain from negative campaigning and protecting the confidentiality of the information source would be ranked highest on the list of ethical principles. However, it should be noted that the problem-solving model presented in this article also requires the organizer to consider whether he or she should resolve the ethical dilemma alone or consult with peers and supervisors. The possible consequences of any decisions considered must also be explored. In this instance, can the organizer be sure that low-income people will suffer if the opposition candidate is elected? What are the possible consequences for the informant if his or her identity becomes known?

Conclusion

Community organization practice is a unique form of social work. Basic practice methods draw on some of the sample principles as other practice modalities. However, much of the work of community organizers takes place outside agency settings and involves using power and influence to achieve social change. Consequently, organizers need adequate tools to resolve ethical dilemmas they encounter in practice.

Recently, community organization as a field of practice has come under pressure to use methods and practices consistent with other areas in social work. Many schools of social work have adopted generalist or multisystems models of practice. Graduates are expected to intervene in diverse systems depending on situational factors (Ryan, DeMasi, Heinz, Jacobson, & Ohmer, 2000). Also of concern is that new community practitioners are less likely to be professional social workers and more likely to be recruited from the ranks of urban planners or public health specialists. Such practitioners are not well equipped to focus on both individual needs and community systems. Consequently, we must make sure that instruction in community organization practice continues to be offered in schools of social work. To remain a vital part of the social work curriculum, we must continue to explore methods for integrating micro and macro practice.

Discussion about how community organization "fits" in the framework of ethical practice is now more critical than ever. The Association of Social Work Boards (ASWB) recently proposed that state legislatures adopt a "Model Social Work Practice Act," which would require that all social workers, not just mental health clinicians, be licensed. The act would apply to any bachelor's or master's degree graduate from a school of social work. State licensing boards would design standardized tests for recent graduates and set continuing education requirements. In addition, the boards would be able to terminate licenses for any individual convicted of a minor felony or found not to be of "good moral character" (ASWB, 2002). Such state regulation of social work practice could lead to the filing of disciplinary action against any social worker engaged in social change activities, especially if such activity involves confrontation with politically powerful individuals.

Consequently, if we are to sustain social work's commitment to social justice, we must strengthen community organization practice. Although the literature describes community organization values in detail, few resources are available for identifying practice skills (Johnson, 1996). One of the more logical steps would seem to be that we better articulate the knowledge base and skills associated with community practice and develop appropriate curriculum (Gamble, Shaffer, & Weil, 1994). We must develop explicit guides and frameworks for the ethical practice of community organization. Organizers should conduct research oriented toward finding out how community organization values, ethics, knowledge, and skills are transmitted to workers in agency settings and in social change organizations. ■

References

Alinsky, S. (1971). *Rules for radicals.* New York: Vintage Books.

Association of Social Work Boards. (2002). *Model social work practice act.* Retrieved October 15, 2002, from http://www.aswb.org/Model_law.pdf

Bailey, R., & Brake, M. (1975). *Radical social work.* London: Routlege & Kegan Paul.

Bull, D. (1989). The social worker's advocacy role: A British quest for a Canadian perspective. *Canadian Social Work Review, 6,* 49–68.

Cohen, M. (1998). Perceptions of power in client/worker relationships. *Families in Society, 79,* 433–443.

Congress, E. (1996). Dual relationships in academia: Dilemmas for social work educators. *Journal of Social Work Education, 32,* 329–338.

Delgado, G. (1997). *Beyond the politics of place: New directions in community organizing.* Berkeley, CA: Chardon.

Delgado, M. (1996). Puerto Rican food establishments as social service organizations: Results of an asset assessment. *Journal of Community Practice, 3*(2), 57–78.

Fisher, R. (1994). *Let the people decide* (updated ed.). New York: Twayne.

Freire, P. (1970). *Pedagogy of the oppressed.* New York: Continuum Books.

Gamble, D., Shaffer, G., & Weil, M. (1994). Assessing the integrity of community organization and administration content in field practice. *Journal of Community Practice, 1*(3), 73–92.
Gutierrez, L., & Alvarez, A. (2000). Educating students for multicultural community practice. *Journal of Community Practice, 7*(1), 39–56.
Gutierrez, L., Parsons, R., & Cox, E. (1998). *Empowerment in social work practice: A source book.* Pacific Grove, CA: Brooks/Cole.
Hardcastle, D., Wenocur, S., & Powers, P. (1997). *Community practice: Theories and skills for social workers.* New York: Oxford University Press.
Hardina, D. (2000). Models and tactics taught in community organization courses: Findings from a survey of practice instructors. *Journal of Community Practice, 7*(1), 5–18.
Hardina, D. (2002). *Analytical skills for community organization practice.* New York: Columbia University Press.
Johnson, A. (1996). The revitalization of community practice: Characteristics, competencies, and curricula for community-based services. *Journal of Community Practice, 5*(3), 37–62.
Kaminski, M., Kaufman, J. S., Graubarth, R., & Robins, T. G. (2000). How do people become empowered? A case study of union activism. *Human Relations, 53,* 53–63.
Lee, B. (1986). *Pragmatics of community organization.* Mississauga, Ontario: Common Act Press.
Lowenberg, F., & Dolgoff, R. (1996). *Ethical decisions for social work practice* (5th ed.). Itasca, IL: F. E. Peacock.
Mondros, J., & Wilson, S. (1994). *Organizing for power and empowerment.* New York: Columbia University Press.
National Association of Social Workers. (2000). *Code of ethics of the National Association of Social Workers.* Washington, DC: Author.
Netting, E., Kettner, P., & McMurty, S. (1993). *Social work macro practice.* New York: Longman.
Parsons, R. (2001). *The ethics of professional practice.* Boston: Allyn & Bacon.
Reamer, F. G. (1998). *Ethical standards in social work* (2nd ed.). Washington, DC: NASW Press.
Reamer, F. G. (1999). *Social work values and ethics.* New York: Columbia University Press.
Reamer, F. G. (2003). Boundary issues in social work: Managing dual relationships. *Social Work, 48,* 121–133.
Reisch, M., & Lowe, J. I. (2000). "Of means and ends" revisited: Teaching ethical community organizing in an unethical society. *Journal of Community Practice, 7*(1), 19–38.
Rivera, F., & Erlich, J. (1998). *Community organizing in a diverse society* (3rd ed.). Boston: Allyn & Bacon.
Robinson, W., & Reeser, L. (2000). *Ethical decision making in social work.* Boston: Allyn & Bacon.
Rothman, J. C. (1998). *From the front lines: Student cases in social work ethics.* Needham Heights, MA: Allyn & Bacon.
Ryan, W., DeMasi, K., Heinz, P., Jacobson, W., & Ohmer, M. (2000). *Aligning education and practice: Challenges and opportunities in social work education for community-centered practice.* Milwaukee: Alliance for Children and Families.
Tropman, J. E. (1997). *Successful community leadership: A skills guide for volunteers and professionals.* Washington, DC: NASW Press.
Warren, R. (1971). Types of purposive social change at the community level. In R. Warren (Ed.), *Truth, love, and social change* (pp. 134–149). Chicago: Rand McNally.

Donna Hardina, PhD, is professor, Department of Social Work Education, California State University, Fresno, 5310 Campus Drive, Fresno, CA 93740; e-mail: donna_hardina@csufresno.edu. An earlier version of this article was presented at the Annual Program Meeting of the Council on Social Work Education, March 2001, Dallas.

Original manuscript received November 18, 2002
Final revision received July 16, 2003
Accepted November 18, 2003

Journal of Progressive Human Services, 21:32–44, 2010

ISSN: 1042-8232 print/1540-7616 online
DOI: 10.1080/10428231003781774

The Social Construction of Social Work Ethics: Politicizing and Broadening the Lens

MERLINDA WEINBERG
School of Social Work, Dalhousie University, Halifax, Nova Scotia, Canada

Structural barriers and the intrinsic paradoxes of practice often lead to a discrepancy between what a social worker would like to do and what that individual actually implements, resulting in ethical tensions. However, the canonical approach to ethics has had a narrow perspective on what constitutes ethics and has tended to treat these issues as peripheral rather than central to the social construction of ethics. This essay provides an explanation of how the construction of ethics evolved and what interests are served by this viewpoint, thereby illuminating the political ramifications of the current social construction. The author suggests ways to broaden the lens of focus.

KEYWORDS ethics, social construction, structure, paradox, history

In social work, at times there is a discrepancy between what a worker would prefer to do ethically and that individual's ability to actualize those preferences in practice (Weinberg, 2007). Practitioners express ethical tension about these incongruities, which are commonly caused by the structural obstacles or the inherent paradoxes that workers encounter in their practice. *Structure* refers to "social regularities and objective patterns external to individual action, intentions, and meanings, and not reducible to the sum of those meanings or actions" (Kondrat, 2002), namely, broad institutional and societal patterns. As examples, stresses emerge from insufficient resources, problematic institutional policies and legal requirements, scarce organizational supports, cost containments, inadequate staffing, frequent reorganizations, and the intense work pace (Aronson & Sammon, 2000; Baines, 2007a,b; Healy, 2000; Smith, 2007). In a 2008 National Association of Social Work study, the greatest stressors for professional social workers were identified as the lack of time to do

Address correspondence to Merlinda Weinberg, School of Social Work, Dalhousie University, 6414 Coburg, Halifax, Nova Scotia, B3H 3J5, Canada. E-mail: merlinda.weinberg@dal.ca the job (31%) and workloads (25%) (Arrington, 2008). At the 2008 Nova Scotia Association of Social Workers' Annual Meeting, the entire focus of the meeting was on ethics, and several speakers addressed issues of expanding needs combined with shrinking resources (Donovan, 2008; Jensen, 2008; Kirby, 2008; Weinberg, 2008c). In a qualitative study, a worker identified that she had $50 a month to distribute to an entire caseload of young new mothers who were living on the streets (Weinberg, 2004a). When a package of diapers costs anywhere from $20 to $30, and one can of powered formula costs a minimum of $15, no matter how conscientiously that worker distributes the discretionary money, there will be a significant shortage, and she will be in the unenviable position of having to determine between the have-nots and the more severely impacted have-nots to determine whom should receive those inadequate funds. When an income assistance worker has 200 people in her caseload (Weinberg, 2008a), how can she behave in a way consistent with her conscience, given the improbability of satisfactorily addressing the needs of that number of service users? In a mixed-methods study, Lonne, McDonald, and Fox (2004) explored the extent to which restructured service delivery was affecting ethical practice. They determined that market-based reforms were having an "often-understated negative effect on ethical practice" (p. 345). Why are those effects often understated? This article looks at how the social construction of ethics contributes to that lack of acknowledgment.

Along with the structural barriers that impinge on ethics, social workers inhabit a world of paradox and are inescapably engaged in conflicting social processes. One paradox is the understanding of the helping profession as involving principled behavior aimed at liberatory activity for service users, and at the same time, workers are members of institutional regimes that require elements of moral regulation. Individuals with expertise have an allegiance to both the political powers that granted them the title of expert and also to the individuals they are authorized to help (Rose & Miller, 1992). The most obvious example of this is the role of Children's Aid workers who, despite obligations to support parents, at times must remove the children from the care of these parents, in part because of workers' mandates to act as agents of the state. Besides the commitment to two opposing actors in society, another component of this conundrum is that the "client" in social work is commonly more than one individual, and each has differing and, at times, conflicting needs (Weinberg, 2004b, 2005a). Take, for example, a mother and child, in a case of child welfare. Protecting a baby because of apprehension may ultimately be positive for the child (although not always) but not constructive for the mother deprived of her child. Consequently, regardless of the "goodness" of the stances taken, harms may be attached (Orlie 1997; Weinberg, 2006), making context, history, and contingent factors essential components when addressing the implementation of ethical decision making (Rossiter, Prilleltensky, & Walsh-Bowers, 2000).

Yet there is a curious theoretical lag in the field of ethics in social work. Although resource limitations and structural dimensions are identified even in traditional approaches (Reamer, 1990, 2006), these issues are often seen as peripheral rather than central in the exploration of ethics in practice. The canonical approach has focused primarily on the one-to-one relationship, and a theoretical-juridical model is taken (Walker, 1998), one that prescribes the correct conduct a practitioner should undertake with clients. This is usually done through a code of ethics, the application of ideals laid out as a series of abstract, universally applicable principles. It is assumed that by applying the code in a prescriptive, linear fashion, in combination with good decision making (Congress, 2000) and a method for tracking harms (Robison & Reeser, 2000), a worker will be able to avoid ethical breaches. Banks (2006) suggests that in the past, the focus of professional ethics has been on "developing lists of principles and how to handle conflict between principles" (p. xiii). The influences of history and the contexts in which ethical dilemmas occur have been secondary. When workers struggle with issues that transcend their interpersonal relationships with service users, they commonly view these struggles as idiosyncratic or outside the lens of ethics. The problem with this perspective on ethics is it tends to see politics as the culprit and the solutions as being beyond the purview of individual practitioners. In one qualitative study, a worker said that fighting structures in her agency with which she disagreed went beyond her responsibility, and that battle was not identified in ethical terms (Weinberg, 2007). When broader solutions are sought, the field is usually based on the premise that the current social arrangements are equitable and that the answers lie more in tinkering with societal structures than in wholesale change. Writing a damning critique of the 2005 Canadian Association of Social Work code of ethics, Mullaly proposes that it "reflects a 'liberal-humanist' approach to social work that seeks to comfort victims of social problems, rather than a critical approach that seeks fundamental social change" (2007, p. 51).

Also, workers' own culpability in the development of those structures may be omitted. For instance, an agency whose mandate is to serve individuals with mental illness contributes to what is taken to be normative behavior and what is framed as ill. Even the construction of mental illness as an illness, rather than, for example, as a gift from the gods or as evil, results in the development of the structures of social science and social services. Each time a worker makes a determination of mental illness, she participates in development of those structures. Who is an insider and who is deviant are also defined, and those definitions reinforce who has the power to make those determinations.

Banks (2006) argues that "if we accept the embeddedness of ethics . . . in social practices, then it is important to study how certain ethical beliefs and qualities of character are constructed and performed" (p. xv). Yet the emphasis in social work ethics is narrowly constructed. When practitioners are so clearly affected by broader issues and the intrinsic paradoxes of the work, why is that the case?

WHAT EXPLAINS THIS SOCIAL CONSTRUCTION OF ETHICS IN THE PROFESSION?

The History of the Profession of Social Work

The history of social work contributes to the constricted social construction of ethics as existing primarily between worker and client, outside of wider structural influences and the inherent contradictions of practice. In the early 1900s, the intransigence of problems in the cities provided a path for community involvement and professional advancement for college-educated, middle-class women entering the new field of social work (Struthers, 1987). One element in the process of professionalization was the need to "build, control, and legitimize an occupational terrain" (Abramovitz, 1998, p. 518). This requirement was particularly acute for the fledgling profession of social work because there were questions about its legitimacy (Flexner, 1915). To gain respectability as a profession, social work embraced a psychoanalytic approach that evolved into a psychologically focused casework model (Kunzel, 1993). The belief was that Freud's theories, which represented the privileged discourse of science (Irving, 1992), were the answer to the "antiquated" approach of early Christian reformers. Simultaneously, it was believed that this scientific advance would help to defeminize a profession that had the more limited prestige accrued by a predominantly female profession. This model emphasized the dyadic relationship between client and worker rather than the broader societal problems as the explanation of why some individuals needed help. By the 1920s, that shift had been accomplished. This move enhanced the status of the profession but was also a route more amenable to change than poverty and social blight. The trend also swung the profession away from explanations of broader causes that impact service users, contributing to a narrow construction of what is ethical practice today.

The Conservatization of the Profession

Wenocur and Reisch (1989) state that professionalization requires an identifiable knowledge base and control of a social service market. They suggest that these needs contribute to the conservatization of professional groups. For social workers, dependency on funders can result in support for maintaining things as they are and not questioning broader patterns of social injustice (Abramovitz, 1998). Also, the state provides much of the professional privilege accrued by social workers, with the consequence that individual practitioners can be "conservative, socialized to comply with employing organizations" (Fook, 2002, p. 25) and state regulations (Hugman, 2005).

Edelman (1988) would argue that when a problem such as poverty persists, the failure to find adequate remedies is the result of the advantages that some groups amass from its continuance. He states (p. 14), "A problem to some is a benefit to others; it augments the latter group's influence . . . the term 'problem' only thinly veils the sense in which deplored conditions create opportunities." By defining social problems as individual, rather than economic or political issues, social workers gain prestige, authority, and financial remuneration in solving those issues. Were those problems socially constructed as macro concerns, social workers might not have the requisite authority or expertise needed to resolve those matters and would lose that piece of the turf, reducing the likelihood that social workers will construct societal problems in broader terms or view ethics through a broader, politicized lens.

Emphasis on the Professional as Being Autonomous and Accountable

One aspect in the narrow construction is the socialization of the helping profession, with the emphasis on the autonomy, accountability, and culpability of each professional. In the Western/European tradition in the modern era, the emphasis has been on the importance of the individual as the unit for arbitrating ethical judgments (Hugman, 2005). The theoretical-juridical model underscores a modernist notion of the practitioner as an autonomous individual (Mattison, 2000) and the use of rational cognitive processes as the means of avoiding ethical breaches. Workers feel individually accountable for any judgments made. The prominence of personal responsibility results in the creation of practitioners who work at developing strong decision-making skills and good rule-following so as to avoid litigation or discipline. Ethical dilemmas that involve structural inadequacies may be viewed as private dilemmas rather than as part of broader societal factors. As a result, social work practitioners often see ethics as being primarily a personal rather than a communal responsibility, supported by codes that place the blame for inadequacies squarely on the shoulders of individuals as independent actors. "A power relation studied in isolation from its cultural and institutional context is easily perceived as an anomaly, and not as part of a larger system," argues Allen (1996, p. 286). By assuming the agentic capacity of individual workers, outside of structural constraints or the inborn paradoxes of practice, the effect of social structures on behavior is lost from view (Arribas-Ayllon & Walkerdine, 2008).

An important factor that influences the construction of ethics in social work is the means by which individual social workers govern themselves. Unlike totalitarian regimes, liberal states do not have the same tools of domination to ensure stability. More subtle methods must be found. Therefore, the state must invoke "the capacities and powers of the self-governing individual while at the same time undertaking to foster, shape, and use those same capacities and powers" (Dean, 1994, p. 163). Foucault spoke about the notion of governmentality, namely the connection between "institutional technologies of regulation and modalities of self-regulation" (Chambon, Irving, & Epstein, 1999, p. 275). These are strategies used by authorities (including social workers) to act on the populace (again, including social workers!) to prevent problems and to affect society positively (Rose, 1996). In the ethics of social work, this is effected through the dominant discourses attached to a juridical-theoretical model, which encourages individual social workers to conduct their one-to-one relationships with clients through the lens of codes of universal abstract principles such as confidentiality and to regulate themselves by being watchful of whether they are consistently abiding by those tenets. Associations of professional organizations, with their subcommittees on discipline, determine whether there have been violations of these codes, and they may censure individual practitioners. These are examples of the complex of technologies that ensure self-government "through . . . allegiance to particular communities of morality and identity" (Rose, 1996, p. 336), in this case that of the social work profession and professional associations. This may not be conscious, but workers, through their support of the dominant discourses in the theoretical-juridical model, enhance their place in the profession while simultaneously regulating their own behavior, thereby aligning "their personal choices with the ends of government" (Rose & Miller, 1992, p. 188). Being positioned in this way results in a point of view that creates a particular moral order (Arribas-Ayllon & Walkerdine, 2008) because, through these discourses, how one ought to behave and what one's powers should be become delineated. The normalizing effect of the theoretical-juridical discourse takes hold, creating the social construction of ethics that dominates in the profession today and can result in social workers' cutting off ideas about other concerns before they even emerge.

The Risk Society and the Blaming Game

The way risk is conceptualized is part of this particular moral order. Collective rights are replaced by individual obligations (Higgs, 2000). Rather than the sinners at the turn of the century, today it is those who are at high risk who are viewed as morally suspect. Hence, social workers' clients are seen as being problematic. Professions that work with those groups can be "contaminated" by the same infection of marginalization and may work to distance themselves, wanting to be different from the groups they serve. Those who have privilege (including professional social workers) tend to think of their successes as having been the result of their own hard work, rather than having been partially the result of the inherent privileges of their positions (Sherwin, 1998). Consequently, they are more inclined to assume others can do the same. This may be true, even for those whose personal journeys began in less privileged beginnings. According to Ryan (1998), a classed ideology emerges, "cloaked in kindness and concern," bearing the "trappings of scientism"

(p. 520) that allows people of good will to "swerve from the central target that requires systematic change" (p. 525) and instead study those affected by social inequality by determining how they are different, but then treating the differences as the explanations of the social problem. These strategies ultimately perpetuate cycles of victim blaming and can be seen in the history of the 1920s, with social work's emphasis not on the causes of problems but on providing a function through a technical service (Abramovitz, 1998).

Perhaps it is not possible to eradicate entirely certain social problems. It is easy to look for someone to blame for the insufficiency of efforts to create a just and civil society. Not only the users but also the providers of services can be held responsible. Because it is a female-dominated profession with limited prestige, status, or clout, social workers also are set up as targets for the frustration about irresolvable societal ills. A system of culpability has been created, and the blaming game occurs (Parton, 1996). The emphasis on calculating risk provides a means of coping (Parton, 1996). The modernist Western/European approach to the individual as autonomous puts the responsibility for self-government of the choices made, and the happiness and success that result, squarely on the shoulders of each person, both worker and client. Accountability and prudence are aspects of risk avoidance that are required of citizens (Rose, 1996), especially those viewed as experts.

However, the forces that impact and limit individual freedom (such as globalization) create anxiety and fear. No amount of risk management can contain the uncertainties of modern life. The result is a risk-saturated society reflecting these anxieties (Beck, 1992). Values rest on ensuring safety, as opposed to ensuring equality or equity. The prominence of high-risk cases, risk-assessment tools, and risk management is rife in social work, requiring professional judgment and sound decision-making skills, the very tools emphasized in the theoretical-juridical model of ethics. Yet the assumption that these dangers can be deduced results in reliance on a positivist standard of science that is often found wanting and inaccurate, leading to more insecurity and increased rigidity in the organizations expected to manage the risk (Parton, 1996). Also, trust in the expertise of those who are to make those determinations (such as social workers) is eroded. And the adequacy of a model of ethics that assumes the suitability of scientism is found to be insufficient as well.

The Economic Effects of Globalization

The current environment of globalization also contributes to the notions of risk. The economic effects of globalization have a profound negative impact on the progressive inclinations of front-line workers and their understanding of what constitutes ethics in the field. Social workers are operating in a climate in which the welfare state is under attack (Ghorayshi, 2004, p. 210). The quality and security of jobs have been eroded and part-time work and contracts have replaced many permanent full-time jobs (Rice & Prince,

2000). These effects are gendered; women in this female-dominated profession are more vulnerable (Dominelli, 2004). Work conditions have deteriorated. Managerialism is on the rise. Individuals (more often men than women) with values arising from the business world have become either the heads of social service agencies or the consultants charged with evaluating those settings. Emphasis centers on the necessity of productivity and documentation and on the dangers of litigation. To manage risk involves calculating it and recording the evasion of it. Social workers spend inordinate amounts of time doing paperwork. Evidence-based and competency-based practices have reduced complex skills to component-measurable parts, and proceduralism has led to the dominance of social work as a rational-technical rather than a practical-moral activity (Parton, 2000) in which practitioners operate as technicians rather than with the autonomy that befits a professional group. Most significantly from the standpoint of ethics, by the emphasizing the value of the marketplace, with efficiency and effectiveness dominating needs and care, the underlying values of social inclusion and entitlements have been eroded (Dominelli, 1999; Lonne, McDonald & Fox, 2004).

The Outcome of These Trends

How do these trends affect social workers' constructions of their responsibilities to solve those problems and hence to the definition of ethics? There is a benefit to carving off ethics from the wide-ranging concerns of structural inequity. It protects individual workers from the duty to engage in the fight to change unjust structures. The historical split in the field of social work into clinical, community, and policy streams contributes to the lacunae in seeing structural constraints as part of social work ethics. The emphasis in direct practice on the dyadic relationship of worker and client, hived off from broader contexts, has aided in the disconnection of ethics from systemic issues. Frontline workers are far removed from wider forces that directly impact their ability to act in ways they might prefer ethically. Those workers may not conceptualize developments such as globalization as being connected to their day-to-day practice. If they do understand the impacts, they still may believe they are impotent when it comes to altering macro-level effects. Social workers also gain privilege and benefits from the status quo, so there may be some reasons to leave those structures unquestioned. To move in the direction of changing structural inequities might require giving up some of social work's power and privilege in the process. Furthermore, as long as social workers frame themselves as victims, like their clients, they are absolved from blame for the way things are (Fook, 2002). This stance keeps social work innocent and infantilized, not answerable for changing the structures of society because to do so is beyond the agency and authority of individual practitioners.

These trends have resulted in several potential responses by workers, including collusion, accommodation, or the possibility of engaging in a rear-guard action to maintain what they have as opposed to fighting for more progressive social change or taking a broader view of the nature of ethics (Dominelli, 1999). The traditional view of ethics thwarts viewing job action, alliances, and social movement responses as opportunities. However, all is not bleak. Because of the freedom in liberal states, there is also the possibility of resistance to the dominant discourses, which can lead to a more expansive definition of ethics in social work.

WHAT SHOULD BE DONE TO BROADEN THE FOCUS OF ETHICS IN SOCIAL WORK?

Social workers would benefit, when constructing their ethical responsibilities, by moving beyond the spotlight on the one-to-one relationship between worker and client. Professional accountability is robust in ethics, but it does not focus on the context of the practice or on the inexorable nature of paradox. Social workers ought to make several shifts (Weinberg, 2005a). Taking into account the broader structures and paradoxes that shape and limit practice would be a starting point. Recognizing the responsibility to question continually the taken-for-granted discourses that frame the development of those structures is also necessary. Social workers must go further and sidestep the dualism of the notions of agency and structure. Practitioners are restricted by structure but they also create structure (Weinberg, 2008b). The ways in which social workers interpret organizational structures, such as the policies and procedures as well as the legislation and funding requirements that lead to those structures, offer opportunities for ethical thinking and behavior. Because practitioners construct the notions of help every time they implement (or resist) such policies (Kondrat, 2002), in those moments there is the potential to shift an organization into more emancipatory directions that foster nonviolative relationships.

The current construction of ethics emphasizes which interactions are ethical and which are not. A further step toward an enhanced construction of ethics in practice would be a greater emphasis on self-reflexivity about the benefits to social workers of keeping the poor poor and the marginalized marginalized (Weinberg, 2005b). In the predominant paradigm, the profession as a whole is generally viewed as being benign, and the benefits of being part of the power elite are downplayed. Questions about privilege and perquisites should be fundamental parts of the social construction of ethics, not sidebars viewed as political difficulties. If workers were able to see ethics as extending to their positioning in social processes and their placement in institutional systems, the social construction of what constituted ethics would shift and there would be the possibility of reversing the historical trend away from a technical function and toward the causes of social problems.

Because they take on the responsibility of determining how normative behavior is defined, social workers invariably contribute to the construction of how, as a society, people ought to live with certain individuals who are disciplined for living otherwise. No emphasis on correct decision making can entirely avert the repercussions of this social obligation. And what goes along with that duty is the potential harm that may follow, not out of intention but because one can never predict the sum total effects of one's actions, especially in a profession in which multiple individuals are impacted by those decisions. Whom does a worker support—the over-stressed adult daughter of a man with signs of dementia who fears for her dad's safety and thus wants him in a nursing home, or the man himself, who abhors the thought of losing his home and perceives, possibly accurately, that he is still capable of looking after himself? Because this is an applied profession, these are not merely theoretical questions. A choice must be made, and supporting one individual's needs and wishes over another's may lead to unintended negative consequences. Social workers unwittingly are engaged in moments of ethical trespass, "the harmful effects . . . that inevitably follow not from our intentions and malevolence but from our participation in social processes and identities" (Orlie, 1997, p. 5).

The current state of affairs in which, to look competent, social workers must act autonomously and on the premise that they know the right thing to do, is problematic to both professionals and service users. Tronto (2001, p. 200) argues that what is required is for "professionals to see their own work in a broader context, to admit their capacity for error, and to accept the nature of their vulnerability." If an ethical framework stressed the ineluctable nature of trespass, isolation could be reduced because the problems would not be perceived as personal inadequacy. The field and the social construction of ethics would be strengthened by the solidarity of a community that recognized the inescapability of trespass, allowing for humility, doubt, and clemency.

REFERENCES

Abramovitz, M. (1998). Social work and social reform: An arena of struggle. *Social Work, 43*, 512–526.

Allen, A. (1996). Foucault on power: A theory for feminists. In S. J. Hekman (Ed.), *Feminist interpretations of Michel Foucault* (pp. 265–281). University Park, PA: Pennsylvania State University Press.

Aronson, J., & Sammon, S. (2000). Practice and social service cuts and restructuring: Working with the contradictions of "small victories." *Canadian Social Work Review, 17*, 167–187.

Arribas-Ayllon, M., & Walkerdine, V. (2008). Foucauldian discourse analysis. In C. Willig & W. Stainton-Rogers (Eds.), *The Sage handbook of qualitative research in psychology* (pp. 91–108). Los Angeles: Sage.

Arrington, P. (2008). *Stress at work· How do social workers cope?* NASW Membership Workforce Study. Washington, D.C.: National Association of Social Workers. Retrieved April 26, 2010, from http://workforce.socialworkers.org/whatsnew/stress.pdf.

Baines, D. (2007a). Anti-oppressive social work practice: Fighting for space, fighting for change. In D. Baines (Ed.), *Doing anti-oppressive practice. Building transformative politicized social work* (pp. 1–30). Halifax: Fernwood.

Baines, D. (2007b). "If you could change one thing": Restructuring, social workers and social justice practice. In D. Baines (Ed.), *Doing anti-oppressive practice. Building transformative politicized social work* (pp. 83–94). Halifax: Fernwood.

Banks, S. (2006). Ethics and values in social work. (3rd ed.). New York: Palgrave Macmillan.

Beck, U. (1992). *Risk society: Towards a new modernity.* London: Sage.

Chambon, A. S., Irving, A., & Epstein, L. (Eds.). (1999). *Reading Foucault for social work.* New York: Columbia University Press.

Congress, E. P.(2000). What social workers should know about ethics: Understanding and resolving practice dilemmas. *Advances in Social Work, 1*, 1–25.

Dean, M. (1994). "A social structure of many souls": Moral regulation, government, and self-formation. *Canadian Journal of Sociology, 19*, 145–168.

Dominelli, L. (1999). Neo-liberalism, social exclusion and welfare clients in a global economy. *International Journal of Social Welfare, 8*, 14–22.

Dominelli, L. (2004). *Social work: Theory and practice in a changing profession.* Cambridge, England: Polity Press.

Donovan, M. (2008, May). *Ethical challenges for social workers working for non-profit and community-based agencies.* Paper presented at the annual general meeting and convention of the Nova Scotia Association of Social Workers, Halifax, Nova Scotia.

Edelman, M. J. (1988). *Constructing the political spectacle.* Chicago: University of Chicago Press.

Flexner, A. (1915). "Is Social Work a Profession?" Paper presented at the National Conference on Charities and Correction, 581, 584–588, 590. Retrieved April 26, 2010, from http://www.uoregon.edu/~adoption/archive/FlexnerISWAP.htm.

Fook, J. (2002). Social work: Critical theory and practice. London: Sage.

Ghorayshi, P. (2004). The discourse of globalization and the alleged inevitability of our global future? In L. Samuelson & W. Antony (Eds.), *Power and resistance* (3rd ed., pp. 201–224). Halifax: Fernwood.

Healy, K. (2000). *Social work practices. Contemporary perspectives on change.* London: Sage.

Higgs, P. (1998). Risk, governmentality and the reconceptualization of citizenship. In G. Scambler & P. Higgs (Eds.), *Modernity, medicine and health* (pp. 176–197). New York: Routledge.

Hugman, R. (2005). *New approaches in ethics for the caring professions.* New York: Palgrave MacMillan.

Irving, A. (1992). The scientific imperative in Canadian social work: Social work and social welfare research in Canada, 1897–1945. *Canadian Social Work Review, 1*, 9–27.

Jenson, L. (2008, May). *Ethical challenges in the field of child welfare.* Paper presented at the annual general meeting and convention of the Nova Scotia Association of Social Workers, Halifax, Nova Scotia.

Kirby, J. (2008, May). *Leveling power: Organizational ethics and you.* Paper presented at the annual general meeting and convention of the Nova Scotia Association of Social Workers, Halifax, Nova Scotia.

Kondrat, M. E. (2002). Actor-centred social work: Re-visioning "person-in-environment" through a critical theory lens. *Social Work, 47,* 435–448.

Kunzel, R. G. (1993). *Fallen women, problem girls: Unmarried mothers and the professionalization of social work, 1890–1945.* New Haven: Yale University Press.

Lonne, B., McDonald, C., & Fox, T. (2004). Ethical practice in the contemporary human services. *Journal of Social Work, 4,* 345–367.

Mattison, M. (2000). Ethical decision making: The person in the process. *Social Work, 45,* 201–212.

Mullaly, B. (2007). The new structural social work (3rd ed.). Toronto: Oxford University Press.

Orlie, M. A. (1997). *Living ethically, acting politically.* Ithaca, NY: Cornell University Press.

Parton, N. (1996). Social work, risk and "the blaming system." In N. Parton (Ed.), *Social theory, social change and social work* (pp. 98–114). New York: Routledge.

Parton, N. (2000). Some thoughts on the relationship between theory and practice in and for social work. *British Journal of Social Work, 30,* 449–463.

Reamer, F. G. (1990). *Ethical dilemmas in social service: A guide for social workers,* 2nd ed. New York: Columbia University Press.

Reamer, F. G. (2006). *Ethical standards in social work: A review of the NASW code of ethics* (2nd ed.). Washington, D.C.: NASW press.

Rice, J. J., & Prince, M. J. (2000). *Changing politics of Canadian social policy.* Toronto: University of Toronto Press.

Robison, W., & Reeser, L. C. (2000). *Ethical decision making in social work.* Toronto: Allyn & Bacon.

Rose, N. (1996). The death of the social? Re-figuring the territory of government. *Economy and Society 25,* 327–356.

Rose, N., & Miller, P. (1992). Political power beyond the state: Problematics of government. *British Journal of Sociology, 43,* 173–205.

Rossiter, A., Prilleltensky, I., & Walsh-Bowers, R. (2000). A postmodern perspective on professional ethics. In B. Fawcett, B. Featherstone, J. Fook, & A. Rossiter (Eds.), *Practice and research in social work* (pp. 83–103). New York: Routledge.

Ryan, W. (1998). Blaming the victim. In P. S. Rothenberg (Ed.), *Race, class and gender in the United States,* (4th ed., pp. 519–529). New York: St.Martin's Press.

Sherwin, S. (1998). A relational approach to autonomy in health care. In S. Sherwin (Coordinator). *The politics of women's health: Exploring agency and autonomy* (pp. 19–47). Philadelphia: Temple University Press.

Smith, K. (2007). Social work, restructuring and everyday resistance: "Best practices" gone underground. In D. Baines (Ed.), *Doing anti-oppressive practice: Building transformative politicized social work* (pp. 145–159). Halifax: Fernwood.

Struthers, J. (1987). "Lord give us men": Women and social work in English Canada, 1918–1953. In A. Moscovitch & J. Albert (Eds.), *The "benevolent" state: The growth of welfare in Canada* (pp. 111–125). Toronto: Garamond Press.

Tronto, J. C. (2001). Does managing professionals affect professional ethics? Competence, autonomy, and care. In P. DesAutels & J. Waugh (Eds.), *Feminists doing ethics* (pp. 187–202). New York: Rowman & Littlefield.

Walker, M. U. (1998). *Moral understandings: A feminist study in ethics.* New York: Routledge.

Weinberg, M. (2004a). *Pregnant with possibility: Reducing ethical trespasses in social work practice with young single mothers.* Toronto: University of Toronto, unpublished doctoral dissertation,.

Weinberg, M. (2004b). Young single mothers: The work of proving fitness for parenting. *Journal for the Association of Research on Mothering, Fall/Winter, 6,* 79–89.

Weinberg, M. (2005a). A case for an expanded framework of ethics in practice. *Ethics and Behavior, 15,* 327–338.

Weinberg, M. (2005b). The mother menagerie: Animal metaphors in the social work relationship with young single mothers. *Critical Social Work, 6.* Retrieved April 26, 2010, from http://www.criticalsocialwork.com/units/socialwork/critical.nsf/8c20dad9f1c4be3a85256d6e006d1089/00a98daf7d49029f85256fd700691579?.

Weinberg, M. (2006). Pregnant with possibility: The paradoxes of "help" as anti-oppression and discipline with a young single mother. *Families in Society, April-June, 87,* 161–169.

Weinberg, M. (2007). Ethical "use of self": The complexity of multiple selves in clinical practice. In D. Mandell (Ed.), *Revisiting the use of self: Questioning professional identities* (pp. 213–233). Toronto: Canadian Scholars Press.

Weinberg, M. (2008a). [Structural barriers in social work practice]. Unpublished raw data.

Weinberg, M. (2008b). Structural social work: A moral compass for ethics in practice. *Critical Social Work, 9.* Retrieved April 26, 2010, from http://www.criticalsocialwork.com/units/socialwork/critical.nsf/982f0e5f06b5c9a285256d6e006cff78/3fc6041e5a0302358525744d0006b1a7?.

Weinberg, M. (2008c, May). *We're all in the same boat: Reasons and solutions for ethical struggles.* Paper presented at the annual general meeting and convention of the Nova Scotia Association of Social Workers, Halifax, Nova Scotia.

Wenocur, S., & Reisch, M. (1989). *From charity to enterprise: The development of American social work in a market economy.* Urbana, IL: University of Illinois.

Australian Social Work
2011, 1–12, iFirst article

Supervision is Not Politically Innocent

Carole Adamson
School of Counselling, Human Services & Social Work, University of Auckland, Auckland, New Zealand

Abstract

This paper argues that the potential tensions within the role, function, and purpose of supervision, potentially magnified by the adoption of the process within a variety of organisational and occupational settings, underscore the importance of supervision being seen as a contextually informed activity. Supervision can be constructed as a professional development activity with processes of reflection that are potentially active contributors to practitioner resilience. It can also be viewed as a developmental tool that assists a worker adapt to the workplace context and to process environmentally located challenges and tensions. Within some workplaces, supervision has an active managerial and risk-management function. Using the lens of resilience theories, this paper addresses key issues for supervision emerging from its different functions and argues that in becoming aware of its contextual location in complex practice and organisational environments, supervision practice itself cannot remain politically innocent.

Keywords: Social Work Supervision; Resilience; Social Work

The practice of supervision in professional contexts has extended beyond social work and into health and human services, education, counselling, and psychotherapy (Davys & Beddoe, 2010). Much of the supervision literature has focused upon the quality of the supervisory relationship (Tsui, 2005); issues for implementing supervision for different disciplines (Davys & Beddoe, 2009); and variations in the delivery of supervision in the light of technological and geographical imperatives such as practice in remote areas of Australia (Lonne & Cheers, 2004), online supervision (Allan, Crockett, Ball, Alston, & Whittenbury, 2007), interdisciplinary accountabilities (Bogo, Paterson, Tufford, & King, 2011; Davys & Beddoe, 2009; Townend, 2005) and so forth. A broad distinction between "micro" and "macro" issues has emerged, with much "micro" focus upon what could be constructed as intra- and interpersonal concerns, the ethics of relationships, and quality-control issues of best practice. This paper offers a contribution to the "macro" focus of supervision practice, workforce, and organisational concerns by addressing the

Correspondence to: Dr Carole Adamson, School of Counselling, Human Services and Social Work, University of Auckland, Private Bag 92601, Symonds Street, Auckland 1150, New Zealand. E-mail: c.adamson@auckland.ac.nz
Accepted 25 August 2011

ISSN 0312-407X (print)/ISSN 1447-0748 (online) © 2011 Australian Association of Social Workers
http://dx.doi.org/10.1080/0312407X.2011.618544

centrality of the contextual dynamics of supervision. Using concepts from resilience literature, the paper argues that supervision within social work is not a politically or organisationally neutral practice but one that must be constantly aware of its context, purpose, and application. In so being, it suggests that the relationship between the practice of supervision and the values and identity of social work can remain vibrant.

Practising Supervision in Context

Supervision never happens in a vacuum. The extension of the role and function of professional supervision throughout and beyond social work has magnified our understanding of the competing tensions that it contains, as different occupational groupings seek to adapt and interpret supervision to meet their specific needs and contexts. Social work literature itself attests to the multiplicity of purposes to which this relational, occupational process can be put.

Early conceptualisations, such as that of Kadushin (1992), identified the potential synergies or disruptions between administrative, education, and supportive functions. Unpacking this further, Kadushin's categories introduced notions of accountability, policies, procedures, and standards; acquisition and expansion of knowledge and skills; and maintenance and strengthening of morale and job satisfaction. Adoption of supervision as a tool for nonmanagerial purposes has led to a growth in understanding about supervision as a professional or consultative, quality enhancement activity that intertwines practitioner reflection and growth with best practice notions of effective clinical skills and positive therapeutic outcomes for clients (Bernard & Goodyear, 1992).

This produces a potentially conflicting range of possible roles, functions, and purposes for supervision, all of which will play out within the various organisational and political environments in which professional practice is supervised. These often competing tensions, highlighted by Hawkins and Shohet (1989) and Beddoe (2010), can be depicted as a "swingometer" (adapted from Chapman's concept, initially applied to election forecasting and described in Easton, 2003) whose pendulum falls at various points between a focus on practice competence and on accountability, dependent upon practitioner or management interpretation or upon policy demands of resource allocation or risk assessment.

On the left of the framework are the professional concerns of practitioner expertise, capturing some of the educational and support functions that Kadushin described, along with developmental notions such as Hawkins and Shohet's (1989) transition from self-centred to process-in-context practitioner and Butler's (1996) development of the practitioner from novice to expert. The emphasis here is on reflective capacity and professional development, which is in harmony with the attention to quality, best practice, and consumer and client rights that can generally be described as having a clinical focus (Bernard & Goodyear, 1992; Feltham & Dryden, 1994; Goldhammer, Anderson, & Krajewski, 1993; Howard, 2008; Tsui, 2005). Overall, these two functions described at the left of the diagram focus on the

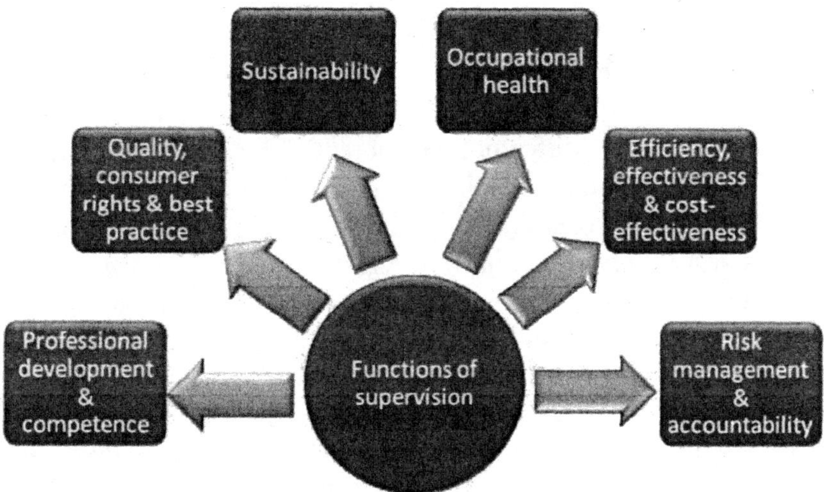

Figure 1 The supervision "swingometer"

relational aspects of the practitioner and the client, embedding their connection within the specifics of the service provided.

The area where the work of Kadushin and these other, relatively early, writers is perhaps the least developed occurs where the pendulum swings further to the right. It first encounters issues of sustainability of practice and of occupational health. It is here that the writings of Brown and Bourne (1996) are widely used in the teaching of supervision practice, as they more actively embed supervision as a practice within an agency context and construct the supervision journey as a development process from induction to connection and on into integration. New social workers progressively develop understandings about their role, the client's world, the team, the agency, and the bigger contextual issues. Issues of resilience and stress are employed in this perspective on supervision, with a person-in-environment recognition of the impact of the work on the worker (Collins, 2007).

The right-hand domains towards which the pendulum can swing describe the activities and purposes of supervision that are determined by managerial requirements, organisationally determined outcomes that are perhaps normative in nature, with a potential to become focused on public accountability within a risk-averse political environment (Beddoe, 2010). These demands upon the supervision process place emphasis on the organisational (as opposed to the clinical, client-focused, or professional) activities and responsibilities of the social worker and are a trend observed in social work supervision by Adams (2007). Collins (2007) referred to the earlier work of Gorman (2000) and Rogers (2001), both of whom suggested that the focus on cost-effectiveness and efficiency reduces a focus on the relational and emotional content of social work. From a constructionist perspective, Hair and O'Donoghue (2009) suggested that this interpretation of the role stems from a modernist construction of supervisor-as-expert and serves to ignore the wider social and political contexts in which supervision occurs. Supervision occurring within these environments may have the most apparent tensions as supervisors and supervisees grapple with the balance between clinical, professional, and managerial accountabilities.

Acknowledgement of these different and potentially competing functions of supervision is, of course, one that is actively negotiated within the construction of supervision contracts and managed skilfully within many supervision settings (Jones, 2004). Supervisors and supervisees constantly juggle performance review functions with support and professional development activities. The argument of this paper is that, once these tensions are recognised, the contextual location of supervision and the resulting dynamics (those that are termed "political" in this paper) cannot be ignored. With this, the imperative to balance risk management with practitioner reflection and development perspectives becomes crucial. It is suggested here that the use of a resilience lens can assist practitioners and supervisors to negotiate this territory.

Using the Lens of Resilience

Arguably, there is no unique theory of resilience as applied to client groups or to ourselves as practitioners. We can chart the evolution of concepts of resiliency from an early focus on pathology, intrapsychic and individual strengths, where both the causes and the solutions to stressors lie within the individual's personality, skills, and resources (Cederblad & Dahlin, 1995). The evolution proceeds through the ascendancy of systems theories (Lewis, 2000) and a greater relational, ecological, or contextual awareness of the power of the environment to determine or limit opportunity (Garmezy, Masten, & Tellegen, 1984; Mackay, 2003) to a current understanding that both individual and collective narratives can interplay with broad community-level and structural factors to create diverse patterns of coping and resilience (Bottrell, 2009; Ungar, 2004, 2008). Such transitions reflect the developments in western perspectives in human services and in social work, where we can trace the shift from pathogenic to salutogenic approaches (Antonovsky, 1996; Bottrell, 2009; Eriksson & Lindström, 2008; van Breda, 2011); from psychodynamic to constructivist constructs; and from reductionist to holistic and strengths perspectives.

Therefore, the development of the concept of resilience for social work has an evolution from a focus on individual characteristics to a greater awareness of contextual and environmental influence and interaction (Bottrell, 2009). Resilience is not currently constructed as dependent upon one dominant factor, but rather as the activation and interaction of an array of possible resources both internal and external to the person.

The importance of tracking this change in the manner in which we understand human strengths and coping mechanisms can be summed up by stating that current conceptualisation of the factors that create resilience recognises that a person becomes resilient through an interplay of individual, relational, systemic, and structural factors that flex and flux over time and place. Luthar and Cicchetti (2000) conceptualised resilience as an adaptive process. This enables a definition of resilience to move from construction as the ability to bounce back from events of adversity to a consideration of a matrix of factors that build the ability to withstand pressure and adapt over time. The development of strengths approaches allows for the description of protective factors that can shield a person or mediate with the environment to lessen the impact of adversity or cumulative pressure. This interactive model can add weight to our understanding of supervision in context.

Collins (2007) suggested that most of the resilience literature has focused on children, with less attention paid to adults. In addition, a small but growing body of research and literature has turned the spotlight of resilience from the "other" (the client) towards the worker in a social work context or system (Russ, Lonne, & Darlington, 2009; van Breda, 2011). It can be argued that this relative paucity of literature is an artefact of the transitional status of the concepts of stress and resilience that continue to move away from a pathological stance (identifying the "problems" in the objects of social worker attention, i.e., clients) towards an interactive and more relational construction of wellness and coping that turns the spotlight equally on the self of the worker. Considerably more literature exists concerning the negative impact of our practice, vicarious and secondary traumatisation, and burnout. There has been less of a specific emphasis on the positive relationship between social work practice and the ameliorative contribution of supervision to the maintenance of best practice and the resilience of the social worker, although some strong studies are now coming through (Collins, 2007; Kinman & Grant, 2011; Mor Barak, Travis, Pyun, & Xie, 2009). While some key arguments can be drawn from this literature, there remains considerable scope to tease out some principles from the resilience literature focused on the "other" and apply them to the workplace and the supervision context. Thus, questions of the correlation and goodness of fit between these principles and supervision provide rich territory for supervision-specific resilience research.

What then can we take from an understanding of resilience that applies to supervision in diverse social work contexts? How does this knowledge guide our awareness of supervision as a contested, political activity with a multiplicity of roles and functions? Using the resilience literature to inform the discussion, this paper tracks the pendulum of the swingometer from consideration of supervision as a reflective tool, focusing upon professional and clinical development and relational expertise that results in effective practice, through a focus upon the sustainability and wellbeing of the workforce, to a consideration of employer and organisational interests in the concept of resilience. In so doing, key issues concerning the link between resilience and supervision in complex environments will be considered.

Supervision in Relation to Professional Development and Best Practice

"Reflection for Resilience"

Current perspectives have suggested that the resilience of an individual at any given time will be a dynamic response to both risk and resiliency factors that brings together their personal history and current environmental demands (Bonanno, Westphal, & Mancini, 2011). With no one universal or dominant characteristic determining hardiness in the face of adversity, this paper suggests that there is potential for supervision to provide a healthy environment for strengthening the professional development and best practice of the supervisee, the left-hand components of the framework. A core element of this function of supervision is that of reflection.

To "take something to supervision" is a term that often refers to the process of creating space within a supervision session in order to address a complex, multi-stranded situation. The process of responding to what Butler, Ford, and Tregaskis (2007) termed "the messy complexities of practice" (p. 285) is the process of reflection, a term that Noble (1999) described as linking the thinking and the doing, and the doing and the thinking. A key role of supervision in social work is the strengthening of a worker's ability to respond to uncertainty and complexity (Askeland & Fook, 2009; Burgess, 2004; Lymbery, 2003; Parton, 1998). The Australian Association of Social Workers [AASW] Education and Accreditation Standards (e.g., AASW, 2008) acknowledged that complex practice situations are responded to by attention to reflective and reflexive practice, structural analysis, critical thinking, and ethical professional behaviour. The notion of "seeing the wood for the trees", of ascertaining what is personal, professional, or political, is core to the supervision process. It is within this space that we explore uncertainty and develop narratives and alternative possibilities.

The relevance of a resilience knowledgebase to this function of supervision is, as Howe (2008) suggested, that the management of emotions underpins resilience. From a psychologically informed theory of resilience, supervision can be constructed as an opportunity for positive reappraisal of complex situations and one's own emotional responses. Collins (2007) constructed supervision as a protective process, with emotional knowledge and positive emotions building up emotional regulation and trait resilience. Referring to Nathan (1993), Collins described reflective thinking as transforming emotional chaos into containable anxiety. Kinman and Grant (2011) suggested that emotional intelligence and aspects of empathy and social competence may be key protective qualities, with reflective ability being "an important predictor of resilience and psychological well-being" (p. 10).

A key strand of reflection for resilience emerges as support for the maintenance and growth of optimism and hope (Collins, 2007; Schwartz, Tiamiyu, & Dwyer, 2007). Similarly, Kinman and Grant (2011) and Morrison (2007) addressed the development of emotional and social competencies, while Stalker, Mandell, Frensch, Harvey, and Wright (2007) considered factors that enable exhausted social workers to maintain satisfaction in their work. Therefore, supervision, as a site for creating a reflective and mediating space for the consideration and comprehension of the emotional impact of experience, can be strongly supported as a process that can maintain and sustain resilience.

With a focus upon the professional functions of supervision, the left-hand side of the swingometer, the synergy between social work values and perspectives with the knowledgebase of resilience appears relatively congruent. Supervision, constructed as a reflective space and activity, is unproblematically linked with supporting resilience in social work. Where the pendulum moves towards workforce (as opposed to practice-focused) functions and managerial need, the relationship with a resilience knowledgebase, although remaining strong, becomes more contestable.

Supervision's Contribution Towards Sustaining and Maintaining the Workforce

Previously in this paper, the developmental models of Hawkins and Shohet (1989), Butler (1996), and of Brown and Bourne (1996) have been acknowledged as being significant to shaping our understanding of the supervision relationship as a developmental process, locating the exploration of these issues within the "sustainability of practice" and "occupational health" foci of the swingometer. These models recognise that the supervisee moves through stages (often sequentially but never perhaps fluidly or directionally consistently) from a beginner in induction through to a practitioner with more highly developed levels of competence and integration. Increasingly, this perspective has incorporated comprehension that it is the supervisory relationship itself that undergoes development (e.g., Kadushin & Harkness, 2002), albeit not without issues of an imbalance of power (Cooper, 2002; Noble & Irwin, 2009).

From both the supervision and resilience literature (Bottrell, 2009; Brown & Bourne, 1996) comes the argument that the environment has a considerable role in facilitating the development of a person in an organisational and supervision context. Attachment theory, relational to its core, informs both supervision and resilience. Bennett (2008) suggested that both embedded and newly created patterns of attachment may determine the outcome of supervisory relationships within the workplace environment. It is the acknowledgement of supervision as a developmental process within a complex and demanding work environment that shifts the use of resilience theory away from a simple interpretation of the importance of reflection to a more critical role of developing reflexive practice and contextual strategies for coping.

There is emerging evidence in the literature that supervision has a crucial role in the wellbeing of early-career social workers (Guerin, Devitt, & Redmond, 2010). Jack and Donnellan (2010) suggested that it is the neglect of the development of social workers through a focus upon knowledge and task completion that erodes their capacity to thrive in complex and demanding roles.

Mor Barak et al. (2009) argued that "effective supervision at the worker's level can contribute to such positive worker outcomes as job satisfaction, organizational commitment, and worker retention" (p. 4). Their meta-analysis considered that effective supervision "is known to serve as a buffer against stressful work conditions, to provide protection from unreasonable job demands, to offer emotional and social support during difficult times, and to guide workers in negotiating the challenges of the job and the organizational context" (p. 4). They suggested that there is organisational benefit in constructing policies and enabling resources focused upon positive supervision relationships and stress the importance of organisational culture and strengthen the case for structuring reflective and reflexive practice as foundations for resilience.

Studies of the resilience of client groups have highlighted a further potential application of theories of resilience to supervision and the wellbeing of social workers. Bottrell (2009) suggested that social and environmental barriers (processes or structures) may inhibit optimal development. While researching young people within a low-income urban environment in Sydney, she found that positive outcomes were impeded or prevented by rigid structures, perceptions, and poor relationships between resources and communities. Applying this notion of resilience to the supervision relationship within an organisational context, barriers to optimum development may take the form of inadequate induction or orientation procedures; lack of clarity in roles and responsibilities; a poor fit with cultural expectations; interdisciplinary confusions or rivalries, and so forth. Whether the barriers are individual, relational, cultural, systemic, or structural, unsuccessful negotiation may result in poor performance and an erosion of the quality of the supervision relationship itself. Supervision's embedded position within the relational dynamics of an organisation necessitates acknowledgement of how barriers such as these may affect development and outcome.

A resilience lens underscores the importance of the relational, both within and external to the supervision relationship. Current concepts of resilience are predicated upon the fundamental assumption that social support is one of the main buffers against stress. For instance, Collins (2007) reflected upon how a team of social workers can provide a protective environment and argued that changes in personnel and management can produce vulnerability for individuals within the system. Supervision needs to be cognisant of relationships and structurally determined patterns of communication external to, as well as within, the supervision. A robust supervision relationship can act as a resilience buffer in a less-than-optimum working environment; similarly, a poor relationship may limit the development of, or access to, wider organisational knowledge or resources.

With the resilience concept of barriers to development comes the risk of normalising a person's behaviour or performance. If barriers are not recognised, the supervisee may be judged according to external norms or expectations. Their inadequate use of resources may be due to poor induction processes rather than to a lack of networking skills.

Our understanding of barriers to the development of resilience is complemented by notions of "hidden" resilience (Ungar, 2004, 2008). Here, supervisee resilience may not be as much impeded by environmental issues external to the person, as much as that they may possess attributes or demonstrate behaviours that either go unrecognised by others or are not recognised as strengths. Within social work, this may be exemplified by a young person missing school. The importance of their role in keeping the family together by caring for a sick parent or siblings may go unrecognised; they may be labelled according to external norms as "failing". Similarly, within the workplace someone whose skills or interests are mismatched with their role requirements may be adjudged a poor performer. For instance, workers selected for cultural expertise may consider their role in community development as taking priority over agency requirements and their behaviour judged as poor time-keeping, absenteeism, or a lack of commitment. A child protection worker may commit comparatively more time to one family, with a view to a therapeutic outcome, than agency targets permit.

Resilience literature cautions us against taking a normative stance in supervision. Bottrell (2009) and Ungar's (2004, 2008) presentation of personal, local, and cultural definitions suggested that a person's resilience can only be assessed through an understanding of their own perceptions, interactions, and contexts. We ignore personal or cultural narratives at our peril. Hair and O'Donoghue (2009) outlined the risks inherent in cultural assumptions within cross-cultural supervision, risks that include not only interpersonal "talking past each other" but assumptions about the process of relationship, culturally specific systems of support, or the structures of supervision delivery compatible within and across cultures or organisational settings.

Noble and Irwin (2009) reflected upon the trend to try out different forms of supervision within social work, considering that this was a result of the managerial and accountability focus of the traditional model of one-to-one supervision and was a demonstration of social workers attempting to move the focus of the process back from organisational demands towards attention to professional practice (the left-hand side of the swingometer). In this way, supervision may become a site of resistance. It is to the issues that confront supervision on the right-hand side of the framework that the discussion now turns.

Implications of Applying Resiliency Theory to Supervision

Resilience in Adverse Environments

Resilience is often defined as an ability to withstand adversity. Within environments that have an undue measure of adverse conditions, the application of concepts of resilience is not without fish-hooks. Kinman and Grant (2011) suggested that "even the most resilient social workers will be unable to thrive under working conditions that are pathogenic" (p. 12). They suggested that this gives us the mandate to pay attention to the structural and systemic issues of social work roles beyond reactive, individualised self-care and stress-management strategies and instead place a focus upon wellbeing and salutogenic environments. From a focus on client resilience, Bottrell (2009) argued that a contextually aware definition of resilience requires us to focus upon bigger picture issues (the "political") of policy demands, competing interests, and organisational conditions. Indeed, it can be argued that a capacity to see the bigger picture and to put issues within a context is in itself a factor that can contribute to resilience.

Matching these core tenets of current resiliency theory to social work values illustrates that, for practitioners, there is an ethical and political imperative to place a spotlight on inequitable conditions for both clients and colleagues. In applying concepts of resilience within supervision, it follows that indicators of stress, inequality, or injustice explored within the supervision relationship also become matters for consideration and ethical inquiry. Beddoe (2010) and Jones (2004) both argued that the construction of the supervisory role will be porous to the social and political tensions in its wider environment. In organisational settings that are risk-sensitive and which have a strong focus on managerial accountabilities, resilience theories within supervision may be applied for purposes of performance management and damage limitation. The construction of a person or team as resilient suggests that key resources may be relocated to apparently more problematic areas with a view to reducing organisational exposure to risk. Being seen to cope may mean being left without the resources with which to do the job, or may entail being given so much more work that competence is threatened. A measurement of competence—such an environmentally sensitive capacity—could potentially erode, rather than strengthen, support.

Conclusion

In conclusion, then, how much adversity should a social worker cope with? There may be risks associated with the adoption of resilience theories without contextual and political awareness. Bottrell (2009) suggested that "resilience building in a neoliberal framework may shift the emphasis from positive adaptation despite adversity to positive adaptation *to* adversity" (p. 334). The conditions that determine resilience may be located outside of the individual social work practitioner and their professional development, supervision relationship, or team. If so, the theories that social work uses to support the provision of supervision (and indeed, the arguments for supervision itself) must be acutely mindful of the contexts in which they are applied. Supervision is not, and should never be presumed to be, politically innocent.

References

Adams, J. (2007). *Managing people in organisations: Contemporary theory and practice.* Basingstoke, UK: Palgrave Macmillan.

Allan, J., Crockett, J., Ball, P., Alston, M., & Whittenbury, K. (2007). 'It's all part of the package' in rural allied health: A pilot study of rewards and barriers in rural pharmacy and social work. *The Internet Journal of Allied Health Sciences and Practice, 5* (3).

Antonovsky, A. (1996). The salutogenic model as a theory to guide health promotion. *Health Promotion International, 11* (1), 11–18.

Askeland, G. A., & Fook, J. (2009). Critical reflection in social work. *European Journal of Social Work, 12* (3), 287–292.

Australian Association of Social Workers [AASW]. (2008). *Australian social work education and accreditation standards.* Canberra, ACT: Australian Association of Social Workers.

Beddoe, L. (2010). Surveillance or reflection: Professional supervision in "the risk society". *British Journal of Social Work, 40* (4), 1279–1296.

Bennett, C. S. (2008). Attachment-informed supervision for social work field education. *Clinical Social Work, 36* (1), 97–107.

Bernard, J. M., & Goodyear, R. K. (1992). Fundamentals of clinical supervision. Boston, MA: Allyn & Bacon.

Bogo, M., Paterson, J., Tufford, L., & King, R. (2011). Interprofessional clinical supervision in mental health and addiction: Toward identifying common elements. *The Clinical Supervisor, 30* (1), 124–140.

Bonanno, G. A., Westphal, M., & Mancini, A. D. (2011). Resilience to loss and potential trauma. *Annual Review of Clinical Psychology, 7* (1), 511–535.

Bottrell, D. (2009). Understanding "marginal" perspectives: Towards a social theory of resilience. *Qualitative Social Work, 8*, 321–339.

Brown, A., & Bourne, I. (1996). *The social work supervisor: Supervision in community, daycare and residential settings.* Buckingham, UK: Open University Press.

Burgess, H. (2004). Redesigning the curriculum for social work education: Complexity, conformity, chaos, creativity, collaboration? *Social Work Education, 23* (2), 163–183.

Butler, J. (1996). Professional development: Practice as text, reflection as process, and self as locus. *Australian Journal of Education, 40* (3), 265–283.

Butler, A., Ford, D., & Tregaskis, C. (2007). Who do we think we are? Self and reflexivity in social work practice. *Qualitative Social Work, 6* (3), 281–299.

Cederblad, M., & Dahlin, L. (1995). Intelligence and temperament as protective factors for mental health: A cross-sectional and prospective epidemiology study. *European Archives of Psychiatry and Clinical Neuroscience, 245*, 11–19.

Collins, S. (2007). Social workers, resilience, positive emotions and optimism. *Practice, 19* (4), 255–269.

Cooper, L. (2002). Social work supervision: A social justice perspective. In M. McMahon & W. Patton (Eds.), *Supervision in the helping professions: A practical approach* (pp. 185–195). Frenchs Forest, NSW: Pearson Australia.

Davys, A. M., & Beddoe, E. (2009). Interprofessional learning for supervision: "Taking the blinkers off". *Learning in Health and Social Care, 8* (1), 58–69.

Davys, A. M., & Beddoe, E. (2010). *Best practice in professional supervision: A guide for the helping professions.* London: Jessica Kingsley.

Easton, B. (2003). The political economy of Robert Chapman. *Political Science, 55* (1), 55–62.

Eriksson, M., & Lindström, B. (2008). A salutogenic interpretation of the Ottawa Charter. *Health Promotion International, 23* (2), 190–199.

Feltham, C., & Dryden, W. (1994). *Developing counsellor supervision.* London: Sage.

Garmezy, N., Masten, A. S., & Tellegen, A. (1984). The study of stress and competence in children: A building block for developmental psychopathology. *Child Development, 55* (1), 97–111.

Goldhammer, R., Anderson, R. H., & Krajewski, R. J. (1993). *Clinical supervision: Special methods for the supervision of teachers* (3rd ed.). Fort Worth, TX: Harcourt Brace Jovanovich.

Gorman, H. (2000). Winning hearts and minds? Emotional labour and learning for care management work. *Journal of Social Work Practice, 14* (2), 149–158.

Guerin, S., Devitt, C., & Redmond, B. (2010). Experiences of early-career social workers in Ireland. *British Journal of Social Work, 40* (8), 2467–2484.

Hair, H. J., & O'Donoghue, K. (2009). Culturally relevant, socially just social work supervision: Becoming visible through a social constructionist lens. *Journal of Ethnic and Cultural Diversity in Social Work, 18* (1), 70–88.

Hawkins, P., & Shohet, R. (1989). *Supervision in the helping professions.* Milton Keynes, UK: Open University Press.

Howard, F. (2008). Managing stress or enhancing wellbeing? Positive psychology's contributions to clinical supervision. *Australian Psychologist, 43* (2), 105–113.

Howe, D. (2008). *The emotionally intelligent social worker.* London: Palgrave McMillan.

Jack, G., & Donnellan, H. (2010). Recognising the person within the developing professional: Tracking the early careers of newly qualified child care social workers in three local authorities in England. *Social Work Education, 29* (3), 305–318.

Jones, M. (2004). Supervision, learning and transformative practices. In N. Gould & M. Baldwin (Eds.), *Social work, critical reflection and the learning organisation* (pp. 11–22). Aldershot: Ashgate.

Kadushin, A. (1992). *Supervision in social work* (3rd ed.). New York: Columbia University Press.

Kadushin, A., & Harkness, D. (2002). *Supervision in social work* (4th ed.). New York: Columbia University Press.

Kinman, G., & Grant, L. (2011). Exploring stress resilience in trainee social workers: The role of emotional and social competencies. *British Journal of Social Work, 41* (2), 261–275.

Lewis, M. D. (2000). The promise of dynamic systems approaches for an integrated account of human development. *Child Development, 71* (1), 36–43.

Lonne, B., & Cheers, B. (2004). Retaining rural social workers: An Australian study. *Rural Society, 14* (2), 163–177.

Luthar, S., & Cicchetti, D. (2000). The construct of resilience: Implications for interventions and social policies. *Development and Psychopathology, 12,* 857–885.

Lymbery, M. (2003). Negotiating the contradictions between competence and creativity in social work education. *Journal of Social Work, 3* (1), 99–117.

Mackay, R. (2003). Family resilience and good child outcomes: An overview of the research literature. *Social Policy Journal of New Zealand, 20* (June), 98–118.

Mor Barak, M., Travis, D. J., Pyun, H., & Xie, B. (2009). The impact of supervision on worker outcomes: A meta-analysis. *Social Service Review, 83* (1), 3–32.

Morrison, T. (2007). Emotional intelligence, emotion, and social work: Context, characteristics, complications and contribution. *British Journal of Social Work, 37* (2), 245–263.

Nathan, J. (1993). The battered social worker: A psychodynamic contribution to practice, supervision and policy. *Journal of Social Work Practice, 7* (1), 73–80.

Noble, C. (1999). The elusive yet essential project of developing field education as a legitimate area of social work inquiry. *Issues in Social Work Education, 19* (1), 2–16.

Noble, C., & Irwin, J. (2009). Social work supervision: An exploration of the current challenges in a rapidly changing social, economic and political environment. *Journal of Social Work, 9,* 345–358.

Parton, N. (1998). Risk, liberalism and child welfare: The need to rediscover uncertainty and ambiguity. *British Journal of Social Work, 28,* 5–27.

Rogers, A. (2001). Nurture, bureaucracy and re-balancing the heart and mind. *Journal of Social Work Practice, 15* (2), 181–191.

Russ, E., Lonne, B., & Darlington, Y. (2009). Using resilience to reconceptualise child protection workforce capacity. *Australian Social Work, 62* (3), 324–338.

Schwartz, R. H., Tiamiyu, M. F., & Dwyer, D. J. (2007). Social worker hope and perceived burnout: The effects of age, years in practice, and setting. *Administration in Social Work, 31* (4), 103–119.

Stalker, C. A., Mandell, D., Frensch, K. M., Harvey, C., & Wright, M. (2007). Child welfare workers who are exhausted yet satisfied with their jobs: How do they do it? *Child & Family Social Work, 12* (2), 182–191.

Townend, M. (2005). Interprofessional supervision from the perspectives of both mental health nurses and other professionals in the field of cognitive behavioural psychotherapy. *Journal of Psychiatric and Mental Health Nursing, 12* (5), 582–588.

Tsui, M. S. (2005). *Social work supervision: Contexts and concepts.* Thousand Oaks, CA: Sage.

Ungar, M. (2004). *Nurturing hidden resilience in troubled youth.* Toronto, Canada: University of Toronto Press.

Ungar, M. (2008). Resilience across cultures. *British Journal of Social Work, 38* (2), 218–235.

van Breda, A. (2011). Resilient workplaces: An initial conceptualization. *Families in Society, 92* (1), 33–40.

Social Work Education
Vol. 28, No. 8, December 2009, pp. 919–933

The Reflective Learning Model: Supervision of Social Work Students

Allyson Mary Davys & Liz Beddoe

A key task for the field education supervisor is to facilitate reflection in beginning practice, and to promote in the student a sense of ownership, mastery and understanding of his or her clinical process. At the same time the supervisor is charged to instruct and guide the student. A major challenge for the supervisor is to balance these two dimensions of supervision and maintain a focus on the student's experience rather than the supervisor's expertise. The authors present a Reflective Learning Model which identifies the importance of both facilitative and didactic interventions within effective supervision. A case study is provided to demonstrate the model in action.

Keywords: Student Supervision; Field Education; Practice Teaching and Learning; Reflective Learning

Introduction

The Reflective Learning Model emphasises the importance of reflection for responsive practice. The ability to reflect however is dependent on the practitioner's level of competence and experience. The skills and interventions employed by the supervisor of a student are thus different from those employed by the supervisor of an experienced practitioner. The model presented here, developed from previous work by the authors (Davys and Beddoe, 2000; Davys, 2001) uses Butler's (1996) stages of competence to consider the skills and processes required when supervising a social work student. The paper presents a case study to demonstrate the model and illustrate how supervision can encourage a student to deepen his or her understanding of the multiplicity of understandings (and misunderstandings) present in a challenging practice scenario.

Allyson Mary Davys, Waikato Institute of Technology, New Zealand & Liz Beddoe, University of Auckland, New Zealand.

Correspondence to: Liz Beddoe, Head of School Counselling, Human Services and Social Work, Faculty of Education, University of Auckland, Private Bag 92-601, Symonds St, Auckland 1035, New Zealand. Tel: +64 9 6238899; Email: e.beddoe@auckland.ac.nz

ISSN 0261-5479 print/1470-1227 online © 2009 Taylor & Francis
DOI: 10.1080/02615470902748662

The Reflective Learning Model rests on the premise that supervision is a forum for learning and that the main vehicle for learning is reflection. Reflection in this context refers to a conscious bringing to the surface of different forms of knowledge, while attending to the thoughts and emotions present in the student both *in situ* and after the experience. This is neatly described by Ruch (2000, p. 108):

> Reflective learning is an holistic, creative and artistic phenomenon which endeavours to hold theory and practice together in a creative tension. It also allows for uncertainty and mistakes and acknowledges the humanity of practitioners and clients. Reflective learning which acknowledges the complexity, diversity and emotionality of situations offers more scope for student practitioners to reach informed decisions which, by embracing the breadth of knowledges which influence decisions, could help avoid defensive, routinised and ritualistic responses.

It is the contention of the authors that students benefit from clear, structured facilitation of their experiences as reflection may not always come easily. As a 'learning process', supervision is driven from the experience of the learner (the supervisee) rather than from the wisdom and knowledge of the supervisor, a view supported by Morrison (2001) who asserts that 'the key to learning and development lies in the ability to engage in, and make use of, the worker's experience' (Morrison, 2001, p. 57). This poses a challenge to the supervisor of a student who must therefore assess what experience a student has, in the broadest sense, and how can that experience can be drawn into learning.

Three fundamental tensions are present in student supervision:

1. The balance between the didactic processes of teaching (information giving and instruction) and facilitation of student learning through reflection.
2. The fostering of reflection in situations where there is limited experience and which are overlaid by anxiety. This anxiety may stem from a number of sources which include the nature of the work and the student assessment process (Ruch, 2002).
3. The management of the dependence–autonomy continuum as students test their new knowledge and skills in "real" work (Beddoe, 2000).

Reflection, Competence and the New Practitioner

The task which lies at the heart of all supervision is to develop student/practitioner competence. Butler (1996), in rejecting models which suggest that competence is developed through an increased repertoire of skills and techniques or through the unconscious imbedding of basic principles, describes a model of performance development based on reflection. His model rests on the assertion that, 'through reflection, performance is transformed. And it is this transformation that brings about improvement in the performance' (Butler, 1996, p. 277). Reflection, however, is not necessarily an easy option for the very new practitioner.

Butler (1996) describes five stages of competence development. For the purposes of this paper we shall focus on the first two stages of this model, novice and advanced beginner, as they reflect the stages of development commonly demonstrated by student practitioners.

Novice, the first stage of Butler's model, describes a context where practitioners (students) are new to the work and have no experience of the situations which might arise. Practice at this level is 'rule governed'. In order to begin to practise the student requires rules to shape and guide practice. The behaviour of novices is 'extremely limited and very inflexible' (Butler, 1996, p. 278).

The second stage of Butler's model, *Advanced Beginner*, is characterised by the practitioner's belief that there is an answer to every problem and that someone will know what to do. The source of knowledge is thus located in someone other than the student and most commonly that person is the supervisor. At this stage the student will have had sufficient experience of practice to be able to identify the main areas of importance but his or her repertoire of interventions will be limited and solutions will be considered either right or wrong. In a similar vein, Loganbill *et al.* (1982, p. 17) describe a beginning practitioner as exhibiting 'naïve unawareness ... narrow and rigid thought patterns' and as having a strong dependence on supervision. It is important however to consider this dependence in context. Lizzio *et al.* (2005, p. 251) remind us that, for the student, dependence may be seen as professional safety and demonstrate appropriate deferral to the expertise of the supervisor and also be an indication of trust and safety within the relationship.

Other challenges are presented for the supervisor. At this beginning stage practitioners are often resistant to reflection in that they are 'generally impatient with complex answers or invitations to think the problem out for themselves' (Butler, 1996, p. 278). Butler concludes that novice and advanced beginners 'can take in little of the complexity of their performance situation, it is too new, too strange, and they have to spend time remembering the rules they have set for them' (Butler, 1996, p. 278). He identifies three requirements for novices and advanced beginners:

- support to understand the performance setting;
- help to set priorities; and
- assistance to learn to reflect on their own performance and become less rigid and more flexible by developing and trusting their own personal practical knowledge (Butler, 1996, p. 278).

Beginning practitioners or students thus require a mixture of interventions which are equally weighted at both ends of the didactic–facilitative continuum. High levels of instruction and information (didactic) are necessary in order that the students have a context and guidelines to begin to undertake the basic tasks of practice and high levels of positive feedback and support (facilitative) are required in order that they can accept the challenge to reflect upon the action taken and the consequences of that action. Without reflection, according to Butler, the practitioner will not progress; however, premature encouragement to reflect can overwhelm the student and create resistance and distress. Yip (2006, p. 781) identifies appropriate conditions for self-reflection which include:

> A supportive environment, social workers readiness to undergo self-reflection, individual space for individual workers to undergo reflective practice, worker's own reflective practice and awareness of one's limits and breaking point.

Yip (2006, p. 787) exhorts 'related parties' to ensure the presence of these appropriate conditions in order that social workers may safely engage in reflective practice. Effective supervision of a student therefore requires preparation, judgement and careful choice of the best way to promote learning within a range of supervisory interventions.

A recurring caution appears in the literature that didactic methods of supervision create over-dependence on the instructions, experience and expertise of the supervisor (supervisor focused) and produce surface learning. Surface learning, often defined as learning as a means to an end, focuses on content rather than underlying purpose and meaning. Clare (2007), discussing the work of earlier educationalists [Marton and Saljo (1976), Gardiner (1984) and Howe (1989) cited in Clare (2007)], describes surface learning as 'extrinsically motivated, passive and reproductive' in contrast with deep learning which is an 'intrinsically motivated process of personalised meaning construction' (Clare, 2007, p. 434).

The didactic–facilitative tension in supervision is usefully explored in a study by Lizzio *et al.* (2005), who investigated supervisee perceptions of the learning processes and outcomes of professional supervision. One of the questions for the researchers was whether 'deep/surface learning, anxiety and self management are salient to supervisees' perceptions of their approach to professional supervision' (Lizzio *et al.*, 2005, p. 243). Lizzio's findings described an 'orthogonal', as opposed to a polarised, relationship between didactic and facilitative approaches to supervision. In other words the use of the one did not exclude the other. They found that supervisors who were perceived by their supervisees to use a facilitative approach used a wide range of interventions which addressed both the content and process of supervision. Didactic interventions to instruct and inform were used within a facilitative approach to supervision.

Significantly Lizzio *et al.* (2005) remind us that it is not the techniques or interventions which characterise a supervisory approach but rather the 'higher order' goals of that particular approach. Where the higher order goals include supervisee learning and development within a supervisee or student focused framework of learning then didactic interventions are not an obstacle to deep learning.

As the student gains experience the need for structure becomes less but the need for encouragement and normalising of feelings and experience increases. The more experienced student needs help to value the learning and growth which comes from making mistakes. This task is complicated when the supervision relationship includes an assessment component which prompts students to promote their competence rather than their inadequacies.

The student supervisor's challenge is neatly summarised by Lizzio *et al.* (2005) who describe the need to find 'an appropriate balance between supervisory authority and supervisee autonomy, between evaluation and support and between transmission of required knowledge and the reflective engagement with the supervisees' experience' (Lizzio *et al.*, 2005, p. 240).

Lizzio *et al.*'s research findings are interesting. Not only do they suggest that facilitative approaches assist (but do not guarantee) deep learning but they also indicate that facilitative approaches reduce student anxiety. Finally, paradoxically, they found that a student learning focus reinforces the supervisor authority and enhances the perception of supervisor ability.

The Reflective Learning Model

The Reflective Learning Model was developed through the need, perceived by the authors, for a practical model of supervision which guided the supervisor from the greetings at the beginning of a supervision session to the farewell at the end. Many models of supervision provide theoretical frameworks which describe developmental stages of supervision (Loganbill *et al.*, 1982;.Brown and Bourne, 1996; Hawkins and Shohet, 2006) or the theoretical (and therapeutic) processes and skills of supervision (Loganbill *et al.*, 1982; Juhnke, 1996; Bond and Holland, 1998; Tsui, 2005; Hawkins and Shohet, 2006) but few provide the new supervisor with a structure which guides the process from beginning to end.

To this end we developed a model which we called the Reflective Learning Model of supervision. This model rests on two premises. The first premise asserts that the main purpose of supervision is to facilitate supervisee learning and development. As such the model is underpinned by an understanding of the principles of adult experiential learning (Kolb, 1984; Schön, 1987). The second premise reflects Butler's (1996) assertion that learning becomes transformational through reflection. As Morrison observes: 'It is not sufficient to have an experience to learn. Without reflecting on the experience it may be lost or misunderstood' [Further Education Unit (1988) quoted in Morrison (1993, p. 45)].

The Reflective Learning Model

This model, whilst promoting the importance of the beginning of the supervision session, 'hello how are you', and the end, 'I will see you next on …', focuses on the process in between these two interactions which is where the 'work' of supervision occurs. It assumes that the supervisor and student will have devoted time and energy to building an effective relationship in the beginning stages of practice learning (Beddoe, 2000).

Beginnings

All supervision sessions begin with an opportunity for the supervisor and the student to catch up and to engage before focussing on the task in hand. We have described elsewhere the specific tasks and themes of the beginning of the supervision session (Davys and Beddoe, 2000). Suffice it to reiterate here that this is an important moment of connection with the student and an opportunity to model the maintenance of ongoing professional relationships. The 'beginning' will include the setting of the agenda, an important task for all supervision and no less so for student supervision. The question of who sets the agenda in student supervision is interesting as a central purpose is to encourage student ownership of his or her work and of the supervision process. The agenda therefore must reflect student concerns and issues. The dilemma of course is that students usually have large areas of 'unknown' which will not find their way onto the agenda. Thus in student supervision it is important that supervisors are alert to the missing elements of the agenda and, where necessary, introduce topics which require attention. When the supervisor and student have established and prioritised the agenda the supervision cycle can begin.

The Reflective Learning Model describes four stages *event, exploration, experimentation* and *evaluation* which are addressed sequentially but allow for the student and the supervisor to move back and forth between the various stages if necessary (see Figure 1). The model mirrors the stages of experiential learning as described by Kolb (1984).

Case Study

Sharon is a third year social work student who is on placement in a government funded community health service. She is an able, enthusiastic student who is keen to get involved in practice and less enthusiastic about the preparatory ground work.

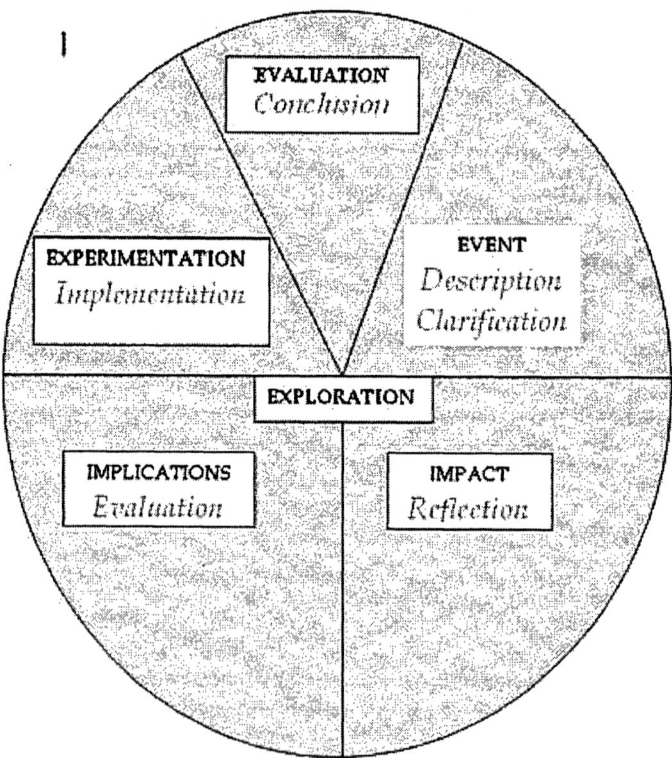

Figure 1 The Reflective Learning Model for Students.

Beginning

Sharon arrives at supervision visibly upset but struggling to present as composed. She has obviously not prepared for supervision and has rushed in from a visit in the community. The supervisor notes all this and chooses, for the start, to attend to Sharon's distress but makes a mental note to raise the issue of preparation with Sharon at some point.

The supervisor comments on Sharon's breathless arrival and observes that she looks upset. Tears begin to flow as Sharon launches into an account of her home visit that morning. 'A disastrous visit, a non-compliant rude service user'; Sharon doubts she is cut out to be a social worker and 'is never going to do another home visit'.

The supervisor listens to this and is sympathetic to Sharon's experience. She then asks Sharon what she wants to talk about in supervision today. Sharon appears surprised that the supervisor should ask and says with a shaky laugh that there is only one thing on her mind at the moment. The supervisor agrees but comments that this visit has obviously brought up a lot of feelings and is dominating her attention at the moment. She wonders if there were other things that Sharon has noted during the week which she wanted to put on the agenda as well. She asks if Sharon has noted anything in her notebook as preparation for supervision as they had agreed when they contracted for supervision. The supervisor does not expect that Sharon has done this but wants to reinforce the expectation of preparation for supervision and to illustrate the fact that critical incidents can dominate and highjack agendas. She is pleased that Sharon's response shows that although she has not recorded anything for an agenda she has remembered their agreement and that she has the ability to contain her immediate distress and name one other issue for the agenda. The supervisor has been reviewing Sharon's case notes and wishes to include case recording as an agenda item.

The agenda thus has three items and Sharon, to the surprise of neither, wants to discuss the morning's visit first.

The Event

Having identified the item of top priority on the agenda, the student and supervisor begin to focus on this item. The task for this stage of the model is for the student and the supervisor to identify the core issue or key question which the student wants to address in supervision about this agenda item.

The student is invited to tell the story. This is an important place for the student to start regardless of how well the supervisor may know the case or situation. Ownership of the situation leads to responsibility for the subsequent intervention and assists the student to gain both confidence and competence. Ford and Jones (1987) suggest that when a supervisor claims any ownership of the case or situation the student's role and sense of responsibility for outcome is proportionally diminished.

The retelling of the story enables the student to hear for him or herself the detail and to re-experience the situation. It enables the supervisor to hear the story from the student's perspective and to hear where the student places emphasis and possibly what the student omits.

The task for the supervisor is to encourage the student to tell enough of the story for both the student and the supervisor to understand the context and issues but not, at this stage, to begin to address the issue.

The supervisor, having listened to the student [Ford and Jones (1987) suggest that the student be uninterrupted during the story telling], may then need to clarify with the student some of the issues, the context and/or the information to ensure that he or she understands the situation. Ford and Jones (1987) suggest here that the supervisor is framing the problem from two perspectives. The first is to get a clear understanding of the problem/issue presented by the student and the second is to hold the student and the problem in a broader context. What is the significance of this particular problem for the student and what might it suggest about the student's stage of knowledge and competence?

The task for the supervisor and the student in the Event stage is to explore the supervision issue sufficiently in order to identify what it is that the student wants from the supervision session. What is the question that the supervisee is bringing to supervision and what does he or she wish to take away from the session?

The Event

The supervisor encourages Sharon to pick up her story of the morning's events but contains it within the context of 'Let us work out how best we can use supervision to help you with this situation. What do you want from supervision?'.

Sharon's visit involved a home visit to a long term woman service user of the agency, Paulette. Paulette's regular worker was going away and had asked that the student make a routine visit. Paulette had been told that a student was coming to see her.

Sharon's task was to make contact with this service user, to engage with her and to discuss whether there were any issues for her at present. As she drove up Sharon had seen a woman enter the house, but when she knocked at the door no one would answer. Sharon stood for five minutes knocking at the door and calling out explaining who she was. Her frustration and embarrassment were exacerbated by the appearance of a neighbour who was obviously curious about her presence and who was all too ready to give Sharon a loud account of Paulette's failings. Paulette finally opened the door and told Sharon in no uncertain terms to get lost. Sharon fled.

The supervisor encouraged Sharon to identify what she wanted from supervision about this situation. Sharon said she wanted to know how she could get this woman to let her into the house and how to deal with manipulative ungrateful service users.

The supervisor knew Sharon to be an enthusiastic student who was respectful of others and polite. She suspected that she would have had little experience in dealing with nosey neighbours and that her inexperience would not have prepared her for an angry rejection by the service user.

The Exploration: Impact and Implications

The Exploration stage of this model is where the work of supervision occurs and where the issue is explored, understood and potential solutions identified. The stage is divided into two phases: impact and implications.

Impact

The impact phase of the Exploration stage is the time where the student is encouraged to reflect on the issue brought to supervision and to consider how this issue has impacted on him or her and what meaning this event has in terms of current or previous experience. How is he or she feeling about the issue? How have these feelings been addressed, accommodated, expressed? How have the feelings affected the work in hand? What ideas, thoughts, judgements or opinions has the student had about the situation? Are there any patterns to these ideas, feelings? Have they been experienced anywhere before? And so on.

The task for the supervisor in this phase is to help the student to locate themselves in the event. How has the situation impacted on them? How have they responded? What meaning does it have to them as student practitioners?

Implications

The second phase of Exploration, implications, moves the student from a focus on themselves to a broader focus on the context of the 'event' or issue. The issue brought to supervision is considered here in terms of broad frameworks such as theory, policy, legislation, treatment protocols, and professional ethics. The phase encompasses Ford and Jones' (1987) evaluative phase and allows the supervisor to assess what knowledge the student possesses and what knowledge he or she requires.

In student supervision this is the phase where the supervisor is most active and where he or she has an opportunity to teach, inform and prescribe, possibly at times even proscribe. In short, it is the place for didactic interventions. It is also a place for feedback, reassurance and affirmation.

During the Exploration stage of the model the student and supervisor may move between impact and implication phases as the issue is explored and uncovered. Reflection on thoughts and feelings may raise questions of a more conceptual nature and theory may be explored. This in turn may prompt a reflection on feelings and actions and patterns may be identified and so the discussion may move back and forth between the two phases and deepen as different aspects are examined and integrated.

The task of the Exploration stage is to reach some decision or understanding about the issue being discussed.

Impact and Implications

The supervisor can see that Sharon is still very upset about the incident and encourages her to talk about how she feels. Sharon describes a range of feelings:

anger, frustration, helplessness and embarrassment. She talks about all her enthusiasm for the visit and how she had looked forward to her first solo home visit. She describes Paulette as 'spiteful' and 'ungrateful'.

The supervisor sympathises with this experience and affirms Sharon for her honesty and courage in owning her strong negative feelings. She observes that it is hard when good intentions and goodwill are rebuffed. She wonders what was going on for Sharon at the time and if Sharon has ever experienced anything like this before. Sharon is able to connect her feelings with an earlier experience in her childhood and is encouraged by the supervisor to recall how she handled that situation.

With support Sharon is able to examine her own position in the situation. She realises that she wanted so badly to do this 'right' and that the presence of the neighbour not only exposed her inability to make a connection with the woman but also embarrassed her by making her a party, however unwillingly, to a criticism of the service user. This compounded her sense of helplessness and, she realises, a sense of incompetence. How can she be a social worker if she can't even get in the door to talk to the service user?

Implications

The supervisor asks Sharon how she would have liked it to be. What was her goal in visiting this home? Sharon is clear that her goal was to make contact with Paulette, begin to establish a relationship and to gather relevant information. What could she have done differently? Sharon is unable to answer this question and becomes stuck in her feelings about the service user and her judgements of her behaviour. Sharon is also unable to imagine what was happening for Paulette when she refused to answer the door.

The supervisor questions Sharon on her preparation before visiting Paulette. Who had she spoken to and what had she read? Sharon admits that she hadn't read the file. She had had a brief conversation with the regular social worker but it was hurried and she felt the visit was routine.

The supervisor recognises this as an important teaching moment in supervision. She reviews with Sharon the purpose of the visit and asks her what process she would follow in preparation for any home visit. The response alerts her to the fact that Sharon did not have any structure for preparation and lacks a framework for assessing potential issues which might arise from a new visit. The supervisor is also concerned that Sharon had made this visit without prior consultation with her supervisor.

The supervisor recognises that Sharon is still distressed about the visit and chooses to address the casework issues before the more procedural concerns. As she knows the service user she is able to summarise some of the information which would have been on Paulette's file. Paulette has a history of mental health problems which are usually well managed but which from time to time need review and remediation. Paulette also has a long history of dealing with official agencies and in the past has had three children taken into care. When she is unwell she can become very suspicious of strangers and fierce about her privacy from interfering social workers and neighbours.

On the basis of this, the supervisor wonders, is Sharon able to hazard a guess at what might have been going through Paulette's mind whilst Sharon was knocking on the door? Sharon is now able to make some thoughtful comments about how Paulette may have been responding to her visit and as she explores this she is able to recognise that her criticism of Paulette is lessening and her criticism of herself increasing. The supervisor applauds her for this shift and encourages her to focus, not on what she has done wrong, but on what she can learn from this situation.

The supervisor again asks what Sharon could have done differently. From her response the supervisor recognises that Sharon is not confident in her knowledge of mental illness and management. She thus spends some time outlining the basic parameters of mental illness management from the agency perspective and gives Sharon a copy of the guidelines for practitioners and other relevant literature and notes that she will follow up on this 'homework'. The supervisor checks out what Sharon is thinking and how she is feeling about this situation now. Sharon is able to recognise her own projected feelings and acknowledges her sense of helplessness and incompetence. She understands more clearly the dynamics at play in the visit and how her newness and lack of preparation have compounded an already complex situation.

The supervisor then addresses the issue of Sharon's acting on a new task without consulting her supervisor. She reminds Sharon of the contract agreement and wonders why Sharon has not followed this. Sharon agrees that she had not followed the procedure but expresses her confusion about the relative status of her supervisor and the senior practitioner who had passed the case on to her. The supervisor accepts this as a legitimate confusion and reinforces the need for Sharon to check out all new work with her.

The supervisor asks Sharon what she is going to do next. Sharon appears a little startled at this and admits she would like to withdraw from the case. The supervisor however believes that Sharon is capable of addressing the situation and encourages her to plan a second visit. As she does this Sharon finds she is able to use the information provided by the supervisor to plan a more careful visit which will include plenty of notice to the service user.

The Experimentation Stage: Implementation

It is our experience that the focus on an issue brought to supervision often ends when a solution has been chosen or when an understanding or insight has been gained. The supervision session will then move on to the next item on the agenda. All too often, in these situations the plan or strategy identified by the supervisee is not put into effect or the insight is not integrated into practice or awareness. Many good ideas from supervision are lost to practice due to incomplete understanding, lack of knowledge and/or lack of confidence. The learning from supervision is lost. In the

Reflective Learning Model, the Experimentation stage explicitly attends to how the student will move forward with the issue.

At this stage of the model the plan or strategy identified through the Exploration stage is tested. Is this the best plan? What are the limitations? What will happen if the plan fails? What resources does the student need in order to put this plan into action? The student is provided with support to consider how he or she will act on the plan and encouraged to identify fears or knowledge gaps which will make the implementation problematic. The supervisor is thus able to consider what extra tuition, support or resources the student may need to promote a successful outcome.

Experimentation

Sharon feels good about her plan and the decision to have a second visit. The supervisor however wants this to be as successful as possible for both Sharon and Paulette. She asks Sharon how and when she is going to do this visit and asks her to imagine the steps. Sharon is able to articulate the early steps of making the appointment but as she contemplates the actual visit she becomes less sure and confesses to being worried about doing this. The supervisor enquires if there was any help she wants. Sharon wonders if someone could go with her. The supervisor has also been thinking along these lines and is happy to agree to accompany Sharon. The supervisor however does not want to take over the case and continues to discuss how Sharon is going to begin her visit. She suggests they role play a possible conversation with Paulette. As they explore this conversation Sharon finds her own words to express what she wants to say and grows more confident in her delivery. The supervisor gives her feedback to this effect.

The supervisor then asks Sharon to consider what she will do if, after all of this preparation, Paulette still refuses to answer the door. Sharon is able to consider this possibility in the context of her new understanding of the service user and within her framework of preparation. She recognises that she does not have total control over events and thinks that, if she has followed through with her preparation, she will have done her best and will be able to withdraw from the situation and consider the next step with her supervisor.

The Evaluation

The Evaluation stage of the Reflective Learning Model brings the student and supervisor full circle to consider whether or not the agenda item has been successfully addressed. Does the student now have sufficient information, knowledge and confidence to move forward? What has the student learned from the reflections and the teaching in the supervision session? What new questions have arisen as a result of the supervision and how and in what time frame will they be addressed?

When this stage is completed the student and supervisor will focus on the next agenda item and begin the cycle once more.

Evaluation

Sharon and her supervisor have now completed the discussion of the issue. The supervisor is keen to establish whether or not the issue is sufficiently addressed for Sharon. On reflection Sharon says she is very happy with the outcome which is more than she had asked for and 'much better'. She has discovered a way to approach meetings with Paulette and along the way has changed her assessment.

The supervisor also enquires what Sharon has learned from talking about this experience. After some thought Sharon says that she realises the importance of preparation. If she had read the file she would have had a better sense of the person she was going to visit and would also have been able to identify in advance the areas where she had little knowledge. She also ventures, tentatively, that she is learning not to beat herself up when she makes an error. The supervisor is warm in her affirmation of Sharon's learning, particularly the last and reinforces the importance of learning from mistakes.

The supervisor then suggests that they focus on the second agenda item.

Endings

> Axiomatically, all good processes have a beginning and an end (Davys and Beddoe, 2000, p. 444).

When the supervisor and the student have addressed all of the items on the agenda or, as is most often the case the supervision time is up, the supervision session ends. The ending of the session is important as it marks the conclusion of this period of learning and teaching. It is useful for both the student and the supervisor to spend a moment reflecting on the themes, progress, challenges and triumphs of the student in his or her work. It is a time when general feedback can be given which assists the student to locate him or herself in the practice-learning journey. The tension of assessment in student placements is real and regular feedback on a student's progress can be reassuring and can assist some students to recognise the areas they must address for successful outcomes.

Ending

Sharon and her supervisor have now addressed all three issues on the agenda and the supervision time is almost up. The supervisor asks Sharon how the session has been and asks if there are any themes Sharon has noted.

Sharon is warm in her appreciation of the session and particularly the help she received in relation to the first issue. She says she feels much calmer but feels really bad about the judgments she now realises she made. Mindful about the stress of assessment, the supervisor reiterates that it is not the mistakes which are of concern but rather whether or not Sharon has learned from them. She asks Sharon to repeat what she has learned from discussing this particular service user and is fulsome in her reinforcement of that learning and her commendation of Sharon's honesty and willingness to explore these issues.

Sharon is unable to identify any other issues or themes. The supervisor however has noted that until this point Sharon has applied a standard interview process and been successful in her interactions with service users. With this confidence she is eager to engage with service users and is often peremptory in her preparation and impatient with information offered by colleagues. More attention to preparation may have prevented the distress of the morning's visit. The supervisor is aware that preparation is a theme of today's session. Sharon was not prepared for supervision, she had not prepared for the visit and when reviewing the case recording of the work Sharon had done to date (the supervisor's agenda item) there was evidence of poor information and rushed recording. The supervisor draws these themes together and comments that this appears to be one of Sharon's next professional challenges and is perhaps a useful focus for future supervision. She sets Sharon two tasks for the next supervision session: to prepare an agenda, and to spend time thinking about her approach to 'preparation' for direct work with service users.

The supervisor rounds off the session with an affirming comment on Sharon's progress to date and they confirm the time and place of the next meeting.

Conclusion

It is recognised here that student supervision cannot rest solely on reflection and that students require parameters, guidelines and information in order to begin to construct their own sense of mastery of the skills and interventions required by practice. This model and the case study presented urge supervisors to find a middle ground between didactic teaching and instruction in supervision on the one hand, and boundary-less reflection on the other. The latter can create anxiety in the student who has little content or context on which to reflect and insufficient experience through which to mediate anxiety and distress. This mix of telling and reflection is well put by Schön (1987) in his description of the conditions for learning professional artistry.

> The freedom to learn by doing in a setting relatively low in risk, with access to coaches who initiate students into the "traditions of the calling" and help them, by the "right kind of telling", to see on their own behalf and in their own way what they need to see. (Schön, 1987, p. 17)

References

Beddoe, L. (2000) 'The supervisory relationship', in *Fieldwork in the Human Services*, eds L. Cooper & L. Briggs, Allen & Unwin, Sydney, pp. 41–54.

Bond, M. & Holland, S. (1998) *Skills of Clinical Supervision for Nurses*, Open University Press, Buckingham.

Brown, A. & Bourne, I. (1996) *The Social Work Supervisor*, Open University Press, Buckingham.

Butler, J. (1996) 'Professional development: practice as text, reflection as process, and self as locus', *Australian Journal of Education*, vol. 40, no. 3, pp. 265–283.

Clare, B. (2007) 'Promoting deep learning: a teaching, learning and assessment endeavour', *Social Work Education*, vol. 26, no. 5, pp. 433–446.

Davys, A. & Beddoe, L. (2000) 'Supervision of students: A map and a model for the decade to come', *Social Work Education*, vol. 19, no. 5, pp. 438–449.

Davys, A. (2001) 'A reflective learning process for supervision', in *Supervision: From rhetoric to reality*, eds L. Beddoe & J. Worrall, Auckland College of Education, Auckland, pp. 87–98.

Ford, K. & Jones, A. (1987) *Student Supervision*, BASW Macmillan, London.

Hawkins, P. & Shohet, R. (2006) *Supervision in the Helping Professions*, 3rd edn, Maidenhead, Open University Press.

Juhnke, G. A. (1996) 'Solution-focused supervision: promoting supervisee skills and confidence through successful solutions', *Counselor Education and Supervision*, vol. 36, no. 1, pp. 48–57.

Kolb, D. (1984) *Experiential Learning as the Source of Learning and Development*, Prentice Hall, New Jersey.

Lizzio, A., Stokes, L. & Wilson, K. (2005) 'Approaches to learning in professional supervision: supervisee perceptions of processes and outcome', *Studies in Continuing Education*, vol. 27, no. 3, pp. 239–256.

Loganbill, C., Hardy, E. & Delworth, U. (1982) 'Supervision: a conceptual model', *The Counseling Psychologist*, vol. 10, no. 1, pp. 3–42.

Morrison, T. (1993) *Staff Supervision in Social Care*, Longman, Harlow.

Morrison, T. (2001) *Staff Supervision in Social Care: Making a Real Difference for Staff and Service Users*, Pavilion, Brighton.

Ruch, G. (2000) 'Self and social work: towards an integrated model of learning', *Journal of Social Work Practice*, vol. 14, no. 2, pp. 99–112.

Ruch, G. (2002) 'From triangle to spiral: reflective practice in social work education, practice and research', *Social Work Education*, vol. 21, no. 2, pp. 199–216.

Schön, D. (1987) *Educating the Reflective Practitioner*, Jossey Bass, San Francisco.

Tsui, M. S. (2005) *Social Work Supervision: Contexts and Concepts*, Sage, Thousand Oaks.

Yip, K. (2006) 'Self reflection in reflective practice: a note of caution', *British Journal of Social Work*, vol. 36, pp. 777–788.

British Journal of Social Work (2005) **35,** 435–452
doi:10.1093/bjsw/bch190
Advance Access publication March 21, 2005

Use of Critical Consciousness in Anti-Oppressive Social Work Practice: Disentangling Power Dynamics at Personal and Structural Levels

Izumi Sakamoto and Ronald O. Pitner

Izumi Sakamoto, Ph.D., is an assistant professor of social work at the University of Toronto, Canada. She received her MA in social welfare from Sophia University, Japan, and her MSW, MS (psychology) and Ph.D. (social work and social psychology) from the University of Michigan, USA. Her research interests include anti-oppressive social work, gender and immigration, cultural influences on the self and identities, and cultural negotiation processes of newcomers.

Ronald O. Pitner, Ph.D., is an assistant professor of social work at Washington University in Saint Louis, USA. He received his MA in psychology from the University of Tennessee, USA, a MSW and Ph.D. (social work and social psychology) from the University of Michigan, USA. His research interests are broadly defined in terms of social cognition, stereotyping, prejudice, race and ethnicity, multicultural social work.

Correspondence to Izumi Sakamoto, Faculty of Social Work, University of Toronto, 246 Bloor St West, Toronto, ON M5S 1A1, Canada. E-mail: *Izumi.Sakamoto@utoronto.ca*

Summary

One of the limitations of anti-oppressive perspectives (AOPs) in social work is its lack of focus at a micro and individual level. AOPs should entail the social worker's addressing the needs and assets of service users, challenging the oppressive social structure and, most importantly, critically challenging the power dynamics in the service-provider/service-user relationship. Critical consciousness challenges social workers to be cognizant of power differentials and how these differentials may inadvertently make social-work practice an oppressive experience. The authors contend that critical consciousness fills in some of the gaps of AOPs, and argue for a fuller integration of critical consciousness into teaching and practice of AOPs. The methods to work toward critical consciousness, such as inter-group dialogues, agent–target distinctions and empowerment, are detailed.

Introduction

As helping professionals, social workers inevitably bring more power to their interactions with service users than vice versa. As a result, the following question seems warranted: Is anti-oppressive social work ever truly anti-oppressive? In an attempt to address this question, the authors suggest the use of critical consciousness in the application of anti-oppressive social work in practice. Developing critical consciousness would help social workers to challenge themselves to be cognizant of power differentials. Originally described by Freire in the 1960s (1997), critical consciousness (Pitner and Sakamoto, in press; Reed *et al.,* 1997) is a concept more recently refined by social-justice-oriented multicultural social work theories in the USA; thus, it was developed under a different historical and political context from anti-oppressive social work. Nevertheless, it has similar goals of eradication of oppression and working toward social justice. Before discussing critical consciousness in depth, let us review what we mean by anti-oppressive perspectives in social work, to lay ground for further discussions.

Brief review of anti-oppressive social work

In the recent years, anti-oppressive and anti-discriminatory perspectives have had significant impact on social work theory, practice and education in the UK (e.g. Burke and Harrison, 1998; Dalrymple and Burke, 1995; Dominelli, 2002; Hatton, 2001; Langan and Day, 1992; Lynn, 1999; Payne, 1997; Thompson, 1997; Williams, 1999; Wilson and Beresford, 2000), as well as in Canada, Australia, New Zealand and other European countries (e.g. Connolly, 2001; Mullaly, 2002; Razack, 1999; Shera, 2003; Valtonen, 2001). Some common features of these anti-discriminatory and anti-oppressive approaches include the influences of Marxist, socialist and radical ideologies, structural/sociological understanding of intersecting oppressions and emancipatory and feminist perspectives (Dominelli, 2002; Payne, 1997). Based on these theories and perspectives, eradication of oppression through institutional and societal changes is seen as an ultimate goal. In fact, these features are the cornerstone of anti-oppressive and anti-discriminatory perspectives, despite there being no consensus among scholars and practitioners on a definitive model of anti-oppressive and anti-discriminatory practice (Lynn, 1999). Focusing solely on the various semantic differences of these perspectives goes beyond the scope of this article. Thus, we forgo this discussion and, instead, use the term 'anti-oppressive perspectives' (AOPs) to refer to those approaches with the aforementioned common features.

Promises of anti-oppressive perspectives

Anti-oppressive approaches in social work emerged in response to the struggles of ethnic minorities, feminists and people with disabilities to challenge the power structures (Langan, 1992; Payne, 1997). Typically, social work practice has been more micro/individually focused. The ability for such a focus to address issues related to oppression was called into question with the rise of radical social work in the late 1960s and early 1970s; radical social work laid the groundwork for AOPs (Lynn, 1999; Payne, 1997). With AOPs, the *structure* of oppression and discrimination has become the centre of analysis. AOPs, as the name suggests, draw attention of social workers to the more focused objective of challenging structural power dynamics in order to eradicate various forms of oppression. In comparison to micro-social work perspectives, AOPs offer a clearer linkage between social work practice and social justice. Most importantly, however, it offers a better conceptual model for understanding the multiplicity of oppression, privilege and power dynamics at a structural level.

AOPs ultimately aim to change the structure and procedures of service delivery systems through macro changes, including legal and organizational transformations (Dalrymple and Burke, 1995; Dominelli, 2002). Unlike more micro-oriented approaches of social work, AOPs suggest that social workers should not buy into the thinking that they are the only ones assuming responsibilities to transform society; rather, it is the state that must assume a much greater role than social workers (Dalrymple and Burke, 1995). In its sociological and structural focus, AOPs provide an effective avenue for analyzing issues at a macro and mezzo level.

Another contribution of AOPs is that it focuses attention on the *diversity* of oppression, unlike radical social work approaches of 1970s, which focused solely on classism, with little or no attention given to sexism or racism (Langan, 1992). AOPs endeavour to incorporate the demands from the autonomous movements by women, ethnic minorities and other oppressed groups.

Limitations of anti-oppressive perspectives

Despite the many promises of AOPs, there are also some limitations. Foremost, as alluded to earlier, the terminology used to describe AOPs is a critical limitation. For example, while some scholars argue about the problems that arise from aggregating anti-oppressive practice and anti-discriminatory practice (Dalrymple and Burke, 1995), others contend that their differences are merely semantic (Thompson, 1997). It seems that the more currency that AOPs acquire domestically and internationally, the more confusion there is about what exactly AOP connotes. Does it refer to a social worker's attempt to eliminate racism, sexism and classism on behalf of service users? Does it refer to a social worker's attempt to eliminate *any isms* in working collaboratively with service users? Does it refer to an attempt to eliminate power differentials across the board? Or, does it create a hierarchy of oppression by viewing one form of oppression (e.g. racism) as more important than another (e.g. ableism)? Clearly, there needs to be greater clarification on what AOPs entail. Similarly, for some social workers, radical social work and AOPs may mean the same thing, whereas for others, empowerment approaches may be regarded as part of AOPs.

Given that it is not entirely clear as to what exactly constitutes anti-oppressive practice, practitioners may not be certain whether their practice can be labelled as such. This lack of 'agreed upon' terminology can invite potential reluctance of practitioners to engage in anti-oppressive work. Furthermore, this could inevitably lead to a 'reliability issue' in our practice, education and research. For example, several articles with anti-oppressive practice/services in their titles do not define exactly which version of AOPs they refer to (Cemlyn, 2000; Langley, 2001; Valtonen, 2001), making it difficult to compare with or build on each other. How can we approach practice, teaching and research from an AOP perspective if we do not have a consensus on the concept?

Moreover, the connotations of anti-oppressive social work can be so negative that, when imposed on practitioners, it could potentially alienate frontline social workers who believe that they have always been practising social work directed at eradicating oppression. Some practitioners may even feel that they are blamed for not doing enough to change social structures. There is, indeed, a criticism that AOPs have been too ideologically and scholarly driven and have not sufficiently incorporated ground-up knowledge, e.g. service users' viewpoints (Wilson and Beresford, 2000). In addition to the negative connotations of the terminology, the ultimate objective of AOPs (i.e. eradication of all forms of structural oppression) can be seen as discouragingly lofty, especially for practitioners who may already have too much on their plate. This could ultimately lead to apathy on the part of the practitioner.

Another major critique of AOPs is its lack of explicit focus on micro practice (Payne, 1997). Although AOPs offer many examples of societal and organizational changes and strategies, it is not as clear how social workers that work directly with individuals and families can utilize AOPs in their daily practice. Some have argued that AOPs have more potential to address 'individual' and 'societal' issues than did radical social work approaches (Lynn, 1999). However, our position is consistent with Payne's (1997) in that we believe that AOPs do not offer enough prescriptions to 'immediate' problems of individuals and families. Clarification in this area will guide training of social work practitioners in micro areas.

Can anti-oppressive social work truly be anti-oppressive?

As mentioned earlier, social workers inevitably bring more power to their interactions with service users than vice versa. Although anti-oppressive social work aims to achieve partnership with service users, one must wonder whether such a partnership is attainable. Dalrymple and Burke (1995) posed the following question: 'Can social work practice *ever* be based on equal power relationships?' (p. 67). If not, then another question becomes pertinent: *Is anti-oppressive social work ever truly anti-oppressive*? Social work, like other helping professions, is, by nature, 'top-down'. By top-down, we refer to the social worker as the expert who imparts knowledge and skills to the service user. In fact, the very nature of the training that social workers receive predisposes them to such power differentials. Although social workers have been reluctant in acknowledging this, social control based on these power differentials has been well embedded in social work since the inception of the profession (Dominelli, 1997, 2002; Margolin, 1997; Matahaere-Atariki *et al.*, 2001; Neubeck and Cazenave, 2001; Payne, 1997; Piven and Cloward, 1993; Sakamoto, 2003; Thompson, 1997; Wenocur and Reisch, 1989). It is our contention that, as an approach of social work, anti-oppressive practice, by default, is vulnerable to the teacher/student trap, i.e. the service user is seen as the student, while the social worker is viewed as the teacher. As Freire (1997) contends:

> The teacher teaches and the students are taught; the teacher knows everything and the students know nothing; the teacher confuses the authority of knowledge with his or her own professional authority, which she and he sets in opposition to the freedom of the students (p. 54).

Thus, instead of moving toward social justice and partnership, the teacher/student trap has a way of forcing social workers to perpetuate and re-inscribe power differentials and social injustice.

When social workers automatically frame service users' problems in terms of oppression (e.g. racism, sexism, heterosexism, ageism, classism, ableism), they may inadvertently do so to the detriment of the needs of the service user. In fact, service users may not define their problems in these same terms. Thus, the service users' (i.e. students') problems become transmuted into a *mission* that social workers (as the teachers) accept in order to address social injustice. If social workers (teachers) impart their knowledge on oppression to teach the 'uneducated' service users, it raises a further question: Who knows more about oppression? Those who teach it or those who live it? In the context of popular education, Freire (1997) contends that helping practice which begins 'with the egoistic interests of the oppressors and makes of the oppressed the objects of its humanitarianism, itself maintains and embodies oppression' (p. 36). Similarly, in her research on deconstructing professional expertise, Fook's observation (2000) was that new social work students tend to be more detached from the service user and to seek 'correct' solutions, 'rather than seeing their own involvement as crucial to the outcome' (p. 113). How can anti-oppressive social workers avoid the teacher/student trap and work in a more anti-oppressive manner?

In the post-colonial context of New Zealand, Matahaere-Atariki *et al.* (2001) argue that in order to overcome our 'false sense of neutrality', social workers must start from the admission that we have failed to be 'anti-oppressive' and maintain that discomfort (p. 131). Continued experience of discomfort signals to social workers that there is more work to be done in order to be anti-oppressive. Such discomfort may also be experienced as anger and, as Bishop (2002) and Mullaly (2002) have suggested, it could be used as a constructive force to make changes toward social justice in various ways. Similarly, Wong (2004) contends that instead of reacting to or combating discomfort itself, social workers' discomfort should be greeted 'with a gentle smile and a friendly hello' (http://www.criticalsocialwork.com) so that social workers can stay in touch with their discomfort.

One way of maintaining discomfort and acting toward changing the oppressive situations is by critically examining the power dynamics within our own profession (cf. Fook, 2000). Instead of the traditional and linear notion of 'therapeutic alliance' between the clinician and the client (Marziali and Alexander, 1991), we believe that anti-oppressive practice could benefit from having a tripartite focus, which would entail the social worker's addressing the needs of the service user, critically challenging social systems and critically challenging his or her own assumptions about the worker's professional role. Such a focus would allow social workers to work toward addressing the needs of the service user, as well as remain cognizant of the potential power differentials in the service-provider/service-user relationship. It also would make them more aware of how their own biases and assumptions affect their interactions with service users.

In the UK and Canada, diversity, social inequality and power differentials have often been addressed in terms of AOPs. However, in the USA, these same issues have generally been framed in terms of multicultural social work (Spencer *et al.*, 2000). Multiculturalism in the UK and Canada may be perceived as an approach in which the dominant group acknowledges only superficial cultural differences, without addressing power differentials (e.g. Bannerji, 2000; Williams, 2001). Moreover, this perspective tends to allocate all aspects of racism to culture and ignore post-colonial influences—by post-colonial, we mean racism as interpreted in the historical contexts—and critically examines the essentialized view of the 'Other' (e.g. Mullaly, 2002). In the USA, multiculturalism encompasses a much broader spectrum of political positions, including radical and critical ones (Bowen and Bok, 1998; de Anda, 1997; Green, 1999; Kivisto and Rundblad, 2000; Spencer *et al.*, 2000; Takaki, 1994). Many authors on multicultural social work analyse racism from historical contexts, although not necessarily articulated in post-colonial terms (e.g. Devore, 2000; Lum, 2004). Further, some authors do view colonialism and neocolonialism at the core of oppression, e.g. for First Nations Peoples (Yellow Bird, 2000). Moreover, the influence of feminist thoughts, Freirean ideology and post-modern perspectives is evident in Gutiérrez and Lewis' work on empowering women of colour (1999). Thus, we believe that a parallel can be drawn from AOPs to some of the more progressive multicultural social work approaches in the USA.

Progressive multicultural social work approaches tend to place heavy emphasis on achieving social justice through overcoming prejudice and discrimination at mainly a micro level (Pinderhughes, 1989; Spencer *et al.*, 2000; Van Soest, 1995). We acknowledge that multicultural social work and anti-oppressive social work practices originate from different historical and political backgrounds. Nevertheless, there are aspects of multicultural social work that can inform our theorizing and pedagogical efforts of anti-oppressive social work. One of those areas is the ways in which a sociological understanding of oppression can be linked to a psychological understanding, thus offering one possibility to enhance micro level practice using AOPs. We believe that critical consciousness offers an avenue to a micro level focus of AOPs.

Critical consciousness

Critical consciousness is the 'process of continuously reflecting upon and examining how our own biases, assumptions and cultural worldviews affect the ways we perceive difference and power dynamics' (Pitner and Sakamoto, in press, p. 2). As was discussed by Reed and her colleagues (1997), this continuous self-reflection must be accompanied by action to address social injustice. The notion of working with the 'consciousness' of oppressed clients, followed by moving this consciousness into practice, is not new, as it was popularized by the feminist movement in the 1970s and thereafter (Fook, 1993). In fact, some scholars have discussed critical consciousness in terms of clients' attempt to understand the structure of oppression that they are experiencing (Fook, 1993). On the other hand, in other scholars' work, this discussion on consciousness has mainly been focused on the social worker's learning to critically interrogate how his or her own identity has been shaped by the dominant ideology. These particular scholars have discussed ways in which an individual can develop critical consciousness (e.g. Gil, 1998; Leonard, 1997; Mullaly, 2002; Schön, 1983). Leonard (1997), for example, refers to this self-interrogation process as reflexive knowledge, suggesting that individuals are gaining more in-depth knowledge about themselves. According to Taylor and White (2000), reflexivity and reflectivity are two different ideas, contending that 'reflective knowledge' is mainly an 'individualized action of separate practitioners' (p. 198), while '(practicing) reflexivity' is a 'collective action of academic discipline or occupational group' (p. 198) through which health and welfare practitioners interrogate their knowledge base and practice. However, articulating the differences between reflexivity and reflectivity is beyond the scope of this article. Thus, we adhere to the brand of critical consciousness that is similar to reflective/reflexive knowledge suggested by Schön (1983), Leonard (1997) and others, since, we believe, such a process is necessary if the social workers are to move toward social change. Within the framework of AOPs, some writers have presented similar concepts, suggesting that social workers need to also develop critical self-knowledge (e.g. Dominelli, 1997; Dalrymple and Burke, 1995).

In the anti-racist practice framework, for example, Dominelli (1997) uses the term 'anti-racism/anti-racism awareness' as 'a state of mind, feeling, political commitment and action' that white people should aim to achieve. On the other hand, in an anti-oppressive framework, Dalrymple and Burke (1995) use the words 'critical self-analysis' (p. 92), which is a process whereby an individual becomes cognizant of his or her own value position in relation to others. Other writings on AOPs have also used words such as 'critical self-reflection' (Mullaly, 2002) and 'reflexivity' (Dominelli, 2002, p. 184) to identify similar processes and concepts. Although these ideas (critical self-knowledge) are often introduced as a significant step in AOPs, it is nevertheless treated briefly and/or at the very end of the books on anti-oppressive social work, suggesting a somewhat marginal treatment within the larger conceptualization of AOPs. Moreover, the ways in which social workers examine him or herself with an analytic lens from multiple identities and oppression are often not articulated in detail, leaving social workers (and students) a challenging task, with few tools. Thus, discussing *how* the *social worker* can also begin to engage in this critical self-examination process is imperative.

When social workers enter helping relationships, they enter with their own biases and prejudices. It is these biases and prejudices that can, and often do, affect how they listen to the problems of their service users and, ultimately, how they proceed to address them. In order to prevent such cognitive biases, social workers must first critically examine their own cultural backgrounds and worldviews. By examining their own assumptions and biases, the social workers may be less likely to impose their own values onto their service users. This self-reflective process has become the mantra in multicultural social work (see Pinderhughes, 1989 and Reed *et al.*, 1997, for examples). In writing this article, it is our hope that this concept will become more fully incorporated in AOPs.

The first step in developing critical consciousness requires an examination of one's various identities, locations and standpoints (Pitner and Sakamoto, in press). We have many *social identities* (race, gender, social class, etc.), which are influenced by historical, socio-cultural and political factors (Reed *et al.* 1997). How we *position* ourselves within these various identity groups affects the way we perceive ourselves and others. These multiple identities also accompany statuses. We are privileged by some identities, yet oppressed by others. For example, a male may be privileged because of his gender, yet oppressed because of disability status. *Standpoint theory* suggests that individuals in oppressed groups develop a different perception of reality than those in non-oppressed groups (Pitner and Sakamoto, in press). Thus, males and females have different perspectives on reality, and disabled and able-bodied individuals have different perspectives. This is because socio-cultural perspectives cause each group to have different narratives about their reality. Standpoint theory suggests that oppressed groups are often more cognizant of their narratives than are non-oppressed groups.

There have been a plethora of writings in the multicultural social work literature that discuss ways in which a social worker can develop critical consciousness (or critical reflexive knowledge) (e.g. Anderson, 1992; Chau, 1990; Iglehart and Becerra, 1995; Pinderghughes, 1983, 1989; Reed *et al.*, 1997; Ridley *et al.*, 1994; Van Soest, 1994, 1995). Comprehensively applying this knowledge base to an anti-oppressive social work paradigm is both instructive and necessary. As social workers, we have received professional training, which has provided us with a level of expertise to help our service users. Moving toward critical consciousness challenges social workers (i.e. the teachers) to question how the dominant ideology has shaped their perspectives about their professional role and about their service users. Moreover, it challenges them to examine how this professional role, itself, may be perpetuating power differentials in the helping relationship.

Critical consciousness and anti-oppressive practice

Scholars contend that liberation of both the social worker and the service user should be the ultimate goal of social work practice (Hopkins, 1986; Pinderhughes, 1989; although not from the social work, Freire, 1997, is useful for the basis of this idea). This requires social workers' overcoming the teacher/student trap. As mentioned, critically reflecting upon one's identities, positionality and standpoints is the first step in this process. However, in any helping relationship, we carry our *professional training schema* with us. Professional training schema may be thought of as a cognitive roadmap that predisposes us to attend to information in a certain way. With AOPs, that schema often guides us to listen for oppression. In order to overcome this, social workers must separate themselves from their professional training. We refer to this as taking a one-down position (Pitner and Sakamoto, in press).

A one-down position means that the social worker recognizes the power differentials in the service-provider/service-user relationship. Thus, the social worker actively becomes a naive investigator, making the service user the narrator of his or her own experiences. In many ways, the social worker becomes the student and the service user becomes the teacher. This requires the social worker's suspending preformed judgments and listening to how their service users describe their own situation. In other words, the social worker truly starts with where the service user 'is' (which is one of the core tenets of social work), instead of starting with where the worker thinks they 'should be'.

Practical ways of moving toward critical consciousness

What steps does an anti-oppressive social worker need to take in order to begin the journey toward critical consciousness? In this article, we present three practical ways of achieving this. First, social workers can start by framing power/oppression issues in terms of target/agent groups (Adams *et al.*, 1997, 2000). Secondly, the training of social work students should utilize classroom exercises that challenge individuals to develop critical consciousness. One procedure that we find very promising is the use of inter-group dialogues. Thirdly, empowerment of social workers should be considered an important step toward reducing social workers' sense of powerlessness, which, in turn, would help them to link their critical consciousness to effective anti-oppressive actions in order to work toward social justice.

Target/agent distinction

As mentioned earlier, the term 'anti-oppressive' has negative connotations. In fact, it is so strong that instead of helping people with privileged social group memberships to understand how they are privileged and how they may become allies to those who have oppressed social identities, it may make them feel guilty and defensive. Inevitably, this could lead to maintenance of status quo and domination. To counter this, it may be useful to identify a focus of change (i.e. what are social workers and service users trying to change?) in a precise yet more neutral way, so that people with certain privileged identities can have a larger societal perspective on their privileges, without just feeling guilty or defensive. This would also potentially increase the chances for people in both privileged and oppressed statuses to work collaboratively toward the goal of social justice.

As mentioned, we have multiple social identities—some privilege us, yet others oppress us. The *agent* is a group of people with greater access to social power and privilege based upon their group membership (e.g. being white or male) (Adams *et al.*, 2000). The agents have been described as the oppressors, or the privileged. The *target* groups, on the other hand, are groups whose access to power is limited due to their group membership (Adams *et al.*, 2000). These groups have often been described as the oppressed. Understanding how one can be both in the agent group and in the target group is important in two ways. First, it helps agent group members to examine power differentials at a structural level and, thus, lowers their resistance to acknowledgement of their own privilege. Secondly, for target group members, this analysis identifies a common goal with the agent group (i.e. eradicating all forms of oppression at every level). It also makes the target group responsible in that they are able to see how their various social group identities may also place them in the agent group role (depending on the social context). Thus, target groups do not simply blame agent groups for owning social power; they join them in working toward social justice. Being able to critically examine how we are both targets and agents allows individuals to feel less threatened and more responsible for working toward social action.

Some may argue that changing the language in AOPs waters down the nature of oppression and privilege. However, we would argue that, as Bishop (2002) and Mullaly (2002) posited, 'the process of becoming an oppressor is hidden from the person' (Mullaly, 2002, p. 208) and that because of our own cognitive and affective limitations, critical self-consciousness may not necessarily allow us to see oppressive parts of our identities (see Pitner and Sakamoto, in press, for a more detailed discussion). It is perhaps important to note that those who promote the words 'agent–target groups' are higher-education teachers in diversity and social justice, who themselves had struggled to teach these concepts to undergraduate students (Adams *et al.*, 2000). Many of us social work practitioners and academics teaching in the area of anti-oppression and diversity are aware that recognizing and continuously confronting oppression is a painful and exhausting process, not only for students 'who don't get it', but for all of us who have long been in the social work profession. Framing this issue in terms of agent and target groups is one way of making the language more accessible and of more readily raising awareness on oppressed and privileged statuses. Needless to say, the use of the terms 'target–agent groups' in no way detracts from the realities of oppression, nor our own responsibilities in interrogating and changing our own oppressive values, attitudes and behaviours. On the contrary, these terms should be seen as a pedagogical and strategic tool for elucidating the complexities of our multiple identities and for increasing alliances between those in oppressed and privileged statuses. Thus, the use of the terms 'agent–target groups' would help social workers and social work students to further develop critical consciousness, which involves a move toward social action.

Inter-group dialogues

There are various pedagogical practices designed to teach cultural diversity and power differentials, and to raise critical consciousness in social work training (Anderson and Carter, 2003; Diller, 2004; Latting, 1990; Lewis, 1993; Nakanishi and Ritter, 1992; Reed *et al.*, 1997). The inter-group dialogue is one technique among them that has been used with different student populations (Schoem, 2003). A model of inter-group dialogue adopted in many universities in the USA (e.g. Arizona State University, University of Illinois, University of Maryland, University of Massachusetts–Amherst, University of Washington) was first developed for undergraduate students at the University of Michigan in the 1980s in response to 'heightened racial and ethnic tensions' on campus (University of Michigan, The Program on Intergroup Relations, Conflict and Community, 2003; Zúñiga and Nagda, 1993). This programme's underlying assumption is that 'systematic education, sustained interaction and dialogue across boundaries' will bring about socially just communities (University of Michigan, The Program on Intergroup Relations, Conflict and Community, 2003). Inter-group dialogues typically provide a learning environment in which an equal number of two self-identified social group members participate in didactic sessions and directed dialogues over a course of a semester (some programmes also offer triad dialogues, such as Latino/African-American/White; and African-American and White inter-group dialogues; Schoem, 2003, p. 219). Often, these dialogues are interracial/interethnic; however, they could comprise any two social group members (e.g. lesbians, gay men, bisexual, transsexual and heterosexual people; women and men; black people and Jews; Schoem, 2003; Zúñiga and Nagda, 1993).

Two peer facilitators who represent both social identities lead the face-to-face dialogue processes and help participants to develop an understanding of their own social identities, learn about how the dynamics of oppression and privilege impact individual lives and develop a commitment to greater personal and social change (Nagda *et al.*, 1999, p. 444; also see University of Michigan, The Program on Intergroup Relations, Conflict and Community, 2003; Zúñiga and Nagda, 1993). The focus of dialogues is on their own social group membership, identity and social position, which produce different statuses of oppression and privilege (Nagda *et al.*, 1999).

Conflicts are seen as part of the dialogue process and students are directed to work constructively through them (Nagda *et al.*, 1999; Schoem, 2003). Through the process of dialogue and conflict resolution (or conflict management), students learn to understand and acknowledge differences within and across groups, form alliances across differences and think creatively about bridging the power differentials toward achieving more socially just communities (Schoem, 2003; University of Michigan, The Program on Intergroup Relations, Conflict and Community, 2003).

Inter-group dialogues have been applied to train social work students at the MSW level (e.g. at the University of Washington, University of Michigan in the USA). In the model used at the University of Washington, the dialogue groups consist of different racial/ethnic groups and teaching modalities include didactic and experiential learning activities, individual and small group discussions and dialogues (Nagda *et al.*, 1999). Several empirical studies have found the inter-group dialogues to be an effective tool for raising critical consciousness (e.g. Yeakley, 1998) and fostering skills necessary for constructive inter-group relations (Nagda and Zúñiga, 2003).

Empowerment

Critical consciousness can contribute to anti-oppressive social work practice and training in that it allows social workers to help to examine not only how they see the world from certain lenses, but also how they themselves may be perceived by the people whom they work with/for, such as service users, communities and organizations. Different parts of social identities will have different saliencies, depending on the contexts for both social workers and service users. For example, complex power dynamics may be played out in a treatment group comprising mostly middle-aged, heterosexual, lower-class, white men and led by a young, lesbian, middle-class, black female social worker. In this example, the social worker has power over the service users because of her professional status and class, but other statuses may or may not discount her credentials in the eyes of the service users and agencies for which she works.

We have discussed earlier that existing literature from AOPs and structural perspectives often, and rightfully, assume that the social worker has absolute or relative power over their service users (e.g. Dominelli, 2002; Mullaly, 2002). However, multiple social identities, with their accompanying multiple privileges and oppressions, could also affect the social worker on professional and personal levels. Social workers can bring with them different vulnerabilities and challenges because of racism, sexism, heterosexism and many other factors. For example, in assuming professional roles, some social workers (more so than others) may be scrutinized under the gaze of the service users and agencies whom they are working with/for.

We believe that social work's mission includes empowerment and liberation of both service users and social workers (Garvin, 1997; also see Freire, 1997). Authors on AOPs often contend that promoting empowerment is an integral part of anti-oppressive/anti-discriminatory practice (Dalrymple and Burke, 1995; Dominelli, 2002; Thompson, 1997). However, empowerment of social workers has not been fully addressed in the AOPs context. Power does not operate as a zero-sum game, i.e. empowerment of social workers does not mean aggravating power differentials between the worker and the service user—it means social workers' being able to choose *when* and *how* to negotiate, relinquish and exercise their power to help service users to empower themselves.

How can social workers who feel vulnerable or marginalized learn to empower themselves? Mullaly (2002) suggests the use of support groups with like-minded people for those social workers and academics who feel marginalized because of their support of sometimes unpopular views on anti-oppressive social work. Similarly, social workers who may feel marginalized or disempowered in their professional capacities because of their social identities could make use of support groups, caucuses of professional organizations, e-mail groups and other forms of group to process their experiences, build coalition with each other, strategize for the next steps and/or take actions to fight against oppression (e.g. for more ideas of empowerment strategies, please see Gutiérrez *et al.*, 1998; Lewis *et al.*, 2001).

In sum, critical consciousness makes social workers aware of power in their professional role which may be oppressive to service users. Used consciously and carefully as allies, this power can help to promote emancipatory changes for service users. At the same time, critical consciousness may also highlight vulnerability of social workers who have certain target group memberships. We argue that empowerment of social workers is crucial because it will help disempowered social workers to (re)gain personal and professional power to effectively perform their role to help service users. Further, if social workers with marginalized identities engage in developing their own critical consciousness and empowerment, then they can be more prepared to turn their dissatisfaction/pain/anger into social action, thus working on anti-oppression.

By utilizing classroom exercises, such as inter-group dialogues, by framing power dynamics in terms of agent/target groups and by explicitly linking critical consciousness to empowerment of both service users and workers, we believe that AOPs can begin to truly be anti-oppressive.

Looking into the future

AOPs in social work should entail the social worker's addressing the needs and assets of the service user, challenging oppressive social systems and, most importantly, critically challenging the power dynamics in the provider/user relationship. Anti-oppressive social work should not start with the social worker's defining oppression of the service user. Rather, 'starting with where the service user is' requires the social worker to relinquish preset beliefs and professional training in order to effectively listen to how their service users describe their own issues. Critical consciousness challenges social workers to be cognizant of power differentials and how these differentials may inadvertently make social work practice an oppressive experience. It is also imperative that social workers link critical consciousness to empowerment within the framework of anti-oppressive social work. Empowerment of both service users and social workers is needed to effectively challenge oppression and bring about positive changes at different levels.

When do we know that we have a sufficient level of critical consciousness? As described earlier, critical consciousness is a process; thus, there is no end point for us to say that we are now a 'good' person, free from oppressive attitudes, thoughts or actions. Critical consciousness inevitably encompasses not only cognition and values, but also actions to correct oppressive conditions. Thus, our work toward critical consciousness is an endless process. As uncomfortable as it may sound, if we are not part of the solution, we are part of the problem; there is no comfortable middle ground where one can be 'neutral' in any of the multiple continua of being oppressed versus privileged (e.g. Thompson, 1997). Accepting this discomfort and taking responsibility for whatever small part of challenging oppression one can take is a significant part of working on critical consciousness (also see Wong, 2004). Effective use of one's privilege as an ally to challenge oppression (Bishop, 2002) is important and often needed for successful systemic change.

As already mentioned, it is important that we have a consistent conceptualization of what AOPs entail. Clarifying this will help us to move toward an evidence-based, anti-oppressive social work practice. Thus, the first step in developing research studies will be to operationalize this term. In doing this, we will have a set criterion for what AOPs should entail. As we have argued, critical consciousness must be considered one important component of AOPs. However, although multicultural social work scholars in the USA contend that critical consciousness is an important practice component, virtually no empirical studies have been conducted to test this claim. As a result, we are left to theorize about the promises of critical consciousness, without much empirical support. More studies need to be focused on examining the role that developing critical consciousness has on anti-oppressive practitioners and practice outcomes.

Our goal for this article was not to construct a research agenda for measuring critical consciousness. Rather, it was to raise the important discussion about the role that critical consciousness plays in anti-oppressive social work. Social workers must remain cognizant of the power dynamics that are inevitably part of the service-provider/service-user relationship. Anti-oppressive social work practice should begin with the social worker's being vigilant of the potential role that such dynamics play in making anti-oppressive practice an oppressive experience for their service users. Critical consciousness, as we have argued, is an effective avenue for examining and understanding such dynamics.

Accepted: January 2004

References

Adams, M., Bell, L. A. and Griffin, P. (eds) (1997) *Teaching for Diversity and Social Justice: A Source Book*, New York, Routledge.

Adams, M., Blumenfeld, W., Castañeda, R., Hackman, H., Peters, M. and Zúñiga, X. (eds) (2000) *Readings for Diversity and Social Justice: An Anthology on Racism, Antisemtism, Sexism, Heterosexism, Ableism and Classism*, New York, Routledge.

Anderson, J. (1992) 'Family-centered practice in the 1990's: A multicultural perspective', *Journal of Multicultural Social Work*, **1**(4), pp. 17–29.

Anderson, J. and Carter, R. (2003) *Diversity Perspectives for Social Work Practice*, Boston, Allyn and Bacon.

Bannerji, H. (2000) 'The paradox of diversity: The construction of a multicultural Canada and "women of color" ', *Women's Studies International Forum*, **23**(5), pp. 537–60.

Bishop, A. (2002) *Becoming an Ally: Breaking the Cycle of Oppression in People*, 2nd edition, Halifax, Canada, Fernwood Publishing.

Bowen, W. G. and Bok, D. (1998). *The Shape of the River: Longer-Term Consequences of Considering Race in College and University Admissions*, Princeton, NJ, Princeton University Press.

Burke, B. and Harrison, P. (1998). 'Anti-oppressive practice', in Adams, R., Dominelli, L. and Payne, M. (eds), *Social Work: Themes, Issues and Critical Debates*, Basingstoke, Hampshire, Macmillan.

Cemlyn, S. (2000) 'Assimilation, control, mediation or advocacy? Social work dilemmas in providing anti-oppressive services for Traveller children and families', *Child and Family Social Work*, **5**(4), pp. 327–41.

Chau, K. (1990) 'A model for teaching cross-cultural practice in social work', *Journal of Social Work Education*, **26**(2), pp. 124–33.

Connolly, M. (ed.) (2001) *New Zealand Social Work: Contexts and Practice*, Auckland, New Zealand, Oxford University Press.

Dalrymple, J. and Burke, B. (1995) *Anti-oppressive Practice: Social Care and the Law*, Buckingham, Open University Press.

de Anda, D. (ed.) (1997) *Controversial Issues in Multiculturalism*, Needham Heights, MA, Allyn and Bacon.

Devore, W. (2000). ' "Whence came these people?": An exploration of the values and ethics of African American individuals, families, and communities', in Fong, R. and Furuto, S. (eds), *Culturally Competent Practice: Skills, Interventions, and Evaluations*, Needham Heights, MA, Allyn and Bacon, pp. 33–46.

Diller, J. (2004) *Cultural Diversity: A Primer for the Human Services*, Australia, Thomson, Brooks/Cole.

Dominelli, L. (1997) *Sociology for Social Work*, London, Macmillan Press.

Dominelli, L. (2002) *Anti-oppressive Social Work Theory and Practice*, London, Palgrave Macmillan.

Fook, J. (1993). *Radical Casework: A Theory of Practice*, Longon, Allyn and Unwin.

Fook, J. (2000) 'Deconstructing and reconstructing professional expertise', in Fawcett, B., Featherstone, B., Fook, J. and Rossiter, A. (eds), *Practice and Research in Social Work: Postmodern Feminist Perspectives*, London, Routledge, pp. 104–19.

Freire, P. (1997) *Pedagogy of the Oppressed*, 2nd edition, New York, The Continuum Publishing Company.

Garvin, C. (1997), *Contemporary Group Work*, 3rd edition, Boston, Allyn and Bacon.

Gil, D. (1998) *Confronting Injustice and Oppression: Concepts and Strategies for Social Workers*, New York, Columbia University Press.

Green, J. W. (1999) *Cultural Awareness in the Human Services: A Multi-ethnic Approach*, 3rd edition, Needham Heights, MA, Allyn and Bacon.

Gutiérrez, L. and Lewis, E. (1999) *Empowering Women of Color*, New York, Columbia University Press.

Gutiérrez, L., Parsons, R. and Cox, E. O. (1998) *Empowerment in Social Work Practice: A Sourcebook*, Pacific Grove, CA, Brooks/Cole.

Hatton, K. (2001) 'Translating values: Making sense of different value bases—reflections from Denmark and the UK', *International Journal of Social Research Methodology*, **4**(4), pp. 65–278.

Hopkins, P. (1986) 'On being a compassionate oppressor', *Pastoral Psychology*, **34**(3), pp. 204–13.

Iglehart, A. and Becerra, R. (1995) *Social Services and the Ethnic Community*, Needham Heights, MA, Allyn and Bacon.

Kivisto, P. and Rundblad, G. (eds) (2000) *Multiculturalism in the United States: Current Issues, Contemporary Voices*, Thousand Oaks, CA, Pine Forge Press (Sage).

Langan, M. (1992) 'Introduction: Women and social work in the 1990s', in Langan, M. and Day, L. (eds), *Women, Oppression and Social Work: Issues in Anti-discriminatory Practice*, London, Routledge.

Langan, M. and Day, L. (eds) (1992) *Women, Oppression and Social Work: Issues in Anti-discriminatory Practice*, London, Routledge.

Langley, J. (2001) 'Developing anti-oppressive empowering social work practice with older lesbian women and gay men', *British Journal of Social Work*, **31**(6), pp. 917–32.

Latting, J. (1990) 'Identifying the "Isms": Enabling social work students to confront their biases', *Journal of Social Work Education*, **26**(1), pp. 36–44.

Leonard, P. (1997) *Postmodern Welfare: Reconstructing an Emancipatory Project*, London, Sage.

Lewis, E. (1993) 'Continuing the legacy: On the importance of praxis in the education of social work students and teachers', in Schoem, D. Frankel, L., Zúñiga, X. and Lewis, E. (eds), *Multicultural Teaching in the University*, Westport, CT, Praeger, pp. 233–48.

Lewis, E., Gutiérrez, L. M. and Sakamoto, I. (2001) 'Women of color: Sources of resilience and vulnerability', in A. Gitterman (ed.), *Handbook of Social Work Practice with Vulnerable and Resilient Populations*, 2nd edition, New York, Columbia University Press, pp. 820–40.

Lum, D. (2004) *Social Work Practice and People of Color: A Process-Stage Approach*, 5th edition, Belmont, CA, Brooks/Cole.

Lynn, E. (1999) 'Value bases in social work education', *British Journal of Social Work*, **29**, pp. 939–53.

Margolin, L. (1997) *Under the Cover of Kindness: The Invention of Social Work*, Charlottesville, VA, University Press of Virginia.

Marziali, E. and Alexander, L. (1991) 'The power of the therapeutic relationship', *American Journal of Orthopsychiatry*, **61**(3), pp. 383–91.

Matahaere-Atariki, D. C., Bertanees, C. and Hoffman, L. (2001) 'Anti-oppressive practices in a colonial context', in M. Connolly (ed.), *New Zealand Social Work: Contexts and Practice*, Auckland, New Zealand, Oxford University Press.

Mullaly, B. (2002), *Challenging Oppression: A Critical Social Work Approach*, New York, Oxford University Press.

Nakanishi, M. and Rittner, B. (1992) 'The inclusionary cultural model', *Journal of Social Work Education*, **28**(1), pp. 27–35.

Nagda, B. A. and Zúñiga, X. (2003). 'Fostering meaningful racial engagement through intergroup dialogues', *Group Processes and Intergroup Relations*, **6**(1), pp. 111–28.

Nagda, B. A., Spearmon, M. L., Holley, L. C., Harding, S., Balassone, M. L., Moise-Swanson, D. and de Mello, S. (1999). 'Intergroup dialogues: An innovative approach to teaching about diversity and justice in social work programs', *Journal of Social Work Education*, **35**(3), pp. 433–49.

Neubeck, K. J. and Cazenave, N. A. (2001) *Welfare Racism: Playing the Race Card Against America's Poor*, New York, Routledge.

Payne, M. (1997). *Modern Social Work Theories*, 2nd edition, Chicago, Lyceum Books.

Pinderhughes, E. (1983) 'Empowerment for our clients and for ourselves', *Social Casework: The Journal of Contemporary Social Work*, **64**, pp. 331–8.

Pinderhughes, E. (1989) *Understanding Race, Ethnicity, and Power: The Key to Clinical Efficacy in Clinical Practice*, New York, The Free Press.

Pitner, R. O. and Sakamoto, I. (in press) 'The role of critical consciousness in multicultural practice: Examining how its strength becomes its limitation, *American Journal of Orthopsychiatry*.

Piven, F. F. and Cloward, R. A. (1993) *Regulating the Poor: The Functions of Public Welfare*, updated edition, New York, Vintage.

Razack, N. (1999) 'Anti-discriminatory practice: Pedagogical struggles and challenges', *British Journal of Social Work*, **29**(2), 231–50.

Reed, B., Newman, P., Suarez, Z. and Lewis, E. (1997) 'Interpersonal practices beyond diversity and toward social justice: The importance of critical consciousness', in Garvin, C. and Seabury, B. (eds), *Interpersonal Practice in Social Work: Promoting Competence and Social Justice*, 2nd edition, Needham Heights, MA, Allyn and Bacon, pp. 44–78.

Ridley, C., Mendoza, D. and Kanitz, B. (1994) 'Multicultural training: Reexamination, operationalization, and integration', *The Counseling Psychologist*, **22**(2), pp. 227–89.

Sakamoto, I. (2003) 'Changing images and similar dynamics: Historical patterning of foreignness in the social work profession', in R. Saunders (ed.), *The Concept of Foreign: An Interdisciplinary Dialogue*, Lanham, MD, Lexington Books.

Schoem, D. (2003) 'Intergroup dialogue for a just and diverse democracy', *Sociological Inquiry*, **73**(2), pp. 212–27.

Schön, D. (1983) *The Reflective Practitioner*, London, Temple Smith.

Shera, W. (ed.) (2003). *Emerging Perspectives on Anti-Oppressive Practice*, Toronto, Canadian Scholars' Press.

Spencer, M., Lewis, E. and Gutiérrez, L. (2000) 'Multicultural perspectives on direct practice in social work,' in Allen-Meares, P. and Garvin, C. (eds), *The Handbook of Social Work Direct Practice*, Thousand Oaks, CA, Sage, p. 131–49.

Takaki, R. (1994) *From Different Shores: Perspectives on Race and Ethnicity in America*, 2nd edition, New York, Oxford University Press.

Taylor, C. and White, S. (2000) *Practising Reflexivity in Health and Welfare: Making Knowledge*, Buckingham, Open University Press.

Thompson, N. (1997) *Anti-Discriminatory Practice*, 2nd edition, London, Macmillan.

University of Michigan Program on Intergroup Relations, Conflict and Community (2003), available online at http://www.umich.edu/~igrc/ (retrieved on 3 June 2003).

Valtonen, K. (2001) 'Social work with immigrants and refugees: Developing a participation-based framework for anti-oppressive practice', *British Journal of Social Work*, **31**(6), pp. 955–60.

Van Soest, D. (1994) 'Social work education for multicultural practice and social justice advocacy: A field study of how students experience the learning process', *Journal of Multicultural Social Work*, **3**, pp. 17–28.

Van Soest, D. (1995) 'Multiculturalism and social work education: The non-debate about competing perspectives', *Journal of Social Work Education*, **31**(1), pp. 55–66.

Williams, C. (1999) 'Connecting anti-racist and anti-oppressive theory and practice: Retrenchment or reappraisal?', *British Journal of Social Work*, **29**(2), pp. 211–30.

Williams, C. C. (2001) 'Confronting the racism in research on race and mental health services', *Canadian Social Work Review*, **18**(2), pp. 231–48.

Wilson, A. and Beresford, P. (2000) '"Anti-oppressive practice": emancipation or appropriation?', *British Journal of Social Work*, **30**(5), pp. 553–73.

Wenocur, S. and Reisch, M. (1989) *From Charity to Enterprise: The Development of American Social Work in a Market Economy*, Urbana, IL, University of Illinois Press.

Wong, Y.-L., R. (2004) 'Knowing through discomfort: A mindfulness-based critical social work pedagogy', *Critical Social Work,* **4**(1), available online at http://www.criticalsocialwork.com

Yeakley, A. M. (1998) 'The nature of prejudice change: Positive and negative change processes arising from intergroup contact experiences', unpublished dissertation, University of Michigan.

Yellow Bird, M. (2000) 'Critical values and first nations peoples', in Fong, R. and Furuto, S. (eds), *Culturally Competent Practice: Skills, Interventions, and Evaluations*, Needham Heights, MA, Allyn and Bacon, pp. 61–74.

Zúñiga, X. and Nagda, B. A. (1993) 'Dialogue groups: An innovative approach to multicultural learning', in Schoem, D., Frankel, L., Zúñiga, X. and Lewis, E. (eds), *Multicultural Teaching in the University*, Westport, CT, Praeger.

Acknowledgements

The authors would like to thank anonymous reviewers for their helpful suggestions, and also Charmaine C. Williams and Usha George for comments on earlier drafts.

Knowing Through Discomfort: A Mindfulness-based Critical Social Work Pedagogy

By

Yuk-Lin Renita Wong, Ph.D

Assistant Professor
School of Social Work
York University
Toronto, Canada

Abstract

Critical social work education has largely focused on engaging students in the conceptual and cognitive processes of learning and reflection. Other forms of knowing and transformation through the body, emotions, and spirit have been submerged under the "discursive rationality" paradigm. Proposing an integrated mind-body-spirit pedagogy in critical social work education, this paper introduces the practice of mindfulness and discusses its transformative potential for critical social work education. In particular, the author discusses how the practice of mindfulness was integrated in a course on identity and diversity in critical social work practice to facilitate students to learn through their feeling of discomfort.

Introduction

Out beyond wrongdoing and rightdoing there is a field. I'll meet you there.
When the soul lies down in that grass, the world is too full to talk about.
Ideas, language, even the phrase 'each other'
Doesn't make any sense.
– Rumi –

Critical social work practice, from its classical Marxist tradition to its recent postmodern orientation, has predominantly privileged conceptual knowing. Critical social work education, therefore, has largely focused on engaging students in the conceptual and cognitive processes of learning and reflection. Other forms of knowing and transformation through the body, emotions, and spirit have been submerged under the "discursive rationality" paradigm that privileges the mind in categorizing and normalizing the world, an epistemic bias of the Enlightenment in European history.

This paper discusses the problems which will emerge for critical social work education if it continues to neglect bodily, emotive and spiritual knowing. It proposes an integrated mind-body-emotion-spirit engagement in critical social work education. More specifically, the transformative potential of the pedagogy of mindfulness for critical social work education will be discussed.

Restoring "Listening" in Critical Social Work

Core to the mission of critical social work is the pursuit of social justice. Critical theories, including Marxist, feminist, anti-racist and anti-oppressive theories, and structural analysis have been the cornerstone of critical social work. The analysis of power, privilege, inequity, discrimination and domination along identities of race, gender, class, sexual orientations, religion, age, and dis/ability underlies its practice. Students are taught the concepts and histories of domination and oppression, the skills of structural analysis, and the attitude of critical reflectivity on their social locations in terms of power (Fooks, 1999; Garcia & Melendez, 1997; Mullaly, 2002; Razack, 1999; Rossiter, 1995). Postmodern and post-structural theories provide further insights into the construction of multiple subjectivities and truths through language. The classroom becomes a pedagogical site of engagement with students in creating an equitable communicative space for dialogues and respectful negotiations among multiple subjectivities and truths (Healy & Leonard, 2002; Leonard, 1994; Nagda et al., 1999; Rossiter, 1996).

Indeed, in a time when diversity of worldviews has increasingly gained legitimacy, how we facilitate meaningful dialogues between people located in both intersecting and conflicting discursive frames becomes more important for the co-construction of a just society for all. Paulo Freire's popular education method, experiential and participatory learning model, border pedagogy, critical classroom events, contracting, and coalition building through group project, to name a few examples, are suggested as some pedagogical methods to facilitate dialogues and understanding across differences in the classroom (Coates & McKay, 1995; Garcia & Melendez, 1997; Garcia & Soest, 1999; Giroux, 1997; Kanpol, 1995; Leonard, 1994; Razack, 1999). Underlying most of these methods is the belief that reflection in the mind will lead to action for change.

The preponderance of multiple voices and discourses in critical social work, however, may have drawn our attention away from "the other side of language" (Fiumara, 1990), that is, the significance of listening in any meaningful dialogue. "To have something to say is to be a person," Carol Gilligan (1993) writes in her early influential feminist work, "But speaking depends on listening and being heard; it is an intensely relational act" (p. xvi). How can we possibly listen to and understand each other if we are all preoccupied with speaking?

In a review of the Western tradition of analytic philosophy and hermeneutics, Gemma Fiumara (1990) uses the work of Heidegger, Wittgenstein, Gadamer, and Ricoeur to restore the "listening rationality" inherent in the semantic of the Greek term " logo ," which is said to be "pivotal" in western thought. "[T]here could be no saying without hearing, no speaking which is not also an integral part of listening, no speech which is not somehow received" (p.1). Nevertheless, this integrated concept of language or logo , with its semantic roots encompassing both listening and speaking, was gradually "reduced-by-half" in the course of Western history to primarily represent "vocalisation," and "sound and voice," which comes to shape all the rational pursuits.

According to Fiumara, in a culture where language is associated only with vocalization and speech, we fall within a "discursive rationality" which makes the world amenable to linguistic and discursive ordering, molding, and systematisation. Any speech act is "potentially normative," Fiumara argues, as "the speech act selects an aspect of reality simply by speaking about it, and whatever is said is then transformed into the statutory basis of a discourse" which "can ultimately result in constraint and epistemic control" (p.24, emphasis in original). In a culture of "discursive rationality," the dominant form of knowledge is one that objectifies, organises, conceptualises, normalizes, and dictates. To "know" the world, we categorize what we see and experience in the world – things, people – into concepts and ideas. Instead of being open to the rich moment-to-moment experiences in our encounters with people and things, we "know" and relate to them primarily through our presumed concepts about them. Such orientation produces a sense of cognitive order and control in our relations to the world. A well-known example is the European empires' extensive categorizing and detailed mapping of the geography, fauna, flora, habitat, and people of their colonies in their effort to rule and control them (Anderson, 1995).

"Listening rationality," on the other hand, functions in the context of "silence." It quiets our mind, takes away our (illusory) sense of security and control, and opens us to the untidiness, contradictions, and richness of being which cannot be bound by conceptual ordering. It invites us to the openness of not knowing and the "risk" of growth. Silence can be "a very fertile way of relating," Fiumara suggests, as it "might indicate a healthy desire to set aside certain automatic defenses that are only intended to fill emotional vacuums" and "a desire to abandon automatic verbal sequences that fill our games [of social interactions]" (p.103). "The highest function of silence," therefore, "is revealed in the creation of a co-existential space which permits dialogue to come along" (p.99). Listening in the context of silence involves "the renunciation of a predominantly molding and ordering activity" (p.123) and represents "the readiness to tear away ideologizing modes of reflection which define and constrict the ways of coexistence" (p.165). It can be "a support to the hermeneutic effort whereby we seek to establish a relationship between our world and a different 'world,' between our own attitude and a different attitude" (p.168).

Listening is also "the attitude which can unblock the creative resources immobilized by the rigidity of traditional 'logical' education" (p.165). It requires considerable "dialogic patience" to give space to the "inexpressible," so that "the inner experience which is less suited to being 'spoken' can be expressed in some way" (p.98). In "listening rationality," the person who knows is someone who transforms him/herself in order to know, rather than objectifies the world in order to recognize her/himself in his/her cognitive conceptual immobility (p.125).

To reach the "highest function of listening silence" for coexistence to be possible, therefore, it is important that we are not confined by the conceptual mind and dominant discourses which categorize, normalize, and exclude. bell hooks (1994) proposes education as "the practice of freedom." I suggest that is also what critical social work education is about: the practice of freedom from the predominant order of things, that is, "to transgress" the mode of "discursive rationality" which privileges the mind and has been governing our production of knowledge and our relations to the world. Like bell hooks, I consider the reunion of mind, body, spirit in our critical social work education an important transgression. It is an attempt to disrupt dominant forms of knowledge premised on the body-mind split, including critical knowledges (Ng, 1998). A few critical social work authors also recognize the limit of the conceptual mind and the significance of bodily and emotive knowledge for critical social work (Piele, 1998; Tangenberg & Kemp, 2002). According to Tangenberg & Kemp (2002), the commitment of social work to social justice demands our recognition that understanding of diversity and social equity must include the experience of difference in its most fundamental form. This inevitably requires attention to the body and bodily knowing, because difference and hence both privilege and marginality are fundamentally inscribed and experienced through the body. Colin Piele (1998) argues that missing in critical theories of change is the importance of bodily and emotive knowledge in governing our actions. Roxana Ng (1998) contends that "the contradiction between what we think and how we act goes beyond a simple theory-practice split" (p.3). It has to do with the fundamental way in which knowledge is organized. Our inability to translate what we know about social and environmental problems into appropriate actions, Heesoon Bai (2001) suggests, is related to the disembodiment of knowledge which replaces our multiple and fluid experiences of the world with restrictive concepts. Both Bai and Ng propose that a re-embodied pedagogy – that is, the reunion of our mind with our body, emotions, and spirit in teaching and learning – is essential to the integration of what one learns and knows with how one acts.

My journey to a mindfulness-based pedagogy for critical social work began with my experience of the limit of traditional critical pedagogical methods which primarily rely on the discursive-conceptual mind in facilitating students' critical reflections. As well, I find problems with the dualistic framing of oppression and anti-oppression in critical social work because it imposes an erroneous conceptual division between oppression and anti-oppression which is usually simplistically associated with the moral categories of bad and good. Such dichotomous conceptual frame allows those who self-identify as anti-oppressive (and hence morally "good") to find comfort in their sense of innocence and to avoid examining their implication in domination and oppression.

In the following pages, I will discuss my first experience of teaching a course on identity and diversity in which I was confronted with the problems I mentioned above. I will then introduce the practice of mindfulness, which I later integrated into the course to support students to befriend their discomfort and internal resistance and look into their participation in systems of oppression, as well as to foster their commitment to social justice.

The Risk of Knowing

Teaching critical and anti-oppressive social work can be a "risky" endeavour. For the most part, neither the teacher nor the students feel safe in the classroom. The teacher, however, is expected to take the full responsibility for creating a safe space for everyone. The image of this safe space provided by the teacher ignores the multiple relations of power operating in the classroom. In a critical reflection on her teaching experience as a minority faculty, Ng (1998) identifies three power axes in the classroom: that between the classroom and the larger academic institution; that between the teacher and the students; and that among the students. Hence, despite the formal authority of the teacher, a minority woman faculty may be challenged more than her white male colleagues because of her minority status in both the academic institution and the larger society. More importantly, anti-oppressive work is inevitably unsafe and uncomfortable because it challenges existing modes of thinking and working (Ng, 1993). What needs to be cultivated in teaching critical and anti-oppressive social work, therefore, is not so much a sense of safety, but more an openness to the feeling of discomfort. The teacher's role is not to promise and guarantee a safe space, but to support and provide a means for students to embrace and learn from their discomfort.

In the winter of 2000, I taught for the first time a course on Identity and Diversity, a core course in my social work program committed to social justice. In this course, students learned to examine how identities and cultures are both socially constructed and personally negotiated in the historical and systemic context of race, gender, class, sexual orientation, age, dis/ability and power relations. Students were encouraged to deconstruct the duality thinking of "us" versus "them," "self" versus "other," and to see how we are all implicated and interconnected in each other's histories of domination and oppression. "Their" history is thus also "our" history, and vice versa. Underlying the design of this course is the belief that understanding the systemic contexts of identities and culture and critically examining one's own social locations in the web of these power relations is of paramount significance for social workers to engage meaningfully with people of different and multiple identifications.

Like some critical social work educators, I consider students' critical reflectivity on their social locations in the web of systemic power relations crucial. Students in this course were asked to keep a journal reflecting on their identities and social locations in light of the course readings and class discussions of the week. To provide students with a (relatively "safe") space to engage in their reflective process, the journals were not graded. Students received marks as long as they handed in the journals. Students were also asked to build learning communities through working together in group projects to learn with and from each other about a particular identity and diversity issue which they were unfamiliar with. In the last three classes of the course, students presented in group to other class members the historical, political, social, economic, and global contexts of the identity and diversity issue they chose to learn about. Each group member also conducted an interview with one individual who self-identified him/herself with the selected identity issue. For their individual final paper, students were asked to reflect on how working on the group project had changed their views on their selected identity issue and how their analysis of the issue was shaped by their own social locations.

The course is inevitably contentious and uncomfortable for many students who are brought to confront their privileges and experiences of oppression. Most of us, especially social workers, are invested in a sense of innocence (Jeffery, 2002; Rossiter, 2001) and sometimes victimhood, as well as the noble vision of social work to help and to do good. We are led to think in the dualistic conceptual frame of oppression versus anti-oppression, and bad versus good. When we are challenged to recognise our participation in systemic domination and oppression despite our best intention, it is not surprising that this state of cognitive dissonance may result in some students' denial, resistance and even hostility towards the teacher. Minority teachers, as discussed earlier, are more likely to be undermined in the classroom (Ng, 1993).

In this course, a minority student wrote in one of her reflective journals about her observation of the classroom power dynamics as well as conversations among students after class. She felt indignant at some white as well as a couple of minority students' blatant discrimination against and intolerance of a minority teacher. She questioned how students could learn and grow to become a critical social worker if they were prejudiced against someone – the teacher – who "looks different." Two white students respectively expressed in their journals their discomfort with the course and criticized it as "white-bashing," despite the emphasis in most of the course readings and class discussions on multiple and interlocking systems of oppression of race, gender, class, and sexual orientations. After reading one of the course readings on the appropriation of Native culture in the white dominant Canadian society, a white student defended fiercely and repeatedly in her journals one of her family member's Native art business as supporting Native artists. A second-generation Chinese-Canadian student could only see Chinese women as submissive and oppressed by "traditional" Chinese culture in both her journals and final paper. At the end of the course, a group of white students who were unhappy about their grade – ranging between "B" and "B+" – organized to meet with the School Director, challenging my authority in grading as well as discrediting the course content and my teaching.

My first experience of teaching this course was unpleasant and anxiety provoking, to say the least. I felt powerless in dissolving the tensions that emerged from the course. I questioned why my experiential-participatory critical pedagogy did not seem to facilitate students' reflections on their social locations. Rather, it invited some students to ride on the dominant racial and gender relations to discredit me as a minority teacher, and to evade from facing the challenges the course had brought them.

Taking the insight from my own spiritual practice of mindfulness, I tried, not without struggles, to stay in touch with my feelings of discomfort and vulnerability and recognised how I also wanted to run away. I began to see that for me to continue teaching anti-oppressive and critical social work while keeping myself hopeful and healthy, I must learn and support my students to learn how to engage and work with my/their discomfort. The key lies in "relaxing into" (Chödrön, 1997) and befriending discomfort (Thich Nhat Hanh, 2000) as an opportunity for openness, learning, and growth. In the following pages, I will introduce the practice of mindfulness and then discuss how I later developed a mindfulness-based pedagogy for the course.

What is Mindfulness?

Mindfulness is the core teaching of Guatama Buddha. Thich Nhat Hanh (1996), a Vietnamese Zen Buddhist monk in exile, a peace activist who was nominated by Martin Luther King Jr. for the Nobel Peace Prize, tells a story which best illustrates the meaning of mindfulness. Once Guatama Buddha was asked, "What do you and your students practice?" He replied, "We sit, we walk, and we eat." The questioner continued, 'But everyone sits, walks, and eats." The Buddha then said, "When we sit, we know we are sitting. When we walk, we know we are walking. When we eat, we know we are eating."

While originating in the teachings of Guatama Buddha, mindfulness has little to do with religion. In recent years, many practitioners in the health and mental health field have adopted the practice of mindfulness in working with clients with chronic pain, stress, depression, and other psychological distress (Deatherage, 1996; Kabat-Zinn, 1990; Linehan, 1995; Segal, Williams & Teasdale, 2002). Mindfulness is about being here, fully present with all our activities and thoughts, with body and mind united, and not in a state of dispersion (Chödrön, 1997; Thich Nhat Hanh, 2000). It means paying attention in a particular way: in the present moment and non-judgementally . This kind of attention nurtures awareness, clarity, and openness to present-moment experience. When we are fully present in the here-and-now, we begin to see how we are often caught in our past, or carried away by our thoughts about the future. We are awakened to the fullness of our moment-to-moment experience, and brought to question our presumed view of the world and our concept of who we are. When we commit ourselves to paying attention in an open way, without being trapped in our likes and dislikes, good and bad, opinions and prejudices, projections and expectations, we have a chance to free ourselves from the constraints of the conceptual mind and predominant discourses. We see new possibilities. Our relation to each other and to the world also opens up. Mindfulness, therefore, is a practice which helps us arrive at the place of listening silence. All in all, it is a practice, not an abstract concept or ideology, of being fully in touch with life.

Going hand in hand with mindfulness is insight: looking deeply into cause and effect and the interconnectedness of all things. For insights to arise, the practice of "resting" and "stopping" is crucial (Thich Nhat Hanh, 2000): stopping our auto piloting, reacting, and ongoing running. In other words, mindfulness facilitates us to quiet our mind from predominant discourses which keep us busy with categorizing and discriminating – our "discursive rationality." Instead, we stay fully present with what is unfolding in the moment. Mindfulness, therefore, is the cultivation of listening silence opening us to dialogic communication and relations.

Mindfulness of Discomfort: Leaving the Comfort Zone for Personal Growth and Social Transformation

Having experienced the quality of openness in mindfulness practice, I decided to develop a mindfulness-based pedagogy when I taught the same course for the second time in the summer of 2000. In the first class, I prepared the students for the discomfort the course might bring up for them. I told the students that this course would probably be very uncomfortable for many of them because it would unsettle many of their old beliefs and conceptions about themselves and the world. Integrating the practice of mindfulness, I asked the students to stay in touch with and embrace their feeling of discomfort, not to judge it wrong and push it away. To encourage the students to relax into and befriend their discomfort, I invited them to take their feeling of discomfort as a teacher and a friend – as a precious opportunity for learning and growth – by greeting their discomfort with a gentle smile and a friendly hello. I encouraged students to "stop" and "rest" when they felt uncomfortable, to listen to what their feeling of discomfort may tell them, instead of busying themselves with reacting, defending or hiding: "What is my feeling of discomfort trying to tell me, about myself, about my social locations in the society?" I also suggested the students to see the place of discomfort as a place where change begins. Only when we feel uncomfortable would we begin to feel the need for change. Social work is fundamentally about change and the possibility of change, individually and collectively. Throughout the course, I introduced simple breathing exercises to facilitate students to pause and go back to their body after some intense class discussions or disturbing videos about systemic oppressions, to allow room for their feelings and for insights to unfold in the moment of "listening silence." Asking student s to stay fully in touch with their thoughts and feelings as they arise in a gentle and non-judgmental way, and to look deeply into what the feelings reveal to them is in fact mindfulness practice. Mindfulness, as Pema Chödrön (1996) puts it succinctly, is about "diving into your real issues and fearlessly befriending the difficult and blocked areas and deep-seated habitual patterns that keep us stuck in ignorance and confusion" (p.301).

In this course, a number of students expressed in their reflective journals how they engaged with their discomfort and noticed their emotional and mental reactivity to the course materials, lectures, and discussions. A student talked about her growing awareness of how she had always tried to run away from her discomfort, rather than facing the challenge of looking into what made her reacted in certain ways. Another student recounted her "uncomfortable" feeling and even "resentment" at "having to rethink her notions" after watching a video which intensely deconstructed the stereotypes of Muslim women in North America. Learning to befriend and engage with her feelings, this student was gradually able to appreciate the experience as "an excellent learning opportunity." Another student took her uncomfortable feeling as "a good thing" when she was confronted with the relations of oppression between the aboriginal people and the dominant (white) Canadians. One student began to recognise how her failing to critically examine the policies and institutions of the society had allowed her "to find comfort in ignorance." For this student, the teachings in the course "have removed the security of ignorance and have illustrated that ignorance is not bliss." Another student recognised how her saying to herself that she had no culture when she felt uncomfortable with class discussions and activities related to culture and race was "just an easy way to escape feeling uneasy with racism." Instead of pushing away her feeling of discomfort, she took it up as "a good place to be in" and opened herself to the questions about her social locations. Her discomfort thus became a "learning opportunity" for her to move out of her "protective cocoon" towards "taking personal responsibility" for her growth as a person and a social worker by inviting her to examine the power and privilege which she "pretend[ed]" she did not have.

In the following year when I taught this course again using the pedagogy of mindfulness, many students similarly identified the moment of discomfort as one of their most important moments in the course which brought about new realisation and change in them. A student commented on how the class not only challenged her "on an intellectual level," but also "on a profound introspective level that often arouses feelings of discomfort." Taking the suggestion of "go[ing] with the feeling" despite having "a hard time" doing so, this student was not only able to recognize her privilege, but also realise how she wanted to "deny" that she "contributed to maintaining that privilege through subscribing to the process of making assumptions and generalisations." Being in touch with her feeling, therefore, this student was able to gain insights into how she participated in perpetuated oppression when she let her mind prevail in making assumptions and generalisations.

Through mindfulness of their feeling of discomfort, these students become conscious of their habitual mental reactivity to issues of domination and oppression. The practice of stopping and non-judging in mindfulness creates room for these students to observe their thoughts and feelings as they arise. In the process, they become aware of how their mind are constantly categorizing and labelling everything they experience, reacting to the experience in terms of what they like and dislike, or judging people and themselves as good or bad.

If we all care to stop and observe the rise and fall of our thoughts and feelings, we will notice how our mind, like the students', is also dominated by the habit of categorizing and judging which often leads us to mechanical reactions. The practice of mindfulness, however, enables us to be a witness to our judging mind. The stance of a witness makes it more possible for us to break away from our habitual mental activities of labelling and judging, as well as the normative dualistic ordering of good and bad, right and wrong. Mindfulness, therefore, is a practice which helps us cultivate "listening silence" – a space where the automatic mental activities of molding, ordering and ideologizing is set aside to make room for our hermeneutic effort to engage in genuine dialogues (Fiumara 1990).

Being fully present with the here-and-now through the practice of mindfulness, we discover the richness and untidiness of the present-moment experience, and notice the limit of the concepts, categories and ideologies we have lived by. When we are not stuck in our categorizing and judging mind, we are more likely to see clearly the flow of our thoughts and emotions: where they came from and where they go. We begin to recognize how our self-identifications are related to the dominant discourses and systemic relations that determine what is good and bad, what is desirable and undesirable in the world we live in. Attending to the source of our thoughts and emotions, we are also brought to touch our deep-seated vulnerability – shame, guilt, fear, despair, and wound – in being part of and caught by these systemic relations. Touching our vulnerability with a gentle and non-judging attention of mindfulness is an important embracing and caring act for ourselves, others, and the world. It helps release us from the grip of our vulnerabilities and supports us to confront our implication in the interlocking systems of power relations, without judging ourselves or others as inherently bad or unworthy, or denying our responsibility in the world.

Mindfulness practice thus enables students to build a new relationship with their discomfort – a feeling they would usually push away – and possibly with others whom they find different and feel uncomfortable with. Being mindful of their mental and emotional reactivity, students learn to realize, not just conceptually, but also emotionally, bodily and spiritually, how their existence and experiences are structured by their location in the larger web of life and relations. Discomfort, therefore, becomes a transformative resource enhancing students' learning and growth, personally and professionally. How students would carry their classroom mindfulness experience into their field practice and actions for systemic change would be a meaningful topic for further study.

Implications for Critical Social Work Education

How we know and what is privileged as legitimate knowing constitute our knowledge about and relation to the world. For critical social work education to challenge the status quo and unsettle the dominant power relations, therefore, it is critical that we problematize and inquire into the very fundamental way of how we know. The commitment of critical social work to social justice demands us to recognize the experience of difference and diversity in its most fundamental form – the many different ways we know, through our mind-intellect as well as through our bodily, emotive and spiritual experiences. It must be made clear, however, that what is proposed in this paper is not about renouncing the conceptualizing mind and privileging other forms of knowing, but more about a reunion of the mind with the body, emotion, and spirit of our being, knowing, and doing.

Acknowledging different ways of knowing means that we provide room for students to explore, discover and nurture their unique creative capacity and resources for learning. Creative classroom pedagogies such as mindfulness exercises and popular theatre that engage students in their bodily, emotive, cognitive, and spiritual knowing and reflection can become significant sites of transgression and decolonization (Smith, 1999). In an advanced course specifically on critical perspectives in social work, I encourage students to "go outside the box," to honour marginalized knowledges, and to bring together their mind, body, emotion, and spirit in presenting and expressing what they have learned and what they aspire to in their assignments. Openness to alternative knowledges is an important attitude for students to cultivate as critical social work practitioners working with people of diverse backgrounds. Over the years, I have had increasing number of students who responded with enthusiasm and excitement in exploring different forms of learning and in expanding their repertoire of knowing. Alongside their analytical writing and presentation, many students also produced video, tapestry, painting, sculpture, mosaic, play script, and poetry for their assignments.

A mindfulness-based critical social work pedagogy also means that we honour listening silence as much as vocalization in our teaching. Fostering students' capacity to listen to others and themselves is therefore as important as encouraging them to speak. Engaging students in breathing and listening exercises as well as in mindfully observing their internal activities and chatters can facilitate students' awareness of the richness of silence and the fluidity of themselves and of others.

A mindfulness-based pedagogy also requires us as teacher to practise what we teach. Only if we actively practise daily mindfulness can we see the limit of "discursive rationality" and understand the struggles students wrestle with, and be effective in cultivating a meaningful dialogic communicative space for the co-creation of a just world for all.

Conclusion

To learn that things and life are more complex than we think is more difficult than staying in the comfort and security of the idea that there is a good or bad, a right or wrong, anti-oppression and oppression, and that we simply need to decide which side we are on. To create a dialogic communicative space, however, it is crucial that we are not preoccupied with categorizing people into good or bad, right or wrong – "us" or "them" – but rather we learn to appreciate the fluidity of being and engage with each other in the openness of "listening silence." Concepts, categories and theories formulated in our discursive-analytical mind may be useful tools and conceptual maps to help us understand our experience and the world around us. But it is important to remember that they are not the experience itself, nor can they fully represent the experience or the world we live in. We must, therefore, not be dictated to by the predominantly ordering and discriminating activities of our mind, but be mindfully open to our bodily, emotive and spiritual knowing in our relation to each other and the world.

References

Anderson, Benedict. 1995. Imagined communities. London: Verso.

Bai, H. (2001) 'Beyond the educated mind: Towards a pedagogy of mindfulness', in B. Hocking & J. Haskell & W. Linds (eds.), Unfolding Bodymind: Exploring possibility through education , Brandon, VT, Foundation for Educational Renewal.

Chödrön, P. (1996) 'No right, no wrong', in M. Dresser (ed.), Buddhist women on the edge: Contemporary perspectives from the western frontier , Berkeley, North Atlantic Books.

Chödrön, P. (1997) When things fall apart: Heart advice for difficult times , Boston, Shambhala.

Coates, J., & McKay, M. (1995), 'Toward a new pedagogy for social transformation', Journal of Progressive Human Services, 6(1), pp.27-43.

Fiumara, G. C. (1990), The other side of language: A philosophy of listening (C. Lambert, Trans.), London, Routledge.

Fook, J. (1999) 'Critical reflectivity in education and practice', in B. Pease & J. Fook (eds.), Transforming social work practice: Postmodern critical perspectives , London, Routledge.

Garcia, B., & Melendez, M. P. (1997) 'Concepts and methods in teaching oppression courses', Journal of Progressive Human Services, 8(1), pp.23-40.

Garcia, B., & Soest, D. V. (1999) 'Teaching about diversity and oppression: Learning from the analysis of critical classroom events', Journal of Teaching in Social Work, 18(1/2), pp.149-167.

Giroux, H. A. (1997) Pedagogy and the politics of hope: Theory, culture, and schooling , Boulder, Westview Press.

Healy, K., & Leonard, P. (2000) 'Responding to uncertainty: Critical social work education in the postmodern habitat', Journal of Progressive Human Services, 11(1), pp.23-48.

Hooks, B. (1994) Teaching to transgress: Education as the practice of freedom , New York, Routledge.

Jeffery, D. (2002) A terrain of struggle: Reading race in social work education , Unpublished Ph.D. Thesis, OISE / University of Toronto, Toronto.

Kabat-Zinn, J. (1990) Full catastrophe living: Using the wisdom of your body and mind to face stress, pain and illness , New York, A Delta Book.

Kanpol, B. (1995) 'Multiculturalism and empathy: A border pedagogy of solidarity', in B. Kanpol & P. McLaren (eds.), Critical multiculturalism: Uncommon voices in a common struggle , Westport, Connecticut, Bergin & Garvey.

Linehan, M. (1995) Treating borderline personality disorder: The dialectical approach [videorecording]. New York: Guilford Publications.

Mullaly, B. (2002) Challenging oppression: A critical social work approach , Toronto, Oxford University Press.

Nagda, B. A., Spearmon, M. L., Holley, L. C., Harding, S., Balassone, M. L., Moise-Swanson, D., & de Mello, S. (1999) 'Intergroup dialogues: An innovative approach to teaching about diversity and justice in social work programs', Journal of Social Work Education, 35(3), pp.433-449.

Ng, R. (1993) ' "A woman out of control": Deconstructing sexism and racism in the university', Canadian Journal of Education, 18(3), pp.189-205.

Ng, R. (1998, April 13-17) 'Is embodied teaching and learning critical pedagogy? Some remarks on teaching health and the body from an Eastern perspective', Paper presented at the American Educational Research Association (AERA) Annual Meeting, San Diego.

Peile, C. (1998) 'Emotional and embodied knowledge: Implications for critical practice', Journal of Sociology & Social Welfare, 25(4), pp.39-59.

Razack, N. (1999) 'Anti-discriminatory practice: Pedagogical struggles and challenges', British Journal of Social Work, 29(2), pp.231-250.

Rossiter, A. (2001) 'Innocence lost and suspicion found: Do we educate for or against social work?' Critical Social Work, 2(1).

Rossiter, A. B. (1995) 'Teaching social work skills from a critical perspective', Canadian Social Work Review, 12(1), pp.9-27.

Rossiter, A. B. (1996) 'A perspective on critical social work', Journal of Progressive Human Services, 7(2), pp.23-41.

Segal, Z. V., Williams, J. M. G., & Teasdale, J. D. (2002) Mindfulness-based cognitive therapy for depression: A new approach to preventing relapse , New York, Guilford Press.

Smith, L. T. (1999) Decolonizing methodologies: Research and indigenous peoples . London: Zed Books Ltd.

Tangenberg, K. M., & Kemp, S. (2002) 'Embodied practice: Claiming the body's experience, agency and knowledge for social work', Social Work, 47(1), pp.9-18.

Thich Nhat Hanh (1996) The long road turns to joy: A guide to walking meditation , Berkeley, Parallax Press.

Thich Nhat Hanh (2000) The path of emancipation , Berkeley, Parallax Press.

Renita Wong, Ph.D can be contacted via e-mail at:
rylwong@YORKU.CA

Neff, K. D. (2012). The science of self-compassion. In C. Germer & R. Siegel (Eds.), *Compassion and Wisdom in Psychotherapy* (pp. 79-92). New York: Guilford Press.

Chapter 6: The Science of Self-Compassion

Kristin D. Neff

When you begin to touch your heart or let your heart be touched,

you begin to discover that it's bottomless, that it doesn't have any resolution,

that this heart is huge, vast, and limitless.

You begin to discover how much warmth and gentleness is there, as well as how much space.

- Pema Chödrön (2001, p. 128)

To understand what is meant by the term *self-compassion*, it is useful to first consider what it means to feel compassion more generally. When we experience compassion, we notice and are moved by the suffering of others. Rather than rushing past a homeless man begging for change on your way to work, for example, you might actually stop to consider how difficult his life must be. The moment you see the man as an actual human being who is suffering, your heart connects with him (compassion literally means "to suffer with;" see Chapter 1). Instead of ignoring him, you find that you're moved by his pain, and feel the urge to help in some way. And importantly, if what you feel is true compassion rather than simply pity, you may say to yourself, "There but for the grace of God go I. If I'd been born in different circumstances, or maybe had just been unlucky, I might also be struggling to survive. We're all vulnerable."

Compassion, therefore, presupposes the recognition and clear seeing of suffering. It entails feelings of kindness, care, and understanding for people who are in pain, so that the desire to ameliorate suffering naturally emerges. Finally, compassion involves recognizing the shared human condition, fragile and imperfect as it is.

Self-compassion has exactly the same qualities—it's just compassion turned inward. In this chapter, I will describe what self-compassion is and isn't, how self-compassion is related to well-being, and how self-compassion contributes to healing in psychotherapy.

What's Self-Compassion?

Drawing on the writings of various Buddhist teachers (e.g., Bennett-Goleman, 2001; Brach, 2003; Goldstein & Kornfield, 1987; Salzberg, 1997), I have defined self-compassion as being composed of three main components: self-kindness, a sense of common humanity, and mindfulness (Neff, 2003b).

Self-kindness

Self-compassion entails being warm and understanding toward ourselves when we suffer, fail, or feel inadequate, rather than flagellating ourselves with self-criticism. It recognizes that being imperfect and experiencing life difficulties is inevitable, so we soothe and nurture ourselves when confronting our pain rather than getting angry when life falls short of our ideals. We clearly acknowledge our problems and shortcomings without judgment, so we can do what's necessary to help ourselves. We can't always get what we want. We can't always *be* who we want to be. When this reality is denied or resisted, suffering arises in the form of stress, frustration, and self-criticism. When this reality is accepted with benevolence, however, we generate positive emotions of kindness and care that help us cope.

Common Humanity

One of the biggest problems with harsh self-judgment is that it tends to make us feel isolated. When we notice something about ourselves we don't like, we irrationally feel like everyone else is perfect and it's only *me* who is inadequate. This isn't a logical process, but a kind of distorted self-centeredness: focusing on our inadequacies gives us tunnel vision so that we can't see anything else but our own feeble, worthless self (see Chapter 3). Similarly, when things go wrong in our external lives, we feel that somehow other people are having an easier time of it, that our own situation is abnormal or unfair. When our experiences are interpreted from the perspective of a separate self, we have trouble remembering the similar experiences of our fellow humans (like the dying 84 year-old man whose final words were "why me?") Self-compassion recognizes that life challenges and personal failures are part of being human, an experience we all share. In this way, it helps us to feel less desolate and isolated when we are in pain.

Mindfulness

Mindfulness is a nonjudgmental, receptive mind-state in which thoughts and feelings are observed as they are, without suppressing or denying them (see Chapter 2). You can't ignore your pain and feel compassion for it at the same time. Of course, you may think that suffering is blindingly obvious. But how many of us, when we look in a mirror and don't like what see, remember that this a moment of suffering worthy of a compassionate response? Similarly, when life goes awry, we often go into problem-solving mode immediately without recognizing the need to comfort ourselves for the difficulties we're facing. Conversely, mindfulness requires that we not be overly identified with negative thoughts or feelings, so that we are caught up and swept away by our aversive reactions (Bishop et al., 2004). This type of rumination narrows our focus and exaggerates implications for self-worth (Nolen-Hoeksema, 1991). The mental space provided by taking a mindful approach to our difficult feelings, however, allows for greater clarity, perspective, and emotional equanimity (Baer, 2003; Shapiro, Carlson, Astin, & Freedman, 2006).

[BEGIN TEXT BOX]

Self-Compassion Phrases

When you're feeling stress or emotional pain— perhaps you are caught in a traffic jam, are arguing with a loved one, or are feeling inadequate in some way— it's helpful to have a set of phrases memorized to help you remember to be more compassionate to yourself in the moment. You can take a deep breath, put your hand over your heart, or gently hug yourself (if you feel comfortable doing so), and repeat the following phrases:

This is a moment of suffering

Suffering is a part of life

May I be kind to myself

May I give myself the compassion I need

[END TEXT BOX]

These phrases capture the essence of the three components of self-compassion. The first phrase helps to mindfully open to the sting of emotional pain. (You can also just say "this is really hard right now" or "this hurts.") The second phrase reminds us that suffering unites all living beings and reduces the tendency to feel ashamed and isolated when things go wrong in our lives. The third phrase begins the process of responding with self-kindness rather than self-criticism. The final phrase reinforces the idea that you both need and deserve compassion in difficult moments. Be experimental with the phrases. Other phrases that may feel more authentic in a given situation are "May I accept myself as I am," "May I forgive myself," or "May I learn to accept what I cannot change." As you may have noticed, this practice is similar to the loving-kindness meditation introduced in Chapter 3.

What Self-compassion is Not

Self-pity

People often avoid taking a compassionate stance toward themselves because they confuse self-compassion with self-pity. Western culture has a strong “stiff-upper-lip” tradition in which we’re taught that we should just carry on without complaint. Self-compassion is very different from self-pity, however. When individuals feel self-pity, they become immersed in their own problems and forget that others have similar problems. They ignore their interconnections with others and act as if they are the only ones in the world suffering. Self-pity emphasizes egocentric feelings of separation and exaggerates the extent of personal distress. Self-compassion, however, allows us to see the related experiences of self and other without distortion or disconnection. When we acknowledge how hard it is for us in the moment, the rest of humanity is automatically included in our concerned attention. Moreover, when we think about what others are going through, we are often able to put our own situation into greater perspective.

Self-indulgence

An even greater block to self-compassion is the belief that it’s self-indulgent to be kind to oneself. Many people think that self-criticism is necessary to motivate themselves, and that if they’re too self-compassionate they’ll just sit around all day watching TV and eating ice-cream. But is this true? A good analogy can be found in how parents motivate their children. When a mother cares about her son and desires his well-being, does she indulge him by letting him do whatever he wants (like sitting around all day watching TV and eating ice-cream?) No. She’ll make sure he does things like eat well, go to school, finish his homework, brush his teeth, and go to bed early—even if he doesn’t want to—because it’s necessary for him to grow and be healthy. Her child will also be more motivated to reach his goals in life when he can count on his mother's encouragement and support even when he fails.

On the other hand, if a mother ruthlessly criticizes her son when he messes up, telling him he's a good-for-nothing failure who'll never amount to anything, how is that going to make him feel? Inspired, motivated, ready to take on the world? Of course not. Constant criticism makes us feel worthless and depressed—not exactly a get-up-and-go mindset. And yet, isn't that how most of us act towards ourselves? We somehow have the notion that self-criticism is a more effective motivator than giving ourselves nurturing, support, and encouragement.

You might say that the motivation of self-compassion arises from love, while the motivation of self-criticism arises from fear. To the extent that self-criticism *does* work as a motivator, it's because we're driven by the desire to avoid self-judgment when we fail. But if we know that failure will be met with a barrage of self-criticism, sometimes it can be too frightening to even try. This is why self-criticism is associated with underachievement and self-handicapping strategies like procrastination (Powers, Koestner & Zuroff, 2007).

Self-criticism is also used as a means of shaming oneself into action when confronting personal weaknesses. However, this approach backfires if weaknesses remain unacknowledged in an unconscious attempt to avoid self-censure (Horney, 1950). For instance, if you have an anger problem but continually blame things on your partner because you can't face up to the truth about yourself, how are you ever going to achieve a more harmonious relationship? With self-compassion, however, we strive to achieve for a very different reason—because we *care*. If we truly want to be kind to ourselves, we'll do things to help us be happy, such as taking on challenging new projects or learning new skills. And because self-compassion gives us the safety needed to acknowledge our weaknesses, we're in a better position to change them for the better.

Self-Esteem

It's also important to distinguish self-compassion from self-esteem. Self-esteem refers to the degree to which we evaluate ourselves positively. It represents how much we like or value ourselves, and is often based on comparisons with others (Coopersmith, 1967; Harter, 1999). In American culture, having high self-esteem means standing out in a crowd—being special and above average (Heine, Lehman, Markus, & Kitayama, 1999). In contrast, self-compassion is not based on positive judgments or evaluations—it is a way of *relating* to ourselves. People feel self-compassion because they are human beings, not because they are special or above average. It emphasizes interconnection rather than separateness. This means that with self-compassion, you don't have to feel better than others to feel good about yourself. It also offers more emotional stability than self-esteem because it is always there for you—when you're on top of the world *and* when you fall flat on your face.

Empirical Data

Okay, but what does the research show? So far, the majority of studies on self-compassion have been correlational and have used the Self-Compassion Scale (Neff, 2003a)—a 26-item self-report measure. (You can take this scale online at www.Self-Compassion.org). However, more recent research has started to examine self-compassion using experimental manipulations or interventions.

Self-Compassion and Emotional Well-Being

One of the most consistent findings in the research literature is that greater self-compassion is linked to less anxiety and depression (see Neff, 2009 for a review). Of course, a key feature of self-compassion is the lack of self-criticism, and self-criticism is known to be an important predictor of anxiety and depression (Blatt, 1995). However, self-compassion still offers protection against anxiety and depression when controlling for self-criticism and negative affect (Neff, 2003a; Neff, Kirkpatrick & Rude, 2007). Thus, self-compassion is not merely a matter of looking on the bright side of things or avoiding negative feelings. Self-compassionate people recognize when they are suffering, but are kind toward themselves in these moments, acknowledging their connectedness with the rest of humanity.

In support of this idea, my colleagues and I conducted a study involving a mock interview task in which participants were asked to write an answer to the infamous question, "Please describe your greatest weakness" (Neff, Kirkpatrick, & Rude, 2007). Not only did self-compassionate people experience less anxiety after the task, they also tended to use more connected and less isolating language when writing about their weaknesses. Similarly, Leary and colleagues (Leary, Tate, Adams, Allen, & Hancock, 2007) investigated the way that self-compassionate people deal with negative life events by asking participants to report about problems experienced over a 20-day period. Individuals with higher levels of self-compassion had more perspective on their problems and were less likely to feel isolated by them. They also experienced less anxiety and self-consciousness when thinking about their difficulties.

Self-compassion is associated with greater wisdom and emotional intelligence (Neff, 2003a; Neff, Rude, & Kirkpatrick, 2007), suggesting that self-compassion represents a wise way of dealing with difficult emotions. For instance, self-compassionate people engage in rumination and thought suppression less often than those low in self-compassion (Neff, 2003a; Neff, Kirkpatrick, & Rude, 2007). They also report greater emotional coping skills, including more clarity about their feelings and greater ability to repair negative emotional states (Neely, Schallert, Mohammed, Roberts, & Chen, 2009; Neff, 2003a; Neff, Hseih, & Dejitthirat, 2005).

Self-compassion appears to bolster positive states of being as well. For example, self-compassion is associated with feelings of social connectedness and life satisfaction—important elements of a meaningful life (Neff, 2003a; Neff, Pisitsungkagarn, & Hseih, 2008). It is also linked to feelings of autonomy, competence, and relatedness (Neff, 2003a), suggesting that self-compassion helps meet the basic psychological needs that Deci and Ryan (1995) argue are fundamental to well-being. Self-compassionate people tend to experience more happiness, optimism, curiosity, and positive affect than those who lack self-compassion (Neff, Rude, & Kirkpatrick, 2007). By wrapping one's pain in the warm embrace of self-compassion, positive feelings are generated that help balance the negative ones.

Self-Compassion, Motivation, and Health

Research supports the idea that self-compassion enhances motivation rather than self-indulgence. For instance, while self-compassion is negatively related to perfectionism, it has no association with the level of performance standards adopted for the self (Neff, 2003a). Self-compassionate people aim just as high, but also recognize and accept that they can't always reach their goals. Self-compassion is also linked to greater personal initiative; the desire to reach one's full potential (Neff, Rude, & Kirkpatrick, 2007). Self-compassionate people have been found to have less motivational anxiety and engage in fewer self-handicapping behaviors such as procrastination than those who lack self-compassion (Williams, Stark, & Foster, 2008). In addition, my colleagues and I (Neff et al., 2005) found that self-compassion was positively associated with mastery goals—the intrinsic motivation to learn and grow—and negatively associated with performance goals—the desire to enhance one's self-image (Dweck, 1986). This relationship was mediated by the lesser fear of failure and perceived self-efficacy of self-compassionate individuals. Thus, self-compassionate people are motivated to achieve, but for intrinsic reasons, not because they want to garner social approval.

Self-compassion also promotes health-related behaviors. For instance, a study by Adams and Leary (2007) demonstrated that self-compassion can help people stick to their diets. Dieters often display a paradoxical tendency—if they break their diet and eat high calorie foods, they tend to eat more afterwards as a way to reduce bad feelings associated with their lapse (Heatherton & Polivy, 1990; see abstinence violation effect, Chapter 16). This study demonstrated that helping women to feel compassionately about blowing their diet attenuated this tendency. Similarly, Kelly, Zuroff, Foa, and Gilbert (2009) examined whether self-compassion could help people stop or reduce smoking. Individuals trained to feel compassionate about the difficulties of giving up smoking reduced their smoking to a greater extent than those trained to reflect upon and monitor their smoking. The self-compassion intervention was especially effective among those who were highly self-critical or resistant to change. Similarly, a study of women's goals for exercising found that self-compassionate women had intrinsic rather than extrinsic motivation to exercise, and their goals for exercising were less related to ego-concerns (Magnus, Kowalski, & McHugh, 2010; Mosewich, Kowalski, Sabiston, Sedgwick, & Tracy, 2011). They also reported feeling more comfortable with their bodies, and had less anxiety regarding social evaluations of their physique. Thus, self-compassion appears to enhance both physical and mental well-being.

Self-Compassion and Interpersonal Functioning

While there is evidence that self-compassion psychologically benefits the individual, there is also evidence that self-compassion benefits interpersonal relationships. In a study of heterosexual couples (Neff & Beretvas, in press), self-compassionate individuals were described by their partners as being more emotionally connected, accepting and autonomy-supporting while being less detached, controlling, and verbally or physically aggressive than those lacking self-compassion. Self-compassion was also associated with greater relationship satisfaction and attachment security. Because self-compassionate people give themselves care and support, they appear to have more emotional resources available to give to their partners.

Research has found that self-compassionate college students tend to have more compassionate goals in relationships with friends and roommates, meaning they tend to provide social support and encourage interpersonal trust with relationship partners (Crocker & Canevello, 2008). Another study (Neff & Yarnell, submitted) found that self-compassionate college students were more likely to compromise in conflict situations with mothers, fathers, and romantic partners, while those lacking self-compassion tended to subordinate their needs to partners. This pattern makes sense given that people with high levels of self-compassion say they tend to be equally kind to themselves as others, but people with low levels of self-compassion say they tend to be kinder to others than themselves (Neff, 2003a). The study also showed that self-compassionate people felt more authentic and experienced less turmoil when resolving relationships conflicts, and reported a greater sense of well-being in their relationships.

An interesting question concerns whether self-compassionate people are more compassionate towards others in general. Cultivating an open-hearted stance towards oneself that recognizes human interconnectedness should theoretically facilitate being kind, forgiving, and empathetic towards others. While there needs to be more research on this topic, preliminary findings suggest that self-compassion *is* linked to other-focused concern, but this link differs somewhat according to age and life experiences.

Pommier (2010) and Neff and Pommier (submitted) examined this question among college undergraduates, an older community sample, and individuals practicing Buddhist meditation. Self-compassion was significantly linked to compassion, empathetic concern for others, and altruism among the community and Buddhist samples, but not the undergraduates. It may be that the sense of interconnectedness facilitating an association between kindness toward self and others does not develop until later on in life. Among all three groups, however, self-compassionate people were more likely to forgive others who had harmed them. They also showed enhanced perspective-taking skills, an important component of wisdom (see Chapter 1).

Similarly, Richie Davidson and colleagues conducted a study with a group of participants who were trained in loving-kindness meditation (which intentionally cultivates compassion for the self and others), and found the training increased self-compassion levels (Davidson, 2007; see also Weibel, 2007). Brain scans were then conducted on participants while showing them images of suffering (such as a child with an eye tumor). Participants who had larger increases in self-compassion experienced greater empathy (as evidenced by increased activity in the insula, a brain area also associated with perspective-taking). This body of research suggests that self-compassion helps engender compassion toward others.

Self-Compassion versus Self-Esteem

The psychological benefits of high self-esteem (such as lessened depression and anxiety) have been touted for decades (McKay & Fanning, 1987). However, psychologists are now starting to question whether self-esteem is all it's made out to be (for reviews, see Blaine & Crocker, 1993; Crocker & Park, 2004). For instance, people with high self-esteem often engage in downward social comparisons with others, meaning they put others down and puff themselves up as a way to feel better about themselves (Tesser, 1999). Self-esteem is also associated with narcissism (Twenge & Campbell, 2009), inflated and unrealistic self-views (Sedikkides, 1993), prejudice (Aberson, Healy, & Romero, 2000), ego-defensive aggression (Baumeister, Smart, & Boden, 1996), and bullying (Salmivalli, Kaukiainen, Kaistaniemi, & Lagerspetz, 1999). The motivation to protect feelings of self-worth can also lead to increased "need for cognitive closure" (Taris, 2000), in which alternative viewpoints are not tolerated. Self-esteem thus seems to work against the development of wisdom. And self-esteem often fluctuates because self-evaluations are continually changing. As the Hollywood saying goes, you're only as good as your latest success (at least when viewing the world through the lens of self-esteem). This type of instability undermines emotional well-being (Kernis, Cornell, Sun, Berry, & Harlow, 1993). Self-compassion, on the other hand, appears to offer many of the benefits of high self-esteem with fewer downsides (Neff, 2011).

Research indicates that self-compassion is moderately associated with trait levels of self-esteem (Leary et al., 2007; Neff, 2003a; Neff, Kirkpatrick, & Rude, 2007), as one would expect given that both represent positive attitudes toward the self. However, self-compassion still predicts greater happiness and optimism as well as less depression and anxiety when controlling for self-esteem (Neff, 2003a). Moreover, the two constructs differ in terms of their impact on well-being.

In a survey involving a large community sample in the Netherlands, self-compassion was shown to be a stronger predictor of healthy functioning than self-esteem (Neff & Vonk, 2009). For one thing, self-compassion was associated with more stability in state feelings of self-worth over an eight month period (assessed 12 different times) than trait self-esteem. This may be related to the fact that self-compassion was also found to be less contingent on things like physical attractiveness or successful performances than self-esteem. Results indicated that self-compassion was associated with lower levels of social comparison, public self-consciousness, self-rumination, anger, and need for cognitive closure, than self-esteem. Also, self-esteem had a robust association with narcissism while self-compassion had no association with narcissism.

These findings suggest that in contrast to those with high self-esteem, self-compassionate people are less focused on evaluating themselves, feeling superior to others, worrying about whether or not others are evaluating them, defending their viewpoints, or angrily reacting against those who disagree with them.

Leary et al. (2007) compared self-compassion and self-esteem using a mood induction. Participants were instructed to recall a previous failure, rejection, or loss that made them feel badly about themselves, and were then asked a series of questions that assessed their feelings about the event. In the self-compassion condition, participants responded in writing to prompts designed to lead them to think about the event in ways that tapped into the three components of self-compassion—self-kindness, common humanity, and mindful acceptance. In the self-esteem condition, participants responded to prompts designed to protect or bolster their self-esteem. Participants who received the self-compassion induction reported less negative emotions when thinking about the past event than those in the self-esteem condition. Moreover, those in the self-compassion condition took more personal responsibility for the event than those in the self-esteem condition, suggesting that self-compassion does not lead to "letting oneself off the hook."

Gilbert and Irons (2005) suggest that self-compassion enhances well-being because it helps people feel a greater sense of interpersonal connection. They propose that self-compassion deactivates the threat system (associated with feelings of insecure attachment, defensiveness and autonomic arousal) and activates the self-soothing system (associated with feelings of secure attachment, safeness, and the oxytocin-opiate system) (see Chapter 18). In contrast, self-esteem is thought to be an evaluation of superiority/inferiority that helps to establish social rank stability and is related to alerting, energizing impulses and dopamine activation. While self-compassion enhances feelings of safety and interconnectedness, self-esteem positions the self in competition with others and amplifies feelings of distinctness and separation.

Self-Compassion in Therapeutic Settings

An exciting area of research concerns the implications of self-compassion for clinical practice (Baer, 2010). People who lack self-compassion are more likely to have critical mothers, come from dysfunctional families, and display insecure attachment patterns than self-compassionate people do (Neff & McGeehee, 2010). Given that therapy clients often have problems related to their family backgrounds, they may be especially likely to benefit from developing greater self-compassion.

It is an interesting empirical question whether self-compassion is implicitly generated in psychotherapy, and is one of the factors underlying effective treatment. This certainly seems to be the case, and may have important implications for understanding the therapeutic process.

My colleagues and I conducted a study that tracked changes in self-compassion experienced by therapy clients over a one-month interval (Neff, Kirkpatrick, & Rude, 2007). Therapists used a Gestalt two-chair technique designed to help clients lessen self-criticism and have greater compassion for themselves (Greenberg, 1983; Safran, 1998). Results indicated that increased self-compassion levels over the month-long period (which were assessed under the guise of an unrelated study) were linked to fewer experiences of self-criticism, depression, rumination, thought suppression, and anxiety.

Paul Gilbert (2009) has developed a group-based therapy intervention called Compassionate Mind Training (CMT). CMT is designed to help people develop skills of self-compassion, especially when their more habitual form of self-to-self relating involves self-attack. In a pilot study of CMT involving hospital day patients with intense shame and self-criticism, significant decreases in depression, self-attacking, shame, and feelings of inferiority were reported after participation in the CMT program (Gilbert & Procter, 2006). Moreover, almost all of the participants felt ready to be discharged from their hospital program at the end of the study. (For more on Gilbert's compassionate mind training and compassion focused therapy (CFT, please see the next chapter as well as Chapter 18.)

Therapeutic approaches that rely on mindfulness, like Jon Kabat-Zinn's Mindfulness-Based Stress Reduction (MBSR) program (Kabat-Zinn, 1982), may also be an effective way for people to develop self-compassion. Mindfulness teaches people to notice the difficult thoughts and emotions that arise in present-moment awareness, so that they can be experienced with kindness, acceptance, and non-judgment. MBSR courses are commonly taught by therapists and other health professionals to help people deal with stress, depression, and other forms of mental suffering. Research has demonstrated that MBSR significantly increases self-compassion (Shapiro, Astin, Bishop, & Cordova, 2005; Shapiro, Brown, & Biegel, 2007). Research also shows that people who practice mindfulness meditation are more self-compassionate than those who are less experienced (Lykins, & Baer, 2009; Neff, 2003a; Orzech, Shapiro, Brown, & McKay, 2009).

Chris Germer, an editor of this book who specializes in mindfulness and acceptance-based psychotherapy, views therapy through the lens of mindful self-compassion. As he notes in the book, *The Mindful Path to Self-Compassion* (Germer, 2009), self-compassion adds another dimension to mindful acceptance. "Whereas acceptance usually refers to *what's happening to us* —accepting a feeling or a thought—self-compassion is acceptance of *the person to whom it's happening*. It's acceptance of ourselves while we're in pain" (p. 33). This is a key insight. When we are soothed and comforted by self-compassion, it becomes easier to relate to painful feelings in a mindful way. Thus, training that explicitly teaches self-compassion in addition to mindfulness skills may be especially useful in therapy.

To this end, Chris and I have recently developed an 8-week training program in Mindful Self-Compassion (MSC), which is designed to explicitly integrate self-compassion and mindfulness training. The program has structural elements similar to Kabat-Zinn's MBSR course (8 sessions, plus a retreat day; formal and informal meditation) and will hopefully provide a useful compliment to it. On the first day of the program we mainly focus on defining self-compassion and explaining how it differs from self-esteem, self-pity, and self-indulgence. During the following weeks, we teach a variety of mindfulness and self-compassion practices for dealing with difficult emotions and challenging relationships in daily life.

We recently conducted a randomized controlled study of the MSC program, comparing outcomes for the treatment group to those in a waitlist control group. Results indicated that participation in the workshop significantly increased self-compassion, mindfulness, compassion for others, and life satisfaction, while significantly decreasing depression, anxiety, stress, and the impact of trauma. The degree to which participants' self-compassion level increased was significantly linked to how much informal and formal self-compassion practice they did over the course of the program. We also explored whether enhanced well-being was primarily explained by increases in self-compassion, or if it was also explained by increased mindfulness. We found that while most of the gains in well-being were explained by increased self-compassion, mindfulness explained additional variance in terms of happiness, stress, and the impact of trauma. This suggests that both self-compassion and mindfulness are key benefits of the MSC program.

An exercise from the MSC program follows; writing a compassionate letter to oneself (see also Shapira & Mongrain, 2010). For more examples of exercises and meditations provided in the MSC program, please visit www.Self-Compassion.org or www.MindfulSelfCompassion.org).

[BEGIN TEXT BOX]

Self-Compassionate Letter

- Candidly describe a problem that tends to make you feel bad about yourself, such as a physical flaw, a relationship problem, or failure at work or school. Note what emotions come up—shame, anger, sadness, fear—as you write.
- Next, think of an imaginary friend who is unconditionally accepting and compassionate; someone who knows all your strengths and weaknesses, understands your life history, your current circumstances, and understands the limits of human nature.
- Finally, write a letter to yourself from that perspective. What would your friend say about your perceived problem? What words would he or she use to convey deep compassion? How would your friend remind you that you're only human? If your friend were to make any suggestions, how would they reflect unconditional understanding?
- When you're done writing, put the letter down for a while and come back to it later. Then read the letter again, letting the words sink in, allowing yourself to be soothed and comforted.

[END TEXT BOX]

We have already conducted one pilot study of the MSC program, and preliminary evidence for its effectiveness is promising. We obtained data for 18 participants both before and after the program, and results indicated significant increases in self-compassion (as measured by the Self-Compassion Scale; Neff, 2003a) and mindfulness (as measured by the Five Facet Mindfulness Questionnaire; Baer et al, 2006). There were also significant reductions in depression, anxiety and stress, as well as significant increases in social connectedness, happiness, and life satisfaction after participation in the program. In some ways, self-compassion practice can be thought of as "portable therapy." We are now conducting a wait-list controlled study of the MSC program.

Whereas clients may learn to relate to their troubles in a healthier way through a relationship with a compassionate therapist, self-compassion practice can help people be their own therapists *between* sessions. Therapists also need self-compassion, of course, especially for the compassion fatigue that can result when outcomes are not necessarily as expected (see next chapter). Not only is self-compassion associated with less compassion fatigue among counselors (Ringenbach, 2009), it is also linked to greater "compassion satisfaction"—the positive feelings experienced from one's work such as feeling energized, happy, and grateful for being able to make a difference in the world.

[DOUBLE SPACE]

In *Toward a Psychology of Being*, Maslow (1968) argued that emotional maturity entails nonjudgmental, forgiving, loving acceptance of oneself. Self-compassion epitomizes this way of being, and may help mental health professionals understand and foster this type of emotional wisdom within themselves and in others.

References

Aberson, C. L. Healy, M.. & Romero, V. (2000). Ingroup bias and self-esteem: A meta-analysis. *Personality & Social Psychology Review, 4*, 157-173.

Adams, C. E., & Leary, M. R. (2007). Promoting self-compassionate attitudes toward eating among restrictive and guilty eaters. *Journal of Social and Clinical Psychology,26,* 1120-1144.

Baer, R. A. (2003). Mindfulness training as a clinical intervention: A conceptual and empirical review. *Clinical Psychology: Science and Practice, 10,* 125-143.

Baer, R. A. (2010). Self-compassion as a mechanism of change in mindfulness- and acceptance-based treatments. In R. A. Baer (Ed.) Assessing mindfulness & acceptance processes in clients (pp.135-154). Oakland: New Harbinger.

Baer, R. A., Smith, G. T., Hopkins, J., Krietemeyer, J. & Toney, L. (2006). Using self-report assessment methods to explore facets of mindfulness. *Assessment*, 13, 27-45.

Baumeister, R. F., Smart, L., & Boden, J. M. (1996). Relation of threatened egotism to violence and aggression: The dark side of high self-esteem. *Psychological Review.* 103, 5-33.

Bennett-Goleman, T. (2001). *Emotional Alchemy: How the Mind Can Heal the Heart* New York: Three Rivers Press.

Bishop, S. R., Lau, M., Shapiro, S., Carlson, L., Anderson, N. D., Carmody, J., et al. (2004). Mindfulness: A proposed operational definition. *Clinical Psychology: Science and Practice, 11,* 191-206.

Blaine, B., & Crocker, J. (1993). Self-esteem and self-serving biases in reactions to positive and negative events: An integrative review. In R. F. Baumeister (Ed.), *Self-esteem: The puzzle of low self-regard* (pp. 55-85). Hillsdale, NJ: Erlbaum

Blatt, S. J. (1995). Representational structures in psychopathology. In D. Cicchetti & S. Toth (Eds.), *Rochester symposium on developmental psychopathology: Emotion, cognition, and representation, Vol. 6* (pp. 1-34). Rochester, NY: University of Rochester Press.

Brach, T. (2003). *Radical acceptance: Embracing your life with the heart of a Buddha.* Bantam Books.

Chödrön, R. (2001). *Start where you are: A guide to compassionate living.* Boston: Shambhala Publications.

Coopersmith, S. (1967). *The antecedents of self-esteem.* San Francisco: W. H. Freeman.

Crocker, J. & Canevello, A. (2008). Creating and undermining social support in communal relationships: The role of compassionate and self-image goals. *Journal of Personality and Social Psychology, 95*, 555-575.

Crocker, J., & Park, L. E. (2004). The costly pursuit of self-esteem. *Psychological Bulletin, 130*, 392-414.

Davidson, R. (2007, Oct.). Changing the brain by transforming the mind. The impact of compassion training on the neural systems of emotion. Paper presented at the Mind and Life Institute Conference, Investigating the Mind, Emory University, Atlanta, GA.

Deci, E. L., & Ryan, R. M. (1995). Human autonomy: The basis for true self-esteem. In M. H. Kernis (Ed.), *Efficacy, agency, and self-esteem* (pp. 31-49). New York: Plenum Press.

Dweck, C. S. (1986). Motivational processes affecting learning. *American Psychologist, 41*, 1040-1048.

Fichman, L., Koestner, R., & Zuroff, D. C. (1994). Depressive styles in adolescence: assessment, relation to social functioning, and developmental trends. *Journal of Youth and Adolescence*, *23*, 315–330.

Germer, C. K. (2009). *The mindful path to self-compassion.* New York: Guilford Press.

Gilbert, P. (2009). *The compassionate mind.* London: Constable.

Gilbert, P. & Irons, C. (2005). Therapies for shame and self-attacking, using cognitive, behavioural, emotional imagery and compassionate mind training. In P Gilbert (Ed.) *Compassion: Conceptualisations, research and use in psychotherapy* (pp. 263 – 325). London: Routledge.

Gilbert, P. & Procter, S. (2006). Compassionate mind training for people with high shame and self-criticism: Overview and pilot study of a group therapy approach. *Clinical Psychology & Psychotherapy, 13*, 353-379.

Goldstein, J., & Kornfield, J. (1987). *Seeking the heart of wisdom: The path of insight meditation.* Boston: Shambhala.

Greenberg, L. S. (1983). Toward a task analysis of conflict resolution in Gestalt Therapy. *Psychotherapy: Theory, Research and Practice, 20*(2), 190-201.

Harter, S. (1999). *The construction of the self: A developmental perspective.* New York: Guilford Press.

Heatherton, T. F., & Polivy, J. (1990). Chronic dieting and eating disorders: A spiral model. In J. H. Crowther, D. L. Tennenbaum, S. E. Hobfoll, & M. A. P. Stephens (Eds.), *The etiology of bulimia nervosa: The individual and familial context* (pp. 133-155). Washington, DC: Hemisphere.

Heine, S. J., Lehman, D. R., Markus, H. R. & Kitayama, S. (1999). Is there a universal need for positive self-regard? *Psychological Review, 106*, 766–794.

Horney, K. (1950). *Neurosis and human growth: The struggle toward self-realization.* New York: Norton.

Kabat-Zinn, J. (1991). *Full catastrophe living: Using the wisdom of your body and mind to face stress, pain, and illness*. New York: Dell Publishing.

Kelly, A. C., Zuroff, D. C., Foa, C. L., & Gilbert, P. (2009). Who benefits from training in self-compassionate self-regulation? A study of smoking reduction. *Journal of Social and Clinical Psychology, 29*, 727-755

Kernis, M. H., Cornell, D. P., Sun, C. R., Berry, A., & Harlow, T. (1993). There's more to self-esteem than whether it is high or low: The importance of stability of self-esteem. Journal of Personality and Social Psychology, 65, 1190–1204.

Kernis, M. H., & Paradise, A. W., Whitaker, D. J., Wheatman, S. R., & Goldman, B. N. (2000). Master of one's psychological domain? Not likely if one's self-esteem is unstable. *Personality and Social Psychology Bulletin, 26*, 1297-1305.

Leary, M. R., Tate, E. B., Adams, C. E., Allen, A. B., & Hancock, J. (2007). Self-compassion and reactions to unpleasant self-relevant events: The implications of treating oneself kindly. *Journal of Personality and Social Psychology, 92,* 887-904.

Lykins, E. L. & Baer, R. A. (2009). Psychological functioning in a sample of long-term practitioners of mindfulness meditation. *Journal of Cognitive Psychotherapy: An International Quarterly, 23,* 226-241.

Magnus, C. M. R., Kowalski, K. C., & McHugh, T.-L. F. (2010). The role of self-compassion in women's self-determined motives to exercise and exercise-related outcomes. *Self & Identity*, *9,* 363-382.

Maslow, A. H. (1968). *Toward a psychology of being*. New York: D. Van Nostrand Co.

McKay, M., & Fanning, P. (1987). *Self-esteem*. Oakland, CA: New Harbinger.

Mosewich, A. D., Kowalski, K. C., Sabiston, C. M., Sedgwick, W. A., Tracy, J. L., *Journal of Sport & Exercise Psychology, 33,* 103-123.

Neely, M. E., Schallert, D. L., Mohammed, S. S., Roberts, R. M., Chen, Y. (2009). Self-kindness when facing stress: The role of self-compassion, goal regulation, and support in college students' well-being. *Motivation and Emotion, 33,* 88-97

Neff, K. D. (2003a). Development and validation of a scale to measure self-compassion. *Self and Identity, 2,* 223-250.

Neff, K. D. (2003b). Self-compassion: An alternative conceptualization of a healthy attitude toward oneself. *Self and Identity, 2,* 85-102.

Neff, K. D. (2011). Self-compassion, self-esteem, and well-being. *Social and Personality Compass, 5,* 1 – 12.

Neff, K. D., & Beretvas, S. N. (in press). *The role of self-compassion in healthy relationship interactions.*

Neff, K. D. (2009). Self-Compassion. In M. R. Leary & R. H. Hoyle (Eds.), *Handbook of Individual Differences in Social Behavior (*pp. 561-573). Guilford Press.

Neff, K. D., Hseih, Y., & Dejitthirat, K. (2005). Self-compassion, achievement goals, and coping with academic failure. *Self and Identity, 4,* 263-287.

Neff, K. D., Kirkpatrick, K. & Rude, S. S. (2007). Self-compassion and its link to adaptive psychological functioning. *Journal of Research in Personality, 41,* 139-154.

Neff, K. D. & McGeehee, P. (2010). Self-compassion and psychological resilience among adolescents and young adults. *Self and Identity,* 9, 225-240

Neff, K. D., Pisitsungkagarn, K., & Hseih, Y. (2008). Self-compassion and self-construal in the United States, Thailand, and Taiwan. *Journal of Cross-Cultural Psychology.*

Neff, K. D., & Pommier, E. (submitted). Self-compassion and other-focused responding.

Neff, K. D., & Rude, S. S., & Kirkpatrick, K. (2007). An examination of self-compassion in relation to positive psychological functioning and personality traits. *Journal of Research in Personality, 41,* 908-916.

Neff, K. D. & Vonk, R. (2009). Self-compassion versus global self-esteem: Two different ways of relating to oneself. *Journal of Personality, 77,* 23-50.

Neff, K. D. & Yarnell, L., (submitted). Self-Compassion, interpersonal conflict resolutions, and well-being.

Nolen-Hoeksema, S. (1991). Responses to depression and their effects on the duration of depressive episodes. *Journal of Abnormal Psychology, 100*, 569-582.

Orzech, K. M., Shapiro, S. L., Brown, K. W., & McKay, M. (2009). Intensive mindfulness training-related changes in cognitive and emotional experience. *The Journal of Positive Psychology, 4*, 212-222.

Powers, T. A., Koestner, R., & Zuroff, D. C. (2007). Self-criticism, goal motivation, and goal progress. *Journal of Social and Clinical Psychology, 26*, 826–840.

Ringenbach, R. (2009). A comparison between counselors who practice meditation and those who do not on compassion fatigue, compassion satisfaction, burnout and self-compassion. *Dissertation Abstracts International.*

Safran, J. D. (1998). Widening the scope of cognitive therapy: The therapeutic relationship, emotion, and the process of change. Northvale, NJ: Jason Aronson.

Salmivalli, C., Kaukiainen, A., Kaistaniemi, L., & Lagerspetz, K. M. J. (1999). Self-evaluated self-esteem, peer-evaluated self-esteem, and defensive egotism as predictors of adolescents' participation in bullying situations. *Personality and Social Psychology Bulletin, 25,* 1268-1278.

Salzberg, S. (1997). *Lovingkindness: The revolutionary art of happiness.* Boston: Shambala.

Sedikides, C. (1993). Assessment, enhancement, and verification determinants of the self-evaluation process. *Journal of Personality and Social Psychology, 65*, 317-338.

Shapira, L, & Mongrain, L. (2010). The benefits of self-compassion and optimism exercises for individuals vulnerable to depression. *Journal of Positive Psychology, 5(*5). 377-389.

Shapiro, S. L., Astin, J. A., Bishop, S. R., and Cordova, M. (2005). Mindfulness-Based Stress Reduction for health care professionals: Results from a randomized trial. *International Journal of Stress Management, 12*, 164-176.

Shapiro, S. L., Brown, K. W., & Biegel, G. M (2007). Teaching self-care to caregivers: Effects of mindfulness-based stress reduction on the mental health of therapists in training. Training *and Education in Professional Psychology, 1*, 105-115.

Shapiro, S. L., Carlson, L. E., Astin, J. A., & Freedman, B. (2006). Mechanisms of mindfulness. *Journal of Clinical Psychology, 62,* 373-386.

Sprecher, S., & Fehr, B. (2005). Compassionate love for close others and humanity. Journal of Social and Personal Relationships, 22, 629–651.

Taris, T. W. (2000). Dispositional need for cognitive closure and self-enhancing beliefs. *Journal of Social Psychology, 140,* 35-50.

Tesser, A. (1999). Toward a self-evaluation maintenance model of social behavior. In R. F. Baumeister (Ed.) *The self in social psychology* (pp. 446-460). New York,: Psychology Press.

Twenge, J. M. & Campbell, W. K. (2009). *The narcissism epidemic: Living in the age of entitlement.* New York: Free Press.

Weibel, D. T. (2007). *A loving-kindness intervention: Boosting compassion for self and others.* Retrieved from Dissertations and Theses database. (AAT 3292869)

Williams, J. G., Stark, S. K., & Foster, E. E. (2008). Start today or the very last day? The relationships among self-compassion, motivation, and procrastination. *American Journal of Psychological Research, 4*, 37-44.

Social Work Education
Vol. 26, No. 4, June 2007, pp. 399–413

'What about Feelings?': A Study of Emotion and Tension in Social Work Field Education

Constance Barlow & Barry L. Hall

Seventy students and field instructors were interviewed in an attempt to identify and understand how upsetting field events were perceived and managed by urban, undergraduate Canadian social work students. The study reports on the emotional impact of the field experience and identifies major sources of tension for *students and* between *field instructors and students.*

Keywords: Social Work; Field Education; Emotion; Tension; Canadian

Introduction

Social work practitioners and field students are repeatedly exposed to the brutal conditions of clients' lives that are often the fallout of oppressive structures in our society. Witnessing painful client circumstances commonly evokes intense emotional responses. An experienced field instructor pointed out that, 'This is how things are. It's part of the job. You just get on with it'. However, as academics with roots in the practice community, we reflected on the incongruity of such an assertion since experiencing intense emotionality while carrying out the work at hand was indeed a complex undertaking. What, we wondered, *was* the emotional impact for our students?

Experiential learning theory, the foundation of social work field education, recognizes both the affective and cognitive nature of learning (Brookfield, 1996; Dewey, 1938; Kolb, 1984) however, affective support for transformation of experience into knowledge is seldom on the classroom agenda, which stresses cognitive and skill development (Coates & McKay, 1995; Rossiter, 1995). Campbell (1999) considered why this was so. She wrote,

> The use of experiential pedagogy carries a concomitant obligation to attend to the sometimes unsettling and disturbing affective response evident among students.

Constance Barlow & Barry L. Hall, University of Calgary, Canada.
Correspondence to: Dr Constance Barlow, Director of Field Education, Associate Professor, Faculty of Social Work, University of Calgary, 2500 University Drive NW, Calgary, Alberta T2N 1N4, Canada. Email: cabarlow@ucalgary.ca

ISSN 0261-5479 print/1470-1227 online
DOI: 10.1080/02615470601081712

> The rationalist nature of most Western educational methods, however, is potentially inconsistent with the affective nature of experiential education. Consequently, academic programs often neglect to support students with the affective aspects of learning. (p. 45)

Not only are emotions a key aspect of learning, they are also a central aspect of human life and the capacity to connect with one's own feelings and the feelings of others is seen as a precondition for growth-fostering relationships (Miller & Stiver, 1997). Empathy is considered the basis of caregiving, and an essential aspect of social work practice.

Recently literature on the effects of repeated exposure to traumatic events or stories of traumatized clients has called attention to the emotional impact of direct practice in the human services. Saakvitne & Pearlman (1996) noted that students were likely to experience strong reactions of grief and outrage in the process of hearing about and witnessing the pain of others. They suggested that the students were possibly responding to their first exposure to human cruelty and indifference.

This paper reports on a research project that set out to consider what Nussbaum (2001) called the 'messy material' that is emotion. With the intent of expanding our understanding of the emotional impact of the student field experience, we set out to learn more about how upsetting field events were perceived and dealt with among urban, undergraduate social work students and field instructors.

Overview of the Literature

Schon (1983) commented that students are faced with epistemological and emotional uncertainty as they move from the 'high hard ground' of the academic classroom to the 'swampy' ground of practice. Rompf *et al.* (1993) found that both undergraduate and graduate students reported high levels of anxiety as they prepared to enter into field practicums. Fook *et al.* (2000) noted that worry related to dealing with anger, violence, and conflict was a recurring theme in student critical incident assignments. In particular, students feared potentially violent male clients who threatened conflict.

An evolving body of research on safety in field placements reports limited dialogue on violence in social work field placements but has served to alert students and faculty to safety hazards (Tully *et al.*, 1993; Elliason, 1996; Mama, 2001). Tully *et al.* (1993) found that, although safety issues received some attention in the classroom, they were seldom directly addressed in field settings, which is puzzling because social workers are frequent victims of violence.

In a replication of Tully *et al.*'s study (1993), Mama (2001) concluded that violence remains a pressing issue for undergraduate students and their field instructors and noted that violence, likely in the form of verbal abuse, can be expected to occur at high rates in field placements. Jayaratne *et al.* (1996) found many social workers, particularly those working in inpatient and outpatient mental health services, lived in fear of violent attacks by clients.

In a national survey of field directors, Reeser & Wertkin (2001) found a dissonance between concerns about violence and the lack of safety policies and related training in many schools of social work. In their study, only 12% of 250 schools surveyed reported having a formal written policy on student safety. Tully *et al.* (1993) pointed out that, even in agencies that had set up safety policies and initiated training opportunities, field placement students were seldom aware of them.

In their study on the impact of female students on working with abused women, Goldblatt & Buchbinder (2003) noted that as students tried to understand and contain their clients' experiences as victims, they experienced emotions such as pain, guilt, shame, helplessness and rage. Barlow & Hall (2003) reported on issues of student vulnerability and how students met the emotional challenges presented by their social work field placements.

Successfully guiding students in direct practice is considered the primary role of the field instructor and pivotal to student satisfaction during their placement experiences (Fernandez, 1998; Knight, 2000). Indeed, the relationship between field instructors and their students is viewed as the central variable in predicting student satisfaction and quality of learning experience (Bogo & Vayda, 2000). In order to optimize coping skills and to model effective self-care that can ultimately enhance their knowledge and capability as practitioners, field instructors must support students who encounter difficult situations (Burke & Harris, 1996). The need for trust is imperative if open, honest, and direct communication is to occur between learner and instructor (Pepper, 1996). The nature of this relationship as viewed through a lens of power, resistance and anti-oppressive practice offers additional data for understanding the emotional impact of social work field education (Barlow & Hall, 2003; Hackett & Marsland, 1997; Preston-Shoot, 1995).

Methodology

This study, initiated on the urban campus of a large Canadian university, involved two groups: 35 students who had, in the prior semester, completed an introductory 300 hours field placement and an unmatched group of 35 field instructors who had just concluded a semester of field instruction with this group of students.

After approval of the study by a university-wide ethics committee, in the following semester, the principle investigators or research assistant made a brief presentation about the research project in social work classes attended by these student. Participants indicated interest in participation by placing their name and telephone number on a sign-up sheet that was circulated after the presentation. All 35 students from a potential pool of 100 students who indicated interest to participate were contacted by telephone to schedule an interview. Thirty-five of the 37 field instructors, who were randomly selected from the field office current list, agreed to participate in the study. The years of association of the field instructors with the University ranged from two to 12 years.

The average age of the 31 female participants and the four male participants in the study was 27.1 years of age. Mandates of the field agencies included mental health, family violence, corrections and child welfare.

The students were asked to describe difficult and/or upsetting experiences in their field placement and reflect on the emotional impact of these experiences. Additionally, they were asked about how they resolved these situations, and to whom they turned to for assistance. Finally they were asked to consider how well the classroom had prepared them for their field placement and whether these upsetting events led them to reconsider their decision to study social work. The field instructors were asked what experiences students may find upsetting, how they informed students about stressors in the agency, what assistance was provided to distressed students, and what they believed to be reasons for student hesitation to seek their support. Additionally, they were asked to comment on how well the classroom prepared students for field work.

The 70 audio-taped, telephone interviews of 30–45 minutes in duration, were transcribed and analyzed by the principal investigators. Although the interview questions offered a beginning structure for data analysis, the dense qualitative data that emerged from the responses were analyzed line by line to create codes according to the principles outlined by Glaser (1992). Coding was initially done independently, by the two researchers, using the inductive process outlined by Strauss & Corbin (1990). Subsequently the two researchers met to cross-code the data, a process that served to enhance definitional clarity and reliability (Miles & Huberman, 1994). The codes were then systematically categorized and the categories were combined into themes.

Findings

The following is a report on what students and field instructors considered to be upsetting. These were related to client circumstances, competency issues, management of potentially violent situations, and agency climate. Although students and field instructors were in general agreement as to the sources of stress, they held differing perceptions of the stressors' impact. For example, students reported feelings of vulnerability, particularly in terms of issues of safety and their relationships with field instructors. In that field instructors were more likely to identify agency politics and unresolved personnel issues on the part of the student as sources of student stress in the social work practicum, the two groups appeared to be out of step.

Theme I: Client Circumstances

Student Views

Witnessing and hearing client stories of betrayal, violence, and the impact of poverty invoked intense responses in students. They reported feeling powerless, uncomfortable, alarmed, overwhelmed, worried, isolated, shocked, upset, humbled, and angry, using expressions such as, 'over my head' and 'out of my league'. Their emotionally laden responses to client circumstances stemmed from witnessing client pain, hearing their painful stories, and struggling with challenges to personal values and beliefs.

Students also reported significant distress when witnessing events such as family arguments, maltreatment of clients, particularly children, and the death of children. One student spoke of her difficulty in observing a father identify the body of his dead son. Another described the agony of speaking to a group of young students about the death of a classmate: 'I'll never forget the looks on their faces'. Hearing painful stories, either directly from clients or by reviewing files that documented a history of child abuse or family violence, was another source of stress.

Another student described how overwhelmed he felt after a client he had seen the week before took his own life. This student reported questioning his own competency in relation to suicide prevention: 'It is in my mind, always in my mind. It really touched my heart. I was stressed and vulnerable'.

Students talked about feeling vulnerable when faced with situations that reminded them of their own past personal pain or when a client encounter called for a re-examination of their personal values and beliefs. For example, one student who had been sexually assaulted as a teenager was not prepared for the possibility of encountering a sexual offender in her social work studies. When her field placement in a youth probation unit required that she work with a young offender charged with sexual assault, she was flooded with unresolved feelings about her own assault.

Being exposed to something not previously encountered can also be disturbing. Prior to one student's first meeting with a pedophile, she had regarded them as 'scum' that 'should be in prison', but after hearing his life story of abuse, she reinterpreted his behavior as a mental illness. Confused about empathizing with this man, she remarked on the tension within her as she tried 'to figure out in my head where it all fit for me'.

Field Instructor Views

Field instructors reported that students would likely be distressed if they witnessed clients in painful situations, comatose, or dying; or if they met children who were victims of abuse or family violence. They also noted that aggressive clients could make matters 'difficult for students and heighten their vulnerability'. One field instructor noted that possibly for the first time in their lives, students may witness 'raw emotion' and experience the 'huge value difference between themselves and their clients'. Another observed that students often experienced what he termed 'moral distress', from wanting to do the right thing but being blocked by organizational barriers.

All 35 field instructors agreed that they may, at times, underestimate the impact on students of client pain and fail to recognize situations that may overwhelm students. One reflected on becoming 'comfortable with the uncomfortable' in the course of her work, and sometimes being complacent about its emotional impact. Another asserted, 'We cannot allow ourselves to forget that what we consider to be normal in our environment is not considered normal by those on the outside. We can't overlook that it has an impact on students'.

Another point where field instructors' perceptions diverged from those of the students was with regard to the impact of student unresolved past issues. Eleven field instructors believed that past personal experiences and interpersonal models of demeanor can unwittingly influence professional responses and create stress, whereas only two students cited personal factors as a source of tension. Several students in the study reported resenting the field instructor's movement into the personal terrain.

Theme II: Perceptions about Competency

Student Views

A second source of tension for students was worry about their competency. Mainly, they were concerned that an error on their part would lead to severe negative consequences for the client and failure in the practicum. Student comments revealed feelings of inadequacy: 'I'm just not skilled enough'; 'What scared me more than anything was doing more harm than good'; 'I felt really, really inadequate'. The students also tended to blame themselves if things did not go well. One, worried that her client's escalation of anger was due to her lack of experience, explained, 'It's like ... being in the position of a student, feeling like maybe he's reacting because I'm not saying something right'.

When students encountered situations that called for a negotiation of competing demands, they also felt ill-equipped to handle them. For example, during an initial child welfare investigation, a young girl with a documented history of lying claimed that her father was abusing her. The student reported, 'I felt really mixed up not knowing whether I should believe her or her parents'.

Many students reported that they believed that the classroom did not and could not adequately prepare them for the demands of the workplace, and that field placement taught them more than they 'could ever learn' in a classroom. They believed that more classroom emphasis could be placed on managing vicarious trauma and educating about grief, bereavement, and how to cope with clients' painful stories.

Field Instructor Views

Field instructors were generally cognizant of the crisis of confidence that students experience during their training in an agency. One noted the stress of negotiating competing demands: 'Sometimes you can be pulled in several different directions with all these persons involved—the resident, the family, and the staff'. Field instructors also recognized that students may feel overwhelmed when faced with 'all they don't know'.

Field instructors described their efforts to enhance their students' sense of competency. For example, while his student was struggling with the structural constraints on effective practice, one field instructor encouraged him to consider ways to work within the limitations: 'At some point you just cut your losses and say, we didn't win this battle, but we live to fight another day'.

Responding to the question of whether they believed students were adequately prepared by the university, the majority of the field instructors indicated that they were 'not sure'. Some felt that students were insufficiently prepared for the intensity of the field placement. Several noted that classroom preparation for the emotional impact of social work was simply not possible: 'Reading about it is one thing; experiencing it in a practicum is another. It doesn't matter how prepared you are; when it is happening in actuality, you are not as prepared as you thought you were'.

Field instructors were able to relate to the students' sense of academic abandonment when unable to apply theories taught in the classroom because they, too, had experienced that problem. In a milieu where abstract knowledge is considered to be of higher value than concrete skills or tacit or inductive knowledge, both the students and field instructors experienced a sense of falling short of the ideal of evidence-based practice. Here the two groups found common ground.

Theme III: Management of Potentially Violent Situations

Student Views

Over one-third of the students reported encountering potentially dangerous situations in their placements. Some had been directly threatened or confronted by clients, as when a mother warned, 'Stay away or I'll hurt you'; and when an angry client began swearing and challenged a student to a fight. Another example of circumstances where a student felt particularly vulnerable occurred during an interview with a mother and her teenaged daughter. Because the office alarm system had been temporarily disconnected, the student had no means of soliciting help when the teenager 'freaked out'. She declared, 'If there would have been an alarm, I definitely would have pulled it'.

Students also cited situations that left them feeling physically at risk, even though they were not directly threatened. Entering clients' homes, not knowing whether 'they are going to be under the influence of alcohol or drugs or if there are going to be any weapons', was one source of tension. Gauging client responses was another: 'I am not sure how well you can actually know people because ... people are unpredictable'.

Students also encountered sexual harassment from clients. One reported feeling extreme discomfort when the prisoners at an adult detention centre turned around and stared at her as she walked in, then surrounded her, asking, 'Can I touch your pants?'.

Field Instructor Views

Although only two field instructors directly identified safety issues as potential student stressors in field settings, they generally structured learning experiences with student safety in mind. One declared that she would never place unsupervised students in situations where she thought they would be unsafe. In order to acknowledge student stress about potentially violent situations, another field instructor shared her own experiences and fears with the student. While discussing harm reduction strategies with students prior to going into the field was seen as a proactive strategy, field instructors were uncertain as to how academic classroom instruction could better prepare students for managing potentially violent situations. 'You can't prepare for everything', noted one field instructor.

Theme IV: Student and Field Instructor Relationships

Student Views

Students in need of direction and support were particularly critical of field instructors who were unsupportive. Ten reported that problematic relationships with their field instructors left them feeling very vulnerable. Relationships with field instructors were strained when students received unsupportive feedback from their field instructors, experienced value differences or interpersonal conflicts with the field instructors, witnessed questionable field instructor and agency practices, sensed they were being assigned inappropriate tasks, and felt uncomfortable with agency mandates.

Unsupportive feedback was a common source of distress. For example, when a student reported that a mentally handicapped client disclosed that someone known to the field agency had raped her, her field instructor suggested that the client had likely 'misinterpreted' the situation and told the student that the agency would handle the matter. Additionally, the student was directed to not pursue the issue further with the client or discuss it with her faculty field liaison or in her university integrative seminar. She reported feeling powerless when the issue was redirected.

Students were also stressed by field instructor practices, agency policies and field assignments that they found questionable. One student had difficulty coping with the authoritarian, militaristic style of her field instructor, quite different from her own. Another reported feeling upset when her practicum supervisor 'did things that I didn't agree with and tried to tell me that's what I need to do'. Privately questioning the values of the agency manager and the practices of its staff enhanced student feelings of vulnerability: 'I was confronted with conflicting and confusing feelings', was how one student summed up her field experience.

Students were distressed if they witnessed their field instructors exhibiting what they viewed as unprofessional behavior in their presence, even if it was not directly client related. For example, when her field instructor began cursing and behaving in a belligerent manner toward 'kids' merely crossing the road in front of her car, a student reported feeling betrayed, disappointed and confused as she witnessed the field instructor 'dropping her act of compassion'.

Another student, while shadowing her field instructor, noted his rude and insensitive behavior towards a weeping client. Confused by her field instructor's apparent attitude of 'get over the crying bit and get with the process' and not trusting his perspective, the student approached other agency personal wondering, 'Is it okay to talk about client feelings?'. This student was seeking responses to the unspoken questions that students face about who determines and who controls a field agency's emotional script.

Data from the study showed that in the face of injustice, many students chose to remain silent. One student commented, 'I didn't want to be labeled one way or another. I just wanted to get the most that I could out of the experience and move on'. Another suggested that she 'would have been opening a can of worms that would have been detrimental to my experience'.

When students felt powerless to redress injustice, they experienced a sense of helplessness. As one stated, 'My supervisor had power over me. So ... I always felt threatened at every moment that she'd be failing me, even though I felt I was achieving'.

Most students valued the opportunity to discuss their feelings with others. As one student noted, 'support is the key'; students however were discriminating in whom they confided. When the field instructors were seen as individuals who could be trusted, they were the initial avenues of support for the student. Nine students reported a positive relationship with their field instructors, describing them as 'amazing', and 'really excellent and supportive'. Twelve students revealed that they consulted with the faculty field liaison and, in most instances, were pleased with the support that they received. However, there were eight who sought support from family members or friends, rather than from field instructors, and five more, in conflict with their field instructors, turned to other agency personnel for support.

Students reported mixed reactions about the value of the university based integrative seminars in terms of a 'safe place to talk'. Four found the seminars to be supportive in terms of discussing field placement issues, while five others determined that they were unhelpful and reported relying solely on peers who were not members of the integrative seminar for support. The remaining students did not view the integrative seminar as a forum for affective expression.

Field Instructor Views

While the students often referred to their stress and feelings of vulnerability in connection with their field instructors, the latter generally underestimated their impact on students and only two field instructors saw themselves as a potential source of distress for students.

Several identified issues of power, control and fear of receiving lower performance ratings as a possible barrier to student learning and support seeking behavior. 'Such a position could be intimidating', conceded one field instructor. Despite recognizing that hierarchy and power imbalance play important roles in the reluctance of students to reveal painful emotions and express vulnerability, some field instructors nevertheless believed it was the students' responsibility to be forthright and open with field educators. All believed that they created a safe environment for students to reflect on the emotional impact of their field experience and that student hesitancy was likely an individual factor related to issues of trust, past negative experiences with supervision or 'maturity issues' on the part of the student.

Many field instructors reported engaging in behaviors that attempted to realign the power relationship, a form of power-with rather than power-over. One strategy was to invite students into a conversation about their feelings. Some field instructors used personal disclosure: 'I tell them about some of the issues that might affect me and how I might deal with them'. One field instructor recognized that student hesitation to seek support was clearly related to their relationship, 'I think that entirely depends on who your supervisor is'. Although most field instructors believed that 'really listening' to the student was very important, several acknowledged times they were inattentive to student concerns.

Theme V: Agency Climate

Student Views

Both students and field instructors considered agency climate as a potential source of tension for students. Students indicated their sense of unease when they experienced the consequences of 'rule breaking' without knowing the rules, poor communication with social work colleagues, and unpleasant encounters with other professionals. In situations where the students did not trust the field instructors or the 'office politics', they felt an acute sense of isolation. One student described the climate of her field agency as 'really cliquey' with 'a lot of backstabbing' and as a result felt discomfort, isolation, and disappointment.

Notably, students wished that they had been given, in the classroom, more information on how to function as a social worker within the bureaucracy of an agency and particularly how to manage office politics and its impact.

Field Instructor Views

Field instructors were more alert than students to the impact of agency climate on student learning. They recognized that students would likely experience conflict in the work environment and that they must learn the 'politics', as well as 'who … the players [are], how they play, [and] how it all works'. One field instructor suggested that 'learning how to manage that type of stress in the work environment is as important as having clinical skills to deal with your families' because one's colleagues are like another client group.

Decision to be a Social Worker

All students reported that the upsetting field experiences did not lessen their commitment to the profession; however, they did question the type of social work they were suited for. Their resiliency in the face of adversity was remarkable. Students spoke about 'taking the good with the bad', shared concerns about burn out, and wondered how to balance caring deeply about clients with maintaining a sense of personal stability. In serving clients facing misfortune, one student reflected that he did not want to be unaffected by the tragedies of others. One student who experienced conflict with her field instructor nevertheless maintained an optimistic outlook: 'It made me more aware of how to handle situations. Because of the lack of support I got, I think I would really watch out for a practicum student of my own'. Another student encapsulated the positive aspects of her field experience: 'What an awesome experience! I want to learn more about this so I can be "more ready". I love my field! I met the most amazing people! I had an amazing supervisor!'.

Summary

Overall, this study demonstrated that students experienced significant stress in field placements and were frequently reluctant to share their emotions with field instructors or faculty field liaisons. When the Oxford Dictionary definition of tension—'mental strain or excitement' or 'a strain state of relationships'—was considered in the data analysis, evidence of numerous sources of tension, that are outlined below, became evident.

Unclear Norms for Emotional Expression

Student narratives were characterized by strong emotionality and tension was intensified when the rules for emotional expression were unclear and unspoken. Tension arose when students were called upon to put on a public face that was incongruent with their private experience. When students experienced emotional distress in a setting where their field instructors were 'comfortable with the uncomfortable', they felt confused and alienated from their field instructors and their own emotional responses.

The literature on emotions in organizations expanded our understanding of this aspect of the student experience. For example, on a cultural level, our Western traditions consider emotions as impediments to knowledge and effective action. Miller (1976) stated, 'We have a long tradition of trying to dispense with, or at least control or neutralize emotionality, rather than valuing, embracing, and cultivating its contributing strengths' (p. 38). Hochschild (1983) noted that a disjuncture between displayed emotions and private feelings produces identity confusion and stress. As a consequence, students may wonder, 'Who am I really? What is real and authentic?'.

The Student–Field Instructor Relationship

Field instructors recognized that students experience emotional distress in their field placements; however only two recognized that they may unwittingly become a source of student stress while over one-third of the students in the study identified their field instructor as a source of distress. Another point of disjuncture between students and field instructors was the belief on the part of field instructors that past personal experiences of students may be a source of distress in their field placements. Only two students cited personal factors as a source of tension. Students in the study reported resenting the field instructors' movement into the personal terrain and in this, they were not unlike students in Knight's study (2000), who regarded field instructors primarily as educators and did not perceive delving into their personal lives as being helpful or enhancing learning. Field instructors venturing into this terrain may find themselves on a slippery slope.

Conflict and Power

The threat of conflict with their field instructors heightened student fears of isolation and condemnation and kept them silent. At first glance, a student's place in the situated power structure appears to be a fact of life; however, Foucault (1980) noted that power is not static but continually being altered and reconstituted. In other words, where there is power, there is resistance. Denying one's emotions, wrote Alice Miller (1986), separates people from their moral sense and makes them obedient and adaptable. Thus, a mechanism for repression is denial of emotions, and a form of resistance is expression of emotion. In this study, students' resistance took several forms: a conscious decision to remain silent 'just to get through', creating alternative alignments, and talking about their feelings.

Safety

The issue of safety, although uppermost in student and field instructor awareness, was often not directly addressed in field placements. Data from the study indicated that the combination of exposure to violence and lack of opportunity to voice one's fears increased tension in field placements. If students are, as Fay (1987) asserts, creatures of tradition constituted out of their cultural inheritances and social environments, female students' safety concerns are congruent with those of women who grow up in a cultural and societal context where physical and emotional violence towards women is visible and common but often not directly spoken about. Research on violence in social work field education suggests a mirroring in field agencies of the cultural milieu related to violence—'it's there but we don't talk about it'.

Hence like most women in our society, students in this study were likely acculturated to the threat of violence and therefore habituated to 'looking over their shoulders', remaining constantly vigilant, and becoming adept at avoiding dangerous situations. As student social workers, however, mobility decisions were not totally in their control and tension arose when they found themselves called upon to enter situations that intuitively they considered to be unsafe.

Integrating Knowledge

Tension was created when students struggled to integrate new knowledge about themselves and still maintain their personal identities within a profession that is not purely technical, but rather guided by value-based thinking that requires adopting certain tenets that may be contrary to what they believe. When they submerged personal values to focus on getting the job done, they experienced frustration and anger.

The study also offered exemplars of emergence of practice wisdom derived from learning that particular beliefs held about people, as in the case of the student who encountered the pedophile, are not always substantiated by experience. This student was challenged to consider multiple meanings and leave behind the habit of imposing one truth across contexts.

Absence of Articulated Practice Guidelines

The students in this study, like those in the study of Fook and her colleagues (2000) experienced tension in the absence of articulated rules of practice. Fook *et al.* (2000) noted that when the goal of field education is to teach students to engage in an inductive process of creating theory that is transferable across contexts, trial and error and the risk of making mistakes are essential aspects of the process. Tension is created for students who are urged to adopt this approach within the structural constraints imposed by evaluation, questions of suitability for practice, and maintenance of program standards. While being encouraged to learn from their mistakes, they are also evaluated on their behavior. The Catch-22 situation can create an environment where students consider hiding some or all of their errors. As well, it has the potential of immobilizing them so that they appear detached and peripheral actors in the field placement.

Conclusion

Attention by field instructors and faculty to the emotional impact of the field experience, often underscored by issues of power, can serve to strengthen the experiential pedagogy of social work field education. When embraced by educators as a critical dynamic of social work field education, it serves to honor the totality of the student learning experience. Considering students' emotional responses to oppression in their field placements can be a beginning point for engaging them in a discourse of anti-oppressive practice and opening up avenues for insight and action (Bishop, 2002; Mullaly, 2002; Fook, 1993). Friere (1970) noted that the oppressed must be their own example in the struggle for redemption.

This study points to tension in social work field settings. Barlow & Hall (2004) noted that traditionally 'trouble' has been depicted as an epiphenomenon, something occurring outside the usual in social work field education. When viewed in this manner, the implication is that field education is smooth and seamless. However, when the concepts of trouble, tension, conflict and power are moved from the margins to a more central position in understanding and implementing social work field education, field educators will be more alert to the need for re-evaluation and change in practices that can ultimately enhance the quality of field education.

Questions arising from this research include the following. How can the schools better prepare students for the reality of practice outside the confines of limited epistemology adhered to by academia? How can students be schooled in the nuances of organizational politics? Along with posing questions for further research, an additional consideration is how students' emotional experiences in their field placements can be used as a springboard for considering larger practice issues, such as vicarious trauma, the role of empathy, and issues of self-care.

References

Barlow, C. & Hall, B. (2003) 'Managing vulnerability in social work field placements: student and field instructor voices', *The New Social Worker*, vol. 10, no. 3, pp. 6–9.

Barlow, C. & Hall, B. (2004) 'Issues of power and resistance in social work field education', *International Journal of Learning*, vol. 10.

Bishop, A. (2002) *Becoming an Ally: Breaking the Cycle of Oppression in People*, 2nd edn, Fernwood Publishing, Halifax, Canada.

Bogo, M. & Vayda, E. (2000) *The Practice of Field Instruction in Social Work: Theory and Process*, 2nd edn, Columbia University Press, New York.

Brookfield, S. (1996) 'Experiential pedagogy: grounding teaching in students' learning', *Journal of Experiential Education*, vol. 19, no. 2, pp. 62–68.

Burke, S. & Harris, R. (1996) 'Violence: a study of ways to support social work students in urban field placements', *The Clinical Supervisor*, vol. 14, no. 2, pp. 147–155.

Campbell, C. (1999) 'Empowering pedagogy: experiential education in the social work classroom', *Canadian Social Work Review*, vol. 16, no. 1, pp. 35–48.

Coates, J. & McKay, M. (1995) 'Toward a new pedagogy of social transformation', *Journal of Progressive Human Services*, vol. 6, no. 1, pp. 27–34.

Dewey, J. (1938) *Experience and Education*, Collier Books, New York.

Elliason, M. (1996) 'Field can be hazardous to your well being: fact or fiction?', *Journal of Baccalaureate Social Work*, vol. 2, no. 1, pp. 79–89.

Fay, B. (1987) *Critical Social Science: Liberation and its Limits*, Polity Press, Cambridge.

Fernandez, E. (1998) 'Student perceptions of satisfaction with practicum learning', *Social Work Education*, vol. 17, no. 2, pp. 173–201.

Fook, J. (1993) *Radical Casework: A Theory of Practice*, Allen & Unwin, Australia.

Fook, J., Ryan, M. & Hawkins, L. (2000) *Professional Expertise: Practice, Theory and Education for Working in Uncertainty*, Whiting & Birch Ltd, London.

Foucault, M. (1980) *Power/Knowledge: Selected Interviews and Other Writings 1972–1977*, The Harvester Press, Brighton, Sussex.

Friere, P. (1970) *Pedegogy of the oppressed*, Continuum, New York.

Glaser, B. G. (1992) *Basics of Grounded Theory Analysis*, Sociology Press, Mill Valley, CA.

Goldblatt, H. & Buchbinder, E. (2003) 'Challenging gender roles: the impact on female social work students working with abuse women', *Journal of Social Work Education*, vol. 39, no. 2, pp. 255–279.

Hackett, S. & Marsland, P. (1997) 'Perceptions of power: an exploration of the dynamics in the student–tutor–practice teacher relationship within child protection placements', *Social Work Education*, vol. 16, no. 2, pp. 44–62.

Hochschild, A. (1983) *The Managed Heart: Commercialization of Human Feeling*, University of California Press, Berkeley.

Jayaratne, S., Vinokur-Kaplan, D., Nagda, B. A. & Chess, W. A. (1996) 'A national study on violence and harassment of social workers by clients', *The Journal of Applied Social Sciences*, vol. 20, pp. 1–14.

Knight, C. (2000) 'Engaging the student in the field instruction relationship: BSW and MSW students' views', *Journal of Teaching in Social Work*, vol. 20, no. 3/4, pp. 173–201.

Kolb, D. (1984) *Experiential Learning: Experience as the Source of Learning and Development*, Prentice Hall, Englewood Cliffs, NJ.

Mama, R. S. (2001) 'Violence in the field: experiences of students and supervisors', *The Journal of Baccalaureate Social Work*, vol. 7, no. 1, pp. 17–26.

Miles, M. B. & Huberman, A. M. (1994) *Qualitative Data Analysis*, Sage, London.

Miller, A. (1986) *Thou Shalt Not Be Aware: Society's Betrayal of the Child*, New American Library, New York.

Miller, J. B. (1976) *Toward a New Psychology of Women*, Beacon Press, Boston.
Miller, J. B. & Stiver, P. I. (1997) *The Healing Connection: How Women form Relationships in Therapy and in Life*, Beacon Press, Boston.
Mullaly, B. (2002) *Challenging Oppression: A Critical Social Work Approach*, Oxford University Press, Toronto.
Nussbaum, M. C. (2001) *Upheavals of Thought: The Intelligence of Emotions*, Cambridge University Press, New York.
Pepper, N. (1996) 'Supervision: a positive learning experience or an anxiety provoking exercise?', *Australian Social Work*, vol. 49, no. 3, pp. 55–63.
Preston-Shoot, M. (1995) 'Assessing anti-oppressive practice', *Social Work Education*, vol. 14, no. 2, pp. 11–29.
Reeser, C. R. & Wertkin, R. A. (2001) 'Safety training in social work education: a national survey', *Journal of Teaching in Social Work*, vol. 21, no. 1/2, pp. 95–113.
Rompf, E. L., Royse, D. & Dhooper, S. S. (1993) 'Anxiety preceding field work: what students worry about', *Journal of Teaching in Social Work*, vol. 7, pp. 81–95.
Rossiter, A. (1995) 'Teaching social work skills from a critical perspective', *Canadian Social Work Review*, vol. 12, no. 1, pp. 9–27.
Saakvitne, K. W., Pearlman, L. A., the Staff of the Traumatic Stress Institute (1996) *Transforming the Pain: A Workbook on Vicarious Traumatization*, W.W. Norton, New York.
Schon, D. A. (1983) *Reflective Practice: How Professionals Think in Action*, Basic Books, New York.
Strauss, A. & Corbin, J. (1990) *Basics of Qualitative Research: Grounded Theory Procedures and Techniques*, Sage Publications, Newbury Park.
Tully, C. C., Kropf, N. P. & Price, J. L. (1993) 'Is field a hard hat area? A study of violence in field placements', *Journal of Social Work Education*, vol. 29, pp. 191–1999.

Accepted October 2005

Australian Social Work
Vol. 63, No. 1, March 2010, pp. 51–66

Epilogues and Prefaces: Research and Social Work and People with Intellectual Disabilities

Ann Fudge Schormans
School of Social Work, McMaster University, Ontario, Canada

Abstract

It is well established that public photographic representations of people with intellectual disabilities strongly influences what we think we know about people so labelled. This paper reports on the unanticipated outcomes of a research project that looked at the ways in which public photographs often construct people with intellectual disabilities as dysfunctional, from the perspectives of the labelled people themselves. Research participants with intellectual disabilities were asked to critique a sample of public photographic images and then, using the computer software program, Photoshop, to change the images to reflect their critique. These changed images were then shown to a number of non-disabled audiences. In this paper, I address the unanticipated outcomes of the project: the effects on participants and non-disabled others resulting from activities arising from the project. These unanticipated outcomes speak to the power of visual imagery, to the empowerment that can take place when people with intellectual disabilities are enabled to have their voices heard, and the ways dialogue between people with and without intellectual disabilities can work towards new understandings. Social work, in its concern for social justice, has a role in enabling the expression of the voices of people with intellectual disabilities and facilitating opportunities for dialogue.

Keywords: Intellectual Disability; Social Work Research; Empowerment; Visual Imagery

> Did you like our work? Did you think I did a good job? How was my reading, was my reading good? (Donna, member of the *PhotoChangers* research group)

The influence of media representations on our understanding of "disability" is well-documented (Elks, 2005; Shakespeare, 2002), yet these images typically construct people with intellectual disabilities as little more than dysfunctional, dehumanising, and oppressive stereotypes (Hevey, 1997). Social workers are not impervious—we are *all* susceptible to the influence of visual and other representations on our determinations of "same" and "different" and the meanings and value we ascribe to others (Derrida, 2001b). Nor are people with intellectual disabilities immune, as they may internalise these constructions, affecting how they come to think about

Correspondence to: Ann Fudge Schormans, School of Social Work, McMaster University, Kenneth Taylor Hall, Room 309A, 1280 Main Street West, Hamilton, Ontario, Canada L8S 4M4. E-mail: fschorm@mcmaster.ca
Accepted 11 October 2009

ISSN 0312-407X (print)/ISSN 1447-0748 (online)
DOI: 10.1080/03124070903464301

themselves. But visual imagery can also be turned on itself and used to reveal how society continues to oppress people with intellectual disabilities. In this paper, I describe the unanticipated outcomes of a research project that attempted to do just that. Donna's (proudly spoken) questioning of the audience at an art gallery presentation of the work she, Bob, Sam, and Robin[1], all adults labelled intellectually disabled, created in a research project on public photographic representations of people with intellectual disabilities, was but one of these unanticipated outcomes, outcomes that attest to the power of visual imagery and of voice. Giving Donna, Bob, Sam, and Robin the opportunity, through the research project, to publicly respond to disabling visual imagery, enabling them to have their voices heard as they challenged this imagery and put forth alternative representations and views, proved to be very empowering, leading to a re-construction—a re-thinking—of themselves. It further led to their initiation of a number of activities stemming from, but subsequent to, the research. As both epilogue and preface, this paper centres on these unanticipated outcomes—the activities that group members engaged in following the research project; how these served to influence their own thinking about themselves as people with intellectual disabilities; and how, through these activities, they used their work with public photographic images to educate and influence what non-disabled others (including social workers) came to think about people with intellectual disabilities.

I will first provide background information on photographic imagery and people with disabilities and on the structure of the research project. A brief description of what happened during the research process will be followed by description and discussion of the unanticipated outcomes and the implications for social work.

Knowing Through Seeing: Photographic Representation and Intellectual Disability

Visual images, as "scenes of instruction" (Mauer, 2005, p. 96) are intricately bound up with knowledge and understanding of the self and the other in contemporary culture. The public photographic image (e.g., newspaper images, charity and retail advertisements, photographic art, documentary, and movie posters) increasingly shapes our world view (Derrida, 2001b). Visual images are critically important to people with disabilities who are, most of all, conceptualised visually (Hevey, 1997) because they are largely presumed to be "true", despite their nature as socially constructed and functional (Derrida, 2001b). Shakespeare (2002) noted the historical distortion of disability in visual images. What we are most often "given-to-be-seen" are dominant fictions (Silverman, 1996): tenacious stereotypes that regard disability as tragedy and lack and present disability in a medical context or as something one "bravely"

[1] The individual members of *The PhotoChangers,* Sam, Bob, Robin, and Donna, insisted upon the use of their own names in this and any other publication. The work that is presented is their work, they are proud of it, and they want readers to know this. They are given the opportunity to review any manuscript I write before it is published and receive copies of all published work. They are also planning a manuscript that we will write together.

overcomes in a struggle to be "normal" (Darke, 1998). Fostering prejudice, these images establish people with disabilities as different—unable, inhuman, undesirable, bad—as the "other" none of "us" would ever wish to be. Their function is to show and construct labelled people in specific ways for specific purposes (e.g., to raise money) (Hevey, 1997). Few alternative scenes are available, especially for people with intellectual disabilities who have yet to make the same political gains as people with other disabilities (Yong, 2007). Yet Phillips (2001) noted neither pity nor spectacle is necessary to disability imagery—they are a choice made by those constructing the images, but, as the central, confirmational images of disability (rarely questioned by non-disabled viewers), they powerfully shape our "knowledge" of disability (Elks, 2005). While many disability scholars address visual disability representations, people with intellectual disabilities are conspicuously absent in this literature, as objects, subjects, creators of, or commentators on, these representations—they have had little control over how they have been represented, visually or otherwise.

The "What's Wrong with this Picture?" Project

At Sam's suggestion, the study came to be called the "*What's Wrong with this Picture?*" project. Its design reflected participatory and inclusive research ideologies (Goodley & Moore, 2000; Knox, Mok, & Parmenter, 2000; Newbury, 1996) and arts-informed research methodologies (Cole & McIntyre, 2004; Knowles & Thomas, 2002; Phillips, 2001). Theoretically, it is grounded in critical disability theory and Emmanuel Levinas' idea of our ethical responsibility to the alterity of the Other. Levinas believed that our most important concern is ethical responsibility towards the Other, the person before you needing your assistance. "Alterity" refers to our uniqueness; we are each unique, different from everyone else. "Difference" (e.g., having a disability) does not create alterity; rather, alterity is what determines difference (Levinas, 2001a, 2001b). From a Levinasian position, social work's emphasis on social justice is achieved, in part, through respect for diversity and the inherent worth of every individual (CASW, 2005), pushing us to re-think disability as devalued difference and, by extension, our (potentially devaluing and disabling) social work relationships with disabled people.

Solomon (2007) wrote of social work as "caring takes thinking and thinking takes caring" (p. 100). To a great extent, social work caring is rooted in a thinking entangled with medicalised, deficit-based notions of disability, in taking care *of the problem* of disability instead of caring *about*, attributing value, and finding a place for people with disabilities. Emphasising diagnosis, this perspective locates disability in the individual, thus ignoring the social, political, economic, and cultural factors involved in creating disability *as a problem* (French Gilson & DePoy, 2002). Instead, regarding disability as a form of social oppression akin to racism, sexism, and heterosexism, critical disability theory locates the causes of disability, not pathologically within the individual, but in society and social organisation (Frazee, Gilmour, & Mykitiuk, 2006), in the entrenched assumptions and practices of "ableism". As such, it demands an analysis of the mechanisms and holders of power, in this case, in photographic representations of intellectual disability. Deemed more consistent with goals of social justice and eradication of oppression, social work is advised to adopt a critical perspective regarding disability (French Gilson & DePoy, 2002). Synonymous with Levinisian thought, social work's responsibility towards oppressed groups is also an ethical one. Thus, the primary purpose of this research project was to extend our knowledge about people with intellectual disabilities by looking critically at one of the ways we have come to know them—public photographic representation.

To make this work more meaningful and relevant, the inclusion of the previously marginalised and absented knowledge of people labelled intellectually disabled was paramount. Hevey (1997) noted that no one has asked the disabled "observed" what they felt about the images in which they figured: "(o)nce again, the entire discourse has absented the voice of those at its centre – disabled people" (p. 335). Similarly, Phillips (2001) argued that what is missing, but is crucial, is the unique and valuable perspective that persons with disabilities bring to their own representations. I used critical disability and Levinasian lenses to inform an ethically responsible social work response: looking at how, through an inclusive research methodology, to give voice to the knowledge, perspectives, and experiences of people with intellectual disabilities as they contend with public photographic representations; and how to use the knowledge gained from this interaction as a means of interrupting what is known about them, to make space for new knowledge, and for alternative social work interactions with people so labelled. Recognising the value of what people with intellectual disabilities have to say, the study provided a space for labelled people to critique public photographic images and challenge the taken-for-granted "truths" of disability inscribed in them, and work towards more complex and nuanced understandings of intellectual disability. As social workers, this search lies at the heart of what we want and need to know for what we understand their experience to be will shape our notions of who they are, what they need, who they can be, and how they should be treated (Trent, 1994; Young & Quibell, 2000).

In addition to seeking their critique, I wondered how people with intellectual disabilities might re-image or alter these public photographs as a pathway to changing the meaning of intellectual disability? And what might happen if these transformed images were shown to people who do not have disabilities? Inherent within photographic work, is its potential for exploring and reconstructing understandings of disability in educational and cultural contexts (Newbury, 1996), so that we might "see" differently (Kratz, 2002). By transforming existing public photographic images to reflect their critique, people with intellectual disabilities can create images that oppose the meanings of disability inscribed in the originals, not to "fix" photographic images, or to determine "correct" disability images (an impossible task in light of the heterogeneity of disability and disability experience), but to render new meanings (Derrida, 1998, 2001a). Photographs that challenge or defy expectations rather than confirming them can be extraordinarily powerful (Newbury, 1996). By inviting non-disabled people to exhibits of the work and engaging them in conversation, a space and opportunity for potentially transformative interactions between people with and without intellectual disabilities is opened (Cole & McIntyre, 2004).

Method

What Happened

I provide here an overly simplistic description of what was a very involved and complex research process. Sam, Bob, Robin, Donna, and I met 1 to 3 times a week for 1.5 to 2 hours for 3 months. For the first step of the project, they selected, from a collection of public photographic images that I provided, 11 images to work with, individually, collectively, or both. I asked a number of questions to facilitate their critical engagement with each picture. For example: What do you think this picture is about? How does the picture make you feel? What do you think the picture is telling you about people with intellectual disabilities? Do you like that story? and What would people *without* intellectual disabilities think about people *with* intellectual disabilities if they saw that picture? Their insights were powerful and heartfelt, emerging from their own lives and experiences, and led to incredibly rich, emotionally, and politically-charged discussions about how to change the images as a means of articulating their critique, telling different stories, challenging and disrupting taken-for-granted notions of intellectual disability, and making visible the plurality of meaning of intellectual disability. We used *Photoshop* (a computer program that enables the user to manipulate photographic images) to transform, or re-image, each photographic image in the manner that Bob, Donna, Sam, and Robin determined necessary. In some instances, they also used a camera to create new images that spoke to the original images and what they read within them.

Let me briefly (for this is not the focus of this paper) offer a description of some of their work with the images. For the most part, they strongly disliked these images. With the exception of three images (from the *Benetton* "Sunflowers" advertising campaign), their reaction was one of disappointment, anger, upset, and opposition. They felt the images revealed that people with intellectual disabilities "are not wanted", neither cared for nor cared about. The images portrayed people with intellectual disabilities as "frightening", "different", unlovable, and powerless—yet unlike any person with a disability they knew. For group members, these images evoked recognition of dominant devaluing attitudes towards people with intellectual disabilities—the disrespect and disregard they experienced daily. However, they did identify some positive attributes of the images. Images in which people with intellectual disabilities were well-dressed, healthy-looking, and smiling were regarded highly by the group: these representations told viewers what people with intellectual disabilities could, and should, look like if properly supported and treated with respect. These images did not make people with intellectual disabilities look "scary", in fact, these were the ways group members, themselves, would like to be represented.

Their visual responses to the images varied. In some instances they changed the image's caption. In others, they took their own photographs: to challenge the original image; to put forth an image they preferred; or to pair with the original in order to change the story of the original. For some, they used Photoshop to add new elements to the original, to transpose parts of the original into another image, or to move things around in the image. The changes were creative, insightful, and powerful. What was important about these transformed images was that they told radically different stories about people with disabilities. For example, rather than powerless victims, new images portrayed strength and resistance. Pity became defiance. Abuse became revenge. Abandonment turned into a loving touch. Empowered to tell their stories visually, the transformations reflected group members' growing politicisation.

The second phase of the research saw Sam, Bob, Donna, and Robin assuming greater control of the research process itself, having an active role in determining the conditions and context of the showing of the work, and the ways in which the audience was invited to experience and make meaning of it (Cole & McIntyre, 2004). The project represented the research component of my PhD studies; consequently, much of the research design was, by necessity, predetermined by me. As noted, this project was intended to be an inclusive one, moving beyond participation only as a "respondent". Towards this end, the research design intentionally left ample room for Sam, Bob, Donna, and Robin to be far more active in the second phase: (a) preparation of the transformed images for exhibition to three different audiences (other people with intellectual disabilities; people sharing a personal or professional relationship with persons with intellectual disabilities; people having little knowledge or experience with labelled persons); (b) determination of the structure of the exhibits (art-gallery styling—each transformed image with selected text fragments was mounted on a white board and hung from the ceiling, corresponding original image lying flat on table below it); (c) methods of engagement with the audiences (dialogically engaging audience members following audience's viewing of the work); (d) recruitment of audiences and; (e) acting as cofacilitators for each exhibit.

The first audience (of other people with intellectual disabilities) responded enthusiastically to the work; sharing their interpretations of the images and stories of their own experiences of oppression. The third audience (of people having no understanding of intellectual disability) was deeply moved. Engaging with the group in open and honest discussion (baring their own prejudices and assumptions), many were moved to tears. The second audience (including many social workers) were silenced by the work and, in personal interviews with me later, admitted that the work disrupted what they thought they knew about people with intellectual disabilities. These responses to the work made apparent to the group the importance and value of their voice. Feeling empowered and in control, they actively sought out ways for the work to continue.

Results

What Happened Next

Atkinson (2005), writing about research as social work, has found that participatory research with people with intellectual disabilities does not always come to a tidy or easy closure. This project was no exception, yet there is also a level of excitement, for me, around what has transpired since the research project officially ended. I wish, now, to outline five key activities the group participated in upon the completion of the project: forming a group; developing a website; teaching social work students; conference presentations; and being featured in the newspaper.

Relationships (emergent and pre-existing) were strengthened by the closeness and personal nature of the work involved in the research project (Atkinson, 2005), facilitating a sense of cohesiveness among the research participants and, to a slightly lesser extent, myself. Developing critical awareness and self-advocacy skills, combined with a shared belief in the importance of the work they were doing, seemed to direct Donna, Sam, Bob and Robin to identify as a group. Formalising this arrangement, they named themselves *The PhotoChangers*—in this sense taking ownership over the "label" assigned to them. Membership in the group has become very important to them and appears to serve a number of purposes. Sakamoto, Chin, Chapra, & Ricciardi (2009), note that empowerment is possible when members of a marginalised population come together to support one another by constructing family-like networks or groups. Social work research, rooted in an empowerment-oriented framework, has the potential to benefit participants beyond the duration of the project itself. *The PhotoChangers*, as a group, began to more actively support and assist each other, inside and outside of group activities. Emotionally, group meetings provide a safe and protective space for members. For example, when one member was being harassed by a group of non-disabled people in the community, other members were quick to provide emotional support: validating her feelings of anger and sadness, giving advice around managing such a situation should it occur again; and offering to accompany her on future visits to that location. Instrumentally, they have helped each other financially and have shared information on services and community supports. Far from being passive victims (Sakamoto et al., 2009), the sense of community fostered by becoming a group provided members greater power to resist and fight against the discrimination and marginalisation they face daily—they understand this to be their task: to help and protect each other and to work together to change people's opinions about them.

From this came the decision to create, and publicly launch, their own website—the *What's Wrong With This Picture* website[2]—as a venue for further self-advocacy: to display their project work, address important issues, showcase creative expressions, and connect with others (both disabled and non-disabled). While not yet able to manage the site themselves, they have complete control over the content of material posted on the site. Here, they have the power to determine how they are

[2] http://www.whatswrongwiththispicture.ca

represented—not the non-disabled social worker or photographer: an atypical experience for people with intellectual disabilities who, historically, have had little control over their "image", over how they are represented visually or textually (Linneman, 2001). Representing themselves visually (with photographs of their own creation and choosing), they are also raising issues that they have identified as important to them. They have written about the importance of having a job and employment discrimination, and of what they regard as the government's determination to keep them poor and dependent. They want to use to site to invite people with and without intellectual disabilities to read these essays, learn from them, and join with them in their efforts to end the discrimination they experience.

The *PhotoChangers* were invited, on two occasions, to speak to graduate level social workers at a university about their work and their lives[3]. With my assistance (providing information about typical graduate class expectations and activities), they determined the structure and content of their presentations. My primary roles were administrative (write down and organise their ideas, work with them to revise these to their satisfaction, type the agreed-upon scripts and prepare power-point slides) and facilitative (introduce the project and their presentation, answer questions they felt unable to answer). This deviates from more typical, top-down social worker/researcher interactions with clients/participants. Once again, group members represent themselves and, in this venue, are able to speak directly to social work students about their experiences and expectations of social work, service providers, the government, and society as a whole.

The PhotoChangers regard any opportunity to teach social workers as critically important to improving the lives of people with disabilities. Keenly aware of the power differential between social workers and clients, they talk often of the role of social workers in their lives, of the power that social workers have over them, and the impact of such on the supports and opportunities provided to them. They do not believe that most social workers understand them, their lives, or the impact of the ways they are treated by social workers and non-disabled people. Nor do they value what they have to say. Teaching social workers affords them the opportunity to flip the traditional "teacher/student" relationships social workers typically impose upon interactions with marginalised clients (Sakamoto et al., 2009, p. 443) allowing for new kinds of learning. Sam stated, "if [non-disabled people] wanted to do people with disabilities as favour, they would appreciate what we say".

Also important is that these presentations took place on a university campus—a location from which people with intellectual disabilities have historically been excluded. Donna and Sam, in particular, rail against an education system that, in relegating people with intellectual disabilities to special education settings, "that don't teach you anything", denies them the opportunity to go to university "like everyone else". Regrettably, on one of their first forays onto the university campus, they were

[3] It must be noted that Robin chose not to participate in any public discussions or have his picture posted on the website—it is my sense that "disabled" is not the identification he chooses to present publicly.

mistaken for vagrants and campus security was called to investigate. Initially outraged (and simultaneously confused and saddened), the incident was smoothed over when the security officers genuinely and profusely apologised. The group has since done much of their work at the university and are establishing a presence there. Robin has noted that it is because people do not know them (the group, and people with intellectual disabilities more generally) that they ignore them or tease them, thus highlighting a useful task for social work: facilitating the occasions for non-disabled people to get to know people with intellectual disabilities is an important step in overcoming the ignorance that perpetuates prejudice (Bogdan & Taylor, 1989).

Barnes (2004) pointed out the value and necessity of having people with disabilities control the dissemination of research by and about them—what is disseminated, how, and to whom—to influencing what we come to understand about disability. Sam suggested *The PhotoChangers* present their work at conferences (another exclusionary site for people with intellectual disabilities). Following discussions as to the types of conferences best suited to their work, and the audiences they wished to reach, we identified a number to apply to. Moving "inside" this other academic space the group, again, disrupted the status quo; challenging assumptions about who belongs where. While often stared at, the group believed themselves to have the right and the responsibility to be in these spaces—these were places where they could talk to people and help them to learn about intellectual disability.

To date, we have presented at local, provincial, and national[4] conferences in the fields of disability and social work. We were also invited to participate in a symposium organised by and held at a local art gallery. The process of preparing and making presentations, my role and the responsibilities of group members, were identical to those for their presentations to graduate students and, once again, placed group members in charge of representing and speaking for themselves. They are increasingly concerned to "spread the word" about their work and what they can do. Interestingly, in presentations they challenge audiences to consider why public photographic representations never show people with intellectual disabilities presenting at conferences! As they learned that people around the world were seeing and hearing about their work, as people in their own communities approached them to acknowledge having seen it, the self-esteem of each member grew—in Donna's words, they were "famous". A lesson for social work research is that each of these opportunities to address an audience impacts both upon their sense of self and on how others perceive them: in evidence are individual empowerment, social empowerment, and social change. Each positive reception to their work and words further empowers and emboldens them to speak out. Each presentation has resulted in non-disabled audience members re-evaluating people with intellectual disabilities, questioning their own assumptions.

---

[4] The work was accepted at an international disability conference in another country. Unfortunately, as all rely on disability benefits as their primary source of income (and we were unable to locate alternative funding sources), not one of *The PhotoChangers* was able to attend. Together we prepared a presentation which I made at the conference on their behalf.

Perhaps the most thrilling opportunity arose when a local reporter was made aware of the project. The reporter interviewed the group and featured their story in a major newspaper. The group, their work, and the necessity of self-advocacy were the focus of the article (my own role and contribution rightfully warranted a mere two lines). The group members were overwhelmed when they realised the numbers of people who would see (for the article included two images) and read about their work. Acutely aware of the power of the media in shaping our understandings of "others", they understand that taking their message public, to a broader and more diverse audience, is a means of working towards social change (Cole & McIntyre, 2004). It was all very exciting—Donna carried a copy of the article in her pocket for months afterward, proudly displaying it to any and all.

Discussion

Cixous (1993) observed that the process of creation is potentially transformative; through the process, all involved are taken to a new place, perhaps even to a new being. Participation in the project, and the activities stemming from it, began to move, not just *The PhotoChangers,* but also some members of their various audiences, to new places and new understandings of themselves and each other.

For the group, some changes were subtle—visible shifts in their carriage, more initiative and direct eye-contact when speaking to an audience, growing confidence, and belief in the value of what they had to say. Afforded the opportunity for self-expression and having their voice heard resulted in a greater sense of self-worth (Freire, 1972; Perring, 2004). They demonstrated pride in their work and in what they were accomplishing through the dissemination of this work. They knew how difficult it could be to escape or change people's ideas about people with intellectual disabilities, "to get them to listen to us and to respect our feelings and opinions", yet they shared an understanding that, through their work, their presentations and website, they were showing the world "the true meaning of disability"—*their* meanings of intellectual disability, not those attributed to them by non-disabled people. Over time, another shift became apparent in the group's perception of ownership of the work. More and more, I was moved into the background. "Ann's research project" became "our research project", "our work", "what we did".

There were other significant changes as well. Bob, Sam, Robin, and Donna were four very different people. What they shared was the label, "intellectually impaired", and far too many experiences of marginalisation, discrimination, and oppression. While able to talk about these experiences and recognise them as unfair, they had all, to greater or lesser degree, internalised dominant, ableist understandings of intellectual impairment as a tragedy, a personal problem, and of people with intellectual disabilities as somehow lesser. None of the group members wanted to have an intellectual disability. They often struggled with their need for support. There was a tension between wanting to feel good about themselves, and dealing daily with prejudice. Donna was most outspoken in this regard, frequently brought to tears as

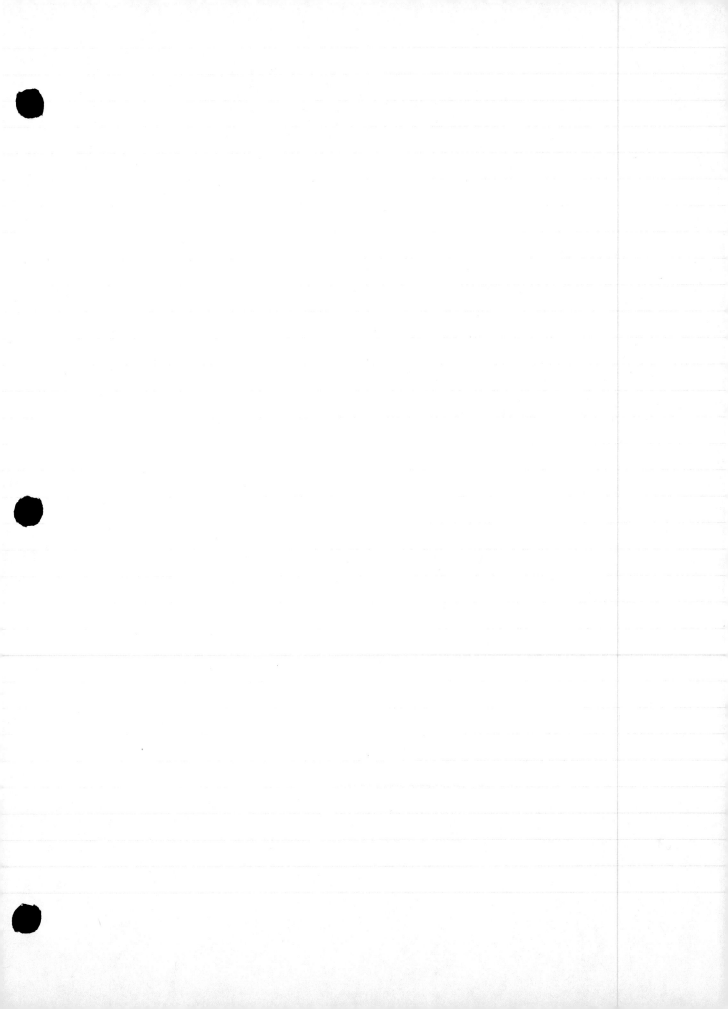

she struggled with the feelings that resulted from being teased and rejected "because we have a disability". She tells audiences, "that's what makes me cry sometimes, that's what really hurts and really bothers me because that's just the way it is".

Reflecting Freire's (1972) conscientisation and empowerment practices, and nudging towards the disability movement's broader goal of emancipation from oppression (both solidly embedded in a social work social justice framework), in being enabled to respond critically and publicly through their work with public photographic images, and to engage with non-disabled audiences, the group moved towards relocating the source of their troubles in oppressive dis-abling structures. This proved a shift for some of them. For example, they began to better understand how social attitudes towards disability—in particular the notion that people with intellectual disabilities had no skills or abilities, nothing to offer society except the burden of their care—were shaped, at least in part, by public photographic images. Images presenting people with intellectual disabilities as child-like, sick, or needing charity, led viewers to regard all people with intellectual disabilities as un-able, as being the same as the people they saw in the images. Yet they repeatedly stressed, "we're not the same as them". Bob and Robin emphasised that public photographic images don't tell the truth about disability, "The pictures do not explain disability. They just tell you the picture is sad." Grappling with public representations, they began to question why they were portrayed in these ways and who was responsible. Sam wrote:

> We just don't know why that the pictures would have to look like this. We need pictures of people with disabilities doing better things. We don't understand why the photographer took these horrible pictures, this is so embarrassing. The people in the pictures must feel embarrassed and humiliated and horrified. They had no right to do that.

As they became better able to articulate how the social world defines and restricts their lives, and to identify prejudice based on disability, they became more explicitly political. Donna wrote a (unanswered) letter to the Premier of the province. The group has been learning about political processes, meeting with members of government. While not entirely abandoning their convictions that intellectual impairment is, itself, dis-abling (Bob believes he will always need his social worker to help him with budgeting and banking because he is "not good at that stuff"), the critical thinking inherent in the research process had begun to move them towards thinking differently about disability. For example, they began to more publicly challenge the message inscribed in many of the images they worked with that represented disability as "the worse thing that could happen"; informing audiences that some people with intellectual disabilities are "quite happy".

Re-making and re-thinking themselves, and people with intellectual disabilities more broadly, through their re-imaging of public photographs and their conversations with non-disabled audiences, the group succeeded, in a small way, of making non-disabled viewers "re-make" and "re-think" people labelled intellectually disabled, to see difference differently.

Let me now offer three stories that, I believe, make these contentions visible. The first story is something that happened at the public launch of the group's website. The launch was well attended, with a mix of people with and without disabilities. As with other presentations, I had scribed for each of *The PhotoChangers* participating a script of what they wished to say, as they were anxious not to forget anything. While increasingly more comfortable speaking publicly, they continued to rely heavily on the scripts (yet they managed questions from audiences independently and successfully). There was an unscripted moment at the launch that revealed how far their skills had developed. Nearing the end of the presentation a particular image of Donna flashed upon the screen; an image of Donna hugging a young child that was her response to the inscriptions of "abnormal", "unable", and "dangerous" that she read in the public photographs and connected to prohibitions against parenting for people with intellectual disabilities. Not being permitted to parent was one of the great tragedies of Donna's life. Upon seeing the image, Donna, out of turn (and, again, completely unscripted), stood and addressed the audience. She spoke passionately and poignantly about what was behind the making of this image—her thoughts, experiences, feelings. It was personal. It was political. It demanded a response. Not content to simply speak her heart and mind, Donna asked questions of the audience, holding them responsible to explain to her why she was oppressed, why people without disabilities did not respect her, why she was excluded, ridiculed, and hurt. From my vantage point at the side of the room, many in the audience squirmed. Most people in the audience remained silent but, by risking and responding, not with excuses but with interest, apologies, and validation, a handful of audience members made Donna feel heard and understood. Skerrett (2000) wrote that the movement towards emancipation starts within individuals; it is by first reflecting on their own lives and the larger world in which they live and then communicating and engaging with others, that change can begin. Many audience members were social workers who, in discussion with myself and the group at the close of the presentation, admitted to their own lack of knowledge about intellectual disability and that they had never considered "disability" as "oppression", as a socially constructed phenomenon.

Variations of my second story occurred at every public presentation of the work, with each of the group members, but for one of the members I found it particularly compelling. What became clear was their growing resistance to the imposition of the dysfunctional, dehumanising, and dis-abling identities inscribed in public photographic images. More and more they began to question societal (and social work) assumptions that disability was the problem it had been made out to be. Donna's scripts began to include the strongly spoken statement, "there's nothing wrong with having a disability!" Having discovered the potential for using the images to effect change, they began to actively seek out platforms from which to be heard. Not content to remain "in their place" (Kitchin, 1998), they resisted with their work with the images and through their engagement with audiences. For some, this resistance was loud and insistent. For others, it was much quieter.

It is generally accepted that in fragmenting and reducing persons with intellectual disabilities to their label, there is little incentive to learn *from them* who they are, their ways of being, and the meanings they attribute to their experiences of the world: the underlay is disbelief in their capacity for insight, memory, and reflexive personal and collective understandings. More than just an inability to articulate their stories, they are presumed devoid of the capacity and means of knowing, unable to analyse their own life situations, to understand who they are and what they may wish to become, and coherently express such to the world (Baum, 1999; Vuletic & Ferrari, 2005). At work there is a presumption of incompetence. One member of the group had a lovely way of quietly, but effectively, turning this presumption on its head. Unable to read well, Bob would ask other group members to read his script for him. Yet he had a way of connecting with the audience, of reaching across the space between them, blurring the perceived divide between dis-abled and non-disabled. Perhaps it was his gentle manner, his soft voice, or his strong faith (for he returned every discussion, critique, and question back to a question of faith). So often, in responding to a question, I could see him drawing the asker of the question towards him: having captured their attention they would physically move towards him, in an almost supplicant gesture. Talking *with* him, one could see the shifting of a presumption of incompetence to an (often surprised) awareness and acceptance of his competence, indeed, to recognition of the value and importance of what he had to share. Lessening both the physical and perceived distance between them, it was a humanising gesture, a valuing of Bob, of his alterity.

Starr (2005) argued that while always "noticed", people with visible or conspicuous differences are not always "seen", for the nature of prejudice is the refusal to look (p. 98). Without looking, without paying attention (Levinas, 2001b), and spending time with people with intellectual disabilities, it is not possible to really see them (Starr, 2005). Such a view has implications for social work practice and research—without forming relationships, without ethically engaging with people with intellectual disabilities and learning from them, we risk being ineffective, if not, indeed, hurtful. It also has political implications for, as Rosemarie Garland Thomson (2007) noted, who, how, and where people appear in public is political.

This was especially apparent at the art gallery symposium, the setting of my third story, where, in more ways than one, *The PhotoChangers* broke out of their allocated spaces (Kuppers, 2003). People with disabilities (especially those with intellectual disabilities) are far more likely to be regarded as objects for non-disabled people to stare or look at than as subjects capable of returning our gaze or of gazing themselves (Fudge Schormans & Chambon, 2009). Sandwiched between highly academic and difficult theoretical analyses, the group's presentation was, I think, unexpected by this audience. The group had not been identified in the symposium program as being people with intellectual disabilities. Nonetheless, the audience was attentive and, at the close of their presentation, group members were deluged with questions as people left their seats and moved up to the table to talk to them more intimately. The response of this and other audiences attests to the power of the visual image and to the power of voice, of enabling marginalised people to speak for themselves and to do so publicly. It is this that can lead social workers (and others) to think differently about disability, to begin to welcome, make space for, listen to, and value people with intellectual disabilities – to respond ethically (Derrida, 2001a; Levinas, 2001a). Thus, it is vitally important that social work create or facilitate the creation of contexts, settings, or situations in which people with intellectual disabilities, who are typically silenced and excluded, are instead, included and given the opportunity to speak for themselves (Ristock & Pennell, 1996).

Conclusion

Synonymous with Levinasian thought and the goals of critical disability theorising, social work has, and continues to, define itself as a profession whose primary responsibility is an ethical one, towards oppressed people (as individuals and as members of social groups), and "located within a story of social advance, of the demonstration of a commitment to social justice, equality, and the struggle against oppression and degradation" (Leonard, 2001, p. 3). As social workers, we understand that change is possible when we work with individuals and that radical change can happen when we listen to oppressed groups. I located this project squarely in a transformative agenda, not in the naïve belief that it would serve to single-handedly dismantle oppressive systems of photographic production or radically alter the social, economic, or political condition of the lives of the participants (it has not—there have been no significant material changes in the lives of *The PhotoChangers*) but rather in the hope that the troubling of "taken-for-granted" meanings and the unburying of multiple meanings of intellectual disability might work towards change, towards the creation of new knowledge, new scenes. The outcomes of this project and its effects on the participants and their audiences, suggests there has been some movement towards this end. Acknowledging the contribution made by the power of the group's work with visual images to the creation of these alternative scenes, facilitating meaningful encounters between people with and without intellectual disabilities was the more important piece and offers social work opportunities for ethical interactions with people with intellectual disabilities. Following Levinas, the *PhotoChangers'* experiences stresses the need to listen and learn from expressions of difference; to value subjugated knowledges; and to rely on less fixed and determined ways of looking and knowing that, in letting us re-think what we think we know, create conditions for the possibility of change.

However, for *The PhotoChangers* this task continues. Two members have left to pursue other opportunities and three new members with intellectual disabilities have come on board. At the time of this writing, we are in the middle of a second research project (initiated by *The PhotoChangers*) wherein the group has identified a number of issues important to their lives (e.g., poverty, parenting, belonging) and are exploring ways to use photography to visually articulate these issues. At the same time, they are learning more about conducting research and thinking about other research questions and methodologies to pursue. Having experienced a sense of the potential power of research, they are eager for more.

References

Atkinson, D. (2005). Research as social work: Participatory research in learning disability. *British Journal of Social Work, 35,* 425–434.

Barnes, C. (2004). Reflections on doing emancipatory research. In J. Swain, S. French, C. Barnes & C. Thomas (Eds.), *Disabling Barriers – Enabling Environments* (pp. 47–53). London: Sage Publications.

Baum, N. (1999). How to break the spell of ill-being and help kids achieve a better quality of life. *Exceptionality Education in Canada, 9,* 129–145.

Bogdan, R., & Taylor, S. J. (1989). Relationships with severely disabled people: The social construction of humanness. *Social Problems, 36,* 135–147.

CASW. (2005). *Social Work Code of Ethics.* Ottawa: Canadian Association of Social Workers.

Cixous, H. (1993). *Three Steps on the Ladder of Writing.* Translated by Sarah Cornell and Susan Sellers. The Welleck Library Lectures at the University of California, Irvine. New York: Columbia University Press.

Cole, A. L., & McIntrye, M. (2004). Research as aesthetic contemplation: The role of the audience in research interpretation. *Educational Insights, 9* (1). Retrieved June 3, 2006, from http://ccfi.educ.ubc.ca/publication/insights/v09n01/articles/cole.html

Darke, P. (1998). Understanding cinematic representations of disability. In T. Shakespeare (Ed.), *The Disability Studies Reader, Social Science Perspectives* (pp. 181–197). London and New York: Cassell.

Derrida, J. (1998). *Right of Inspection.* New York: The Monacelli Press, Inc.

Derrida, J. (2001a). *On Cosmopolitanism and Forgiveness,* English translation (Transl. by Mark Dooley and Michael Hughes). New York: Routledge.

Derrida, J. (2001b). *Jacques Derrida: Deconstruction Engaged: The Sydney Seminars.* In P. Patton, & T. Smith (Eds.). Sydney: Power Publications.

Elks, M. A. (2005). Visual indictment: A contextual analysis of *The Kallikak Family* photographs. *Mental Retardation, 43,* 268–280.

Frazee, C., Gilmour, J., & Mykitiuk, R. (2006). Now you see her, now you don't: How law shapes disabled women's experience of exposure, surveillance, and assessment in the clinical encounter. In D. Pothier & R. Devlin (Eds.), *Critical Disability Theory: Essays in Philosophy, Politics, Policy, and Law* (pp. 223–247). Vancouver: UBC Press.

Freire, P. (1972). *Pedagogy of the Oppressed.* Baarn: Anthos.

French Gilson, S., & DePoy, E. (2002). Theoretical approaches to disability content in social work education. *Journal of Social Work Education, 38,* 153–165.

Fudge Schormans, A., & Chambon, A. (2009, accepted). "Please don't let me be like this!": Un-wounding photographic representations by persons with intellectual disability. In J. Hladcki, & S. Brophy (Eds.), *Embodied Politics in Visual Autobiography.*

Goodley, D., & Moore, M. (2000). Doing disability research: activist lives and the academy. *Disability & Society, 15,* 861–882.

Hevey, D. (1997). The enfreakment of photography. In L. J. Davis (Ed.), *The Disability Studies Reader* (pp. 332–347). New York & London: Routledge.

Kitchen, R. (1998). "Out of place", "knowing one's place": Space, power and the exclusion of disabled people. *Disability & Society, 13,* 343–355.

Knowles, G. J., & Thomas, S. M. (2002). Artistry, inquiry, and sense-of-place: Secondary school students portrayed in context. In C. Bagley & M. B. Cancienne (Eds.), *Dancing the Data* (pp. 121–132). New York: Peter Lang.

Knox, M., Mok, M., & Parmenter, T. R. (2000). Working with the experts: collaborative research with people with an intellectual disability. *Disability & Society, 15*, 49–61.

Kratz, C. A. (2002). *The Ones That Are Wanted, Communication and the Politics of Representation in a Photographic Exhibition.* Berkeley, CA: University of California Press.

Kuppers, P. (2003). *Disability and Contemporary Performance, Bodies on Edge.* New York: Routledge.

Leonard, P. (2001). The future of critical social work in uncertain conditions. *Critical Social Work, 2*, 1–7. Retrieved March 24, 2001, from http://www.criticalsocialwork.com/01_1_future_leonard.html

Levinas, E. (2001a). Vocation of the Other. In J. Robbins (Ed. & Trans.), *Is It righteous to be?: Interviews with Emmanuel Levinas* (pp. 105–113). Stanford: Stanford University Press.

Levinas, E. (2001b). Being for the Other. In J. Robbins (Ed. & Trans.), *Is It righteous to be?: Interviews with Emmanuel Levinas* (pp. 114–122). Stanford: Stanford University Press.

Linneman, R. D. (2001). *Idiots, Stories about Mindedness and Mental Retardation.* New York: Peter Lang Publishing.

Mauer, B. M. (2005). The Epistemology of Cindy Sherman: A Research Method for Media and Cultural Studies. *Mosaic, 38*, 93–113.

Newbury, D. (1996). Reconstructing the self: photography, education and disability. *Disability and Society, 11*, 349–360.

Perring, G. (2005). The facilitation of learning disabled arts, A cultural perspective. In C. Sandahl & P. Auslander (Eds.), *Bodies in Commotion, Disability and Performance* (pp. 175–189). Ann Arbor, MI: The University of Michigan Press.

Phillips, C. (2001). Re-imagining the (dis)abled body. *Journal of Medical Humanities, 22*, 195–208.

Ristock, J. L., & Pennell, L. (1996). *Community Research as Empowerment: Feminist Links, Postmodern Interruptions.* Toronto: Oxford University Press.

Sakamoto, I., Chin, M., Chapra, A., & Ricciardi, J. (2009). A "normative" homeless woman?: Marginalisation, emotional injury and social support of transwomen experiencing homelessness. *Gay and Lesbian Issues and Psychology Review, 5*, 1–19. Retrieved September 13, 2009, from http://admin.psychology.org.au/Assets/Files/GLIP%20Review%20Vol%205%20No%201.pdf#page=5

Shakespeare, T. (2002). Art and lies? Representations of disability in film. In M. Corker & S. French (Eds.), *Disability Discourse* (pp. 164–172). Buckingham & Philadelphia: Open University Press.

Silverman, K. (1996). *The Threshold of the Visible World.* New York and London: Routledge.

Skerrett, D. (2000). Social work – a shifting paradigm. *Journal of Social Work Practice, 14*, 63–73.

Solomon, B. (2007). Taking "guilty knowledge" seriously: Theorizing, everyday inquiry, and action as "social caretaking. In S. L. Witkin & D. Saleebey (Eds.), *Social Work Dialogues, Transforming the Canon in Inquiry, Practice, and Education* (pp. 94–112). Alexandria, VA: Council on Social Work Education Press.

Starr, A. (2005). Looking in the mirror: Images of abnormally developed infants. *Journal of Medical Humanities, 26*, 97–106.

Thomson, R. G. (2007, October). *Extraordinary Bodies: Transnational Images of Disability.* Paper presented at Ontario Institute for Studies in Education, University of Toronto, Toronto, Canada.

Trent, J. W. Jr. (1994). *Inventing the Feeble Mind, a History of Mental Retardation in the United States.* Berkeley, CA: University of California Press.

Vuletic, L., & Ferrari, M. (2005). A transfer boy: About himself. In J. Rak (Ed.), *Auto/biography in Canada: Critical Dimensions* (pp. 129–143). Waterloo, ON: Wilfrid Laurier University Press.

Yong, A. (2007). *Theology and Down Syndrome, Reimagining Disability in Late Modernity.* Waco, TX: Baylor University Press.

Young, D. A., & Quibell, R. (2000). Why rights are never enough: Rights, intellectual disability and understanding. *Disability and Society, 15*, 747–764.

THEORETICAL APPROACHES TO DISABILITY CONTENT IN SOCIAL WORK EDUCATION

Stephen French Gilson
University of Maine

Elizabeth DePoy
University of Maine

This article presents an analysis of disability theory and content in the social work curriculum and advances a theoretically expansive approach to disability that is consistent with social work's commitment to diversity and the elimination of oppression. A careful examination of relevant social work literature reveals that disability is generally discussed and treated from a diagnostic perspective. We suggest shifting the approach to disability content in social work curricula from one that emphasizes individual deficiency to one that addresses disability as the interaction of a medical condition or diverse conditions with disabling environments.

OVER THE PAST SEVERAL DECADES, theoretical perspectives on disability have undergone a major paradigm shift. Traditionally viewed as a deficit, disability is now more commonly understood as an element of human diversity. Concurrently, on university campuses, definitions of disability have been revised to locate disability within the discourses of multiculturalism and diversity. However, despite the foundational focus on diversity and social justice in the social work curriculum, discussion and analysis of disability in social work courses typically occur through a deficit-treatment lens. In this article disability is defined as the interplay of diverse human conditions with environmental barriers to full community inclusion. This contemporary view of disability, although consistent with the mission and values of social work, receives limited attention in social work curricula (DePoy & Miller, 1996; Liese, Clevenger, & Hanley, 1999). Beginning with a review of the literature on disability and the positioning of disability theory within academic discourse, this article goes on to examine disability content in social work curricula and literature. Finally, a framework is presented to guide social work educators in addressing disability as an element of human diversity.

Literature Review

Disability Perspectives

Historically, disability has been explained and understood from a variety of perspectives. These views of disability span a continuum from a diagnostic-medical perspective to a complex, interactive person-in-environment perspective (Stiker, 1999). Simply put, the diagnostic-medical explanation of disability places the locus of disability internally, within an individual who has experienced illness, insult, or anomaly. This internal focus results in an interpretation of the disabled individual as defective with reference to normative physical, behavioral, psychological, cognitive, or sensory being. The interactive, person-in-environment lens, on the other hand, looks at the interaction of internal and external factors in an individual's life that creates a disabling condition. Between these two views, numerous other explanations and understandings of disability exist, including spiritual demonization or glorification of individuals with disabilities (Gilson & DePoy, 2000b). Contemporary theorists, influenced by pluralism, a perspective which posits the phenomenon of multiple realities (DePoy & Gitlin, 1998), view disability within the complex and diverse universe of human experience, and from this perspective understand disability as a multilevel social justice concern embedded within particular cultural, sociopolitical, economic, and relational environments (Gilson & DePoy, 2000b; Linton, 1998; Oliver, 1996; Scotch, 1984). Contemporary legislation and protection prohibiting segregation and externally imposed control over the lives of people with disabilities have emerged from this perspective (Americans with Disabilities Act of 1990, 1990; Rehabilitation Act of 1973, 1978). But even these laws advance diverse definitions of disability. For example, Social Security defines disability as the inability to engage in remunerative employment as a result of a disabling condition (Kiernan & Stark, 1986), whereas the Americans with Disabilities Act (ADA) defines disability more broadly as limitation in life activities due to impairment .

The literature reveals the complexity and conceptual confusion regarding definitions and understandings of disability. However, two broad definitions of disability predominate: one locating disability as internal to individuals, and one identifying disabling factors in environments external to individuals. Therefore, we propose that social work students be introduced to these two distinct ways of conceptualizing disability.

The Diagnostic Approach to Disability

The diagnostic approach to disability is based on medical explanations of individual human conditions. In this perspective disability is defined as a long-term to permanent physical, behavioral, psychological, cognitive, or sensory impediment that renders individuals less able than those who are free of such impediments, or those with impediments from which they can recover (Mackelprang & Salsgiver, 1997). This perspective both essentializes disability and locates it within the individual (Shakespeare, 1996). Interventions provided by disability services are designed to be curative. That is to say, services are aimed at remediating the disability (Mackelprang & Salsgiver, 1997).

In large part, the diagnostic approach is based on the historic notion of illness advanced by Parsons in the early 1950s. According to Parsons (1964), illness releases the sick person from compliance with socially enforced behavioral norms. In exchange for release from behavioral obligations, the individual who is ill is expected to be compliant with, and appreciative of, medical intervention designed to cure. Not unexpectedly, the diagnostic approach to disability does not bode well for those with conditions that cannot be cured, modified, or changed by professional intervention (Quinn, 1998, p. xix). In this view, the individual who cannot be "fixed" remains deficient in the sense that the person appears to function in ways outside of socially acceptable norms (Longmore, 1997; Mackelprang & Salsgiver, 1997). The diagnostic approach to understanding disability, then, classifies an individual as a deviant or as noncompliant with conventional behaviors.

The concept of rehabilitation underlying a wide variety of interventions is firmly situated within the diagnostic approach, in that most interventions are aimed at improving the function and well-being of individuals with medical diagnoses (Granger & Fiedler, 1997). While fields such as occupational therapy and vocational rehabilitation are concerned with the elimination or alteration of environmental barriers that impede individual function, these fields are still based on the diagnostic approach to disability. This orientation is apparent in these fields' concern with addressing diagnostic-functional abnormality (developmental disability, psychosis, and so forth), regardless of the locus of the interventions. An individual is referred to rehabilitation because of what is perceived to be a medical condition that limits function, and this view of disability frames the work of the rehabilitation professional, even if modification of the individual's environment is the intervention. Within this perspective, rehabilitation practice can range from adapting an environment to fit individual limitations to working with individuals to adapt to an environment and exhibit more normative function (Johnston, Steinman, & Velozo, 1997).

Disability as a Construct

From a constructionist approach, disability is viewed as a phenomenon constructed by factors and forces in the external environment rather than as a physical, behavioral, psychological, cognitive, or sensory inadequacy (Shakespeare & Watson, 1997). For many people with disabilities, while physical, behavioral, psychological, cognitive, or sensory anomalies are acknowledged, they are not necessarily seen as undesirable, in need of remediation (Quinn, 1988), or even relevant to understanding the circumstance and experiences of disabled people. Central to this approach is the notion of human diversity. A fundamental question raised by constructionist approaches to disability is why a condition such as impairment of an individual's ability to walk, which requires the use of adaptive equipment, is perceived as a disability, and a condition such as mild nearsightedness, which also requires the use of adaptive equipment, is not. In constructionist approaches to disability, language or the terms that one calls oneself are determined by the disabled person reflecting that individual's interpretation of his or her connection to the social, political, economic, physical, cognitive, and sensory environment. Because disability is seen as a social "construction" rather than a condition which is located "with" an individual, the admonitions by professionals, and even scholarly writing venues, for those not using person-first language are not appropriate. The individual is "disabled" by a socially created set of circumstances and has the right to declare or define himself or herself as "disabled" by an environment rather than living with a disability (DePoy & Gilson, 2001).

Unlike the rehabilitation approach, which can also address the environment as the needed locus of change, constructionist approaches to disability attribute an individual's incapacity to function to a disabling environment in which barriers are socially erected and maintained (Hahn, 1993). Negative attitudes, limited or nonexistent physical and communication access, and the denial of rights and privileges are examples of just some of the barriers that interfere with a disabled individual's potential to actualize desired social roles such as student, partner, parent, etc. (Barnes, Mercer, & Shakespeare, 1999). Thus, disability is seen as inequity in how an environment responds to and interprets human diversity, rather than as a deficit to be cured, remediated, or fixed (Barnes et al., 1999). It is not surprising that individuals with disabilities have advanced this notion of disability in direct response to models that devalue them (Oliver, 1996).

Within constructionist conceptualizations of disability, there are many different emphases, each of which has been posited as a model of disability in and of itself. For example, in the view of those who see disability as a political construction, the barrier creating the disabling condition is disempowerment caused by unequal earning opportunities for individuals with conditions that are socially constructed as disabilities. Discrimination and exclusion from the workplace limit the disabled individual's capacity to exchange earned resources for privileges, goods, and services. For disabled people political life is an economic life wherein the discrimination, exclusion, and disenfranchisement are experienced as an increased probability of substandard wages and poverty. According to Oliver (1996), the political understanding of disability, and we would suggest an economic understanding of disability, while not equivalent to policy, legislation, or social change, does provide direction for future political action.

Another important focus within constructionist approaches to disability is the view of disability as culture. This focus suggests that all individuals who define themselves as disabled belong to a unique group, which shares circumstances, experiences, tacit rules, language, and discourse. In this view, the notion of disability is one of group belongingness and distinction from other groups who do not share the disability identity (Mackelprang & Salsgiver, 1997). That is to say, anyone who identifies as disabled is disabled. Who belongs and does not belong to the culture is therefore not based on diagnosable condition, since diagnosis is irrelevant in this approach to determining who is disabled and who is not. Those individuals who perceive themselves to be unfairly treated and perceived as undesirable by dominant social institutions are therefore members of the culture of disability in that they share disadvantage and curtailment of civil rights (Linton, 1998). Within this framework, issues involving race, class, gender, sexual orientation, and disability identification are important determinants of the shared experiences that bind people together in single, identifiable communities of concern (Charlton, 1998). Linton (1998) notes,

> we [disabled people] are bound together, not by . . . [a] list of our collective symptoms but by the social and political circumstances that have forged us as a group. We have found one another and found a voice to express not despair at our fate but outrage at our social positioning. (p. 4)

This outrage is tied not only to the political position of disabled people, but from a materialist analysis, which identifies the "economic restrictions imposed on the individual that disable him or her" (Rioux, 1994, p. 5).

Disability Content in Social Work Curricula

For the most part, the academy has taken the diagnostic approach to disability, viewing disability as a medical phenomenon to be understood by professionals and treated through the provision of services and supports that counterbalance personal deficits. Thus the primary study of disability has been limited to such academic disciplines as education, health, and human services. And, according to Linton (1998), the current division of disability into specialized applied fields in higher education (e.g., rehabilitation, special education, health, and so forth) perpetuates the view of disability as pathology.

One way to assess disability content in social work education is to look at the Council on Social Work Education's 1992 *Curriculum Policy Statement* (CPS) and the 1994 *Handbook of Accreditation Standards and Procedures*. Both reveal an ambiguous approach to disability definition and content requirements. Prior to the most recent CPS, social work programs were guided to organize their curricula around either populations or problem areas. In this taxonomy, disability was included under problem areas, while other vulnerable groups were included in populations. Thus disability was seen as an individual deficit rather than as a group characteristic.

The 1992 CPS reflected some attempt to more thoughtfully or progressively address the issue of disability. However, in addition to the term "disability," the use of phrases such as "populations at risk" (B6.6), which deny positive experiences of disability and position it within a medical and pathological perspective continued to be used without further positioning disability in the category of diverse populations along with other devalued "at risk groups." Placing disability solely within the category of at risk groups leads one to question, "at risk for what?" The implicit answer is that the condition of disability places one "at risk" for failure in one or more essential life functions as a result of an intrinsic pathological condition. Thus, services and protection from professionals are asserted as necessary by the categorical placement of disabled people in anticipated jeopardy even when no such condition should be ascribed.

It is of great concern that disability in social work curricula is primarily presented and examined through a diagnostic lens, not only because of the current academic trends towards pluralism, but also because of the fundamental commitment of social work to eradicating oppression, promoting equal opportunity, and advancing self-determination. While we do not suggest that the diagnostic approach to disability be entirely eliminated from social work education, we offer an educational model below that critically examines each perspective of disability and applies it thoughtfully to the curriculum areas of human behavior in the social environment, practice, research, and policy.

Model Disability Curricula

As presented in Table 1, the two views of disability correspond to different theoretical, methodological, and action approaches in the primary social work curriculum areas. The social work curricular content areas on which we focus are human behavior and the social environment (HBSE), social work practice, social welfare policy and services, and research. We have not included a section on the field practicum, due in part to the great number of practicum settings in which students are placed, and because this educational component tends to have an experiential rather than didactic focus. Our discussion considers baccalaureate and foundation-year master's content.

The Diagnostic Approach to Disability and Social Work Curricula

Human Behavior and the Social Environment. As mentioned above, the diagnostic approach to disability defines disability as a long-term or permanent, physical, behavioral, psychological, cognitive, or sensory impediment to be treated by working with individual recovery or adaptation, or both (Longmore, 1997; Mackelprang & Salsgiver, 1997; Shakespeare & Watson, 1997). Given this definition, disability can be examined in the HBSE curriculum area through developmental, psychodynamic, biological, behavioral, and psychopathological theories. That is to say, these theories provide the "normal backdrop" from which disability can be distinguished. By "normal backdrop," the authors are referring to the set of norms that provide the boundaries for what is considered to be typical as well as acceptable. Anything existing outside of those boundaries is therefore deviant. Medical model theories that are studied within the HBSE curriculum provide a foundation for assessing functional adequacy and providing intervention for individual improvement. This foundation provides a framework for viewing individuals in direct practice, policy practice, and research practice.

The theoretical frameworks studied in HBSE courses posit normative behaviors that differentiate age-related phases from one another. Those who do not fit within the norms are labeled on a continuum from eccentric or odd to deviant or dysfunctional. These theo-

TABLE 1. Diagnostic and Constructionist Approaches to Disability Content across Four Major Curriculum Areas

	HBSE	Practice	Policy	Research
Diagnostic	Developmental	Clinical intervention	Rational models	Clinical, outcomes oriented
	Psychodynamic	Case management		
	Psychopathology			
	Behavioral			
	Biological			
Constructionist	Systems	Problem Solving	Rational and nonrational models	Integrated
	Sociohistorical/economic context	Community/group organization		Critical theory approach
	Social construction			Participatory
	Humanistic	Psychoeducational		Ethnography
	Multiculturalism	Legislative intervention		
		Direct action (e.g. lobbying, civil disobedience)		

ries serve to identify those who are in need of professional guidance at the clinical or institutional levels and provide a set of normative outcomes to which an individual should be professionally directed.

Social Work Practice. Guided by the diagnostic approach, direct practice education would center on teaching clinical strategies to "normalize" or "fix" disabled individuals to the degree possible. These strategies may be collaboratively developed with clients, but also may be determined as best practice by the social worker, professional team, or both.

To illustrate we focus on a typical sequence of hospital-based practice, followed by rehabilitation settings, and specialized clinical community outpatient service experienced by a young adult who has sustained a closed head trauma. This vignette or illustration reflects a composite characterization of individuals with brain trauma with whom one of the authors worked. The hospital social worker is involved primarily as educator to the family, and secondarily to the individual, and as discharge planner. Within a diagnostic model, social work practice would focus on the individual's adjustment to the illness experience and the family's adjustment to the change in the status, role, and functioning of the individual. If the social worker is practicing from a family strengths perspective (Freedman & Boyer, 2000), it is likely that the family would be perceived in the role of caregiver and, by extension, as a part of the treatment team (particularly in the presence of severe disability). Social work direct practice tasks might typically involve assisting the individual and family with the acquisition of equipment, social service supports, educational interventions, and linkages to specialized clinical community outpatient services and support groups. Rehabilitation would focus on teaching compensatory skills to the individual with the head injury, modifying the environment to accommodate the individual's condition, and, to the extent possible, restoring normative roles. Additional practice modalities guided by the diagnostic-based model include community case management and case coordination (Gilson, 1998; Gilson & Casebolt, 1997; Netting, Kettner, & McMurtry, 1998).

Social Welfare Policy and Services. In the social welfare policy sequence, rational models of policy, practice policy, or policy implementation analysis and development are often taught. Rational models of policy development, implementation, and analysis tend to approximate both linear-based reasoning and an ideologically conservative framework of thought. While this characterization may not always be an absolute, these models tend to share more commonalities with traditional medical models of analysis and determination than a nonrational model (Jansson, 1994; Netting et al., 1998). These models of policy and administrative management analysis, development, and implementation are grounded on assumptions that: (a) the individuals exchange productivity for privilege and (b) individual self-interest is a given. Because of this exchange, the social worker would advance policy to promote maximum function for disabled individuals but would also maintain clinical contact as a mechanism to supervise the continuation of valued productive function on the part of the disabled individual. Within disability practice, the social worker would therefore advance policies through an approach to agency management that promotes the maximum functioning of a disabled individual for the least social/economic cost, while maintaining clinical models of professional intervention.

On an agency level, macro practice may take the form of working to extend individual and family services for a specific individual, family, or a subset of individuals with disabilities, such as individuals diagnosed with developmental or mental disabilities or individuals with multiple sclerosis.

For the micro-focused social worker, policy concerns are commonly limited to a program and agency base of practice. Practice policy guided by the diagnostic approach takes the form of advocating for goods and services for the immediate need(s) of individuals and families. Examples of this approach include working with third-party payers to purchase a wheelchair, medications, secure educational or vocational evaluation and services, or modify the home environment to improve function.

Research. In the diagnostic approach, research methods that examine disability from a researcher-driven perspective are emphasized in the research sequence. In particular, clinical outcome research relying on predetermined, standardized testing is indicated. Social work students are taught strategies such as single case study designs, experimental, quasi-experimental, and nonexperimental approaches to examining client and family outcome (Yegidis, Weinbach, & Morrison-Rodriguez, 1999). Research methods to maintain accountability and measure the outcomes of interventions are emphasized, along with cost-benefit investigation strategies.

The Constructionist Model of Disability and Social Work Curricula

Human Behavior and the Social Environment. As discussed above, in the constructionist model, while an individual's anomalous physical, behavioral, psychological, cognitive, or sensory conditions may be acknowledged, they are not necessarily perceived as undesirable, in need of remediation (Quinn, 1988; Shakespeare & Watson, 1997), or even relevant to disability. Rather, individuals are perceived to be disabled by marginalization, oppression, and hostile environments—those characterized for example by a lack of ramps, limited attention to alternative formats for printed material, and a severe shortage of sign language interpreters, as well as any number of forms of social, political, and economic devaluation.

Taught from the constructionist view of disability, the HBSE curriculum would be informed by several perspectives. A broad systems perspective extending beyond individuals and their families to their interactions with multiple sociocultural systems would be most useful in examining disability as a construct. These interactions with sociocultural systems would be examined to discover the extent to which they are disabling to particular groups and individuals. Targets of change would be the negative attitudes, discrimination, oppression, limitations in civil rights, devaluation, and limited access to resources, privilege, and community life experienced by individuals and groups stigmatized on the basis of anomalous physical, behavioral, psychological, cognitive, or sensory conditions. Several theories would serve as lenses through which to examine disability and the marginal social/cultural positioning assigned to individuals and subgroups whose physical, behavioral, psychological, cognitive, or sensory conditions are perceived as "disabilities." These would include social learning theory, social construction, pluralistic perspectives, and multiculturalism. A specific focus on social, economic, political, cultural, and environmental barriers that prevent individuals from full community participation might be a point from which to define and examine disability (Hutchison, 1999). Further examination of disability as minority culture would not only include analysis of members of disabled groups as marginalized, but also would include looking at disability, race, gender, and class as interactive factors that serve as barriers to civil rights and social justice. In such an examination disability would be located within the larger discussion of domination and oppression experienced by marginalized cultural groups.

An example of how social work practice might unfold if approached from a constructionist view of disability can be seen by reconsidering the individual who has been hospitalized after sustaining a closed head injury. A social worker practicing from this perspective would use medical information to understand the conditions of head injury. With that knowledge, attitudes towards individuals with head injuries, their recovery environments, and their social limitations would be examined through the lenses of systems theory (Chetkow-Yanoov, 1992), social learning theory (Gambrill, 1997), and postmodern constructionist and deconstructionist theories (Pease, 1999). These views would inform a broad understanding and analysis of the social positioning, advantage, and disadvantage likely to be experienced by the disabled individual.

Social Work Practice. Practicing from a constructionist perspective a social worker might engage in advocacy, assurance of civil rights, and elimination of oppression. Whether in a central or peripheral role, the social worker's practice model would be based on theory in which disability is seen as a social construction within oppressive systems (Chetkow-Yanoov, 1997). Practice education would therefore include problem solving, emancipatory approaches (Gambrill, 1997) in which multiple systems would be challenged, and culturally competent methods to eliminate barriers to community inclusion and social justice for disabled individuals (Longres, 1995). Moreover, practice would be client/consumer driven or directed, with the social worker acting collaboratively as facilitator and liaison to eliminate barriers, advance opportunity and choice for individuals, families, and groups of disabled individuals, and link disabled people together in arenas which promote the healthy celebration of disability identity and the advancement of self-determination (Gilson & DePoy, 2000a).

Systems change and political action would be important elements of practice within the constructionist framework of disability. Intervention would be carried out through teamwork with other professionals, politicians, family, and community members who are involved in the life of the disabled individual. Intervention techniques might involve advocacy, psychoeducational groups, sharing of information with client systems, policy change, and collaborative political action.

Social Welfare Policy and Services. Policy and services work framed within a constructionist model of disability would focus on a continuum ranging from rational to nonrational approaches, and would be carried out at multiple system levels (Stone, 1997). Work might begin at the local agency level and progress to the larger community, state, and federal systems levels. As described above, the rational model of policy analysis suggests a planned and linear approach to the development of policy. In contrast, in the nonrational perspective policy creation is viewed as a series of complex and nonlinear events and phenomena. Multiple and often competing value-based interests are viewed as important influences on the creation and revision of policy. Stone's (1997) model is based on the assumption that policy development, modification, and overturn occur within a paradoxical political environment in which personal values and stake-holding supercede evidence-based, reasoned policy change. The nonrational model focuses on social values, political decision making, community interests, and the *polis*.

A more conservative rational approach within the constructionist framework would involve social workers assuring that disabled individuals could be included within existing services and supports of a particular client system. A social worker's analysis or interpretation of intervention and change strategies would combine a rational model (e.g., Jansson, 1994; Netting et al., 1998) and a nonrational model (e.g., Stone, 1997). While the rational approach would explain the reasoned, evidence-based foundation for policy, the introduction of a nonrational perspective would provide the social worker with an expanded view of social, civil, economic, and legal experiences of disabled people and communities of disabled people. Consistent with Schneider and Netting's (1999) call for social workers to "embrace ambiguity and to connect the often-invisible struggles of individuals with the more public actions of decision makers in powerful positions" (p. 349), this viewpoint would help the worker begin to appreciate the multiple and competing meanings of social welfare policy and services as they affect individuals and communities.

Considering disability as culture, Netting and colleagues (1998) suggest that policy work involves (a) identification of target population, (b) determining community characteristics, (c) recognition of differences, and (d) identifying structure. Further, the authors of this article believe that the addition and synthesis of Figueira-McDonough's approach (1993) provides a complementary policy analysis and practice perspective guiding the social worker to promote the acknowledgment of disability as a marginalized culture in need of protective efforts such as the ADA.

Research. For students to be able to examine disability from pluralistic and multilevel viewpoints, both experimental and interpretive research methods (DePoy & Gitlin, 1998) would be taught. Experimental-type models of research yielding quantitative findings might be most useful in concert with interpretive approaches. Using mixed methods would allow for the measurement of service needs and outcomes to be synthesized with a qualitative understanding of the attitudinal social context in which these needs and outcomes occur. These two important areas of knowledge would inform and advance social change in multiple social, political, and economic arenas. Research from a critical theory perspective—which is conducted for the purpose of political change—would guide inquiry towards the production of knowledge for social, political, and economic change (DePoy & Gitlin, 1998). Studies undertaken from this epistemological perspective would enhance understanding of power relationships and action strategies designed to provoke change. Traditional methods of ethnography (see Babbie, 2001) hold the members of a culture as experts in their own lives and experiences and, thus, the investigator would look to cultural members to answer questions about language, rules, traditions, rituals, etc. that would inform social work knowledge and practice in disability. Along with ethnographic approaches, participatory action research would be useful in identifying areas and methods for cultural and social change.

Conclusion

Disability content in social work education is taught largely from a diagnostic perspective. However, this approach is seriously outdated and does not encourage social workers to engage in practice, thought, inquiry, and policy change aimed at the eradication of social injustice resulting from discrimination towards disabled individuals. As indicated in the literature, disability coexists with poverty, limitations in civil rights, prejudice, and devaluation. In concert with social work's mission to advance social justice and eliminate oppression are conceptualizations of disability which fall broadly within the constructionist approach. It is critical that these conceptualizations of disability be included in social work curricula so that students can develop an informed, contemporary understanding of disadvantage resulting from disabling environmental factors.

In this article we have examined multiple explanations for disability and have illustrated how the social work curriculum can be revised to integrate a diagnostic approach into the broad perspective of disability as constructed by social, cultural, political, and economic factors. The knowledge, theory, and skills that would emerge from this complex, multifaceted, and contemporary treatment of disability would reflect social work's professional commitment to social justice and locate discussions of disability within the larger discourse on diversity.

We do not deny that content on various physical, behavioral, psychological, cognitive, or sensory conditions is necessary to an understanding of disability. However, we assert that decreasing the emphasis on the diagnostic approach to disability and increasing the emphasis on constructionist approaches are essential if social work is to actualize its mission and values. Moreover, adopting an approach to studying disability that is similar to the approach that has been taken by other vulnerable groups is an important step in advancing civil rights for those who currently belong to this group and those who do not. Dissimilar to other groups such as women and ethnic minorities, the boundaries of the disability community are permeable. Anyone can become a member at any time, whether through injury or illness. Integrating disability into the dialogue on diversity and oppression therefore has a wide application for those who are currently disabled as well as for those who are not.

References

Americans with Disabilities Act of 1990, Pub. L. No. 101-336, 104 Stat. 327 (1990).

Babbie, E. (2001). *The practice of social research* (9th. ed.). Belmont, CA: Wadsworth.

Barnes, C., Mercer, T., & Shakespeare, T. (1999). *Exploring disability: A sociological introduction.* Cambridge: Polity Press.

Charlton, J. I. (1998). *Nothing about us without us: Disability oppression and empowerment.* Berkeley: University of California Press.

Chetkow-Yanoov, B. (1992). *Social work practice: A systems approach.* Binghamton, NY: Haworth.

Council on Social Work Education. (1992). *Curriculum policy statement for baccalaureate and master's degree programs in social work education.* Alexandria, VA: Author.

Council on Social Work Education. (1994). *Handbook of accreditation standards and procedures* (4th ed.). Alexandria, VA: Author.

DePoy, E., & Gilson, S. F. (2001, July). *Sticks, stones and language.* Paper presented at the Society for Disability Studies Annual Meeting, Winnipeg, Manitoba, Canada.

DePoy, E., & Gitlin, L. (1998). *Introduction to research: Understanding and applying multiple strategies* (2nd ed.). Chicago: Mosby Yearbook.

DePoy, E., & Miller, M. (1996). Preparation of social workers for serving individuals with developmental disabilities: A brief report. *Mental Retardation, 34*(1), 54-57.

Figueira-McDonough, J. (1993). Policy practice: The neglected side of social work intervention. *Social Work, 38*, 179-188.

Freedman, R. I., & Boyer, N. C. (2000). The power to choose: Supports for families caring for individuals with developmental disabilities. *Health and Social Work, 25*(1), 59-68.

Gambrill, E. D. (1997). *Social work practice: A critical thinker's guide.* New York: Oxford University Press.

Gilson, S. F. (1998). Case management and supported employment: A good fit. *Journal of Case Management, 7*(1), 10-17.

Gilson, S. F., & Casebolt, G. M. (1997). Personal assistance services and case management. *Journal of Case Management, 6*(1), 13-17.

Gilson, S. F., & DePoy, E. (2000a, February). *Disability as culture: Four didactic curriculum areas.* Paper presented at the Council on Social Work Education Annual Program Meeting, New York, NY.

Gilson, S. F., & DePoy, E. (2000b). Multiculturalism and disability: A critical perspective. *Disability and Society, 15*(2), 207-218.

Granger, C. V., & Fiedler, R. C. (1997). The measurement of disability. In M. J. Fuhrer (Ed.), *Assessing medical rehabilitation practices: The promise of outcomes research* (pp. 103-126). Baltimore: Paul H. Brookes.

Hahn, H. (1993). The politics of physical differences: Disability and discrimination. In M. Nagler (Ed.), *Perspectives on disability* (2nd ed., pp. 37-42). Palo Alto, CA: Health Markets Research.

Hutchison, E. D. (1999). *Dimensions of human behavior: Person and environment.* Thousand Oaks, CA: Pine Forge.

Jansson, B. S. (1994). *Social policy: From theory to policy practice* (2nd ed.). Belmont, CA: Wadsworth.

Johnston, M. V., Steinman, M., & Velozo, C. (1997). Outcomes research in medical rehabilitation: Foundations from the past and directions for the future. In M. J. Fuhrer (Ed.), *Assessing medical rehabilitation practices: The promise of outcomes research* (pp. 1-42). Baltimore: Paul H. Brookes.

Kiernan, W. E., & Stark, J. A. (1986). *Pathways to employment for adults with developmental disabilities.* Baltimore, MD: Paul H. Brookes.

Liese, H., Clevenger, R., & Hanley, B. (1999). Joining university-affiliated programs and schools of social work: A collaborative model for disabilities curriculum development and training. *Journal of Social Work Education, 35*, 63-69.

Linton, S. (1998). *Claiming disability: Knowledge and identity.* New York: New York University Press.

Longmore, P. K. (1997). Conspicuous contribution and American cultural dilemmas: Telethon rituals of cleansing and renewal. In D. T. Mitchell & S. L. Snyder (Eds.), *The body and physical difference: Discourses of disability* (pp. 134-160). Ann Arbor: University of Michigan Press.

Longres, J. F. (1995). *Human behavior in the social environment*. Itasca, IL: F.E. Peacock.

Mackelprang, R. W., & Salsgiver, R. O. (1997). *Disability: A diversity model approach in human service practice*. Pacific Grove, CA: Brooks/Cole.

National Organization of Disability. (1994). *N.O.D./Harris survey of Americans with disabilities*. New York: Louis Harris and Associates.

Netting, F. E. (1992). Case management: Service or symptom? *Social Work, 37*, 160-164.

Netting, F. E., Kettner, P. M., & McMurtry, S. L. (1998). *Social work macro practice* (2nd ed.). New York: Longman.

N.O.D./Harris. (2000). *The 2000 N.O.D./Harris Survey of Americans with Disabilities: Survey program on participation and attitudes* [Online]. Available at http://www.nod.org.

Oliver, M. (1996). Defining impairment and disability: Issues at stake. In G. Barnes & G. Mercer (Eds.), *Exploring the divide: Illness and disability* (pp. 39-54). Leeds, UK: Disability Press.

Parsons. T. (1964). *Social structure and personality*. Free Press.

Pease, B. (1999). *Transforming social work practice: Postmodern critical perspectives*. New York: Routledge.

Quinn, P. (1998). *Understanding disability: A lifespan approach*. Thousand Oaks, CA: Sage.

Rehabilitation Act of 1973, Pub. Law No. 93-112, 87 Stat. 335 (1973) (codified as amended at 29 U.S.C. § 701, 797 [1978]).

Rioux, M. H. (1994). New research directions and paradigms: Disability is not measles. In M. H. Rioux, & M. Bach (Eds.), *Disability is not measles: New research paradigms in disability* (pp. 1-7). North York, Ontario, Canada: Roeher Institute.

Schneider, R. L., & Netting, F. E. (1999). Influencing social policy in time of devolution: Upholding social work's great tradition. *Social Work, 44*, 349-357.

Scotch, R. K. (1984). *From good will to civil rights: Transforming federal disability policy*. Philadelphia: Temple University Press.

Shakespeare, T. (1996). *Disability, identity and difference*. In G. Barnes & G. Mercer (Eds.), Exploring the divide: Illness and disability (pp. 94-113). Leeds, UK: Disability Press.

Shakespeare, T., & Watson, N. (1997). Defending the social model. *Disability and Society, 12*, 293-300.

Stiker, H. J. (1999). *A history of disability*. Ann Arbor, MI: University of Michigan Press.

Stone, D. A. (1997). *Policy paradox: The art of political decision making*. New York: W.W. Norton.

Yegidis, B. L., Weinbach, R. W., & Morrison-Rodriguez, B. M. (1999). *Research methods for social workers*. Boston: Allyn & Bacon.

Accepted: 10/01.

Stephen French Gilson is associate professor, School of Social Work, and **Elizabeth DePoy** is professor, School of Social Work, and coordinator of research and evaluation, Center for Community Inclusion, University of Maine.

Address correspondence to: Stephen French Gilson, University of Maine, 5770 Annex C, Orono, ME 04469; email: stephen_gilson@umit.maine.edu.

/

Social Inclusion as Solidarity

Rethinking the Child Rights Agenda

Introduction

A few months back a story came to me across cyberspace attached to an e-mail message. The story goes like this:

In Brooklyn, New York, CHUSH is a school that caters to learning disabled children. Some children remain in CHUSH for their entire school career, while others can be mainstreamed into conventional schools. At a CHUSH dinner, the father of a CHUSH child delivered a speech that would never be forgotten by all who attended. After extolling the school and its dedicated staff, he cried out, "Where is the perfection in my son Shaya? Everything God does is done with perfection. But my child cannot understand things as other children do. My child cannot remember facts and figures as other children do. Where is God's perfection?" The audience was shocked by the question, pained by the father's anguish and stilled by the piercing query. "I believe," the father answered, "that when God brings a child like this into the world, the perfection that he seeks is in the way people react to this child." He then told the following story about his son Shaya:

One afternoon Shaya and his father walked past a park where some boys Shaya knew were playing baseball. Shaya asked, "Do you think they will let me play?"

Shaya's father approached one of the boys in the field and asked if Shaya could play. The boy looked around for guidance from his teammates. Getting none, he took matters into his own hands and said, "We are losing by six runs and the game is in the eighth inning. I guess he can be on our team and we'll try to put him up to bat in the ninth inning."

Shaya's father was ecstatic as Shaya smiled broadly. Shaya was told to put on a glove and go out to play short center field. In the bottom of the eighth inning, Shaya's team scored a few runs but was still behind by three.

In the bottom of the ninth inning, Shaya's team scored again and now with two outs and the bases loaded with the potential winning run on base, Shaya was scheduled to be up. Would the team actually let Shaya bat at this juncture and give away their chance to win the game?

Surprisingly, Shaya was given the bat. Everyone knew that it was all but impossible because Shaya didn't even know how to hold the bat properly, let alone hit with it. However as Shaya stepped up to the plate, the pitcher moved a few steps to lob the ball in softly so Shaya would at least be able to make contact.

The first pitch came in and Shaya swung clumsily and missed. One of Shaya's teammates came up to Shaya and together they held the bat and faced the pitcher waiting for the next pitch. The pitcher again took a few steps forward to toss the ball softly towards Shaya. As the pitch came in, Shaya and his teammate swung at the bat and together they hit a slow ground ball to the pitcher. The pitcher picked up the soft grounder and could easily have thrown the ball to the first baseman. Shaya would have been out and that would have ended the game. Instead, the pitcher took the ball and threw it on a high to right field, far beyond the reach of the first baseman.

Everyone started yelling, "Shaya, run to first. Run to first."

Never in his life had Shaya run to first. He scampered down the baseline wide-eyed and startled.

By the time he reached first base, the right fielder had the ball. He could have thrown the ball to the second baseman who would tag out Shaya who was still running. But the right fielder understood what the pitcher's intentions were, so he threw the ball high and far over the third baseman's head. Everyone yelled, "Run to second, run to second." Shaya ran towards second base as the runners ahead of him deliriously circled the bases towards home. As Shaya reached second base, the opposing short stop ran to him, turned him in the direction of third base and shouted, "Run to third." As Shaya rounded third, the boys from both teams ran behind him screaming, "Shaya run home."

Shaya ran home, stepped on home plate and all 18 boys lifted him on their shoulders and made him the hero, as he had just hit a "grand slam" and won the game for his team.

"That day," said the father softly with tears now rolling down his face, "those 18 boys reached their level of God's perfection."

I was very moved by this story. One of the lines that struck me most was the father's belief that "perfection" lies not in his son, or in any child, but in the ways people react to his child. This insight shifts our view about what matters. We turn from a child's disability to the ways in which he is recognized by others, to the way others "react" and know him. The shift in view the story records is central, I believe, to understanding what social inclusion is all about. My aim in this paper is to formulate a notion of social inclusion that could help to advance a political and public policy agenda for the well-being of children in Canada, with a particular focus here on children with disabilities and their families.

The paper is organized around the following contentions. Social inclusion is more a normative than descriptive term. I suggest that one of its core notions is that societal institutions should be organized to provide *valued recognition* to diverse groups, to the 'others' often marginalized by a dominant political culture. Calls for inclusion as valued recognition are growing as the dilemma of the 'rights revolution' becomes clear – a context where rights are expanded and exclusion is entrenched.
A social inclusion agenda could address this dilemma by promoting social solidarity across expanding social, ethnic and cultural differences that increasingly characterize and divide so many societies, often in destructive ways.
I argue that policy analysis should reveal ways that social, economic and political arrangements systematically undermine social solidarity by devaluing certain people and groups, even though their rights are assured. Fostering solidarity across differences in our society is an important step in creating a culture where the citizenship rights people hold can be more fully realized in their daily lives.

In the final section of the paper, I show how a social inclusion analysis could be applied to the exclusions facing children with disabilities to generate a public agenda for change. It would bring to light a number of the rules and practices by which the devaluation of children with disabilities is constructed. Stereotyping of children, practices to 'cleanse' the human genome of genetic disability, and indicators for measuring and monitoring child development at a population level that equates disability with ill-health and abnormal development, are the priorities that I suggest for analysis.

1. Calling for inclusion, and facing the dilemma with the rights revolution

Defining social inclusion

A large body of literature on social exclusion details various ways in which particular population groups are denied participation in, and access to, benefits and advantages of political, social and economic institutions. Social inclusion names a goal that brings exclusion into view and into question. It expresses an aspiration that the arrangements between us be inclusive – whether in our personal relationships, a neighbourhood baseball game like the one Shaya joined, or in our social, political and economic institutions in the public and private sector. 'Social inclusion' names an ideal that arrangements not disadvantage certain 'others' because they are different from the dominant norm; that arrangements not allocate benefits, status and advantages in ways that misrecognize, devalue or stereotype certain groups in relation to others. It means that arrangements should not foster or fund forms of recognition that deepen and entrench the social distance between certain groups (e.g. residential and education segregation of disabled persons would not survive such a test). Socially inclusive arrangements would help to nurture paths of mutual recognition that close the distance in ways that bring respect and value for the differences that define us.

When social inclusion is viewed in this way, we can understand how the term might sometimes be used as a political claim for full citizenship, or as an ideal to which societal organizations and institutions should aspire, or as a way to name the process of reform of such arrangements. There are many institutional arrangements to which the claims, ideal, and process of social inclusion could apply – for example, early childhood development services, recreation services, education, family support services, labour market training, arrangements that provide benefits through the tax system and by other means, and even those institutions that regulate, fund and undertake social and health research on human populations (e.g. the Human Genome Project), etc. Simply stated, such institutional arrangements should be inclusive, we should be able to examine the extent of their social inclusivity, and we should be able to launch a process of reform that we might call social inclusion.

Calls for inclusion from the disability rights movement

Disability rights movements have helped to formulate this understanding of social inclusion. Over the past few years there have been many calls from disability movements nationally and internationally to advance a new agenda of inclusion with its variants of education inclusion (Bunch and Valeo, 2000), labour market and workplace inclusion (The Roeher Institute, 1993), or community inclusion (The

Roeher Institute, 2000a; 2000b; 2001a). A call for inclusion is particularly resonant in the disability movement because it speaks directly to the problem of recognition and misrecognition of others. Many are seeking not only the 'integration' of children with disabilities in the education system (usually a mix of regular and 'special' or segregated classes and schools), but their 'inclusion'. This means an understanding of the child as a child first; full education in regular classrooms; valued recognition that we expect all children to obtain from teachers and peers; inclusion in the activities and personal relationships in which children come to be known personally and the needed physical, curricular and other accommodations to make this happen. It also means that difference and diversity will be taken seriously – systems will be developed that enable communication among children, even when some children do not communicate through spoken or written language. In this sense, social inclusion is not an agenda for homogenization, it is one that seeks to bring to the forefront the challenges of articulation and alliance and communicative capacities across the social, physical and communicational differences that define us.

Similarly, with labour market and workplace inclusion the issue is not simply provision of paid work opportunities to working-age adults with disabilities. Sheltered workshops have provided that for a number of years, but at the cost of many adults, particularly those with intellectual disabilities, not being recognized as capable of participating with co-workers in regular workplaces and the labour market, nor as deserving of basic labour rights. In this context, inclusion is the process of adapting workplaces, accommodating individuals, and ensuring that labour market information is provided to individuals with disabilities in ways that enable their access to training and paid work opportunities in the mainstream.

'Community inclusion' has been conceptualized as a multi-faceted process with personal, institutional and societal dimensions. It is the process of fostering 'valuing' personal relationships for people marginalized by a disability status, securing rights protections, ensuring economic and educational inclusion and reconstructing community institutions (education, recreation, social services, etc.) to enable full participation by people with disabilities (The Roeher Institute, 2000b).

The vision of citizenship that a call for inclusion appeals to goes beyond the exercise of political rights, and social and economic claims on the state. It demands social, cultural, political and economic participation in all institutions of society. The calls expand the arena for realizing citizenship from state provision to include civil society (that sphere of association, free press, public forums and community institutions), "emancipatory inasmuch as it liberates the individual from entrenched social hierarchies and allows interaction across formerly separated spaces" (Chandoke, 1995 p. 198). Calls for educational, workplace and community inclusion are consistent with the shifts in theories of citizenship that Kymlicka and Norman (1994), Young (1990, 2000), Chandoke (1995, 1999), and others point to – citizenship is fundamentally about full and democratic participation and inclusion in the institutions of society. Such calls speak to a desire to go beyond the juridically defined individual of liberal theory whose rights are realized but may still encounter exclusion. The calls from the disability movement for inclusion envision forms of social identity, reciprocity and solidarity that provide a foundation for rights to be realized in relation to others, for a life well-lived in community.

Why call for inclusion now? Dilemma of the 'rights revolution'

Why these calls now? In their historical context, calls for inclusion appear at the cusp of the disability rights movement, mobilized most strongly in Canada over the past two decades. Part of the answer, it seems to me, lies in the assumed relationship between rights granted and valued recognition realized. In his recent tracing of "the rights revolution", its history and current achievements, Ignatieff (2000) suggests that the "political and social history of Western society is the story of the struggle of all human groups to gain inclusion" in a political community where everyone has an equality of rights (p. 140). It is true that an impressive framework of constitutional and statutory rights has been established in Canada at the federal, provincial and territorial levels. Canadians now have protections to equal benefit and advantage of the law without discrimination on the basis of disability written into our constitution. We have rights to freedom from discrimination on the basis of age, disability, gender, race, etc. – in access to employment, housing and services available to the public – written into our provincial/territorial and federal human rights codes. International human rights instruments have also expanded. *The Universal Declaration on Human Rights*, and various subsequent conventions, hold the promise that the state's granting and protection of human rights will redress economic and social inequality and denial of freedoms. For children, the 1989 *UN Convention on the Rights of the Child* signifies the recognition of children as full citizens – deserving of comprehensive human rights protection.

This array of rights, Ignatieff suggests, requires of us all the "recognition, empathy, and if possible, reconciliation" with others who we understand bear equal rights to our own. Yet Ignatieff seems a little more sanguine than I am in assuming that the institutionalization of rights will bring recognition and empathy across the boundaries of gender, race, ethnicity, religion and ability that continue to divide us. We have secured inclusion for many under the banner of human rights, but have we gained full inclusion for those who, nonetheless, through various policies and practices seem to be less recognized and valued than others? That the extension of human rights is a condition of valued recognition, does not mean that valued recognition necessarily follows. This dilemma – of rights *without* recognition – is what we might call the dilemma of the 'rights revolution'.

Evidence abounds that exclusions persist for many groups despite an expansion of rights. For example, there exists a litany of exclusions of children and youth with disabilities and their families, including: endemic discrimination faced in access to life-saving treatments, to health care, to childcare services, to education (The Roeher Institute, 2000a); the sexual abuse of children and youth with disabilities – 50 percent of children and youth who are deaf; 60 percent of young women with an intellectual disability (The Roeher Institute, 1988; Sullivan, Vernon and Scanlon, 1987); access to the justice system denied because they are often not considered credible witnesses to their own victimization (The Roeher Institute, 1995); inadequate integration into national child development schemes in many countries – children miss out on key developmental opportunities, and are often not seen as worthy of the investment (Alur, 2000); continual downgrading of parents' labour force participation – for many to unemployment because they cannot obtain the workplace flexibility or outside supports they need (Irwin and Lero, 1997; The Roeher Institute, 2000c); the overrepresentation of children with disabilities among those neglected and maltreated and who are in the child welfare system (Trocme, et al., 2001), etc.

For children and adults with disabilities, and their families, a rights-based approach to citizenship finally gives people a claim to press on the state, finally gives a promise of equality to challenge the violence, the poverty, the education exclusion so many face. But like so many others the members of this group face the harsh realities of the rights revolution of the latter part of the 20th century. We have largely been getting what we asked for in terms of human rights instruments – but people are still excluded. The advances in social and economic rights and human rights law for children, for people with disabilities and others, have come with three main problems.

First, exit systems are in place where the law imposes obligations on the state and others to secure human rights for people with disabilities, granting to governments, employers and providers of services ways of exiting from their responsibilities and obligations when the costs seem too high – for instance, when inclusive education imposes an 'undue hardship' on the school board, or when the rights of children with disabilities under Article 23 of the *UN Convention on the Rights of the Child* are limited to the extent that states have resources to deliver on them.

Second, in the Canadian legal context at least, the application of human rights law tends to provide individual compensation rather than systemic and proactive policy change. As human rights are more and more institutionalized, fewer cases based on disability are coming forward. A small subset of disability cases are proceeding, usually not those related to developmental or intellectual disability.[1] Remedies in the cases are individualized – compensation for discrimination, rather than the systemic change that this movement has been calling for. For those who do persist with a complaint, the process is long, and the outcome often provides little in return – certainly not "inclusion" as the disability movement expresses that ideal. Often the discrimination is based on stereotypes and devaluing attitudes which the individual compensation does little to address.[2]

Third, human rights laws are still fragile structures when it comes to addressing discrimination and disadvantage faced by people with disabilities. These laws still need embedding in our legal and political cultures, and in our policy frameworks if they are to be instruments of change. In Canada, children with disabilities have no entitlement to the disability-related supports they require to live at home with their families, though a medical diagnosis might give them an entitlement to long-term institutional care. Moreover, attempts to institutionalize greater entitlements meet resistance and those won remain fragile. For example, the Government of Ontario repealed the provincial *Employment Equity Law* when the Conservative Party came into power in the 1990s. This law required that large employers simply identify and plan to address the workplace barriers to employment of people with disabilities, women, racial minorities and Aboriginal or First Nations peoples, that they provide reports on the progress of removal of barriers, and report on the numbers of people among these four groups who were employed in their organizations. This fragility is as true in the western industrialized countries as it is in the south. Writing in the Indian context, Sheth (1991) suggests that political, social and economic rights provisions, as advanced as they might be on paper, prove of "limited utility for those without entitlements and outside of the organized sectors" (p. 34).

For many in the disability movement these exit systems can only be resolved if we make integral to securing citizenship and human rights the process of recognizing and supporting others in ways that make their inclusion possible and valued. But how do we get there from here? How do we confront the dilemma of the rights revolution where rights granted do not mean recognition secured? If universal human rights provisions on their own do not secure inclusion for all among those who are recognized with value and status, and if our inclusion and value depends to a significant extent on recognition from others (e.g. school teachers, employers, community service providers, other citizens), the first step is to better understand this process of denial and the granting of the recognition we seek.

2. Jurisprudence and theories of equal recognition

How is it that children with disabilities come to be recognized as something less than fully human, less deserving of the same moral and legal status as others? How are we to understand what is at the root of the various forms of exclusion, the various ways in which children with disabilities are misrecognized? Where do we turn if a human rights strategy cannot on its own address these exclusions? In *Making All the Difference: Inclusion, Exclusion, and American Law*, Minow (1990) suggests that the social and economic boundaries that define status according to class, race, age, ability, sexual orientation, etc. – are rooted in some way in law. While statutory and case law define and grant rights, they also define conditions for exercising those rights, and for being known and recognized as a person or group able to exercise those rights. This is where the formula that equates the granting of rights, with securing equal and valued recognition, breaks down. Along with the rights granted, the exit systems the law also establishes can, in fact, mobilize the kind of recognition that devalues certain groups. We cannot fully understand the nature of exclusion of children, and of children with disabilities in particular, or how we might secure their inclusion among those fully valued, unless we bring into view this relationship between human rights, law and state policy, and the forms of knowledge and recognition they command.

Social inclusion as valued recognition – what the jurisprudence suggests

Issues of recognition by others, and who is included among those obtaining valued recognition and who is not, are central issues in recent jurisprudence in Canada concerned with interpreting constitutionally-protected equality rights. In the 1989 *Andrews v. Law Society of British Columbia* case, for example, a non-Canadian citizen argued that a provincial statute regulating the legal profession infringed on his equality rights because it restricted him from practicing law in Canada, simply on the grounds that he had not received his legal education in Canada. His nationality, he claimed, was used by a Canadian institution to recognize him and his capacities in devaluing ways. Writing the majority opinion for the Court and striking down the provision, MacIntyre J. wrote that equality rights under the Canadian *Charter of Rights and Freedoms* require:

> *the promotion of a society in which all are secure in the knowledge that they are recognized at law as human beings equally deserving of concern, respect, and consideration.*[3]

In the 1998 *Vriend v. Alberta* case, a man brought a human rights complaint on the basis that he had been fired from a teaching position because he was gay. The Supreme Court of

Canada eventually ruled on the case, where the Court quoted a minority judgement in the *Egan* case:

> *A discriminatory distinction is one "capable of either promoting or perpetuating the view that the individual adversely affected by this distinction is less capable or less worthy of recognition or value as a human being or as a member of Canadian society, equally deserving of concern, respect, and consideration.*

In the *Law v. Minister of Human Resources Development* (1999) case a 35-year-old woman, denied a surviving spouse pension under the Canada Pension Plan because she was not 65, claimed she had been discriminated against on the basis of her age. In a judgement rejecting her claim, the Supreme Court of Canada reviewed cases under the equality rights section of the *Charter*, and wrote:

> *It may be said that the purpose of s. 15(1) [the equality rights provision in the Charter] is to prevent the violation of essential human dignity and freedom through the imposition of disadvantage, stereotyping, or political or social prejudice, and to promote a society in which all persons enjoy recognition at law as human beings or as members of Canadian society, equally capable and equally deserving of concern, respect, and consideration.*

These cases suggest that what we come to know of one another, how we come to know it, and the institutionalized distinctions on which our views of one another rest, matter fundamentally. We might call the process of securing the equal value recognition characterized in these judgements as the process of social inclusion – inclusion among those recognized and valued "as a human being or as a member of Canadian society, equally deserving of concern, respect, and consideration."

Guided by the language of the *Law v. Minister of Human Resources Development* case, this process of social inclusion is one of constructing forms of knowledge, and institutional rules and boundaries that confer recognition and respect on individuals and groups as valued members of society, and that do not systematically undermine that respect.

We cannot take for granted that rights instituted means that valued recognition follows. Despite the legal requirements to ensure equal recognition under human rights law there are instructive cases where exclusions seem enforced because of whose knowledge is given status, whose act of recognition matters. For example, in the *Eaton v. Brant County Board of Education* case[4] , the Supreme Court of Canada ruled that a school board was not required to accommodate Emily Eaton in a regular classroom because of the extent of her communication and other needs, and that a segregated environment did not impose a burden on Emily. In the Court's view, what came to be defined as Emily's physical, intellectual and communication competencies marked her as so different than other children that the instruction she was deemed to require was considered impossible in a regular classroom. Segregation was thereby justified.[5] The Court ruled that knowledge about Emily's "actual characteristics" resides only with those who know by the means of a bio-medical account of disability – where a 'characteristic' comes to light only by its deviation from what is presumed to be 'normal'.[6] Moreover, this particular form of knowledge was validated as the only foundation for defining best interests of the child in this case, and for making the educational placement. The knowledge of Emily Eaton's parents was consigned to the category of parental preference and choice. The struggle over whose knowledge, whose form of recognition of Emily was to count, and questions about the extent to which different forms of recognition bring dignity, were not addressed, were not adjudicated. Nonetheless, the court did decide whose knowledge of Emily was to be valued, what attitudes about Emily mattered, and what forms of recognition were to count in determining where she would go to school.

Resolving the dilemma of the rights revolution – at least in theory

If there is no simple equation between rights granted and forms of recognition that secure value and inclusion, then what other variables matter? In his analysis of the rights revolution, Ignatieff suggests that recognition of others

> *is something more than a process of concession and negotiation alone. Properly considered, recognition is an act of enlargement that enables both sides to envisage new possibilities of living together. We don't simply recognize each other for what we are; we recognize what we could become together (p. 136).*

Honneth (1995) seeks to articulate a theory of recognition to make explicit how this 'enlargement' happens. He does so by making problematic the ways in which, and the practices with which, we come to know one another. He does not assume that rights possessed lead simply to valued recognition. Rather, he understands an extension of human rights as one strategy in weaving bonds of recognition in society. In developing a multi-layered theory of recognition, he begins with the assertion that the value of "human dignity" emerges as a mobilizing force throughout history in response to forms of personal degradation. In asking what then must constitute human dignity, Honneth suggests that it depends upon intersubjective, mutual recognition. Hegel's and Mead's theories of intersubjectivity provide the starting point for Honneth – the self develops in "a process in which the individual can unfold a practical identity to the extent that he is capable of reassuring himself of recognition by a growing circle of communicative partners" (1995, p. 249). He proceeds to identify three distinct forms of degradation and disrespect, and corresponding forms of recognition.

Physical maltreatment of another person's body – sexual exploitation, trafficking in children, torture, other forms of physical abuse – is the first and most basic. Such actions by others bring many harms. For Honneth, one of the most profound is denying the person a recognition that personal control over and care for his or her body is, to others, worth preserving. Its converse is a form of mutual recognition that gives one self-confidence from an early age. It comes in the attachment to one's intimate circle and brings an understanding that one's physical and emotional needs can be heard and responded to by others; that others will take care with respect to one's body and grant respect to the boundaries it establishes. Such forms of recognition are granted by one's "concrete others" (Benhabib, 1987), those in a relationship of personal knowing and attachment. Honneth calls this form of recognition simply – love. But, as we have seen, love is not enough to make sure that a child can get into school, or that an adult will have a job, friends in the community, or exercise the right to vote.

So Honneth turns to the history of a second kind of disrespect – a disrespect that denies a person possession and enjoyment of legally established rights within a society. Refusing to recognize a person as a full member of society, as "a full-fledged partner in interaction who possesses equal moral rights" (p. 251), can bring a loss of self-respect. It denies the opportunity to view oneself, according to Honneth, from the standpoint of the "generalized other" in Mead's terms who is institutionalized in established rights. The corresponding form of mutual recognition is a condition in which a person "learns to see herself from the perspective of her partners in interaction as bearers of equal rights" (p. 254). As we have seen, even as people obtain their rights as citizens, they face exclusion. Such forms of recognition are not enough.

A third form of disrespect comes from others devaluing the ways in which persons or groups realize themselves, the form of life they establish or participate in, "within the horizon of the cultural traditions of a given society" (p. 251). Such a denial of recognition for the social contributions and forms of life of others undermines the value that a person or group can attach to their own abilities, their own ways of life. Honneth sees the counterpart form of mutual recognition as "solidarity" – an approval for "unconventional lifestyles" and valuing of people's uniqueness and difference. Such approval across cultural, racial, linguistic and genetic differences, for example, provides individuals and groups with a cultural vantage point from which to affirm and value their own differences, and those of others.

These three types or "patterns" of mutual recognition – love, right and solidarity – each correspond to different levels of society: those concrete others in intimate relation to a person; the institutional framework of a society and, the broader set of cultural values and social forces. I find in Honneth's framework a key source for conceptualizing social inclusion as a multi-faceted and dynamic process for constructing at interpersonal, institutional, and societal levels the valuing forms of knowledge and recognition the Supreme Court of Canada suggests are central to realizing human dignity and equal recognition of worth.

Towards a social inclusion as solidarity agenda

I would argue for a social inclusion agenda that focuses more clearly than it has on Honneth's third level of recognition – of building a social solidarity that can bring value and recognition across differences of gender, language, communication, culture, age, ability, etc. This is not to leave aside a concern for fostering capacities and conditions for nurturing and attachment (level 1 in Honneth's framework), or for strengthening protection, participation and provision rights for children (level 2). Rather, it is to acknowledge that the solidarity that brings recognition across deeply divided social spaces is weak in certain respects in Canadian and other societies. Formulated in this way, 'solidarity' is not simply about coalition building, or forging alliances for a particular political struggle. Following Honneth, it is much more about bringing to critical light the extent of recognition granted to different forms of life, the breadth of diversity that a particular set of cultural and institutional arrangements allow, and the forms of knowledge that fortify exclusionary divides.

Advancing solidarity – in the way that Honneth defines the term – as valuing forms of life characterized by many social differences including race, ethnicity, language and disability, can be read as a guiding purpose in recent political philosophy. In *Inclusion and Democracy* (2000), for instance, Young suggests that solidarity is now a goal we need to pursue in order to secure inclusion for disadvantaged groups defined by culture, race, gender and disability in the benefits and resources allocated by state and society (housing, for example). She also advances solidarity as a goal to guide strategies and designs for political inclusion in processes of decision-making in local, regional, national and international governance. She frames the ideal as "differentiated solidarity" to account for the fact that valued recognition of others can mean supporting groups to form and support one another on the basis of particular affinities of race, ethnicity, etc. For Young, solidarity creates an obligation to "constitute and support institutions of collective actions organized to bring about relations of justice among persons" – where she defines justice as obtaining the conditions for self-development and self-determination (p. 224). By bringing focus to solidarity as the test for the inclusiveness of social, economic and political institutions, Honneth and Young provide a vantage point for thinking about the possibilities and limitations of granting rights protections. Human rights can also serve as a test of inclusiveness – i.e., do all individuals and groups have adequate rights protections to enable them to access social, economic and political institutions? The test of solidarity shifts the obligation for securing inclusion exclusively from those who must press their rights claims in order to get access to the education system, or to paid employment, or to the political process. A focus on solidarity puts the obligation on others to enable those claims to be made and realized. It establishes the obligation, for example, to create education systems where all children can be included and fully recognized by others in ways that value them, and thereby thrive.

A conception of solidarity can also be rooted in the intellectual contributions to understanding societal recognition of different groups made by Canadian philosophers. For instance, Taylor (1994) called the politics of our times a 'politics of recognition'; Tully (1995) refers to the 'politics of cultural recognition' in his study of the constitutional misrecognition of First Nations peoples in Canada; Kymlicka's (1995) study advances proposals for securing recognition of diverse and disadvantaged cultural communities through constitutional and legal protection of minority rights and O'Neill's (1994) study of children demonstrates their absence from the visions of liberal political theory. Honneth's work, and that of Canadian political philosophers are informing theories and proposals for recognition of diverse and marginalized religious, ethnic, and cultural communities in the U.S. (Gutmann 1994), in India (Chandoke 1999), and in the European Community (Habermas 1998) to name a few of the applications. Much of this work seeks to account for the 'struggle for recognition' of diverse groups in a political age so defined by individual rights.[7]

Solidarity is O'Neill's answer to the question about what can ground a full citizenship for children in an age defined by liberal individual rights. As he writes in *The Missing Child in Liberal Theory*, "any form of sustainable society is grounded in a vast lore/law that requires us to extend ourselves in a community of civic obligation towards others whose recognition simultaneously affords us our own moral worth" (1994, p. 86). And, he confirms, solidarity is a means by which this kind of recognition is mobilized in a society, it is the basis of "any adequate concept of citizenship" (p. 111).

Solidarity is also one way of answering Tully's question about the "spirit" appropriate to an age of cultural diversity. After his detailed analysis of the conventions for a constitutionalism that could account for that diversity in the Canadian context, and after his argument that "mutual recognition" among cultures must be a guiding convention for such a constitutionalism, he quotes Vaclav Havel to answer his question: "if the world today is not to become hopelessly enmeshed in ever more terrifying conflicts, it has only one possibility: it must deliberately breathe the spirit of multicultural co-existence into the civilization that envelops it." Still quoting, Tully writes "the 'basis' of this 'new spirit' is for different peoples, religions, cultures' to learn to 'respect each other', to 'respect and honour each others' differences'" (p. 212).

Taylor suggests that in the midst of our contemporary diversity, what makes us equally worthy of respect is a "universal human potential, a capacity all humans share. This potential, rather than anything a person may have made of it, is what ensures that each person deserves respect." Moreover, "our sense of the importance of potentiality reaches so far that we extend this protection even to people who through some circumstance that has befallen them are incapable of realizing their potential in the normal way" (1994, pp. 41-42). Taylor argues that this "presumption" of equal worth should guide our "approach" to others different from us, and help guide us through the contemporary struggles and "politics of recognition". With Habermas, I would say that solidarity names the acts of approaching, recognizing, and honouring others in ways that bring an equal worth and respect, even to the strangers in our midst:

> *Equal respect for* everyone *is not limited to those who are like us; it extends to the person of the other in his or her otherness. And solidarity with the other* as one of us *refers to the flexible "we" of a community that resists all substantive determinations and extends its permeable boundaries ever further. This moral community constitutes itself solely by way of the negative idea of abolishing discrimination and harm and of extending relations of mutual recognition to include marginalized men and women... The "inclusion of the other" means... that the boundaries of the community are open for all... and most especially for those who are strangers to one another and want to remain strangers (Habermas, 1998, pp. xxxv-xxxvi).*

There is yet an adequate study to be done in political philosophy that would consider how people with disabilities might be viewed as a cultural community whose status is deserving of the recognition, collective rights and constitutional protections that Kymlicka, Taylor, Tully, Chandoke and others consider necessary for other cultural communities more conventionally defined. In studies extending the analysis beyond ethno-racial-cultural-linguistic communities, there should be no simple equation with differences defined by gender as Wolf (1994) has argued, and I suspect the same is true for disability. But there are useful links and equivalencies to be drawn. Certainly, the negative stereotyping and construction of people with disabilities as diseased, as deficits, as abnormal, to be rehabilitated, or genetically cleansed, suggests disadvantages and cultural harm similar in scale to other groups for whom claims to cultural and political recognition have become so urgent. And certainly within the disability movement claims for recognition of rights to self-determination, to escape institutional confinement, etc. echo the calls of other groups in many ways. Moreover, without more collectively defined rights to needed disability-related supports and accommodations in education, the labour market, etc. there is little doubt that the citizenship of this group remains diminished and neglected.

There is no uniform answer to the constitutional and human rights guarantees necessary to recognize cultural diversity, and indeed the solution is undoubtedly place and nation specific. While they disagree to some extent on what the rights regime might look like, and some focus on actual proposals more than others, Taylor, Tully, Chandoke, Honneth, Habermas, Young, and others look beyond particular frameworks of rights for solutions to the misrecognitions and failures of recognition in our age of diversity. They theorize and seek to establish principles for the acts of solidarity, the modes of dialogue, the cultural means of recognition which might ground and help to negotiate an adequate framework of rights in different settings. Either implicitly or explicitly they distinguish the recognition that comes with rights granted, from the social solidarity and political culture that makes those rights manifest and that hold a promise for cultural recognition. It is an atrophied or absent "spirit" and political culture of recognition, or solidarity, that helps to explain the negotiation of an unjust framework of rights and a daily disrespect in so many lives.

I believe that useful implications for a social inclusion agenda for children with disabilities can be drawn from Honneth's analysis of how institutionalized rights are inadequate *on their own to ensure valued recognition.* Understandings of other theorists in social and political philosophy about the need for solidarity and mutual recognition to ground a just framework of rights can also contribute to such an agenda. Collectively, their work brings me to an assessment and to a question: The current frameworks of constitutional and statutory rights do not yet secure inclusion for Emily Eaton among classmates in a regular school where possibilities for her valued recognition might have a fighting chance. So what other strategies might a broader solidarity agenda point toward?

3. A 'social inclusion as solidarity' agenda for children with disabilities

Given the dilemma of rights and recognition I have outlined above, I would argue that we need a focused public agenda to advance solidarity with children with disabilities and their families. Undoubtedly, there are numerous issues to confront. But the analysis I have laid out in this paper suggests the challenge is to build a broadly-based valued recognition in society of children with disabilities on which the numerous issues can then be better addressed; and on which the full citizenship of children with disabilities will rest. Otherwise, the citizenship of all of us – who withhold that solidarity – will be diminished. In Ignatieff's terms, our sense of self and community will not be 'enlarged' to the extent it might have been if we had more widely woven the bonds of recognition and reciprocity.

I suggest three priorities for a public agenda to build 'solidarity for social inclusion' of children who are marginalized and devalued because they do not measure up to physical and intellectual norms. These priorities are distilled from three aspects of exclusion that the current rights discourse has not fully addressed: i) institutionalized forms of knowledge that stereotype and objectify on the basis of disability; ii) misrecognition and devaluing of different forms of physical and intellectual life (i.e. genetic differences read as genetic deficiencies and abnormalities) and iii) a 'naturalizing' of certain kinds of capacities and developmental paths over others (i.e. particular, dominant forms of communication and mobility that devalue other forms of communication or mobility, and thereby undermine justifications for investment in developing alternative capacities). Formulated in this way, these issues go beyond education, or the need for disability supports, or child poverty per se. When the question is about the forms of recognition that result in various exclusions of children with disabilities then new, and I believe deeper, issues rise to the surface.

Stereotyping and objectification in public policy

It is clear that Emily Eaton was excluded from

a regular classroom because of the way in which the conflict over different forms of knowledge was adjudicated. Forms and technologies for producing knowledge based on a typology of disorders and capacities which constructs disability as a fixed and absolute quantity ruled the day. The social and economic relations by which those technologies were deployed were occluded in the adjudication (the professional interests, the institutionalized requirements for an either/or educational placement process, the history of the constructs that informed the categorical assessments of Emily). Thus disability came to be seen as an ontological feature of an individual life rather than a social relation, a status ascribed by others. In another case put before the Supreme Court of Canada, which dealt with a right to interpreter services in order to effect the right to access health care services, this social construction of disability was a central element of the ruling and led to a very different conclusion by the Court:

> *It is an unfortunate truth that the history of disabled persons in Canada is largely one of exclusion and marginalization. Persons with disabilities have too often been excluded from the labour force, denied access to opportunities for social interaction and advancement, subjected to invidious stereotyping and relegated to institutions. The historical disadvantage has to a great extent been shaped and perpetuated by the notion that disability is an abnormality or flaw. As a result, disabled persons have not generally been afforded the "equal concern, respect and consideration" that s.15(1) of the Charter demands. Instead they have been subjected to paternalistic attitudes of pity and charity, and their entrance into the social mainstream has been conditional upon their emulation of able-bodied norms.*[8]

The conflict over whose knowledge should matter and how is at the core of what moral philosopher Lorraine Code (1987) refers to as "epistemic responsibility" – the moral responsibility for knowing others well. She suggests this requires that we do not objectify others beyond recognition as humans. We have a responsibility not to use stereotypes in knowing others – because that is the source of hate, of devaluation of others (Code, 1989). She suggests, along with other philosophers MacIntyre (1981), Taylor (1989), Benhabib (1986), Kearney (1998) that we can only know another well if we know them narratively – or through their personal story. We become valued in the eyes of others, and our 'self' is born – only in stories written and rewritten by ourselves and those who know us – stories of the past, of hopes for a future. Research has shown, in fact, that people's attitudes about those with disabilities change most clearly when they come to know them personally, and coming to know someone personally is to know them through their personal stories of struggle, of hope, of pain, of misfortune, of likes and dislikes, of family and friends (The Roeher Institute, 2000a).

Kearney (1998) writes of the 'moral-transformative' nature of witnessing the personal narratives of others in public spaces and forums. In their witnessing, such narratives are the source of empathy and the stuff of new social bonds. In the stories heard lies a critique of structures of domination that exclude. In the moral visions they point to are utopias for the future. The recent report of the Law Commission of Canada (2000) on abuse of children in institutions considers whether such an approach – through a Truth Commission, for example – might be needed to bring about valued recognition of and restitution for victims of abuse. Truth and reconciliation commissions in South Africa, the Nuremburg trials and the work of the War Crimes Tribunal in gathering testimony from refugees fleeing Kosovo, are all examples of the work of building solidarity on which a new foundation for affirming and asserting rights was established, even if in the midst of horrific abuses of those rights.

Knowledge is not a neutral affair, and state and other interests in regulating the status of different accounts about a child with a disability are determinative in a child's life and possibilities. A social inclusion as solidarity agenda for children must confront the question of whose knowledge counts in public policies regulating educational placement, and other allocation decisions (such as triaging of health services for children whose projected quality of life might be considered inadequate to justify heart surgery; long-term institutionalization of children). It must also consider how to nurture new forms of social knowledge that bring to life the narratives of those systematically excluded by disability, by poverty, by institutionalization. I suggest three possible directions to explore in such an agenda.

First, clear principles are needed to guide public policy to ensure that personal, narrative knowledge of a child's capacities, hopes, forms of communication, needs – often the knowledge with which parents and family members have the most expertise – is granted priority status in educational placement decisions for children with disabilities.

Second, there is a need to critically examine and revise eligibility criteria for access to needed health and social supports at home, in the community, and at school in order to question the forms of knowledge-making that require parents to have their children labelled with 'severe' deficits and syndromes as a condition of gaining access to any supports at all. In the education system, the examination might look at the 'catch 22' many parents encounter: have a child labelled as severely as possible in order to gain access to supports, but then face the prospect that the child may not be placed in a regular classroom because those responsible for gathering knowledge to determine educational placements will likely find the child too severely disabled to benefit from, or to be accommodated into, a regular classroom. Efforts to restructure relationships and status between different forms of knowledge would be driven by the insight that children with disabilities will come to be known by others as children first, only if they are borne through personal narratives about their possibilities, and not confined by labels and stereotypes.

Third, consideration might be given to the creation of a public sphere where children, youth and adults with disabilities (including the disproportionately high proportion who live in poverty), and their families, can document and widely share their own personal stories (their hopes, their accomplishments, the barriers they face in accessing services, jobs, food, adequate income). The forums and public media that might help constitute such a public space could help shape a political culture strong enough to advance a full citizenship agenda for people with disabilities and their families (through reforms in social assistance, income tax, labour market policy - e.g. paid leave for caregiving - and disability supports policy, for example). Without such a public sphere, Canadians are unable to witness and come face-to-face with the realities of a growing proportion of the population. The creation of an inclusive public sphere does not replace the need for a human rights agenda. A social inclusion as solidarity strategy would supplement the agenda. It would focus on the apparent lack of political will to advance anti-poverty and social support policies; on the need to foster a more supportive political culture; and on the need to form bonds of solidarity to nurture such a culture. That solidarity is only possible if Canadians come to hear and witness the faces and stories of disability and poverty in Canada. One might argue that Canadians have heard, and they won't listen, but such an argument should not be accepted uncritically. It may be that our strategies for solidarity-building – for giving testimony and witnessing – have not been compelling enough, and that they need rethinking.

Public policy and genetic value

There are growing concerns in the disability movement about the eugenic potential of the genetic technology revolution, and the implications for public policy are just now being articulated. As standards of good prenatal care in some jurisdictions now require publicly funded genetic testing (Weir, 1996) and as the (in part) publicly financed Human Genome Project draws the boundary around what it means to be genetically 'human', the status of those with genotypes outside of the norm comes into question, and human value tends to be reduced to genetic makeup (Wolf, 1995). Recent legal judgments confirm such outcomes. Damages for 'wrongful birth' are being awarded to parents of children born with disabilities, because the mother's physician did not make available the genetic testing that would have identified Down's syndrome, for example, or give the woman information on which to base a decision about selective abortion. Genetic screens and tests are technologies for knowing others as genetically deficient and therefore as something less than human. As technologies for knowing and judging the possibilities and shape of human life, they should be a central concern in an agenda for the valued recognition and status of all children. The information they generate can present a divide in social solidarity that is difficult to overcome without a conscious rethinking of how the knowledge is produced and used. Otherwise, the technologies will sustain and supplement forces of exclusion. Their very existence, for example, has been used by insurance companies to suggest that parents who knowingly bear a child with so-called 'genetic deficiencies' should not be eligible for the extended benefits for that child (Wolf, 1995). The possibilities of genetic knowing makes the bearing of a child with a disability a private affair, and therefore makes the financial responsibility for care a private matter as well.

Who benefits from the genetic technology revolution? The biotechnology research and development industry clearly benefits with the equation of genetic normalcy and good maternal health care. The value of 'gentech' stocks skyrocket, and health care systems in Canada and elsewhere absorb the burgeoning costs of purchasing genetic screens, and physician charges for applying the tests. The insurance industry benefits as it divests itself of responsibility for the costs of care where women make decisions to bear children who might have a disability. The industry also benefits as the costs of medical insurance balloon in the wake of recent decisions like that of the highest appeal court in France to award damages against a physician that did not genetically test a fetus for Down's syndrome prior to the child's birth.

But at what cost? The cost, the disability rights movement and some ethicists are arguing, is the perpetuation of the stereotype of disability as abnormal, as a burden, as a genetic failure that should be cleansed (Asch and Geller, 1996; Wolf, 1995; Cole 2001). Just as decisions to selectively abort on the basis of sex are understood to do harm beyond the fetus involved, to do harm to women as a whole, so too selective abortion on the basis of disability has been argued to bring harm to people with disabilities as a whole. The availability of the technology and its systematic use threaten a eugenics that makes mutual recognition across the differences between us that much more difficult to nurture.

What might a social inclusion as solidarity agenda entail were it to address the divides being established among humans on the basis of their genotypes and screened genetic conditions? Caulfield, et al. (2001) suggest the need for an analytic framework of "tests" to determine whether public funding or access to a genetic test is justified. The first analytic test determines whether a particular genetic service is "morally acceptable". Such a framework provides a useful place to begin, depending of course on how the criteria for 'moral acceptability' are determined. To deal with the concern that 'disability' might be left as morally 'irrelevant', a framework to regulate both research and applications in the health care system might also require that groups who may be adversely affected by genetic research or applications (e.g. through the stereotypes it might perpetrate, or through the inattention in research to the ethical and legal questions genetic technologies raise) be part of the ethics approvals process. This could be fairly simply addressed by requiring that representatives of national or regional disability rights organizations be part of ethics review committees at major research institutions (universities, Canadian Institutes for Health Research), and be part of any technology assessment process that guides development of purchasing and practice guidelines in the health care system. Their participation would ensure that the perspectives of people with disabilities are part of the ongoing dialogue about the potential for a new eugenics that genetic research and testing/screening raises, and about the guidelines to be developed for minimizing such risks.

Ensuring an inclusive design for the national monitoring mechanisms on genetic research and applications in Canada, called for under the recent UNESCO *Declaration on Human Rights and the Human Genome* to which Canada is a signatory, could also help to advance solidarity across the genetic divides now being etched. The monitoring mechanisms should engage disability, First Nations, and other groups who stand to be substantially disadvantaged through basic and applied genetic research (e.g. by 'patenting' of genetic sequences, or by the hierarchy of human value that comes with the enterprise to establish normal and abnormal genotypes). The national monitoring mechanisms could be structured to ensure that groups are resourced to participate in the monitoring of impacts of genetic technologies, and in the consideration of regulatory frameworks to ensure that the research accords with the commitments in the UNESCO Declaration to ensure a recognition of and respect for human diversity, dignity, and human rights. Solidarity emerges through understanding that often comes with face-to-face dialogue. Ongoing dialogues between geneticists and people with disabilities could be organized to resist the genetic reductionism that has come with much of the new wave of genetic research under the Human Genome Project.

These specific strategies would not address all of the citizenship and inclusion issues raised by the spectre of the genetic revolution. A human rights agenda is also clearly needed to ensure that adequate protections are in place to prevent discrimination on the basis of genetic differences – in access to insurance coverage, health care, education, training and the paid labour market, etc. But, on their own, such human rights provisions will likely be as inadequate in securing full citizenship as are existing human rights provisions in ensuring equality and prevention of discrimination on other grounds. A social inclusion as solidarity agenda would help to bridge the gulf of understanding between the scientific community and the truths it bears (which often seem invulnerable to human rights provisions), and the disability community whose members bear the narrative knowledge of human life well-lived in the midst of genetic diversity. At its core, the solidarity agenda must confront the forms and technologies of knowledge-making used to establish hierarchies of human value, and give greater status to forms of knowledge borne by those near the bottom of the hierarchy.

Measuring healthy child development

Psychoanalytic theory, theories of cognitive development and social psychology all emphasize that healthy, "normal" development occurs as infants, toddlers, young children and adolescents reach and pass through certain developmental stages or benchmarks. Failure to reach certain stages (in terms of language and communication abilities, cognitive, and motor skills and ego and identity formation) is usually regarded as a sign of "abnormal development". When failure is first noticed, assessments are often called for to determine nature of disability, and to assign a particular bio-medical status.

The systematic exclusion of children with disabilities from a conceptual and monitoring framework of healthy child development is evident in a growing body of literature on the importance of ensuring that adequate investments are made in the 0-6 age group so that they are "ready to learn" at school age (McCain and Mustard, 1999). Indicators of readiness to learn usually include:

- physical well-being and appropriate motor development
- emotional health and a positive approach to new experiences
- age-appropriate social knowledge and competence
- age-appropriate language skills
- age-appropriate general knowledge and cognitive skills.[9]

Many children with disabilities are simply unable to meet some of these developmental outcomes. They may communicate in different ways than the majority of children raised in a hearing and English- or French-speaking culture. They may not be able to move in the same ways or have the same kinds of agility as those who fall within the statistically "normal" range. When viewed from the perspective of children with disabilities, the cultural bias of these outcomes is clear. They mark a group of children that education systems, in their current design, are most able to include and educate. They are based on a narrow theory of development in which verbal language skills are associated with cognitive development, readiness to learn and healthy development.

Establishing a framework of developmental outcomes is not simply an exercise of academic value. With the recent adoption by the federal and provincial/territorial governments of the 'Early Childhood Development Agreement', the federal government has committed a transfer to provinces and territories of $2.2 billion a year for five years for early childhood services. Both levels of government have committed to monitoring their investments in early child development and the outcomes for children. How outcomes are conceptualized, and the benchmarks selected for developmental progress, will help to determine which children are seen to most benefit from investments. Concerns have been expressed that some children with developmental and other disabilities are losing access to early childhood services such as speech and language therapy because these children are considered unable to adequately benefit from this investment. It is believed that the scarce dollars and services would be better invested in other children. [10]

Mackelprang and Salsgiver (1999) review some of the intellectual foundations for a broader view of developmental theory that would begin to address the cultural biases of predominant approaches, and make possible the development of a more inclusive set of outcomes and indicators. This work suggests we need to shift from measuring the gap between age and expected developmental achievements, to focus on the conditions that enable people with disabilities to carry out "developmental tasks", that are culturally shared and defined. To be able to communicate with others, for instance, is a developmental task whose achievement need not be measured by verbal language skills in the dominant language. Moving into adulthood need not be defined by the capacity for independence, which would exclude from successful adult achievement those who require ongoing personal supports. It can also be defined by the control one is given over one's supports, and the opportunity to develop and pursue a wider range of goals.

A more inclusive developmental framework for children would pay more attention to conditions which enable access to needed resources and which structure opportunities for development, for social interaction and for exercising control over one's environment. Novick, drawing on the work of the Laidlaw Foundation's *Children at Risk Programme* and a wide body of research in the field, suggests that an adequate theory of child development must incorporate an understanding of the various domains which structure opportunities, social interaction, control and access to resources. He includes the structural domain (broad societal cultural forces), institutional, personal, familial and communal domains.[11] This approach shifts the focus from one of strict age-related developmental stages to be achieved, to an understanding that every child has a unique "developmental path" (or unique ways of realizing different developmental tasks whether they be managing communication and interaction with others, developing personal identity, moving from adolescence into adulthood). The task of public policy, social investment and community development is to ensure that children have access to the life chances they need to pursue and realize their unique path across all domains of development. How different domains structure and distribute life chances, in ways that account for differences of sex, race, economic class and disability becomes a subject for research and a matter of public monitoring. [12] Taylor's formulation, of each person's unique potential as the basis of worth and equal respect, provides the ethical foundation for a public policy that values diverse developmental paths. It provides an ethical foundation for choosing self-anchored indicators in measuring a child's development. [13]

How could a social inclusion as solidarity agenda be struck to confront the divides structured in a developmental investment strategy that values children with certain physical, intellectual and developmental characteristics over others? First, it is essential that an inclusive framework of developmental outcomes be established as the basis of public investments and monitoring. Second, population survey instruments are needed to gather data on indicators consistent with outcomes and domains of development incorporated into the framework, with a particular emphasis on the extent to which children obtain the needed supports and opportunities to develop and exercise communicative and other capacities. Third, disability organizations could be supported to engage in the public monitoring of child outcomes so that perspectives of children and youth with disabilities are adequately represented. Population survey instruments could then be designed to incorporate evolving understandings of needed supports and the various ways children develop and exercise learning, communicative and other capacities. Finally, given the importance of communicative capacities to a child's intellectual and social development, it is essential to critically review the breadth of communication systems funded and used in early childhood services and the education system (e.g. written and spoken language, sign language interpretation, augmentative communication technologies and use of a child's unique gestural and behavioural sign systems where spoken language is not used).

A social inclusion as solidarity agenda asks *what* knowledge, *whose* knowledge, and which communicative competencies are left outside of public sphere and public discourse. Bridging social, economic and cultural differences that bring valued recognition to those who are devalued and excluded, requires that we promote dialogue and understanding across public spaces previously silent to their voices and their realities. The agenda *would not* be about ensuring everyone's access to every benefit and advantage Canadian institutions have to offer. Rather, it would ask that distinctions made in the rules and practices of institutions, services and organizations not systematically undermine the recognition and status of any group based on their age, capacity, sexual orientation, gender, etc. Moreover, it would be about fostering forms of knowledge and recognition that value others, and about questioning forms of recognition that distance, that devalue, that cast aside. At an institutional level it would add to the rights protections associated with citizenship, a prescription to identify and transform policies and practices that violate human dignity through stereotyping and discrimination. At a personal level it would call for a 'virtue' of citizenship practised through knowing and recognizing others in ways that bring human dignity.

Conclusion: Policy Implications

Women's movements, disability rights activists, poverty action groups[14], First Nations' members and various groups based on distinct ethno-racial-linguistic differences increasingly claim exclusion of one form or another. These are important voices. They speak from outside institutions and organizations of power, privilege and advantage in Canadian society. They tell us something about ourselves, about how we are 'reacting' to the differences in our midst, about our collective state of imperfection. At their roots, these claims of exclusion are about the denial of valued recognition in Canadian society, and speak back to the ways that some come to be known by others. The denial of valued recognition is organized in concrete ways through our political culture, legal systems, public policies and practices.

In this paper I have suggested that we can usefully understand social inclusion as a political claim, as an ideal for social institutions and as a process for building solidarity and valued recognition across diverse persons and groups in the spaces structured by the state and civil society – schools, labour markets, health care institutions, community associations, public governance, etc. Social inclusion is about rewriting the rules, recasting our cultural images and resources and instituting practices to bring equally valued status to those who have been assigned a place of lesser value and status in Canadian society. Social inclusion does not demand that we assimilate and homogenize social and cultural differences in our education, health care, political and other systems. Valued recognition of others entails respecting their differences and identities in ways that enable them to speak their voices, exercise their rights, and secure their own path to well-being. Social inclusion also demands reciprocity. Groups who seek status and public space, but whose mission and practice involves stereotyping and devaluing others, are not deserving of equally valued recognition and status by their broader society.

What are the policy implications of this understanding of social inclusion for advancing the well-being of children in Canada? First, it brings focus to the ways in which knowledge about children, and about certain groups of children is made. It asks about the status that different kinds of knowledge are given in gaining access to these different settings and institutions. Forms of knowledge that stereotype children as so different than other children that they are refused access to education, for instance, are challenged in such an agenda.

Secondly, an agenda for social inclusion raises a challenge to create new public spaces where the lives and realities of children and their families can be witnessed, where testimony can be given, where a new commitment to invest can take root. It is in these acts of recognition that the other, Kearney argues, comes to make an ethical difference, where new social bonds can be woven across the differences that divide. Surely this is the promise of a citizenship that values belonging, dignity, reciprocity and respect - where rights claims and aspirations obtain not only legal but broad social recognition and commitment. Only then are needed policy investments likely to follow. I believe the analysis outlined above applies not only to issues facing children with disabilities and their families; they have provided a case study with which to explore the notion of social inclusion as solidarity. The analysis, it seems to me, applies also to other issues affecting children. Persistent, deepening child poverty in Canada, for example, is not a consequence of a lack of resources, or labour markets and policies that cannot be restructured. It results from a lack of will and commitment, where the fact of poverty does not seem to matter enough. A social inclusion as solidarity agenda focuses, for example, on building a much wider recognition of the realities of children and families who are poor, of making their realities matter to all Canadians in a way that commitment to address the structural roots of poverty will follow. A solidarity agenda does not on its own put bread on the table. It creates the public consciousness and commitment for public policies and practices to make sure it gets there.

A social inclusion as solidarity agenda should be paramount if we are to move forward on the kind of covenant for children that O'Neill (1994) calls for, and address the exclusions that persist. The covenant does not need to be written. It is already expressed in many national and international human rights instruments – most clearly for children in the *Convention on the Rights of the Child.* It could be articulated anew, but the sources for its expression and for legal and moral obligation are there. What is missing is the commitment to realize it. What is missing is the process of social inclusion that will bring all children within the ambit of moral consideration, worthy of securing the personal and collective obligations they are due. So many children and families are absent from the public sphere – children with disabilities and their families, aboriginal children, children growing up in poverty, victims of abuse and violence. Commitment for the covenant will grow only as their testimonies are more widely witnessed, their realities and possibilities more clearly documented in population surveys and by other means, and in ways that make their concerns and aspirations resonate in Canadian political culture. By these means we might shed better light on the absences in our collective social imaginations.

Social inclusion as solidarity does not deny the need for a strong framework of rights for children. It does require that we look at how children and youth come to be known, at the policies and practices of genetic differencing, of educational segregation, of communicational straightjacketing. A solidarity agenda would not seek to eradicate diversity. It would make problematic the organization of advantage and disadvantage across the differences that define us. With such an agenda we would not be satisfied with a simple extension of rights, safe in the knowledge that children and adults can then press claims to battle the walls that exclude them. It would demand that 'citizenship virtues' of reciprocity, or knowing others well, be actively fostered. It would sound a call to mobilize personal and collective forms of recognition that bring dignity and value to all children.

I have sought throughout this paper to draw the links between human rights, full citizenship, social inclusion and solidarity. The notion of citizenship and what it requires has evolved historically through many political and intellectual struggles. The calls for social inclusion have been made in its shadow – calls to be included as citizens from those not yet seen in the light it sheds. Hence, the strategies for social inclusion have evolved and changed as the concept of citizenship has been rewritten. In the past 50 years, a human rights agenda has been the most compelling strategy to advance inclusive citizenship. While that agenda has clearly not yet been fulfilled, it is becoming increasingly clear that, on its own, it still leaves some in the shadows. I have suggested that a solidarity agenda should now constitute a major agenda for socially inclusive citizenship – one that fully accounts for and recognizes all children in equally valuing ways. In the arguments I have laid out here a solidarity agenda need not depart from a human rights agenda. Rather, they represent different orders of analysis and criticism in a common cause to secure valued recognition of devalued groups.

Institutionalizing human rights has been one means to fuel the social inclusion of devalued groups among those who obtain valued recognition and citizenship in society's institutions. Solidarity agendas must also be struck to complement establishment of human rights if we are to more fully confront the refusal by some to include others in ways that bring value, respect and dignity. Social inclusion is not the aim. Valued recognition, respect and dignity that make full social, economic and political participation possible, name the core elements of citizenship and the aspirations to which human rights instruments intend. Social inclusion names social and political struggles to realize these aspirations in the lives of people and groups so often misrecognized, devalued and denied. It offers an ideal for institutional arrangements. Criteria for inclusivity could also help guide institutional reform.

In these times we find ourselves in, a commitment to social inclusion must involve steps to bring understanding across the divides that establish race, language, gender, ability, creed, genotype, economic class and nationality as grounds of status and value. To bring inclusion where it has so often been denied, we must forge a solidarity that listens across these divides of status and then questions their roots in law and in domestic and foreign policy. We must question the institutionalized refusal to know and respect others well. Thereby, the daily realization of children's rights might become a much deeper concern and commitment for governments, communities and other citizens. The evidence makes clear that a solidarity and political culture valuing all children is certainly not a given in our society; it is yet to be woven.

Endnotes

1 This may be because the link between reason and citizenship remains firmly entrenched in our political culture, statutory law and legal reasoning making human rights claims by people with intellectual disabilities that much harder to press.

2 See Judith Mosoff, "Is the Human Rights Paradigm 'Able' to Include Disability? Who's In? Who Wins? What? Why?," Queens Law Journal 26 (2001).

3 Andrews v. Law Society of British Columbia, 1 S.C.R. 143 at 171 (1989).

4 Eaton v. Brant County Board of Education, 1 S.C.R. 241 (1997).

5 For a detailed analysis of this case see the Canadian Association for Community Living, Intellectual Disability and the Supreme Court: The Implications of the Charter for People who have a Disability, (Toronto, 1999).

6 In contrast, a "social model" of disability is being advanced by those who find in the bio-medical account a reductionist tendency – reducing the disability to individual characteristics defined as deficits (Barnes, 1991; Rioux, 1994; Oliver, 1996). In a social model, disability arises from the discrimination and disadvantage individuals experience in relation to others because of their particular differences and characteristics. This shift in thinking finds a primary source in feminist theories of difference where the challenge is to recognize differences of gender, race, sexual orientation, physical and intellectual characteristic, etc. without assigning social or economic value on the basis of these differences (Minow, 1990).

7 Kymlicka's (1989) analysis of liberal and communitarian theories of the self helped enormously in resolving the theoretical impasse between liberal accounts of the political and ethical primacy of the individual, and communitarian accounts of the person that emphasize the importance of community, tradition and culture (e.g. MacIntyre, 1981; Sandel, 1982). Kymlicka addressed the impasse by revealing the link between the self-development and self-determination that liberal political philosophy so values, and the availability of cultural resources that a community provides an individual – resources of language, modes of thought, horizons of meaning, etc. Recognizing the centrality of community and culture to individual self-development and freedom begs the question of how to provide recognition and protection for diverse communities, some of which may be threatened by cultural genocide, which face systematic discrimination by dominant cultures, or which come into being with the massive dislocations and migrations that are unlikely to subside in these times.

8 Eldridge v. British Columbia (Attorney General), 141 D.L.R. (4th) 577 at 613 (1997). In confronting the issue of recognition of people with disabilities in Canadian society directly, the court moved to clearly articulate a "right to effective communication" in this case, establishing that in order for deaf citizens in Canada to access their right to health care, they were entitled to interpreter services in the health care system.

9 See G. Doherty, Zero to Six: The Basis for School Readiness (Ottawa: Human Resources Development Canada, 1997).

10 Examples of children who lost access to such services were reported in a series of consultations conducted by The Roeher Institute. See The Roeher Institute, Moving In Unison into Action (Toronto, 2001(b).

11 See Marvyn Novick, "Prospects for Children: Life Chances and Civic Society" (Toronto: Laidlaw Foundation, 1997).

12 The Roeher Institute has drawn on this work and related literature, as well as a series of consultations with disability and family organizations, children's services providers and government policy analysts, to reconceptualize a framework of healthy child development for monitoring public investments and their impact on children. The framework includes a set of seven developmental outcomes, framed to be inclusive in their basic conceptualization (e.g. all children could meet the developmental targets with adequate supports). The outcomes include: physical well-being, emotional and mental well-being, social well-being (membership, participation, social relationships), spiritual well-being, communicative capacity, learning capacity and a positive future for a child envisioned by others. The 'domains of development' which should provide support and opportunity for children to pursue and reach these outcomes include family, school, community, paid labour market (for parents), public policy (for investment in needed developmental supports). This framework is presented and discussed in The Roeher Institute, Toward An Inclusive Approach To Monitoring Investments And Outcomes In Child Development And Learning: Draft Discussion Document (Toronto, 2001c).

13 Self-anchored indicators measure a child's progress in reaching their own potential. Rather than measuring a child against a fixed norm or criterion of capacity, self-anchored indicators measure a child's progress over time in meeting his or her unique communicational, motor, relational, learning and other goals. Self-anchored indicators are already in use in some population surveys. For example, the National Population Health Survey asks people to rate their own health status. Such a survey leaves the definition of health up to the respondent. For a discussion of self-anchored indicators and a critique of norm-referenced assessments as the sole basis for assessing child development, see The Roeher Institute, Toward An Inclusive Approach To Monitoring Investments And Outcomes In Child Development And Learning: Draft Discussion Document (Toronto, 2001c).

14 I am not suggesting here that 'poverty' represents a difference that should be valued, or that those living in poverty constitute a unique cultural identity of their own choosing. We need a sustained attack on poverty that addresses its systemic roots in inequitable access to education, labour markets, income support, health care, social supports, transportation and decent housing. I am arguing, however, that those living in poverty tend to be constituted by others in stereotyped and devaluing ways, where their poverty is seen as an individual rather than structural problem. Building a much broader solidarity with those living in poverty is required, I suggest, in order to foster a political culture where the will might be borne to address the systemic roots of poverty. Until people living in poverty matter more to Canadians in general, the political and cultural forces that demonize them and justify political inaction will win the day.

References

Alur, Mithu. 2000. Inclusion for Children with Disabilities in India. In *International Scan of Issues: Children with Disabilities and Their Families.* A discussion document for the Sixth International Congress on the Inclusion of Children With Disabilities in the Community. Toronto: The Roeher Institute.

Asch, Adrienne, and Gail Geller. 1996. Feminism, bioethics, and genetics. In *Feminism & Bioethics: Beyond Reproduction,* edited by Susan Wolf. New York and Oxford: Oxford University Press.

Barnes, Colin. 1991. *Disabled People in Britain and Discrimination.* London: Hurst & Co.

Benhabib, Seyla. 1986. *Critique, Norm, and Utopia: A Study of the Foundations of Critical Theory.* New York: Columbia University Press.

________ . 1987. The Generalized and Concrete Other. In *Feminism as Critique,* edited by Seyla Benhabib and Drucilla Cornell. Minneapolis: University of Minnesota Press.

Bunch, G. and A. Valeo. 2000. Educational Inclusion of Children with Disabilities. In *International Scan of Issues: Children with Disabilities and Their Families.* A discussion document for the Sixth International Congress on the Inclusion of Children With Disabilities in the Community. Toronto: The Roeher Institute.

Canadian Association for Community Living. 1999. *Intellectual Disability and the Supreme Court: The Implications of the Charter for People who have a Disability.* Toronto.

Caulfield, T., M. Burgess, and B. Williams-Jones. 2001. Providing Genetic Testing Through the Private Sector: A View from Canada. *Isuma: Canadian Journal of Policy Research 2, no.3* (autumn): 65-71.

Chandoke, Neera. 1995. *State and Civil Society: Explorations in Political Theory.* Delhi: Sage.

________. 1999. *Beyond Secularism: The Rights of Religious Minorities.* New Delhi: Oxford University Press.

Code, Lorraine. 1987. *Epistemic responsibility.* Hanover, NH: University Press of New England.

________ . 1989. Experience, Knowledge and Responsibility. In *Feminist Perspectives in Philosophy,* edited by Morwenna Griffiths and Margaret Whitford. London: MacMillan.

Cole, Audrey. 2001. *Genetic Discrimination: Looking Back to the Future?* Occasional Paper, The Roeher Institute, Toronto.

Doherty, G. 1997. *Zero to Six: The Basis for School Readiness.* Ottawa: Human Resources Development Canada.

Gutman, Amy, ed. 1994. *Multiculturalism: Examining the Politics of Recognition.* Princeton, NJ: Princeton University Press.

Habermas, Jurgen. 1998. *The Inclusion of the Other: Studies in Political Theory.* MIT Press, in Cambridge, Mass.

Honneth, Axel. 1995. *The fragmented world of the social: Essays in social and political philosophy.* Edited by Charles W. Wright. Albany, NY: State University of New York.

Ignatieff, Michael. 2000. *The Rights Revolution.* Toronto: Anansi.

Irwin, S.H., and D.S. Lero. 1997. *In our way: Child care barriers to full workforce participation experienced by parents of children with special needs – and potential remedies.* NS: Breton Books.

Kearney, Richard. 1998. *Poetics of Imagining: Modern to Post-modern.* New York: Fordham University Press.

Kymlicka, Will. 1989. *Liberalism, Community, and Culture.* Oxford: Clarendon Press.

________ . 1995. *The Rights of Minority Cultures.* Oxford: Oxford University Press.

Kymlicka, Will, and Wayne Norman. 1994. Return of the Citizen: A Survey of Recent Work on Citizenship Theory. *Ethics* (January): 352-81.

Law Commission of Canada. 2000. *Restoring Dignity: Responding to Child Abuse in Canadian Institutions.* Ottawa.

Mackelprang, Romel, and Richard Salsgiver. 1999. *Disability: A Diversity Model Approach in Human Service Practice.* Pacific Grove, CA: Brooks/Cole Publishing.

MacIntyre, A. 1981. *After Virtue.* London: Duckworth.

Marshall, T.H. 1965. *Class, Citizenship and Social Development.* New York: Anchor.

McCain, Margaret, and Fraser Mustard. 1999. *The early years study: Reversing the real brain drain.* Toronto: Ontario Children's Secretariat.

Minow, M. 1990. *Making All the Difference: Inclusion, Exclusion, and American Law.* Ithaca: Cornell University Press.

Mosoff, Judith. 2001. Is the Human Rights Paradigm 'Able' to Include Disability? Who's In? Who Wins? What? Why? *Queens Law Journal* 26.

Novick, M. 1997. *Prospects for Children: Life Chances and Civic Society.* Toronto: Laidlaw Foundation.

Oliver, Mike. 1996. Defining Impairment and Disability: issues at stake. In *Exploring the Divide: Illness and Disability,* edited by C. Barnes, and G. Mercer. Leeds, UK: The Disability Press, University of Leeds.

O'Neill, John. 1994. *The Missing Child in Liberal Theory: Towards a Covenant Theory of Family, Community, Welfare and the Civic State.* Toronto: University of Toronto Press, in association with the Laidlaw Foundation.

Rioux, Marcia. 1994. Towards a Concept of Equality of Well-Being: Overcoming the Social and Legal Construction of Inequality. In *Disability is Not Measles: New Research Paradigms in Disability,* edited by M. Rioux, and M. Bach. Toronto: The Roeher Institute.

The Roeher Institute. 1988. *Vulnerable: Sexual Abuse and People with an Intellectual Disability.* Toronto.

________. 1993. *On-Target? Canada's Employment-Related Programs for Persons with Disabilities.* Toronto.

________. 1995. *Harm's Way: The Many Faces of Violence and Abuse against Persons with Disabilities.* Toronto.

________. 2000a. *International Scan of Issues: Children with Disabilities and Their Families.* A discussion document for the Sixth International Congress on the Inclusion of Children With Disabilities in the Community, Toronto.

________. 2000b. *Towards Inclusion: National Evaluation of Deinstitutionalization Initiatives.* Toronto.

________. 2000c. *Labour Force Inclusion of Parents Caring for Children with Disabilities.* Toronto.

________. 2001a. *Community Inclusion Initiative: Participatory Action Research Final Report – 2000-2001.* Toronto.

________. 2001b. *Moving In Unison into Action.* Toronto.

________. 2001c. Toward An Inclusive Approach To Monitoring Investments And Outcomes In Child Development And Learning. Draft Discussion Document. Toronto.

Sandel, Michael. 1982. *Liberalism and the Limits of Justice.* Cambridge: Cambridge University Press.

Sheth, D.L. 1991. An Emerging Perspective on Human Rights in India. In *Rethinking Human Rights,* edited by S. Kothari, and H. Sethi. New York: New Horizons Press: 31-6.

Sullivan, P.M., M. Vernon, and J.M. Scanlon. (1987). Sexual Abuse of Deaf Youth. *American Annals of the Deaf* 32, no. 4: 256-62.

Taylor, Charles. 1989. *Sources of the Self: The Making of the Modern Identity.* Cambridge: Harvard University Press.

________. 1994. The Politics of Recognition. In *Multiculturalism: Examining the Politics of Recognition,* edited by Amy Gutman. Princeton, NJ: Princeton University Press.

Trocme, N., B. MacLaurin, B. Fallon, J. Daciuk, D. Billingsley, M. Tourigny, M. Mayer, J. Wright, K. Barter, G. Burford, J. Hornick, R. Sullivan, and B. McKenzie. 2001. *Canadian Incidence Study of Reported Child Abuse and Neglect: Final Report.* Ottawa, ON: Minister of Public Works and Government Services Canada.

Tully, James. 1995. *Strange multiplicity: Consitutionalism in an age of diversity.* Cambridge: Cambridge University Press.

Weir, Lorna. 1996. Recent developments in the government of pregnancy. *Economy and Society* 25 (3): 372-392.

Wolf, Susan. 1994. Comment. In *Multiculturalism: Examining the Politics of Recognition,* edited by Amy Gutman . Princeton, NJ: Princeton University Press.

________. 1995. Beyond "Genetic Discrimination": Toward the Broader Harm of Geneticism. *Journal of Law, Medicine & Ethics* 23: 345-53.

Young, Iris Marion. 1990. *Justice and the Politics of Difference.* Princeton: Princeton University Press.

________ . 2000. *Inclusion and Democracy.* Oxford: Oxford University Press.

FIS

Assessment and Formulation: A Contemporary Social Work Perspective

Ruth G. Dean & Nancy Levitan Poorvu

ABSTRACT

Assessment and formulation, the gathering of information about a client, and the conceptualization of the client or situation are the essential elements that mark a thoughtful approach to client care. This process has been shaped over time by changes in orientations to knowledge, new theories, new practices, and political and institutional pressures. Currently, there is an intense debate concerning the nature of social work practice, especially the assessment and formulation process. In this context, we review traditional approaches to formulation in light of contemporary understandings and trends. We present a model for formulation that highlights multiple ways of knowing and includes ecological, cross-cultural, psychodynamic, systemic, biological, and spiritual components. Social justice is the value that is foundational to the process.

This is a time when researchers, educators, and practitioners are debating the essence of social work (Gambrill, 2006; Graybeal, 2007; Sellick, Delaney, & Brownlee, 2002; Witkin & Harrison, 2001). The clinical practices of assessment and formulation are at the center of this debate. The form that clinical social work practice takes in the future will be strongly influenced by the way that social work educators and practitioners conceptualize the processes of assessment and formulation. As teachers of practice, and as practitioners ourselves, we wish to enter the debate and offer a model of assessment and formulation for the consideration of educators, students, and practitioners.

The model is comprehensive and multidimensional. It highlights several knowledge areas considered important in the process of understanding a client or situation. The domains that we have selected are not new; they have long been the ways that social workers think about clients. We consider it especially important in a time of change to review traditional practices and reconfigure them in light of contemporary theories and approaches. The model will help clinicians hold on to full, rich, and complex understandings of clients and clinical work.

In this material we first define what we mean by the terms *assessment* and *formulation*. Then we discuss the nature of current challenges and show how they emerge from historical trends in social work. Having explored current and past themes, we present our model and demonstrate its application with a case example.

Defining Terms—The Language of Social Work

Work with a client begins with eliciting information considered relevant to the issue with which the client presents

 DOI: 10.1606/1044-3894.3822

(Mattaini & Kirk, 1991). We refer to this process as the assessment. We define formulation as a focused, brief conceptualization of the client or situation, based on the assessment. It highlights the central issues, offers a tentative understanding of them, and sets the groundwork of the plan for intervention that follows (Madsen, 2007; Perry, Cooper, & Michels, 1987; Ross, 2000). Assessment is an ongoing process that leads to inferences and hypotheses that contribute to the developing relationship between worker and client as they reflect on themes and increase their understanding of an issue or problem (Germaine & Gitterman, 1996). In most models of contemporary practice, the way social workers formulate their cases is developed in collaboration with clients, privileging their views and supporting their strengths (Madsen; Parton & O'Byrne, 2000).

Models for assessment developed in the fields of psychiatry, psychology, and family therapy have made important contributions to the ways social workers formulate their cases. Social workers must be able to speak the languages of the *Diagnostic and Statistical Manual of Mental Disorders* (*DSM-IV-TR*; American Psychiatric Association, 2000) and psychodynamic, developmental, behavioral, and family systems theories, to name a few current influences. But borrowed understandings leave out interests essential to social work. Our model integrates multiple perspectives, some of which originated in other disciplines, within an orientation that is consistent with the values, theories, practices, and language of social work. This approach, highlighting multiple ways of knowing, falls within a constructionist perspective. Forces in social work representing different views would challenge this choice. We now consider some of these current challenges.

Current Challenges

Powerful intellectual and political and social forces are challenging the social work practices of assessment and formulation. In the academy, two very different orientations to knowledge have been the source of strong debates that began in the 1960s with critiques of the ideal of objective truth and an objective scientific methodology (Irving, 1999; Sellick et al., 2002). These orientations are variously referred to as modern and postmodern, empiricist and postempiricist, and realist and constructionist (Iversen, Gergen, & Fairbanks, 2005). They have powerful implications for social work education and practice; they also direct the ways in which assessment and formulation are conceptualized and enacted.

Those steeped in empiricist models, such as the advocates of evidence-based practice, argue for a research-based, scientific orientation to assessment and treatment planning (Gambrill, 2006; O'Hare, 2005; Rosen, 2003). Scales and assessment instruments may be used to help name the problem being treated and to offer a baseline for assessing change (O'Hare). In this model, although clients' views are considered, the worker's expertise and responsibility for assessment and treatment planning is stressed (O'Hare).

The postmodern or constructionist orientation emphasizes the shifting, evolving, contextual, and fluid aspects of knowledge, and this orientation questions whether objectivity is at all possible in selecting the information that goes into a formulation (Dean, 1993; Iversen et al., 2005; Parton, & O'Byrne, 2005). Multiple perspectives are utilized, based on the belief that all views are partial and that no single theory or perspective has a monopoly on the "truth" of a situation. Clients' understandings and meanings are privileged, and the process of formulation involves collaboration between workers and clients (Madsen, 2007).

In addition to pressures emanating from these ideological differences, political and institutional changes in the United States have altered the context in which social work practice occurs with implications for the assessment process. The conservative political turn that has gripped the United States in the past 30 years has led to dismantling the safety net established by President Franklin Roosevelt during the New Deal (Krugman, 2007). This has meant decreased support for social services, tighter agency budgets, and pressure to limit workers' hours to those spent in direct client contact (Barlas, 2006; Schneider, Hyer, & Luptak, 2000; Stoil, 2001). The management of care by third-party payers requires medical (psychiatric) diagnoses. Formulations are often limited to *DSM-IV-TR* diagnostic categories, determinations of risk, problem lists, and the specification of measurable outcomes (Cohen, 2003; Furman & Langer, 2006; Mishne, 2004; Schneider et al., 2000).

In this stressful practice climate, strongly held differences have emerged among social workers concerning the priorities of the evaluation process. Some emphasize measurable behavioral change; some focus on "strengths"; others focus on culture, context, ecological factors, political inequalities, social injustices, intrapsychic phenomena, and systemic issues. Tensions inherent in these differences have at times resulted in oversimplified assessments that represent the views of a single camp. Although most social workers agree that some form of inquiry and assessment is needed, what this should consist of is unclear.

We do not wish to take sides in this debate, for each side has something to contribute to a discussion of assessment and formulation. Like the empiricists, we see the need for establishing a baseline formulation of the problem that will guide the interventions that follow and make it possible to evaluate outcomes. But, in agreement with the constructionists, we believe that any view is tentative and will (and should) dissolve or shift as the work proceeds. Although we see the necessity for using words and categories to organize thinking, we also believe, with the constructionists, that words construct rather than reflect the ways we see the world. The words we use to construct a client can be morally evaluative and negatively affect the ways that others see him or her (Urek, 2005). These words have serious, damaging effects and forever obscure the person he or she is. Therefore, we must choose the words we use in a formulation very carefully, and hold them lightly, always ready to be changed. We prefer descriptive to diagnostic terms and, if possible, the use of clients' words to describe their plights. We support a collaborative effort in which clients' views are primary (constructionist). But we also see the need for the worker's expertise to guide the process (empiricist). Thus, we see the work of assessment proceeding within the tensions of differing intellectual traditions. These tensions have existed throughout the history of the profession.

The History of Assessment and Formulation in Social Work

From early in its history, social work has struggled to lose its association with friendly visiting and be recognized as a profession. In 1917, Mary Richmond's seminal book, *Social Diagnosis*, set in motion assessments that involved investigative studies of clients and their families and, based on these studies, the development of diagnoses that defined treatment. Although strongly influenced by the medical model, Richmond incorporated ideas of community context and individual and family strengths into her view of diagnosis.

Since these early beginnings, changes in the assessment and formulation process can be divided into three categories: shifts related to ideological differences, the influence of new practice models and approaches, and recurrent themes. In the material that follows we highlight each area.

Conceptual Shifts

Whereas early evaluations employed a linear, cause-and-effect view of problems, an appreciation for multicausality gradually emerged (Hollis & Woods, 1981). The need to collect a large number of facts about a client or situation was tempered by recognition of the importance of the meaning that events and situations had for clients. A focus on relationships and the client's relational history was prominent early on (Graybeal, 2007; Perlman, 1979); in the past 20 years, there has been more interest in problems, solutions, and behavior (de Shazar, 1985; Madsen, 2007).

Interest in developing a scientific base for the profession moved social work beyond the earliest forms of assessment, which were based on determinations of worthiness (Brill & Taler, 1990; Canda & Furman, 1999; Richmond, 1917). However, there have been strong differences as to the ways that science is defined, along with notions of how scientific interests should affect the process of assessment and treatment (Graybeal, 2007; Witkin & Harrison, 2001).

Assessments became more sensitive to the impact of race, culture and ethnicity, gender, and sexual orientation (Boyd-Franklin, 1989; Laird & Green, 1996; McGoldrick, 1998; Panos & Panos, 2000; Pinderhughes, 1989). The impact of immigration, whether recent or in an earlier generation, has become a more current focus, along with greater understanding of the strain of acculturation and of intergenerational conflicts in immigrant families (Mirkin, 1998; Mock, 1998).

Understanding of the role of social injustices and oppression as causal factors in people's troubles and the need to assess their impact has always been part of social work thinking. Issues of reform and community solidarity raised by Reynolds (1973) in the 1930s evolved into later models of empowerment that focused assessments on the strengths of individuals and the resources in their communities (Lee, 2001; Reynolds; Weinberg, 2006).

Influence of New Theories, Models, and Approaches

As new theories, models, and approaches emerged in the human sciences, they were taken up by social work and were influential in assessment and formulation. Psychoanalytic theory, as it took hold in the United States in the 1940s, turned social workers' attention to intrapsychic causes and personal history (Hollis & Woods, 1981). This psychoanalytic focus was followed in the 1970s by a wave of family therapies that focused on larger systems, groups, and family interactions and structures (Brill & Taler, 1990; Minuchin, 1974; Shulman, 1992). The psychodynamic and systemic methods spawned many schools and therapies, which were readily absorbed and then discarded by social work programs (H. Goldstein, 2001). Each new model prioritized something slightly different in the evaluation and treatment process.

Social work's basic interest in context, expressed early in the "person-in-environment" configuration, was broadened with the introduction of the ecological model (Germaine & Gitterman, 1996). Increasingly, there has been a turn toward a risk and resilience form of ecological model that allows workers to conceptualize a problem at multiple levels and consider the internal or external risk and protective factors (Corcoran & Nichols-Casebolt, 2004).

Recurrent and Expanded Interests

In a reaction to the deterministic and diagnostic directions of Freudian theory, humanistic concerns with individual will and people's strengths emerged at different historic times, as seen in the Functional School in the 1930s (Robinson, 1930), and the "strengths perspective" in the 1990s (Saleeby, 2005). Belief in the importance of focusing on health instead of pathology changed the direction of assessments (Saleeby, 2005; Weick, 1986). The biological part of a "biopsychosocial" formulation was broadened to include considerations of health, fitness, genetic endowments, predispositions, and "normal" changes associated with life phases, such as aging. The concept of able-bodiedness reshaped consideration of physical challenges. New understandings of mind–body connections led to an awareness of the relationships between spirituality and religious beliefs to well-being and the importance of including these areas in assessments (Griffith & Griffith, 2003; Perry, 1998).

Finally, the debate about the relationship of science to social work practice has been recurring and, at times, sharp and divisive. It is currently represented by the evidence-based practice movement (O'Hare, 2005). The practices of assessment and treatment that this movement supports collapse models of research and practice, so that the process of formulation becomes problem analysis (O'Hare). Problems are rendered in the form of research questions and then used to search the professional literature for interventions supported or informed by controlled experiments. Evidence-based practices currently available are studied in terms of their applicability and appropriateness in a particular situation and modified as necessary to the situation at hand. Outcomes are defined operationally and then assessed according to standardized outcome measures (Rosen, 2003).

Ongoing Tensions

Tensions observed in these conflicting approaches have carried forward in current practice. These include conflicts inherent in balancing the profession's commitment to strength-based assessment with models or settings that require diagnosis of illness, deficits, or risks. There are additional conflicts between a commitment to a collaborative approach with clients and situations that require the social worker to render an "expert" or diagnostic opinion (e.g., assessment of suicidality). Finally, there are strong differences regarding ways to ensure the effectiveness of social work practice. These ongoing strains are not necessarily resolvable since responses to them emanate from very different knowledge orientations. We believe they add to the vitality of the profession.

Components in Social Work Assessments and Formulations

Social work practice has been shaped by interests and necessities that fluctuate over time. But the values of the profession are foundational. They have remained constant, but their meaning has evolved as social work practitioners have become more cognizant of the dimensions of power, oppression, and difference.

Social Justice Perspective

A primary social work value is the belief that all human beings should be treated as unique individuals with certain basic rights including the right to self-determination. The profession's commitment to social justice emphasizes that many peoples' problems reflect the difficulties of living in an unjust and oppressive society. These values are reflected in social work formulations that include the uniquely individual characteristics that affect a person's well-being and the institutional and political dimensions of people's problems.

Thus, formulation begins with a social justice perspective that takes into account the ways in which social forces and conditions constrain clients' lives and affect the ways we see them. These forces include the devastating effects of poverty and violence along with prejudices enacted in relation to gender, race, age, class, ability, sexual orientation, and other differences. A social justice perspective that is sensitive to power and social inequities also focuses social workers on their social identities and power in relation to clients. This sensitivity to differences can make it less likely that oppression will be unwittingly repeated in the worker–client relationship.

Ecological Perspective

An ecological perspective emphasizes the dynamic transactions between people and the multiple social systems, subsystems, and environments in which they participate. This understanding requires careful observation of the actual places where clients spend their time (homes, schools, communities, and streets) to determine if clients' interactions with their environments are enriching and supportive, or limiting and destructive. It includes using structural data that provide a demographic understanding of the resources and challenges of clients' neighborhoods, with attention to community-based indicators of well-being (Ung, 2004). An ecological assessment begins with clients' assessments of their communities and includes their creative solutions to community challenges. An empowerment approach engages diverse resources to enable clients to find solutions, expand their capacities, and enhance the possibilities of their communities.

Diversity and Cross-Cultural Sensitivity

Since the 1970s, social work literature has been particularly attentive to the impact of culture, race, and ethnicity on peoples' identities (Atkinson, Morten, & Sue, 1979; Boyd-Franklin, 1989; McGoldrick, Giordano, & Pearce,

1996; Pinderhughes, 1989; Staples, 1978; Sue, 1981). Early clinical approaches to diversity, coming from a modernist orientation, used more static and essential views of ethnicity, culture, and race.

In contemporary practice when a postmodern frame is used, the changing, evolving, contextual, and interactive nature of identities is stressed (Laird, 1998). Social workers are encouraged to appreciate the limits of their knowledge and work from a "not-knowing" and curious position, one that supports empathic attunement and learning what it is like to be in another's shoes (Anderson & Goolishian, 1992; Dean, 2001). Clinicians need to be aware of the prejudices, attitudes, and distortions they carry in regard to other groups and to be self-critical and open to new understandings (Comas-Diaz & Jacobsen, 1991; Hamilton-Mason, 2004; Perez Foster, 1999). Sensitivity, respectful curiosity, openness, and self-awareness are the hallmarks of a formulation undertaken from a cross-cultural perspective.

Systemic Approaches

A systemic perspective focuses specifically on the systems in a client's life such as the family, workplace, church, or community. The art of formulation lies in making a determination of the size of the client system to be approached and the necessary scope of the inquiry. The work might be with a family subsystem, the nuclear family, or members of the extended family; it might include several families in the same community who have a mutual interest, or several community groups (e.g. teenagers, their parents, and the police). The focal system could change as issues improve in one area and become apparent in another.

There are a multitude of systemic theories and approaches to understanding small groups and families. The direction of the formulation and clinical work depends on which theories are used. The field has moved from a focus on assessing structures (Minuchin, 1974) to understanding interactive processes (Lowe, 2004). More recently in narrative approaches, attention is being given to clients' stories. If a client's story is problem-saturated, there is an effort to help the client replace it with stories of strengths and resilience, often located at the margins of a client's awareness (Anderson & Goolishian, 1992; White & Epston, 1990). Clients and social workers become partners in co-constructing new narratives.

A systemic perspective focuses on external, observable patterns and processes, as well as articulated stories. To understand the client's problem from a psychological perspective, the focus turns to intrapsychic phenomena.

Psychological Perspective

A psychodynamic approach posits that life events, situations, and early relationships are internalized and influence ongoing behavior (E. Goldstein, 1995; Hollis & Woods, 1981). There have been many psychodynamic "schools"; each highlights different aspects of behavior and development and shapes the lens of the formulation process accordingly. Some focus on conflict and resolution; others, on early relational experiences that shape ongoing behavior; and still others, on self-development or attachment. All assume that development occurs in stages—each phase with its own challenges and opportunities—and that the way that these challenges are managed affects a person's ongoing development and behavior (Erikson, 1950; Perry et al., 1987). Individual responses are seen as adaptive and as representing the best possibility for the person at the time they occur, even if they become maladaptive later in life. The relationship between the social worker and client is considered an additional source of insight regarding the client's relational style and patterns.

In this discussion of factors to be considered in formulation we have moved from a broad view of political and institutional forces to a consideration of neighborhood environments, family systems, and individual psychology. At the individual level, two additional aspects of human functioning to consider are biology and spirituality.

Biological Perspective

The biological component of a biopsychosocial formulation has gained importance, with genetic factors receiving particular attention at present. Patterns of substance abuse and family history of mental illness are included in a biological assessment, along with indicators of well-being or illness (Bisman, 2001). Cultural beliefs about health, disease, and healing need to be understood; it is important that Western biases not be imposed on clients from diverse cultures (Panos & Panos, 2000). Past and present sexual behavior and attitudes, as well as sexual dysfunction, would be appropriate subjects for a formulation if relevant to the issues for which the client is seeking help.

Assessments of persons with disabilities need to distinguish between impairment, the "physical, sensory, cognitive, or systemic condition that directly imposes a reduction in certain functions," and disability, "those barriers and reductions in function imposed by the physical and psychosocial environment" (Olkin, 1999, p. 89). The locus of impairment is in the person whereas the locus of disability is in the sociopolitical environment (Olkin).

Spiritual Perspective

Clinicians have not always explored the spiritual component in clients' lives (Gotterer, 2001; Thayne, 1998). Yet the lack of assessment of this dimension can prevent clients and clinicians from using the full array of resources that have been shown to be helpful (Canda & Furman, 1999; Gotterer; Perry, 1998). Information about a person's spiritual perspective and religious beliefs offers insight into the ways they see themselves and the world (Thayne). Definitions of spirituality differ and may or may not be connected to a person's membership in a formal religious group (Canda & Furman; Gotterer). Recent writers have offered ideas about sensitive ways to conduct a spiritual and religious assessment (Griffith & Griffith, 2003; Pargament, 2007). Although spiritual and religious beliefs can serve as sources of strength, they can also be problematic for clients.

We have identified seven potential components of a social work assessment: social justice, ecological, cross-cultural, systemic, psychodynamic, biological, and spiritual. Now we will present a model that shows how these areas are woven together into a formulation.

Model for Formulation: Process and Format

Work with clients inevitably begins with an inquiry guided by the reasons for referral. During the assessment phase, information is collected and recorded in a number of domains including environmental factors, relevant systems (i.e., family, school, work, etc.), cultural background, and developmental history. The social worker observes the client's appearance, affect, behavior, and ways of relating and telling his or her story. The client's strengths are highlighted. Information collected during the assessment phase that is considered most important to understanding the client or situation is then briefly summarized in the formulation.

The formulation, as written or presented, begins by repeating the client's identifying demographic information and includes relevant identifying information about the worker. Each of the parties brings aspects of identity to the interaction that will affect the relationship, the possibilities for understanding, and the work they do together. Including information about the worker makes it possible to note and highlight differences, similarities, and the interactive possibilities and challenges.

Information collected during the assessment phase that is considered most important to understanding the client or situation is then briefly incorporated in a discussion of the issues from any of the perspectives that pertain: social justice, ecological, cultural, systemic, psychodynamic, biological, and spiritual. The co-constructed formulation continues with a statement of goals and a plan of interventions consistent with these goals. There can be a consideration of aspects of the clinical relationship that might be helpful or problematic. If research is available to guide the treatment planning, it is cited in the formulation as part of the justification of the intervention to be used. The formulation concludes with a specification of desired outcomes and a plan for evaluating results. When possible, goals are stated in measurable terms, but we would not restrict goals to those that can be quantified.

The scope of the inquiry and the depth of the formulation are dependent on the client's concerns, the function of the agency in which the client is seen, and the time available for the work. Although the worker is guiding the inquiry, a collaborative approach should be maintained. There needs to be a balance between the worker's use of questions and space for clients to tell their stories in ways that are natural and holistic. At the end of the process, the worker and client together make decisions about priorities. The following example of a client with whom one of us worked (Poorvu) is provided to demonstrate the process of assessment and formulation as illustrated in Figure 1.

Figure 1. *Assessment and formulation outline.*

I. Identifying demographic information regarding client and worker: reason for referral, agency context, presenting problem, and history of the problem.
II. Summary of relevant biopsychosocial information: This may include client's history, environmental situation, cultural background, class, family, work and other systems, individual psychological factors including developmental history, biological factors, and spirituality.
III. Formulation: Brief conceptualization of the issues from social justice, ecological, cultural, systemic, psychodynamic, biological, and spiritual perspectives as relevant.
IV. Exploration of literature for evidence-informed interventions.
V. Goals, interventions to be used, and justification for these choices.
VI. Advantages and challenges in the clinical relationship.
VII. Plan for evaluation.

Example

Presenting Problem

Angela, a 20-year-old White Irish woman, is referred for support by her son's pediatrician, when 10-month-old Brian is diagnosed with malabsorption and severe chronic bowel disease and admitted to the hospital. She reports that Brian has always been difficult to feed despite her efforts at trying different types of bottles and formulas. Brian has numerous stools each day, increasing the money spent on disposable diapers because Angela does not have time to wash cotton ones. Angela admits that her frustration often renders her tearful and hopeless about being an adequate mother for Brian. She states, "I just thought Brian was small and troublesome. I didn't think he was really sick." The hospitalization has added to her stress, despair, and difficulty sleeping.

Summary of Biopsychosocial Information

Angela, a single mother, was abandoned by the baby's father, her high school boyfriend, after telling him she was pregnant. She is determined to manage Brian's care alone. Angela lives with her son and mother in a rented apartment (a two-bedroom, third-floor walk-up) in a working-class, tightly knit, mostly Irish neighborhood in Boston. In addition to her responsibilities as a mother, Angela is also caring for her mother, who is frail, has chronic emphysema, and requires oxygen and an array of other services. This means that Angela cannot stay overnight with Brian at the hospital. Her father, an alcoholic, is homeless, unemployed, and in minimal contact with the family. Angela's girlfriends help out, but she knows that her mother really wants only her. Thus, she feels torn between the needs of her mother and her son.

Angela had heard stories from her immigrant grandparents about prejudice against the Irish that they encountered upon arriving in Boston. She expects similar treatment, saying that Irish Catholics should "stick to their own kind." Her mother insists that one doesn't share one's business outside of the family. Angela has become increasingly uncomfortable with the growing Hispanic population in her neighborhood and with the gang of boys who hang out at the corner convenience store.

Angela is unemployed. She and Brian have the support of several government assistance programs, including Temporary Assistance for Needy Families; the Special Supplemental Nutrition Program for Women, Infants, and Children; and Medicaid. She wonders if her poverty will prevent Brian from getting the treatment he needs at the hospital clinic. His condition requires that he be fed with breast milk that has to be bought at a high cost. Angela states, "That must be for rich people; how will I ever afford it?"

Angela has many close relationships with women friends and a positive relationship with her mother. Demonstrating her capacity for insight, Angela says that her early negative experiences with her father made her untrusting of men in general. She fears that Dr. Smith might judge her for being a "welfare mom" and refuse to be Brian's pediatrician.

Angela has never seen a social worker and states, "Strong people shouldn't need help." Angela wonders how it will be to talk to a non-Catholic social worker. Comforted by her worker's being the same age as her mother, Angela decides to give the relationship a try. The clinician is aware of her maternal and protective feelings toward Angela, as she remembers what it was like to be a new mother.

Formulation

This 20-year-old new mother and her family contend daily with the effects of poverty, poor health, and inequities in the health care system. Her social worker, a 50-year-old married Jewish mother of three adult children, lives in comfortable circumstances and takes for granted access to good health care. It is important that the worker be mindful of these differences in circumstances.

Angela lives fearfully, concerned about the shifting demographics of her neighborhood and the increase in gun violence and gang-related crime. She has been raised with core beliefs about sticking to one's own kind, and she expects to be misunderstood by others. She has few models of women empowered to make beneficial changes, since she has been surrounded by women who share her circumstances and sense of a lack of power. She is easily intimidated by hospital staff and fears criticism from the doctor. Angela appears to have a secure relationship with her mother. But she is stressed by being in charge of a multigenerational family with serious needs, at an age when she might benefit from nurturing. While she is able to advocate well for herself, and to negotiate difficult welfare systems, the frustrations at times overwhelm her and exhaust her problem-solving ability. Her identity as an Irish American appears to be a source of pride. Likewise, her strong religious beliefs and rituals sustain her.

Angela seems to be having difficulty taking in the seriousness of her child's illness. She continues to think that he is just a fussy, colicky baby.

Relevant Writing and Research

The literature concerning social work practice with families of pediatric patients, which is anecdotal and not research based, supports the importance of developing an empathic relationship and validating the parents' identity as parents and the decisions they have made. The ongoing assessment needs to consider the problems that existed before the child's illness (Dungan, Jaquay, Reznik, & Sands, 1995).

Goals and Interventions

1. Assist Angela in managing the stress of Brian's hospitalization. It is important that the social worker and staff understand the stress Angela experiences in being the sole caregiver for her mother and her son. The possibility of providing parking and food service vouchers and of arranging for a visiting nurse for her mother will be explored. Offering these services, as needed, will be helpful in building a relationship with Angela and in enabling her to recognize that her needs are important to the staff.
2. Assist Angela in developing a new view of her son and his future, as well as her own future. The use of support and clarification will enable the social worker to provide a relationship within which Angela can grieve the loss of the child she expected and develop a bond with Brian, as he is. Angela has suggested that she has conflicted feelings about men, having been abandoned by her father and her boyfriend. If she is willing, it could be helpful to explore her feelings about men and how she imagines it will be to raise a male child in a changing neighborhood that doesn't feel safe. The social worker will explore the ways in which having this baby derailed other plans she might have had for herself and evaluate how she is adjusting to the loss of that anticipated life.

3. Support Angela's strengths. The social worker will encourage Angela's current level of functioning by having her continue to make arrangements for the concrete services needed upon discharge, including contacting the Worcester Breast Milk Bank. The social worker will encourage ongoing use of her church and friends for support.
4. Referral to a support group for mothers of children with gastrointestinal disorders. Participation in such a group might support Angela in her ongoing struggles with Brian's care. It could also help her develop an awareness of social injustices and inequities in the health care system and help her advocate for better health care for herself and others like her.
5. Continue to investigate research specific to helping parents of children with gastrointestinal disorders. A search of the Social Work Abstracts database using the keywords "Pediatric G.I. Disorders" uncovered the following citation: Hathaway, P. (1989). Failure to thrive: knowledge for social workers. *Health Social Work, 14*(2). Since such disorders might initially present as failure to thrive, a keyword search using this term elicits 37 more articles.

Treatment Relationship

Mindful of her maternal feelings toward Angela, the worker will be careful to empower her by not taking over. It will also be important to be curious about Angela's experience of growing up Irish and to encourage her to express concerns about religious and ethnic differences between herself and the social worker. Showing empathy for the strain of being torn between her mother's needs and those of her son will help Angela to feel trusting and safe; this will enable the sharing of strong feelings.

Plan for Evaluation

Signs of success will include the following:

1. Decreased anxiety and sadness could be measured by depression scales at the beginning, middle, and end of the treatment.
2. Increased comfort on the unit and trust in the staff would be measured by self-reports and observations of multiple staff members.
3. Increased comfort in managing Brian's care would be measured according to a decrease in anxious phone calls and increased instances of advocating for Brian's care and making follow-up calls and arrangements.
4. Increased confidence in her own judgment and efforts would be evidenced by decreased requests for support from the worker and increased reports of her successful management of situations.

Conclusion

Every clinical situation is unique and leads to the collection of information and development of a formulation specific to the particular circumstances of that situation. At the same time, the values and interests of the social work profession require a broad approach to assessment and formulation that integrates social justice, ecological, systemic, biological, cultural, spiritual, and psychological perspectives. At this time in the history of social work, there are pressures to reduce, simplify, and reconfigure the assessment and formulation process in ways that will redefine practice. We advocate a model for assessment and formulation that is broadly conceived. It contains components historically important in social work; our model reconfigures them in the light of contemporary theories and approaches. With a comprehensive model for assessment and formulation, we can sustain the richness of multiple orientations and understandings that best inform our work.

References

American Psychiatric Association. (2000). *Diagnostic and statistical manual of mental disorders* (4th ed., text revision). Washington, DC: Author.

Anderson, H., & Goolishian, H. (1992). The client is the expert: A not-knowing approach to therapy. In S. McNamee & K. Gergen (Eds.), *Therapy as social construction* (pp. 25–39). Newbury Park, CA: Sage.

Atkinson, D. R., Morten, G., & Sue, D. W. (1979). *Counseling American minorities: A cross cultural perspective* (3rd ed.). Dubuque, IA: Brown.

Barlas, S. (2006). Mental health budgets take another hit. *Psychiatric Times, 23*(5), 22.

Bisman, C. D. (2001). Teaching social work's bio-psycho-social assessment. *Journal of Teaching in Social Work, 21*(3/4) 75–89.

Boyd-Franklin, N. (1989). *Black families in therapy: A multisystems approach.* New York: Guilford Press.

Brill, M., & Taler, A. (1990). A spiral model for teaching psychosocial assessment. *Journal of Teaching in Social Work, 4*(1), 67–83.

Canda, E., & Furman, L. D. (1999). *Spiritual diversity in social work practice: The heart of helping.* New York: Free Press.

Cohen, J. A. (2003). Managed care and the evolving role of the clinical social worker in mental health. *Social Work, 48*(1), 34–43.

Comas-Diaz, L., & Jacobsen, F. M. (1991). Ethnocultural transference and countertransference in the therapeutic dyad. *American Journal of Orthopsychiatry, 61*(3), 392–402.

Corcoran, J., & Nichols-Casebolt, A. (2004). Risk and resilience ecological framework for assessment and goal formulation. *Child and Adolescent Social Work Journal, 21*(3), 211–235.

de Shazar, S. (1985). *Keys to solution in brief therapy.* New York: Norton.

Dean, R. G. (1993). Constructivism: An approach to clinical practice. *Smith College Studies in Social Work, 63*(2), 127–145.

Dean, R. G. (2001). The myth of cross-cultural competence. *Families in Society: The Journal of Contemporary Human Services, 82*(6), 623–630.

Dungan, S. S., Jaquay, T. R., Reznik, K. A., & Sands, E. A. (1995). Pediatric critical care social work: Clinical practice with parents of critically ill children. *Social Work in Health Care, 21*(1), 69–80.

Erikson, E. (1950). *Childhood and society.* New York: Norton.

Furman, R., & Langer, C. L. (2006). Managed care and the care of the soul. *Journal of Social Work Values and Ethics, 3*(2). Retrieved November 5, 2007, from http://www.socialworker.com/jswve/content/view/39/46/

Gambrill, E. (2006). Evidence-based practice and policy: Choices ahead. *Research on Social Work Practice, 16*(3), 338–358.

Germaine, C. B., & Gitterman, A. (1996). *The life model of social work practice.* New York: Columbia University Press.

Goldstein, E. (1995). *Ego psychology and social work practice* (2nd ed.). New York: Free Press.

Goldstein, H. (2001). *Experiential learning: A foundation for social work education and practice.* Alexandria, VA: Council of Social Work Education.

Gotterer, R. (2001). The spiritual dimension in clinical social work practice: A client perspective. *Families in Society: The Journal of Contemporary Human Services, 82*(2), 187–193.

Graybeal, C. T. (2007). Evidence for the art of social work. *Families in Society: The Journal of Contemporary Social Services, 88*(4), 513–523.

Griffith, J. L., & Griffith, M. E. (2003). *Encountering the sacred in psychotherapy: How to talk with people about their spiritual lives.* New York: Guilford Press.

Hamilton-Mason, J. (2004). Psychodynamic perspectives: Responding to the assessment needs of people of color. *Smith College Studies in Social Work, 74*(2), 315–332.

Hollis, F., & Woods, M. E. (1981). *Casework: A psychosocial therapy.* New York: McGraw-Hill.

Irving, A. (1999). Waiting for Foucault: Social work and the multitudinous truth(s) of life. In A. S. Chambon, A. Irving, & L. Epstein (Eds.), *Reading Foucault for social work.* (pp. 27–50). New York: Columbia University Press.

Iversen, R. R., Gergen, K. J., & Fairbanks II, R. P. (2005). Assessment and social construction: Conflict of co-creation. *British Journal of Social Work, 35,* 689–708.

Krugman, P. (2007). *The conscience of a liberal.* New York: Norton.

Laird, J. (1998). Theorizing culture: Narrative ideas and practice principles. In M. McGoldrick, (Ed.), *Re-visioning family therapy* (pp. 20–36). New York: Guilford Press.

Laird, J., & Green, R. (1996). *Lesbians and gays in couples and families: A handbook for therapists.* San Francisco: Jossey-Bass.

Lee, J. A. B. (2001). *The empowerment approach to social work practice: Building the beloved community.* New York: Columbia University Press.

Lowe, R. (2004). *Family therapy: A constructive framework.* Thousand Oaks, CA: Sage.

Madsen, W. C. (2007). *Collaborative therapy with multi-stressed families* (rev. ed.) New York: Guilford Press.

Mattaini, M. A., & Kirk, S. A. (1991). Assessing assessment in social work. *Social Work, 36*(3), 260–266.

McGoldrick, M. (Ed.). (1998). *Re-visioning family therapy: Race, culture, and gender in clinical practice.* New York: Guilford Press.

McGoldrick, M., Giordano, J., & Pearce, J. K. (Eds.). (1996). *Ethnicity and family Therapy* (2nd ed.). New York: Guilford Press.

Minuchin, S. (1974). *Families and family therapy.* Cambridge, MA: Harvard University Press.

Mishne, J. (2004). Managed mental health care, suicidal despair, and countertransference: A clinical tragedy. *Psychoanalytic Social Work, 11*(2), 55–70.

Mirkin, M. P. (1998). The impact of multiple contexts on recent immigrant families. In M. McGodrick (Ed.), *Revisioning family therapy: Race, culture and gender in clinical practice* (pp. 370–383). New York: Guilford Press.

Mock, M. (1998). Clinical reflections on refugee families: Transforming crises into opportunities. In M. McGodrick (Ed.), *Revisioning family therapy: Race, culture and gender in clinical practice* (pp. 347–369). New York: Guilford Press.

O'Hare, T. (2005). *Evidence-based practices for social workers: An interdisciplinary approach.* Chicago: Lyceum Press.

Olkin, R. (1999). The personal, professional and political when clients have disabilities. *Women and Therapy, 22*(2), 87–103.

Panos, P. T., & Panos, A. J. (2000). A model for a culture-sensitive assessment of patients in health care settings. *Social Work in Health Care, 31*(1), 49–62.

Pargament, K. I. (2007). *Spiritually integrated psychotherapy.* New York: Guilford Press.

Parton, N., & O'Byrne, P. (2000). *Constructive social work: Towards a new practice.* New York: St. Martin's Press.

Perez Foster, R. (1999). An intersubjective approach to cross-cultural clinical work. *Smith College Studies in Social Work, 69*(2), 269–292.

Perlman, H. H. (1979). *Relationship: The heart of helping people.* Chicago: University of Chicago Press.

Perry, G. F. (1998). The relationship between faith and well-being. *Journal of Religion and Health, 37*(2), 125–136.

Perry, S., Cooper, A. M., & Michels, R. (1987). The psychodynamic formulation: Its purpose, structure, and clinical application. *The American Journal of Psychiatry, 144*(5), 543–550.

Pinderhughes, E. (1989). *Understanding race, ethnicity, and power: The key to efficacy in clinical practice.* New York: Free Press.

Reynolds, B. (1973). *Between client and community: A study in responsibility: Social case work.* New York: Oriole.

Richmond, M. E. (1917). *Social diagnosis.* New York: Russell Sage Foundation.

Robinson, V. (1930). *A changing psychology in social casework.* Chapel Hill: University of North Carolina Press.

Rosen, A. (2003). Evidence-based social work practice: Challenges and promise. *Social Work Research, 27*(4), 197–208.

Ross, D. E. (2000). A method for developing a biopsychosocial formulation. *Journal of Child and Family Studies, 9*(1), 1–6.

Saleeby, D. (2005). *The strengths perspective in social work practice* (4th ed.). Boston: Allyn & Bacon.

Schneider, A., Hyer, K., & Luptak, M. (2000). Suggestions to social workers for surviving in managed care. *Health and Social Work, 25*(4), 276–280.

Sellick, M. M., Delaney, R., & Brownlee, K. (2002). The deconstruction of professional knowledge: Accountability without authority. *Families in Society: The Journal of Contemporary Social Services, 83*(5/6), 493–498.

Shulman, L. (1992). *The skills of helping individuals, families and groups.* Itasca, IL: Peacock.

Staples, R. (1978). *The black family: Essays and studies.* (2nd ed.). Belmont, CA: Wadsworth.

Stoil, M. J. (2001). Bush budget winners and losers. *Behavioral Health Management, 21*(3), 9–10.

Sue, D. W. (1981). *Counseling the culturally different: Theory and practice.* New York: Wiley.

Thayne, T. R. (1998). Opening space for clients' religious and spiritual values in therapy: A social constructionist perspective. *Journal of Family Social Work, 2*(4), 12–23.

Ung, T. (2004). *Demographic mapping: Using ecoscans to enhance student application of ecological perspectives to practice.* Unpublished manuscript.

Urek, M. (2005). Making a case in social work: The construction of an unsuitable mother. *Qualitative Social Work, 4*(4), 451–467.

Weick, A. (1986). Issues in overturning a medical model of social work practice. *Social Casework, 67*(9), 551–559.

Weinberg, M. (2006). Pregnant with possibility: The paradoxes of "help" as anti-oppression and discipline with a young single mother. *Families in Society: The Journal of Contemporary Social Services, 87*(2), 161–169.

White, M., & Epston, D. (1990). *Narrative means to therapeutic ends.* New York: Norton.

Witkin, S. L., & Harrison, W. D. (2001). Whose evidence and for what purpose? *Social Work, 46*(4), 293–297.

Ruth G. Dean, PhD, LICSW, is professor, Simmons College School of Social Work. **Nancy Levitan Poorvu,** MSW, LICSW, is adjunct professor, Simmons College School of Social Work. Correspondence regarding this article may be addressed to the first author at ruth.dean@simmons.edu or at 300 The Fenway, Boston, MA 02115.

Manuscript received: March 16, 2007
Revised: December 19, 2007
Accepted: January 22, 2008

Clinical Reasoning for Child and Adolescent Mental Health Practitioners: *The Mindful Formulation*

SOPHIE S. HAVIGHURST
University of Melbourne, Australia

LAUREL DOWNEY
James Cook University, Australia

ABSTRACT

This article outlines a systematic approach to the formulation of clinical problems for practitioners working with children and their families. Whilst assessments in child and adolescent mental health often use a range of theoretical and practical approaches for data collection, there are relatively few resources to assist the clinician in integrating this information to develop a formulation that leads to a well considered intervention plan. The formulation approach presented here was designed to assist in training child and adolescent clinicians in a method that facilitates the process of understanding complex cases. This is done by examining the patterns of strength and difficulty identified during an assessment and systematically providing an explanation for these using 'the Four Ps' – predisposing, precipitating, perpetuating, and protective factors – to structure the clinician's thinking. Interventions that address patterns of strength and difficulty for each of the 'Four Ps' are recommended when working with complex clients. This formulation approach may take more time than merely summarizing the case, but the benefits are a more comprehensive understanding of the client. This means that problems often associated with working with complex cases can be identified and addressed, reducing the risk of drop out, poor engagement or treatment failure.

KEYWORDS

assessment, child and adolescent mental health, clinical reasoning, formulation, intervention planning

Introduction

HOW DO WE UNDERSTAND the presentation of the clients we see? How do we make sense of the stories families tell about their lives in the context of extensive theoretical and empirical literature about development, relationships, and personality functioning? What are the best approaches for training new clinicians who are attempting this

Clinical Child Psychology and Psychiatry Copyright © The Author(s), 2009.
Reprints and permissions: http://www.sapepub.co.uk/journalsPermissions.nav
Vol 14(2): 251–271. DOI: 10.1177/1359104508100888 http://ccp.sagepub.com

challenging task? Having a framework for the systematic link between knowledge and practice is essential for delivering effective and appropriate interventions. This article outlines a series of steps which may be useful for those seeking to learn clinical formulation.

The Mindful Formulation has been specifically designed for infant, child, adolescent and family mental health contexts; however, it is likely to be useful in other settings. Our review of the clinical literature has shown that there are very few resources to systematically help the clinician to take the information gained in an assessment and use it to formulate an explanation about what is happening in the case. As a result, there is little consistency across clinical services. The approach that we have developed aims to explain patterns of difficulties and strengths through a rich understanding of the case history and current dynamics – instead of just a description of symptoms as so often occurs in practice. Linking the hypothesized explanation for these patterns to the intervention plan was an important step we felt was lacking in the empirical and clinical literature. We also wanted to ensure that intervention planning addressed the breadth of the presenting difficulties across the child's ecological system and to ensure the interventions addressed the predisposing, precipitating, perpetuating and protective factors. Finally, we wanted to ensure that this approach to formulation would incorporate the developmental and contextual factors that are essential for determining interventions with children, and which are often not adequately attended to in formulations targeting adult clients.

Contextual basis for a formulation framework

At *Mindful*, a range of training programmes are offered to clinicians specializing in child and adolescent mental health. As part of the training programmes we offer, in particular in the Developmental Psychiatry Course[1], clinicians are taught a process by which they integrate information collected in an assessment into a formulation. The experience of teachers in the programme has been that developing skills in formulation poses one

---

ACKNOWLEDGEMENTS: This article is a result of a partnership project between *Mindful*, at the University of Melbourne and Take Two, Berry Street Victoria. Sadly, during this the time of writing this article Dr Howard Cooper, the Director of *Mindful*, was killed in an accident. We wish to acknowledge the wonderful guidance and leadership that Howard provided to us both over the time that we worked with him.

SOPHIE S. HAVIGHURST is a child clinical psychologist and senior lecturer at the University of Melbourne where she teaches child and adolescent mental health practitioners from around Victoria, Australia. She is the Principal Investigator and an author on the *Tuning in to Kids* parenting programme. She also works as a clinical psychologist in private practice and at the Melbourne Children's Court Clinic.

CONTACT: Sophie S. Havighurst, Mindful: Centre for Training and Research in Developmental Health, University of Melbourne, Building C, 50 Flemington Street, Flemington, Melbourne 3031, Australia. [E-mail: sophie.h@unimelb.edu.au]

LAUREL DOWNEY is a family therapist currently working on a child protection and placement research and training project at James Cook University in Far North Queensland. She was previously the Manager of Practice Development and Training for Take Two, a Berry Street programme. Laurel has also worked as the Senior Family Therapist at the Eagle Unit, Victoria's Child Psychiatry inpatient unit.

of the most challenging tasks to training clinicians. To date, teaching about how to formulate has not been as systematic as we would have hoped for, nor has there been an adequate structure for teachers to follow or trainees to use. Supervisors also tell us of the difficulty they have in teaching/supervising new clinicians as they learn to develop formulations, and trainees speak of the confusion arising from a range of supervisors all with different ideas about what a formulation should be.

Generally, it is advocated that a bio-psycho-social model that considers the predisposing, precipitating, perpetuating and protective factors (the Four Ps) in the formulation is used in Child and Adolescent Mental Health Services (Broder & Hood, 1983; Herbert, 2001; Weerasekera, 1996). The Four Ps, and how they are used in formulations, are not always logical, and the leap between knowledge of historical events and the impacts on personality, relationships and functioning is often unclear. *The Mindful Formulation* attempts to break down and operationalize those steps through a series of worksheets, where data is collected and organized before any causal deductions or assumptions are made about the client or family. The model involves steps in reasoning that track from the assessment to a comprehensive formulation. Any intervention plan developed from this process should then reflect this depth.

The need for more sophisticated tools for formulation and intervention planning was also highlighted by the creation of Take Two, a new Victorian state-wide intensive therapeutic service designed to meet the needs of infants, children and adolescents who have been traumatized by child abuse and neglect. Take Two brought together a large group of clinicians with a variety of skills, experience and knowledge. The development of Take Two highlighted a need for a comprehensive practice framework that drew on current literature and research to develop a preferred range of intervention strategies which would adequately meet the needs of this complex client group. *The Mindful Formulation* is one part of that framework. In working on this project for Take Two we found that *The Mindful Formulation* needed little modification to be useful to a wide range of mental health practitioners, and that it was also applicable to other settings, particularly CAMHS – Child and Adolescent Mental Health Services, where highly complex cases are often seen.

An experienced clinician draws on the evidence base (both empirical and practical) along with clinical wisdom and intuition to construct a formulation about the infant, child or adolescent and family they see. The ability to construct a formulation in the mind of an experienced clinician is the result of years of training and experience, knowledge of theory, and the clinician's own personal qualities. The capacity for reflexivity, including awareness of one's own assumptions, motives, cultural attitudes and approaches to interpretation are crucial for good clinical reasoning (Dallos, Wright, Stedmon, & Johnstone, 2006). It has been said that the personal qualities of the clinician are eight times more likely to impact on clinical reasoning than theoretical orientation and clinical training (Mahoney, 1991). This is a hard fact to accommodate when teaching formulation. Formulation skills take years to acquire, hence the challenge in teaching new clinicians. Further, within the child and adolescent mental health field there appears to be some conflict about the benefits and uses of engaging in this process when there are significant case load time pressures. In some countries where cost-cutting to child and adolescent services has occurred, formulation gets lost, treatment gets briefer and interventions are at times perceived to be less effective (Conner & Fisher, 1997).

The framework presented here is intended for use primarily as a learning tool. It takes new clinicians through logical steps to synthesize the information gathered during assessment into a coherent statement that sums up the predicament facing the child and family. Experienced clinicians do this quickly and accurately, using their knowledge, skills, experience and intuition to form their coherent statement. It is hoped that in breaking down the process of formulation, even though this may take some time for a new clinician, it will assist in fast tracking their skill development.

The Mindful Formulation does not advocate any particular theoretical orientation and can be used by clinicians using cognitive-behavioural, psychodynamic, systemic or other frameworks. It explicates a process that many experienced clinicians go through automatically, or intuitively, based on their knowledge and experience. By presenting this model we provide new clinicians with a structure to follow as they begin to organize and reflect on what and how their clients present during assessment. It may also provide a fresh way of approaching assessment and clinical reasoning for the more experienced clinician.

The approach we take in this article uses a modernist framework where causal mechanisms are examined and intervention aims to reduce symptoms and improve social and emotional wellbeing. We understand that the field of child and adolescent mental health has diversified and improved with the advent of postmodern interventions, including narrative, solution focused, and social constructivist therapies. These approaches take a different structural view of children and their families where formulation may not have as central a role. These ways of working are both interesting and exciting, but as yet untested in child and adolescent mental health settings where more traditional therapies hold sway. Consequently, we have not accommodated these ways of thinking into this formulation framework.

The Mindful Formulation has a strengths and difficulties orientation, to steer the clinician's information gathering away from a narrow problem focus. It includes equal attention to the three domains of functioning: the child's experience of self and other, the child's day to day interactions and relationships, and those people and agencies who have influence in the child's life (e.g., school, Protective Services). *The Mindful Formulation* attends to individual processes within the child and within significant others. We advocate for both a child-focused and a family-systems-focused approach to assessment, formulation and intervention. The formulation has been designed in this way to assist the clinician's intervention planning to cover a range of domains in a child's life. This approach has similarities to Weerasekera's (1996) model of formulation that integrates individual and systemic factors into the predisposing, precipitating, perpetuating and protective factors, while including attention to the individual's coping style.

In broadening the formulation process to include all three domains of a child's life we also want to promote an understanding of the intergenerational nature of many human problems, particularly trauma and attachment disruption. In doing so we wish to avoid the common traps in child and adolescent work, neither locating blame for problems in the child, nor in the parent. We believe that a solid systemic foundation, backed up by compassion and wisdom, provides the optimal approach to support and challenge all involved in the child's life, including the child, in addressing the presenting difficulties.

What is a formulation?

A formulation is the clinician's hypothesis about the intra- and inter-personal dynamics that underlie the client's difficulties. It is the process by which the clinician integrates all of the information known about a client and their environment with clinical knowledge and theory, in order to understand their presenting difficulties, the history of these difficulties, and how they are maintained (Herbert, 2001; Johnstone & Dallos, 2006). A good formulation is also collaborative, accounting respectfully for the client's own hypotheses about the problem (for more in-depth exploration of this idea see Dallos et al., 2006). The formulation becomes a working hypothesis that directs the clinician's choice of intervention and assists them in predicting issues that may impede or assist in efforts to bring about change. Good formulation helps the clinician obtain a broader and deeper understanding of the client, guides selection of one treatment modality over another, assists in prediction and understanding of non-compliance, treatment failure and setbacks, and enables the clinician to understand and work within the therapeutic relationship (Persons, 1993).

In some clinical settings, a diagnostic formulation is the end point of a clinical assessment. While this allows for certain problems to be categorized enabling a link to specific forms of treatment, we advocate for a broader formulation that is individually tailored to the client and which can give more accurate predictions about how they will respond to the intervention. Further, in the current climate of clinical services, where comorbidity and case complexity are now the norm, interventions often require multiple modes of therapy involving multiple systems if they are to produce effective and lasting change. This diversity has been met by a range of approaches to formulation across different modalities of therapy (for further exploration of this see Eells, 2007).

The link between assessment and formulation

The process of assessment will not be considered in depth here; however, a number of key aspects of the assessment are necessary for developing a sound formulation. These include:

- A thorough assessment involving the child/young person, family/carers, including the roles of significant extended family, childcare/kindergarten/school, the peer group, and the wider social and cultural context should occur.
- Enquiry into the presenting problem and events occurring around the presenting problem is needed with a focus on the onset, development and maintenance of the problem.
- Strengths should be explored as well as difficulties.
- Aspects of medical and biological functioning should be explored.
- A thorough history of the family, including the intergenerational family history and the child's developmental history are necessary.
- The clinician's observations of presentation and of interpersonal dynamics in the clinic setting should be included as data.
- If assessment is conducted in an outreach context, in the client's home or school, this information should be recorded similarly to information collected in the clinic, and the rationale for such outreach should also be documented.

Fathers are often under-represented in both the assessment and intervention phases of a case. We highlight the necessity of involving fathers, as they are always an important part of the child's life. The marginalization of fathers from therapeutic services limits opportunities for change, and has the unintended outcome of leaving mothers carrying all the responsibility for family difficulties.

Services vary in the depth and breadth of information collected in an assessment – meaning the formulation will vary. Traditionally, CAMHS staff in Victoria conduct three assessment sessions followed by a feedback of the formulation and treatment plan. However, a study by staff at the Maroondah Hospital found that experienced clinicians typically conducted an assessment that provided sufficient information for formulation and treatment planning in two one-hour sessions followed by a feedback session (Luk, Birleson, Wong, & Manders, 1998). Other services advocate for a longer assessment process, while the Royal Australian and New Zealand College of Psychiatrists suggests an assessment can be conducted in one hour (The Royal Australian and New Zealand College of Psychiatrists, 2006). Take Two clients, who frequently experience multiple foster placements, family difficulties and a range of mental health problems, often require a much longer assessment process because it can be difficult to gain enough trust early in the therapeutic relationship to be able to collect sufficient information to make a clear formulation and intervention plan. Family members of children and young people in out-of-home care can be difficult to locate, have often had negative experiences in the past of 'helping professionals', and are often angry and distressed at the loss of their child. Young people who are clients of Take Two often have a similar reluctance to engage with clinicians. Therefore Take Two has stated an optimum assessment period of six sessions to gain as much information as possible, while accepting it may not be everything. Often engagement and the beginning of therapeutic intervention occur during this phase.

Historically, clinicians have been trained to develop formulations from the first point of contact with the client: the referral letter. A hypothetico-deductive method of assessment posits that the clinician establishes a series of hypotheses from the referral that are then evaluated in the assessment process. But this method has been criticized because it may prematurely and possibly incorrectly direct the clinician's attention in the wrong place (Ward & Haig, 1997). Clinicians, especially those new to the field, are prone to a series of biases and common mistakes that make this method of formulating from the first moment problematic. A confirmation bias, where the clinician's first impressions are often resistant to alternative explanations despite new evidence, illustrates potential pitfalls in the clinician's 'first impressions' (Dumont, 1993; Salovey & Turk, 1991). The 'Anchoring Effect' is where a tentative explanation has taken hold in our minds, and information to the contrary may produce not corrections but elaborations of the explanation. Deductions and hypotheses can be wrong and can be based on our own cultural biases and prejudices. Further, in a clinical context where ever increasingly severe cases are seen, the anxiety clinicians experience often creates a need for certainty in our explanations. By utilizing a systematic approach to thinking through a case, the clinician can have some confidence in their clinical reasoning, thereby reducing their anxiety. This provides them with the confidence to state an opinion based on empirical reasoning, while also being open to the possibility of other explanations. It seems clear that this combination of humility, confidence and clarity is a difficult attribute to gain, but without it clinicians tend to both de-emphasize their own knowledge and make tentative, somewhat meaningless, formulations, or boldly assert judgements which are not carefully considered inferences based on thoroughly collected data.

Grounded theory, a qualitative approach to theory generation, advocates that all data is collected and patterns deduced from these data before these patterns are compared and evaluated against existing theory and explanations (Glaser & Strauss, 1967). This approach to theory generation has been applied to clinical assessment and formulation to strengthen the accuracy and treatment utility of case formulation (Ward & Haig, 1997). We advocate for a similar process, especially for the trainee clinician.

While the assessment serves the twin purposes of engagement and the gathering of information, this process should remain relatively objective, although it will be influenced by the subjectivity of the clinician. Formulation on the other hand is the clearly subjective process of making sense of the information gathered to better inform both the mode (CBT or psychodynamic therapy, individual or group/family therapy) and the content of therapy (what is worked on).

Steps in the formulation process: *The Mindful Formulation*

Once all the assessment material is collected, we advocate for a structured process by which this information is integrated with theoretical explanations in order to construct a plausible formulation. We have structured this process in three steps:

1) The first step involves drawing in all the pertinent data using an 'assessment worksheet'.
2) The second step involves identifying patterns of strength and difficulty for the child, significant others, within and amongst significant relationships, and across the system – the 'patterns worksheet'.
3) The third step is where the patterns of strength and difficulty are explained using information from the assessment worksheet and clinical and theoretical knowledge to articulate the predisposing, precipitating, perpetuating, and protective factors in the written formulation.

Step 1: Assessment worksheet – context and history

The first step is to organize the information gathered under a series of headings in the assessment worksheet (Table 1). This information is drawn from clinical assessment, psychometrics, consultations and all other modes of data collection.

Table 1. Assessment worksheet

Presenting problem(s)	List all presenting problems for the identified child and for other family members
Relationships, home & social environments	List all information collected that pertains to family and community context, family history, current and past family/parent relationships, out-of-home care experience and relationships, relationships with peers, relationships with authority figures, school/education situation, community activities, membership of clubs, groups etc. List who the client identifies as significant persons in their life. Describe the home and social environment.
Experience of adverse events	List all events and experiences which could be termed adverse, e.g. abuse, neglect, accidents, disasters, illnesses, medical interventions, losses, etc.
Experience of attachment	Describe early attachment relationships to parents/carers, extended family, others including degree of attunement, perceptions of connection, experiences of separation, loss and neglect – physical and emotional.
Developmental history	List developmental history.
Other developmental factors	List any factors which may affect development, such as temperament, physical or intellectual disability, developmental delays, sight or hearing impediments, speech and language delays, learning difficulties, organic problems.
Safety concerns	Describe any concerns about the client's safety, either danger to them from others, danger to them from themselves, or danger they may be to others. Also include issues of emotional safety, and experiences the client may have of being uncontained in any setting, either emotionally or physically. Describe any other aspects of the clients system where there is a lack of safety.
Resilience factors	List all positive features, interests, ambitions, personal qualities and attributes, skills, talents and positive attributes of aspects of the client, their system, both family and wider community.
Missing information	E.g. information about current relationship between parents, information about the family's connection to community.

Step 2: Patterns worksheet

The second step is to describe the clients' strengths and difficulties across the dimensions of:

- child functioning;
- parents/carers/siblings/significant other's functioning;
- relationships – with the child and among significant others; and
- relationships – with and among community.

Across each of these four dimensions elements of affect, behaviour and cognitions are described to form a matrix from which patterns emerge (Table 2). These patterns, or

Table 2. Patterns worksheet

Child's functioning	*Parents/Carers/Siblings Significant others functioning*	*Relationships – with the child and among significant others*	*Relationships with and among community*
Affective responses	*Affective responses*	*Affective responses*	*Affective responses*
List the client's emotional/affective responses as they relate to self, e.g.:	List the relevant emotional/affective responses of others, e.g.:	List the client's/family system's affective responses as they relate to each other, e.g.:	List the client's emotional/affective responses as they relate to others in the wider system, and affective responses within the system e.g.:
Becomes anxious when faced with new situations	Mother has experienced low mood since the birth of her son	Is warm and affectionate with mother	Becomes emotionally distraught when criticized at school
Finds it difficult to regulate affective arousal when angry or sad	Sister struggles with social anxiety	Becomes sad and withdrawn on returning from contact visits with father	Anxiety in people in the wider system whenever client absconds
Responds warmly to affection from carers	Father has a long standing difficulty with affect regulation	Emotionally cold marital relationship	School staff like and support the client
Is able to calm down after an angry outburst	Mother expresses pleasure at her child's achievements	Is happy when visiting grandmother for contact	
Behaviours	*Behaviours*	*Behaviours*	*Behaviours*
List relevant behaviours as they relate to self, e.g.:	List relevant behaviours of significant others, e.g.:	List relevant behaviours toward/among relationships with significant others, e.g.:	List relevant behaviours as they relate to others in the wider system, and between others in the system, e.g.:
Self-harms, i.e., cuts arms when overwhelmed by emotions	Older brother involved in criminal activity	Intense conflict between maternal and paternal grandparents	Becomes aggressive with peers when losing a game
Engages in risk taking behaviours such as drinking and then driving	Father has alcohol and substance use problems	Coercive behaviour patterns	Is easily led into delinquent behaviours with older peers
Is eating less than recommended for age and development	Mother becomes violent when angry	Is impulsive and distractible at home	Is impulsive and distractible at school
Behaves appropriately at school, but is oppositional at home	Mother has some compulsive and ritualized behaviours	Parents often engage in verbal conflict	Collaborative relationship between all members of the care team
Takes care of younger siblings when mother is ill	Grandmother supports the family by looking after the children while mother works	Parents support each other in relation to client's difficulties	

Table 2. continued

Cognitions	*Cognitions*	*Cognitions*	*Cognitions*
List relevant thoughts and beliefs about self, e.g.:	List relevant thoughts and beliefs of significant others, e.g.:	List relevant thoughts and beliefs about/ among relationships with significant others, e.g.:	List relevant thoughts and beliefs as they relate to others in the wider system, e.g.:
Thinks she is 'bad'	Mother believes child's problems are due to genetic inheritance	Believes that mother will return and he will live with her again	Believes a peer from school is following him
Believes herself to be fat even though has lost significant weight	Mother holds core beliefs about ineffectiveness and herself as a failure	Thinks her mother loves her sister more than her	Thinks Child Protection removed him from home because he is bad
Believes herself to be stupid	Parents believe client is capable of overcoming his difficulties	Mother believes she is powerless to control children	School principal believes the intervention is futile
Believes that school achievement is worthwhile		Father believes mother is solely responsible for parenting	School principal believes the child should not have returned to mother's care
Auditory hallucinations that reflect core fears of being unloved			

phenomenon as they are often referred to in psychiatric literature, encompass areas which formulation will explain and intervention will target. Patterns include typical behaviours, beliefs, schemas, affective expression, skills, relational patterns, actions and responses. Patterns may be symptoms but may be broader than this in order to provide a rich description of the child within their context. Examples of patterns of difficulty may include limited attention, negative beliefs about oneself in social interaction, aggressiveness when feeling threatened, perceiving self as inept, repetitive washing in response to fear of contamination, or coercive cycles of conflict between a parent and child. Patterns of strength may be confidence with friends, an engaging warm interpersonal style, an ability to take other people's perspective, the ability to distract when under significant stress, or school staff being able to contain the child's violent outbursts. Patterns of difficulty are generally the targets of our interventions, but patterns of strength may be the capacities of the child and their system to enact changes.

We have divided the patterns worksheet into those that are affective responses, behaviours and cognitions, and then into those that involve the self, those that involve significant others, relationships with and amongst close others, and those that involve the wider system. While we initially separated the patterns of strength from those of difficulty on the worksheet, we have amended this because strengths may also be a difficulty depending on the context and the informant.

Step 3: The summary and formulation

The third step in the process is to use the previous two worksheets to construct the written formulation. *The Mindful Formulation* begins with a summary and then uses the 'Four Ps' (predisposing, precipitating, perpetuating, and protective factors) to give the formulation structure. We recommend that new clinicians use a separate paragraph to explain each of the 'Four Ps'. The formulation is not a summary or a rehashing of the history, but an integration of how the case history/facts may have shaped patterns of difficulty and strength including protective factors. This is the point where objective assessment and data gathering shifts to subjective theorizing. The theoretical orientation and training experiences of the clinician will play an important role in the explanations that are made about how these patterns arose and are maintained.

The summary At the start of the formulation there should be a summary paragraph of the case (Table 3). This should include the name, age, referral issues and presenting difficulties of the child including (if relevant) current diagnosis and (if relevant) risk of harm/dangerousness/suicide. The summary should read something like:

Table 3. The summary

The summary
[Name] is a [age & gender of child] who has been referred to the [name of service] to explore [client's and system's predicament – statutory case management details, referral question, referrer's desired outcomes]. During assessment the main presenting problems were . . . The client currently meets criteria for [diagnosis where appropriate]. They are currently deemed at low/medium/high risk for . . . [only if appropriate]

Thereafter, follow the four paragraphs outlining the predisposing, precipitating, perpetuating, and protective factors in the formulation.

The formulation: Predisposing factors In the first paragraph, the clinician draws on their information about the case history (assessment worksheet), and theoretical and clinical knowledge to explain how the patterns (patterns worksheet) might have arisen (Table 4). This paragraph weaves a chronological account about how the early years appear to have contributed to patterns in relating/behaving/thinking/feeling in the child and family/carers. This section should begin to draw on concepts from different theories that help to explain the child/family functioning. For example, attachment theory, trauma theory, family systems theories, cognitive-behavioural theories and psychodynamic theories.

Table 4. Predisposing factors

Explain how these patterns have developed – predisposing factors. Use the information from the Assessment worksheet and theoretical/developmental knowledge to explain how you think this history may have predisposed the client/family to these patterns of difficulty (Patterns worksheet).

Discuss how the birth/pregnancy/early environment (in terms of context and the expected or demonstrated effects of this environment) affects the child/family's functioning and family relationships. Include the influence/role of service providers and others in the child's early years. How have these experiences engendered these patterns of difficulty (i.e., methods of affect regulation, coping skills, social skills, intimacy patterns, ability to protect and care etc). For example:

'The pattern of affective dysregulation has arisen in the context of trauma following repeated witnessing of domestic violence where his mother was severely beaten by his father.'

'A strong biological family history of anxiety along with the modelling of avoidant and self critical responses appears to have contributed to early difficulties with social phobia for this child.'

'The pattern of lacking a sense of connection to family or others has arisen as a consequence of early neglect and abuse followed by multiple placements in out-of-home care.'

'Maternal drug use during pregnancy, along with maternal and paternal intellectual disability may have predisposed the child to learning difficulties and developmental delays.'

The formulation: Precipitating factors In the second paragraph, the clinician considers how recent events have contributed to the child/family's current presentation (Table 5). Once again, the case history information (assessment worksheet), predisposing factors, and clinical/theoretical knowledge are integrated to explain these patterns of difficulty (patterns worksheet). For example, triggers to anxiety problems, effects of sexual abuse and family denial of post-traumatic stress disorder symptoms.

Table 5. Precipitating factors

Explain how recent events and predisposing factors have precipitated the current patterns of difficulty and the presentation of the client now.

Discuss how these early patterns of difficulty have been affected by recent events. How do these events and ways of thinking/feeling/behaving/relating explain the presenting difficulties? How have events and patterns of difficulty culminated in presentation for help at this time? For example:

'A lack of adaptive coping resources and social supports, in the context of the recent loss of paternal employment and death of the maternal grandmother, has triggered this mother's depressive episode. Her emotional unavailability appears to have contributed to an escalation in her son's demands for her attention and aggression when she fails to provide this.'

'The death of a paternal uncle has intensified this child's fear of illness and parental abandonment setting off a pattern of refusal to attend school and a belief that he must protect his mother.'

'As this girl moves into adolescence, issues of sexual maturity and identity development have triggered traumatic memories of early abuse, which she attempts to repress by restricting her eating.'

The formulation: Perpetuating factors In the third paragraph, the clinician considers how these patterns are maintained by drawing upon different explanatory theories (Table 6). For example, the coercive pattern of parent–child conflict; avoidance maintaining social functioning difficulties; depressed thinking style contributing to a failure to engage in pleasurable, rewarding experiences. Once again this is where theory explains patterns of difficulty and how these patterns are maintained.

Table 6. Perpetuating factors

Drawing on theoretical knowledge and information about current interactions, explain how these patterns of difficulty are perpetuated/maintained.

How are the patterns of difficulty, and the underlying factors that have shaped them, perpetuated? What are the patterns that maintain current functioning and prevent more adaptive patterns of functioning? What do these patterns suggest for future functioning? Explain the ways in which these patterns of difficulty may continue without intervention? Explain how these patterns of difficulty may manifest within the treating system? What safety risks are posed by the perpetuation of these patterns of difficulty? For example:

'The pattern of affective dysregulation is maintained by the difficulty his mother and the school have in containing his aggressive outbursts. Instead they become accusatory and punitive which exacerbates his angry feelings and fails to help him to regulate his difficult behaviour.'

'The pattern of conflict between Child Protection and the Fostercare Agency undermines collaboration and increases friction between the child and her foster-carer, resulting in splitting of workers into "good or bad" roles and oppositional behaviours by her.'

'The pattern of a lack of sense of connection is maintained by the frequency of placement changes and the lack of an attachment figure who can provide security and continuity.'

'Without intervention in this pattern of aggression this boy is likely to be expelled from school, reducing the involvement of any other supportive attachment figures.'

This paragraph will also make some prediction about what might happen for the child/family without intervention. Predictions always need to be made with the anticipation that they may be incorrect, but will be guided by the history of the child/family. This paragraph on perpetuating factors will also consider how the pattern of interaction between the child/family and the system may be perpetuated in efforts to intervene (i.e., the family's pattern of withdrawal from services when crises subside then results in professionals feeling helpless and giving up – this has resulted in few options for help being available). Consideration of how the interaction between the family and the system contributes to patterns of difficulty may include thinking about how the system contributes to the family's problems, how the client/family may contribute to the clinician's responses, and what factors will need to be considered when planning the intervention so as not to perpetuate the patterns of difficulty. This section of the formulation may articulate how the maintenance of these patterns contributes to the safety risk for the child/family (and is then clearly addressed at the start of the recommendations).

The formulation: Protective factors In the fourth paragraph, the clinician considers how patterns of strength have developed and how they act protectively in the child/family (Table 7). Once again, the case history information (assessment worksheet) and knowledge about how events may have contributed to patterns of strength (patterns worksheet) are used in this paragraph. Patterns of strength will often be central to intervention planning because they highlight the resources of the child/family/system which, if further strengthened, may provide the catalyst for change.

Table 7. Protective factors

Explain how patterns of strength are protective and might be drawn upon in intervention planning.
What factors act in this child/family's favour? What are the strengths and how might these offer some point of protection or promote change in an intervention? For example:
'The pattern of warmth and affection has arisen due to significant positive early attachment with his mother and grandmother. Increasing activities that give the opportunity for enjoyment and affection will strengthen these relationships.'
'Her awareness of her own strengths academically have assisted her in the past to solve difficult problems, and are likely able to contribute to a self belief that she is capable of making change.'
'When in a supportive play setting, the boy can engage in social interaction that involves sharing and prosocial behaviour, and such settings may increase his confidence with peers.'

Intervention planning

The intervention plan should address the Four Ps from the formulation by targeting the key patterns of difficulty while taking into consideration the patterns of strength (Table 8). It should include a plan for addressing the patterns through work with the child, the family, and the wider system. Issues of safety should always be prioritized as the first of the recommendations. In particular when there is a complex case to be considered, it is imperative to include the wider system, and thought needs to be given to comprehensive planning that values collaboration and team work.

The intervention plan must also consider each of the Four Ps. Often, an intervention will only address the perpetuating factors that maintain the difficulties. The result is often that there is only minimal symptom reduction, the family re-present again later with the same or a different constellation of symptoms, or no progress is made. We believe that

Table 8. Intervention planning

Addressing predisposing factors: There may be some things in this category not appropriate for intervention, as they are historical, however examples may include:

Therapy for mother to assist in changing her long standing perception that she is incapable of changing anything in her life.

Help parents maintain consistency and predictability to improve attachment relationships.

Assisting the child to explore issues of trust, mastery, authority, and industry not previously experienced at earlier stages of development. This may occur in individual therapy, dyadic work, and/or occur through working with the parents.

Family work to explore grief at parental separation.

Individual or dyadic child therapy to integrate past trauma. This may occur after initially addressing some of the previous recommendations.

Addressing precipitating factors examples may include:

Mediation between child's carer and grandmother to reduce child's anxiety during access.

Work with parents to accept responsibility for the abuse of the child.

Work with mother on issues of unresolved grief/fear of illness, to improve child's capacity to feel safe and secure with her.

Addressing perpetuation factors examples may include:

Individual therapeutic work to address depression and factors underlying this.

Assist both mother and school with behavioural interventions to contain child's aggressive outbursts. These might involve consistent clear rules, warnings and consequences for misbehaviour, and containing strategies for times of difficult behaviour.

Teaching the child stop, think, do to manage impulsive behaviours as well as emotion understanding and affect regulation skills.

Addressing protective factors examples may include:

Increase supportive relationships outside the family and assist the boy to return to school.

Increasing time spent with grandmother with whom the child has a loving relationship. This might involve advocacy with Child Protection services to enable access to occur.

a failure to take into account factors contributing to the current presentation, namely the predisposing and precipitating factors, may result in a failure to address the key factors driving the problem. It is often necessary to address issues of attachment (within the individual and the system), a trauma history, developmental milestones not achieved and issues of separation, loss or grief, before the current patterns of difficulty can begin to be alleviated. Integration of this knowledge is the seminal contribution and strength of a good multi-component assessment implemented by child and adolescent mental health services. That said, not every intervention requires this level of depth, but we often find with increasingly complex cases a failure to address predisposing and precipitating factors in the intervention is the weak point of the work.

It is also important to consider the resources available for interventions, both the external resources of the treating system (Dallos et al., 2006) and the internal resources of the family, which include financial resources. It is not wise to recommend a wide range of interventions which may not be available in the local area or which the family may not be able to afford. It is also important not to weigh the family down with too many weekly appointments for therapeutic intervention. The intervention plan should be discussed with the family to streamline interventions.

Case example

The following is an example of a fictitious case using *The Mindful Formulation*. Cassie is a nine-year-old girl who presents to Child and Adolescent Mental Health Services with symptoms consistent with Obsessive Compulsive Disorder. She lives with her parents Tim (43 years) and Andrea (39 years), and her younger brothers, Cody (5 years), and twins Jack and Judd (2 years). Cassie was referred by her GP with symptoms of continuous washing of her hands related to a fear of germs, with other compulsive rituals around food and clothing. The GP reported that the middle child also has behaviour problems and separation anxiety. Tables 9, 10 and 11 show the use of the worksheets for this case.

Assessment worksheet

Table 9. Assessment worksheet case example

Presenting problem(s)	Cassie presents with a six month history of increasing symptoms of OCD, which include a fear of germs, resulting in frequent washing, the need to have her food individually wrapped, her clothes washed separately, and her underwear wrapped in plastic until worn. Her parents are quite distressed about her condition and are requesting help. Cassie has a history of infant sleeping and feeding difficulties, separation anxiety first noted at aged three years on attendance at crèche, kindergarten and first year of school. Cassie has some current separation difficulties and stays home from school regularly after voicing somatic complaints. Cassie's school performance is affected by her symptoms, as she struggles to complete work due to perfectionism.
Relationships, home and social environments	Father comes from a second generation English migrant family; family history of anxiety and depression; his own father was hospitalized after WW2 with combat related neurosis. Father suffers from diagnosed depression and anxiety. Mother has a history of childhood sexual abuse, perpetrated by her older brother. She has current PTSD symptoms. Both parents have had treatment, both pharmaceutical and therapy. The marital relationship is generally good although there is an avoidance of conflict. Cassie's relationship with mother is more comfortable than with father; mother gives in to her demands and participates in her rituals to avoid conflict; father gets irritated with her and thinks she is being 'silly', and thinks mother is too soft. Cassie has a good relationship with brother Cody, but finds the twins irritating, noisy, messy and demanding of mother's time. Family financial difficulties due to the birth of twins; mother is not working as childcare is too expensive, and this causes tension and worry for both parents. Cassie's academic achievement is below her capacity; she is very bright but perfectionism gets in the way of completing work, and she is often behind the class in finishing. She has a group of friends although tends to be bossy and dominating with them.

Table 9. continued

	The family are very involved in school and kindergarten communities, and have friends in their suburb. Mother is actively involved with school parents' organization. Family are connected to father's family and see his parents and siblings regularly, but apart from one sister are not connected to mother's family, due to the disclosure of sexual abuse and her parents' denying the abuse and supporting her brother. The birth of twins two years ago, who were premature and have some ongoing health problems, including asthma, has increased stress for the family.
Experience of adversity	No particular adverse events known for Cassie. Mother suffered sexual abuse from age 9 to 11 years.
Experience of attachment	Mother's relationship with Cassie was characterized by anxiety. Mother reports not feeling very well attuned to Cassie, and often feeling she wasn't meeting her needs. She could not turn to her own mother for assistance, and had few people around to ask advice. She describes Cassie as clingy and not wanting to be put down, which she found very tiring and annoying. Mother was also somewhat preoccupied by her own feelings about her family during this time. Mother also describes delighting in Cassie as time went on, as she was a bright and lively baby. Based on history, attachment style was most likely in the insecure-ambivalent category.
Developmental history	Although the pregnancy had been normal, Cassie's birth had been a difficult two-day labour resulting in a high forceps delivery. Mother found establishing breast feeding difficult and bottle fed from day two. Cassie was an irritable baby who cried a lot, fed poorly and slept poorly. Mother was very tired and stressed, but not depressed. Mother sought help when Cassie was 9 months old, as the family was not sleeping and Cassie was underweight. She and Cassie spent three days at a mother–baby centre, where a sleeping pattern was established. Cassie's physical milestones were within normal limits, crawling at 9 months and walking at 13 months. Cassie had some words at 18 months and was talking in sentences by two and a half years. Toilet training was uneventful and complete by two and a half years. Cassie exhibited some separation anxiety from age three years, when she had difficulty attending crèche, kinder and then school. Cassie still has separation anxiety and often stays home from school.
Other developmental factors	None known.
Safety concerns	No obvious safety concerns.
Resilience factors	Cassie is able to maintain friendships, and has many pleasurable interactions at home and school. She gets on well with brother Cody, and generally has a close and warm relationship with her mother. Cassie is a lively and likeable girl. Good parent marital relationship Paternal familial support/connections. Strong community links. Supportive teacher and school. Parents view therapy as positive and are committed to getting help. They are concerned for Cassie and want to help in any way.
Missing information	None.

Patterns worksheet

Table 10. Patterns worksheet case example

Child's functioning	*Parents/Carers/ Siblings/Significant others own functioning*	*Relationships (for child and among significant others)*	*Relationships with and among community*
Affective response	*Affective response*	*Affective response*	*Affective response*
Cassie becomes very angry when not able to complete rituals. She is observed to often look sad, but does not speak of sadness. She has happy times on family outings, enjoys swimming at pool or beach and does not worry about germs at such times.	Mother has a history of PTSD, currently has intermittent anxiety, flashbacks and nightmares, causing fatigue and irritability. Father has anxiety problems, depressive episodes and chronic insomnia. Five year old brother has mild separation anxiety with behaviour problems.	Cassie becomes irritated easily with two year old twin siblings. She can play happily with five year old brother. She exhibits anxiety and sometimes distress at separation from mother. Parents both feel helpless and overwhelmed by Cassie's problems.	Cassie becomes upset and tearful if criticized at school. Members of local school community express care and concern about Cassie and her family. Cassie enjoys basketball, and participates well.
Behaviours	*Behaviours*	*Behaviours*	*Behaviours*
Cassie has a number of compulsive rituals, including repeated hand washing; needing her food to come straight from a wrapper; needing her clothes to be washed separately. She has perfectionism with school work, constant rubbing out of writing/drawing. Occasional aggression, screaming when she is unable to complete a ritual.	Mother when upset and tired due to own and family stress becomes resigned and withdrawn, 'going through the motions'. Father is irritable at times when anxious and worried. Brother Cody is occasionally aggressive and oppositional at home with either parent. He is also upset and tearful on separation from mother.	Cassie can be controlling and bossy with father, brothers and friends. Mother gives in to her demands, placates and collaborates in her rituals. Mother brings her lunch to school, with each item individually wrapped. Mother washes clothes separately and helps Cassie sort and fold clothes, wrapping underwear in plastic. Parents are warm and affectionate toward each other, but avoid points of conflict.	Cassie is often distracted at school due to worry. She is well behaved at school generally, and has a small group of friends, although is often bossy with them.
Cognitions	*Cognitions*	*Cognitions*	*Cognitions*
Cassie has a range of obsessive thought patterns, which include a fear of germs and becoming ill due to contamination; worry about bad luck; worry about bushfire. She is concerned about her mother while she is at school. She believes her schoolwork is not good enough, which interferes with her concentration.	Father believes that Cassie has inherited his problems with anxiety. Father is often thinking about financial problems. Mother believes that her problems during Cassie's infancy have caused her current difficulties, and ruminates about her own family of origin issues. Mother is angry about rejection from her family.	Parents are joined in their concern about Cassie and want the best for her.	School principal and teacher are concerned that Cassie is not achieving her potential academically, due to perfectionism, and that she has trouble concentrating and finishing her work.

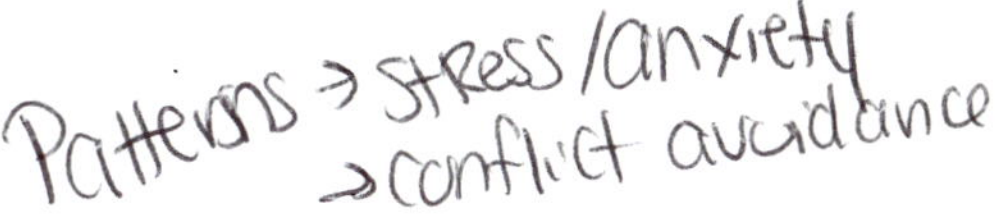

Formulation worksheet

Table 11. Formulation worksheet case example

Explain how these patterns have developed predisposing factors. Use the information from sheet one and theoretical/developmental knowledge to explain how you think this history may have predisposed the client/family to these patterns of difficulty (sheet two).

Patterns of anxiety in the family have contributed to Cassie's lack of trust in the world as a safe place.

Patterns of father's anxiety and his family history of anxiety lead him to avoid confronting any potential conflict in the family.

Patterns of mother's pre-occupation with family of origin issues including a sexual abuse history, and rejection by her family, which have led to poor attunement with her child in infancy.

Explain how recent events and predisposing factors have precipitated the current patterns of difficulty and the presentation of the client now?

Patterns of increasing stress and anxiety caused by financial concerns and the ongoing health problems of the twins have exacerbated existing and long standing anxiety to produce an environment currently saturated with worry, concerns and anxiety.

Pattern of parents' tendency to avoid conflict has led to a concerted effort to placate Cassie to keep the peace in the family.

Drawing on theoretical knowledge and knowledge of current interactions, explain how these patterns of difficulty are perpetuated/maintained?

Current patterns of both parents feeling stressed and anxious are maintained by their real concerns re money and health and these patterns tend to maintain a sense of helplessness and inability to resolve difficulties.

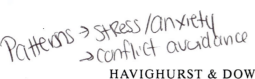

The patterns of conflict avoidance make solving problems more difficult as there is an avoidance of taking a stand, giving advice or changing routines, to avoid the potential for conflict which may arise.

The above patterns maintain a level of stress which impacts on Cassie and heightens her anxiety levels, perpetuating her OCD.

Cassie's parents' inability to help her soothe herself maintains a situation which is difficult for them to help her to reduce her need for rituals.

Explain how patterns of strength are protective and might be drawn upon in intervention planning?

Patterns of family connection, within the marital relationship and to extended family and community allow for support to come from outside the immediate family.

Patterns of warmth and affection in the family allow for the designing of interventions which will reduce stress and increase family play and fun.

Cassie's patterns of likeability and her capacity to interact with others may help her draw support from those around her.

The school environment is very supportive of Cassie, giving her added resources to draw on.

The written formulation

This should read something like:

Cassie X, a nine-year-old girl, has been referred to the Metropolitan Child and Adolescent Mental Health Service to explore ways of intervening and assisting her to manage her high levels of anxiety, obsessional thoughts and compulsive behaviours. She was referred by the Guidance Officer at her school. She has a history of Separation Anxiety from age three years, and a six month history of increasing obsessive-compulsive thoughts and behaviours. During assessment, obsessional thoughts followed by compulsive ritualized behaviour were noted. She currently meets diagnostic criteria for Obsessive Compulsive Disorder. Her symptoms are currently quite severe.

Predisposing factors

While there is strong evidence to suggest genetic factors in the development of OCD, high levels of anxiety in families can be considered a predisposing factor. Cassie's early environment was influenced by her mother's stress, due to pre-occupation with issues from her family of origin, particularly sexual abuse by her brother and the resulting rejection of her by her family following disclosure. This pre-occupation was intense at the time of Cassie's birth, and was coupled with PTSD symptoms of flashbacks and nightmares. The resultant difficulty in attunement with Cassie as an infant was exacerbated by Cassie's own irritability, with poor sleeping and feeding. The father's anxiety about his child's health also contributed to an anxious, stressed environment. The resulting anxious attachment style of the family may have contributed to Cassie's ongoing difficulty in soothing herself or regulating her affect when besieged by worries and doubts. This has presented in the past as a difficulty in separating from either parent. Both parents acknowledge difficulties in facing conflict, and tend to avoid confrontation, which encourages them to give in to Cassie and meet her demands, thus not encouraging her to manage her anxiety herself.

Precipitating factors

Over the last two years, since the birth of the twins, there has been increased stress for the family. The twins were born prematurely and there were concerns about their health, which have continued to the present. They are often unwell, particularly with asthma. In addition, Cassie's mother has had to delay returning to work, as child care for two children is too expensive. This has diminished the family income considerably, adding financial strain. These concerns have heightened the level of anxiety in the family, and have become caught up with the ongoing tendency on the part of both parents to avoid conflict, leading to further efforts, particularly by Cassie's mother, to placate Cassie by engaging and assisting in her rituals. In general these patterns have reduced Cassie's capacity to solve her own problems, soothe herself when distressed and cope with the academic and social demands of school.

Perpetuating factors

The above mentioned patterns of an environment of anxiety and worry about finances and health, as well as a pattern of avoidance of conflict, are perpetuating Cassie's difficulty in managing her own anxiety, influencing an increase in anxiety related symptoms. The atmosphere of anxiety also at times promotes a further sense of anxiety in Cassie, who then tends to worry about external events (such as illness or bushfires) damaging her family. Her parents' difficulty in supporting her to manage anxious feelings also contributes to this increase in symptoms. Her mother often participates in Cassie's rituals and frequently allows her to stay home from school with somatic complaints, rather than risk a tantrum. When Cassie cannot complete her rituals, or is thwarted from them in some way, she can become very angry and aggressive, hitting, screaming and biting others. Her parents are at a loss as to how to manage her during these episodes, which perhaps increases her level of anxiety.

Protective factors

There are many protective factors for Cassie and her family. Cassie is a likeable and engaging child who speaks willingly about her difficulties. Her family has good extended family and community supports, and her school teachers are also supportive. Cassie has the capacity to enjoy the company of other children including her brother. Cassie's parents are currently very worried about her and willing to seek help and to be involved in therapeutic endeavours. They also recognize some of the ways their own patterns contribute to Cassie's difficulties, and want assistance to change these.

Intervention plan

The following recommendations were made for intervention (see Table 12). They are the most comprehensive list possible, and are followed by a priority list that was made after discussion with the family.

Table 12. Intervention plan case example

Addressing predisposing factors:
Individual therapy for mother to address family of origin issues.
Individual therapy for father to address long standing anxiety problems.
Addressing precipitating factors:
Assistance for the family in resolving financial difficulties – referral to local services for financial counselling.
Assistance for health problems of the twins, such as asthma support group or relevant support group for parenting twins.
Couple counselling for parents to strengthen their capacity to tolerate conflict with each other and conflict with Cassie. This work should include work on united parenting.
Addressing perpetuation factors:
Assistance for the family to reduce the atmosphere of tension and stress, such as family quiet times, with relaxation methods.
Assistance for parents to manage five year old Cody's oppositional and aggressive behaviours through understanding and helping him resolve his anxieties and through setting limits.
Parent therapy for both parents to work on a planned approach to helping Cassie manage her anxiety and reduce the need for rituals. This approach may include setting limits on the amount of participation mother allows herself in maintaining the rituals.
Family therapy to address anxiety sequences as they occur in the relationships between family members and to work on relaxation methods.
Individual therapy for Cassie, using a CBT approach, to assist her to manage OCD symptoms.
Addressing protective factors:
Draw on family's capacity to engage in community relationships, particularly to assist mother to get support with the twins.
Utilize parent's desire for better family functioning to collaboratively make plans for change.
Draw on Cassie's capacity to engage in therapy.
Draw on the school's willingness to help by encouraging them to assist in any management plan for Cassie.

After discussing the assessment and formulation with the family, with the suggestions for intervention, it was decided that the priorities for intervention were:

- Individual therapy for the mother, who located an experienced counsellor at the local Centre Against Sexual Assault. The centre was able to find low cost child care for the twins to support this.
- A series of four, weekly, parent/couple therapy sessions to discuss tolerating conflict within the context of setting limits for the children. The parents felt that separate couple's therapy was beyond their resources at that time, due to child care and financial restraints. The father's mother agreed to look after the children during these sessions.
- After the initial series of parent/couple sessions, introduce fortnightly sessions, alternating family therapy and parent therapy.
- Weekly individual therapy for Cassie, which her father agreed to bring her to.
- The mother was able to join a support group for parents of twins, which was conducted in a town one hour's drive from the family's home. She found this supportive enough to compensate for the travel, and formed close friendships with the other mothers.
- The family also accessed financial counselling at the local Family Resource Centre, which helped them better manage their resources and to plan for the future.

The Mindful Formulation for training clinicians

To date, over 200 clinicians attending the Developmental Psychiatry Course, Take Two training, and the Child and Adolescent Psychiatry Course have been taught *The Mindful Formulation*. These new clinicians report that it provides them with a series of useful steps for integrating the assessment material into a theory about what is happening for the child and family, which assists in constructing a comprehensive intervention plan. Feedback has been that the steps are logical, but the process continues to be difficult in the early stages of training, and it takes time before the structure starts to become clearer and the technical terminology is integrated. We continue to find it a challenge to teach clinical reasoning – in many ways because formulation is a developmental skill for the clinician that time and experience will shape.

Conclusion

With the increasing pressure for clinicians to offer time-limited treatment with maximum effectiveness, a comprehensively structured approach to designing intervention is needed. In settings where infants, children, adolescents and their families are presenting with increasing complexity, a failure to tailor the intervention to meet this complexity may lead to repeated re-presentation of the client, and little change. *The Mindful Formulation* offers a systematic approach to developing a clinical formulation which addresses patterns of strength and difficulty across the child's ecological system. These patterns are explained using information from the assessment as well as clinical and theoretical knowledge to articulate the predisposing, precipitating, perpetuating, and protective factors in the written formulation. The intervention plan addresses the key patterns of difficulty while taking into consideration the patterns of strength. In doing so, the goal is to offer effective and efficient intervention to children and their families. We acknowledge that the formulation process advocated for here may take longer than is customary in clinical practice. However, the level of depth and comprehensiveness that we recommend in this article is critical for teaching new clinicians. In doing so, it is more likely that errors in judgement often occurring with inexperienced clinicians can be avoided. It also ensures a rigorous process for clinical reasoning in complex cases which may assist in more accurate delivery of intervention, stronger client engagement, lower drop out levels and more successful treatment. These are central if the needs of complex clients we see in CAMHS and services like Take Two are to be adequately met.

Note

1. The Developmental Psychiatry Course is a one-year postgraduate certificate for allied health professionals working in CAMHS and related services that focuses on assessment and clinical formulations skills with children, adolescents and families.

References

Broder, E.A., & Hood, E. (1983). A guide to the assessment of child and family. In P.D. Steinhauer, & Q. Rae-Grant (Eds.), *Psychological problems of the child in the family* (2nd ed., pp. 25–55). New York: Basic Books.

Conner, D.F., & Fisher, S.G. (1997). An interactional model of child and adolescent mental health clinical case formulation. *Clinical Child Psychology and Psychiatry*, *2*(3), 353–368.

Dallos, R., Wright, J., Stedmon, J., & Johnstone, L. (2006). Integrative formulation. In L. Johnstone, & R. Dallos (Eds.), *Formulation in psychology and psychotherapy: Making sense of people's problems*. Hove, UK: Routledge.

Dumont, F. (1993). Inferential heuristics in clinical problem formulation: Selective review of their strengths and weaknesses. *Professional Psychology: Research and Practice*, *24*(2), 196–205.

Eells, T.D. (Ed.). (2007). *Handbook of psychotherapy case formulation* (2nd ed.). New York: The Guilford Press.

Glaser, B.G., & Strauss, A.L. (1967). *The discovery of grounded theory: Strategies for grounded research*. Chicago, IL: Aldine.

Herbert, M. (2001). Clinical formulation. In T. Ollendick (Ed.), *Children and adolescents: Clinical formulation and treatment* (Vol. 5, pp. 25–55). Amsterdam: Pergamon.

Johnstone, L., & Dallos, R. (2006). Introduction to formulation. In L. Johnstone, & R. Dallos (Eds.), *Formulation in psychology and psychotherapy: Making sense of people's problems*. Hove, UK: Routledge.

Luk, E.S.L., Birleson, P., Wong, L., & Manders, J. (1998). Assessment in child and adolescent psychiatry: Does training and years of experience count? *Australian Psychiatry*, *6*(3), 128–142.

Mahoney, M.J. (1991). *Human change processes: The scientific foundations of psychotherapy*. New York: Basic Books.

Persons, J. (1993). Case conceptualization in cognitive-behavior therapy. In K.T. Kuehlwein, & H. Rosen (Eds.), *Cognitive therapies in action: Evolving innovative practice*. San Francisco, CA: Jossey-Bass.

Salovey, P., & Turk, D.C. (1991). Clinical judgement and decision-making. In C.R. Snyder, & D.R. Forsyth (Eds.), *Handbook of social and clinical psychology* (pp. 416–437). New York: Pergamon.

The Royal Australian and New Zealand College of Psychiatrists. (2006). *The Clinical Examination*. Retrieved December 2008, from www.ranzcp.org

Ward, T., & Haig, B. (1997). Abductive reasoning and clinical assessment. *Australian Psychologist*, *32*(2), 1–8.

Weerasekera, P. (1996). *Multiperspective case formulation: A step towards treatment integration*. Malabar, FL: Krieger.

Patricia A. Sharpe, PhD MPH ■ Mary L. Greaney, MPH
Peter R. Lee, MPH ■ Sherer W. Royce, MPH

Assets-Oriented Community Assessment

SYNOPSIS

Determining how to promote community health requires that community health workers first assess where the community stands. The authors maintain that Healthy Communities initiatives are better served by assets-oriented assessment methods than by standard "problem-focused" or "needs-based" approaches. An assets orientation allows community members to identify, support, and mobilize existing community resources to create a shared vision of change, and encourages greater creativity when community members do address problems and obstacles.

Dr. Sharpe, Ms. Greaney, and Ms. Royce are with the Prevention Research Center at the University of South Carolina School of Public Health. Dr. Sharpe is Research Associate Professor. Ms. Greaney and Ms. Royce are Research Assistants with the Center and doctoral candidates in the Department of Health Promotion and Education, School of Public Health. Mr. Lee is Senior Associate for Healthy Communities at the Medical Foundation, Boston.

Address correspondence to Dr. Sharpe, Prevention Research Center, School of Public Health, USC, Columbia SC 29208; tel. 803-777-4253; fax 803-777-9007; e-mail <pasharpe@sph.sc.edu>.

With the growing interest in community participation and self-determination—both central to Healthy Communities principles—the standard "problem-focused" or "needs-based" approaches to community health have come under criticism. Problem-focused theories and planning models share a common focus on problem identification and have permeated government, the media, professional training of all sorts, as well as funding agencies and organizations.[1] Kretzmann and McKnight contend that deficiency-based approaches can have negative effects even when positive change is intended because they force community leaders to highlight their communities' worst side in order to attract resources.[1] Needs-focused perspectives may also unintentionally create one-dimensional images that characterize communities and the individuals within them based on disease risk profiles or social problem categories, such as "low income," "welfare mom," "the handicapped," or "high crime neighborhood." In contrast, the movement toward promoting greater community participation is grounded in theories, perspectives, and planning frameworks that focus on communities' strengths or give balanced attention to strengths and needs.

Community asset assessment is a method for collecting information about a community. Assessing a community's assets means identifying, supporting, and mobilizing existing community resources and capacities for the purpose of creating and achieving a shared vision. In the process of doing a self-assessment, community members also identify problems and obstacles that must be addressed in order to achieve their dream of a healthy community. An assets orientation does not imply ignoring problems and needs or throwing out rational, strategic planning; rather, a key distinction between assets-based approaches and needs-based approaches is the rallying point for bringing citizens together. In both needs-focused and assets-focused approaches, hard realities must be faced. By involving community members in visual, intuitive, and non-linear processes of self-assessment and discovery, assets-oriented approaches invite more creativity in assessment and planning than collection and perusal of statistical data alone can engender.

How to Assess a Community's Assets

Community health workers' choices of techniques for identifying community assets reflect multiple philosophical and practical influences. The techniques described below can be used to identify both needs and assets, even though the focus of this discussion is on assets as an emerging concept in community work. It should be noted that no particular technique for collecting information holds inherent power to build community capacities or create a participatory framework for action. The community assessment process can be ultimately empowering or exploitive regardless of technique; however, because the techniques described below involve community members in the assessment process, they can set the stage for future community-generated changes.

Windshield and walking tours of communities. Professional and lay researchers conduct driving and/or walking tours of a geographic area at varying times of day and days of the week to observe and record information about community characteristics. Preferably, these tours take place within community-designated boundaries rather than geopolitical boundaries; or if geopolitical boundaries are used, community self-designations are also noted. Observers can easily conduct windshield tours with an observational guide or checklist. While this technique is ideal for introducing outsiders to a community in which they will be working, community members can be actively involved in driving and walking tours, both as tour guides and as observers/auditors.

> **For community assessment purposes, key informants include people in both formal and informal leadership roles.**

Working in pairs or small groups (one driver and one or more observer-recorders), observers make notes, take photos, and make videotapes (where appropriate) about community characteristics. These might include the location and characteristics of recreational areas, transportation and traffic patterns, landmarks, housing, commons and informal gathering places, terrain and greenspaces, safety, businesses, churches, and health and social services facilities. In addition, Walters[2] and Anderson and McFarlane[3] have included boundaries, signs of development/decay, religion and churches (including spiritual and folk healers), and art/media. Wilson and Mitrano[4] have assessed community values through attention to community symbols evident in graffiti, billboards, T-shirt slogans, and lawn ornaments.

Windshield and walking tours can broadly document a community's assets, resources, and concerns, or they can focus on specific environmental and social factors related to a particular objective. For example, in Sumter, South Carolina, coalition members conducted walking tours using community survey tools to assess the "walkability" of their neighborhoods.[5,6] Written narratives, tables and diagrams, collages, slide shows, or maps (see also "Assets maps" below) summarize and display tour results.

Key informant/key leader interviews. The key informant interview is a one-to-one interviewing technique for qualitative data collection with a long history of use in ethnographic studies. The term *key informant* implies that an outsider is conducting the interview, which may be the case for research. However, when community coalition members initiate the assessment or work with outsiders to conduct it, many of the key informants or key leaders are, in fact, the coalition members themselves and their neighbors. For community assessment purposes, key informants include people in both formal and informal leadership roles representing diverse stakeholder groups, amateur community historians, and community caretakers[4]—those trusted people who keep track of the everyday events in a neighborhood and are often at the center of informal helping networks.

Identification of key leaders usually begins with community coalition members generating a list. It is essential that this list contain more than the community members who hold political power. The list expands through a snowballing process of referral, with each key informant naming others he or she thinks ought to be interviewed. The goal is to cover the range of opinion in a community. Examples of potential topics include:

- how the community has met challenges or accomplished goals in the past;
- sources of community pride;
- who gets things done in the community;
- the nature of social connectedness, cohesion and affiliation among neighbors (social capital);[7–9]
- the level of trust between citizens and local government, business, financial, and social service institutions;
- the array of community values and interest groups;
- and perspectives on what a healthy community is.

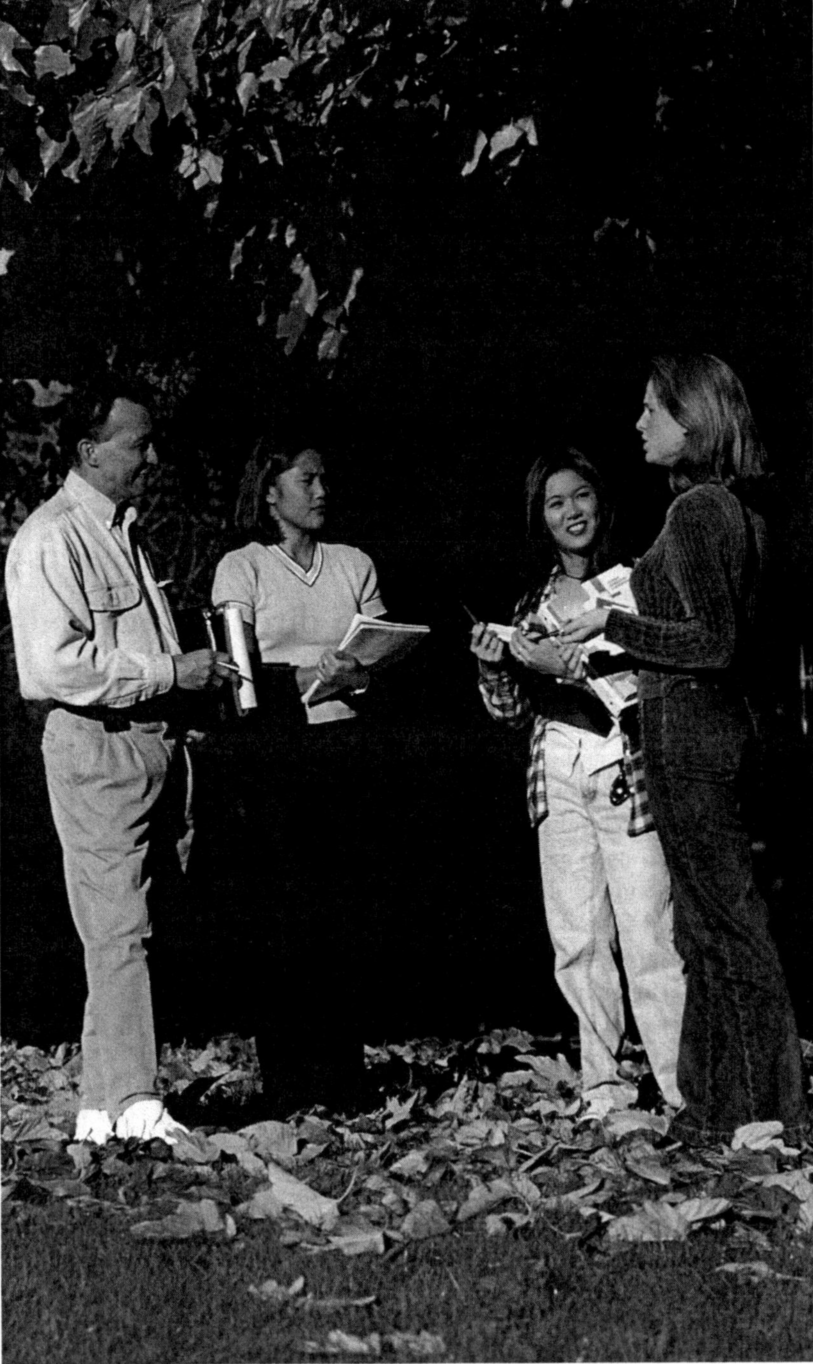

Responses are compiled in narrative form and/or in summary charts, along with a roster of names of community leaders.

Assets maps. An assets map is a geographic map on which physical assets such as schools, landmarks, playgrounds, public gathering places, churches, schools, airports, and recreation areas may be designated. When the community has already determined a focus for its initiatives, more than one map might be created: a global one and one highlighting characteristics of special relevance (for example, all the factors of special significance to children's health and safety). Wilson also suggests identifying *human activity settings*, locations within the community in which people carry out day-to-day activities of living, such as where they work, play, shop, go to school, congregate, worship, get health care and services, and so forth.[4] These features are observed and assessed in terms of the meanings the community assigns them and the participants' values, roles, and purposes in everyday human interaction.[10,11] For example, assets mapping in a Columbia, South Carolina,[12] neighborhood revealed that almost none of the members of a particular church (a potential asset) lived in the surrounding neighborhood, and residents did not feel any connection to the church. Prior to assets mapping, outsiders' assumptions about the church's significance as a venue for community gatherings would have been in error.

An advantage of creating an assets map is that community members can be directly involved in the map's creation and interpretation, can identify desirable and undesirable patterns, and can use the map as a springboard for creating a healthier vision in dialogue with city planners and officials. Sources of input for an assets map include key informant interviews; coalition meetings and other community forums; windshield and walking tours; archival data from city, county or state government; existing community directories and inventories; and research. Community groups can create assets maps with simple materials. Land use maps are often available from city or county government, and coalition members can use simple adhesive symbols or push pins to designate community characteristics and assets. Recently developed community planning and evaluation software tools include the capability to import or scan maps and save bitmapped images for assets mapping. The user adds icons to the map to represent community assets.[13]

An advantage of creating an assets map is that community members can be directly involved in the map's creation and interpretation, can identify desirable and undesirable patterns, and can use the map as a springboard for creating a healthier vision in dialogue with city planners and officials.

For communities that wish to undertake a detailed geographic study of community assets, Geographic Information Systems (GIS) software provides a powerful tool for working with spatial data.[14,15] GIS technology allows the user to examine the locations and distribution of specific features of a geographic area and to display data in map form. Data layers may include features such as population distribution, road networks, school district boundaries, and the locations of health care facilities. Communities can use this technology to examine where people live in relation to where community resources are located, to look at patterns in the distribution of resources and services throughout the community, or to answer questions about the relationships between specific features and community attributes.

Data for creating data layers are available through government or private agencies or can be developed. Remote Sensing and Global Positioning Systems (GPS) are tools used in creating data layers.[16] Airplane and satellite remote sensing systems are commonly used to obtain information about an object, feature, or area by abstracting data collected with a device not in contact with the feature being studied. For example, a user may take a handheld device and walk the boundaries of a park or along a trail or sidewalk to collect data on the geographic location. Remote Sensing and GPS data can be imported into the GIS system for analysis and mapping. Although GIS, Remote Sensing, and GPS involve specialized expertise and some expense, their use is becoming common enough that community organizations could partner with government or academic institutions for access to this technology.

Focus groups and dialogue groups. The focus group has become a widely used method in community assessment and evaluation. A skilled moderator uses open-ended questions to lead a group of five to 12 people in a discussion of about an hour to an hour and a half's duration. Questions for use in a general discussion of community assets might include:

- What would you say are some of this community's strengths?
- What are some of the gifts and talents of the people here?
- What is the community's greatest source of pride?
- Who are the people in the community who take care of others when it is not part of their jobs? For example, who makes sure that children are safe; who makes sure that families have food?

- What groups, clubs, or associations in the community make a difference in the well-being of the community?
- To what extent do people in this community know their neighbors?

A number of guides to conducting focus groups are available.[17–21] In community settings, groups should take place among a wide variety of constituencies so that the entire domain of ideas and viewpoints is tapped. Because effective focus group discussions require a degree of skill on the part of the moderator, this technique has been under the purview of professionals; however, Krueger and King have written a guide to developing focus group skills among community members.[22] Focus group discussions are usually tape-recorded and transcribed, although careful note-taking during the discussion may be adequate for some purposes. Researchers often use qualitative data analysis packages to examine the transcripts and identify important themes. Reports include narrative summaries with illustrative quotes and summary tables or diagrams.

Discussion groups need not strictly conform to the guidelines for focus groups research. For the Healthy Communities Agenda project, Norris and Howell suggest having a team convene community dialogue events with groups of five to 500 participants in a variety of settings.[23] A hybrid event that combines elements of focus groups, nominal group process,[24] or community forums, may be appropriate in some communities.

In visioning, skilled facilitators bring people together for a full day or more and pose questions to guide participants in visualizing their greatest desires for how their community will look some years into the future.

Inventories. Assets and capacities inventories are documents that catalogue and describe individual and organizational capacities. With adequate mechanisms in place for connecting capacities to opportunities for action, inventories can be the first step in putting untapped potential to work. Capacities inventories of individual community members assess talents, skills, and experiences that might lead to employment, volunteering, community activism, bartering systems, or microenterprise opportunities.[1] This process draws attention to the often overlooked talents of children, older residents, and labeled or stigmatized people.[25] People may have difficulty identifying their own range of talents and assets. Wilson leads community groups in an exercise called an assets auction, in which participants identify assets they own or skills they possess, and then involves them in bartering with their neighbors.[4] Families can benefit from doing inventories to identify their strengths and sources of mutual support and connection within the community.[12]

Useful inventories of associations and organizations include information about a group's goals and mission, membership, impact on community health, projects in progress, and potential for partnering with others in promoting community health.[1] Inventories stretch traditional definitions of who can be a partner in community health enhancement projects. An inventory can be a tool for creating new links among diverse groups that may not have traditionally worked together or considered their work, hobbies, or pastimes as having the potential to positively affect community health. The information for the inventory comes from key informant interviews; windshield tours; printed sources such as community directories, Yellow Pages, and local libraries' reference sections; and telephone interviews with associations' contact people.[1,26]

Visioning. Visioning is a process whereby a group of community stakeholders collectively define a shared dream of what their community can become. The degree of formality for conducting visioning varies; a retreat or workshop format has been used in some communities.[27,28] In general, skilled facilitators bring people together for a full day or more and pose questions to guide participants in visualizing their greatest desires for how their community will look some years into the future, how people will interact, what daily life will be like, and how all sectors of the community will operate to contribute to a healthy community environment. Working in small groups, participants illustrate and describe their vision creatively with words, drawings, or collages. The groups reconvene and discuss their images and categorize or summarize the elements in the images. A smaller core group may follow up on the retreat by creating a document to return to the participants. Follow-up meetings may be held to refine the collective vision and to develop plans for incorporating it into a planning process. Because the visioning process puts no limits on participants' dreams, it can be powerfully motivating.

Wilson has used a visioning process called *community buildout*. In developing countries, community members have used modeling materials (clay, for example) to build models of their community visions. In Columbia, South Carolina, children have used craft materials to build a healthy community model (Personal communication, K Wilson, Institute for Families in Society, University of South Carolina, September 1996).

Creative assessment. Creative assessment refers to the use of techniques for documenting community members' perceptions of their community, its assets and its problems. Community groups use photography, film, theater, music, dance, murals, puppet shows, storytelling, or drawings for multiple purposes: to portray a problem and its solutions; to enact a community vision; to celebrate cultural and civic pride; to protest; and to grieve. Creative techniques provide an acceptable forum of expression for community emotions and a mode for reaching diverse groups of community members who may be uncomfortable with structured assessment methods. For example, Wang and Burris[29,30] put cameras into the hands of women in rural China to create a participatory process of assessment, analysis, and action. Wallerstein involved New Mexico adolescents in visits to, and interviews at, emergency rooms and jails to observe and explore the experiences of people involved with alcohol and drugs.[31] Creative assessment activities stimulate conversation and may provide triggers that can be incorporated into a process of dialogue, reflection, and action.

The Challenges of Conducting Assets-Oriented Community Assessment

Even though the language of assets and capacities is spreading, the question of whether community participation is real or represents tokenism in most initiatives remains.[32] Giving attention to assets is not the same as fostering community participation. Numerous examples of token community advisory boards or outright exploitation of community assets for furthering agencies' agendas exist.[32] Many, if not most, funding sources remain categorical in focus and require a problem-focused grant application. Additionally, giving attention to assets is not the same as ignoring problems, but there is the potential for misappropriating an assets orientation to justify funding cuts by using the argument that assets-rich communities must have no need for dollars and resources from the outside. While communities may have tired of constantly having their problems highlighted,[33] they may also look with suspicion on the rhetoric of assets orientation unless a groundwork of mutual respect and trust has been established. As new perspectives emerge and rapid changes occur in public health, health care, and civic life, articulation of unspoken assumptions and values in research and service projects and constant self-reflection[32] will be necessary.

The authors thank Regina Fields, CHES, Dwayne Porter, PhD, Nancy Whittle, MSW, and Linda Neff, MSPH, for their assistance in the preparation of the manuscript. This work was supported in part by Prevention Research Center grant number U48/CCU409664 from the Centers for Disease Control and Prevention. Its contents are solely the responsibility of the authors and do not necessarily represent the official views of the Centers for Disease Control and Prevention.

References

1. Kretzmann JP, McKnight JL. Building communities from the inside out: a path toward finding and mobilizing a community's assets. Chicago (IL): ACTA Publications; 1993.
2. Walters SR. Community assessment: application of multiple methodologies. Presented at the Annual Prevention Center Directors Meeting, US Centers for Disease Control and Prevention; 1995 Feb 17; Atlanta, GA.
3. Anderson ET, McFarlane JM. Community as client: application of the nursing process. Philadelphia (PA): Lippincott; 1988.
4. Wilson K, Mitrano T. An assets-based approach to neighborhood and community development. Columbia: University of South Carolina, Institute for Families in Society; 1996.
5. Pollack PB. Liveable communities: an evaluation guide. Washington: AARP Public Policy Institute; 1999.
6. Partnership for a Walkable America. Walkable America checklist [cited 2000 Apr 14]. Available from: URL: **http://www.nsc.org/walk/wkcheck.htm**
7. Putnam RD. Bowling alone: America's declining social capital. Current 1995;73:3-9.
8. Potapchuk WR, Crocker JP, Schechter WH. Building community with social capital: chits and chums or chats with change. National Civic Rev 1997;86:129-39.
9. World Bank Group. Social capital for development [cited 2000 Apr 4]. Available from: URL: **http://www.worldbank.org/poverty/scapital/index.htm**
10. Gallimore R, Goldenberg CN, Weisner TS. The social construction and subjective reality of activity settings: implications for community psychology. J Community Psychol 1993; 21: 537-59.
11. O'Donnell CR, Tharp RG, Wilson K. Activity settings as the unit of analysis: a theoretical basis for community intervention and development. J Community Psychol 1993;21:501-20.
12. Sharpe PA. An assets approach to healthy families and communities. Presented at the Minority Health Issues Conference; 1998 Dec 7; Columbia, SC.

13. Gold RS, Koeppel PT, Grossman W, Bilton M, Biletnikoff J, Green T, Wray L. Outcomes Toolkit: the results-oriented system for community improvement [software]. San Francisco: The Health Forum; 1998. Also available from: URL: **http://www.act-toolkit.com**
14. Clarke KC. Analytical and computer topography. Upper Saddle River (NJ): Prentice-Hall; 1995.
15. Clarke KC. Getting started with geographic information systems. Upper Saddle River (NJ): Prentice-Hall; 1997.
16. Lillesand TM, Kiefer RW. Remote sensing and image interpretation. New York (NY): John Wiley and Sons; 1979.
17. Stewart DW, Shamdasani PN. Focus groups: theory and practice. Thousand Oaks (CA): Sage Publications; 1990.
18. Krueger RA. Moderating focus groups. Thousand Oaks (CA): Sage Publications; 1997.
19. Krueger RA. Developing questions for focus groups. Thousand Oaks (CA): Sage Publications; 1997.
20. Morgan DL. Planning focus groups. Thousand Oaks (CA): Sage Publications; 1997.
21. Community Tool Box. Tools. Table of contents. Part A: Promoting awareness of health and community development issues and community resources. Chapter 2: Assessing community needs and resources. Section 4: Berkowitz B. Focus groups [cited 2000 May 1]. Available from: URL: **http://ctb.lsi.ukans.edu**
22. Krueger RA, King JA. Involving community members in focus groups. Thousand Oaks (CA): Sage Publications; 1997.
23. Coalition for Healthier Cities and Communities. Community library. Search the resource section of the library. Enter keyword(s): "dialogue guide." Healthy people in healthy communities: a dialogue [cited 2000 Jun 19]. Available from: URL: **http://www.healthycommunities.org**
24. Gilmore GD, Campbell MD. Needs assessment strategies for health education and health promotion. 2nd ed. Madison (WI): Brown and Benchmark Publishers; 1996.
25. McKnight JL, Kretzmann JP. Mapping community capacity. In: Minkler M, editor. Community organizing and community building for health. New Brunswick (NJ): Rutgers University Press; 1998. p. 157-72.
26. Community Tool Box. Tools. Table of contents. Part A: Promoting awareness of health and community development issues and community resources. Chapter 2: Assessing community needs and resources. Section 6: Berkowitz B, Wadud E. Identifying community assets [cited 2000 May 1]. Available from: URL: **http://ctb.lsi.ukans.edu**
27. Grossman W, Norris T. Healthier communities action kit: a guide for leaders embracing change. San Francisco: Healthcare Forum Leadership Center's Healthier Communities Partnership; 1993.
28. Johnson K, Grossman W, Cassidy A. The Healthcare Forum. Collaborating to improve community health: workbook and guide to best practices in creating healthier communities and populations. San Francisco: Jossey-Bass; 1996.
29. Wang C, Burris MA. Empowerment through photonovella: portraits of participation. Health Educ Q 1994;21:171-86.
30. Wang C, Burris MA. Photovoice: concept, methodology, and use for participatory needs assessment. Health Educ Behav 1997;24: 369-87.
31. Wallerstein N, Sanchez-Merki DL. Freirian praxis in health education and community organizing: a case study of an adolescent prevention program. In: Minkler M, editor. Community organizing and community building for health. New Brunswick (NJ): Rutgers University Press; 1998. p. 195-211.
32. Minkler M, Pies C. Ethical Issues in community organizing and community participation. In: Minkler M, editor. Community organizing and community building for health. New Brunswick (NJ): Rutgers University Press; 1998. p. 120-38.
33. Ammerman A, Parks C. Preparing students for more effective community interventions: assets assessment. Fam Community Health 1998;21:32-45. ■

Commentary

The Diagnostic Strengths Manual?

Dennis Saleebey

As influential as it is, the DSM-IV (the DSM-IV-TR has just been published and has approximately 100 additional pages of text on disorders—primarily because of the increased enumeration of criteria and specifiers) of the American Psychiatric Association (1994) poses some dilemmas and tensions for practitioners and, therefore, for clients and patients who are diagnosed under its protocols and schematics. Volleys of criticism of DSM-III, -III-R, and -IV have come from many fronts, based on a variety of concerns: that the DSM fails to provide convincing evidence for the reliability and validity of diagnostic criteria and standards that other medical specialties ostensibly require (Kutchins & Kirk, 1997), and that it provides an insufficient and hard-to-operationalize conceptualization of mental disorder (Wakefield, 1992). In addition, this lack of a clear definition permits an ever-widening net of definition of disorder so that all manner of common human foibles, annoying traits, and bad habits are captured as mental disorders (Wolin & Wolin, 1993); it has an extensive white male bias and a history of developing diagnostic categories that are inimical to some racial groups and to women (Tavris, 1992); and through its numeric system of taxonomy and the numerical anonymity of the patients who appear in the "casebook," the DSM subtly encourages objectification of individuals with mental disorders (Cutler, 1991). Whatever its weaknesses and whatever the character of its construction of human frailties and foibles, the DSM is enormously popular, and its influence would be hard to understate. It is the lingua franca of mental health professions. Insurance companies and the enormously powerful pharmaceutical industry rely on it heavily for very different reasons. (Goleman, 1994; Kutchins & Kirk, 1997)

Finally, the social, medical, scientific, and political processes that have nourished the development of an influential document like DSM reflect an evolving social norm (and its attendant practices) and cultural dynamic of "progressive infirmity." Such a norm decrees that an expanding range of behaviors, internal emotional and mental states, and human conditions come to be labeled as deficiencies requiring medication, sequestering, treatment and, in some cases, imprisonment. This has the cumulative effect of producing a rapidly developing social hierarchy in which a growing number of individuals and professions, employing the lexicon of deficit, have the power to evaluate and act on those who are identified as not measuring up, weakening more communal understandings and melioration of human trials, troubles, and tribulations; and "enfeebling" the sense of self of those who fail under the terms of the new normative lexicon (Gergen, 1994).

Obviously, the DSM has a host of individual, disciplinary, professional, and institutional supporters. Its intent to create, like Emil Kraepelin 70 years before (Andreasen, 1984), an encyclopedic, descriptive manual that clearly distinguishes a given disorder, through specific and behavioral criteria, from every other disorder reflects the intent of medicine generally. It must be pointed out, however, that other branches of medicine are interested as well in underlying pathology (causality) because locating and understanding that particular cellular, physiological, or biochemical dynamic is a key to effective treatment, cure, or prevention (Walker, 1996). The framers of DSM seem curiously uninterested in cause.

There are two particular problems with DSM-IV that I think are especially disturbing, and both have profound and too often adverse

CCC Code: 0037-8046/01 $3.00

effects on people who seek the help of mental health professionals.

It's All in Your Head!

Many, if not most physical illnesses, serious and slight, often yield cognitive, emotional, and behavioral changes as part of the symptom picture. In some of these illnesses, the emotional and cognitive changes are the first thing that might be observed by family members or a psychiatrist. Perhaps as many as 80 or 90 physical illnesses have depression, for example, as a part of the symptom picture (Gold, 1987). To embark on a process that hurries one to a diagnosis of major depressive episode when the individual is in the initial throes of systemic lupus erythematosus or in the first stage of hypothyroidism is a disaster poised. Walker (1996) reported the case of "Danny." A bright, mischievous 9-year-old, Danny had been identified by school officials as having attention deficit hyperactivity disorder (ADHD) because of extreme fidgetiness, disruptive classroom behavior, and persistent learning problems. However, he was a leader on the playground and an accomplished class clown. Especially troubled by his academic achievements, his parents came to Dr. Walker hoping for a prescription for Ritalin™ to control Danny's hyperactivity and maybe improve his classroom performance. Careful examination revealed some interesting findings. Danny's whorl (the swirl of hair at the crown of the head) was in the middle of his crown rather than on the side opposite from his dominant hand. Dr. Walker also discovered that Danny used his right hand for writing but kicked footballs with his left foot and used his left hand for eating. Danny had trouble distinguishing right from left, and his left eye was the dominant one. He sometime reversed letters in reading and sometimes began to read from the wrong side of a written page. Walker concluded, after further examination, that Danny was suffering from "mixed dominance" in which neither hemisphere of the brain is dominant. Mixed dominance can cause reading and writing difficulties. Compensating for the stress caused by mixed dominance might have contributed to some of the behaviors that got Danny into trouble in the first place (for example, his classroom difficulties). Danny subsequently went to a reading clinic where he learned several techniques for dealing with his nondominance. In eight weeks he was back in class and eventually became a top student.

To continue with ADHD, the following physical illnesses or mental conditions can reproduce some of the so-called symptoms of that disorder: sleep apnea, lead poisoning, pinworms, caffeinism, hyperthyroidism, learning disorders of various kinds, diets heavy in glucose and other sugars, and hyperinsulinism. And as Kovel (1981) pointed out, the label hyperactivity may be an indicator that a school classroom has little tolerance for normal fidgetiness and the activity levels of well, and appropriately energetic eight- and nine-year-olds.

Where's the Rest of Me? Missing Virtues

The DSM-IV and long-standing diagnostic habits make it virtually impossible to consider or make an accounting of the assets, talents, capacities, knowledge, survival skills, personal virtues, or the environmental resources and cultural treasures such as healing rituals and celebrations of life transitions that a person might possess—despite or, in some cases, because of their difficulties and trauma. To ignore these things is to disregard the most important resources in helping a person recover, adapt to stressful situations, confront environmental challenges, improve the quality of life, or simply adjust to or meliorate the effects of a devastating, chronic condition.

Conclusion

In this regard I have two proposals for further discussion and work. The first arose out of a student's concern with the five axes of the DSM. The last axis is the global assessment of functioning (GAF), and in its brevity is meant to catch, not only poor functioning but also competent functioning as well. But the latter is defined primarily in terms of the relative absence of symptoms and difficulties in a person's life. The GAF also is extremely spare in description and explanation, with little capacity to paint the picture of individual virtues or distinctive aspects of being. The student proposed that the DSM should include an Axis VI. On this axis the clinician and clients together are obliged to make a strict accounting of the merits and strengths of clients and the resources in their environment. These strengths can be skills (for example, gardening, caring for children, speaking Spanish, and doing budgets); talents (for example, playing the bagpipes, gardening, juggling, and cooking); personal virtues and traits (for example, insight, patience, self-discipline, a capacity for relationships, and a sense of humor); interpersonal skills (for example, comforting the sick, mediating conflict, and reducing tension between groups); interpersonal and environmental resources (for example, extended family, ethnic associations, strong intimate relationships, and good neighbors); cultural knowledge and lore (for example, healing ceremonies and rituals, stories of cultural perseverance, and the modeling of cultural heroes); family stories and narratives (for example, overcoming obstacles, migration and settlement, falls from grace and redemption, important family members, and instructive family lore); knowledge gained from struggling against adversity (for example, how one came to survive and surmount barriers and how one developed and maintained faith and hope); knowledge from one's occupational or parental roles (for example, caring for others, planning events and celebrations, and tending to the dying); spirituality and faith (for example, a transcendent system of meaning to rely on and a declaration of purpose beyond the self); and hopes and dreams (for example, personal, familial, social, and occupational goals and vision, and positive expectations about a better future). I ask students who are in appropriate placements always to "fill out" an Axis VI even if it is simply a matter that passes between them and those they are helping, unless they do not feel comfortable. I also encourage students at staffings to bring up at least one strength of a client with whom they are familiar, the purpose being to consider how this capacity or resource might be used in a treatment plan.

Let us envision a day in which the language of our virtues and estimable qualities is rich and trips off the tongue with the alacrity that our current dictionary of sometimes invalidating and alien language does. In that spirit I offer the beginnings of a

DSM—Diagnostic Strengths Manual— I

Code 300: Estimable Personal Qualities

301.00 Trustworthiness

A. For at least six months, nearly every day, the individual has exhibited at least three of the following:
- has done what he or she promised
- kept at a task that had many snares and difficulties
- did not reveal a confidence
- stuck by a relative, friend, or colleague during a rough time
- did more than expected.

B. This is not better explained by codependency or a pathological desire to please.

C. Such behavior must have improved the lives of other people.

D. Rule out the possibility of a self-seeking desire to cash in on these loyalties later.

302.00. Patience

A. For at least six months, nearly every day, the individual has exhibited at least three of the following:
- held his or her own wishes in abeyance while allowing a young child or a dependent to struggle to master a behavior
- demonstrated forbearance in the face of a serious delay, not of his or her own doing, in achieving an important goal
- calmly endured serious challenges and stresses occurring in the environment
- exhibited tolerance and understanding when confronted with a personal situation that defied personal values and standards of taste
- maintained equilibrium and steadfastness in the midst of a situation of rapid change and transition.

B. This is not better explained by sedative, hypnotic, or anxiolytic abuse.

C. Such behaviors have a positive, calming effect in stressful situations.

D. Such behaviors do not interfere with taking assertive action when it is required.

303.00 Initiative

A. For at least 12 months, the individual has demonstrated a sustained capacity to engage in two or more of the following behaviors:
   - a willingness to and an interest in solving problems
   - bringing difficult personal, interpersonal, or occupational problems to a satisfactory conclusion
   - taking responsibility for dealing with problematic situations that others avoid
   - planning for future outcome and taking the initial steps to realize goals and objectives
   - working diligently to do the initial things to ensure the success of any projects that are undertaken.

B. This capacity is typically based on disappointments early in life.

C. This is not better explained by obsessive compulsive disorder.

D. The individual typically does not see these traits as a problem.

304.00 Insight

A. For at least six months, the individual has demonstrated a capacity to understand self and others including at least three of the following:
   - the capacity for honest and deep self-reflection
   - the capacity to read others motives clearly and without bias
   - the ability not to leap to conclusions but to wait until there is sufficient information
   - the confidence to rely on his or her own thoughts and perceptions
   - the devotion to seek and to face the truth
   - the strength to see difficulty and disappointment honestly.

B. Insight is not used to harm others but may have its roots in harm done to the self by others.

C. This is not better explained by delusional disorder.

D. These symptoms typically benefit others and produce positive changes in the individual's self-knowledge or self-esteem.

Conclusion

Although the proposal for a DSM of strengths may seem a tad precious, maybe even a bit frivolous, the intent is serious. The number of people who suffer from disorder and disorganization in their mental and interpersonal life suffer enough without having to experience an iatrogenic push toward chronicity and a social nudge toward alienation. As social workers, given our value commitments, we must do what we can to leaven the intense preoccupation with symptoms and labeling with an equally intense preoccupation with understanding life's real problems and the virtues of the people who suffer them. The work of constructing an institutional edifice of the possible and the promising, of virtues and visions, must begin now and must be taken seriously. ■

References

American Psychiatric Association. (1994). *The diagnostic and statistical manual of mental disorders* (4th ed.). Washington, DC: Author.

Andreasen, N. (1984). *The broken brain.* New York: Harper & Row.

Cutler, C. E. (1991). Deconstructing the DSM-III. *Social Work, 36,* 154–157.

Gergen, K. J. (1994). *Realities and relationships: Soundings in social construction.* Cambridge, MA: Harvard University Press.

Gold, M. S. (1987). *The good news about depression: Cures and treatments in the new age of psychiatry.* New York: Villard.

Goleman, D. (1994, December 14). Helping family doctors spot psychiatric problems. *New York Times,* p. B8.

Kovel, J. (1981). *The age of desire: Reflections of a radical psychoanalyst.* New York: Pantheon.

Kutchins, H., & Kirk, S. A. (1997). *Making us crazy—DSM: the psychiatric bible and the creation of mental disorders.* New York: Free Press.

Tavris, C. (1992). *The mismeasure of woman.* New York: Simon & Schuster.

Wakefield, J. C. (1992). Disorder as harmful dysfunction: A conceptual critique of DSM-III-R's definition of mental disorders. *Psychological Review, 90,* 238.

Walker, III, S. (1996). *A dose of sanity: Mind, medicine, and misdiagnosis.* New York: John Wiley & Sons.

Wolin, S. J., & Wolin, S. (1993). *The resilient self: How survivors of troubled families rise above adversity.* New York: Villard.

Dennis Saleebey, DSW, *is professor, School of Social Welfare, University of Kansas, Lawrence, KS 66045; e-mail: denniss@ukans.edu.*

Original manuscript received March 12, 1999
Final revision received September 15, 1999
Accepted January 12, 2000

Editorial

Whose Evidence and for What Purpose?

Stanley L. Witkin and W. David Harrison

Evidence-based practice (EBP) is one of the predominant new ways of thinking about what social workers should do in their practice and how they should decide to do it. EBP involves using the "best available" evidence, often interpreted to mean research-based "knowledge," about specific types of practices with particular problems. Although its advocates tout EBP as an imperative for social workers, others have raised questions regarding potential drawbacks of this approach. This editorial is intended neither to advocate nor to oppose EBP, but rather to identify issues that we believe social workers should consider.

Origins and Characteristics of EBP

Before there was EBP, there was EBM—"evidence-based medicine"—a didactic approach first used with medical students in Canada and later applied to the solution of clinical problems. Widely adopted in the United Kingdom, and increasingly in the United States, EBM is used to determine the most desirable ways to promote health and especially to treat illnesses. Its more general form, EBP, has become a major dimension of professional education in the United Kingdom and a way of attempting to arrive at a consensus about what collective bodies of research findings have to recommend. Gambrill's (1999) thoughtful and informative article advocating EBP in social work documents some of these fundamental and influential British sources.

The medical origins of EBP are evident in the value placed on randomized clinical trials, similar to what social workers call experimental designs. Information generated by randomized clinical trials is taken to be the "gold standard" of evidence. Although results from studies using less traditional research controls such as case accounts are used by EBP, they occupy a lower status in the hierarchy of credible evidence. Judgments about evidence also are based on systematic reviews of treatment–outcome studies and meta-analyses that aggregate several research studies statistically. Assessing such evidence is a complex process requiring a high level of research sophistication and knowledge of the subject matter. For example, even with a large group of randomized clinical trials on a topic, small alterations in the definitions of problems or "interventions" can lead to changes in what is considered best practice. A review of readily accessible online reports of EBP or evidence-based medicine studies (see, for example, Research Triangle Institute, 2000) shows that various types of "psychosocial" treatments are sometimes aggregated across studies, and that medically precise definitions of "outcomes" may be hard to reconcile with social workers' espoused views of taking into account all relevant aspects of a social situation.

Social Work and EBP

Today, EBP has become a common term in many professions, including social work. Attempts to deal seriously with systematic evidence as a way to reduce uncertainty and improve practice have a long history in social work, as anyone familiar with the extended and legally oriented presentation concerning evidence as a basis for social work in Mary Richmond's *Social Diagnosis* (1917) will recall. Similarly, social surveys historically have provided evidence of the existence and effects of structural inequalities in society, often with suggestions for reform and documentation of the social benefits of reforms. The contemporary social work version of EBP (like its predecessor, empirical clinical practice) is focused more on weeding out ineffective therapies and practices and recommending interventions that logically are related to predetermined changes.

Social workers' current advocacy or adoption of EBP can be thought of as an expression of the profession's recent attention to research activities and ways of thinking. The idea of systematically basing our practice on scientific evidence is appealing in our "tell me what works" society. Paralleling medicine to a degree not seen in years,

CCC Code: 0037-8046/01 $3.00 © 2001

recent concerted efforts to place social work in the mainstream of scientifically oriented professions can be considered the enactment of cultural beliefs about what a profession should do and be. If only we have enough evidence, based on accurate specification of conditions, outcomes, and interventions, we should be able to solve our problems. What remains unclear is the range and types of problems for which the "what works" formulation is helpful. For example, it may be a useful formulation for problems that are believed to exist stably across time and contexts, where problems and interventions can be specified (operationalized) and replicated in other practice settings, where they exist in deterministic relationships to one another, and where outcome measures are seen as reflecting rather than generating the problems they address. It seems less useful for a world characterized by shifting, multiple identities and relational constructions, in which an "outcome" is at most the beginning of something else, or where the production and evaluation of knowledge for practice are considered mutual activities between professionals and people who use their services.

At its heart, EBP involves using the best evidence available to help practitioners make decisions and conduct their practice in concert with professional values. Ideally, "best evidence" would include integrating knowledge gained from practice experience with knowledge gained through research, a position that even some EBP advocates accept (see, for example, Sackett, Rosenberg, Muir Gray, Haynes, & Richardson, 1996). Practitioners should be able to understand, critically assess, and apply evidence that is relevant to the tasks and missions they undertake. They should be able to do so while appreciating the complexity and meaning of the situation to the people with whom they hope to reshape the situation in mutually desired ways.

Social work has produced few studies that exemplify randomized clinical trials. One reason for this may be the complex ways in which social workers understand their practice. Social workers see the heart of their practice as "person in situation," in expanding problem understanding to include social and environmental elements. Social work practice involves seeing people as much for their differences as for anything that links them to classifiable problems or diagnoses. It values the often subjugated perspectives of the people we serve and attempts to understand their individual and collective narratives of their situations and conditions. We learn to work with moral narratives, the "morass of goods and bads, rights and wrongs, evils and virtues, bearing little resemblance to the diagnostic labels or the balance sheet of assets or liabilities that the client inevitably earns" (Goldstein, 2000, p. 349). These interactive accounts of people in their situations are not just tools for understanding, but the essential components of the individual's experience of social problems, medical conditions, and behavior. We learn to listen for discrepancies between the public discourse of disadvantaged people dealing with more powerful systems and the internal discourse within groups and individuals that frequently offer different understandings. In this sense, social workers often are cultural bridges, able to deal in multiple worlds of understanding. Sometimes this involves using the logic of EBP with clients when there is credible evidence of some relevant knowledge available. Other times, however, the most important work is in educating decision makers or those who have control of resources about how irrelevant the best scientific evidence is to the world of people whose experiences brought them into contact with the professionals.

It is interesting to note that in the United Kingdom significant debates have arisen concerning the place of EBP in the professions. Even the *British Medical Journal*, where a great deal of EBP advocacy was centered, recently included a series of articles on "narrative based medicine" (for a good example, see Greenhalgh & Hurwitz). Thoughtful critiques also have begun to emerge in British social work, citing EBP's narrow approach to practice and the fact that social work remains contested philosophically. Webb (2001) offers a particularly thought-provoking caution that uncritically embracing the basic assumptions of EBP would be incompatible with the reality of social work practice, which is a reflexive, interactive, and rather unpredictable rather than regular and "rational-technical" process.

Language and EBP

Words like "evidence" and "outcome" are just that, words. They do not point to any pre-existing entities in the world. Rather, their meaning is derived from their use in particular contexts. In situations where being able to provide the grounds for one's beliefs or actions is normative, having "evidence" for a position provides a stronger warrant for that position than not having evidence. Evidence is the name given to a culturally preferred reason for an existential claim or the performance of an action. In the first case evidence functions as proof, in the second as justification.

But a claim of evidence must fit the rules of the social situation in which it is used and be negotiated with those who have the power to legitimate the claim. Therefore, what counts as evidence and the value of different types of evidence tell us much about cultural beliefs and power relations as about what is real. We are familiar with these notions in legal proceedings, where what can be entered "into evidence" is governed by rules and the determination of a judge, and where such decisions may determine the outcome of a case.

These notions are no less important to practice. Definitions of evidence, and their presumed relation to professional practice, support particular assumptive and ideological positions. By restricting the types of information to be used as evidence and defining the relationships among these types of evidence (for example, information from a randomized clinical trial versus practice experience), EBP supports certain practices (for example, those claiming to be "empirical") and undermines others.

Fortunately, because the social work world functions only some of the time like a court room, we are not bound by the meanings ascribed to these terms by any particular group. The value of particular meanings can be contested and alternative meanings and values considered. We might examine EBP from several perspectives. For example, consider the question of who gains and who loses by the adoption of an EBP approach? If you subscribe to the meaning of evidence as used in EBP and its importance to the justification of practice, then you might respond that clients gain and irresponsible practitioners lose. Alternatively, by keeping social work practice a highly complex technology that can be mastered by relatively few experts, adherence to EBP may weed out some incompetent practitioners, but also rid the profession of many people who are doing excellent work, dissuade potentially creative practitioners from entering the field, or create (or render invisible) new kinds of incompetence.

Different sources of evidence (for example, researchers, practitioners, and clients) also might be considered. EBP seems to presume a context in which practitioners do something to clients. This "doing" is considered to be most effective (and ethical), if based on "evidence." But what if practice is viewed as a mutual activity in which what is best (not necessarily effective) is co-generated by clients and practitioners? What is the relative value of different sources and types of evidence in this scenario? (Of course, clients will not ordinarily use the word evidence to justify or prove something, putting them at a disadvantage in a setting where evidence already is afforded high status.) These are merely a few examples of the type of inquiry we encourage social work practitioners to conduct as they wrestle with this important issue.

Conclusion

Evidence-based practice envisions a scientifically based social work that uses the best available evidence to guide practice decisions. It also aligns social work with other, more prestigious professions like medicine. Determining whether these are desirable directions for the profession presents social workers with considerable technical and conceptual challenges. Even social workers who like the idea of EBP need considerable expertise in how to evaluate research design, methodology, and analysis lest they accept on faith others' judgments about the "best evidence" (a position that would be inconsistent with EBP). But such evaluations, although important, are not sufficient. They are confined to criteria presumed important by EBP and may not address other issues that are important to social workers.

EBP, like all approaches, is ideological in the sense that it assumes certain beliefs and adheres to certain values. Understanding these assumptions, beliefs, and values requires examining EBP through a variety of lenses (for example, social reform) and questioning what is taken for granted or considered unproblematic. For example, we might question whether there are parallels between EBP's current affiliation with medicine and social work's affiliation with psychiatry in the early part of the 20th century. What do (did) we gain and what do (did) we lose by this association? Or we might inquire about what EBP-informed social work practice is actually like. How does it position the profession vis-a-vis its social values? What effect will it have on issues of relationship that are so central to social work practice?

It seems to us that social work in today's society is largely reactive in that it responds to social forces for the efficient management of lives rather than building communities, helping people determine their own goals and destinies, and standing with unpopular or unrecognized people. Much of practice is oriented to blending into the mainstream, going with the flow of professional acceptability where the prevalent, if unspoken, values and tasks center on diagnosing and treating people who are personally experiencing society's problems or coping with human conditions. Social work's social control functions have been reflected in the language of "servicing" people, assessing their "needs" for them, and, despite the widespread use of the term "empowerment," in conformity with the conventions of medical and legal descriptions of people and the work of the profession.

Given our view, we want to be mindful that the power of the ideas encompassed in EBP can be used in a variety of ways. These ideas are so compatible with other dominant professional trends and cultural narratives about how people and society function that they may be taken for granted and thus may lead to social work's losing its traditional emphasis on understanding people in context and understanding that individual problems and social problems are inseparable. Is it a coincidence that EBP is favored by managed care providers pushing practice toward an emphasis on specificity in problem identification and rapid responses to the identified conditions? Social work's vision of EBP must not be limited to a medicalized view of social problems and a clinical view of responses to them. Rather, as social workers seek to develop more credible practice, we hope they will be mindful of Gambrill's (2001) challenge to use EBP principles for purposes of mutuality and empowerment. If EBP is to have any lasting value in social work, it will involve helping the profession take a more critical stance to all knowledge, including knowledge grounded in what is considered to be the best available evidence. ■

Stanley L. Witkin, PhD, is professor, Department of Social Work, University of Vermont, and W. David Harrison, PhD, is dean, School of Social Work and Criminal Justice, East Carolina University, Greenville, NC.

References

Gambrill, E. (1999). Evidence-based practice: An alternative to authority-based practice. *Families in Society, 80,* 341–350.

Gambrill, E. (2001). Social work: an authority-based profession. *Research on Social work Practice, 11,* 166–175.

Goldstein, H. (2000). Joe the King: A study of strengths and morality. *Families in Society, 81,* 347–350.

Greenhalgh, T., & Hurwitz, B. (1999). Narrative based medicine: Why study narrative. *British Medical Journal, 318,* 48–50.

Research Triangle Institute. (2000). Assessing "best evidence": Grading the quality of articles and rating the strength of evidence [Online]. Available: www.rti.org/epc/grading_article.html.

Richmond, M. (1917). *Social diagnosis.* New York: Russell Sage Foundation.

Sackett, D. L., Rosenberg, W. M. C., Muir Gray, J. A., Haynes, R. B., & Richardson, W. S. (1996). Evidence based medicine: What it is and what it isn't. *British Medical Journal, 312,* 72–73.

Webb, S. A. (2001). Some considerations on the validity of evidence-based practice in social work. *British Journal of Social Work, 31,* 57–79.

Professional Psychology: Research and Practice
2010, Vol 41, No 3, 202–209

0735-7028/10/$12.00 DOI 10.1037/a0018445

Mental Health Professionals' Adaptive Responses to Racial Microaggressions: An Exploratory Study

Pilar Hernández
Johns Hopkins University

Mirna Carranza
McMaster University

Rhea Almeida
Institute for Family Services, Somerset, New Jersey

This study examines adaptive responses that mental health professionals of color use to cope with racial microaggressions in their professional lives. Twenty-four mental health professionals from diverse ethnic backgrounds in the United States and Canada participated in focus groups discussing their experiences with racial microagressions and how they cope with them. Results of the analysis indicated that 8 primary coping themes illustrated strategies used by the participants. These include: identifying key issues in responding to racial microaggressions, self-care, spirituality, confrontation, support, documentation, mentoring, and collective organizing. Suggestions for mentoring professionals of color are offered.

Keywords: racial microaggressions, training, professional development, resilience, coping

Recent developments in the study of racial microaggressions at university campuses (Solórzano, Ceja, & Yosso, 2000; W. A. Smith, Allen, & Danley, 2007), in the counseling process (Constantine, 2007; L. Smith, Constantine, Graham, & Dize, 2008, Sue et al., Copodilupo, 2007) and among faculty in university environments (Constantine, Smith, Redington, & Owens, 2008) have shed light into the everyday impact of modern forms of racism towards ethnic minorities. Sue (2003) posited that racial microaggressions are more complex and difficult to identify, examine, and confront. Moreover, they also have a more sustained and detrimental impact on those who are regularly affected by them. Sue, Copodilupo, et al. (2007) defined them as "brief, everyday exchanges that send denigrating messages to people of Color because they belong to a racial minority group" (p. 273). They developed a typology of racial microaggressions identifying the following categories: microassault, microinsult, and microinvalidation at both environmental and interpersonal levels. Sue, Copodilupo, et al. (2007) argued that examining racial microaggressions is necessary to identify, respond, and prevent the threats and harm that they pose in today's society. Solórzano et al. (2007) and Sue, Copodilupo et al. (2007) called for research that investigates how people of color adaptively respond to these everyday aggressions and how to increase the awareness and accountability on those who perpetrate them.

The purpose of this study is to respond to the first issue: how do people of color adaptively respond to this contemporary form of racism? Specifically, how do mental health professionals of color (psychologists, social workers, counselors, and family therapists) engaged in teaching and/or clinical practice adaptively respond to racial microaggressions while performing their professional duties? To date leading authors in this field (Constantine, 2007; Constantine, Smith, Redington, & Owens, 2008; L. Smith et al., 2008; Sue, 2008; Sue, Copodilupo, et al., 2007) have offered a conceptual framework to understand racial microaggressions, examined perceptions of racial microaggressions among African American supervisees in cross-racial dyads (Constantine & Sue, 2007), explored the experiences of Asian Americans (Sue, Bucceri, et al., 2007), African Americans (Sue et al., 2008) and African American counseling faculty in academia (Constantine, Smith, Redington, & Owens, 2008), discussed the implications of this contemporary form of racism in professional psychology training settings (L. Smith et al., 2008), and proposed applications in organizational consultation (Sue, 2008). However, the question of how mental health professionals adaptively respond to racial microaggressions in their daily professional lives is a new dimension in need of exploration. This issue has key practical implications on the professional development and mentoring of mental

Pilar Hernández received her PhD in counseling psychology from the University of Massachusetts at Amherst. She is associate professor and director of the Clinical Community Counseling program in the Department of Counseling and Human Services at Johns Hopkins University. Her areas of research and practice include traumatic stress and resilience, clinical supervision and training, critical postcolonial therapy models, and domestic violence.

Mirna Carranza received her PhD in marriage and family therapy from the University of Guelph. She is assistant professor in the Department of Social Work at McMaster University. Her research interests include immigrant and refugee families issues, grief, ambiguous losses, war and torture, social justice issues and forced migration, children's and women's rights in Latin America.

Rhea Almeida received her master's in social work from Columbia University School of social work and her PhD in Social Anthropology from Makerere University. She is the director of the Institute for Family Services, Somerset, New Jersey and creator of the cultural context model. Her areas of practice include the development and implementation of the cultural context model, domestic violence, and cultural equity.

Correspondence concerning this article should be addressed to Pilar Hernández, Department of Counseling and Human Services, Johns Hopkins University, 2800 North Charles Street, Baltimore, MD 21218. E-mail: pilarhw@jhu.edu health professionals in contemporary training and practice settings where standards of cultural competence are expected.

Because of the novelty of this area of study and the need to develop a conceptual framework grounded in mental health professionals' experiences, we chose a qualitative inquiry as the best method for our investigation. We formulated a preliminary description of how professionals of color adaptively respond in environments where racial microaggressions are a part of their everyday life through a phenomenological and grounded theory analysis and offer practical recommendations for training, mentoring, and support.

Racial Microaggressions

Sue, Copodupulo, et al. (2007) defined *microaggressions* as "brief and commonplace daily verbal, behavioral, and environmental indignities, whether intentional or unintentional, that communicate hostile, derogatory, or negative racial slights and insults that potentially have harmful or unpleasant psychological impact on the target person or group" (273). They proposed three major categories identifiable in larger social contexts and in interpersonal relationships: microassaults, microinsults, and microinvalidations. Briefly, these authors defined *microassaults* as explicit behaviors intending to hurt a person of color such as name calling, avoidance, and discrimination. Examples in a mental health professional setting include White supervisors calling Chinese supervisees "chink" (Hernández, Taylor, & McDowell, 2009). Microinsults refer to communications conveying a hidden insult demeaning a person's racial heritage, for example, a comment by a White psychologist to a Latino American psychologist from South America about his negative views of people from his country based on his experiences working in the prison system with Latinos. Microinvalidations are characterized by denial, exclusion, and invisibility of a person of color's thoughts, feelings, and experiences as they relate to his or her ethnic heritage. This form of microaggression involves experiences, in which the opinions of professionals of color are typically not taken seriously, especially as they relate to their own ethnic groups. For example, a Latina faculty may find herself teaching in a mental health training program with a training clinic serving Latinos. She may experience that a common response to her efforts to integrate ethnic minority psychology in the curriculum involves acknowledgement about the relevance of this content, yet no one discusses her ideas with depth and moves to explore how to make possible changes to the curriculum.

Studies conducted thus far in the fields of education and counseling psychology have involved qualitative- and mixed-method methodologies Qualitative studies used purposive sampling and focus group interview formats. They coincide in identifying various forms of racial microaggressions and their negative impact on the lives of those who suffer them. In their pioneer study on racial microaggressions, Solórzano, Ceja, and Yosso (2000) examined the impact of racial microaggressions on the campus' climate in undergraduate education at three predominantly White research university campuses. The authors identified how experiences of racial microaggressions within academic and social spaces impact life on campus in general as well as the academic performance and social interactions of the participating students. Racial microaggressions that occurred in classrooms and in interactions with White peers and faculty involved lower expectations, negative assumptions about the ability to perform academically, and beliefs that their presence on campus was the result of some form of affirmative action. A major effect of this climate on students was feeling drained as a result of the intense scrutiny and offenses faced in everyday life. Students also reported increased self-doubt, frustration, and isolation. The students' response to this climate involved the creation of counter spaces within and outside the classroom. Some of these spaces included study groups, fraternities and sororities, and Black student organizations

Another qualitative study conducted by Sue, Bucceri, Lin, Nadal, and Torino (2007) explored experiences of racial microaggressions among Asian Americans. Focus groups were conducted with 10 self-identified Asian American students and working professionals from various backgrounds (Chinese, Filipino, Korean, Japanese, and Asian Indian). The following themes were identified: alien in own land, ascription of intelligence, denial of racial reality, exoticization of Asian American women, invalidation of intelligence differences, pathologizing of cultural values and communication styles, second class citizenship, and invisibility. The authors reported that participants had difficulty determining whether a microaggression occurred given that most of the racial microaggressions experienced came from peers, neighbors, friends, or authority figures. They also expressed conflict about whether to respond to microaggressions because they deemed them as unintentional and possibly outside the level of awareness of the perpetrator. Alleyne (2005) explored the impact of racial microaggressions towards ethnic minorities in the work place in England. She interviewed 30 participants mostly from African descent. The participants' narratives concluded that racial aggressions can be verbal or nonverbal, subtle, stunning, and result in shame and hurt. The narratives described workplace cultures that covertly fostered collusion of management and subtly abusive practices with Black workers. For example, one of her participants stated, "they know they just can't get rid of you ... the law wouldn't allow it these days ... so they put pressure on you to make damn sure you don't cope" (p 288). In her view, racial microaggressions continue to wound the psyche of those whose collective history involves carrying the legacy of slavery. Like Sue (2003), Alleyne spoke about the conspiracy of silence; however, she linked it to a legacy of traumatic stress and explained it in terms of the relationship between the traumatic legacy of slavery, structural oppression, and everyday forms of racial aggression toward African Americans.

In the counseling field, Constantine & Sue (2007) and Constantine (2007) conducted studies to examine the impact of racial microaggressions in various aspects of the counseling process. A qualitative study (Constantine & Sue, 2007) explored the occurrence of racial microaggressions towards Black supervisees in supervisory relationships with White supervisors. They found the following themes: invalidation of racial–cultural issues, making stereotypic assumptions about Black clients, making stereotypic assumptions about Black supervisees, reluctance to give performance feedback for fear of being viewed as racist, focusing primarily on clinical weaknesses, blaming clients of color for problems stemming from oppression, and offering culturally insensitive treatment recommendations. In addition, Constantine (2007) conducted a mixed-method study to test a path model examining the various relationships among African American clients' perceptions of racial microaggressions in counseling by White therapists, the therapeutic working alliance, the clients' perception of the counselors' general and multicultural counseling competence, and the clients' counseling satisfaction. Her findings indicated that African American clients' perceived racial microaggressions were negatively associated with their perceptions of the therapeutic working alliance and White therapists' general and multicultural counseling competence. As in previous studies, it emerged that the racial microaggressions identified could be seen as relatively subtle manifestations of bias or could be considered to be ill defined and vague. She posited that unconscious racial hostility in the therapeutic relationship would negatively impact the working alliance and can potentially be more harmful to the client because it is coming from someone who is supposed to help.

W. A. Smith et al. (2007) argued that in academic contexts there is a need to understand and manage universities' academic policies, historical legacies of racial exclusion, racial behaviors inside and outside the classroom, and to find mentors and support systems. Likewise, professionals of color working as faculty, clinical directors, and therapists in colleges and universities, hospitals, community mental health agencies, government health agencies, and the like need to pay systematic attention to understanding and responding to the ways in which these organizations are structured to maintain contemporary forms of racism.

This study explores how mental health professionals of color in the United States and Canada (psychologists, social workers, counselors, and family therapists), engaged in teaching and/or clinical practice, adaptively respond to racial microaggressions while performing their professional duties. We formulate a preliminary description through a phenomenological and grounded theory analysis. This study does not intend to generalize its findings to all ethnic minorities but to examine the accounts of the participants from the vantage point of meaning construction and interpretation based on personal experience. In addition, we believe that this kind of analysis is similarly applicable to other covert and structural discriminations, such as those based on gender, sexual identity, class, ability, age, or religion.

Method

This qualitative, exploratory study was guided by grounded theory (Glaser & Strauss, 1967; Lincoln & Guba, 1985; Padgett, 1998), and interpretive phenomenological analysis (Creswell, 1998; Moustakas, 1994). It was conducted through a combination of focus groups and individual follow-up interviews. The following guidelines for trustworthiness in qualitative research were followed: interview guideline pilot, data analysis triangulation, transferability, dependability, and data analysis saturation (Denzin & Lincoln, 2005; Lincoln & Guba, 1985; Marshall & Rossman, 1999). The research team included three ethnic minority female doctoral level mental health professionals involved in training and clinical practice in the United States and Canada and two masters' level family therapy interns, a heterosexual Jewish man and a lesbian White woman, both in their early 30s. Interns were trained in grounded theory and interpretive phenomenological data analysis prior to the study. An external reviewer, an ethnic minority doctoral level mental health faculty, examined the data analysis and its results at the end of the process.

Participants

Participants in this study were ethnic minority professionals with master's and doctoral degrees in mental health who were teaching mental health related courses at universities or training institutes, or/and had a clinical practice (counselors, psychologists, social workers, and marriage and family therapists). Forty nine potential participants were invited to participate in the study. Twenty four responded, no one was excluded and no one refused to participate in the study before or during the focus groups. There were 13 participants from the United States (seven women and five men): four Latinas, one Asian, two Asian Americans, and five African Americans. There were 11 participants from Canada (six women and five men): four African Canadians, three Asian Canadians, three Latina Canadians, and one Kurdish Canadian. Ages ranged from 28 to 55 years of age. Fourteen participants worked only in clinical settings, nine participants worked in teaching/training and clinical settings, and one worked in an academic training setting only. Years of practice as clinicians ranged between 5 and 15 years, while practice in teaching/training ranged from 3 to 10 years. Practice settings included counseling (doctoral and masters), marriage and family therapy (masters), and psychology (doctoral and undergraduate) training programs, private practice settings, and outpatient clinics. All participants categorized their current class status as middle class.

The selection of participants was based on (a) intensity sampling that uses the selection of information-rich cases that manifest the phenomenon profoundly; (b) chain sampling, used to identify participants through people who know people who know what cases are information-rich; and (c) politically important cases sampling that involves the selection of sites and participants according to the particular usefulness and interest of a political dimension in the study (Patton, 2002).

Participants were invited on the basis of their public work (publications, presentations, participation in community, and professional activities) in matters of diversity and mental health. They were recruited through professional networks in which the investigators had membership and were referred by colleagues of the investigators who considered the ways in which their backgrounds and interests were suitable to the study. The investigators provided a general overview of the study in their preliminary contact with potential participants via email or phone. If they were interested, an email with a complete description of the study—providing the definition of racial microaggressions offered by Sue, Capodilupo, et al. (2007) but without using this term—a consent form, possible times to schedule a focus group, and a location were sent. Three focus groups were conducted in the United States (San Diego, CA; Baltimore, MD; Sommerset, NJ) and three focus groups were conducted in Canada (two in Kitchener, ON; one in Hamilton, ON) by the principal investigators, who were all trained and experienced in facilitating focus groups. Follow-up interviews were conducted with two participants in San Diego and one participant in Baltimore because they did not have enough air time to share in detail their stories in the focus groups. Debriefing was offered after the focus group and/or interviews were conducted.

Measure

Data was collected through a brief demographic questionnaire (ethnicity, gender, age range, occupation, and education) and a semi-structured interview protocol (see Appendix). The protocol was developed based on previous studies on racial microaggressions (Solórzano et al., 2000; Sue, Burcceri, et al., 2007; Sue, Copodupolo, et al., 2007). All questions were open-ended and aimed at eliciting the participants' experiences with racial microaggressions, and how they found ways to respond to them. Focus groups lasted between 1 and 1½ hr, and were facilitated by each of the investigators. They were audio- and videotaped. Three follow-up interviews were conducted to get the full stories that some of the participants could not share fully because of time issues. These individual interviews did not follow a specific format. Data from these follow-up interviews was only included in the analysis when it was supportive to the domains emerging from the focus group data.

Procedure

Data analysis was guided by grounded theory (Glaser & Strauss, 1967; Lincoln & Guba, 1985; Padgett, 1998), and interpretive phenomenological analysis (Creswell, 1998; Moustakas, 1994). Prior to data collection the three leading researchers and the two family therapy interns discussed their personal histories involving identity privilege and oppression (i.e., Latinas and heterosexual, White and Lesbian, South Asian and heterosexual, and Jewish and heterosexual). They also discussed their interests, and biases relevant to the topic of the study to make visible their preferences, feelings, and potential close connections to the data. For example, the leading researchers discussed their immigration histories and the relationships between immigration and career choice, teaching and research in multicultural counseling. With regard to their biases, they believe that professors/clinicians of color, and gay or lesbian professors/clinicians would report varying levels of stress, frustration, and sadness associated with experiencing racial microagressions in the workplace. They also discussed various ways in which professors/clinicians cope with microaggressions in general and racial microaggressions in particular. These involved seeking support from family, friends, and colleagues, confrontation, channeling their energy into positive endeavors, withdrawing from engagement and withdrawal.

Transcripts were coded for each individual interview into domains that were agreed on by consensus within the team. The consensus process involved individual review of each other's analysis, face-to-face meetings and conference calls to discuss how all researchers identified domains. Areas of disagreement were further discussed until all parties felt that their views were included in the analysis. Domains developed were audited by all team members and core ideas were identified for all material within each domain for each individual case; finally, a cross analysis of categories to describe consistencies in the core ideas within domains across cases was performed.

Triangulation methods. The process of corroborating evidence from different individuals, types of data, data collection techniques, and data analysis is used in qualitative research to strengthen accuracy and credibility (Lincon & Guba, 1985). Data triangulation consisted of multiple-focus groups and follow-up interviews conducted in three cities in the United States. Three focus groups were conducted in two cities in Ontario, Canada. Investigator triangulation involved a research team including the authors and an external reviewer. The initial coding on what constituted what kind of racial microaggression was based on the typology outlined in Sue, Capodupolo, et al. (2007). Coding for themes, domains, and core ideas was performed by team members until reaching consensus. An independent auditor revised the data analysis and suggested clarification of themes. As a result of this feedback, the research team discussed and implemented modifications to the data analysis.

Data analysis. A sample of two focus group transcripts was transcribed and used to develop an initial set of basic categories about racial microaggressions, their impact, and coping. The narratives from the transcripts were analyzed along the following domains: (a) identifying racial microaggressions, (b) illustrations of racial microaggressions, (c) impact of racial microaggressions, and (d) coping responses to racial microaggressions. This paper elaborates on the analysis of item (d).

Results

The data analysis resulted in the identification of eight themes emerging from the participants' accounts about how they cope with racial microaggressions. These themes are interconnected and they have been categorized, described, and illustrated with direct quotes from interview transcripts. Data did not reach saturation in regards to age differences and gender. Differences regarding country of residence are noted.

Theme 1: Identifying Key Issues in Deciding How To Respond To a Racial Microaggression

All participants ($n = 24$) indicated that they follow a processes by which they identify their thoughts, feelings, and responses to a perceived racial microaggession. This process involves multiple steps and decision points. At times, each individual must respond to her or his personal need for self-care and choose how and when to respond to a microaggression individually, collectively, and/or for the protection of others. Participants noted that they must balance their knowledge that racism exists while taking distance from a situation that they may deem as racist or potentially racist. They remind themselves not to interpret every situation as racial. If a situation occurs that is ambiguous enough to require pondering whether it was a microaggression or not, a decision is made as to whether it is worth it to invest energy in pursuing its understanding and possibly responding. However, if appraisal deems it necessary to respond, a decision is made to reflect on the situation alone or with others. An African American female described this process as follows:

> I take a deep breath and sit with it for a minute and second guess myself. Did they really say that to me?! Think about it. Is there any other way I can interpret this other than racism? Is there any other way I can rationalize this and extend this person a little bit of grace before I tell them exactly what my experience is and how I experienced that situation. If it is possible, I want to confront it directly as I am dealing with this person. Another way of coping for me has been to find someone that is going to understand and process it with them whether it be my partner, whether that be a close friend, or whether that means snatching the first African American person I can find on the campus. Processing with somebody who can confirm that I am still sane, that I am not crazy, and that I am not hypersensitive or overreacting or any of that stuff. Then I have a thought process where I think about these

persons and whatever my history is with them and see how this goes with their character and what I expected of them.

Participants posited that being able to talk with others who are supportive and may concur with one's interpretation of situations involving microaggressions is essential to maintain perspective not only in how events are interpreted but also in determining what to do about it in the context of assessing current power structures. In addition, understanding of the possible implications of any decision is a part of a process of strategizing with the support of friends, colleagues, and family.

Theme 2: Self-Care

All participants ($n = 24$) reported that they are mindful of the need to take care of themselves on a regular basis to detoxify from frequent forms of racial microaggressions they experience in their jobs. Self-care involved exercise, meditation, visualizations, acupuncture, chiropractic treatment, taking time off, thinking positively and avoiding negative thoughts, and taking pride in one's ethnic heritage. For example, an Asian American female explained: "My daughters built a labyrinth in our backyard to help me deal with the stress in my department. I use it regularly to meditate and center myself. It helps me release all the bad energies." Two Latinas shared that they used energy work to help each other to regain balance after stressful events with White clinicians at their center. A male African Canadian discussed his involvement in sports and others commented on the benefits of exercise in their lives.

Theme 3: Spirituality

Participants for whom spirituality was relevant in their lives ($n = 18$) explained that their faith played a major role in overcoming frustrations brought up by racial microaggressions. Meditation, prayer, and rituals helped them channel their feelings towards a higher purpose and ponder various perspectives in regards to the aggressor and the situation. This dimension had a practical aspect for most participants including rituals that helped them face challenging situations. For example, an African American female said,

> When I sought advice from a Native American friend, I was advised to do a ritual before I go into the domain of this people. That was really helpful to me. As soon as I pull my car into the parking lot and before I walked to the office, I make an offering and call my ancestors to shield me, to be with me, to protect me from any negative energy, and to allow me to connect with my students.

Theme 4: Confronting the Aggressor

More than half ($n = 16$) participants examined ways in which they challenge aggressors in professional settings. Various responses were discussed involving direct responses to microinsults and microassaults, verbalizing that an issue needs to be addressed and discussed, and being proactive about educating others. An African American female described one of her responses as follows:

> We can have a dialogue if you want so I get engaged with them and connected, but I don't let them get away with it. That to me is the best victory—to not do what they do but to rise above that and call it out, and out of my example, tell you that it is not right, and we can have a dialogue about it.

An African American male used humor to confront racial aggressions:

> I was working as a program director and founded a program for working with HIV African American men, and we had this art show this White man said to me, "Wow, we are reading about you all over the newspapers You have done a lot of things. Pretty soon you're going to get your Cadillac!" And I just say, "Oh no, I am a Volvo kind of guy."

Theme 5: Seeking Support From White Allies

More than half of the participants ($n = 15$) discussed how they sought support from White allies in critical situations involving decision making and leadership roles. They noted that it is important to have the support of other clinicians and faculty when they raise challenging issues, have a stake in decision-making processes and lead others in matters of policy, training, and service. When anticipating the possibility of being challenged, they seek support from allies to strategize how to respond. A Latina explained,

> I have very good relationships with White gay colleagues and a White heterosexual faculty. They have lived abroad or traveled a lot and understand issues of privilege and oppression. I regularly talk with them to seek validation and support. There was a time when my White peers challenged my nomination to an important committee. They stood by my side, talked to the dean and took the heat for some of the conflict that emerged

Theme 6: Keeping Records and Documenting Experiences of Microaggressions

More than half of the participants ($n = 16$) reported being mindful about documenting their experience at their workplace. There were country of residence differences, with more U.S. professionals ($n = 10$) speaking to this issue. They noted that although it was time consuming, it allowed them to see patterns of events in time and keep a paper trail. Documenting the history of microaggressions became useful to strategize new responses to further aggressions. An Asian American said,

> I document even the nonverbal communication! I create a paper trail of documentation of my work in case they want to minimize it. When the time comes, I communicate with my supervisor. I create a space to develop my own voice.

Theme 7: Mentoring

All participants ($n = 24$) identified mentoring as a highly valuable endeavor in any setting An African American female indicated that discussing these issues must be done tentatively and delicately to understand the concerns as accurate as possible and to validate the students' needs.

> I can only talk about my experience. I always look to describe the scenario to someone else to see if they see it in the same way I do. I trust their reaction to what I describe, so if they say, "You are really overreacting It could have been this or this," I let it go. But if they say, "No, that was really clearly racism," I go with that. So I explain

> how I have handled it in my life, and what I have found is effective for me and hope that would be helpful and encourage them to be prepared, because sooner or later, I would expect that to happen It's not getting resolved. It's not disappearing That's the best that I can do—share my experience with them and give them the heads up

Theme 8: Organizing Public Responses

Most of the participants ($n = 22$) recognized the importance of developing strategies to organize others in similar situations. They stated that individual responses are helpful but limited, and that change requires group effort and public awareness. A Latina explained,

> We created a diversity committee and 10 or eight of us that were directly involved with that incident and that had been noticing the ones calling out certain things going on in the school. We are getting together, we're venting, and supporting each other, but we're also making recommendations to our principle and to people at the district office

Participants also noted the importance of professional publications and research in the area of racial microagressions to articulate the issues and provide individual and collective support for their concerns in work settings and interactions with other professionals. A male African American participant explained how he used scholarly literature to support a long standing issue with White colleagues in his department, "I identified what I experienced using the micraggressions typology, highlighting context and patterns in my department. Although the discussion was tense, this allowed me to be heard."

Discussion

This study identified individual and collective adaptive responses that mental health professionals of color (psychologists, social workers, counselors, and family therapists) engaged in teaching and/or clinical practice use to cope with racial microaggressions while performing their professional duties. Although these adaptive responses are described in this paper as a matter of fact existing in the repertoire of these individuals, they evolved over time with regular practice and while experiencing a life time of racism. They illustrate multiple ways to self-regulate emotions and actions that have proved successful in dealing with the perniciousness of subtle racism. However, an examination of the dynamic interplay involving the stress brought by racial microaggresions and how individuals respond to it is needed. It has been documented that stable stress may elicit feelings of hopeless and resignation in people (Czopp, Monteith, & Mark, 2006), thus, the responses from this study's participants may be considered highlights in a continuum of coping in which emotional pain and other responses are a part of dealing with racism.

Implications for Professional Development

Participants in this study identified mentoring as a highly valuable endeavor in any setting precisely because they learned to cope over time and with the help of others who guided the way. Based on the results of this study, we suggest general guidelines to help navigate professional settings at an interpersonal level.

1. Voice and share your interest in addressing the challenges that professionals of color in the mental health field face in training, research, and clinical practice. We found that as a result of our focus groups, some of the participants were able to express for the first time some of their experiences and connect with others.
2. Faculty and clinicians must challenge racial privilege and its effects by confronting comments that minimize or deny issues related to students and professionals of color. Czopp, Monteith, & Mark's (2006) research corroborates that confronting racism reduces its frequency in the long term.
3. Question the theories and clinical practices you use in regard to the way they address how power, ethnicity, and the other isms intersect. Prepare a video and bibliography that can be handed to colleagues and students as a reference.
4. Use current research and theoretical approaches to racial microaggressoins to articulate your own experience and advocate for yourself.
5. Anticipate difficult dialogical exchanges about multiple identities by understanding your own identity and being accountable with respect to your own power position and privileges.
6. Organize with colleagues and students to create projects, support groups, and task forces to address navigating the professional mental health field from the vantage point of the person of color.

Methodological Limitations

The exploratory nature of this research invites reflections on the methodology and consideration of directions for future research on the topic. We were aware that the results of the study would be significantly shaped by the choice of interview questions. The selection of questions was rooted in the literature on racial microaggressions, and the experiences of professionals of color such as us, who had accounts but no identifying label for them. We attempted to account for our own biases by including an external auditor and using triangulation techniques. The findings should also be considered in light of the limitations presented by the methodology. Although the sample size is consistent with the standard in the field (Lincoln & Guba, 1985), generalizability is limited.

Another issue related to trustworthiness in qualitative research involves credibility (Lincoln & Guba, 1985). Credibility refers to the development of credible findings and interpretations based on the research design, participants, and context of the study. Credibility was established by using investigator and data triangulation. However, this study could have been strengthened by involving the participants' in reviewing the findings and providing feedback in the writing of the results.

Conclusions

The results of this study illustrate how professionals of color cope with racial microaggressions. Although helpful, these individual and interpersonal responses must be connected to the social contexts that both promote and challenge racism. As we advance multicultural and social justice initiatives in the mental health professions, improvements in training and service settings can be accomplished by expanding our understanding of racism and racial microaggressions. A key dimension in this endeavor involves addressing White privilege, its misuse and abuse. It can be argued that this is what makes possible and sustains overt and subtle racism (Almeida, Dolan Del-Vecchio, & Parker, 2007). As the literature on those whose societal position is at the margin grows with its focus on empowerment, so should the literature on those whose societal position is of dominance grow with a focus on accountability (Cook & Simpson, 2007). Future studies should focus on how to increase the awareness and accountability on those who perpetrate racial microaggressions.

References

Alleyne, A. (2005). Invisible injuries and silent witnesses: The shadow of racial oppression in workplace contexts. *Psychodynamic Practice, 5,* 283–299.

Almeida, R., Dolan Del-Vecchio, K., & Parker, L. (2007). *Transformative family therapy.* Boston, MA: Allyn & Bacon

Constantine, M. (2007). Racial microaggressions against African American clients in cross- racial counseling relationships. *Journal of Counseling Psychology, 54,* 1–16.

Constantine, M., & Sue, D. W. (2007). Perceptions of racial microaggressions among black supervisees in cross-cultural dyads. *Journal of Counseling Psychology, 54,* 142–153.

Constantine, M., Smith, L., Redington, R. M., & Owens, D. (2008) Racial microaggressions against black counseling and counseling psychology faculty: A central challenge in the multicultural movement. *Journal of Counseling and Development, 86,* 348–355.

Constantine, M., & Sue, D. W. (2007). Perceptions of racial racial microaggressions among black supervisees in cross-racial dyads. *Journal of Counseling Psychology, 54,* 142–153.

Cook, L., & Simpson, J. (2007). *Whiteness, pedagogy, performance: Dis/placing race.* Lanham, MD: Lexington Books.

Creswell, J. W. (1998). *Qualitative inquiry and research design: Choosing among five traditions* Thousand Oaks, CA: Sage.

Czopp, A. M., Monteith, M. J., & Mark, A. Y. (2006). Standing up for a change: Reducing bias through interpersonal confrontation. *Journal of Personality and Social Psychology, 90,* 784–803.

Denzin, N., & Lincoln, Y. (2005). *The Sage handbook of qualitative research.* Thousand Oaks, CA: Sage.

Glaser, B. G., & Strauss, A. L. (1967). *The discovery of grounded theory: Strategies for qualitative research.* Chicago, IL: Aldine.

Hernández, P., Taylor, B., & McDowell, T. (2009). Listening to ethnic minority AAMFT approved supervisors: Reflections on their experiences as supervisees. *Journal of Systemic Therapies, 28,* 88–100.

Lincoln, Y., & Guba, E. (1985). *Naturalistic inquiry.* Thousand Oaks, CA: Sage.

Marshall, C., & Rossman, G. B (1999) *Designing qualitative research.* Thousand Oaks, CA: Sage.

Moustakas, C. (1994). *Phenomenological research methods.* Thousand Oaks, CA: Sage.

Padgett, D K. (1998). *Qualitative methods in social work research: Challenges and reviews* Thousand Oaks, CA: Sage.

Patton, M. Q (2002). *Qualitative evaluation and research methods.* Thousand Oaks, CA: Sage.

Smith, L., Constantine, M., Graham, S., & Dize, C. B (2008). The territory ahead for multicultural competence: The "spinning" of racism. *Professional Psychology: Research and Practice, 39,* 337–345.

Smith, W. A., Allen, W. A., & Danley, L. (2007). Assume the position . . . you fit the description: Psychosocial experiences and racial battle fatigue among African American male college students. *American Behavioral Scientist, 51,* 551–578

Solórzano, D., Ceja, M., & Yosso, T. (2000) Critical race theory, racial microaggressions and campus racial climate: The experiences of African American college students. *Journal of Negro Education, 69,* 60–73.

Sue, D. W. (2003). *Overcoming our racism: The journey to liberation.* San Francisco, CA: Jossey-Bass.

Sue, D. W. (2008). Multicultural organizational consultation: A social justice perspective. *Consulting Psychology Journal: Practice and Research, 60,* 157–169.

Sue, D W., Bucceri, J., Lin, A. I., Nadal, K. L., & Torino, G C. (2007). Racial microaggressions and the Asian American experience. *Cultural Diversity & Ethnic Minority Psychology, 13,* 72–81.

Sue, D. W, Capodilupo, C. M, Torino, G. C., Bucceri, J. M, Holder, A. M, Nadal, K. L., & Esquilin, M. (2007). Racial microaggressions in everyday life: Implications for clinical practice. *American Psychologist, 62,* 271–286

Sue, D. W., Nadal, K. L., Capodilupo, C. M., Lin, A. L., Torino, G. C., & Rivera, P. (2008). Racial microaggressions against black Americans: Implications for Counseling *Journal of Counseling and Development, 86,* 330–338.

Appendix

Racial Microaggressions Group Interview Guideline

Guidelines for group facilitation:

1. Identify a type or types of racial microaggression that you have experienced consistently in your professional life. Please describe the experiences and their impact on you (emotional, physical, cognitive, relational, occupational, financial, etc.).

2. Are there racial microaggressions that you feel have more or less impact in you? What distinguishes the less from the more harmful?

3. How do you cope/manage with the racial microaggressions that you have experienced consistently in your life?

4. How do you resist them and protect yourself while in a hostile environment?

5. What helps you do this?

6. How do you make sense of these encounters?

7. What helps you to keep going with your life?

8. Do you incorporate the wisdom learned from coping and resistance in your mentoring, training, and clinical practice? How?

9. Is there anything else you would like to add?

Received March 29, 2009
Revision received August 6, 2009
Accepted November 3, 2009 ■

Progressive Until Graduation? Helping BSW Students Hold onto Anti-oppressive and Critical Social Work Practices

Critical Social Work 11(2)

Jennifer M. Poole [1]

[1]Ryerson University

Acknowledgements: I would like to thank Dr. S. Wehbi for her feedback on this text and the class of SWP 50/51 (2006-2007) for pedagogical inspiration.

Introduction

> Former BSW student: I'm really worried about this job interview. I know they are going to think I am too critical, too passionate, too much. How can I dumb myself down Jennifer? How do I get in the door so I can do the work I want to do? Maybe staying quiet will get me the job I need...maybe I should shut up about AOP?

This was part of a conversation I had last week, with a passionate, anti-oppressive and critical former undergraduate student who had been told, on more than one occasion, that she was just "too much" for the 'mainstream' social work organizations to which she had been applying for employment. It was not the first time one of my graduates had shared such worries, for many had reported negative workplace reactions to their critical and anti-oppressive stance, nor would it be the last. As the literature reminds us, social workers are now labouring in a post-welfare context where critiques of power, racism, ageism, sexism, heterosexism and ableism will not make 'best practice' lists unless they also save money and increase productivity (Baines, 2007; Hugman, 2001). As Donna Baines writes,

> ...neoliberal management models emphasize the importance of 'efficient' and 'effective' work practices, 'flexible' workforces, and the application of measures aimed at improving individual workers' performance. The way these goals play out in everyday social work practice is through standardization, fragmentation, deskilling, increased stress and higher workloads. (Baines, 2007. p. 11-12).

She adds, practices that do not serve these functions, practices that may be critical and anti-oppressive, "are discouraged or penalized" (Baines, 2007. p. 14).

Given this context, how do social work educators teach not only to transgress (hooks, 1994), but to weather the "discouragement" and "penalty" that may face the social work graduate steeped in anti-oppressive (AOP) and critical practices once they enter the workforce? Inspired by authors Wehbi and Turcotte (2007) as well as Sinclair and Albert (2008), in this paper I will think through this question along with some concerns about the process attached to teaching AOP and critical social work practices. I ask, what will my students hold onto 'out there' in this post-welfare world? Will they go on and use critical and anti-oppressive notions in their work or will they become what I call P.U.G.S., progressive until graduation only to be beguiled by post positivism, dragged down by managerialism and silenced by the corporate culture that seems to permeate many social service agencies these days.

I approach these questions as a critical post structuralist (Harris, 2001). Following social work scholars such as Jan Fook, Bob Pease, Adrienne Chambon and Ken Moffatt, my stance demands a particular philosophical lens. This is not the morally relativistic, "anything goes" lens often equated with 'pomo' but one that pushes me to disrupt the familiar, to ask questions about power, how things come to be possible and who benefits. It also means I have read far too much Foucault.

In addition, I approach these questions as a critical community worker, one who earned her stripes working with the new social movements that drive grassroots self-help/mutual aid organizing in this country. That work was always fuelled by what is now known as anti-oppressive social work practice. It was also driven by a lifelong concern with issues that sit under the umbrella of mental health and social exclusion.

With these lenses made clear, the paper has been organized into four sections; a brief tour of the terrain that is anti-oppressive and critical social work practice, some of the challenges and strengths that are attached to this way of work, what some former BSW students had to say on the issues and finally, suggestions for a pedagogical plan that may better help students hold onto anti-oppressive and critical practices whether as researchers, community organizers, policy makers or even outside the 'discipline' that is social work.

A Brief Tour of the Terrain

The literature on anti-oppressive practice is rich, as is that on critical social work (Fook, 2002; Healy, 2000; Ife, 1997; Rossiter, 1996). Elsewhere, scholars have provided detailed explanations of what this practice entails (see Adams, Dominelli and Payne, 2002 or Baines, 2007 for example). They have provided definitions of oppression as any inhumane treatment based on affiliation to a group. They have also outlined anti-oppressive practice as:

> ...a form of social work practice which addresses social divisions and structural inequalities in the work that is done with people whether they are users or workers. AOP aims to provide more appropriate and sensitive services by responding to people's needs regardless of their social status. AOP embodies a person-centred philosophy...a

methodology focusing on both process and outcome; and a way of structuring relationships between individuals that aims to empower users by reducing the negative effects of social hierarchies..." (Dominelli, 1994, p. 3)

Arguing that a critical social work approach begins with these ideas but then adds pieces developed by post structuralists, scholars such as Fook (2002) have made clear that critical social work practitioners are not only concerned with domination, oppression and inequality but also recognize that knowledge is always socially constructed and that positivism must be critiqued. In my classroom at an urban university in Toronto, these critical and anti-oppressive social work practices take centre stage, their combination meant to more thoroughly prepare graduating BSW students for what may be to come in the field.

Reflecting on the texts I teach and take up, I have come to understand critical and anti-oppressive social work practices as broad, relatively new and frequently attacked. I understand them as a stance, a process, an ethos birthed by structural, anti-racist and feminist work, a reaction to neoliberalism and what the British call 'competency-driven social work'. They are organizing tools, social work identities, discourses both dominant and subversive (Millar, 2006). Through their concern with the use and abuse of power in relation to individuals and broader social structures, I understand them as space making, change creating but according to psychiatric survivors Wilson and Beresford (2000), sometimes flawed and exclusionary. In fact, I see the field of 'critical AOP' as a contested terrain, and if we look to the work on hierarchies of oppression (McDonald & Coleman, 1999), the institutionalization of AOP and the jockeying around how to do it 'right' (Barnoff & Moffatt, 2007), we come to understand why some students might let it all go once they have crossed the convocation stage.

Thinking through the very same before I began to teach anti-oppressive practice in the academy, I went to the literature, to what had been put to paper. Speaking to the strengths of the approach, I found comfort in Mullaly's (2001) article on "confronting the politics of despair". Making clear what "the new anti-oppressive discourse and framework" can do, what its strengths are, he argues that it "offers an explanation for social problems that fits the lived reality of millions of people who find themselves in difficult circumstances because of social forces that are beyond their control" (2001, p. 313). "It eliminates any claim or pretence that social work is not a political activity", it helps to expose the "euro-centric biases of traditional welfare and social work, and it "depathologizes" seemingly "psychotic behaviours on the part of members of subordinate groups by understanding that such behaviours are often defence and coping mechanisms" (Mullaly, 2001, p. 313). Most intriguing is the possibility that this framework can be the bridge between structuralists and post structuralists. It might be big enough for us all.

However, far more common in the literature was talk of the tensions and challenges that AOP presents, especially with respect to teaching. Burke and Harrison (2002) argue "the driving force of anti-oppressive practice is the act of challenging inequalities, as opportunities for change are created by the process of the challenge" (p.133). However, these confrontations are not always successful and may be painful for those being challenged or doing the challenging. Similarly, Gillespie et al. (2002), tackle the issue of white women teaching about privilege and social action. I keep coming back to their admission that doing this kind of social work involves a particular kind of labour, the courage to sensitively sift through various acts of resistance to the material but also the courage to be on guard around the desire to be 'liked' by your students. As Heron argues (2005), we want to be seen as particular kinds of women, particular kinds of social workers and particular kinds of anti-oppressive educators. Who does that really benefit? Additionally, I come to Razack's writing about the classroom where she admits;

> Many articles tell us what to teach but tend not to deal with the major challenges the teacher and students face... what about the anger students display, the guilt, the competitiveness, the feelings of the minority students in the classroom...What support does a staff member need in order to continue to face such emotions in herself and others? (Razack 1999, p. 233).

Then there is Audre Lorde (1994) and her reminder that the focus of change must be "that piece of the oppressor which is planted deep within each of us" (cited in McDonald & Coleman, 1999. p. 24). That writing leads me back to post structuralism and what often happens when resistance becomes power, when experts are made, pedagogical rules put in place and the oppressed ask if some marginalized communities are actually being left behind by anti-oppressive practice (Wilson and Beresford, 2000)? It is why Chambon (1999) suggests we take the time to break "self-evidence" and explore the ways in which progressive, resistance based discourses can be controlling. All of these challenges and more sit with me in the classroom.

Former BSW Students Speak Out About Anti-Oppressive and Critical Practices

Yet how do they sit with (former) BSW students once they *leave* the classroom? In hopes of addressing this question, I have been asking former students, long after the marks are in and convocation is over, to speak back to the field of AOP and critical social work, to the strengths, weaknesses and what they have taken with them.

On the strengths I have heard that this approach to social work "made space for my personal experience", and "it made clear privilege, raising my own consciousness, however hard". I have been told that "it starts to push at the traditional student/teacher binary, setting a climate where we can teach each other", and "it allows us to resist the image of the 'nice, feminine and suitably dressed' social worker". For a graduate now working in gerontology, she argued that practicing social work without the anti-oppressive framework would limit clients from receiving truly holistic care. Another claimed that the most useful piece has been Fook's (2002) critical social work question, "who is the problem a problem for?" (p. 119). A third argued that the grounding in critical self reflexivity had been central, second only to her new found theoretical awareness. Wherever I am she said, whatever I do, I now think "things can always be otherwise".

On the challenges of holding onto critical and anti-oppressive practices, former students have talked about "the neglect of the margins within the margins", "the competitiveness" and "the dissonance between classroom performance and actual belief change". They also talked about fear, fear of sounding naïve, calling oppressive acts when others have turned a blind eye and selling out when the job market is so fierce and finances are so fragile. In the words of one my graduates, "AOP taught me how to fight however it did not give me the first aid kit with which to clean my wounds once I have been boxed to the ground".

Helping Undergraduate Students Hold On: Towards a Pedagogical Plan

Clearly, the field that is critical and anti-oppressive social work practice is far from perfect, nor is it going to 'stick' with every student or educator, but it is the ethos with which many critical educators work at this time. Thus, in the hopes of making available both the "boxing gloves" and a small first aid kit, in this section I share teaching practices that could help students hold on to some of the notions that critical and anti-oppressive practitioners hold dear. Informed by my post structural stance and guided by 'road tested' suggestions from Fook's text, *Critical Theory and Practice* (2002), these are steps towards a pedagogical plan that acknowledges the probability of "discouragement and penalty" on the road to social change.

That road begins with clarity, for I must make visible to students why we are using/teaching/ working with AOP and critical practices at this point in social work's long history. Thus we begin our course with discussions around where these practices came from, why they came, what birthed them, what they have produced and what they entail. We go to history, to theory, to social movements, neoliberalism, resistance and discourse, to name a few destinations. We acknowledge that to take up the social construction of knowledge is to turn our attention to the social construction of critical and anti-oppressive thought.

Then we talk about the talk. In the classroom, I must elucidate the words that are attached to AOP discourse, the theoretical positions that inform how those words come to be and the deeply material effects of those words. We must take up the term 'AOP' itself, hold it up to the light, examine its power and effects. The discursive formation of AOP has produced certain phrases, metaphors, practices, 'rules' and texts, so, following Radford's (2003) explanation of discursive formation, I ask my students to;

> ...imagine yourself standing in front of [a] library bookshelf. Just by looking at the titles on the spines, you can see how the books cluster together. You can see which books belong together and which do not. You can identity those books that seem to form the heart of the discursive formation and those books that reside on the margins...you see those books that tend to bleed over into other classifications and that straddle multiple discursive formations. You can physically experience the domain of a discursive formation... (Radford, 2003 p. 3)

In the same vein (and however introductory it may appear), I must teach students how to do a critical reading of a text. Demonstrating a critique of positivism and objectivity, I must ask who funded the article/project/report we read, what do we know about the author/social worker and what theory appears to be driving the analysis? Making clear that authors are not untouchable gods tucked behind glass walls, I have also encouraged students to contact scholars directly with concerns, challenges and questions.

I do this because I welcome arguments in the classroom. As a post structuralist, I maintain that papers, presentations, proposals, policy analyses, research findings and class lectures are essentially arguments, little performances crafted for specific audiences. If I am teaching students to be critical, to, according to Thomas (1993), "describe, analyze and open to scrutiny otherwise hidden agendas, power centers, and assumptions that inhibit, repress and constrain" (cited in Glesne, 1999 p. 12), then I must make space for the same process in the classroom. The 'gaze' must be turned on all texts and practices, including my own.

I also make clear that there is no one way to 'do' critical and AOP practice. There is no set format, just a collection of texted practices, hits and misses in the name of challenging inequality (Burke & Harrison, 2002). Neither are AOP and critical practices specific to social work. With my own professional 'story' I show students how these practices can be taken outside traditional disciplinary borders and into policy analyses in public health for example. In return, students show me how they 'challenge inequality' in retail, marketing and even manufacturing.

Indeed, the broader the definition of what social work is, the less pain and burnout there may be (Fook, 2002, p.158). Yes, the work includes community organizing and advocacy, but it is also possible through clinical, policy, research and teaching practice in addition to community education, program development and fundraising.

Central too is assuming the work of social change will always be unfinished. Indeed the task of challenging inequality is intrinsically unmanageable, so *transcend* helplessness and *ground* action by choosing a piece to focus on now (Fook, 2002 p. 159). My students tell me it might be working with one client, crafting one critical paragraph in a paper or sharing one 'smoke' with a consumer/ survivor outside the drop-in, but each moment counts towards an anti-oppressive and critical approach to the work.

Then there is paying special attention to what Belenky et al. (1986 cited in Fook, 2002, p. 154) call texts and subtexts because naming disconnects between them is central to challenging inequality and modeling how to hold onto AOP. If texts are lecture notes, performance evaluations and policies, subtexts are the messages, the climate and tones that attach themselves to how those texts are presented. They also leave the most lasting impressions and can be the most 'cutting', so in our effort to make anti-oppressive and critical social work practices applicable, we must examine the subtexts and details of our teaching such as the ways in which classrooms and offices are arranged, what we do with our bodies, artifacts and voices, the way we silence with a cough or boost with a look.

Additionally, I teach a re-theorizing of the crusader. Fook (2002) asks us to consider if, on certain topics, we might think of ourselves as correct crusaders, as the sole inhabitants of the "moral mountain" (p.152). From this stance, blaming 'the enemy' (such as psychiatry) may protect us from doing the messy, fractious work of education across difference, yet re-theorizing the crusader means we must critically reflect on what we gain from being 'right', and what we lose from being let "off the hook".

Most important however is the creation of microclimates (Fook, 2002), warm fertile greenhouses of allies in the "discouraging" storm. Because I could not continue without the friends I made during my social work education, because we still meet each month, I encourage students to do the same, to carve out the space and time to 'grow together'. I also model how to show weakness and uncertainty in this process, those moments of unknowing when I have silenced, made mistakes or simply not seen, moments which, if unpacked collaboratively, can become central critical incidents brimming with pedagogical and practice possibilities.

Concluding Thoughts

After presenting some of these ideas at a recent social work conference, I was asked a variety of questions. Could I speak to the elements of 'good' AOP teaching, could I outline what should be included in an AOP-guided curriculum and most intriguing of all, could I sketch out what the *ideal* AOP student looks like? As a post structuralist, I quietly balked at the questions, knowing full well that to box anti-oppressive and critical social work into a set of 'best practices' or 'characteristics' is to succumb to the neoliberal forces I attempt to resist. I also felt a touch of what Baines called 'discouragement' and 'penalty'. Yet these questions forced me to consider a number of issues. First, they confirm that although many educators work in critical and AOP spaces, those spaces are often ringed, threatened and infiltrated by interests that welcome evidence-based and other modernist inventions meant to limit, control and prescribe. Consequently, when reflecting on how I present my pedagogical process, I realize that to modernist ears, these flawed, unfinished and subjective ponderings read like a list, a recipe for certain pedagogical success. It follows that those listeners (and readers) would want me to box the work, making it easier to translate and of course, test and apply. It is what we do in the name of science and productivity, what we have all been taught to accept as 'normal'.

In addition, I am mindful of how my list looks. Going back to my own admission about post structural performativity, how is my own desire to be liked by students informing how I teach? How is my desire to appear critical and anti-oppressive informing how I write these lines? Do students sense the same in so-called critical and anti-oppressive classrooms?

In response, I will say that although I certainly believe in critical and AOP approaches, I argue that this work is not above critique itself. It brings with it multiple opportunities for resistance but also for the perpetuation of power imbalances, privilege and the benefits that come from knowledge territories. However, discourses such as AOP are always productive and repressive. Indeed,

> Discourses are not once and for all subservient to power or raised up against it...We must make allowance for the complex and unstable process whereby discourse can be both an instrument and an effect of power, but also a...point of resistance and starting point for an opposing strategy... (Foucault, 1988b p. 102).

Indeed, if critical and AOP social work is part of an 'unstable' discourse-a point of resistance and an 'instrument' of power- then so are the pedagogical practices that go along with this discourse. We cannot ensure that students hold onto 'it' after convocation nor guard against the production of 'P.U.G.S'. We can only continue to examine our practices, dialogue with our students and 'challenge inequalities' where we find them, both in and outside the classroom.

References

Adams, R., Dominelli, L. and Payne, M. (2002). *Anti-oppressive practice.* Basingstoke: Palgrave MacMillan.

Baines, D. (2007). Anti-oppressive social work practice. In D. Baines (Ed.) *Doing anti-oppressive practice: Building transformative politicized social work.* Halifax: Fernwood.

Barnoff, L. and Moffatt, K. (2007). Contradictory tensions in anti-oppression practice in feminist social services. *Affilia*, 22 (1): 56-70.

Burke, B. and Harrison, P. (2002). Anti-oppressive practice. In R. Adams, L. Dominelli and M. Payne (Eds.) *Anti-Oppressive Practice.* Basingstoke: Palgrave MacMillan: 227-236.

Chambon, A. (1999). Foucault's approach: Making the familiar visible. In A. Chambon, A, Irving and l. Epstein (Eds.). *Reading Foucault for social work.* New York: Columbia.

Chand, A., Clare, J. and Dolton, R. (2002). Teaching anti-oppressive practice on a diploma in social work course: Lecturers' experiences, students' responses and ways forward. *Social Work Education*, 21 (1): 7-22.

Dominelli, L. (1994). Anti-racist perspectives in the social work curriculum. In L. Dominelli, N. Patel and W. Bernard (Eds.). *Anti-racist social work education: Models of practice.* UK: SSSU.

Dominelli, L. (1996). Deprofessionalizing social work: Anti-oppressive practice, competencies and postmodernism. *British Journal of Social Work*, 26: 153-175.

Fook, J. (2002). *Social work: Critical theory and practice.* London: Sage.

Foucault, M. (1988). *The care of the self: Volume 3 of the history of sexuality.* Translated from the French by Robert Hurley. New York: Vintage.

Gillepsie, D., Ashbaugh, L. and DeFiore, J. (2002). White women teaching white women about white privilege, race cognizance and social action: Toward a pedagogical pragmatics. *Race, Ethnicity and Education*, 5(3): 237-253.

Glesne, C. (1999). *Becoming qualitative researchers: An introduction.* Don Mills, Ontario: Longman.

Harris, P. (2001). Towards a critical post-structuralism. *Social Work Education*, 20(3): 335-350.

Healy, K. (2000). *Social work practices.* London: Sage.

Heron, B. (2005). Self-reflection in critical social work practice: Subjectivity and the possibilities of resistance. *Reflective Practice*, 6(3): 341-351.

hooks, b. (1994). *Teaching to transgress: Education as the practice of freedom*. New York: Routledge.

Hugman, R. (2001). Post-welfare social work? Reconsidering post-modernism, post-Fordism and social work education. *Social Work Education*, 20(3): 321-333.

Ife, J. (1997). *Rethinking social work: Towards critical practice*. Melbourne: Addison-Wesley Longman.

McDonald, P. and Coleman, M. (1999). Deconstructing hierarchies of oppression and adopting a 'multiple model' approach to anti-oppressive practice. *Social Work Education*, 18(1): 19-33.

McLaughlin, K. (2005). From ridicule to institutionalization: Anti-oppression, the state and social work. *Critical Social Policy*, 25(3): 283-305.

Millar, M. (2006). 'Anti-oppressiveness': Critical comments on a discourse and its context. *British Journal of Social Work* :1-14

Mullaly, B. (2001). Confronting the politics of despair: Toward the reconstruction of progressive social work in a global economy and postmodern age. *Social Work Education*, 20(3): 303-320.

Radford, G. P. (2003). Trapped in our discursive formations: Toward an archaeology of library and information science. *The Library Quarterly*, 73(1): 1-18.

Razack, N. (1999). Anti-discriminatory practice: Pedagogical struggles and challenges. *British Journal of Social Work*, 29: 231-250.

Rossiter, A. (1996). A perspective on critical social work. *Journal of Progressive Human Services*, 7(2): 23-41.

Sinclair, R. and Albert, J. (2008). Social work and the anti-oppressive stance: Does the emperor really have new clothes? *Critical Social Work*, 9 (1).

Wehbi, S. and Turcotte, P. (2007). Social work education: Neoliberalism's willing victim? *Critical Social Work*, 8(1).

Wilson, A. and Beresford, P. (2000). 'Anti-oppressive practice': Emancipation or appropriation? *British Journal of Social Work*, 30: 553-573.

Anti-oppressive Practice in Mental Health

Grant Larson

ABSTRACT. This article identifies the challenges to incorporating an anti-oppressive practice approach in the field of mental health, which has traditionally utilized a discourse and perspectives of a bio-medical model. Schools of Social Work often teach anti-oppressive and social justice approaches which make it difficult for students to link theory and practice in fields such as mental health. In this article, seven principles of practice are presented as a framework for working with people with disabling conditions of mental health. Specific strategies for implementing these principles are presented.

KEYWORDS. Mental health, anti-oppressive, social justice, empowerment, practice principles

INTRODUCTION

In recent years, many North American and British schools of social work have introduced courses and curricula on anti-oppressive practice. Some view this as a return to the social justice roots of the profession and others as a "way of rethinking, redefining and reconstructing social work in a time of dramatic change" (Canadian Association of Schools of Social Work, 2005). Regardless of the interpretation of this change, it is apparent that in some fields of social work, anti-oppressive perspectives remain

Grant Larson, PhD, is Dean of the School of Social Work and Human Services at Thompson Rivers University, Kamloops, BC, Canada.

Address correspondence to: Grant Larson, School of Social Work and Human Services, Thompson Rivers University, Kamloops, BC, Canada V2C 5N3 (E-mail: glarson@tru.ca).

Journal of Progressive Human Services, Vol. 19(1) 2008
Available online at http://jpro.haworthpress.com

doi:10.1080/10428230802070223

distant and incongruent with the dominant discourse and practice models used by helping professionals. Practice involving people who have disabling conditions of mental health is one such area.

A review of the literature focusing on social work in mental health reveals, for the most part, continued reliance on medical and bio-psycho-social perspectives. Many textbooks used in educating mental health practitioners include extensive information about diagnosis and assessment, classification systems such as the Diagnostic and Statistical Manual IV, medical interventions, and clinical counseling roles focused on the amelioration of pathological conditions and deficits. Although some attention is given in the literature to antipsychiatric, critical, empowerment, and strengths perspectives (Jackson, 2001; Morley, 2003; Repper & Perkins, 2003; Sullivan, 1997), as well as to the roles of education, advocacy, and interdisciplinary action (Sands & Angell, 2002), much less attention is paid to the ways in which these progressive concepts are actually implemented in practice.

For the most part, then, anti-oppressive concepts remain abstract and peripheral to the actual practice of social work in mental health. There is a lack of fit between general anti-oppressive, structural, and feminist frameworks taught in social work education and the literature and practice used in mental health settings. This sets the stage for dissonance between the domains of education and practice. A translation of anti-oppressive concepts into actual behaviors and principles of practice is needed so as to link theory and practice in the realm of mental health intervention.

The practice principles presented in this article are the result of work generated by one social work faculty member and undergraduate social work students at a Canadian university. The focus of the work was on the discipline of social work in mental health, yet the specific themes and ideas generated are applicable to other mental health disciplines and, in fact, to any progressive human service worker. Students in two sections of a course on social work and mental health were asked in small discussion groups to generate ideas about how social workers might work with people with disabling conditions of mental health to fulfill the social justice, empowerment, and structural goals of the profession. They were asked to keep in mind that the dominant discourse in mental health organizations is the medical model (or a bio-psycho-social model at best), which is imbued with hierarchy, patriarchal structures, and power differentials. Once students' ideas were generated and recorded, the faculty member collated the responses by both classes and redistributed them to the students for further discussion, clarification, and analysis. The students and instructor identified themes and patterns that emerged from the data and organized the themes into several practice principles. Once the students were satisfied with their articulation of the principles, the faculty member interviewed three practicing social workers in mental health settings to solicit their feedback on the principles. Although the practicing social workers did not change the general principles articulated by the students, they did identify some of the challenges, complexities, and barriers to implementing them fully in mental health organizations. These challenges are noted throughout the article.

DEFINING ANTI-OPPRESSIVE PRACTICE

Jennifer Martin (2003) has suggested that the key features of anti-oppressive practice are making a commitment to social justice and challenging existing social relations that highlight social injustice, particularly in forms that are reproduced in social work practice. She has further indicated that anti-oppressive practice challenges the notions of professionalism and focuses on power sharing and egalitarian relationships based on shared values. Dalrumple and Burke's (1995) work addresses the notion of developing a clear theoretical framework that informs a value base, which is then translated into a set of practice behaviors that are anti-oppressive. "Anti-oppressive practice, then, means recognizing power imbalances and working toward the promotion of change to redress the balance of power" (p. 15). This process involves self-reflection, an understanding of power and oppression and one's place in that oppression, and a constant evaluation of one's relationships and behaviors. Anti-oppressive practice is much more, then, than simply adopting a set of behaviors or skills that are congruent with this particular paradigm. "It involves an awareness of the social worker's location and how this can contribute to the oppressiveness of the intervention through classism, racism, sexism, ableism, heterosexism, and other ways that all of us as human beings unfairly judge, rank, and deal with others" (Moosa-Mitha and Turner, 2005, p. 3).

Dalrumple and Burke (1995) suggest that it is not enough to recognize power imbalances; one must actively work toward change, or risk perpetuating inequality. Martin and Younger (2000), in a study of nursing care of people with dementia, suggest that it is useful to think of oppression in terms of the ability of a powerful group (health care professionals) to make decisions for and possibly against the wishes of a less powerful group (patients/clients). For the purposes of this article, then, anti-oppressive practice is defined as a commitment to social justice that includes the following key elements:

- a clear theoretical and value base that promotes egalitarianism and power-sharing;
- an understanding of one's social location and how it informs relationships and practice behaviors;
- a challenge to existing social relationships in which powerful groups maintain power and influence over less powerful groups; and
- specific practice behaviors and relationships that minimize power imbalances and promote equity and empowerment for users of service..

Although all of these elements are addressed in this article, the primary focus is on the last element, which attempts to link anti-oppressive theory and mental health practice.

DOMINANT DISCOURSE AND PRACTICE IN MENTAL HEALTH

A premise of this article is that the dominant perspective used in the field of mental health is the medical model (Stromwell, 2002) or at best, a bio-psycho-social perspective. Adherents of psychosocial rehabilitation often suggest, however, that social and ecological factors take second place to biological explanations and interventions. Mental health services are generally organized within primary or tertiary health care organizations where the majority of helping professionals are medically trained psychiatrists and psychiatric nurses. Desai (2003, p. 95) states that "when it comes to intervention, social workers commonly feel overwhelmed and debilitated by medical practitioners who claim much more expertise on mental health issues." Social workers in these settings are likely to be more interested than their non-social-work colleagues in the social and environmental factors related to mental health, but one could contend that the basis of care in mental health organizations, as well as the interventions and the organizational structures, typically emanate from a medical model. Medical terminology is used (e.g., mental illness, mental disorder, diagnosis, and patients); medically oriented diagnostic and assessment processes are employed; organizations are structured such that medical disciplines maintain power over other disciplines and consumers; interventions are often medicalized (psychotropic medications are the first order); mental health legislation typically gives power to physicians rather than to consumers; and little attention is paid to issues of stigma, social exclusion, and social justice.

Tews (2002) suggests that the dominance of biomedical approaches has offered little space for the articulation of more holistic alternatives, and that there has been a tendency to conflate a social perspective with only the practice issues that impact a person's life, such as benefits and housing. This tends to relegate social and environmental issues to secondary concerns in the treatment of disabling conditions of mental health. Tews (2002) further states that there is little evidence so far that biomedical strategies have been successful in promoting longer term recovery rates, even for such disabling conditions as schizophrenia. Research has indicated that only a small percentage of people from non-Western cultures utilize mental health services (Li & Browne, 2000; Martin, 2003; Naidoo, 1992; Stefl & Prosperi, 1985). At the same time there is evidence that some ethnic groups and women are overrepresented in psychiatric facilities and that they often experience exclusion and infringement of their civil rights (Desai, 2003; Levine, 1989; Martin, 2003). From these two extremes one might speculate that Western medical perspectives are neither sensitive to nor helpful with culture and gender differences, yet at the same time they are used to further the social inequality of some groups. Desai (2003) suggests that "race" and psychiatry are inextricably linked, and that in the United Kingdom Black African Caribbean people have been disadvantaged and abused in mental health settings. Others have written about the medicalization of women's issues (Martin, 2003) and the place of racism, classism, and ethnocentrism in mental health systems (Desai, 2003 Solomon, 1976). Although some have written about culturally appropriate methods, Western medical notions of mental health and well-being predominate in mainstream psychiatric care, and there has been little room for more holistic strategies and culturally sensitive approaches.

PRINCIPLES OF ANTI-OPPRESSIVE PRACTICE IN MENTAL HEALTH

The creative ideas of students and feedback from practitioners, along with the literature, have been used in the developing the following principles of practice for social workers working in mental health settings who wish to incorporate an anti-oppressive practice approach. It should be noted that these principles are not listed in order of importance and are not mutually exclusive. Operationalizing any one of these principles undoubtedly involves the implementation of others. It should also be noted that social workers practicing in mental health settings were particularly helpful in identifying the real challenges and obstacles to using these principles in mental health organizations.

Inviting Service Users to be Full Participants in all Aspects of Mental Health Service

There is general agreement in the literature that the empowerment of service users is enhanced when professionals facilitate conditions by which service users can take control of their own circumstances (Jackson, 2001 Staples, 1999). This facilitation requires that service users and their families be invited to participate fully in all aspects of service delivery, even areas that are traditionally reserved for the expertise of professionals and managers. This involves the sharing of power and the development of egalitarian relationships and structures whereby the hierarchy of mental health organizations is reduced. Full participation at a practical level may involve, for example, listening to and taking seriously what people say about their own mental distress and experience—that is, (treating them as experts in their own experience (Tews, 2002)); involving service users in all decision making about their care; sharing information and providing access to clinical records (Anthony & Crawford, 2000); inviting service users to participate in agency activities at all levels, including staff meetings and their own case conferences (respecting confidentiality of course); policy development, research, education, and governance (Staples, 1999); and reducing the us-and-them distinctions between service users and professionals (Tews, 2002). These distinctions often locate expertise with professionals and marginalize and exclude service users and their families (p. 144).

These examples are all critical aspects of anti-oppressive practice, which requires that practitioners and managers critically reflect on the paternalism of their organizations and the location of service users and families within that organization. It is not enough to relegate empowerment and participatory strategies to self-advocacy and external consumer groups; service users must become full participants in all aspects of service. Truman and Raine (2002, p. 7) conclude their research on user involvement by stating that "active involvement in mental health services may draw people who have felt excluded as a result of their illnesses back into community life, and may be one means of combating the discrimination and exclusion typically experienced by this group."

The practitioners consulted about this principle indicated that organizational context often creates barriers to the full participation of service users. Agency policies, privacy regulations, the degree of agency formality and professionalization, and the positioning of specific disciplines in the organization create challenges for those who promote egalitarian relationships and user participation at all levels. Although tensions among disciplines may result, practitioners agreed that much more could be done by individual social workers to mitigate these organizational factors and to use existing opportunities for the participation of service users in their individual situations. The practitioners also stated that a key to implementing this principle was encouraging workers to reflect on their own contributions to the paternalism of the organization and to act in ways that not reinforce such attitudes and behaviors.

Using Language and Discourse That Is Respectful, Egalitarian, and Empowering

One of the themes that students identified most strongly as being essential to anti-oppressive approaches was the use of language and communication styles that do not stigmatize service users or increase the power of professionals over service users. Mullaly (2002) suggests that both language and discourse become powerful mechanisms of oppression. The term *discourse* describes the larger frameworks (paradigms) of political assumptions, linguistics, and attitudes that are often communicated through language. The dominant discourse is deconstructed subsequently. Here, the focus is on using language that is not oppressive. Mullaly (2002, p. 89) indicates that "language reflects culture, particularly the dominant culture, and if the culture is oppressive, then one of the ways of changing it is to avoid words that reflect and/or reinforce the oppressive element of that culture." Language is used to construct and maintain oppression, but it may also be used to resist and challenge it. Many practitioners would agree that the medical terminology used in mental health settings focuses on pathology and puts service users in less powerful positions. The language of anti-oppressive professionals might include referring to service users by name rather than by the term *patient or client* or by diagnostic category; asking service users how they would prefer to be addressed;

using vocabulary and tone that are respectful and are understood by service users; refraining from speaking about mental illness and mental disorder; and actively seeking to educate others about the power of appropriate use of language.

Although students recognized the value of using consistent and common terms when communicating about mental health issues, they clearly suggested that professionals needed to be sensitive to the negative connotations, symbolism, and power attached to specific terms and kinds of language and discourse. Desai (2003, p. 99) affirms this idea by stating that "if social work is to make an impact in mental health it needs to engage in other discourses, rather than solely relying on the medical discourse."

Consultation with current practitioners about this principle validated the students' thinking about the importance of language and the need to be vigilant in not adopting agency discourse. One practitioner illustrated the effectiveness of using this principle by explaining how she had seen a slow but progressively positive change in the language utilized by her coworkers in the agency because of her consistent use of and modeling of anti-oppressive language. Operationalizing this principle in unobtrusive and nonconfrontational ways was viewed as being the most effective means of introducing change into discourse.

Actively Deconstructing the Medical Model With Service Users and Their Families and Encouraging Alternative Healing Perspectives and Strategies

As suggested earlier, one of the elements of anti-oppressive practice is a clear theory and value base that promotes egalitarianism and power sharing. Inherentin the application of this principle to social work in the field of mental health is the need to deconstruct the medical model and reduce its dominance in discourse and practice. Dominant discourses are powerful social control mechanisms that cover up or contradict the interests of subordinate groups (Mullaly, 2002). In fact, professions like social work "often contribute to oppression by controlling the discourses of their practices in which pathological, diagnostic, and professional vocabularies exclude and disempower the service user" (p. 92).

The medical model often used in mental health settings represents a hierarchical structure that ascribes power to professionals as experts who diagnose pathology and prescribe treatment to passive clients (Stromwell, 2002). Anti-oppressive approaches move away from reliance on biomedical theories and incorporate holistic, strength-based, and structural perspectives. These approaches work to empower service users and their families and to create change in structure, policy, and attitude. When deconstructing the biomedical model, social workers must explore with service users the larger injustices and stigmas they face rather than relying on individualistic pathological explanations. As well, they should explore structural barriers to services (such as the requirement of a psychiatric diagnosis for eligibility), work with people in holistic ways (Tews, 2002), explore support networks and community resources, and question policy and practice approaches that are pathologizing and rely on conventional singular biomedical explanations and treatments. Deconstructing the dominant discourse means bringing its oppressive underpinnings to light so that a counterdiscourse, one that critiques the ruling discourse and points the way toward more egalitarian social relations, practices, and processes, may be developed (Mullaly, 2002, p. 92). Engaging in these practices undoubtedly creates tension between social work practitioners and other mental health workers who embrace the medical model (Bland & Renouf, 2001).

This is a complex issue, and the practicing mental health social workers indicated that of all the principles, this is the one they struggle with the most. They agreed theoretically with the need to deconstruct the medical model but argued that they often felt they had little choice in agency contexts about the degree of use of the model, and that they needed to choose their battles carefully when attempting to create change in this area. Specifically, practitioners indicated that although they actively sought to depathologize mental health issues in their individual work with clients and in teamwork by drawing attention to the larger social injustices and factors in people's lives (poverty, discrimination, and so forth they would not go so far as to actively challenge the medical structures, policies, and hierarchy of the agency except in extreme circumstances. The practitioners gave examples of their attempts to voice anti-medical-model sentiments in their settings and noted that doing so simply marginalized them and antaganized their coworkers in the agency. The practitioners agreed that there is often a price to pay for the pursuit of these larger goals, but that attempts to do so must be made in intelligent and strategic ways that do not alienate social workers from other professionals in the organization.

Establishing Just Working Relationships

Staples (1999) emphasizes the establishment of "working relationships with services users and families that are based on trust, power sharing, informality, and collaboration and are committed to minimizing the power associated with the formal expert helping roles." Moosa-Mitha and Turner (2005) indicate that anti-oppressive practice begins with an understanding of the social worker's social location and how that contributes to the development of oppressive relationships and interventions. Self-awareness is critical to developing genuine relationships in which both the real and the perceived power of professionals is understood and diminished. Stromwell (2002) articulates well the difference between relationships based on the medical model and those based on empowerment theory. Students and practitioners identified many practical ways in which social workers in mental health could move away from formal relationships and work on a person-to-person basis rather than professional-to-client basis. They include:

- avoiding the use of titles, positions, and educational qualifications in referring to self and other professionals;
- not using judgments in the form of diagnostic categories and labels;
- using appropriate self-disclosure so as to relate person to person;
- not pretending to competence and knowledge when they are not present;
- providing and explaining all relevant information to service users so as to demystify mental health practice;
- not making decisions for people but inviting them to be part of every decision, focusing on strengths and uniqueness, not on pathology and roles as service users;
- assuring service users that they have the right to ask questions and to feel as they choose to feel;
- asking service users for feedback regarding the oppressive and non-oppressive features of the service and the relationship;
- providing an informal and user-friendly environment for interviews and sessions.

One cannot emphasize strongly enough the importance of relationships in good practice and particularly in good anti-oppressive practice. As with the use of language, the practicing mental health social workers strongly concurred with the use of the principle of relationship in real practice settings and suggested that awareness of one's own social location and need for power most strongly influenced the ability to form anti-oppressive relationships. The practitioners recognized that it was their own commitment to minimizing the power they were often vested with that helped to create egalitarian relationships with service users. Many progressive educators insist that the only mechanisms to assist students in developing these types of relationships are transformative pedagogical approaches in which students are encouraged to explore their personal experiences of oppression and difference and to challenge their own values, beliefs, knowledge, and attitudes about oppression and injustice (Hughes, Chau, James, & Sherman, 2003).

Promoting Education

The promotion of antistigma education and anti-oppressive professional development for practitioners, service users, and community groups is another important principle. In keeping with the theme of creating larger social change and broader understandings of the disabling conditions of mental health, it is important that anti-oppressive practitioners actively participate in appropriate professional development. An informal scan of the professional development opportunities for mental health practitioners in British Columbia, Canada, revealed that none focused on social justice issues or anti-oppressive approaches and that most included traditional medical and psychosocial approaches to treatment. Anti-oppressive social workers need to seek out and organize professional development activities that actively support anti-oppressive beliefs and practices. Also, as part of their ongoing professional responsibilities, social workers should challenge oppressive attitudes, policies, and practices of coworkers and agencies. Schools of social work, nursing, and medicine should be urged to include anti-oppressive content in their mental health curricula. As Sheehan and Ryan (2001) recommend in their study of Australian schools of social work, more explicit attention should be paid to antiracist and anti-oppressive agendas in social work mental health curricula.

At the same time, it is essential that social workers engage in antistigma and antidiscrimination education regarding mental health in the community in general and also with in specific relevant groups. Public schools, justice systems, social services, health systems, recreation organizations, religious organizations, and the media are all prime examples of venues suitable to this type of education. Social workers, with their extensive training and experience in community development, are well positioned to facilitate specific education strategies tailored to the needs of the local community.

One clear limitation to the involvement of practicing social workers in these activities was articulated—the lack of time and opportunity. Practitioners commented that in their settings, little time was available for public community education and little opportunity existed for professional-development workshops concerning anti-oppressive behavior. These activities were often viewed as the role of other mental health organizations that included advocacy as one of their specific mandates. Most agreed, however, that they could do more and that a shift in practitioners' attitudes toward the importance of education and professional development was needed.

Embracing Cultural Diversity and Strengths Perspectives in Practice

Several authors have written about the need to include the perspectives of cultural diversity and strength when working with users of mental health services (Spearman, 2005; Sullivan, 1997; Waxler-Morrison, Anderson & Richardson, 1990). Rather than relying solely on Western understandings of mental health, social workers should actively embrace the culture, spirituality, and strengths of service users' contexts. Anti-oppressive workers must engage in open inquiry with service users to understand and interpret their experiences of mental distress on the basis of their worldviews, values, cultures, and historical contexts. The history of oppression of Canadian First Nations people, for example, may provide a much broader and deeper understanding of the disabling conditions of mental health in aboriginal peoples than would individualistic pathological explanations. Responding to such concerns from the frameworks of the dominant society may, in fact, further perpetuate the oppression of an already marginalized group.

Bainbridge (1999) has indicated that tools such as the Diagnostic and Statistical Manual of Mental Disorders have little relevance or applicability to non-Western cultures; diagnostic categories are generally assigned after acculturation processes have occurred. Mental health services are usually organized in ethnocentric ways that pay little attention to culturally appropriate services and programs. There is also extensive research and writing on the experience of mental health in non-Western societies, where observable behaviors are understood, valued, and interpreted in ways that differ from the perspectives of the dominant North American society (Lee, 1986). This clearly supports the idea that mental health concepts are socially constructed. Specifically then, anti-oppressive practitioners must show an active interest in learning about other cultural ways, suspend understandings and assessments when they are based on lack of familiarity with a given culture and history, and encourage the use of culturally appropriate as well as relevant spiritual strategies for intervention. Waldegrave (1990), National Indian and Inuit Health Representatives Organization (2003), Morrisseau (1998), and Mussell, Nicholls and Adler (1993) provide some specific suggestions about ways of including Maori and Canadian aboriginal traditions of mental health treatment and how to build on the resiliency and strengths of those cultures and histories. This principle calls not just for culturally sensitive and appropriate methods, but also for an embracing of the culture and strengths of diverse populations in responding to mental health concerns. The practitioners consulted for this paper agreed that reliance on culture-bound syndromes (American Psychiatric Association, 1994) simply does not suffice to create anti-oppressive practice in diverse cultures and stated that their organizations were actively involved in pursuing strategies to incorporate diverse cultural perspectives in practice.

Promoting Principles of Social Justice

Bland and Renouf (2001, p. 239) state:

> At the level of social justice, social work is concerned with issues of stigma and discrimination, of political freedoms and civil rights, of promoting access to necessary treatment and support services, and of promoting consumer and carer rights to participation and choice in mental health services. It is concerned with making all human services more accessible and responsive to the specific needs and wishes of people with mental illness and their family carers.

In some ways, promoting social justice may be the most difficult principle to actualize, but it is at the root of anti-oppressive approaches. It is not enough for practitioners to give intellectual assent to the principles of social justice. They must become partners with service users and their families in political action directed at people's political freedoms and civil rights rather than just being concerned about the care and treatment of those with disabling conditions of mental health (Bland & Renouf, 2001; Moosa-Mitha & Turner, 2005). Popular writers such as Nunes and Simmie (2002) and Capponi (2003) espouse the experiences of those suffering with mental distress in a society where the subject is still largely taboo. It is the principle of social justice that urges anti-oppressive practitioners to "walk and talk" their professional beliefs, values, and ethics. In sum, this principle demands that practitioners become active participants in social action and reform.

Some specific ways in which practitioners can become involved in social justice and reform include taking public stands on the rights of users of mental health services; actively pursuing changes in legislation and public policies that disenfranchise those with disabling conditions of mental health; joining with consumer groups to advocate on behalf of this disadvantaged group; seeking funding to support the work of advocates and social activists; and using every opportunity to join antistigma campaigns.

It is interesting to note that when the practicing mental health social workers were asked to provide feedback on this principle, they indicated that the social justice role of social workers in their organizations was expected by the other disciplines, so it tended to cause less tension and opposition than attempts to use some of the other principles. They stated that nurses and physicians had commented that they thought social work was about human rights and social justice, and that they viewed such activities as specific contributions social work could make to mental health practice that other professions often did not make. The practitioners felt that other disciplines actually deferred this activity to social workers and expected them to take strong positions on the rights of those with disabling conditions of mental health.

CONCLUSION

Social work in mental health faces a huge challenge in putting into practice the essential features of an anti-oppressive approach to practice. This means operationalizing alternative perspectives in a context in which many of the features of a modernist, positivistic, paternalistic paradigm abound, and in which the marginalization and pathologization of those with disabling conditions of mental health continues. As an educator, I fear that schools sometimes create a paradox for beginning practitioners by instilling general empowerment, anti-oppressive, feminist, and structural philosophies and then leaving students and workers to determine for themselves how they will take these frameworks into settings that do not support them. This article is an attempt to begin to articulate in specific behavioral terms the meaning of an anti-oppressive approach to practice in mental health, thus bridging the gap between theory and practice in this important field.

REFERENCES

American Psychiatric Association. (1994). *Diagnostic and statistical manual of mental disorders* (4th ed.), Washington, DC: Author.

Anthony, P., & Crawford, P. (2000). Service user involvement in care planning: The mental health nurse's perspective. *Journal of Psychiatric and Mental Health Nursing, 7*, 425–434.

Bainbridge (1999). Competing paradigms in mental health practice and education. In B. Pease & J. Fook (Eds.), *Transforming social work practice: Postmodern critical perspectives* (pp. 179–194). London: Routledge.

Bland, R., & Renouf, N. (2001). Social work and the mental health team. *Australasian Psychiatry, 9*(3), 238–241.

Canadian Association of Schools of Social Work. (2005). *Reimagining social work: Seeing both forest and trees*. London, ON: Author.

Capponi, P. (2003). *Beyond the crazy house: changing the future of madness*. Toronto, ON: Penguin Books.

Dalrumple, J., & Burke, B. (1995). *Anti-oppressive practice: Social care and the law*. Buckingham, UK: Open University Press.

Desai, S. (2003). From pathology to postmodernism: A debate on race and mental health. *Journal of Social Work Practice, 17*(1), 143–155.

Hughes, J., Chau, C., James, P., & Sherman, S. (2003). Controversies, tensions, and contradictions: Antioppression and social justice in the social work curriculum. In W. Shera (Ed.), *Emerging perspectives on anti-oppressive practice* (pp. 349–362). Toronto, ON: Canadian Scholars' Press.

Jackson, R. (2001). The *clubhouse model: Empowering applications of theory to generalist practice*. Belmont, CA: Wadsworth/Thomson Learning.

Lee, R. N. F. (1986). The Chinese perception of mental illness in the Canadian mosaic. *Canada's Mental Health, 34*(4), 2–4.

Levine, H. (1989). The personal is political: Feminism and the helping professions. In A. Miles & G. Finn (Eds.), *Feminism: From pressure to politics* (pp. 233–267). Montreal, Quebec: Black Rose Books.

Li, A., & Browne, A. (2000). Defining mental illness and accessing mental health services: Perspectives of Asian Canadians. *Canadian Journal of Community Mental Health, 19*(1), 143–159.

Martin, G. W., & Younger, D. (2000). Anti-oppressive practice: A route to the empowerment of people with dementia through communication and choice. *Journal of Psychiatric and Mental Health Nursing, 7*, 59–67.

Martin, J. (2003). Mental health: Rethinking practices with women. In J. Allan, B. Peace, & L. Briskman (Eds.), *Critical social work: An introduction to theories and practices*. Crows Nest, NSW, AU: Allen & Unwin.

Moosa-Mitha, M., & Turner, D. (Eds.), (2005). *Challenge for change: An anti-oppressive approach to conflict resolution*. Victoria, BC: School of Social Work, University of Victoria.

Morley, C. (2003). Towards critical social work practice in mental health. *Journal of Progressive Human Services, 14*(1), 61–84.

Morrisseau, C. (1998). *Into the daylight: A wholistic approach.* Toronto, ON: University of Toronto Press.

Mullaly, B. (2002). *Challenging oppression: A critical social work approach.* Don Mills, ON: Oxford University Press Canada.

Mussell, W. J., Nicholls, W. M., & Adler, M. T. (1993). *Making meaning of mental health challenges in First Nations: A Freirean perspective* (2nd ed.). Chilliwack, BC: Saltshan Institute Society.

Naidoo, J. C. (1992). The mental health of visible ethnic minorities in Canada. *Psychology and Developing Societies, 4*(2), 165–187.

National Indian and Inuit Community Health Representatives Organization. (2003). *Mental health and wellness in aboriginal communities: In touch.* Kahnawake, Quebec: Author.

Nunes, J., & Simmie, S. (2002). *Beyond crazy: Journeys through mental illness.* Toronto, ON: McClelland & Stewart.

Repper, J., & Perkins, R. (2003). *Social inclusion and recovery: A model for mental health practice.* Edinburgh, UK: Bailliere Tindall.

Sands, R. & Angell, B. (2002). Social workers as collaborators on interagency and interdisciplinary teams. In K. Bentley (Ed.), *Social work practice in mental health: Contemporary roles, tasks and techniques.* Pacific Grove, CA: Brooks/Cole.

Sheehan, R., & Ryan, M. (2001). Education for mental health practice: Results of a survey of mental health content in bachelor of social work curricula in Australian schools of social work. *Social Work Education, 20*(3), 351–361.

Solomon, B. (1976). *Black empowerment: Social work in oppressed communities.* New York: Columbia University Press.

Spearman, L. (2005). A developmental approach to social work practice in mental health: Building on strengths. In T. Heinonen & A. Metteri (Eds.), *Social work in health and mental health.* Toronto, ON: Canadian Scholars' Press.

Staples, L. H. (1999). Consumer empowerment in mental health systems: Stakeholder roles and responsibilities. In W. Shera & L. Wells (Eds.), *Empowerment practice in social work* (pp. 119–141). Toronto, ON: Canadian Scholars' Press.

Stefl, M. E., & Properi, D. C. (1985). Barriers to mental health utilization. *Community Mental Health Journal, 21*(3), 167–178.

Stromwell, L. K. (2002). Is social work's door open to people recovering from psychiatric disabilities. *Social Work, 47*(1), 75–83.

Sullivan, W. P. (1997). On strengths, niches, and recovery from serious mental illness. In D. Saleebey (Ed.), *The strengths perspective in social work practice* (2nd ed., pp. 183–197). White Plains, NY: Longman Publishers USA.

Tews, J. (2002). Going social: Championing a holistic model of mental distress within professional education. *Social Work Education, 21*(2), 143–155.

Truman, C., & Raine, P. (2002). Experience and meaning of user involvement: Some explorations from a community mental health project. *Health and Social Care in the Community, 10*(1), 1–8.

Waldegrave, C. (1990). Just therapy. *Dulwich Centre Newsletter,* 1, 5–48. Adelaide, South Australia, AU: Dulwich Centre Publications.

Waxler-Morrison, N., Anderson, J., & Richardson, E. (1990). *Cross-cultural caring: A handbook for health professional in western Canada.* Vancouver, BC: University of British Columbia Press.

British Journal of Social Work (2013) **43**, 1312–1329
doi:10.1093/bjsw/bcs056
Advance Access publication April 26, 2012

Overt and Covert Ways of Responding to Moral Injustices in Social Work Practice: Heroes and Mild-Mannered Social Work Bipeds

Marshall Fine* and Eli Teram

Marshall Fine, Ed.D, is a Professor at the Faculty of Social Work, Wilfrid Laurier University, Waterloo, Ontario, Canada. His research interests are in social work ethics, family experiences with child welfare systems, couple and family therapy, and family therapy/social work supervision. Eli Teram is Professor at the Faculty of Social Work, Wilfrid Laurier University, Waterloo, Ontario, Canada. His main research interests relate to the organisational, interprofessional and inter-organisational contexts of social work practice.

*Correspondence to Marshall Fine, Professor, Faculty of Social Work, Wilfrid Laurier University, 120 Duke Street West, Kitchener, Ontario, Canada, N2H 3W8. E-mail: mfine@wlu.ca

Abstract

This article explores overt and covert actions taken by social workers against perceived moral injustices in their work organisations. Covert and overt actions are defined and examples of these actions from a research study of social work ethics are presented. The paper argues that both covert and overt actions ought to be considered heroic in light of what appears to be timidity on the part of many social workers to act against perceived moral injustice in their workplaces. The concepts of multiple institutional logics and embedded agency are used as a means of moderating and contextualising the concerns social workers might have about acting in either covert or overt ways to address moral injustices, and to examine the potential pitfalls and merits of each type of action. The article concludes by encouraging social workers to consider more systematically avenues for overt actions to address perceived moral injustice, as basic social work values of client care can be paradoxically found even in the logics of dominantly neo-liberal organisations. If overt action is not possible or may have the potential of causing more harm to the client, covert actions can be morally justified.

Keywords: Covert and overt actions, ethics, heroism, moral injustice, multiple institutional logics, resistance

Accepted: March 2012

Introduction

> I think it's very important to know what you consider to be right and very important to speak up when you think something is not right and to explore it and to be willing to sort of be one of the few voices and not just go with the flow because everyone else is comfortable with it... (aa3a).

While social work is expected to stand up for social justice, little is known about the actions and motivations of social workers' attempting to address what they observe as moral injustices related to their organisation's policies and practices (Musil *et al.*, 2004; Papadaki and Papadaki, 2008). Based on a study of the ethical issues experienced by social workers in their everyday practices, this paper examines the courage required to take particular actions, and analyses the different types of risk faced by social workers choosing to act in the face of moral injustice. The different risks depend, in part, on whether their actions to address perceived moral injustice in the workplace are carried out in an overt or covert manner. To facilitate informed comparisons between the potential risks and requisite courage related to involvement in these two types of actions, we integrate in our analysis of philosophical writings on heroism with current thinking about the institutional pluralism that characterises human service organisations.

This integration is intended to expand the analytical frameworks used by those who consider action to correct the perceived harm caused by their organisations. Since the analysis of the situation is one of the determinants for ethical action/inaction by individual social workers (Banks, 2004), we hope that this paper will improve the quality of this analysis by critically and reflexively considering the contexts in which their contemplated actions might happen. To act against moral injustice is a principle clearly expressed in many social work Codes of Ethics: for example, 'Social workers promote social fairness and the equitable distribution of resources, and act to reduce barriers and expand choice for all persons, with special regard for those who are marginalized, disadvantaged, vulnerable, and/or have exceptional needs' (Canadian Association of Social Workers, 2005, p. 5). However, it is naive to expect that social workers will act unquestionably to confront the organisation and right the perceived wrongs produced by its policies and practices. For workers in the helping professions, acting against moral injustices perpetuated against clients can be complicated and risky (Stanford, 2011). Banks (2004) suggests that the decision for action/inaction is complex and is determined by considerations that go beyond the analysis of the situation; these considerations include courage, commitment to certain ideals, career stage, family circumstances, type of job and employment agency, and the availability of support. Thus, contemplating such action can involve going through a period of moral distress, which, according to Austin *et al.* (2005), 'is experienced when, as humans, we believe we know how we should act, know what the right thing to do is, but find we cannot do it' (Austin *et al.*, 2005, p. 199).

Although we know little about what social workers do when confronted with moral injustice, with a few exceptions (e.g. Aronson and Smith, 2010; Baines, 2007; Stanford, 2010, 2011), the scant research literature tends to imply that many social workers choose not to address injustices in their places of work (Musil *et al.*, 2004; Papadaki and Papadaki, 2008). There may be a number of reasons for this. Stanford (2010), for example, referring to neo-liberal risk-based societies, notes that:

> It appears that fear, the undermining of trust and the need to control have overtaken and undermined discussions about the creative impetus and courage required to take risks in practice (Parton, 2001; Alaszewski and Alaszewski, 2002; Titterton, 2006). Hence, the argument of the critical social work risk literature is that social workers have adopted a more defensive and morally timid position in response to the pervasive and insidious political and moral conservatism of neo-liberal risk society (Stanford, 2010, p. 1067).

Papadaki and Papadaki (2008) note a similarity in their findings with those of Musil *et al.* (2004) in that 'social workers who try to change conditions that cause the dilemmas in social service organizations are rare' (Papadaki and Papadaki, 2008, p. 176). This reluctance to change conditions is what we refer to as *inert* action and we, along with others, primarily view inert action as attempts to refrain from making decisions that would pit the professional against the workplace (Lipsky, 1980; Musil *et al.*, 2004; Papadaki and Papadaki, 2008). These actions do not respond to the needs of clients, but attempt to shelter the social worker from potential sanction, because such 'pitting' could, for example, have pragmatic repercussions on their future statuses and livelihoods. Whereas inert actions might imply an absence of moral courage, actions directed towards dealing with moral injustice, imply a presence of such courage (Austin *et al.*, 2005; Hugman, 2005; Strom-Gottfried, 2007), particularly in light of the potentially negative consequences for those who take action (Fine and Teram, 2009; Lonne *et al.*, 2004; McAuliffe and Sudbery, 2005; Musil *et al.*, 2004; Papadaki and Papadaki, 2008).

With respect to our current study and in contrast to the concern regarding inert actions, a number of study participants talked specifically about taking actions to address perceived moral injustices in the work setting. We distinguished between two primary types of action: overt and covert. Whereas overt actions dealt with the perceived injustice directly and openly, covert actions addressed the contested issue through less visible means that subverted agency policies by taking actions not sanctioned by the organisation in order to achieve what social workers considered an ethically preferred outcome for their clients.

The distinction between covert and overt actions provides a means to gain a nuanced understanding of the respective risks associated with each type of action through the lenses of institutional pluralism. Specifically, we will argue that, under certain conditions, taking overt actions such as challenging the organisation's deviations from its mission through personal or lobbying activities, while seemingly heroic, may be less risky than taking covert actions. Since such identity conflicts are typically within the constitutional framework of the organisation and are 'for' it (Kraatz and Block, 2008, p. 255), they can be defended as something done for the good of the organisation. Covert actions, which are implicitly outside the constitutional framework of the organisation, can hardly be defended on this ground. A proper understanding of these distinctions is a good starting point for encouraging overt actions, which are more likely to lead to organisational change than covert actions, which, notwithstanding their benefits for individual clients, tend to mask and smooth organisational inadequacies. Refined analyses of the complex choice between overt and covert actions will also help us generate ideas with respect to how professionals can be encouraged and supported to act as advocates in the institutional settings that encompass much of social work practice.

The advocate role is important, for two primary and related reasons:

(1) The social service environment appears to become increasingly neoliberal and managerial in perspective, which, by its nature, does not necessarily cater to social work values (Lonne *et al.*, 2004; Noble and Irwin, 2009; Pollack and Rossiter, 2010).

(2) Institutions tend to have different purposes from practitioners, as noted by MacIntyre (1985, p. 194, cited in Banks and Gallagher, 2009), such that the 'common goods of the practice is always vulnerable to the competitiveness of the institution' (MacIntyre, 1985, p. 47).

Methodology

The findings presented herein are from a study exploring social workers' experiences of ethical issues in their practices (Fine and Teram, 2009). Aspects of this section are taken from Fine and Teram (2009), in which we focus on how the participants related to the code of ethics. Based on a different subset of the study's database, this article explores a different theme.

The study received approval from the authors' university as being ethically sound. Prior to submitting any paper from our study for journal review, participants are e-mailed a copy of the paper for feedback.

Grounded theory was employed to conduct the study and analyse the data (Greenwood and Levin, 2000; Teram *et al.*, 2005). Thus, there were two steps to the project. The first step involved the collection of data through in-depth interviews followed by data analysis. The second step consisted of five group consultation sessions with social work stakeholders in various cities in Ontario, representing a broad range of practice settings. The stakeholders were members of various regional social work associations in Ontario. The researchers presented the findings to the stakeholders and they were asked to comment and offer practice suggestions based on the findings.

The interview data were analysed using the constant comparative method that fits the discovery-based and in-depth nature of the study (Bogdan and Taylor, 1975; Denzin and Lincoln, 1998). All data were coded using Nvivo 6™. The first author initially coded six interviews to develop a tentative list of open codes for subsequent coders. Three additional coders, the primary one being the project co-ordinator, then continued the open coding process, adding new codes as they became apparent. Regular meetings were held with coders to review the evolving codes and refine and modify the process over time. After the interviews were open coded, we reduced, refined, combined and organised the codes. For a detailed explanation of the methodology, see Fine and Teram (2009).

The sample

Social work participants were recruited from a list provided by the Ontario Association of Social Workers (OASW). Five hundred and sixty-three letters and/or e-mails of invitation were sent to all OASW members living in five cities within Ontario. The cities were chosen as they represent a range of social-geographical factors such as: rural–urban, diversity of population, closeness to the USA, Francophone and Indigenous influences. Ninety-three individuals responded to the invitation and fifty-six social workers agreed to, and participated in, individual interviews. Two focus groups within south-central Ontario consisting of fifteen participants were also conducted and those data are included in this study. The total social work participant sample composed fifty-one women and twenty men. Sixteen participants identified themselves as members of a minority group. Years of social work practice experience ranged from two to forty-three and the average social work years of experience was 18.5. Participants in individual interviews worked in hospital and health services ($N = 12$), private practice ($N = 12$), mental health ($N = 8$), child welfare ($N = 8$), community development ($N = 5$), addictions ($N = 4$), family services ($N = 3$), academia ($N = 2$), sexual assault services ($N = 1$) and correction services ($N = 1$). One focus group consisted of children's mental health residential social workers and the second group consisted of hospital social workers.

Overt ethical responses to perceived moral injustices

As a starting point for our discussion, we offer examples of overt and covert ethical actions at the managerial and front line levels that emerged from the interviews with participants. These participant examples and others will serve to support our positions related to addressing moral injustices.

Managerial-level action

> [I] was being asked to do something and take over an agency, which I did not agree with because I thought it would undermine the whole child welfare system in a community. Umm, because the Minister wanted to take over an agency. Umm... I said no and I could have lost my job over that... I mean it was really overt when you've got a Minister saying I want you to do something that you really believe ethically is wrong in terms of best practices or services for a community (Et7u).

Even though this participant considered his job to be at stake, he stood up to the government minister who was 'explicitly' asking him to take over a community agency. He refused to act in a way that he thought would result in an injustice. He did not, in the end, lose his job, but was prepared to do so.

Front line-level action

Administrators, of course, are not alone with regard to ethical challenges. The following front line worker opted to speak out about what she saw as a moral injustice in her work setting:

> ... when you're talking with a manager who's made a decision ... they don't always react kindly when you're sort of saying, 'well, first of all, you're violating the law, and second of all ... is that really appropriate to be doing to this individual [not informing him of his rights]?' (aa3a).

This participant was speaking out about the fact that, because of the local public outcry and notoriety regarding one adult offender who had just come to live in the residence, another offender, who was at the time unable to fully understand his rights, was not informed of and, in one instance, was denied his legal rights to leave the premises unaccompanied. To add salt to the wound, he was even denied the right to go on an outing accompanied by a guard. As in the above takeover example, the moral issue in this instance might not have been viewed as compelling in the public eye. Indeed, as it turns out, the situation was not even a concern for some professionals who worked in the residence:

> And I had quite a few staff members ... saying, 'He's just an offender, why are you so concerned about his rights and his, y'know, the limitations, like, who cares?' (aa3a).

In both the managerial and front line situations, the social workers were addressing openly the persons/systems seen as potentially responsible for the perceived injustices. In the former situation, the participant refused to act in a way he saw as unjust. He was straightforward and able to convince the minister to back down from a takeover. In the latter situation, the participant had approached her superior openly, but to no avail. She also talked with the offender whose rights she felt were being violated. By using such overt ethical actions to address injustices, these professionals lived knowing that their jobs, or at least their comfort within their jobs, might have been placed in some jeopardy.

Covert responses to perceived ethical injustices

Managerial-level action

> I always found many ways to manipulate the formal rules so that the money was spent on children in order to provide support that they needed . . . there were many, many other managers who simply wouldn't do that . . . (cf2a).

This particular manager considered that funds were not always allocated to services he thought would benefit clients—in fact, he determined that some funds were misallocated. He viewed this as a moral issue and would reallocate money in areas that he thought would benefit, in an ethical way, the well-being of clients. His superiors were not informed of his actions. He suspected that he would have to pay a price if his superiors found out.

Front line-level action

In a similar covert manner, a front line social work participant attended to what she perceived as unjust. The participant was asked quite some years ago to work with a young woman identified as being lesbian. Two issues concerned the participant. The first was that she knew very little about the lesbian community and experience. The second was that she worried that the goal of the hospital was for her to 'cure [the client] of her homosexuality', which was particularly problematic for the participant, who at first did not know how to proceed:

> . . . but I knew a former student at the School of Social Work who was lesbian, who was very active and was now a social worker and I asked her if she would come to meet with this client and me. Which she did and I sneaked her in because I wasn't the least bit sure the hospital would be the least bit comfortable with me having a social worker from someplace else come in and tell this underage client how to make connections with other young lesbians in the community. So I didn't like that feeling that I'm, that I could get in trouble that I might be doing something here that wasn't what the higher ups thought I should be doing and that I would be forced to be practicing in ways that didn't feel right, [as] that is a major reason I am here (mf3c).

Given the attitudes towards homosexuality at the time this event occurred, we strongly suspect that the participant was taking a significant risk by attempting to prevent harm to the client. The harm could have come from two sources: the fact that the participant knew little about the lesbian community or 'lesbianism', which relates to an issue of cultural awareness; and the treatment of the day that aimed at 'curing' homosexual clients from what was then considered a form of psychiatric disorder. Asking the institution to attend to her concerns would have been questionable particularly given the institutionalised psychiatric/medical logics at that time and the power difference between social workers and medical professionals. As with the other participants in our study who took covert action, she thought she would have suffered serious consequences if discovered.

The two participants in these examples of covert ethical actions did not address openly the persons/systems they considered responsible for the perceived injustice, but acted in ways that diminished the unjust impact of current practices. They acted in a manner that Aronson and Smith (2010) would term 'expanding entitlements', through which they 'sought to stretch or disorganize narrow definitions of need and eligibility in order to move forward what they saw as the proper social objectives of their organizations' activities' (Aronson and Smith, 2010, p. 540). Nonetheless, the participants in our study tended to feel isolated in that there was no safety and formal support for open talk about their concerns and actions. In addition, the possibility of discovery constrained them from divulging and discussing their actions, which is consistent with the findings of McAuliffe and Sudbery (2005).

Will the real morally responsible professional please stand up!

Since there are many individual and systemic 'enticements' to avoid overt or covert actions that address moral injustices (Fine and Teram, 2009), we wondered what attitudes the participants might have held that led them to act courageously. The article's opening quote, and the following participants, provide some general sense about their constitutions in relation to standing up:

> And a manager has to do more than just pay lip service, a manager has to be willing to challenge rules and break rules that are simply wrong because they are motivated by a system need or whatever, . . . the manager needs to bring to the workers' attention these contradictions and these sorts of difficulties and say, really, I'll support you to do work in this way (cf2a).

> Our responsibility is to stand up and tell the truth; you stand up and tell the truth (aa8a).

> ... I think maybe I'm pretty severe on that issue when I see another colleague doing something that's out of line, I don't turn the other way (mf8n).

We observe as common among all of the participants above what seems to be a very robust sense of knowing what ought to be done and a drive to act accordingly. It is almost as if there is simply no question about any avoidance. That is not to say that the participants are blind to the pitfalls:

> There is always a cost. Always estimating the cost. Always. There is an economic cost and there is personal cost.... When you're dealing with principles and ethics ... when you're facing a dilemma, either side of the coin there is always a personal and economic cost (cf1a).

Although the costs articulated by this participant may be masked by the conviction and firmness of the participants' narratives, it would be naive to suggest that their actions are clear-cut and the process to reach their decisions painless:

> I really didn't like even being an employee of an organization that was conducting themselves illegally. Really, you know, and I had to do a lot of soul-searching, you know, like,... should I just quit? And, you know, when you have bills to pay and whatnot, it's really difficult to just quit without having something else and as well, in fact, my colleague is a psychologist, he said, actually,... if you quit, you're not going to be able to help this guy, whereas if you stay, you're more likely to be more help, because you can continue to advocate (Aa3a).

The above quote highlights one final aspect that appears to be at the core for all of the above participants: the welfare of the client. The following participant, a manager who went to arbitration in order to try and prevent a worker whom he felt was not competent from being promoted, brings this point home:

> I literally took it off the wall, and went through arbitration and the whole bit and it was because if I let it go by, it would make that person a case manager. I wouldn't wish that person a case manager on anyone and I would not do that to our clients. So that one I took right to the mat, we took it to arbitration. You know, that one I wouldn't give up on because it related to clients and client service (et7u).

Unfortunately, our data do not provide an opportunity to look more closely at whom these people are. We can only say that they seem to defy the norm and speak out based on courage that appears to come from a conviction to be truthful and faithful to what they perceive as moral justice for clients (see Stanford (2011) for other observations on likeminded social workers). MacIntyre's (2007) reflections on courage describe this virtue well:

> We hold courage to be a virtue because the care and concerns for individuals, communities and causes which is so crucial to so much in practices requires the existence of such a virtue. If someone says that he cares for some individual, community or cause, but is unwilling to risk harm or danger on his, her or its own behalf, he puts in question the genuineness

> of his care and concern. Courage, the capacity to risk harm or danger to oneself, has its role in human life because of this connection with care and concern (MacIntyre, 2007, p. 192).

On superheroes and heroes

If reporting and acting upon moral injustices, as noted above, is rare (Papadaki and Papadaki, 2008; Musil *et al.*, 2004) and the consequences for those who do are potentially serious (Bauman, 1993), we agree with Austin *et al.* (2005), Hugman (2005) and Strom-Gottfried (2007) that it takes courage to address moral injustice. The participants above seem to have such courage.

If standing up against moral injustice is courageous, and yet is expected of social workers in relation to their code of ethics, does that mean that social workers have to 'possess' courage as a basic human characteristic in order to do their jobs properly? Is doing social work only for the lionhearted, particularly given that moral issues arise almost daily, many of which are related to conflicts between the professional and the organisation (McAuliffe and Sudbery, 2005)? Are social workers who stand up against moral injustices superheroes?

According to Loeb and Morris (2005), superheroes are special beings possessing extraordinary capabilities—far above what any human could possibly achieve. Enjoying such qualities then begs the following question: 'What is so heroic about stopping an armed robbery if your skin is bullet proof and your strength is irresistible by any ordinary, or even extraordinary, street thug?' (Loeb and Morris, 2005, p. 12). Loeb and Morris go on to point out that, even though they might not have to fret bodily harm (Kryptonite and such excepted), superheroes demonstrate other qualities that earn them the 'hero' in superhero. For example, despite the potential to live any life they might wish, they fight evil at great cost to themselves (Brenzel, 2005), by making sacrifices such as leaving family and forfeiting social lives (Loeb and Morris, 2005). Some hold great secrets regarding their identities, which can lead to isolation, loneliness and lack of recognition. They fight for truth, justice and morality. Does this not sound similar to our participants? They all made potential sacrifices whether in terms of job security, stressful collegial relationships and possible marginalisation (see also Fine and Teram, 2009).

It is clear that humans cannot be superheroes. However, the metaphor of the superhero has been with us as far back as one can see, each character seeming to fit with the socio-political contexts of the times (Waid, 2005). And we surmise, as do Loeb and Morris (2005), that there are reasons for our ongoing relationship with superheroes; primary among those are that superheroes provide us with inspiration to rise above and do what we consider the right thing, even though and particularly because, unlike superheroes, we have no apparent protective gear. They stir and inspire us to keep going 'when the going is very tough' (Loeb and Morris, 2005, p. 19) or provide us with 'ethical will', as Stanford (2011, p. 1516) might state. And what could be tougher and who could be more in need of inspiration than social workers attempting to soften and advocate against the deleterious impact of rapidly expanding neo-liberal policies on the lives of clients? Indeed, inspiration is particularly warranted in this climate, as it appears many social workers may be feeling downcast (Stanford, 2011).

There is another reason we find the superhero image useful. As noted above, humans do not have the extraordinary protective gear that superheroes possess; however, perhaps they have more protective gear than they might realise. For social workers, as we have implied above, this protective gear lies within an understanding of institutional pluralism and multiple logics, which we speak to below. First, however, we address the notion of the hero.

Being a hero implies struggling for moral justice even though, and particularly when, it is against the mainstream and there is potential for a great deal to lose (Loeb and Morris, 2005). This definition sounds like quite a feat, and yet there may be more heroes out there than we might initially imagine. Indeed, given the basic charge of social workers and other social and health care workers, these professionals, by the very nature of their work, as noted by Loeb and Morris (2005), could be considered heroes:

> People in these jobs are often able to rise above the universal and altogether natural concern for the self, with its interests, and put the needs of others first on their list of priorities. They fight for human health, safety, growth, and excellence. They are the warriors of everyday life whose sacrifices and noble deeds benefit us all (Loeb and Morris, 2005, p. 13).

Well, that is at the essence of our concern. Are we indeed heroes just because we do this type of work? The answer, we believe, given our concern that apparently many social workers do not stand up against injustice, is not necessarily. But are those engaged in overt and covert actions heroes?

Overt and covert heroes within institutionalised pluralism

Is it more risky to speak out about perceived injustices or to do something covertly to right perceived organisational wrongs? Is it more heroic to openly resist injustice than to take covert corrective actions to reduce the potential harm of unjust organisational practices for clients? Variants of these questions are likely to occupy the minds of many who experience moral distress.

Given their deceptive nature, covert actions may not be considered heroic because they do not entail direct confrontation with the organisation. Indeed, such actions may perpetuate current policies by smoothing the deficiencies of the system, masking society's ambiguities towards addressing the needs of vulnerable groups (Hoggett, 2006) and preventing proper public debates (Lipsky, 1984). Moreover, covert actions can signify both dissatisfaction regarding particular organisational practices, and willingness to continue and enjoy the benefits received from the organisation. As such, covert actors, it would appear, can hardly be sung as heroes.

This understanding of heroism, however, is incomplete, as it separates the contributions and the risks associated with overt and covert heroes from the pluralist context of human service organisations (HSOs). Since HSOs typically operate within *multiple institutional spheres* (Kraatz and Block, 2008), workers and managers have to make decisions within an internally pluralist environment that originates from and reinforces conflicting community values and shifting attitudes towards social problems and groups with special needs (Hasenfeld, 2000; Hoggett, 2006). Within this context, even overt resistance that appears radical and heroic may paradoxically contribute to the legitimacy of the organisation.

For example, a study of a merger between agencies working with youth-in-trouble (Teram, 2010) identified two equally legitimate discourses regarding the transformation of a kitchen in one of the group homes to food services. Pointing out the need to prepare hundreds of meals for the clients served by the merged entity, management's discourse centred on the cost savings generated by this change. Staff's discourse, on the other hand, highlighted the many social, educational and rehabilitative functions served by the kitchen and the harm caused to youth by its removal. In this open discursive resistance, managers were portrayed as villains, who are willing to 'remove the heart of the house' for financial reasons. Managers used this antagonistic portrayal of them to support their selves as rational and moral. In the managerial discourse, workers' resistance to change provided 'an opportunity to accentuate management's openness, flexibility and ability to make tough decisions in order to save the organization' (Teram, 2010, p. 50). Thus, while we encourage tempered radicalism (Meyerson, 2001) and the open expression of alternative positions, we do not consider overt actions that can draw legitimacy from one of the multiple logics of an organisation extremely risky. We also think that such overt actions can provide as much legitimacy to the system as covert actions that smooth its deficiencies. However, overt conflicts can also move the organisation forward by facilitating talk about both what the organisation should do and what it should be or aspire to (Kraatz and Block, 2008).

The scope of these discussions is not limitless, as overt conflicts are embedded within the particular framework that encompasses its logics. Battilana and D'Aunno (2009) refer to this limitation as embedded agency, which they conceptualise as:

> ... a temporally embedded process of social engagement, informed by the past (in its habitual aspect), but also oriented toward the future (as a capacity to imagine alternative possibilities) and toward the present (as a capacity to contextualize past habits and future projects within the contingencies of the moment) (Battilana and D'Aunno, 2009, p. 47).

Overt actions are driven by the imagination of better alternatives, or, as noted above, what Aronson and Smith (2010) call 'expanded entitlements', within the logics of the system within which social workers are embedded. As such, these actions do not push for radical changes and are not as risky as covert actions that reject and violate current institutional arrangements. The manager who refused to act on the minister's directive, for example, could explain his decision based on the principles of best practices in social service, particularly the welfare of clients, which is a prima facie mandate of the ministry.

Finally, with respect to overt actions, we would add that much of the risk and anxiety related to taking overt actions against perceived injustice are related to moral ambiguity, which is a product of institutional pluralism. As such, and as demonstrated in the kitchen story above, given the multiple institutional logics their organisations have to consider, and the diverse stakeholders they have to satisfy, the injustices social workers observe are more likely to be morally ambiguous rather than clearly illegal. This ambiguity presents both avenues and obstacles for action.

Covert actions are necessary when the perceived injustice cannot be addressed within the institutionalised logics of the organisation, multiple as they may be. These actions are a product of the realisation by social workers that great energy and time are required to change large systems and, most importantly, the potential harm for clients waiting for the system to change. Although covert actions do not change systems, they do affect the lives of individuals who are being 'un-served' by these systems, as demonstrated by the manager who covertly rechanneled funds to clients whom he felt were most in need, and the front line participant who ensured that her lesbian client would receive properly informed and capable service.

Another example from our research might serve to further the point. A participant chose not to 'hear' a client when he claimed that he was earning extra money above his disability payments—if reported, the client's disability allowance would have to be reduced to the point at which getting by would be very tough. For the social worker, this was an issue of social justice. She saw herself working for a system that can foster an uneven socio-economic playing field by constraining clients from attempting to 'get out from under'. Clearly, confronting the system overtly to be more flexible would not have benefitted the client.

Covert actions have also been reported by Austin *et al.* (2005). A psychologist in their study felt compelled to act 'secretly' to ensure proper treatment for a patient who was becoming increasingly at risk regarding his own safety and mental well-being in the institution. After a number of pleas to other professionals within the institution, the psychologist realised that "*interinstitutional politics*" (Austin *et al.*, 2005, p. 204) were preventing a necessary transfer to an appropriate facility. Seeing that nothing would happen within the institution and that directly confronting the issue with the institution would lead to delays and high costs for the client, the psychologist made an anonymous call from outside the institution to a group that could advocate for the patient. Within very short order, the external advocacy group contacted the institution with the anonymous concern. In response, the institution transferred the client to another facility where the psychologist thought the patient would receive the required treatment. The psychologist's action is referred to by Austin *et al.* as 'acting in secret' (Austin *et al.*, 2005, p. 205), which is analogous to what we call covert action. In this situation, overt confrontation of the system would have been at the expense of the welfare of the patient.

Clearly, this is a situation that, according to the psychologist, needed to be addressed in an immediate way and would likely have led to harm if the psychologist had attempted to continue to confront the system openly. We believe that the psychologist's acting in a 'disloyal' way against his institution in order to protect the rights and health of a patient is heroic, as well as judicious. Indeed, the action does not change the system, but we suspect that this action and the others above fit with Loeb and Morris's (2005) notion that such care professionals are heroic because they put others first—particularly others who are disadvantaged—and because, if they are caught, the consequence could likely be severe.

While Austin *et al.* (2005) would question the contribution of covert actions to a healthy ethical environment, we argue that covert actions are heroic. In relation to our understanding of heroism, covert action is resistance with a cost—possibly at the cost of losing one's job if caught—but certainly at the cost of fear of discovery, isolation and condemnation, as our earlier analysis has noted (Fine and Teram, 2009). The deceptive nature of these actions means that they cannot be justified within the current institutional logics, and can therefore be formally penalised without adverse consequences for the legitimacy of the organisation.

Since moral actions are ultimately personal (Bauman, 1993), once one chooses to act covertly and/or overtly as opposed to inertly, the challenge is to make a judicious choice between overt and covert actions. The most heroic action, with the greatest potential for social change, would probably be overt actions that go beyond the institutionalised logics of a particular organisation.

Before taking any covert action in a situation that the social worker believes, through a reflexive process, is morally unjust and important to pursue, all possible legitimate avenues for addressing the issue overtly within the organisation ought to be explored. If these explorations fail, as it did with the social worker who informed her superior that he was breaking the law by not informing a client of his rights, then potentially going public or acting covertly are options. If one chooses to take overt action, then it is helpful for the social worker to remember that, when the harm is very clear and the organisation violates its own institutionalised logics, even overt actions that publicise injustice may be immune to formal retaliation. Therefore, a good understanding of institutional pluralism in general, and the multiple logics of one's organisation in particular, may expand the zone of relatively safe overt actions that professionals may consider. This safety is limited, however, to formal consequences, as superiors and co-workers can be very creative with informal retaliations against overt actors.

In some situations, professionals may be way ahead of their organisations in imagining alternatives that are outside of the current organisational logics. In these situations, overt actions may be fruitless and possibly detrimental for clients. In the example of the social worker who was concerned about 'curing lesbianism', overt action would have been unproductive, as the hospital was not yet ready for change in this area. Indeed, it was outside their organisational logics in terms of the psychiatric thinking with regard to the treatment of persons who were labelled as 'homosexual'. Overt action in this case would have yielded institutional resistance and possibly the assignment of a new worker—one who may not have taken into consideration the complex ethical implications of the situation. Thus, resorting to covert action manifests the realisation by the worker that her ethical logic, and what she thought was best for the client, could not be readily accommodated within the institutional logics of her organisation.

Similar realisation guided the covert actions of other participants, whose clients' immediate needs could not be subjected to the prolonged process of changing institutional logics and the uncertainty of its outcome. In the instance of the client who was earning extra money under the table, it is highly unlikely that the monolithic social assistance system was going to turn on a dime and sanction increased payments to all deserving clients. The psychologist, too, realised that fighting the system would get him and the client nowhere. The manager who was reallocating funds would also most likely have been stymied.

While covert actions seem a useful way to prevent injustice in such instances, they do not release the professional from trying to have an influence overtly on the way the institution handles such situations. Covert actions can work to 'right' a particular 'wrong', but we agree that they do not change systems. Indeed, covert actions can reinforce systems and the status quo, allowing things to run smoothly by not requiring the system to deal openly with its ambiguities (Lipsky, 1984; Hoggett, 2006). As for overt actions, we believe, as already suggested, that they should occur ideally whenever possible. Given that social workers do not possess superhero capabilities, they cannot fight every battle and, as such, they need to prioritise what they speak out for. However, considering the multiple logics of HSOs, we think that social workers have a wide range of options for relatively safe overt actions. The social worker who informed her superior that he was denying the rights of an offender, for example, acted within the institutionalised logics of her organisation, which would be to act in accordance with the law and, as such, she would be 'protected' in her action. However, while institutional pluralism provides formal protection for those who act overtly within the multiple logics of their organisation, as our stakeholders groups informed us, it does not provide protection against the informal hostility targeted at them if their actions upset the supporters of the dominant logics.

We believe that much more research is required in order to address in a more refined and informed way our speculations about the use of covert and overt actions. At this point, we would offer a general and tentative opinion: address overtly perceived injustice particularly when the overt action fits one of the multiple logics of the organisation. When the overt action is beyond the current institutionalised logics to the extent that pursuing it would potentially cause an immediate and potentially deeper harm to the client's welfare, covert action could be justified. In these latter situations, a social worker could be lobbying more generally for changes in the policies that allow moral injustices.

Conclusion

Pollack and Rossiter (2010), in a keen critique of neo-liberalism, consider neo-liberal policies, as implicated in the 'erosion of social work as a justice-based practice' (Pollack and Rossiter, 2010, p. 168). They maintain that feminists and social workers need to resist 'neoliberalization by rejecting assumptions about neoliberalism as a limited, neutral, economic realm and exposing the insidious and hidden ways in which neoliberal ideology is embedded within state (and private) structures, discourses, policies, and goals' (Pollack and Rossiter, 2010, p. 167). It could be argued that a number of the injustices in this article are linked to the increasing dominance of neo-liberalism. This is all the more reason for social workers to find the courage to preserve and strengthen the very essence of social work—social justice.

In an ideal world, with proper support, heroic figures, ethical champions and organisational practices that allow safe spaces for discussions about moral justice and moral distress, we might not need to speak of heroes, but rather mild-mannered social work bipeds: doing the job in a way that supports moral justice would be expected and honoured. However, we do not work in ideal situations. The world is complex, social and political structures do not necessarily favour the concerns of our clients, and resources are scarce. While we should not let those factors block continuous work towards social justice, there will be many times when mild manners need to be transformed into bold and heroic actions.

Acknowledgements

This research was funded by a grant from the Social Science and Humanities Research Council (SSHRC) Grant No. 410-2003-0203. We express our appreciation to all participants, without whom this study would not have been possible.

References

Aronson, J. and Smith, K. (2010) 'Managing restructured social services: Expanding the social?', *British Journal of Social Work*, **40**, pp. 530–47.

Austin, W., Rankel, M., Kagan, L., Bergum, V. and Lemermeyer, G. (2005) 'To stay or to go, to speak or stay silent, to act or not to act: Moral distress as experienced by psychologists', *Ethics & Behavior*, **15**(3), pp. 197–212.

Baines, D. (ed.) (2007) *Doing Anti-Oppressive Practice: Building Transformative Politicized Social Work*, Halifax, Fernwood Publishing.

Banks, S. (2004) *Ethics, Accountability and the Social Professions*, Houndsmills, UK, Palgrave Macmillan.

Banks, S. and Gallagher, A. (2009) *Ethics in Professional Life: Virtues for Health and Social Care*, Houndmills, Basingstoke, Hamshire, Palgrave Macmillan.

Battilana, J. and D'Aunno, T. (2009) 'Institutional work and the paradox of embedded agency', in T. Lawrence, R. Suddaby and B. Leca (eds), *Institutional Work: Actors and Agency in Institutional Studies of Organization*, Cambridge, UK, Cambridge University Press.

Bauman, Z. (1993) *Postmodern Ethics*, Oxford, UK, Blackwell.

Bogdan, R. and Taylor, S. (1975) *Introduction to Qualitative Research Methods: A Phenomenological Approach to the Social Sciences*, New York, John Wiley & Sons.

Brenzel, J. (2005) 'Why are superheroes good? Comics and the ring of gyges', in T. Morris and M. Morris (eds), *Superheroes and Philosophy: Truth, Justice, and the Socratic Way*, Chicago, Open Court.

Canadian Association of Social Workers (2005) *Code of Ethics*, Ottawa, ON, Author.

Denzin, N. K. and Lincoln, Y. S. (1998) 'Introduction: Entering the field of qualitative research', in N. K. Denzin and Y. S. Lincoln (eds), *Strategies of Qualitative Research*, Thousand Oaks, CA, Sage.

Fine, M. and Teram, E. (2009) 'Believers and skeptics: Where social workers situate themselves regarding the code of ethics', *Ethics & Behavior*, **19**(1), pp. 60–78.

Greenwood, D. J. and Levin, M. (2000) 'Reconstructing the relationships between universities and society through action research', in N. K. Denzin and Y. S. Lincoln (eds), *Handbook of Qualitative Research*, 2nd edn, Thousand Oaks, CA, Sage.

Hasenfeld, Y. (2000) 'Organizational forms as moral practices: The case of welfare departments', *Social Service Review*, **74**(3), pp. 329–51.

Hoggett, P. (2006) 'Conflict, ambivalence, and the contested purpose of public organizations', *Human Relations*, **59**(2), pp. 175–94.

Hugman, R. (2005) *New Approaches in Ethics for the Caring Professions*, New York, Palgrave Macmillan.

Kraatz, M. S. and Block, E. S. (2008) 'Organizational implications of institutional pluralism', in R. Greenwood, C. Oliver, K. Sahlin and R. Suddaby (eds), *The Sage Handbook of Organizational Institutionalism*, London, Sage.

Lipsky, M. (1980) *Street-Level Bureaucracy: Dilemmas of the Individual in Public Services*, New York, Russell Sage Foundation.

Lipsky, M. (1984) 'Bureaucratic disentitlement in social-welfare programs', *Social Service Review*, **58**(1), pp. 3–27.

Loeb, J. and Morris, T. (2005) 'Heroes and superheroes', in T. Morris and M. Morris (eds), *Superheroes and Philosophy: Truth, Justice, and the Socratic Way*, Chicago, Open Court.

Lonne, B., McDonald, C. and Fox, T. (2004) 'Ethical practice in contemporary human services', *Journal of Social Work*, **4**(3), pp. 345–67.

MacIntyre, A. (2007) *After Virtue: A Study in Moral Theory*, 3rd edn, London, Gerald Duckworth & Co.

McAuliffe, D. and Sudbery, J. (2005) '"Who do I tell?": Support and consultation in cases of ethical conflict', *Journal of Social Work*, **5**(1), pp. 21–43.

Meyerson, D. E. (2001) *Tempered Radicals: How People Use Difference to Inspire Change at Work*, Boston, MA, Harvard Business School Press.

Musil, L., Kubalíková, K., Hubíková, O. and Neasová, M. (2004) 'Do social workers avoid the dilemmas of work with clients?', *European Journal of Social Work*, **7**(3), pp. 305–19.

Noble, C. and Irwin, J. (2009) 'Social work supervision: An exploration of the current challenges in a rapidly changing social, economic and political environment', *Journal of Social Work*, **9**(3), pp. 345–58.

Papadaki, E. and Papadaki, V. (2008) 'Ethically difficult situations related to organizational conditions: Social workers' experiences in Crete, Greece', *Journal of Social Work*, **8**(2), pp. 163–80.

Pollack, S. and Rossiter, A. (2010) 'Neoliberalism and the entrepreneurial subject: Implications for feminism and social work', *Canadian Social Work Review*, **27**(2), pp. 155–69.

Stanford, S. (2010) '"Speaking back" to fear: Responding to the moral dilemmas of risk in social work practice', *British Journal of Social Work*, **40**, pp. 1065–80.

Stanford, S. N. (2011) 'Constructing moral responses to risk: A framework for hopeful social work practice', *British Journal of Social Work*, **41**, pp. 1514–31.

Strom-Gottfried, K. (2007) *Straight Talk about Professional Ethics*, Chicago, Lyceum Books.

Teram, E. (2010) 'Organizational change within morally ambiguous contexts: A case study of conflicting post-merger discourses', *Journal of Applied Behavioral Science*, **46**(1), pp. 38–54.

Teram, E., Schachter, C. L. and Stalker, C. A. (2005) 'The case for integrating grounded theory and participatory action research: Empowering clients to inform professional practice', *Qualitative Health Research*, **15**, pp. 1129–40.

Waid, M. (2005) 'The real truth about superman: And the rest of us, too', in T. Morris and M. Morris (eds), *Superheroes and Philosophy: Truth, Justice, and the Socratic Way*, Chicago, Open Court.

CHAPTER FIVE

Supportive Skills

THE SKILLS OF HELPING that facilitate engagement with clients; put them at ease; establish a trusting and empathic working relationship; provide comfort, understanding, compassion, and encouragement; and further facilitate the implementation of the assessment and intervention are referred to here, for the sake of simplicity, as *supportive skills*. As noted earlier, the research on the working relationship and basic counseling skills is voluminous, and the evidence for the importance of a sound working relationship is impressive (e.g., Hill, Nutt, & Jackson, 1994; Hill & O'Brien, 2004; Horvath & Greenberg, 1989; O'Hare, 2005; Orlinsky & Howard, 1986; Orlinsky, Grawe, & Parks, 1994; Rogers, 1951; Truax & Carkhuff, 1967). Implicit in the ability to develop and maintain a good working relationship and to engage and motivate clients in the change process is the need for practitioners to master basic interviewing skills (Hill & O'Brien, 2004; Shulman, 1999; Sommers-Flannagan & Sommers-Flannagan, 2003). Although practitioners and theoreticians of good will often disagree about the meaning or theoretical significance of the working relationship, most social workers agree that a sound supportive relationship and essential interviewing skills are a critical dimension of effective care.

The Basic Elements of Supportive Skills: Listening and Communication Skills

Interviewing skills are, perhaps, the most elemental of the helping skills. They are not only essential for the effective use of supportive, therapeutic coping, and case management skills but also necessary to conduct valid assessments and evaluation. Thus, basic interviewing skills lay the foundation for effectively implementing all social work practice functions. Basic interviewing skills include asking important questions, listening accurately, seeking clarification, accurately identifying feelings, and recounting client experiences. Skillful interviewing creates a level of discourse that encourages clients to be forthcoming about their difficulties, enhances collaboration, and enhances clients' adaptive capabilities. To better understand clients, practitioners must make their best efforts to enter and understand the client's subjective world to better understand who they are, what experiences they have had, how they see themselves and others, how they understand their current difficulties, what they want to achieve, and what they need to do to improve their lives.

At all stages of service provision, from first contact to last, interviewing skills (1) develop and maintain a working relationship with the client; (2) help obtain as accurate a picture as possible of what the client thinks, feels, and does; (3) deepen the practitioner's understanding of the role of people and events that affect the client, both through the client's eyes and by interviewing significant others; (4) encourage the client to engage in the intervention process; and (5) assist the client in monitoring his or her own progress and evaluating the impact of the intervention as best as he or she can. How interviewing skills are used may vary from client to client on the basis of age, the client's presentation style, the client's psychological and intellectual capacities, and the practitioner's own personal style. Nevertheless, there are some basic interviewing skills that have been well researched and honed by years of practice experience. They will be briefly reviewed here before considering other supportive and facilitative skills.

Types of Questions Used in the Helping Interview

There are different types of questions one can use to help clients generate personal narrative and obtain the information necessary for understanding a client's difficulties and adaptive capabilities. A good general approach is to ask questions initially that are somewhat general and then work toward more specific questions that focus on greater detail. This deductive trajectory from the general to the specific is helpful not only in the first few interviews when the practitioner conducts a thorough assessment but also in later interviews when clients are actively engaged in working toward solutions to their problems. Most of what follows regarding basic skills applies to older adolescents and adults. This chapter will also address adapting essential supportive skills to working with children.

Open-ended questions are quite general and allow clients wide latitude to talk about themselves and their situations. By using minimal prompts and little structure, open-ended questions provoke clients to take the initiative to discuss what they think is important. In the first visit, for example, a practitioner may simply begin, "So, what brings you into the clinic today?" For some clients, this opener may be more than enough. At some point, the practitioner may have to interject some modest amount of structure in the discussion to obtain necessary information to conduct the formal assessment (see appendix B). However, for verbally active clients, a little structure and occasional prompts ("So, tell me a little more when you first felt depressed") may be sufficient.

Closed-ended questions offer a more limited range of answers and encourage clients to provide more definitive answers to specific topics. "So, did you drink alcoholic beverages this weekend?" may be a follow-up to a client's vague report on how he or she has been coping since being discharged from a rehabilitation facility. If the client responds in the affirmative, closed-ended, follow-up questions might include "So, how many drinks did you have?" With a court-ordered client, a practitioner might ask: "Have you tried to see your spouse since she had a restraining order taken out on you?" Closed questions are intended to limit the range of possible answers, in this case, to yes or no.

Specific questions are intended to focus the interview in greater detail on important subjects regarding the client's thoughts, feelings, behaviors, or details of a situation or event. These questions are intended to fill in the gaps of a general narrative about especially important events (e.g., "When did your husband hit you? Was this the first time? No? Then, how many times had it happened before? How did he hit you? Was it a slap or a punch? Did he ever use an object or a weapon? What kind of injury did you sustain? What happened after the event was over? Did you call the police? Was anyone else there to witness what happened?). Although in some situations, the interview may sound a bit like an interrogation, this is typically not the case if a sound working relationship has been formed with the client and the practitioner communicates empathic concern. The details of clients' problems and experiences may be critical to understanding exactly what has been going on for them. At times, talking about the events out loud may be the first time a client has had a chance to process thoughts and feelings about a stressful or traumatic event. The opportunity to discuss the events in detail in the presence of an empathic and trusted listener can be inherently therapeutic.

Detailed querying is also critical when recounting a client's experiences in implementing the intervention outside of the fifty-minute hour. Most effective interventions involve a client's active participation in the treatment during everyday life, whether the purpose is working on communication skills with his or her partner, improving parenting skills with an oppositional child, taking one day at a time to stay clean and sober, or trying to master social anxiety. When client and practitioner meet in session, recounting the client's efforts to implement the intervention in everyday life usually involves some reconstruction of events to gauge whether the client is making progress (e.g., "What opportunities did you make to work on your social anxiety this week?" "For how long did you carry on your conversation with that new woman in your office?" "Did you ask her out for a cup of coffee?" "How did your lunch date go?" "Did you ask her about what she likes to do in her free time?" "What did she say?").

Some counseling texts refer to interviewing styles as either directive (structured) or nondirective (unstructured). The fact is that effective interviewing requires a thoughtful use of both. Nondirective interviewing relies more on open-ended questions, creates ambiguity regarding expectations of the practitioner, and gives clients free rein to take the discussion where they want to go. A directive style introduces more structure into the interview, uses more closed questions that limit response options, and is more purposeful to the task at hand. As for the client recently discharged from rehabilitation, mixing closed and open questions might sound like the following: "So, you had about fifteen drinks on Saturday afternoon. Can you tell me what was going on with you emotionally at that time?" (open question). Then, "Did you make any attempt to cut short your relapse?" (closed question) and "How did you feel about your slip the next day?" (open question). Using only one interviewing approach or the other makes little sense in social work practice. The exclusive use of a nondirective approach would result in puzzling ambiguity and leave many clients eventually wondering what the purpose of the intervention was. Conversely, an exclusive reliance on a directive style would likely leave some clients wondering if the practitioner were even interested in what they thought or felt or were simply carrying out some predetermined agenda of his or her own. Directive and nondirective approaches should be mixed and follow both an inductive (broad information gathering) and deductive (drawing cause-effect conclusions) pattern. The purposes of each interview are guided by the goals of the intervention (previously negotiated between practitioner and client) and the phase of the intervention: completing the assessment, implementing the intervention, or conducting the evaluation. In general, sessions with clients should probably begin on an open-ended note and

move toward a more structured purpose linked to treatment goals. Imbuing each interview with that kind of rhythm helps keep the purposes of the intervention at the forefront.

Adopt a Relaxed and Attentive Posture

Helping a client feel at ease is the result of several processes and is closely intertwined with good interviewing skills: careful listening so the client feels that he or she is being understood accurately, carefully delineating both the practitioner's and client's role; and being relatively nonjudgmental and focusing on an agenda to solve problems and enhance coping in everyday life. Practitioners must be genuine, authentic, and come across in a way that is congruent with who they are so that their professional demeanor does not come across as contrived. Clients feel more at ease when they understand the purpose of meetings and feel they have some input into the treatment agenda. Even court-ordered clients can be given some degree of choice and a sense of control over methods and treatment goals. Clients will also feel more at ease when they feel assured that the practitioner will uphold the informed-consent and confidentiality aspects of ethical practice (see chapter 3). Clients feel more at ease when practitioners communicate that they are knowledgeable, competent, and confident that they have the skills to help the client. Finally, clients feel more at ease when they sense that the purpose of the meetings is to focus exclusively on the agreed-on goals of the intervention and that there is no other competing agenda insinuated into the meeting. Said another way, the express purpose of the meetings is to help the client achieve his or her goals.

Most clients are at least a little nervous when interviewed by a social worker, particularly for the first time. They may suffer from a psychiatric disorder, be investigated for alleged abuse, struggle with a drug problem, or have recently been released from prison. The client may be relieved to have the opportunity to be seen, may be guarded or angry at being coerced into the visit, or may be indifferent. Some clients may suffer from psychoses and be somewhat delusional about the purpose of the meeting, and others may be so depressed they are almost unable to respond to questions. In general, it helps to begin by appearing relaxed and attentive. This presentation will communicate to the client that the practitioner is alert, ready and willing to be of assistance, and interested in hearing what the client has to say. Depending on the cognitive and emotional state of the client, practitioners should be ready to expend the necessary level of energy it takes to engage each client depending on how much initiative the client takes in the interview. The client recently court-ordered to the interview, for example, may be hostile and give only one-word answers, provoking the interviewer to work harder to engage the client in the assessment. An anxious client may speak rapidly, obsess over every minute detail of a story, or jump from one subject to the next. Practitioners might need to help these clients structure their presentation and focus on more substantive matters. The depressed client may be almost mute, necessitating that the practitioner work hard just to excavate even basic background information. Practitioners should consider being relaxed and attentive a good starting point, but they should be flexible and ready to engage the client according to his or her needs, abilities, and expectations.

Nonverbal Communication

For the most part, in Western cultures, making eye contact is a powerful form of communication in that it demands the other person's attention and communicates a form of psychological engagement. When you look into the client's eyes, it says that you are paying attention to them. However, not all clients are comfortable being stared at for a lengthy period of time. Clients who are shy or otherwise anxious, feel unduly scrutinized, are ashamed, or are hiding something they feel uncomfortable about may begin to chafe under a social worker's unwavering gaze. In some cultures, it may be simply impolite or even an affront to make steady eye contact. Practitioners should take notice to determine whether a client is comfortable making consistent eye contact; if not, practitioners should perhaps break off the constant gaze by taking occasional notes or looking down or away from the client between questions or points of discussion. Some practitioners have been known to position their chairs in such a way that they need not look directly at the client if the client seems uncomfortable. Being flexible about seating arrangements and providing choices for clients can help them be more comfortable during the interview.

If one pays attention to everyday conversation (in line at the check-out counter, at home with family, with friends, or at work), one would readily become aware that much of what passes for conversation is nonverbal. *Nonverbal behaviors* refer to nonword vocalizations and physical gestures that convey fairly specific meaning in everyday discourse. Nonverbals are, essentially, powerful shorthand vocalizations and gestures that facilitate communication. The classic *uh-huh* encountered in popular media portrayals of therapy is, indeed, a common utterance. It is simple, easily recognized in everyday conversation (though not in all languages), and is

infinitely flexible to provide nuanced indication of interest in what the client is saying. *Uh-huh* can suggest keen interest, boredom, humor, disapproval, concern, or compassion with the slightest inflection. The same can be suggested about *hmm*, *aha*, or other nonverbal expressions. Practitioners should pay careful attention to these almost automatic utterances and note how clients respond to them, as their meaning can be ambiguous.

Other nonverbal utterances include facial expressions, another powerful form of communication. Generally, social workers do not receive the kind of training that, for example, professional actors do. So they may not be keenly aware of what they are communicating through facial expressions. But facial expressions can clearly communicate any of the following, often in a more primal and compelling way than words can: concern, compassion, disgust, anger, sarcasm, pity, ridicule, alarm, fear, and so forth. Spending some time in front of the mirror may not be a bad way for a practitioner to examine how he or she expresses the full range of emotions, and being aware of how one wears one's feelings on his or her face is critical to becoming aware of communicating emotional responses to clients. For example, after several months of this author working with a depressed young woman going through a divorce with an apparently difficult man, she remembered little about what I had said during our sessions but recounted in her last session: "All I had to do while talking about how things were going at home was to look at your face, and I knew that I wasn't the crazy one!" Fortunately, my ingenuous communications of alarm and puzzlement at their encounters validated for her that her husband's behaviors were somewhat extreme, unfair, and sometimes hostile, and that the failure of the marriage was not all her fault.

But nonverbal behaviors go well beyond facial expressions. Sitting back, relaxed with one's legs crossed comports with the earlier suggestion to be relaxed and attentive. At some point, however, such a posture would seem bizarre, when, for example, a client recounts a time when he or she was sexually assaulted or contemplating suicide. Physical posture communicates an emotional response, and practitioners must be aware of what they are trying to say with their physical presentation. Again, practicing in front of a mirror may help beginning practitioners define extra concern (e.g., leaning forward in a chair to listen with extra care), such as reeling back slightly with a single clap of the hands to express surprise at a fortuitous outcome or joy at a client's courageous breakthrough. Leaning sideways in one's chair and scratching one's head to communicate a bit of confusion can be an effective way of saying, "Your version of the story seems to contradict what you were telling me last week. Perhaps I'm not getting this right." Although traditional approaches to psychotherapy long extolled the virtues of adopting a somewhat impassive, blank-slate posture on which clients would project (displace) their deepest feelings about others in their life, this posture not only can seem contrived and artificial but also can be easily interpreted by some clients as apathy. Because most social work encounters are relatively brief (e.g., three to twelve visits), there is little benefit in creating such a level of ambiguity and confusion. When it comes to communicating with clients, practitioners should assume that everything they say or do, even silence, is a form of communication. The question is, What is it you are trying to say to your client, and is it in his or her best interest (i.e., does it help the client move toward intervention goals?)?

Reflection, Tracking, and Clarifying

Effective communication between two people is generally considered a process of developing mutual understanding of each other's thoughts, feelings, intentions, and behaviors. Most theoretical communication models are represented as feedback loops: one person communicates a message, and the other person receives it, analyzes it, and sends back a communication. The first person acknowledges the response and demonstrates that he or she understood the second person's response—and the cycle continues. Understanding someone you know well or are especially close to can seem almost automatic. At times, you feel that you can anticipate what that other person is about to say. Sometimes friends, family members, or intimate partners can communicate and be fully understood with a gesture. People sometimes talk at each other simultaneously (breaking all the rules of good communication), or finish each other's sentences and, amazingly, can still find mutual understanding at a deep level.

Working with clients is another story, and little should be taken for granted about clear communications. The helping relationship is a professional and somewhat contrived one whereby relative strangers are expected to divulge personal information in a relatively short amount of time at scheduled intervals. As such, professional helping interviews are a special kind of relationship and require more purposeful communication skills. Understanding what your client is trying to tell you and helping them understand your responses can be much more difficult, and these skills must be cultivated with much practice. Helping the client feel understood is a task that often must be accomplished in a relatively short amount of time, not over weeks, months, and years. Practitioners facilitate communication by demonstrating that they really comprehend what the client is trying to get them to understand. Practitioners are primarily responsible

for seeing that the communication feedback loop is completed on a consistent basis. In addition to careful listening, the practitioner can ensure that the communication process is complete by consistently testing the clarity of the signal between practitioner and client.

Reflecting, tracking, and clarifying are related communication skills that are used to focus on one major goal: to gradually string together a clear, accurate, and understandable client narrative and to help the client confirm for him- or herself that you have understood. Reflecting, tracking, and clarifying are three related skills used to continually test the hypothesis that you, as practitioner, understand what the client says. *Reflecting* simply means repeating in a somewhat different way what the client said to see if your meaning is congruent with the client's meaning. This, of course, may take a bit of practice and may require a process of gradual approximation. Clients generally appreciate that you make the effort to accurately reflect what they say before you move the conversation forward. One way to quickly lose a client's tenuous commitment to the working alliance is to behave as though you knew what the client meant when, in fact, you did not. The client might sense that you did not understand him or her and failed to make an effort to clarify what was said because of apathy or distraction. Making a concerted effort to understand exactly what the client meant shows respect, empathy, and a real commitment to helping the client. Clients have to feel, first and foremost, that you are willing to try hard to listen and understand what they are saying from their point of view. Practitioners may develop their own points of view, and may later (after a working relationship has developed) share their perspective with the client. But, especially early in the helping process, practitioners must demonstrate that they are willing and able to listen and reflect back to the client an accurate understanding of what the client is trying to say.

Accurate reflection is more challenging with some clients than with others. Young children, for example, might not have the verbal capacity to express their thoughts and feelings or to describe others' behaviors or intentions clearly or accurately. Adolescents may use language that is comprehensible only to their immediate social group. Many clients may struggle with their host country's language. Other clients may have difficulties expressing themselves verbally as a result of poor education, learning disabilities, or other developmental disabilities. Clients suffering from serious mental illnesses might use idiosyncratic language or have difficulty expressing themselves because of a thought disorder. Practitioners, whatever the circumstance, should be prepared to be flexible and resourceful in finding ways to communicate with clients. In many circumstances, such as with younger children, people who primarily rely on a nonnative language, or people with specific problems with verbal expression, practitioners should be prepared to obtain specialized training so they can fully communicate with clients.

After demonstrating that you can accurately reflect what the client is saying, track what the client says, which means demonstrating that you can follow the narrative along from one point to the next. For clients who express themselves in clear, organized, linear fashion, tracking the narrative may be relatively easy. However, many clients encountered in social work practices struggle with emotional distress or cognitive impairments as a result of substance abuse, mental disorders, or other learning disabilities. Tracking what clients say may involve more than just following along, but it may take considerable effort on the part of the practitioner to help clients construct their narrative both temporally (i.e., connecting time and dates related to key events) and sequentially (i.e., sequencing cause and effect over time). This process of helping the client track the time line and causal sequence of events often requires some directive interviewing but must be done with a minimum of interference.

Clarifying combines the best of both reflection and tracking. Clarification is accurately communicating to the client that you understand not only specific facts or expressions of feelings but also how the client's experiences evolved over time and across situations. When practitioners clarify, they do not simply make sure that they understand each individual fact of the client's narrative; they show that they are beginning to get the big picture (i.e., put the facts in a broader context) and to connect the dots. The elements of your clients' experiences are related to all facets of their experience: thoughts, feelings, behaviors, and situations, especially those involving other people in their lives. As a result of clarification and understanding, an intricate picture of a client's experience begins to emerge. To use a more contemporary metaphor, accurate clarification of a client's experiences is similar to the emergence of a picture from a digital camera: the clearer is the electronic signal (i.e., the more pixels), the clearer is the whole picture. Clarification is, essentially, a descriptive exercise, not an interpretive one. A good test of whether you have achieved clarification is an unambiguous confirmation from the client, such as when he or she exclaims, "Yes, that's exactly what I mean!"

At times, practitioners must confront clients with known facts or the practitioner's professional opinion regarding something that potentially affects the client's well-being or the well-being of others. The term *confrontation* often brings to mind the stern or disapproving admonishments of an authority figure. In the working relationship, confrontation skills give

clients accurate feedback for several purposes: (1) the practitioner might have information that points out incongruities or apparent falsehoods in what the client has stated and maintained (e.g., evidence of child abuse, drug use, violence toward a partner, other harmful or unethical behaviors); (2) the practitioner might feel the need to point out something about the client's behavior that puts him or her at risk (e.g., repeating behaviors that put the client at risk of harm in a relationship, behaviors that put the client at greater risk of relapse with drugs or psychiatric symptoms). There are many other reasons why practitioners sometimes have to express opinions to clients that they may resist accepting. For confrontation to be effective, however, a sound working relationship must be in place. For example, if a young woman with a history of dating verbally and sometimes physically abusive men says, "I know he's been violent before, but I really think I can change him!" the practitioner might respectfully muster the relevant facts of the client's past relationships and present them in a straightforward manner: "Abbey, from our previous discussions, it sounds to me like you're about to make the same mistake you've made several times before. Each time, you thought you could change abusive men by loving them. And each time, you have ended up being disappointed or, even, abused again. I think we need to examine more closely why you seem to believe you have this power to change abusive men and why you confuse their efforts to control you with love or passion. Maybe we should talk about this some more before you plunge ahead. What do you think?"

For a young man struggling to abstain from alcohol and other drugs, confrontation may take the following form: "Joe, you've been in and out of rehab three times now. Each time, you've made an attempt to hang out with the same group of guys that like to party a lot. How is this time going to be different?"

Practitioners should develop their own styles with regard to confrontation. However, confrontation is a skill to be implemented with a balance of straightforward honesty and sensitivity. Being ambiguous, tentative, or overly sensitive is likely to be both confusing and ineffective. Real compassion requires the ability to be honest and explicit when the practitioner judges that the client is ready to receive accurate feedback. Being sensitive does not mean being ineffectual. Navigating the path toward an effective confrontation takes practice, and confrontations should be used sparingly and only after a sound working alliance is established. Although the client role brings with it some expectation that the client will receive some feedback from their practitioner, that feedback needs to be communicated in a way that shows empathy for the client's ongoing struggle.

Adapting Basic Interviewing Skills to Work with Children

As a function of age and cognitive development, children see the world differently than do adults. Thus, interviewing children requires special skills and a solid understanding of what cognitive competencies they have at each age. Practitioners who work with young children should especially have a solid grasp of modern child developmental psychology. Particularly young children (younger than age six, more or less) often have very different ideas about human relationships, the passage of time, and difficulty sorting out the concrete from the abstract. Children may have good memories of specific events, but the experience of the interview itself may significantly affect the retrieval and understanding of the memories. Children also have many fears and anxieties, some realistic and some not. They are quite susceptible to the vagaries of their imaginations in response to things they are told by others, see on television, hear in bedtime stories, or see in the movies. The phenomenology of young childhood is quite different from that of older children, adolescents, and adults.

It should also be understood that there are different purposes to interviewing children in social work practice: clinical assessment (to describe the problem and understand the factors related to the problem to prepare an intervention) and forensic assessment (to determine whether a crime has occurred). Many of the basic principles of interviewing described in relation to adults apply to children as well: careful listening, empathic attunement, putting them at ease, reflecting, tracking, and clarifying are all essential skills for interviewing a child. However, perhaps even more critical information is obtained through observation of children not only in the consulting room but also in the classroom, at day care, and during structured after-school activities. Possibly the most critical information is acquired from parents, guardians, and other adults (e.g., teachers, coaches, other responsible caretakers) who have ample opportunity to observe the child.

Nevertheless, there are some essential data that can be obtained from young children in the traditional one-on-one interview. Focus on their agenda, not yours. Listen with minimal prompts as needed and allow the child to communicate his or her inner world and version of events from his or her own point of view. Wilson and Powell (2001) suggest some ground rules for basic listening, tracking, and clarifying with children. Practitioners should take care to communicate to a child the following: "Let me know if I misunderstand you," "Tell me everything you can about what happened," "Let me know if you don't understand something I've said and I'll try again using different words," "Saying 'I don't know' or 'I don't remember' is OK," "Tell me everything you remember but don't guess; just tell me what you are sure about," "Even if you think I already know something, tell me anyway," "Only talk about things that you know really happened," "You may use whatever words you want to use," "I promise I'll not get upset or angry at anything you say to me" (pp. 35–36).

A variety of aids can be enlisted to facilitate interviewing with a child, including the use of games, toys, and dolls (Morrison & Anders, 1999). When playing with children, use figures or toys that do not overly constrict play or themes that they might elicit. Put children at ease, get down on the floor at their level, and participate in a way that encourages them to play. Be a participant observer. Build rapport with the child, explore general themes, and then delve into promising areas with increasingly greater specificity. Be flexible in the way you approach the interview. Young children are not usually linear in communicating their story.

Research on the validity of using these methods suggests that simple games or activities that put children at ease and enhance communication with the practitioner are helpful. These activities include playing games or using dolls to re-create or remember events which may be a cause for concern (e.g., physical abuse, sexual abuse). However, practitioners should avoid drawing firm conclusions from children's utterances in response to symbolic play. Young children are suggestible, can be easily led, and often do not understand the significance of what the practitioner is driving at. Interpreting a child's unconscious motives or inferring abuse from symbolic play with toys, games, or drawings is risky, and there is little evidence that such interpretations are valid. Interpreting children's play or artwork is no substitute for more objective evidence when attempting, for example, to determine some external cause of their depression, anxiety, or other behavioral problem. As discussed in chapter 4, only through the collection of multidimensional data from multiple sources can a practitioner begin to make reasonable but tentative hypotheses about allegations of abuse, neglect, or other events that may negatively affect a child's mood or behavior.

Wilson and Powell (2001) provide some guidelines for the structure of the basic interview with children that reflect a similar approach to interviews with adults: establish a basic rapport, introduce the topic for discussion, elicit a free narrative account using open-ended questions, and use prompts minimally to keep the conversation on track. Practitioners should use simply worded, specific questions to clarify inconsistencies and obtain sufficient detail. The interviewer should then close with a brief summary and the interviewer should make an effort to provide the child with a chance to correct any mistakes or misunderstandings.

Putting Basic Interviewing Skills to Work: Developing the Working Alliance and Facilitating Change

Communicating Positive Regard and Respect

To successfully engage clients in a working alliance, communicating basic respect for them is essential. Treating a client with positive regard means that the practitioner communicates in words and behavior that he or she believes the client to have inherent value as a human being. Treating the client with respect means communicating through one's words, intonation, and other nonverbal expression that the client has inherent dignity and is worthy of concern and assistance. This assumption on the part of the practitioner may seem, at face value, to be an obvious prerequisite for practicing social work. However, practitioners, at times, should expect to find this assumption a challenging one to maintain with every client.

It has been commonly observed in the helping professions that some practitioners find that clients who are more verbal, better educated, and have better incomes seem to be more appealing to work with than are clients who are more marginalized or stigmatized in society. Voluntary, educated, and self-sufficient clients tend to be more personally engaging, are better socialized into the purposes and processes of psychotherapy services, are less likely to have serious mental illnesses, tend to place a priority on relationship problems, and are generally less stressful to work with. It is understandable that many practitioners cultivate their practice with clients who appear more amenable to voluntary, private social work services.

Some practitioners view clients who are less economically and educationally advantaged, are less sophisticated in the ways of talk therapy, are more likely to have serious mental health problems and chronic addictions, or have perhaps run afoul of the law as less desirable to work with. Many of these clients are considered involuntary, are less amenable to the role of client, and are more likely to be considered resistant and difficult to treat. Many of these clients have been in prison, and some have committed serious crimes, including domestic violence, physical and sexual abuse of children, rape, assault and battery, and gun related offenses. Some practitioners may find that maintaining a position of positive regard and respect for clients who have engaged in serious antisocial behaviors or are otherwise stigmatized is very challenging indeed.

Practitioners, particularly those starting out in their social work careers, should be honest with themselves if they experience a strong degree of ambivalence regarding work with difficult-to-treat or antisocial clients. To work with involuntary clients, it is essential that practitioners sort through that ambivalence early on and be willing to distinguish clients' harmful behaviors from their inherently good qualities as people. Understanding the contributions of genetic risk factors, the developmental impact of years of physical or sexual abuse, and the enduring effects of other environmental stressors can sometimes promote empathy and help practitioners maintain respect and positive regard for the client. At some point, the client may have been a good son or daughter, friend, or parent or may have contributed to the community in some meaningfully positive way. However, differentiating people from behaviors (while holding them accountable for their offenses) may not be easy for some practitioners. Beginning practitioners who choose to work with clients who have engaged in harmful and antisocial behaviors should honestly explore their feelings about working with such "unattractive" groups and admit any serious reservations they might have. The social work profession serves many needy populations, and practitioners should work with clients with whom they can establish a commitment and consistently maintain a feeling of respect and positive regard.

Being Genuine and Authentic

Genuineness and authenticity are achieved when one's professional persona is congruent with who one really is as a person. Many clients can instinctively sense when a social worker is not being him- or herself, comes across as playing a role, or presents an image that simply does not ring true. Being authentic and genuine, however, does not mean self-confession or self-disclosure with a client. Being honest does not mean saying everything on one's mind. Such excesses on the part of the practitioner can actually make the client uncomfortable (e.g., "Who is the client here anyway?"). All practitioners are somewhat different in the way they present themselves, in their sense of humor, in their comfort level with different clients, and in their style of professional decorum (formal vs. informal). What matters most is that a practitioner maintains good boundaries with the client, communicates a genuine empathy, and keeps the professional purposes of the work together clearly in mind.

Communicating Empathy, Compassion, and Understanding

Communicating empathy means demonstrating verbally and nonverbally that you understand, as best you can, how the client feels. Clients are likely to sense whether what you say and how you say it truly communicates empathy. Empathy should not be confused with agreeing with what the client says or condoning a client's behavior. Empathy should also be distinguished from compassion, an expressed feeling that reflects a sense of shared, often painful human experience. You may express empathy for a man who has acted violently toward his family ("I can understand your sense of frustration and sense of powerlessness") without communicating compassion. On the other hand, a practitioner may be more likely to feel and communicate compassion for a client who has just lost a child to a terminal illness. Compassion goes beyond empathy, beyond merely communicating an understanding of the client's feelings and experience. Expressing compassion lets the client know that, as a person, you can imagine sharing in disappointment, loss, or other source of emotional distress.

Engendering Trust through Consistency and Attending to Client Needs

Many clients have had negative experiences with people in their lives. Many clients have been physically and sexually abused by people they otherwise trusted, betrayed by someone with whom they had an intimate relationship, abandoned by a mother or father, financially exploited, discriminated against, victimized by crime, rejected by fellow citizens after risking their lives for them in combat, or deeply harmed in some other way. Why should they expect a social worker to be any more reliable? Mutual trust is a condition between two people that must be developed, cultivated, and nurtured over time. It is not an assumed condition of the relationship between social worker and client. Trust implies constancy and congruency. Clients are more likely to trust social workers when they say what they mean clearly and directly, do not hide behind vague answers or use ambiguous, pseudo-professional language (i.e., psychobabble), do not pretend to know things for which they cannot give a well informed answer, and consistently focus on clients' needs.

Practitioners can engender trust in a client by empathizing with the client's feelings regarding experiences in which he or she has been betrayed and by being trustworthy as a practitioner. Being worthy of trust means being consistent, reliable, and honest with your client, and always keeping the client's well-being in mind by keeping the main purpose of the intervention in the forefront.

Providing Encouragement and Enhancing Motivation

Clients come to receive social work services with different levels of motivation and readiness to make changes. Many clients experiencing personal

problems, mental illnesses, substance use disorders, eating disorders, family problems, and the like, generally do not feel enthusiastic about asking for help. Some may not feel they have a problem and resent having been coerced into social work services through the child welfare, mental health, or criminal justice system. Some clients may be difficult to engage initially but often participate more when they feel they have some say in how the intervention will progress and realize that participation may yield some personal benefit.

Other clients are highly motivated: they want to feel better and want their situation to improve. Such clients are more readily engaged in the beginning, though considerable ambivalence might emerge later as they realize they may have to work hard to make some changes to feel better. Seriously depressed clients may have a hard time even getting out of bed in the morning, but they might feel the need to work hard because of obligations to those who depend on them. The person struggling with an addiction wants to stop drinking or using other drugs, but the initial success is often short lived. A young angry adolescent might be tired of getting into trouble but also does not want to give in to the demands of adults around him or her. The mother investigated by child welfare struggles with her commitment to give up smoking marijuana daily but does not want to lose custody of her children. All these clients know that they must make an effort to improve their situation, know that change might be hard, and struggle with their commitment to change.

In recent years, practice researchers have focused their efforts on reaching difficult-to-engage clients. Because of an increased emphasis in social work on work with involuntary (e.g., court referred, treatment mandated) clients, practitioners are more likely to deal with clients who do not believe that they have a problem, do not believe that psychosocial interventions are of any value, or simply disagree with practitioners about the nature of the problem or necessity for intervention. They may feel strongly (rightly or wrongly to some degree) that it is the system that is unfair.

Supportive and facilitative skills that focus on enhancing motivation are now considered essential for engaging clients in the early process of change (Miller & Rollnick, 2002). Perhaps one of the better-known assessment frameworks for identifying a client's readiness to change is that developed by James Prochaska and colleagues (Prochaska & DiClemente, 1984; Prochaska, DiClemente, & Norcross, 1992) at the University of Rhode Island. Their research team stipulates five stages of change: precontemplation, when clients do not agree that they have a problem, may see others as the cause of their difficulties, or may feel coerced into treatment by the courts or significant others; contemplation, when a client is aware of a problem and may want to find out whether therapy can help; preparation, when the client takes some initial steps toward change; action, when a client may take more significant steps toward working on the problem and actively seek help in the change process; and maintenance, when clients have already made changes with regard to a problem and have sought treatment to consolidate previous improvements. Clients may cycle through these stages of change or proceed in a trajectory of one step forward, two steps back. The stages-of-change model has been employed with a range of problems including smoking cessation, substance abuse, and other mental health and health-related problems.

As the stages of change imply, clients are usually not clearly in one stage or another and may feel considerable ambivalence in the change process (O'Hare, 1996). If stages of change suggest when clients are ready, motivational enhancement methods (designed to help clients move beyond ambivalence and through the stages of change) suggest how to help clients engage in the change process (Miller & Rollnick, 2002). Readiness to change is particularly relevant for working with involuntary clients, those more or less coerced into receiving social work services who practitioners often label as "resistant," "hard to reach," "hostile," and "unmotivated" (Rooney & Bibus, 2001). However, the voluntary versus involuntary dichotomy is far from absolute and is better considered a continuum. Strategies designed to help clients move through the stages of change include the following:

- Accept clients' initial reluctance: Empathize with clients' ambivalence about engaging in treatment or making changes, acknowledge that they may have been treated somewhat unfairly without suggesting that you think they are blameless with regard to their current difficulties, and acknowledge that not everyone benefits from social work intervention. Above all, do not argue or try to sell clients on the benefits of treatment.
- Avoid premature confrontation: Again, do not quarrel. Get the facts from clients and other relevant sources. Practitioners should objectively present their summaries to clients and give them a chance to respond and explain their point of view.
- Clarify one's dual role within the social service and/or criminal justice system: Be up front with clients. Let them know you empathize with the situation and want to help with concerns. However, you collaborate with the criminal justice system because a particular client has been convicted of child abuse, drug possession, domestic assault, or some other antisocial act. Communicate the expectation that clients have an obligation to acknowledge the behavior (assuming the accusations are well founded), take responsibility for the behavior, and change the behavior. Social workers not only have an ethical obligation to protect society but also should use contingencies of the courts as therapeutic leverage to help clients meet agreed-on goals of the intervention (i.e., therapeutic jurisprudence).
- Explore clients' perspective on the problem: Encourage clients to suggest intervention goals and ways to pursue them. Recruiting clients as collaborators this way can provide them with some sense of control and choice in developing the intervention plan.
- List problems by priority: Start with one or two that are more readily resolved; then break each individual problem and objective down to manageable steps.
- Employ behavioral contracting: Collaborate on agreements, keep them specific, and track them to completion.
- Avoid overemphasis on clients' irrelevant self-disclosures: Gauge each client's need to open up but do not make it a condition of pursuing intervention goals.
- Anticipate obstacles to treatment compliance: Look down the road with clients and help them identify scenarios that may interfere with successfully reaching agreed-on goals.
- Involve significant others when at all possible: Encourage clients to recruit people in their lives who have a vested interest in the client's compliance with intervention goals.
- Actively enhance motivation: Help clients visualize the benefits of working toward intervention goals and consequences of returning to the previous problem behaviors, list the pros and cons of changing versus not making progress, and empathize with the difficulties of change but communicate optimism about positive change and the benefits that might accrue.

Enhancing Clients' Confidence and Morale

Improving self-confidence, overall morale, or self-efficacy with regard to coping with some specific problem is not something that a practitioner can readily impart to a client. Clients must earn that feeling from graduated experiences of success. Relating positive testimonials of other clients struggling with similar difficulties or reporting relevant outcome-research findings might be helpful ("You mean, I'm not hopeless?"), but there is no substitute for success. For positive success experiences to occur, however, practitioners must be skilled in clearly identifying the problem and helping clients break it down into manageable objectives. The intervention methods used must be targeted toward achieving modest but substantive objectives so clients can gradually gain back a true sense of confidence. This linking of client behavior and increased self-efficacy (i.e., the belief that one can cope in a given situation) is where the practitioner's ability to cultivate a supportive working relationship facilitates effective therapeutic coping skills. The working relationship, in many cases, makes it possible for clients to take the risks necessary to make real changes and experience success. The practitioner and the working relationship he or she cultivates become a catalyst for change.

Clarifying Roles of the Practitioner and the Client

The practitioner has the primary responsibility of being the expert; that is, the practitioner, not the client, is the one who has the requisite credentials, gets paid for the service, is liable for providing services within established standards of care, and is held accountable for delivering ethical and effective interventions. Clients expect social workers to be knowledgeable about the problems they treat and skilled in the interventions they provide. Thus, in the practitioner-client relationship, the practitioner is responsible for certain roles: conducting informed assessments, implementing interventions that have been shown to be effective in current outcome research, and evaluating the results of those efforts.

Although practitioners bear much of the responsibility for implementing professional services, clients have responsibilities as well. They should be expected to show up on time, make an effort to participate constructively in treatment, and cooperate with arranging for insurance and initially agreed-on out-of-pocket payments. Also, clients can forfeit their rights to confidentiality and informed consent when they threaten to harm themselves or other people during the course of the intervention.

Clarifying the role of the practitioner and that of the client, however, can be confusing at times. For example, for most social work agencies, maintaining fiscal integrity (i.e., balancing the budget) is critical for the agency to continue serving the public. Sources of income for agencies can span the continuum from private to public funding and often combine both sources. The manner in which these conditions influence practitioners, however, can influence intervention planning decisions. For example, in a busy clinic where a combination of state funding and private insurance pays for services, should the extent of coverage determine, in part, clients' length of stay? Even with the most ethical of behavior (e.g.,

avoiding conflicts of interest) on the part of practitioners and administrators, there are external influences that have a subtle but real impact on how social workers define their role in relation to clients.

Defining the client's role can be difficult at times. A more challenging situation concerns involuntary referrals. *Voluntary* and *involuntary* is a matter of degree—perhaps representing a level of willingness to engage in treatment. If a court-diversionary program, for example, offers a client the choice of drug treatment or jail, who is the client? The overloaded criminal justice system or the person who arrives for treatment? If a distraught and depressed middle-aged woman arrives for her first session, and it becomes clear that she is there because she does not know what to do about her alcohol-addicted husband but wants to get him to come for treatment, who is the client? If a young woman is referred for mental health treatment as a condition of having child custody reinstated by the courts via the approval of child welfare and mental health professionals, who is the client? Practitioners can help clients define their role by helping them sort out the reasons why they sought treatment and how those reasons are contingent on the behavior of other people in their lives or other institutions. Although many of these circumstances involve mixed motives in the client, these must be drawn out: "Is there any reason why you don't want to be here?" "Do you feel that you are being forced here against your will?" "Is there any reason why you think this might be helpful to you despite the fact that you don't really want to be here?" Helping clients sort out mixed agenda can go a long way toward helping them define their role as client, a necessary step in defining mutually agreed-on intervention goals and engaging in the change process.

Collaborating with the Client on the Assessment, Intervention, and Evaluation Plan

Defining practitioner and client roles also necessitates determining shared responsibilities. One of the most supportive aspects of effective helping is cultivating a shared feeling of collaboration, the sense that client and practitioner are "in this thing together." True, one does not want to ignore the power differential: the practitioner has the responsibility to implement effective care and has some prerogatives that the client does not (e.g., the practitioner can hospitalize clients against their will; the practitioner can breach confidentiality should a client threaten to harm him- or herself or others; the practitioner may be bound to report client information to the courts). However, the practitioner can underscore the importance of collaboration in the following manner: "We both agree that you want to work on

Topic A, and that we will first do that by trying Intervention B and then see how it goes." To transcend some of the ambivalence about receiving social work services, clients must feel that, on some level, they voluntarily participate in (and take responsibility for) the course of the intervention. This collaborative relationship, again, does not obviate the power differences in the relationship, but it does establish a common ground on which practitioner and client can base a productive working relationship.

As part of the intervention, however, the practitioner also recruits the client into activities. Clients provide the information to complete the assessment. Clients might also spend some time on their own completing assessment instruments, such as self-report scales, charts, or diaries to help with the assessment and monitor treatment progress. Practitioners might also have clients carry out some of the intervention during the time when they are not in session. For example, people struggling with addictions may attend mutual help meetings, psychoeducational classes, or a family gathering (later on in recovery)—at which they know family members are likely to drink—to practice relapse-prevention coping strategies. A family with a conduct-disordered adolescent may have to spend time in brief family meetings to negotiate guidelines for doing homework and increasing prosocial activities. Clients, in effect, become collaborators with practitioners to implement interventions successfully. They are not passive recipients of treatment. The shared feeling that exists between practitioner and client that they are collaborating on the assessment, intervention, and evaluation plan together is the glue that holds the working alliance together.

Maintaining Clear Boundaries

Defining clear boundaries and collaborating effectively on the intervention requires that the practitioner take the responsibility for maintaining clear professional boundaries over the course of the intervention. Boundaries are best kept in sight not by maintaining a pseudo-professional, aloof posture but by continuing to communicate empathy and respect and by continually focusing on the goals of the intervention contract. To stay on track, good working questions for every practitioner are, Is what I am doing in the meeting with the client today likely to enhance this client's progress? and, Am I helping the client move toward the agreed-on goals? Practitioners also need to model behavior that reinforces good boundaries to reassure the client about the respective roles of practitioner and client. Clients should be encouraged to express their feelings, participate in the intervention during the session, put what they have learned into action

outside of sessions, and help evaluate whether things are getting better. In other words, for both practitioner and client, the mutual focus should be on getting the work done together.

Clients sometimes have strong feelings about their practitioner. How should practitioners handle these feelings? For a variety of reasons, the helping relationship creates, at times, an ambiguity about the nature of the relationship whereby the client may interject a variety of feelings (e.g., love, hate, anger, envy, jealousy, gratitude) into the relationship. The client may communicate these feelings in a variety of ways, both directly and indirectly. These feelings may spring from a variety of sources. In the psychodynamic tradition, feelings displaced or projected onto the practitioner (i.e., transference) were often assumed to be feelings that the client felt about his or her mother or primary caretaker in the past. Although one's parents may be a source of such feelings, there are many other possible sources as well, including how the person actually feels about the relationship with the practitioner (e.g., the client may be justified in feeling angry with the practitioner). Other sources of these feelings may stem from experiences the client had with some other person with whom they had or currently have a close relationship (e.g., spouse, friend, employer). Other legitimate feelings may be evoked from racial, cultural, or socioeconomic differences and tensions. A young African American man who has had negative experiences with white authority figures may feel suspicious and resentful about a white social worker; a woman who has been abused by men in the past may be predisposed to feel a mixture of anger and shame or other feelings toward a male practitioner; an older client may feel either nurturing or resentful feelings toward a younger social worker; a male client from a culture where women are dissuaded from achieving educational or professional success may feel disdain toward a female social worker. Because a professional helping relationship is not a naturally occurring relationship (e.g., friendship, marriage, parent-child, coworkers), ambiguities abound and clients will find a way to fill in those ambiguities, accurately or otherwise. It is the practitioner's job to explore those ambiguities and help clients deal with them realistically and with minimal distortion.

Likewise, practitioners make interpersonal misattributions (O'Hare, 2005) toward some clients. Practitioners can experience a range of feelings that potentially obstruct the helping process. These may include anger, disgust, sexual attraction, a parental need to nurture, and so on. Mild feelings of genuine affection or caring are usually not a matter of concern and may enhance the helping process. However, other feelings toward clients can become a serious obstacle to effective intervention. Anger can lead to punitive behavior toward a client, premature termination, or abandonment; attraction or infatuation can lead to overtures for sexual relations. Practitioners are obliged to identify for themselves what they feel, determine whether the way they deal with their feelings helps or hinders the working relationship, and take responsibility for feelings and subsequent behaviors toward the client. Practitioners often sort these matters out for themselves or in discussion with colleagues; if the problem is not readily resolved, the practitioner can seek professional consultation. Whatever method practitioners use to cope with these matters, keeping the client's well-being in mind should be the foremost priority. Maintaining clear boundaries means continually returning to the key question: Is what I am about to say or do in the client's best interest?

Summary

Supportive and facilitative skills incorporate basic interviewing methods in the service of cultivating a sound working alliance, enhancing motivation, and helping the client engage in a collaborative change process. However, although supportive skills are essential for establishing the working alliance, the practice process research has clearly shown that they are usually not sufficient for helping clients with more serious and complex problems. To conduct more advanced interventions with clients with moderate to severe psychosocial disorders, expert use of therapeutic coping skills is essential.

doi 10 1093/cdj/bss023
Advance Access publication 7 September 2012

Bold but balanced: how community development contributes to mental health and inclusion

Patience Seebohm*, Alison Gilchrist and David Morris

Abstract This article explores the positive contribution that community development (CD) can make to mental well-being by providing close but critical support to individuals and community-led initiatives. The emphasis on self-determination, collective action and empowerment within the CD approach inspires hope and recovery from mental distress. Drawing on a recent study of CD practice across varied UK settings, we demonstrate how practitioners use their skills to break down barriers, build relationships, manage group dynamics and tackle prejudice. They 'connect and include' people experiencing mental health difficulties with community activities and mainstream services, increasing opportunity and choice. We note that a skilfully balanced, empathetic but bold CD approach requires professional capabilities, flexible management and participative forms of evaluation. It fits the current UK policy emphasis on empowerment and engagement and responds to the growing evidence that personal networks and social equality correlate with health and well-being. However, its impact tends to be limited by workplace context, insufficient resources and a failure by health providers and others to recognize its potential.

Introduction

Community development (CD) supports people in communities to generate their own initiatives and networks while also supporting them to

*Address for correspondence: Patience Seebohm, Cavehall Cottage, Wyddial, Buntingford, Herts SG9 0ER, UK, email: patienceseebohm@btinternet.com

work with public and voluntary services. In this article, we argue that the principles of self-determination, collective action and empowerment which underpin a bold but balanced CD approach help to enhance well-being, inclusion and recovery from mental ill-health. In examining issues arising from practice, we draw upon recent literature, especially our own *Connect and Include* (Seebohm and Gilchrist, 2008), an exploratory study of the role CD can play in the UK mental health context.

We show how a skilfully balanced, empathetic but bold CD approach provides close but critical support to community-led groups, the organizations that grow out of them, the networks that link them and the public agencies that engage with them. We discuss the dilemmas facing CD practitioners working in a mental health context, including the challenge to gather persuasive evidence of their impact. We conclude that CD deserves greater recognition and investment as part of a wider strategy to bring about more equal, healthy societies. It aligns well with international policies on well-being but remains under-used.

Connect and Include (Seebohm and Gilchrist, 2008) examined the contribution of CD practice in the mental health field, drawing on a literature review, survey and interviews in eight sites across the United Kingdom. Here we refer to two examples from that study, Beat the Blues (Box 1) and the Upper Teesdale Agricultural Support Services (UTASS) (Box 2) as well as the Hamdard group for Muslim women based within Sharing Voices, a mental health CD organization working with black, Asian and minority ethnic communities (Box 3). All quotes are from *Connect and Include* unless otherwise stated.

Box 1. Beat the Blues Stockport (www.beattheblues-stockport.co.uk)

Postnatal depression affects thousands of women but many reject medical treatment. Health visitors and a mental health CD practitioner explored scope for a peer support group. Women were reluctant until the practitioner adopted a slower, personal approach, encouraging women to set up *Beat the Blues* in their own way. Now the group runs many activities including monthly meetings attracting fifteen to twenty people, complementary therapy, information, family fun sessions, service user involvement and awareness raising. CD support initially included help with funding, venue and networking but then the practitioner stepped back, remaining available when needed.

'Beat the Blues made me realise that I was not insane. . . . I don't like to think where I would be without it. I have found some courage to go back to college and retrain.'

Box 2. Upper Teesdale Agricultural Support Services (UTASS) (www.utass.org)

Upper Teesdale is a remote area where farmers find it hard to cope with the recurring crises and bureaucracy of today's agricultural industry. People were isolated from health, social, leisure and advice facilities until, after an unprecedented number of suicides, local people adopted a CD approach to researching the sources of stress. They subsequently set up UTASS modelled on its recommendations, now run by local staff, volunteers and 1600 members.

UTASS aims to improve the well-being, economic status and quality of life of local people. As a community hub, it delivers services and supports smaller groups, facilitating training, information exchange, social and cultural activities. People access emotional and practical help in non-stigmatizing settings. UTASS also enables young people to gain a voice, influence and place in society.

'Often the setting in which people are placed is part of the problem, and so by working within that setting you are most likely to be able to help with that problem.'

Box 3. Hamdard at Sharing Voices, Bradford (www.sharingvoices.org.uk)
Source: Seebohm *et al.* (2005)

Hamdard is the Urdu word for 'someone who gives support'. A Muslim woman with experience of personal difficulties set up the group to provide a holistic approach to mental health and well-being, taking into account the daily experiences of Muslim women. At weekly meetings, women share experiences of family tensions and other pressures in a friendly, confidential setting. They participate in creative, spiritual and learning activities and service-user consultations. Participants from different cultural backgrounds (including English) have often been to the doctor for depression, self-harmed or come from psychiatric wards. A female Muslim practitioner at Sharing Voices, a mental health community development project, provides support when needed.

'Hamdard's made me speak up – it's built my confidence ... now I'm thinking about the future.... I'd like to get a job'.

Mental health and community context

Well-being, recovery, inclusion

Some people experiencing mental health difficulties may have a clinical diagnosis such as schizophrenia, while at the other end of the mental health spectrum some receive little or no help from their doctor for the unrelenting stress in their daily lives. Regardless of their clinical status, people can achieve positive mental health or well-being, terms we use interchangeably; functioning well, they can work, contribute to their community and enjoy a sense of purpose (Friedli, 2009).

People using mental health services developed a new and now widely adopted concept of 'recovery' to describe their journey from distress to well-being. This involves regaining hope, a positive and purposeful sense of self and taking control of their life, whether or not symptoms of ill-health continue (Wallcraft, 2005). Recovery can bring greater social interaction and 'inclusion', a term which describes

> ... the degree to which citizens or community members are able to participate in, and benefit from, the activities and services generally available in society. The capacity to influence decisions is crucial to inclusion. (Morris and Gilchrist, 2011, p. 7)

The combination of close 'bonding' relationships, looser 'bridging' connections across social groups and the ability to influence decision-making through links across levels of society, commonly described as 'social capital', is associated with well-being (Friedli, 2009). Social capital is not always benign: Siisiainen (2000) finds that Bourdieu highlights the conflict and domination within and across groups (e.g. Bourdieu, 1986), while McKenzie, Whitley and Weich (2002) note that tight, closely knit communities can be intolerant of deviant behaviour, with serious implications for those who are mentally unwell. CD, underpinned by values of equality and social justice, helps to identify and challenge oppression. It enables people from groups who are often marginalized to participate in community activities in ways that reduce stigma and exclusion, creating opportunities to mix, think and act more freely.

Community-led initiatives

Self-determination and empowerment are at the heart of well-being and recovery; they also underpin collectively owned and run initiatives like the UTASS:

> It was an issue raised by local people, on behalf of local people, local people were involved in controlling it.... This is the practical result and it is held by the community.
>
> CD practitioner

Researchers including Munn-Giddings and Borkman (2005) describe community-led initiatives as 'self help' and 'mutual aid'; community participants may use different terms, but the common features in the academic literature on self-help are widely agreed to be that:

- they are run for and by people who share the same health or social issue;
- their primary source of knowledge is based on sharing direct experience; and
- they occur as voluntary collectives predominately in the third sector of society as opposed to the statutory or private sectors (Munn-Giddings and Borkman, 2005, p. 139).

Chamberlin (1997), a mental health activist, describes how people are empowered by coming together to talk about their shared predicament, to critically reflect on the social, political and economic structures around them and subsequently reinterpret their situation: an educative process which replaces self-blame with self-esteem. Horton, in her work with Gypsies and Travellers, describes the liberating impact of this process:

> The realisation that everyday existence is due, or at least can be traced to, legislation, political or historical factors, is liberating... people [gain] the confidence to critique and challenge images of themselves they encounter in the local health, education or police service. (Horton, 2007, p. 31)

Participants may become accepting and proud of complex or stigmatizing identities, increasing their capacity to integrate with others (Gilchrist, Wetherell and Bowles, 2010) and act collectively (Ledwith, 2011). Many of the Muslim women attending the Hamdard group gained the confidence to study, work and engage with service providers.

While some community-led groups remain small and informal, others acquire a formal presence by campaigning for better public services or delivering services themselves. They fill the gaps left by public services or operate as complementary to them (Archer and Vanderhoven, 2010). Initiatives run by black groups facing racism and cultural ignorance often address deep distress within their communities (Keating, 2002). Munn-Giddings and Stokken (2012) describes how groups are shaped by their social, economic, cultural and policy context. She distinguishes between the 'predominately single issue groups' of North America, Canada, Scandinavia and Europe, where importance is attached to individual autonomy and more 'community-oriented' groups in areas of acute hardship or non-Western cultures. Among the respondents to *Connect and Include*, we found both 'single issue' and 'community-oriented' initiatives.

Regardless of their function, the ethos and impact of community-based or user-led initiatives differ from those which are philanthropic or professionally managed (Keating, 2002; Munn-Giddings and McVicar, 2006). Decision-making and accountability remain with group members, who exercise influence that is often lacking in other spheres of their life. Expertise based on their lived experience is prioritized over professional and clinical training. Members both receive and give help. Such initiatives are life-enhancing but often fragile; they need support that respects their ethos and independence. The CD approach is uniquely equipped to respond.

The CD approach

CD has taken different forms over time and place, but retains some core principles (Craig *et al.*, 2011). As Henderson and Vercseg (2010, p. 4) observe: 'the origins and structures of community development reflect the societies of which they are a part... [but] the fundamental architecture of community development is the same'. CD is 'the bottom-up stimulus and facilitation for people to become involved through their own priorities' (Fisher, 2011, p. 5). CD practitioners, guided by a commitment to social justice and equality, act as catalysts bringing people together to identify, discuss and act upon shared problems (Department of Communities and Local Government, 2006). Freire (1972) and others describe how collective reflection and action around a common purpose builds shared capacity and increases influence so that ultimately communities and individuals are able to gain greater control over the decisions that affect their lives. CD practitioners participating in *Connect and Include* held diverse roles in a range of settings, including housing, health, regeneration and leisure. The scope of their work varied but many adopted this approach. CD differs from 'community engagement', which usually refers to the way authorities seek to consult or involve people in activities and decision-making on an agenda that is set externally.

There is a history of CD contributing to health improvement in the United Kingdom, for instance within community care (Barr *et al.*, 2001) and in mental health services as a cornerstone of the Delivering Race Equality in Mental Health (DRE) programme (Department of Health, 2005). Many DRE practitioners focused on influencing strategic activities (Walker and Craig, 2009; Craig *et al.* in this special issue). However, the central focus here is on work at community-level to support collective action. We make the case for a bold, balanced but critical approach to CD, based on enhanced sensitivity to the mental health difficulties facing community members. By this, we mean that CD practitioners who seek to empower and enable people affected by distress need to find the right balance between close support and a 'hands-off' approach which leaves control with the people.

CD practitioners need to know how to be bold and critical in challenging discriminatory assumptions and practices across community and statutory sectors while seeking to maintain supportive, trusting relationships.

Bold but balanced approach

Taking time

In some communities, the reluctance to admit to stress or despair lies deep within social traditions. Hill farmers of Upper Teesdale often prefer to be stoical (Shaw, 1997), while people from black and Asian communities may associate mental ill-health with spiritual or social shame (McCabe and Priebe, 2004; Sainsbury Centre for Mental Health, 2002). CD practitioners interviewed in *Connect and Include* described how they used various strategies to build up trust and credibility before they turned conversations to mental health. They said that personal skills and a shared heritage, language or faith helped, but judging the right time was crucial. It was six months before the practitioner at UTASS asked about stress and suicide:

> You have to be very careful; you can't walk into something like that. The community has to accept me.... I was tested almost like an animal, literally at the mart, where the farmers would go. I would go to the bar, I went to the farms, so everybody was really familiar with me before I started.
>
> CD practitioner

Once trust is established, relationships need to be maintained. Practitioner interviewees felt that long-term relationships helped them to sustain community participation and revisit established groups whose future becomes jeopardized. Managers who fail to understand the unpredictable nature of community involvement and the cycles of group dynamics can put such activity at risk.

Enabling and challenging

There is a widespread misconception that CD practitioners work only with groups. Individual community interviewees in *Connect and Include* described how CD practitioners identified and nurtured their talents, creating opportunities for participation and leadership that were sensitive to but not limited by their support needs. Their self-esteem and aspirations grew as they took up roles that challenged and interested them. At Beat the Blues, UTASS and Hamdard, participants with experience of mental health difficulties were supported to set up their own groups and move into committee, volunteer and employee positions. Some moved on to other work situations. Participants spoke of immense pride in these achievements:

> I get a sense of achievement and satisfaction that it is a group that started from nothing, and now it is successful and helping the women. I'm just so proud of Beat the Blues.
>
> Community participant

Practitioners described how they balanced being a bit 'pushy' in challenging community participants to take on new responsibilities, with standing back, letting people find their own way of doing things. By doing tasks alongside participants, practitioners model how they might be done; they 'do *with*' not 'do *for*' (Henderson, 2001). In contrast to many mental health workers who operate within a framework of risk-avoidance and low expectations, CD practitioners focus on strengths, not afraid of setbacks. As this participant says, they do not judge:

> I never felt judged by her. She never ever judged. She just knew what support was needed.
>
> Community participant

Blurring boundaries

Within CD, relationships often become multifaceted and reciprocal. The distinctions between paid practitioner, activist, volunteer or friend become blurred, in contrast to the professional (and protecting) boundaries between clinicians and clients.

People with mental health difficulties interviewed in *Connect and Include* told us that practitioners listened because they cared, not because it was their duty; practitioners were 'on a level', not separated by status or position. Practitioner interviewees spoke of valuing the friendships they made with those they supported, often living nearby, with a shared identity and background, such as being a Muslim in the United Kingdom. Dealing with sensitive, emotionally charged issues required courage, integrity and management support. Many interviewees felt they wanted appropriate guidance from their employers and argued that practitioners working alongside people in acute distress needed additional emotional supervision. This was provided at UTASS, Sharing Voices and Beat the Blues but often lacking for DRE practitioners (BRAP, 2010). Some practitioners working in close-knit communities established sufficient distance to ensure they were perceived as impartial: neither caught up in the web of local relationships, nor accountable solely to their employers.

On tap, not on top

Taylor *et al.* (2007) found that community-led initiatives valued the help of an expert facilitator whose roles included confidence-building, broadening horizons, critical friend, mediator, broker and someone to turn to in a crisis.

CD practitioners delivering this help need to find the right balance between 'light-touch' and 'in-depth' support. They need to be close to the action: 'on tap, but not on top'.

Being on hand but not in control is no easy task. Our study found practitioners need strong personal and professional skills to be both 'enabler' and 'facilitator' in complex, often politically sensitive social settings (Seebohm and Gilchrist, 2008). One group member complained that their practitioner could be too dominant:

> Sometimes [the practitioner's] influence is overbearing You have to get the balance.
>
> Community participant

A practitioner interviewee contrasted the light-touch support she gave Beat the Blues with her more directive approach with a group of people discharged from long-term institutions, to ensure that their participative but anarchic meetings kept the group on track. She encouraged groups to develop participatory practices, challenging them but remaining pragmatic, intervening neither too little, nor too much. Taylor *et al.* (2007, p. 2) note that more intensive support is needed 'where there is a long history of disadvantage'. The mental health system fosters dependency but we found CD practitioners sought to give participants the opportunity to use their skills and take control:

> I make the assumption that they want to be in control, and it becomes contagious so they realise that they are in the driving seat.
>
> CD practitioner

Several practitioners in *Connect and Include* described how they brought people together to identify and address shared problems, exchange coping strategies and learn about health and support services. They helped to build trust and confidentiality in friendly, supportive gatherings, gradually moving conversations from talking about healthy living to sharing experiences of acute distress:

> Out there you don't know who to trust and who will talk. I can talk here and I go away knowing that my load has been lightened
>
> Community participant

Chamberlin (1997) found that people with mental health problems feel empowered as they define, develop and mobilize their own groups, gaining more power and influence together than they could ever achieve on their own. Several participants interviewed for *Connect and Include* spoke of the boost they gained from helping others with similar experiences:

> It has helped me to help someone else. It has given me the satisfaction of knowing that someone else won't go through what I did.
>
> Community participant

> It made me feel I wasn't isolated any more. It gave me the confidence to show someone else, *you* are not isolated any more.
>
> Community participant

Creating vibrancy

Creating and nurturing networks between people and organizations is a fundamental component of CD (Gilchrist, 2009). Networks link individuals and groups to a range of other people, resources and opportunities, enabling social movement and change. One practitioner interviewed for *Connect and Include* described how she supported people from stigmatized groups to use leisure services, which in turn became more welcoming. Another interviewee explained how UTASS invited support and advice services into their premises giving the farming community easy, non-stigmatizing access to help. Another drew mental health service user groups away from institutional settings by encouraging them to meet in voluntary sector premises:

> We don't live our life in bunkers or ghettos – we need to look at integration with other parts of the community and other community groups.
>
> CD practitioner

We found some practitioners had boldly broken down social and cultural divisions by encouraging groups to make unexpected connections and widen their social networks. Historically divided faith and cultural groups came together for celebrations, learning or exercise activities. Informal networking made people feel differently about their neighbourhood:

> At first I was thinking they might say, oh no, I don't want to go there, but they were really happy, you wouldn't think they were two different cultures or religions Sometimes you need to give the opportunity to do that.
>
> CD practitioner

Beat the Blues and UTASS became vibrant, well-connected and influential, linking with arts, leisure and a range of statutory agencies. Practitioners also informed or directly helped groups, for instance with advice about funding and practical resources such as venues or specialist expertise.

Bridging the gap

Language barriers, differences of perspective, lack of trust and an imbalance of power can divide mental health services from the communities they serve. In addition to obvious hindrances to communication, there were more deep-rooted social barriers. Economic, social or spiritual understandings of mental ill-health found in non-Western communities (McCabe and Priebe, 2004) mean that clinical labels have no equivalence in those cultures and may fail to resonate with many people in the United Kingdom. CD practitioners interviewed for *Connect and Include* described how they worked to bridge this gap. They supported health workers to run innovative sessions, for instance for South Asian women on depression, hearing voices and medication. They explained to health workers how to adjust their practice to suit the communities they are working in:

> It's about getting information across to people in a way that they are able to absorb it, and there needs to be a lot of flexibility.
>
> Mental health professional

> An awful lot of people who work in services are deeply institutionalised and are afraid of the communities.... Sometimes we can open doors.
>
> CD practitioner

Communities and clinicians were encouraged to co-produce support and solutions, providing vital and reciprocal links between people in crisis and recovery. For example, UTASS created 24-hour telephone access to local doctors, who in turn referred patients back for voluntary work. Henderson and Vercseg (2010, p. 132) note that 'CD can shift the locus of control and power from service provider to the user of community'. By enabling health services to understand and adapt to community circumstances, practitioners contributed to that shift.

Challenges

Perspective and influence

The *Connect and Include* study found that several generic CD practitioners understood mental ill-health in mainly clinical terms, viewing it as irrelevant to their work despite dealing daily with people distressed by life's pressures. Some DRE practitioners dismissed non-Western models of mental health described above that were prevalent within the communities they were meant to support, unaware that increasing numbers of psychiatrists were themselves challenging Western dominance within established practice (e.g. Bracken and Thomas, 2005; Fernando, 2010). Those with a more critical understanding of psychiatric services were able to help clinicians reflect on their assumptions. The study concluded that practitioners should increase understanding of the impact of racism and the value of community-based solutions to distress, but clinicians may not be receptive: Fountain and Hicks (2010) found some mental health professionals lack interest in community perspectives.

· Practitioners often have to balance their commitment to community empowerment and self-determination with professional obligations within a public service hierarchy. To manage this complex accountability, they need space for reflection, integrity and the capacity to question authority without closing down the dialogue. Effective challenge becomes difficult where statutory sector managers misuse 'community development' to implement top-down policies (Ledwith, 2011). Practitioners' influence with decision-makers can be further diminished by their deliberately low profile and community orientation. Consequently, their role risks being under-valued and their skills are overlooked when set against the high status of clinical roles and medical expertise. Medically trained managers can find the lack of clear timeframes, control and uncertain objectives difficult to tolerate (Gerrard, 2000). In four of the eight sites visited for *Connect and Include*, statutory staff were said to lack understanding or were sceptical of CD.

Evidence

Tensions are exacerbated by the contrast often made between the strong positivistic evidence-base for medical interventions and the 'more nebulous activities' of CD (Gilbert and Russell, 2006). An increasing body of scientific literature suggests that strengthening social networks improves the well-being of its participants (Gilchrist, 2009), but this cannot be verified through random controlled trials, clinicians' preferred research methodology. Similarly, the varied pace and unpredictability of outcomes is hard to fit within the monitoring frameworks that guide health managers. These may be intangible and unexpected, and appear long after an intervention has ended.

CD has been accused of lacking a plausible theory of change setting out a causal explanation of how specific interventions result in intended consequences (e.g. Miller, 2010). Miller argues that although CD urgently needs impact and outcome measures that have credibility with clinically trained commissioners, a robust and systematic approach is hindered by a lack of directly related statistics, dilemmas around attributing credit in partnership work and short-term funding.

Where mental health service users participate in a community-led initiative, it is possible (but not easy) to demonstrate variations in service use during their participation, but data-collection processes tend to be alienating and intrusive. With more diverse groups, there may be no appropriate set of indicators. Miller (2010) argues that a range of measures could be set up across a locality where practitioners support networks of groups but this may be expensive, bureaucratic and inflexible, ignoring the changes that matter to participants themselves. Participatory methodologies avoid these pitfalls and fit well with CD (Seebohm *et al.*, 2005) but their interactive processes tend to lack credibility with clinicians. The findings are regarded as potentially distorted by communities' own hopes and therefore overly subjective.

Qualitative research, particularly case studies, usefully complements quantitative evidence. In much CD, qualitative research will provide a more accurate picture of what has happened than statistical data, for instance, from questionnaires. Qualitative research helps to *illustrate* and *explain* the impact which statistics fail to do. *Connect and Include* provides an exploratory, not a representative, picture. Nevertheless, interviews with community participants suggested CD practitioners were helping to change lives:

> Most probably I would still be drinking, most probably dead by now. It has made a big difference to my life. Even my family look at me differently.
>
> Community participant

All these approaches require resources, time and guidance. CD practitioners should work with health managers to agree the reporting mechanisms needed to capture evidence of the effects of their work.

Conclusions

We have shown how a bold but balanced CD approach helps people to gain well-being, inclusion and recovery from mental ill-health by promoting core components of positive mental health: namely, self-determination, interaction and empowerment. With CD support, people come together in their own groups and networks, gaining more control over their lives, giving and receiving help using expertise grounded in shared experiences. These community-led initiatives may complement statutory services but can never be replicated by them. With CD support, excluded people are included as both participants and leaders. Within the groups and across the networks, relationships spread horizontally across the community and grow vertically into public agencies, increasing statutory sector understanding of local needs and opportunities. This creates the conditions for a range of solutions to mental distress to emerge using different kinds of expertise.

Not all CD practitioners have the capacity for this approach. We have noted they need to work closely with communities, using their skills to facilitate, enable and support people in distress alongside mental health professionals. Courage and a critical perspective help them to challenge oppressive practices in communities and services. Management support for practitioners, commitment to a community-led approach and long-term investment are essential.

Connect and Include found that statutory services often fail to appreciate the potential of CD. Its accountability to the community as well as to the state and its lack of clinical measures do not fit comfortably within a service culture of risk-avoidance and tight outcome measurement. Too often, CD roles are constrained by statutory bodies, implementing top-down policies (Ledwith, 2011). However, *Connect and Include* identified mental health managers and commissioners who believe that the bold, balanced and critical approach to CD such as described here makes a vital contribution to healthy, cohesive communities. A CD practitioner sums up its potential:

> By connecting people together, which is what community development is about, you are putting in place an informal support system which is probably going to be more effective and long term than drugs.

Turning to the policy implications, the role of CD in promoting self-determination, collective action and empowerment aligns well with the United Kingdom's mental health and broader government policies. The Department of Health's DRE programme (2005) seemed to recognize this with funding for 500 CD workers, but many felt undervalued and misunderstood (Walker and Craig, 2009; Craig *et al.* in this special issue). CD has a warmer reception in Scotland, where its National Health Service funds the Community Health Exchange (CHEX) to support strategic and operational collaboration between policy-makers, CD practitioners and community-led initiatives.

Mental health policy in England has often neglected the community dimension of people's lives. Exceptions include the National Social Inclusion Programme (NSIP), which adopted a strategic approach from 2005 to 2010 in seeking to create new kinds of relationships between service providers and communities, reducing barriers to community participation in a range of life domains and encouraging co-production of support. NSIP sought to challenge stigma and discrimination, which inhibit inclusion and remain a central policy concern (Department of Health, 2011).

The financial burden of mental ill-health has increased interest in prevention and well-being. The link between well-being and inclusion is recognized by the World Health Organization (Friedli, 2009), European Commission (2010), South Australian Social Inclusion Board (2007) and Mental Health Commission for Canada (2009), among others. However, these rarely acknowledge the potential of CD to support well-being initiatives. UK policy recently advocated interpersonal networks to help reduce vulnerability (Department of Health, 2010) based on evidence of how connecting and giving contributes to well-being (Foresight Mental Capital and Wellbeing Project, 2008). Henderson and Vercseg (2010) find levels of mutual support in eastern and central European countries insufficient for a mental health agenda at this juncture, and their CD must therefore focus on generic community needs. As mentioned earlier, CD and community-led initiatives are shaped by their social and political context. For greatest impact, CD must be part of a wider political strategy to reduce economic and social inequalities: even modest reductions in economic inequality can significantly improve our health (Wilkinson and Pickett, 2009).

Community empowerment policies could make better use of CD to stimulate the co-production of support services whereby communities and professionals work closely together on equal terms to achieve the desired outcomes – in this case, mental well-being and recovery. This approach has attracted international interest (Needham, 2009), but expansion in the United Kingdom may be hampered by institutional resistance, funding cuts and a reduced emphasis on collaboration. Austerity measures and government ideology indicate a shift away from public provision towards greater social responsibility for localized service delivery. This presents an opportunity for change but questions arise. Will communities be resourced and supported to address their own priorities? Who will ensure social justice and equality for minority groups? Will community activists and organizers charged with galvanizing local collective action have the skills and long-term investment needed to deliver a bold, balanced and critical approach? As Henderson and Vercseg (2010) wryly note, the capacity of CD to redistribute power seems to threaten the control exercised by public authorities. Policy-makers, intent on predictable and easily measurable targets, may prefer the rhetoric to the reality.

The CD approach outlined in this article could help UK policy-makers to translate their rhetoric of community empowerment, self-help and collective action into practice, which would in turn improve mental health and well-being for our many communities. It may also have relevance for other national contexts.

Acknowledgements

The authors thank all the participants and the advisory group members who contributed to *Connect and Include*. The study, carried out by the Community Development Foundation (CDF), included a literature review; survey with thirty-one respondents; and semi-structured interviews in eight sites with nineteen CD practitioners, fifteen people with mental ill-health and five mental health professionals.

Funding

The study was funded by the National Social Inclusion Programme, Department of Health, UK.

Patience Seebohm is an independent researcher, Cavehall Cottage, Wyddial, Buntingford, Herts SG9 0ER, UK.

Alison Gilchrist is an independent community development consultant, Kendal, LA9 7HU, UK.

David Morris is Professor of Mental Health, Inclusion and Community and Director of Inclusion Institute, School of Health, University of Central Lancashire, Preston PR1 2HE, UK.

References

Archer, T. and Vanderhoven, D. (2010) *Growing and Sustaining Self Help: Taking the Big Society from Words to Action*, Community Development Foundation, London.

Barr, A., Stenhouse, C. and Henderson, P. (2001) *Caring Communities: A Challenge for Social Inclusion*, Joseph Rowntree Foundation, York, UK.

Bourdieu, P. (1986) The forms of capital, in J. G. Richardson, ed., *Handbook of Theory and Research for the Sociology of Education*, Greenwood Press, New York, NY, pp. 241–258.

Bracken, P. and Thomas, P. (2005) *Postpsychiatry: Mental Health in a Postmodern World*, Oxford University Press, Oxford, UK.

BRAP (2010) *Great Expectations: The Value of the Community Development Worker Role in Mental Health*, Yorkshire and Humber Improvement Partnership, BRAP, Birmingham, UK.

Chamberlin, J. (1997) A working definition of empowerment, *Psychiatric Rehabilitation Journal*, **20** (4), 43–46.

Craig, G., Mayo, M., Popple, K. *et al.* (2011) *The Community Development Reader: History, Themes and Issues*, The Policy Press, Bristol, UK.

Department of Communities and Local Government (2006) *The Community Development Challenge*, UK Department of Communities and Local Government, Wetherby, UK.

Department of Health (2005) *Delivering Race Equality in Mental Health Care: An Action Plan for Reform inside and outside Services and the Government's Response to the Independent Inquiry into the Death of David Bennett*, UK Department of Health, London.

Department of Health (2010) *A Vision for Adult Social Care: Capable Communities and Active Citizens*, UK Department of Health, London.

Department of Health (2011) *No Health without Mental Health: A Cross-Government Outcomes Strategy for People of All Ages*, UK Department of Health, London.

European Commission (2010) *European Year for Combating Poverty and Social Exclusion*, European Commission, accessed at: http://www.2010againstpoverty.eu/?langid=en (26 August 2011).

Fernando, S. (2010) *Mental Health, Race and Culture*, 3rd edn, Palgrave Macmillan, Basingstoke, UK.

Fisher, B. (2011) *Community Development in Health - A Literature Review*, accessed at: http://www.healthempowermentgroup.org uk/files/project_papers/Literature_review_Nov_11.pdf (13 August 2012).

Foresight Mental Capital and Wellbeing Project (2008) Final Project Report, The Government Office for Science, London.

Fountain, J. and Hicks, J. (2010) *Delivering Race Equality in Mental Health Care: Report on the Findings and Outcomes of the Community Engagement Programme, 2005–2008*, International School for Communities, Rights and Inclusion, University of Central Lancashire, Preston, UK.

Freire, P. (1972) *Pedagogy of the Oppressed*, Penguin, London.

Friedli, L. (2009) *Mental Health, Resilience and Inequalities*, World Health Organization, Copenhagen, Denmark.

Gerrard, N. (2000) An application of a community psychology approach to dealing with farm stress, *Canadian Journal of Community Mental Health*, **19**, 89–100.

Gilbert, T. and Russell, G. (2006) Primary care graduate mental health workers: an evaluation of the contribution of a cohort of graduate workers in their first year, *Primary Health Care Research and Development*, **7**, 230–240.

Gilchrist, A. (2009) *The Well-Connected Community*, 2nd edn, The Policy Press, Bristol, UK.

Gilchrist, A., Wetherell, M. and Bowles, M. (2010) *Social Action and Identities: Connecting Communities for a Change*, Open University Press, Basingstoke, UK.

Henderson, P. (2001) Doing with, not doing for, *Mental Health Today*, November 2001, 22–24.

Henderson, P. and Vercseg, I. (2010) *Community Development and Civil Society: Making Connections in the European Context*, The Policy Press, Bristol, UK.

Horton, M. (2007) Health and home place: close contact participatory research with Gypsies and Travellers, in A. Williamson and R. DeSouza, eds, *Researching with Communities: Grounded Perspectives on Engaging Communities in Research*, MuddyCreekPress, Auckland and London.

Keating, F. (2002) Black-led initiatives in mental health: an overview, *Research Policy and Planning*, **20** (2), 9–19.

Ledwith, M. (2011) *Community Development: A Critical Approach*, The Policy Press, Bristol, UK.

McCabe, R. and Priebe, S. (2004) Explanatory models of illness in schizophrenia: comparison of four ethnic groups, *British Journal of Psychiatry*, **185**, 25–30.

McKenzie, K., Whitley, R. and Weich, S. (2002) Social capital and mental illness, *British Journal of Psychiatry*, **181**, 280–283.

Mental Health Commission (2009) *Toward Recovery and Well-being: A Framework for a Mental Health Strategy for Canada*, Mental Health Commission for Canada, accessed at: http://www.mentalhealthcommission.ca/SiteCollectionDocuments/boarddocs/15507_MHCC_EN_final.pdf (26 August 2011).

Miller, C. (2010) *The Impact of Health Related Community Development and Engagement Projects*, Health Empowerment Leverage Project, accessed at: http://www.healthempowermentgroup.org.uk/files/project_papers/impact_of_health_related_comm_dev&engagement_project.pdf (26 August 2011)

Morris, D. and Gilchrist, A. (2011) *Communities Connected. Inclusion, Participation and Common Purpose*, Royal Society of Arts, London.

Munn-Giddings, C. and Borkman, T. (2005) Self-help/mutual aid as a psychosocial phenomenon, in S. Ramon and J. E. Williams, eds, *Mental Health at the Crossroads*, Ashgate Publishing Ltd, Aldershot, Hants, UK, pp. 137–154.

Munn-Giddings, C. and McVicar, A. (2006) Self-help groups as mutual support: what do carers value? *Health and Social Care in the Community*, **15** (1), 26–34

Munn-Giddings, C. and Stokken, R. (2012) Self-help/mutual aid in nordic countries: introduction to the special nordic issue. *International Journal of Self Help and Self Care*, **6** (1), 3–9.

Needham, C. (2009) Co-Production: An Emerging Evidence Base for Adult Social Care in Transformation, SCIE Briefing 31, Social Care Institute for Excellence, London.

Sainsbury Centre for Mental Health (2002) *Breaking the Circles of Fear*, Sainsbury Centre for Mental Health, London.

Seebohm, P. and Gilchrist, A. (2008) *Connect and Include: An Exploratory Study of Community Development and Mental Health*, Community Development Foundation and National Social Inclusion Programme, London.

Seebohm, P., Henderson, P., Munn-Giddings, C. *et al.* (2005) *Together We Will Change: Community Development, Mental Health and Diversity*, Sainsbury Centre for Mental Health, London.

Shaw, S. (1997) Sources of Stress in Upper Teesdale, Unpublished Report for County Durham and Darlington Health Authority, Darlington.

Siisiainen, M. (2000) 'Two concepts of social capital: Bourdieu vs. Putnam', paper presented at the International Society for Third Sector Research Fourth International Conference, 5–8 July, Dublin, Ireland.

South Australian Social Inclusion Board (2007) Stepping Up: A Social Inclusion Action Plan for Mental Health Reform 2007-2012, South Australian Social Inclusion Board, accessed at: http://www.socialinclusion.sa.gov.au/files/Stepping_Up-_mental_health_action_plan.pdf (26 August 2011).

Taylor, M., Wilson, M., Purdue, D. *et al.* (2007) *Changing Neighbourhoods: Lessons from the JRF Neighbourhood Programme*, The Policy Press, Bristol, UK.

Walker, R. and Craig, G. (2009) Community Development Workers for BME Mental Health: Embedding Sustainable Change, Report to the National Institute for Mental Health in England, National Workforce Programme and the UK Department of Health Programme for Delivering Race Equality in Mental Healthcare, NIMHE, London.

Wallcraft, J. (2005) The place of recovery, in S. Ramon and J. E. Williams, eds, *Mental Health at the Crossroads*, Ashgate Publishing Ltd, Aldershot, Hants, UK, pp. 127–136.

Wilkinson, R. and Pickett, K. (2009) *The Spirit Level: Why More Equal Societies Almost Always Do Better*, Allen Lane, London.

Journal of Progressive Human Services, 23:1–17, 2012

ISSN: 1042-8232 print/1540-7616 online
DOI: 10.1080/10428232.2011.606736

ARTICLES

Deconstructing Neoliberal Community Development Approaches and a Case for the Solidarity Economy

CARISSA VAN DEN BERK-CLARK
Department of Social Welfare, University of California–Los Angeles, Los Angeles, California, USA

LORETTA PYLES
School of Social Welfare, University at Albany, State University of New York, Albany, New York, USA

The solidarity economy movement is a burgeoning global justice movement that focuses on economic justice, sustainability, and democratic processes. Social workers care about alleviating poverty, but they generally adhere to neoliberal strategies and ignore transformative approaches to economic justice such as solidarity economics. Recent neoliberal community-development efforts center on approaches such as asset development, human capital building, and social capital enhancement. Solidarity economy seeks to boost economic and social development that promotes shared ownership, sustainable production/consumption, and fair distribution. In this article, we launch a critique of current approaches to community development and argue for a solidarity economy approach.

KEYWORDS economic justice, solidarity economy, community development, social capital, poverty

Address correspondence to Carissa van den Berk-Clark, Department of Social Welfare, Luskin School of Public Affairs, University of California–Los Angeles, 3250 School of Public Affairs Building, Box 951656, Los Angeles, CA 90095-1656, USA. E-mail: cvandenberk@ucla.edu

Community development and poverty reduction have been at the heart of many social work interventions. Recent approaches have centered on the roles that social capital enhancement (Brisson & Usher, 2007; Saegert, 2006); human capital building (Zhan, 2007); and asset development (Johnson & Sherraden, 1992; Zhan, 2007) can play in decreasing poverty. The emphasis on such approaches on the part of social workers is arguably a natural result of neoliberal attempts to destroy the social safety net infrastructure in the United States and other countries. Socially stratified neighborhoods and marginalized communities are experiencing a host of deleterious outcomes, whether it is unemployment, high incarceration rates, violence, poor health, or low educational achievement (Sastry, Pebley, & Zonta, 2002). As a solution, social capital approaches affirm the role that networking and trust building can play in alleviating such poverty and concomitant social problems (Saegert, 2006). Similarly, theories of human capital posit that educational advancement and job-related training will result in greater levels of economic well-being, and asset building such as home ownership will yield analogous results (Zhan, 2007). However, without access to financial capital and legitimate democratic engagement in economic processes, economic stratification persists (DeFilippis, 2001).

The social work profession acknowledges that poverty results not only from economic dynamics but also from social and political dynamics (National Association of Social Workers, 2009). Social work has held a critical interest in the economic well-being of individuals, families, and communities in their environments. Historically, Jane Addams favored widespread progress over individual progress. This was reflected not only through her settlement-house work but also in her work with children, public parks, adult education, and labor organizing (Lasch, 1965). Yet today the actual number of social workers engaged in economic justice work appears to be extremely small when compared to the number of social workers engaged in clinical and administrative work (Specht & Courtney, 1994). The quality and quantity of social work engagement in development, organizing, and advocacy efforts related to economic justice, particularly in the context of the recent economic crisis, leaves much to be desired.

Given a declining interest in economic justice in the profession, coupled with a growing interest in the ideas of social capital, asset building, and human capital development, we wonder just what role new ideas about solidarity economics can play in the field of social work, especially when it comes to program development, community organizing, and policy practice. In this article, we analyze some of the current arguments that favor approaches focused on social capital, assets, and human capital development. Drawing from a social constructionist tradition of analysis and aligned with the critical tradition, we deconstruct the rhetoric and discourses of contemporary approaches to community development (Pyles, 2009). We present the philosophical underpinnings and provide examples of solidarity economy organizing. We then consider social work in relation to some important dimensions of solidarity economy (SE) and seek to offer some provisional answers to the question How can the social-work field make use of the ideas being developed through the solidarity economy movement?

NEOLIBERALISM AND THE PROBLEMS WITH CURRENT COMMUNITY DEVELOPMENT APPROACHES

Neoliberalism is a term that has been used globally since the 1980s to describe the economic philosophy and practices associated with the contemporary globalized economy in the form of corporatization (Chomsky, 1999). The neoliberal philosophy adheres to a belief in unfettered market growth and deregulation, with social welfare retrenchment as its hallmark. There is mounting evidence that the practices of neoliberalism are having detrimental consequences across the globe, with its victims being workers, women, the environment, food systems, and indigenous peoples (National Labor Committee, 2004). High prices for food and oil, continuing war, threats presented by climate change, lack of access to health care and education, rising debt, and unemployment have led to vast resentment of the neoliberal model (Chatterton, 2005). Neoliberalism appears to have little genuine concern with universal poverty alleviation or ecological sustainability. Instead, neoliberalism seeks to undermine economic equality in order to increase the growth of a small minority (Chomsky, 1999).

Recent social work interventions in the area of economic and community development are often focused on the neoliberal term *social capital*. Social capital, as defined by political scientist Robert Putnam (2000), is a prerequisite for group membership and action; this membership, in turn, produces wealth. Social capital arises out of networks of trust, the meeting of obligations, and reciprocity. This trust arises as a consequence of informal values and norms within a community (Fukuyama, 1999). There are three types of social capital that are constructed on the basis of connections among differing races, classes, ethnic groups, and so forth, all of which are assumed to be positive. They include bonding (connections among people of the same race, class, etc.); bridging (connections among people of different races, classes, etc.); and linking (connections between poor people and institutions; (Lang & Hornburg, 1998; Putnam, 2000). There are also concepts that are used as measurements of social capital, which include cohesion, trust, social networks, and the tendency to exchange goods and services. Studies have shown that such concepts actually do exist, but whether or not they serve to eliminate poverty is debatable.

Scholars have criticized the wisdom of the social capital theory that affirms the belief that increasing social capital results in better individual and community outcomes, noting instead that the theory ignores global economic trends, scientific measurement, moral miniaturization, and histories of oppression (Defillipis, 2001; Fukuyama, 1999; Grootaert, 1998). Social capital, after all, exists in many groups, such as the Ku Klux Klan, gangs or mafias, and many corporate lobbying groups. This social capital serves to increase poverty and inequality by disregarding democracy and increasing division and fear among Americans. In the end, it can be argued that social capital generally can make for a much more unhealthy American civil society. However, we believe that this is not the case. The reason for the current confusion and arguments about social capital is that no distinction between negative and positive social capital has been established in the literature. Instead, studies tend to determine the positivity or negativity of bonding, bridging, or linking social capital. For example, studies have shown that the existence of bonding social capital among poor people does not necessarily decrease poverty and lead to social or neighborhood advantage; indeed, it can actually make things worse (Cairns, Cairns, Neckerman, Gest, & Gariepy, 1988; Dawkins, 2006; Friedman et al., 2007; Hays & Kogl, 2007). Studies concerned with bridging and linking social capital have generally concluded that bridging and linking, although potentially leading to decreased poverty, rarely happen because of vast societal stratification by race, class, or ethnicity (Butler & Robson, 2001; Hays & Kogl, 2007; Musso, Weave, Oztas, & Logas, 2006). Such findings signal a fundamental problem with the assumptions that positive or negative social capital can be determined by group membership. This assumption, unfortunately, disregards the fact that all forms of social capital are subject to power differentials, whether they are gender, time in the neighborhood, or ability to use force. Thus, we conclude that social capital that is negative is inherently undemocratic. Positive social capital, on the other hand, takes place through groups that are democratically self-governed and that have social values that extend beyond the accumulation of wealth.

Human capital approaches to poverty alleviation are premised on the idea that the lack of access to educational opportunity is largely responsible for poverty, so remedying this problem is best achieved by creating opportunities for individuals to develop their knowledge and skills, thereby leading to higher wages. This idea has been prevalent in the welfare reform literature as a response to the public policy emphasis on work-first approaches to welfare that began in the 1970s and culminated with the implementation of the Temporary Assistance to Needy Families (TANF) program in 1996 (Zhan & Pandey, 2004). One study by Zhan and Pandey (2004) exemplifies some of the findings in this area, namely that having education, especially post-secondary education, significantly improves the economic well-being of single mothers, much more than does past work experience. Unfortunately, such findings tend to reify the false belief that lack of human capital alone causes poverty.

The asset development approach is grounded in a reasonable critique of welfare policy approaches that overemphasize the role of income and underemphasize the impact that capital accumulation plays on people's overall economic well-being. With this approach, however, we see very little analysis of neoliberal attempts at free market deregulation and elimination of social safety nets as some kind of warped opportunity for poor people. Advocating these individualist, market-driven approaches contradicts the concern for community that has been characteristic of social work. Social workers partnered instead of critiqued homebuilders, realtors, and banks during President George W. Bush's ownership society. When housing markets surged, social work researchers were so enthusiastic about the "relationship" between poverty and homeownership or saving that they rarely considered or even attempted to understand the riskiness of subprime mortgages, the costliness of home ownership, the hardships of saving on substandard wages, or the instability of low-income jobs (Johnson & Sherraden, 1992; Scanlon, 1998).

The use of neoliberal approaches to help poor people puts poor people and even middle-income workers at a substantial disadvantage, either by expecting them to rely only on themselves (individualism) or to rely on the "generosity" of wealthier interests. Social movement studies and community organizing scholarship have shown that redistribution of wealth, power, and resources is more likely to occur when poor and middle-income people have collectively resisted the interests of the wealthy, instead of creating partnerships with them (Scott & Fruchter, 2009). Social workers have gotten caught up in this neoliberal logic, when really, we argue, they should be trying to change it. In the end it would seem that the values and discourses that justify the various neoliberal theories of poverty alleviation (e.g., home ownership, partnerships, etc.) run counter to the interests of those in poverty. Interventions grounded in social capital theory, asset building, and human capital development basically preserve the status quo.

Solidarity Economy

Environmental activists and economic justice philosophers are noting a global Great Turning, that is, a movement from an industrial-growth society to a life-sustaining society that values the sharing of and preservation of resources for future generations (Korten, 2006; Macy & Brown, 1998). One of the manifestations of this Great Turning is the SE movement, which upholds the belief in a more just, sustainable, and democratically operated economy. With origins in Latin America and Europe, SE organizing is taking root in the United States and offers some potentially important implications for social work.

SE organizing focuses on all aspects of economic life, including production, distribution, and consumption. The SE may best be understood as an organizing strategy that democratizes economic relations so that participants are connected by the values that imbue their activities (Lewis & Swinney, 2008). It is a set of practices that emphasizes environmental sustainability, cooperation, equity, and community well-being over profit. The SE is concerned with the means by which communities stand in solidarity in order to live sustainably and to attain full human functioning. These communities are creating institutions that are self-governing and proactively anti-oppressive, that is, non-hierarchal, environmentally sustainable, and so forth. Current examples of these types of institutions are numerous, from the factories that have been collectivized in Argentina, Uruguay, Bolivia, and Venezuela to cooperative businesses, such as the Evergreen Cooperative Laundry (ECL) in Cleveland, Ohio, the Black Bear Bakery in St. Louis, Missouri, and Algoma Steel in Sault Ste. Marie, Ontario, Canada (Bertucci, da Silva, & Schiochet, 2009; MacLoad, 1997). Such businesses may, on the surface, appear to the wholesale or retail consumer to be like any other company. ECL, for example, provides laundry services to the health care industry in Cleveland, Ohio. What is different, though, is its commitment to environmental sustainability and to investing in local community development. It is entirely worker-owned, and employees receive training in operations, sustainability, and ownership principles.

The term *solidarity economy* has been relatively unknown in the United States until recently. It is closely allied with global justice movements, including the Social Forum movement. The U.S. Solidarity Economy Network (SEN) was strengthened by its organizing work at the U.S. Social Forum, which was held in Atlanta in 2007. At the forum, the solidarity economy was described as "an alternative development framework . . . grounded in practice" (www.populareconomics.org). The SE generally rests on the following principles: solidarity and cooperation; equity in all dimensions (race, ethnicity, gender, class, etc.); social and economic democracy; and sustainability, pluralism, grassroots-level organizing, diversity, and putting people and the planet first (Allard, Davidson, & Matthaei, 2008; Moulaert & Nussbaumer, 2005). One of the key points of SE is to affirm the many types of economies already in existence (such as subsistence farming, informal economies, fair trade, etc.). These economies go beyond the limited and false dichotomy of a capitalistic economy (unplanned) versus a socialist economy (planned); the point is to continue to grow and advance these alternative economies as a strategy for development and social change.

Overall, the SE is a new way of conceptualizing a variety of transformative economic values, practices, and organizations with the goal of enhancing democracy and distributing resources more equitably. The idea of SE is rooted in a broader Marxian critique of corporate power and, more recently, it has emerged through an analysis of globalization and neoliberalism. For example, SE advocates contest the existence of corporate personhood, the benefits accrued to absentee owners, the marginalization of workers, the fetishism of commodities, and the negative impact of expanding markets to the environment and indigenous peoples. SE advocates argue for and engage in practices that favor worker ownership and empowerment, sustainable consumption, and fair distribution.

Although SE has its roots in indigenous communities and is arguably thousands of years old, some of the earliest efforts at SE organizing as an intervention strategy occurred in the United States in the late 1800s. The Farmers' Alliance formed as an amalgamation of various farmers' unions and alliances between the 1860s and the 1890s (Hicks, 1931). These alliances, which formed as a direct result of corporate monopolies and inequitable banking conduct in the crop-lien system, were established to create unity among farmers. This unity was used to form cooperatives that could take back the farming economy by controlling grain storage, milling, warehousing, meat and fruit curing, leatherwork, brick making, and the creation of general stores. The unity ensured higher commodity prices for the farmers and helped to protect them from powerful groups that were unsympathetic to farmers, such as monopolies and certain government officials (Hicks, 1931). In San Luis Obispo, California, a very active chapter of the Farmers' Alliance was able to force the Southern Pacific Railroad to lower its shipping rates because the cooperatives created increased competition in the marketplace (Magliari, 1995). The Farmers' Alliance also strengthened the social and economic conditions of rural Americans (Hicks, 1931). The alliances advocated for a more equitable tax structure, regulation of commerce by Congress, progressive income taxes, and the abolition of national banks and monopolies (Hicks, 1931). By the 1890s, the People's Party had created a populist foundation that further decreased poverty by representing farmers and influencing state and national policy throughout the 1900s (Hicks, 1931).

Fifty years later in Spain, a Basque Catholic priest, Father Don Jose Arize, sought to decrease unemployment through a series of study circles and workshops (Morrison, 1990). These circles concluded that building institutions that put workers first would reduce poverty. Today, those circles have evolved into Mondragon, which is made up of more than 100 cooperatives and 100 subsidiaries, amounting to revenues of $24 billion as of 2007 (Mondragon, 2008). Mondragon cooperatives manufacture a wide range of products and services, including computer chips, alternative energy, food, health care, housing, communications, and financial services (Mondragon, 2008). Mondragon ensures democratic representation through a one-member, one-vote policy for members of the cooperative. The town, as a result, also experiences an equal distribution of revenues, resulting in a solidly middle-class citizenry (Mondragon, 2008; Morrison, 1990).

Recently, researchers and activists have begun the task of mapping the SE as a way to affirm existing SE practices. The preliminary findings of a study in Boston revealed SE activities in the areas of food (e.g., community-supported agriculture, caterers); banking/investment (e.g., credit unions, community currencies); housing (community land trusts, housing co-ops); clothing (clothing swaps, fair-trade clothing); transportation (Zip Car, bike co-ops); bookstores/presses (used bookstores, South End Press); media/information (Dollars and Sense, Weekly Dig); education/training (Haley House, South End Technology Center at Tent City); retail (Ten Thousand Villages, freecycling); childcare/eldercare (parent-childcare co-ops, cooperative home care); energy/environmental health (Coop Power, Mass Green Jobs Coalition); health care (free energy work); and social movement/solidarity organizing (Boston Workers' Alliance, Jobs with Justice) (Matthaei & Nagin, 2009).

Social Work and the Solidarity Economy

U.S. civil society has a rich history of associationalism (Anheier, 2005) that has promoted community responsibility for educational, cultural, social, and welfare responsibilities. Philanthropy in the United States was deeply intertwined with associations, which led to social movements like the abolitionist movement and the women's movement. This has resulted in a liberal model of civil society, a model in which there is low government spending for social welfare and a large non-profit sector, which engages in service delivery and advocacy. Within this model is a high respect for the de Tocqueville view of the capacity of voluntary associations to promote egalitarianism and social development and to constrain tyrannical rule. By the mid-1950s, according to Anheier (2005), the culmination of these associations and their institutional innovations (which included philanthropic foundations, privately endowed universities, charities, voluntary associations, etc.) came to be known as the third sector. This third sector was independent of the first sector (business) and the second sector (government) of the economy and had the ability to create an organizational infrastructure for social movements that crossed class and race lines (Anheier, 2005).

Increased federal government programming did not adulterate the independence of the third sector until it was devolved and privatized in the 1980s. This led to a number of third-sector organizations like non-profits running first- and second-sector institutions. The remaining third sector, which will be referred to later, does not seek to follow the rules of either of the other two sectors. Rather, there is a definite focus on social values, which also increases economic development. Organizations that fit into this third sector are SE organizations. These SE organizations have the mission to serve their members or community, not shareholders (Lewis & Swinney, 2008). They are self-governed, which means they are independently managed and democratic; decisions represent all members, community residents, or stockholders (Anheier, 2005). These organizations are value imbued, meaning that their purpose is to promote social objectives.

TABLE 1 Social Work in the Three Sectors of Solidarity Economy.

Sector	Program
First Private and profit-oriented	IDA, microenterprise/microfinance, financial education, home ownership, education/promotion, job training (human capital), small-business education/assistance, affordable housing using TIF/ mixed-income affordable housing, Section 8, marriage initiatives, father involvement
Second Public service/ planned provision	Medicare/Medicaid, Social Security, unemployment insurance, prisons, substance abuse, mental illness, education, crisis intervention, international relations, including foreign aid, immigrant/refugee assistance, youth programming, child welfare environmental and worker protection
Third Self-help, reciprocity, and social enterprises	Time-dollar programs, community development, community self-help, community/neighborhood college programs, settlement houses, youth programs in the context of community development programs, CDCs, neighborhood associations/community action programs, Head Start programs, community gardens, Habitat for Humanity (sweat equity programs), individual self-help groups (AA/NA, etc.), political/social/economic advocacy (unions can be included here), coalition building

AA = Alcoholics Anonymous; CDC = community development corporation; IDA = individual development accounts; NA = Narcotics Anonymous; TIF = tax increment financing.

Table 1 shows the social work organizations that fit this third-sector category. It also distinguishes them from adulterated social work organizations that fit first- and second-sector categories. In many ways, these social work organizations correspond to de Tocqueville traditions in promoting egalitarianism while still promoting economic development and increasing poverty. Characteristics of SE thus represent a positive form of social capital in which groups form around democratic and social principles in an attempt to increase the economic prospects of their members.

On the other hand, adulterated organizations must adapt to value-based ideologies, namely, the "deserving" versus the "undeserving" poor as well as cost-benefit analyses, which favor the first sector of the economy in order to survive (Anheier, 2005; Dinitto, 2007). Policies that favor these programs usually focus on preserving economic stability by promoting self-sufficiency whenever possible, even though there is much evidence from social workers and other social scientists that this is ineffective (Dinitto, 2007). Thus, much of the policy provisions are focused on who is able to work and who is not. This is especially obvious in TANF program as well as in more recent policies concerning immigrant assistance. For individuals who have disabilities and children, there is an attempt to create stabilization for the cheapest price possible through the child welfare system, the mental health system, and more recently through the prison system (Rice, Kelman, & Miller, 1992; Steurle, Reynolds, & Carasso, 2007). Other programs could not exist without their simultaneous ability to bring revenue to the first sector of the economy, like food stamps or Section 8 housing (Dwyer & Mayer, 1975), or increase involvement with it, like microenterprise, homeownership, and job training (Johnson & Sherraden, 1992).

In the current political climate of social welfare retrenchment, effecting change in the arena of governmental policy can be challenging for social workers. Social workers' access to political power at this point in history is limited. Currently, only 10 federal legislators are or have been social workers (National Association of Social Workers, 2007), and politicians rarely rely on information from NASW to make decisions; instead, they rely on information from economists, business interests, journalists, medical doctors, lawyers, and others from more "respected" fields (Golden, 1998). Because of our obvious point of view and our declining interest in grassroots community organizing and connection to people in poverty as well as social work's attempt to retain alliances with the first and second sectors, we have lost the leverage to push through the goals not only of a viable social safety net but also of innovative solutions that could transform economic and social relations. The research on social programming has shown overwhelmingly that decreased funding has increased poverty along with concomitant social ills (Rank, 2006). Shifts from an industrial economy to a service economy; global outsourcing, which has lowered wages, along with increasing deregulation; and the destruction of the social safety net are also responsible for increasing poverty in the United States (Chomsky, 1999; Sweet & Meiksins, 2007).

Social workers, at least in the rhetoric, have resisted efforts on the part of government to devolve and fragment social safety nets to promote work-first policies, knowing full well that these policies require vulnerable people to take substandard wages and put their loved ones at risk for further marginalization. Social workers, however, remain pragmatic and have attempted to make the best of the narrow funding streams that provide resources to those considered particularly vulnerable and deserving (second sector) or that create programs for the able-bodied that promote individual self-sufficiency or increase the wealth of the first sector. These interventions essentially break people into two groups: people who can work and people who cannot work. Those who cannot work are subject to second-sector policy, which distinguishes between the deserving and the undeserving. Those who can work are subject to either first-sector or third-sector programming. The first sector, stimulated by government revenue, may have shown mild success but could help only a few people because of high costs, in the case of individual development accounts (Flacke, Grossman, & Dailey, 2000; Rohe, Gorham, & Quercia, 2005), which showed the costs of creating individual development account programs; or did not equip people adequately to compete in an increasingly competitive job market, in the case of human capital job training programs (Banerjee, 2002) or in the market itself, in the case of microenterprise (Sanders, 2002). These interventions stem from the assumption that people can pull themselves up by their bootstraps, and by the power of their own individualism can compete against large corporate conglomerations that control wages and prices.

There is also the traditional third-sector notion of communities' pulling themselves up by their bootstraps, as is evident in Habitat for Humanity programs, local 12-step groups, community-development non-profits, community development corporations, neighborhood college programs, time-dollar programs, and Head Start. In many ways these programs also correspond to the third sector of the economy and can be considered part of the SE. These programs are steeped in social work traditions and have been highly successful when funded properly (McKey, 1985; Richey, 2007). There has been some coalition building among these groups, but committed political advocacy simply cannot take place because of lobbying restrictions on 501(c)(3)s and the stronger emphasis on service delivery. Thus coalition building must involve 501(c)(4) tax status, which simultaneously lacks access to certain grants for service delivery and economic development.

Increased conservatism among social workers is a likely explanation for social workers' having avoided SE interventions, according to Reisch and Andrews (2002): "The lack of a strong class consciousness and its organizational manifestations, such as trade unions; the myth of equal opportunity and political pluralism and the individualistic and materialist aspirations they foster" (p. 228). Reisch and Andrews (2002) also think social workers have avoided ideas that could be considered radical because of their focus on specific needs rather than on universal rights as well as their concentration on professionalism. Fukuyama (1999) argues that both the left and the right wing concentrate on excessive individualism at the expense of community (the left emphasize lifestyle, the right, money). This has led to a much smaller, more polarized radius of trust, closed selfishness, and diminished communal responsibility, which result in the moral miniaturization of group participation and brings little positive social capital or, in our belief, the potential for SE.

Social workers' investment in what some have referred to as "the nonprofit industrial complex" (Incite, 2007) may also be responsible for the lack of interest in the SE movement. Instead, social workers focus on programs and services that are fundable in lieu of grassroots endeavors that might contribute to the goals of SE. The pressures of maintaining funding streams and fee-for-services activities and engaging in service provision are key forces that have served to depoliticize social work.

Nueva Esperanza: Solidarity Economics in Action

One can point to Nueva Esperanza in Holyoke, Massachusetts, as a type of intervention in which the social work profession should be front and center when it comes to organizing for affordable housing and poverty reduction. Nueva Esperanza is a community land trust (CLT), a model for affordable housing that seeks to create shared wealth and responsibility for land by separating ownership of land from permanent structures like buildings, co-ops, and apartment buildings. The city of Holyoke, which was suffering significant white flight and disinvestment, planned to phase out residential and commercial facilities in favor of industrial facilities, resulting in increased numbers of absentee landlords (Meehan, 1996, p. 96). In an atmosphere of protest, local citizens formed a community development corporation, Nueva Esperanza, which pushed CLTs into the forefront (Meehan, 1996). The result has been important because the CLT could buy houses more cheaply in a depressed market and sell them at reasonable rates without being concerned with profit making. The homes were kept affordable by CLT lease agreements, which led to a more sustainable form of development.

Through CLTs, a new business model is evident; it is commensurate with the aims of social work but, unfortunately, has not been addressed by the field adequately. Community members were able to find affordable housing and the stability that comes with it as well as have the opportunity to build a meager but altogether more stable form of equity, which is dependent on long-term participation in the community (Foldy & Walters, 2004). The CLT does not require poor people to gamble on the housing market; it expects them to work together to protect the interests of one another by taking away the incentives to flip properties or leave them behind in foreclosure or disinvestment. The CLT does more than try to promote asset development or community cohesion; rather, it aims to redistribute wealth and promote self-governance (Foldy & Walters, 2004).

CONCLUSION

Creating organizations, collaborating with organizations, and creating organizational collaborations are precisely the activities of social workers. So one has to wonder why social workers have not dared to touch on the economic-development potentials of creating more democratic distribution alternatives that workers own and control in order to ensure that their best interests are considered. Creating non-profit, collective, or cooperative infrastructures for the production and distribution of goods would seem to be the first step toward providing increased opportunity to contribute truly and to influence economic structures that are more powerful at this point than programs based on bootstrap capitalism (Stoesz, 2007).

Social workers have historically battled the anti-regulatory tendencies of unfettered capitalism, which produced vast inequalities, by helping clients, colleagues, and communities become more aware of their resources (Reisch & Andrews, 2002). However, it is unclear whether the last few generations of social workers have been attuned to the effects of global corporatization or, rather, to the effects of too extreme a focus on the first sector of the economy. Walmart, for instance, has been shown to decrease economic prosperity substantially, especially in the geographic areas in which stores are built (Basker, 2007; World Bank, 2005). On the other hand, business models like those in Mondragon lead to much more sustainable economic growth, which substantially decreases poverty. Social work practitioners and researchers pay little attention to Walmart or Mondragon, even though their effects are clear. It is the job of evidence-based practitioners and researchers to point out these phenomena, analyze the ways those economic structures affect communities and individuals, and present alternative policies and programs. Thus, it is necessary that social work practitioners and researchers increase their understanding not just of the economics taking place through social programming but also of the economics that occur through deregulation and alternative models of economic development. Furthermore, social work curricula could focus on topics that would further the development of the SE. Such topics would include the impact of global capitalism on communities and the role that democratic organizational structures can have on outcomes. In addition, it is vital to create environments in which community members, students, practitioners, and scholars can engage in critical analyses of the basic assumptions of current community development approaches and social work organizational structures. Finally, it is necessary that social workers make efforts to improve the lobbying power of their organizations. For-profit organizations can engage in unlimited lobbying and now face no limits when it comes to campaign contributions. This inability to influence government policy should be seriously considered by social work organizations, researchers, and other organizations advocating for the needy.

It is the role of social workers not only to enhance the safety net but also to ensure access to economic structures for the most marginalized in society. When social workers find there is limited access to those structures, those systems must be changed and alternatives must be envisioned. Social workers must realize that we are dealing not only with a dwindling social safety net, which hampers our abilities as social workers, but also with a very empowered corporate elite that aims to decrease economic and social equality and exploit natural resources in order to increase their profit margins and with an unempowered majority that seeks access to economic and social development. In order to fight oppression, we must consider all three. It is not clear to what extent social workers will embrace SE, given a cultural context of individualism and an economic backdrop that focuses on growth and profit. However, in an environment in which localism and green jobs are gaining greater attention, in which dissatisfaction with unregulated capitalism has become more evident, and in which globalization and rising energy costs have made jobs more difficult to get and keep, it is evident that social workers must promote new ways of bringing sustainable economic development programs to the increasing numbers of working and non-working poor (Gaiger, 2004). The window of opportunity is here, and it would seem that social work as a field is in a position to be a critical agent of change.

REFERENCES

Allard, J., Davidson, C., & Matthei, J. (Eds.). (2008). *Solidarity economy: Building alternatives for people and planet*. Chicago, IL: Changemaker Publishing.

Anheier, H. K. (2005). *Nonprofit organizations: Theory, management policy*. New York, NY: Routledge.

Banerjee, M. M. (2002). Voicing realities and recommending reform in PROWA. *Social Work, 47*, 315–328.

Basker, E. (2007). The causes and consequences of Wal-Mart's growth. *Journal of Economic Perspectives, 21*(3), 177–198.

Bertucci, J. D. O., da Silva, R. M. A., & Schiochet, V. (2009, February). Solidarity economy system of information: Visibility and strengthening of solidarity economy in Brazil. Solidarische Oeconomie Kongress: Vienna, Austria.

Brisson, D., & Usher, C. L. (2007). The effects of informal neighborhood bonding social capital and neighborhood context on homeownership for families living in poverty. *Journal of Urban Affairs, 29*(1), 65–75.

Butler, T., & Robson, G. (2001). Social capital, gentrification and neighborhood change in London: A comparison of three South London neighborhoods. *Urban Studies, 38*, 2145–2162.

Cairns, R. B., Cairns, B. D., Neckerman, H. J., Gest, S. D., & Gariepy, J. L. (1988). Social networks and aggressive behavior: Peer support or peer rejection? *Developmental Psychology, 24*, 815–823.

Chatterton, P. (2005). Making autonomous geographies: Argentina's popular uprising and the Movimiento de Trabajadores Desocupados (Unemployed Workers Movement). *Geoforum, 36*, 545–561.

Chomsky, N. (1999). *Profit over people: Neoliberalism and the global order*. Boston, MA: Seven Stories Press.

Dawkins, C. J. (2006). Are social networks the ties that bind families to neighborhoods? *Housing Studies, 21*, 867–881.

DeFilippis, J. (2001). The myth of social capital in community development. *Housing Policy Debate, 12*, 781–806.

Dinitto, D. M. (2007). *Social welfare: Politics and public policy*. Boston, MA: Pearson Education.

Dwyer, D. T., & Mayer, J. (1975). Beyond economics and nutrition: The complex basis of food policy. *Science, 188*(4188), 566–570.

Flacke, T., Grossman, B., & Dailey, C. (with Jennings, S.). (2000). Individual development account program-design handbook: A step-by-step guide to designing an IDA program. Washington, DC: Corporation for Enterprise Development.

Foldy, E., & Walters, J. (2004). The power of balance: Lessons from Burlington Community Land Trust. New York, NY: New York University Research Center for Leadership in Action.

Friedman, S. R., Mateu-Galabert, P., Curtis, R., Mustow, C., Bolyard, M., Sandoval, M., & Flom, P. L. (2007). Social capital or networks, negotiations and norms? A neighborhood case study. *American Journal of Preventative Medicine, 32*(68), S160–S170.

Fukuyama, F. (1999). *The great disruption: Human nature and the reconstitution of social order*. New York, NY: The Free Press.

Gaiger, L. (2004). The solidarity economy and the alternative globalization proposal. *Dados-Revista de Ciencias Sociais, 42*, 799–834.

Golden, M. M. (1998). Interest groups in the rule-making process: Who participates? Whose voices get heard? *Journal of Public Administration Research and Theory, 8*(2), 245–270.

Grootaert, C. (1998). Social capital: The missing link. Washington, DC: World Bank.

Hays, R. A., & Kogl, A. M. (2007). Neighborhood attachment, social capital building and political participation: A case study of low and moderate income residents in Waterloo, Iowa. *Journal of Urban Affairs, 29*(2), 181–205.

Hicks, J.D. (1931). *Populist revolt: A history of the Farmers' Alliance and the People's Party*. Minneapolis: University of Minnesota Press.

Incite! Women of Color Against Violence (Ed.). (2007). *The revolution will not be funded: Beyond the non-profit industrial complex*. Cambridge, MA: South End Press.

Johnson, A., & Sherraden, M. (1992). Asset based social welfare policy: Home ownership for the poor. *Journal of Sociology and Welfare, 19*(3), 65–83.

Khader, N. (2008). Introduction to the economics of liberation: An overview of PROUT. In J. Allard, C. Davidson, & J. Matthaei (Eds.), *Solidarity economy: Building alternatives for people and planet* (pp. 83–90). Chicago, IL: ChangeMaker Publications.

Korten, D. C. (2006). *The great turning: From empire to Earth community*. Bloomfield, CT: Kumarian Press.

Lang, R. E., & Hornburg, S. P. (1998). What is social capital and why is it important to public policy? *Housing Policy Debate, 9*(1), 1–16.

Lasch, C. (Ed.). (1965). *The social thought of Jane Adams*. New York, NY: Bobbs-Merrill.

Lewis, M., & Swinney, D. (2008). Social economy and solidarity economy: Transformative concepts for unprecedented times? In J. Allard, C. Davidson, & J. Matthaei (Eds.), *Solidarity economy: Building alternatives for people and planet* (pp. 9–22). Chicago, IL: ChangeMaker Publications.

MacLoad, G. (1997). *From Mondragon to America: Experiments in community economic development*. Sydney, Canada: University College of Crepe Breton Press.

Macy, J., and Brown, M. Y. (1998). *Coming back to life: Practices to reconnect our lives, our world*. Gabriola Island, Canada: New Society Publishers.

Magliari, M. F. (1995). What happened to the populist vote? A California case study. *Pacific Historic Review, 64*, 389–412.

Matthaei, J., & Nagin, R. (2009). Sectors of the solidarity economy. Unpublished manuscript.

McKey, R. H. (1985). The impact of HeadStart on children, families and communities: Final report of Head Start. Washington, DC: Administration for Children, Youth and Families, Head Start Bureau.

Meehan, J. (1996). *Reinventing real estate: The CLT and the social market in land*. [Dissertation]. Boston, MA: Boston College.

Mondragon. (2008). Annual report. Mondragon, Spain: Mondragon Corporation.

Morrison, R. (1990). *We build the road as we travel*. Philadelphia, PA: Library Company of Philadelphia.

Moulaert, F., & Nussbaumer, J. (2005). Defining the social economy and its governance at the neighborhood level: A methodological reflection. *Urban Studies, 42*, 2071–2088.

Musso, J. A., Weare, C., Oztas, N., & Logas, W. E. (2006). Neighborhood governance reform and networks of community power in LA. *American Review of Public Administration, 36*(1), 79–97.

National Association of Social Workers. (2007). Social workers in Congress. Washington, DC: Author.

National Association of Social Workers. (2009). Issue fact sheet: Poverty. Washington, DC: Author.

National Labor Committee. (2004). Trying to live on 25 cents an hour. Retrieved from http://www.nlcnet.org/campaigns/archive/chinareport/costoflivingdoc.shtml

Putnam, R. (2000). *Bowling alone: The collapse and revival of American community*. New York, NY: Simon & Schuster.

Pyles, L. (2009). *Progressive community organizing: A critical approach for a globalizing world*. New York, NY: Routledge.

Rank, M. (2006). *One national underprivileged: Why American poverty affects us all*. New York, NY: Oxford University Press.

Reisch, M., & Andrews, J. (2002). *The road not taken: A history of radical social work in the United States*. New York, NY: Brunner-Routledge.

Rice, D. P., Kelman, S., & Miller, L. S. (1992). The economic burden of mental illness. *Hospital Community Psychology, 43*, 1227–1232.

Richey, S. (2007). Manufacturing trust: Community currency and the creation of social capital. *Political Behavior, 29*, 69–88.

Rohe, W. M., Gorham, L. S., & Quercia, R. G. (2005). Individual development accounts: Participants' characteristics and success. *Journal of Urban Affairs, 27*, 503–520.

Saegert, S. (2006). Building civic capacity in urban neighborhoods: An empirically grounded anatomy. *Journal of Urban Affairs, 28*(3), 275–294.

Sanders, C. K. (2002). The impact of microenterprise assistance programs: A comparative study of program participants, non-participants, and other low-wage workers. *Social Service Review, 76*, 320–340.

Sastry, N., Pebley, A. R., & Zonta, M. (2002). *Neighborhood definitions and spatial dimensions of daily life in LA*. Los Angeles, CA: Rand.

Scanlon, E. (1998). Low-income homeownership policy as a community development strategy. In M. S. Sherraden & W. A. Ninacs (Eds.), *Community economic development and social work*. Binghamton, NY: Haworth Press.

Scott, J., & Fruchter, N. (2009). Community resistance to school privatization. In R. Fisher (Ed.), *The people shall rule: ACORN, community organizing, and the struggle for economic justice* (pp. 180–205). Nashville, TN: Vanderbilt University Press.

Specht, H., & Courtney, M. (1994). *Unfaithful angels: How social work has abandoned its mission*. New York, NY: Free Press.

Steurle, C. E., Reynolds, G., & Carasso, A. (2007). *Investing in children*. Washington, DC: Urban Institute.

Stoesz, D. (2007). Bootstrap capitalism: Sequel to welfare reform. *Families in Society, 88*, 375–378.

Sweet, S., & Meiksins, P. (2007). *Changing contours of work: Jobs and opportunities in the new economy*. Thousand Oaks, CA: Pine Forge Press.

World Bank. (2005). World development indicators database. Washington, DC: World Bank.

Zhan, M. (2007). Assets, human capital development, and economic mobility of single mothers. *Families in Society, 88*, 605–615.

Zhan, M., & Pandey, S. (2004). Post secondary education and economic well-being of single mothers and single fathers. *Journal of Marriage and Family, 66*, 661–673.

Journal of Progressive Human Services, 23:110–126, 2012

ISSN: 1042-8232 print/1540-7616 online
DOI: 10.1080/10428232.2012.666725

ARTICLES

A Community of Strangers: Supporting Drug Recovery Through Community Development and Freirean Pedagogy

DAVID BECK
School of Education, University of Glasgow, Glasgow, Scotland

This article explores the educational journey of one man from leaving school in the mid-1970s, at the age of 14, through a period of chaotic drug use, and on to developing his career helping other chaotic drug users back into a "normal" life. Although focused on someone with drug dependency as part of his history, the article exposes issues that potentially underlie the experiences of many learners within working-class communities. In particular, it examines the role of formal and informal education, considers education's ability to liberate or domesticate (Freire, 1972), and examines approaches to learning that support recovery and transformation.

KEYWORDS *community development, drug recovery, Freirean approaches, informal education*

This article is the distillation of a series of informal conversations, formal dialogues, and joint studies of emergent issues that occurred between Colin and me over a period of several weeks. We met when he joined a community project which I had set up to train people who had been unemployed for more than a year so they could learn community development skills, with a view to their moving on to paid employment. Through the program and beyond, we developed a friendship and discovered that we had a shared passion for working with people to achieve personal and social change and that

Address correspondence to David Beck, University of Glasgow, School of Education, St. Andrew's Building, 11 Eldon Street, Glasgow G3 6NH, Scotland. E-mail: dave.beck@glasgow.ac.uk we favored approaches that blended critical reflection and action to achieve those ends. We had a lot in common. We were both born in Govan and were roughly the same age and yet we had traveled very different journeys.

Having worked on a number of joint projects, we decided to coauthor a paper for an international conference in London (Beck & Callahan, 2001); at that point I was a lecturer at the University of Glasgow and he was an addiction worker with the local authority, working in Govan. This is a reworking of that paper, which focuses on Colin's educational journey.

In tracing this journey we explore the impact of the school system, the misuse of drugs, the experience of community-based education and development, and how they link with the world of higher education and Freirean pedagogy, which informed both Colin's and my educational philosophy and practice. Its context is Govan, an area of Glasgow that lies on the banks of the Clyde, about 3 miles from the city center. It is an area that was widely renowned for its shipbuilding industry. At its height, at the beginning of the 20th century, it had a population of 95,000, which has declined to approximately 25,500 at present. The effects of the decline in the shipbuilding industry and the depopulation of the area have been factors contributing to the sense of hopelessness and powerlessness within some sections of the community.

Govan has many of the problems associated with inner-city living: high unemployment levels, high crime rates, problems of drug and alcohol abuse, and, of course, poverty, which underpins all of the above. The Local Development Company (Govan Initiative, 2004), highlights Govan's position in Scotland's most deprived areas. It is the 23rd most income-deprived, 8th most work-deprived, 8th most health-deprived, 6th most learning-deprived, and 10th most housing-deprived neighborhood in Scotland. In 2002, only 8% of Greater Govan school-leavers progressed to higher education; this is less than half the proportion of Glasgow school-leavers (20%) and less than a third of the Scottish average (31%). From this it can be seen that the community's learning aspirations are very clearly circumscribed.

METHODOLOGY

This research takes a qualitative approach: qualitative researchers seek to understand how people account for, take action concerning, and otherwise manage their day-to-day situations (Miles & Huberman, 1994). Rhodes (2000) describes qualitative research in the field of addictions as a process that seeks both to describe the social meanings that participants attach to drug use and the social processes by which such meanings are created, reinforced, and reproduced. In this approach to research, findings cannot be generalized or portrayed as representative of drug users in general; rather, it seeks to obtain a deeper and more contextualized understanding of the subject's life and experiences (Neale, Allen, & Coombes, 2005).

In this particular research, the relationship between Colin and me was well established. He joined a community-development training program I was running in 1997. This project was informed by Freirean pedagogy, described below, which has a focus on coinvestigation and the shifting of power balances. This approach led us to undertake joint projects and training in the field of addiction work. Eventually, we both decided to conduct a formal study that focused on his life history as a way of understanding the issues that lead to drug addiction and recovery and how different pedagogies influence this process so we could encourage a conversation between educators and addiction workers that would promote more holistic approaches. There are advantages to carrying out research with a subject who is well known to the researcher. As Neale et al. (2005) discuss, feelings of trust and rapport that arises between the researcher and research participant facilitates discussions about intimate information. Many of the issues explored were both intimate and painful, and not all of them are appropriate to include in this study. Anne Grinyer (2005) highlights the emotional impact of research on both the researcher and the subject. The feelings generated by this work were fully discussed as part of the research process but are not recorded here. As a coproducer of the material explored in this article, Colin wanted his own name to be used rather than a pseudonym.

A possible weakness of qualitative research is the potential for bias and misrepresentation. The integrity and honesty of drug users' responses to interview questions are often doubted, along with their ability to recall events and emotions. For example, a subject may simply report those beliefs and behaviors that he or she feels the researcher wishes to hear. I believe that this danger is lessened by the long-standing nature of our relationship and the levels of trust that have been generated as well as the variety of reflective processes that we went through.

Webb, Campbell, Schwartz, and Sechrest (1966) note that the particular dynamics of any given researcher/subject interaction can create, as well as measure, attitudes. This was an intentional part of this research process and links to Freirean approaches to research, as described by Cornwall and Jewkes (1995).

> Affirming that people's own knowledge is valuable, these approaches regard people as agents rather than objects: capable of analysing their own situations and designing their own solutions. A central thread which runs through these approaches is an emphasis on changing the role of the researcher from director to facilitator and catalyst. Through a process of mutual learning and analysis, which takes place throughout research rather than at distinct stages, people are brought into the research as owners of their own knowledge and empowered to take action. (p. 1670)

This research does not claim to be objective and detached; indeed, it could be considered a process of cogenerative dialogue, an intentional, democratic dialogue that forms a praxis of collective sense-making (Roth, 2006). It is the product of coinvestigation by two people with a deep critical curiosity about how different forms of education impact addictions. Because Freirean education informs much of what follows, I begin by outlining the key features of that approach.

Freirean Education

A Freirean approach to education is underpinned by some basic assumptions, as outlined in the *Pedagogy of the Oppressed* (Freire, 1972). They are the possibility of humanization, the historical reality of dehumanization, and the belief that dehumanization occurs as a result of an unjust social order. This belief in humanity's potential to become more fully human gives rise to Freire's philosophy of hope and the pedagogy of liberation (Ledwith, 2005).

In its understanding of the world, the Freirean approach takes a structural analysis, recognizing that all social phenomena are produced by the complex interplay of opposing structural forces: labor/capital, rich/poor, and oppressor/oppressed. In its understanding of people it takes a materialist analysis, theorizing that people's subjectivities are constructed by the complex interrelationship between themselves and their material conditions—their environments, social conditions, and social relations. Finally, in its examination of education, it takes a political analysis; no education is neutral. Education either domesticates and shapes people to function within the given social order, leading to "banking education," described by Margaret Ledwith (2005) as an act of cultural invasion; or it liberates, causing people to act for change through critical analysis, which leads to Freirean or "problem-posing" education within which, "Knowledge emerges only through the restless, impatience, continuing, artful inquiry men pursue in the world" (Freire, 1972, p. 45). The problem-posing approach of Freirean education seeks to develop critical consciousness, a state in which people see themselves and their lives in the context of their social realities and become capable of acting for change. They cease to be objects and become writers of their own stories (Jesson & Newman, 2004).

Dialogue lies at the heart of this process of humanization. This involves horizontal communication among equals involved in critical inquiry (Ledwith, 2005) through which knowledge becomes so well integrated and assimilated that it becomes located within our subjectivities and, thus, in addition to being known, it is felt, or subjectively experienced, as a type of lived compassion and commitment (Allman, 2001). This democratic, personal, and emotional process of knowledge building (Beck & Purcell, 2010) was at the heart of the approach taken both in the research and in the community development project that Colin and I were involved with. His experience of mainstream education was very different from that.

SCHOOL

The promise of the education system is described by Richard Waller (2004) as offering individuals the chance to develop intellectually, equip themselves for work, and add to their sense of personal fulfilment while increasing their knowledge and understanding. He goes on to say, however, that the reality for many is that schools are a time of personal trauma when people feel devalued or excluded. This is indeed the experience Colin had in many of his encounters with formal education.

Three main elements contributed to his not thriving in school: the culture of the community; peer and family influences; and the beliefs and practices of the school.

The culture of the community was such that the connection between working hard at school and going on to a good job was never made, either by parents or teachers (Kinder, Kendall, Halsey, & Atkinson, 1999). This was partly because in Govan in the mid 1970s, although the unemployment rate was 16% (University of Manchester, 1971), low-skilled jobs were perceived to be relatively abundant at that time, and the expectation was that a job would be secured and that educational qualifications would have no bearing on that. In fact, this proved to be the case because Colin was able to secure employment immediately after leaving school, even though he had no qualifications. However, the employment was short-lived, which is in accord with the pattern seen in 1970s Britain (Organisation for Economic Co-Operation and Development [OECD], 1998). Paradoxically, the existence of many unemployed people in the community also undermined the motivation to work at school. Colin knew many people who were living reasonably happy and comfortable lives on the dole, and this represented yet another career path that required no academic qualifications.

By the time of this research, Colin had reflected on his childhood and had become clear that his community affected his attitudes toward school. His conclusion is reflected in the literature, which suggests that there is a clear link between poor communities and low levels of pupil attainment (Bickle, Smith, & Eagle, 2002; Brody et al., 2001). Despite that empirical evidence, it is not always the lived experience of people. For example, in another study of pupil attitudes carried out in Merseyside, a working-class area in England, pupils stated that the neighborhood had no effect at all on their attitude toward school (Kinder et al., 1999). This may reflect the dominant discourse that states that individual pathology is the main determinant of lack of educational attainment (Sparkes, 1999). Freire would say that they had internalized their failure because of the lack of the opportunity to reflect critically on the social conditions that contributed to it (Freire,

1972). Colin's critical reflection on his life as a result of Freirean education perhaps gave him a more ecological viewpoint, which recognizes the discordant fit between people and their social and physical environments (Bostock & Beck, 1993).

In school, he was unable to express interest in any subjects for fear of being bullied and ostracized by his peers. One incident in particular typifies this dilemma. After staying off school for several months he was forced to return to class on the day an English exam was being held. When the results were given the following week, the teacher made a great show of the fact that Colin had produced an excellent piece of work for which he was given a mark of 94%. He had been "made to look clever in front of the Neds."[1]

Although he did not want to be part of the Ned world—his tactic for survival had been to keep a low profile—this incident made him look as if he were better than they. As a result, it was safer to stay away from school. This experience is echoed by Charlesworth (2000), in whose work subjects discuss their inability to show anything that could be considered to be weakness. The Neds' response echoes Freire's (1972) "fear of freedom," a state in which prescribed roles have been internalized, rendering people afraid of the autonomy and responsibility that must be taken on if that role were to be rejected. Someone else's success might suggest that the oppressor's reality of living is not the only one that exists. This challenge to a perceived, static reality could be very threatening and uncomfortable.

Finally, there was the impact of teachers and the school regime itself. In primary school Colin had a teacher whom he felt he could trust; she saw through his boisterous behavior and saw the real Colin. It felt as if there were a human bond and not just a functional teacher-pupil relationship. The secondary school experience was very different. His recollections of teachers were that they kept attention by using the belt rather than making the subject matter of interest to the pupils. He remembered some teachers' being drunk. However, the most basic discord stemmed from a clash of cultures. The school was middle-class in approach, language, and ethos and was not seen as being relevant to the lives of people from the community (Bernstein, 2003; Elliot, 1996). The upshot of all of this was that Colin settled into a pattern of nonattendance at school.

His family life acted as no challenge to that ongoing situation. His mother had died when he was very young, so he was raised by his father who was himself an alcoholic and ill equipped to bring up a child. Colin's older sister tried to fill the maternal role. He went through the pretence of getting up in the morning and going out to school, but when his father left for work, he would return and spend the day at home. This was a

[1] "Ned is a derogatory term applied in Scotland to hooligans, louts or petty criminals" [http://en.wikipedia.org/wiki/Ned_(Scottish)]

very comfortable existence. He knew he was not thick, he could read and write, and there were no challenges. Parental collusion is also a factor here. Despite being aware of Colin's nonattendance at school, it was only when a truancy officer got involved that his father insisted on his going to school. This experience is supported by the literature, which suggests that parental attitudes are contributing factors to how pupils understand school and the value they attach to it (Payne, 2002).

This lack of engagement in school, coupled with low expectations about employment prospects, laid the foundation for his life as a "career drug user," as described below.

Drugs

The journey into drug addiction is a long and complex one: "You don't just wake up one morning and decide to be a drug addict" (Burroughs, 1969, p. xxxviii).

Colin's experience of the journey toward heroin addiction began with the use of glue, pills, and alcohol in his early teens, and the practice was widespread within his peer group. It developed into the use of cannabis, the sniffing of heroin and, eventually, the regular injecting of heroin. He felt at every stage that he could stop if he wanted to. He just did not want to. In fact, heroin addiction became problematic only after he lost his job some 2 years after he had become addicted. Up until that point he had been able to support his habit through his wages and some black market activities. Losing his job meant no money; he therefore had to resort to petty crime in order to get drugs. The lack of work also caused a lack of structure and direction in his life; in this vacuum, drugs became the dominant force in his life.

The experience of taking drugs is a pleasant one in itself—at least initially—but that is not the only thing that keeps the habit going. There is a strong sense of community and high levels of bonding as social capital (Putnam, 2000) that are generated by this common experience, which sets the addict outside the rest of society. The esoteric language, image, and lifestyle had a hold on the Colin long after the chemical dependency had been dealt with. This in itself would indicate that approaches to drug rehabilitation that focus solely on dealing with chemical dependency are unlikely to be successful. If drug taking is about culture and identity, these issues must feature centrally in any recovery process. Kawachi, Kennedy, and Glass (1999) suggest that the development of social capital could be beneficial in recovery programs by providing affective support and acting as the source of self-esteem and respect.

In the latter stages of addiction, drugs became the dominant force in every aspect of Colin's life. Addiction took the place of career, giving purpose and shape to the day. As Bourdieu (2000) observes, there is no worse deprivation, perhaps, than that of the losers in the symbolic struggle for recognition, for access to a socially recognized social being, in a word, to humanity" (p. 242), and so with nothing to fill the gap, drugs win by default (Burroughs, 1969). Colin stated:

> You wake up, do some shoplifting, sell the goods, score the drugs, and get stoned. It defines who you will spend time with. You are part of a community of strangers although primarily loners joined by this common obsession.

Prison provided an opportunity to stop or at least reduce drug taking on a regular but temporary basis. It provided a safe place where the pressure was off for a while but did not provide long-term motivation to kick the habit altogether. This finding contradicts the findings of Council of Europe study (European Public Health Committee, 1980) that identified prison as a motivating force to stop using drugs. More recent work carried out by the World Health Organization (2010) also indicates that prison serves as no motivation for stopping drug misuse, because "The rate of acute drug-related mortality, or overdose deaths, among prisoners in the immediate postrelease period is unacceptably high" (p. 3). People are released from prison and immediately return to their former drug use. However, because their tolerance for the drug has been reduced while in prison, the usual doses can, in some cases, be fatal.

In the end, it was a variety of internal and external factors that came together to produce that motivation. First, Colin stated, "I was worn down physically and emotionally by the lifestyle and I felt bad about myself. The life of a 'career drug addict' is one which forces you to do things that you are deeply ashamed of." Finally, he saw his peers, at the age of 28, doing well in life while he was not.

It was at this time that he came upon a methadone program. Although initially attracted by "free drugs," this program became the trigger for a major turnaround in his life. He hoped methadone would stabilize his life for him. But he still did not want to stop taking drugs, just manage their use more effectively. However, after a couple of months he began to realize that there was an opportunity for him to live drug free and achieve something better in his life. And so it can be seen that despite some of the negative experiences of maintenance programs (European Public Health Committee, 1980) they can in some instances provide a springboard back into "normal" life. This is in line with developments in Glasgow which support, with caution, the development of methadone prescribing programs (Greater Glasgow Drug Action Team, 1999).

The Council of Europe (European Public Health Committee, 1980) suggests that recovery from drug addiction is a linear process marked by appropriate interventions at each stage: medical, then psychological, then social. However, it seems clear from Colin's experience that it is a far less neat process and, in fact, all three of these elements must come together to effect change. This is also confirmed by the work of Prochaska, DiClemente, and Norcross (1992) who propose a nonlinear cycle of change in addictive behavior that includes thinking and acting but also lapse and relapse in the process of recovery.

At the time when he was emerging from his chaotic drug use, Colin came into contact with community-based education. Before going on to describe this encounter, I outline some theoretical underpinnings of this work.

Community-based Education and Community Development

Community-based education is part of the wider approach of community development; an approach to working with people based on a common set of values and principles. In the United Kingdom, the values of community development work are defined as a commitment to social justice, self-determination, working and learning together, sustainable communities, and participation and reflective practice (PAULO, 2003). Margaret Ledwith describes a radical form of community development:

> An approach begins in people's lives and community reaches beyond the symptoms of injustice to the root causes by making critical connections between personal experiences and the oppressive political structures that perpetuate discrimination. Collective action is the process by which people join together to bring about change. If we fail to take practice beyond the good work that goes into local issues and local projects, we fail to realise this potential and the work is good but not transformative (Ledwith, 2005, p. 7).

Henderson (1995) highlights an aspect of the community development approach, community service approaches, as being particularly appropriate in the delivery of services to people recovering from addiction. Its features are that it is needs-based; participative; and interorganizational. This approach is applicable to community-based learning projects, working not only at the level of the individual but also developing the community's collective understanding of drug issues. This increases their capacity to engage usefully in the debates and responses to local drug issues (Barr, Purcell, & Ross, 1995).

Colin's first contact with community-based education was through a chance conversation with his partner's sister, who was the cleaner in the local community center. She had been thinking of joining a childcare and crèche work course based in Govan and run by the Community Education Service of Glasgow City Council. He felt that he had nothing to lose, "no penalty to benefits. It was not formal and I didn't need to disclose anything about my past life—just turn up." Also, it was a short course, which meant no long-term commitment. And so they went together.

The course was held in the local community center. It was a very small group of eight women, but he felt quite comfortable, even though he was the only man there. The way the initial session was run was a key to his successfully participating in the course. Although everyone felt a bit uncomfortable, they talked about their experience; it was stressed that everyone has valuable experience and that meant that he had something to contribute. In this way, the model of passive education was, to a small extent, undermined and Colin's confidence as a learner began to develop. Within a week or two of completion, he got paid for sessional crèche work. This period allowed him to ground what he had learned in practice and to observe and discuss the work with qualified and experienced workers. It was also the first step toward his seeing himself as a worker.

His next step was to join a Basic Youth Leadership course. "It felt like the next logical step and there was the suggestion that sessional work might be available on successful completion of the course." He reports a major turning point of the course:

> I asked a question about positive stroking: "What is that?" No one else asked, and I assumed that they all knew. I asked the question, got a simple explanation for the term and said, "Why don't you just say that?" Lots of other people said, "Thanks for asking, we didn't know either." I grew in confidence and now always ask questions.

Initially activated and motivated by dissatisfaction with his current lifestyle, he identifies several key features of the process that enabled him to sustain change through this form of education:

- a relational introduction and a collective response; he heard about the program from his partner's sister and went with a friend;
- local provision;
- an educational approach that values the learner's experience;
- short-term commitment initially required;
- immediate application of new skills and opportunity to link theory to practice;
- changed status through employment;
- clear opportunities for progression;
- opportunities to challenge existing knowledge and practices.

Although this was not radical community development, as described earlier, it did begin to shift both his material conditions in terms of employment and his sense of himself as a learner. This foundation was built on during his experience of Freirean-based education, as described below.

Freirean Education

The next stage in Colin's educational journey was a year-long program that linked paid work and completion of a Certificate in Community Work at the University of Glasgow. This project was informed by the work of Paulo Freire (1972). McLaren and Leonard (1993) outline 10 key values that underpin the Freirean approach to education, among them, that they are situated in the learner's own thought and language: democratic; dialogic; transforming social roles within learning; challenging discrimination; having an action focus; and embracing the affective as well as the cognitive domains. Using the definitions of McLaren and Leonard (1993), Colin reflects, in his own words, on the outworking of some of those values in his experience of Freirean learning.

Situated

The course material was situated in student thought and language, beginning with their words and understanding of the material and relating back to their material conditions.

> We were invited to think about our lives, read and analyze newspapers, and talk about our experience of oppression. This meant moving from one subcultural use of language and values to another; from the familiar, comfortable, and well practiced to the uncertainty, risk, and the insecurity that comes through change.

Democratic

Students have equal speaking rights as well as the right to design and evaluate the curriculum.

> Initially, equality was felt amongst fellow students, fostered by a strong affinity with the local community and shared values. However, in joint sessions with a different group of students the gulf in experience created a fear of speaking freely, which highlighted lack of confidence within the group. This could have been a barrier to learning. However, in general the learning group enabled me to create an environment in which to develop and link theoretical knowledge to practice and to take responsibility for shaping my future career.

Dialogic

The class is structured around problems posed by teachers and learners.

> This model of dialogical exploration was non-threatening, challenging, inclusive and conducive to my own personal learning needs. This style

> focussed more on the process of the journey between a) and b), through asking questions, challenging perceptions, critical analysis and awareness of the issues up for discussion. 'In Dialogical action the educational process reunites ourselves with the world. Yes, we have been shaped by our social context, but in naming and understanding that context we are in a position collectively to reshape it and ourselves.' (Prince, 1997)

Desocialization

This aspect of Freirean learning challenges the socialized roles of learners as passive and authority-dependent, and teachers as dull and domineering.

> My experience of school served as an inoculation against any future aspirations of participating in formal education, but the cultural differences between school and Freirean education changed my perception of learning. School was about: being collectively labelled; individual learning needs not being recognised; no choice in decisions; prescribed curriculum; peer pressure to conform and banking without explanation. Freirean education was about the liberation of being an individual; individual learning needs catered for; participation in decision-making process; increased personal responsibility; working in partnership to negotiate the curriculum; peer support for learning; exercising choice; being invited to challenge and focus on process rather than outcome.

Multicultural

Freirean education takes a critical attitude toward discrimination and inequality and examines the cultures of dominant and nondominant groups.

> As a starting point to becoming critically aware, previously unrecognised feelings of oppression were identified and explored; it is then impossible to ignore your own discriminatory attitudes and behaviour. This was a difficult learning experience.

Activist

The learning experience is active through problem posing. It also envisages that action is the end product of the educational exchange.

> In adopting this new value base and belief system, which encourages critical thinking and self-awareness of your own position in society, the natural progression is to challenge, ask questions, reason, and search for solutions.

AFFECTIVE

The problem-posing dialogic method embraces the affective as well as cognitive domains.

> Using dialogical methods facilitated issue-based discussion and promoted sharing of personal experiences, both practical and emotional. However, what must be taken into account is the depth of personal feelings, anxieties, fears, and conflicts which were exposed. This requires sensitive facilitation and great awareness of the implications of the empowerment process.

The impact of this educational encounter can be seen not only in Colin's career and personal life but also in his approach to working within the addiction field. Using a similar approach when working with recovering drug addicts, he is creating opportunities for people to reflect on and transform their lives through learning and work.

CONCLUSION

This journey, which was initially blighted by failures within the school system, the community, the family, and the individual himself, is by no means uncommon. Given that, there may well be themes that are applicable to the journeys of others.

This study suggests that effective drug recovery programs that blend individual desire for change with opportunities to recast oneself through critical reflection, education, and employment are able to effect lasting change. This must be a challenge to contemporary responses that set recovery programs as a compulsory alternative to custodial sentences and focus only on addiction issues. Eley, Gallop, McIvor, and Yates (2002), exploring the use of the Drug Treatment and Testing Orders introduced by the British government in 1995 as an alternative to custodial sentencing, note that drug users report a drop in but not cessation of drug use during the six months they are in the program.

The evidence in this story is supported by the Alcohol and Public Health Research Unit, Auckland (1999), Sowers, Garcia, and Seitz (1996), and White (2004), in suggesting that community-based education can provide a useful vehicle to aid the journey of people who are rebuilding their identities and lives after an experience of drug addiction. This study suggests that relational approaches to inducting participants into programs are effective. Introduction should be easily accessible, use well-known local venues, and require short-term commitment. Educational approaches should value the learners' experiences and allow for immediate application of new skills and the opportunity to link theory to practice, enabling learners to assimilate new learning. A learning context in which there are opportunities to challenge existing knowledge and practices further enables an epistemological shift where learners become not just passive recipients but, rather, creators of new knowledge (Allman, 2001). If this process of identity change by career drug addicts is to be secured, clear progression opportunities that enable changed material and social conditions through securing meaningful employment must be made available.

There may also be lessons to be learned by schools from this study. The subject in this case study left school with no qualifications and yet was able to gain a Certificate in Higher Education from the University of Glasgow successfully. The causes of the lack of thriving and the truant behavior are many, so a multistrand response to improving the situation will be required (Morris, Nelson, Stoney, & Benefield, 1999). It could include targeted outreach work; focus on the individual, perhaps using mentoring schemes; interagency work, which provides alternatives to mainstream curricula; and the provision of clear, individually negotiated progression routes, as well as radical review of the mismatch between the culture of the school and that of the community. Nick Lawson (2005), writing on the subject of Citizenship Education as part of the National Curriculum, suggests drawing on Freirean approaches in schools to develop an active pedagogy of criticism and political literacy that can begin to impact the culture of schools and of teaching throughout the curriculum.

One implication of adopting Freirean approaches would be the development of a negotiated curriculum. Perhaps the innovative work developed in the Italian province of Reggio Emilia in creating a negotiated curriculum in early-year education has something to say to the school system in general about the integration of teachers, parents, and learners and their lived experience. Within this approach:

> The curriculum is not child centred or teacher directed. The curriculum is child originated and teacher framed. . . . We have given great care in selecting the term 'negotiated curriculum' instead of emergent or child centred curriculum. We propose that 'negotiated curriculum' better captures the constructive, continual and reciprocal relation among teachers, children and parents and better captures the negotiations among subject matter: representational media and the children's current knowledge. (Fyfe & Forman, 1996).

This approach values the knowledge of both learners and teachers, promoting a mutual respect and a context for learning. This seems to be in full accord with Freire's ideas of coinvestigation. Too often we think that children need to be adapted to fit the school. Perhaps we should rather be asking how we adapt the school to fit the children.

REFERENCES

Alcohol and Public Health Research Unit. (1999). *Advice for purchasing strategy on public health issues: Health of older adults*. Auckland, New Zealand: Author.

Allman, P. (2001). *Critical education against global capitalism: Karl Marx and critical revolutionary education*. Westport, CT: Bergen and Garvey.

Barr, A., Purcell, R., & Ross, C. (1995). *Strong communities effective government: The role of community work*. Glasgow, Scotland: Scottish Community Development Centre.

Beck, D., & Callahan, C. (2001, July). *Poacher turned gamekeeper*. Paper presented at the Standing Conference on University Teaching and Research in the Education of Adults, London, UK.

Beck, D., & Purcell, R. (2010). *Popular education practice for youth and community development work*. Exeter, UK: Learning Matters.

Bernstein, B. (2003). *Class, codes and control*. London, UK: Routledge.

Bickel, R., Smith, C., & Eagle, T. (2002). Poor, rural neighborhoods and early school achievement. *Journal of Poverty*, *6*, 89–108.

Bostock, J., & Beck, D. (1993). Social enquiry and action. *Journal of Community and Applied Psychology*, *3*, 213–214.

Bourdieu, P. (2000). *Pascalian meditations*. Cambridge, UK: Polity Press.

Brody, G., Ge, X., Conger, R., Gibbons, F., Murry, V., Gerrard, M., & Simons, R. (2001). The influence of neighborhood disadvantage, collective socialization, and parenting on African American children's affiliation with deviant peers. *Child Development*, *72*, 1231–1246.

Burroughs, W. (1969). *Junkie*. London, UK: New English Library.

Charlesworth, S. (2000). *A phenomenology of working class experience*. Cambridge, UK: Cambridge University Press.

Cornwall, A., & Jewkes, R. (1995). What is participatory research? *Social Science and Medicine*, *41*, 1667–1676.

Eley, S., Gallop, K., McIvor, G., & Yates, R. (2002). *Drug treatment and testing orders, evaluation of the Scottish pilots*. Edinburgh, Scotland: Scottish Executive Social Research.

Elliot, J. (1996). School effectiveness research and its critics: Alternative visions of schooling. *Cambridge Journal of Education*, *26*, 199–224.

European Public Health Committee. (1980). *Treatment of drug dependence*. Strasbourg, France: Council of Europe.

Freire, P. (1972). *Pedagogy of the oppressed*. London, UK: Sheed and Ward.

Fyfe, B., & Forman, G. (1996). The negotiated curriculum: Innovations in early education. *The International Reggio Exchange*, *3*(3), 4–7.

Govan Initiative. (2004). *Poverty in greater Govan*. Retrieved from http://www.govan-initiative.co.uk/FileAccess.aspx?id=118

Greater Glasgow Drug Action Team. (1999). *Tackling drugs together in greater Glasgow*. Glasgow, Scotland: Glasgow City Council.

Grinyer, A. (2005). Personal agendas in emotionally demanding research. *Social Research Update*, *46*. Retrieved from http://sru.soc.surrey.ac.uk/SRU46.html

Henderson, P. (1995). *Drugs prevention and community development: Principles of good practice*. London, UK: Central Drugs Prevention Unit.

Jesson, J., & Newman, M. (2004). Radical adult education and learning. In G. Foley (Ed.), *Dimensions of adult learning: Adult education and training in a global era* (pp. 251–264). Maidenhead, UK: Open University Press.

Kawachi, I., Kennedy, B. P., Glass, R. (1999) Social capital and self-rated health: A contextual analysis. *American Journal of Public Health, 89*, 1187–1193.

Kinder, K., Kendall, S., Halsey, K., & Atkinson, M. (1999). *Disaffection talks.* Berkshire, UK: National Foundation for Educational Research.

Lawson, N. (2005). *What lessons does the pedagogical approach of Paulo Freire have for the development of citizenship as a national curriculum subject?* Retrieved from citizED: http://www.citized.info/index.php?l_menu=students#reflect

Ledwith, M. (2005). *Community development: A critical approach.* Bristol, UK: Policy Press.

McLaren, P., & Leonard, P. (1993). *Paulo Freire: A critical encounter.* London, UK: Routledge.

Miles, M. B., & Huberman, A. M. (1994). *Qualitative data analysis: An expanded source book* (2nd ed.). London, UK: Sage.

Morris, M., Nelson, J., Stoney, S., & Benefield, P. (1999). *Disadvantaged youth: A critical review of the literature on scope, strategies and solutions.* Nottingham, UK: DfEE Publications.

Neale, J., Allen, D., & Coombes, L. (2005). Qualitative research methods within the addictions. *Addiction, 100*, 1584–1593.

Organisation for Economic Co-Operation and Development. (1998). *Overcoming failure at school.* Paris, France: Author.

PAULO. (2003). *National occupational standards for community development work.* Retrieved from http://www.fcdl.org.uk/publications/documents/nos/Standards%20040703.pdf

Payne, J. (2002). *Attitudes to education, and choices at age 16: A brief research review.* London, UK: DfEE Publications.

Prochaska, J. O., DiClemente, C. C., & Norcross, J. C. (1992). In search of how people change: Applications to addictive behavior. *American Psychologist, 47*, 1102–1114.

Putnam, R. (2000). *Bowling alone: The collapse and revival of American community.* New York, NY: Simon & Schuster.

Rhodes, T. (2000). The multiple roles of qualitative research in understanding and responding to illicit drug use. In G. Greenwood & K. Robertson (Eds.), *Understanding and responding to drug use: The role of qualitative research* (pp. 21–36). Lisbon, Portugal: European Monitoring Centre for Drugs and Drug Addiction.

Roth, W. (2006). Editorial: Responsibility, solidarity, and ethics in cogenerative dialogue as research methods. *Forum Qualitative Sozialforschung/Forum: Qualitative Social Research, 7*(2). Retrieved from http://www.qualitative-research.net/index.php/fqs/article/view/122

Sowers, W., Garcia, F., & Seitz, S. (1996). Introduction: Community-based prevention: An evolving paradigm. *The Journal of Primary Prevention 16*, 225–231.

Sparkes, J. (1999). *Schools, education and social exclusion.* London, UK: Centre for Analysis of Social Exclusion, London School of Economics.

University of Manchester. (1971). *Census: Small area statistics*. Manchester, UK: Registrar General for Scotland.

Waller, R. (2004). 'I really hated school, and couldn't wait to get out!': Reflections on 'a wasted opportunity' amongst Access to HE students. *Journal of Access Policy and Practice*, *2*(1), 24–43.

Webb, E. J., Campbell, D. T., Schwartz, R. D., & Sechrest, L. (1966). *Unobtrusive measures: Nonreactive research in the social sciences*. Chicago, IL: Rand McNally.

White, W. (2004). *The history and future of peer-based addiction recovery support services*. Washington, DC: Substance Abuse and Mental Health Services Administration.

World Health Organization. (2010). Prevention of acute drug-related mortality in prison populations during the immediate post-release period. Retrieved from http://www.euro.who.int/__data/assets/pdf_file/0020/114914/E93993.pdf

British Journal of Social Work (2014) **44**, 2078–2094
doi:10.1093/bjsw/bct091
Advance Access publication May 12, 2013

Critical Practice for Challenging Times: Social Workers' Engagement with Community Work

Catherine Forde* and Deborah Lynch

Catherine Forde is a lecturer in youth and community work at the School of Applied Social Studies, University College Cork. Deborah Lynch is a senior lecturer in social work at the School of Social Work and Human Services, University of Queensland, Australia.

*Correspondence to Catherine Forde, Lecturer, School of Applied Social Studies, University College Cork, Cork, Republic of Ireland. E-mail: *c.forde@ucc.ie*

Abstract

The contribution that social workers make to communities is integral to the principles and values of the profession but is often 'hidden' and unacknowledged. This paper is an exploration of social workers' engagement with community work approaches in a range of settings in the Republic of Ireland, where managerialism and a climate of austerity pose particular challenges for social work practice. By exploring the findings of qualitative interviews with social work practitioners, the paper examines themes and issues that emerge in the context of their practice settings and considers how community work ideas are enacted in contemporary social work practice. These ideas challenge dominant discourses and emphasise a process of active engagement with communities to counter inequality and injustice and seek change at both community and societal levels. The concept of 'creative activism' is developed to explore the idea of critical practice and the different forms of collective action that social workers undertake. The use of these ideas to strengthen the links between theory, research and practice on a postgraduate qualifying social work degree is discussed. The paper seeks to re-emphasise the place of community work within social work research, theory, practice and professional education.

Keywords: Community discourse, community work, critical practice, activism

Accepted: April 2013

Introduction

A succession of high-profile child abuse cases in the UK and elsewhere has accentuated social work interventions with children and families within a child protection context. Media portrayals have sought to attribute blame to individual social workers for failing to protect children from abuse, and have focused much negative attention on the profession. Examples include the Baby Peter Connolly case in England (see Parton, 2011) and the Roscommon case in Ireland (see O'Brien, 2012). Review processes in the aftermath of such tragic events have refocused government on child protection and the role of social work within it (Parton, 2011, p. 154; see Munro, 2011; Ryan, 2009), and have deflected attention from social work activity at the community and collective levels.

In UK and Irish policy frameworks, there has been a renewed emphasis on individualism and a shift of responsibility away from the state towards civil society (Ellison, 2011; Powell and Geoghegan, 2007). In the UK, the 'Big Society' has been posited as a return to moral and civic values of individual responsibility, mutuality and obligation (Cameron, 2009) as part of a 'new' communitarian arrangement where the focus is on the agency of individuals within their communities, 'community action' and citizen responsibility and empowerment (Szreter and Ishkanian, 2011). Lister (2011), however, argues that notions of citizenship in 'the age of responsibility' are more about the obligations of citizens on the margins of society than their human rights. For example, it has been suggested that the new personalisation agenda for adult care is more aligned with individualist and consumerist ideas than egalitarian and social justice principles (Lymbery, 2012). Moreover, public sector and welfare cuts under governments' austerity programmes in both the UK and Ireland have had a regressive impact on policy implementation and third-sector activity across a range of areas, affecting those who are most disadvantaged and marginalised in society (Featherstone *et al.*, 2012; Lloyd, 2010; Lloyd-Hughes, 2010; Kirby and Murphy, 2011; Parton, 2011; Lymbery, 2012). Under such conditions, it is argued that the 'Big Society' reforms will have a very limited impact (Stepney and Ford, 2012).

Critiques of the political, economic, social policy and organisational contexts of contemporary social work practice have emphasised the neo-liberal and New Public Management (NPM) agenda within human service organisations and its impact on social work (Featherstone *et al.*, 2012; Harlow *et al.*, 2012; Marston and McDonald, 2012; Parton, 2011). In Ireland, this agenda has led to an increasingly bureaucratic social work practice environment with 'high priority placed on tangible outputs' and less regard for 'relationship- and principle-based work' with children and families (Buckley, 2008, p. 23). In England and Wales, the reform process advocated by the *Munro Review of Child Protection* (Munro, 2011) has sought to reduce bureaucratic constraints on social work practice; however, there are concerns that, in the current neo-liberal policy context and climate of fiscal tightening, these wide-ranging reforms will not ameliorate inequalities and injustices at the societal level (Featherstone *et al.*, 2012; Parton, 2011). This poses a significant challenge to social work to respond to the complex and deepening problems that face individuals, families and communities.

According to the International Federation of Social Workers (2000), social workers are 'change agents' for communities and society as well as for individuals and families. Social work practitioners and educators consistently endeavour to assert the relevance of community work approaches to social work practice (Dixon and Hoatson, 1999; Ife, 1998; Skehill, 1999; Heenan, 2004; Lynch and Forde, 2006; Stepney and Popple, 2008; Mendes, 2007, 2008; Barron and Taylor, 2010; Ingamells *et al.*, 2010; Healy, 2012), but how these ideas are conceptualised and used in practice varies between settings (Ife, 1998; Stepney and Popple, 2008; Healy, 2012). The term 'community social work' (Stepney and Popple, 2008; Harrison, 2009; Teater and Baldwin, 2012) is typically associated with ideas of self-help, voluntarism and facilitating access to local services. Mantle and Backwith (2010) refer to 'community-orientated social work' as a locally based, collective and empowering approach to combating poverty. While not eschewing these ideas, Ife (1998) advocates a form of community-based social work which locates practice within a *community discourse*. This is a community development approach characterised by an organic 'bottom-up' engagement with communities, contrary to the operation of the dominant discourses of managerialism and professionalisation in social work. The community discourse is consistent with the social work value base in emphasising social justice, community empowerment and the rights of marginalised groups (Ife, 2008). Crucially, it is underpinned by a critical perspective and practice that seeks social change at both community and societal levels (Stepney, 2006), and informed by critical social work, a theoretical perspective that 'seeks social transformation as forms of justice and emancipation' (Gray and Webb, 2009, p. 77). Critical practice therefore involves a structural analysis and engagement with the root causes of social exclusion and injustice (Stepney, 2006; Gray and Webb, 2009; Gray *et al.*, 2012). It encompasses an understanding of the complexities of power and how it functions (Stepney and Ford, 2012), a willingness on the part of practitioners to challenge existing power structures and to encourage and enable service users to do the same by facilitating their participation in the decisions that affect them. Social workers can engage in critical practice without moving outside their regular conceptual frameworks and ways of working (Ife, 1998; Stepney, 2006; Fook, 2012). For example, Stepney (2006), Stepney and Ford (2012) and Fook (2012) underline the importance of alliance-building and collective approaches to practice. This paper explores how these ideas are expressed and enacted in contemporary social work practice and the challenges that practitioners encounter in pursuing a community work approach.

Study and methodology

This paper is based on a research project undertaken in 2009–10. The objective of the research was to strengthen the links between theory, research and practice in the teaching of community work on the Master of Social Work (MSW) at University College Cork. The MSW is a two-year full-time postgraduate qualifying professional social work programme. The project aimed to undertake qualitative research into social workers' use of the community discourse in their practice and to use the findings to incorporate contemporary practice themes and dilemmas into the teaching of the community work module.

The study sought social work practitioners or 'good informants' (Flick, 2009) who were using community work approaches in their practice. A combined purposive and snowball (Sarantakos, 2005) sampling strategy was used to reach a target of fifteen interviews. Social workers were sought by an e-mail that was distributed via the mailing list of the Irish Association of Social Workers (IASW). Of the eighteen social workers who expressed interest in participating, interviews were conducted with nine who were using community work approaches in varying practice contexts and geographical areas. In addition, a number of social workers from the authors' professional networks were invited to participate and asked to recommend other practitioners who were working with communities. A further six participants were recruited using this method. In total, fifteen interviews were completed. Prior to commencement of data collection, the research was approved by the University Social Research Ethics Committee.

The interviews were conducted between December 2009 and April 2010. Prior to the interviews, participants were asked to complete a consent form and a brief questionnaire eliciting information on their employment and social work training. Structured interviews with open-ended questions were used. This allowed in-depth exploration of participants' work with groups and communities, the challenges posed by engaging in community work and their attitudes towards critical practice and social action or campaigning. The interviews were audio taped and transcribed. This yielded rich qualitiative data which were analysed using an inductive (Charmaz and Henwood, 2008) and iterative process. NVivo8 software was employed to code and group the data into broad categories based on the interview themes, and for cross-coding to identify relationships between themes, thereby enabling their refinement and the identification of emerging themes.

Profile of interviewees

All of the participants were qualified social workers with the exception of one, who was an accredited social work practice teacher. The majority (twelve) were female and most were established in their positions for more than six years. Six worked in generic community work contexts within specific geographical areas, while eight worked in more specialised settings including child protection and family support, community drugs projects, disability services, advocacy in mental health and probation services. One social worker was a member of a voluntary environmental activist group. Eight interviewees were employed by the state and seven were working with voluntary agencies or groups. Seven of the interviewees were based in cities, six in large towns and two in rural contexts.

Social workers' experiences of using community work approaches

Interviewees described a broad range of collective activities in diverse practice contexts. These contexts include social inclusion projects in urban settings, generic community development work within a geographical catchment area, a neighbourhood youth project, an initiative to build relationships with the Roma community, a support project for the children and families of prisoners, a drop-in facility for people who misuse drugs and alcohol, an advocacy initiative with mental health service users and youth work for children with disabilities.

Community development may be envisaged as a process that is cyclical rather than linear in nature. Engagement with communities, collaborative endeavour and networking are integral dimensions of this process (Federation for Community Development Learning, 2009; see Gilchrist and Taylor, 2011), as well as building effective relationships between and across sectors, and collective action (Kenny, 2011). In discussing their practice, interviewees described key elements of the community development process. For example, a practitioner working in an inner-city context explains how she became involved in the initial stages of contact making and engagement with the community:

> One of the first things that I got involved in was bringing a group of people together to look at the need for some kind of response intervention project . . . that would address the needs of . . . vulnerable children and families . . . it meant going and knocking on doors and making contacts and . . . there were lots of people that were very interested in developing some kind of response (Interview 11, social worker in community work context).

This initial contact making resulted in the establishment of a children and family project that has been running for a number of years. The same practitioner underlines the importance of collaborative working and networking in developing 'a co-ordinated and integrated response' to issues affecting the community.

These activities describe a process of change that builds from the smaller to the larger scale, involving greater numbers of people as it proceeds. This transformative potential distinguishes community development as an approach (Ledwith and Springett, 2010). Transformational practice is value-based, democratic and collaborative, and links the local with the global. It resists the 'onslaught of managerialism' (Houston *et al.*, 2005; see Ferguson and Woodward, 2009) and avoids an undue focus on the technical aspects of the work. A practitioner considers how this perspective characterises his work:

> I suppose for me community work is about a transformative action based type response to issues rather than sort of where do we get funding, how do we find the funding, how do we manage the funding .... Community work always in a nutshell boils down to how do we involve people in the process of change as well (Interview 1, social worker in a neighbourhood youth project).

The consistency of social work and community development values is of significance for social workers who engage in community development work, regardless of the context in which they are working. A number of practitioners spoke about the interconnectedness of social work and community development work:

> ... without community work, without community development, without community projects, we can't do social work (Interview 13, social worker in child protection).

> I think all of the social work values and principles around empathy, empowerment, working in partnership and all of those values are carried into community work (Interview 10, social worker in community work context).

Transformative practice can only take place when practitioners become aware of their own power and how it may be unintentionally used to reinforce inequality (Ife, 1998; Ledwith and Springett, 2010). This theme was present in our findings. One practitioner observed:

> ... I think language can be very divisive, disempowering of people as well ... very often people will intuitively from their experience know, for instance social injustice but they don't label it as such (Interview 4, social worker and environmental activist).

Practitioners in the study underlined the important process of building relationships with service users and communities. As one practitioner expressed:

> Trust is a huge thing obviously to everybody but especially when you work in a drug using homeless community, it is a massive issue. You just need that space where you just can go and create those relationships ... sometimes that can take loads of time (Interview 12, social worker in a community drugs project).

An inclusive approach, a readiness to hear others' voices and the sharing of knowledge are fundamental to collaborative working (Dominelli, 2010). This form of dialogue with communities develops an impetus that feeds a cyclical process of engagement, building 'steadily outwards, from issue to project, from project to alliances/networks, gathering momentum towards movements for change' (Ledwith and Springett, 2010, p. 16; see also Ledwith, 2005). This process is both slow and time-consuming, which is not always understood by employing organisations, particularly in Ireland, where most social workers work in statutory settings within the context of child protection (National Social Work Qualifications Board, 2006). This problem draws attention to the contextualised or embedded nature of practice and the challenges that it presents for social workers. These challenges are explored in the next section.

Challenging dominant discourses in social work practice settings

Much has been written about the contextual nature of social work practice and the potential of the organisational context to facilitate or limit 'the realisation of the humanitarian values to which social workers are committed' (Healy, 2005, p. xiii). The practitioners in this study work within diverse practice contexts and organisational settings. The contextual or embedded (Martin *et al.*, 2007) nature of their practice was clearly evident as interviewees discussed their engagement with communities within the organisational context in which they were working. Their responses demonstrated awareness of the influence of context and practice location on the kinds of community development activities that were pursued:

> ... I think that it is very easy for the work to be just prescriptive and just task-driven ... so I think as social workers we have to be very careful ... there is probably more scope in the voluntary agencies where campaigning can be a feature of the work (Interview 4, social worker and environmental activist).

This highlights the constraining effects of top-down organisational structures on developing community development approaches to practice. Discourses 'construct the boundaries of practice, suggest what is to count as good practice, and most importantly, define and legitimise relationships of power between various actors' (Ife, 1998, p. 40). Practitioners spoke about the influence of dominant discourses in the workplace on the position of community development. A social work practice teacher referred to his organisation's initial interest in community development but eventual distancing from the community discourse and concentration on individual work:

> So they (the statutory agency) become more and more distant from the community and the community aspect became just a word, something that was accepted in theory but not in practice (Interview 3, practice teacher in a community drugs project).

In this context, it was the leadership displayed by an individual senior social worker that enabled re-engagement with a community development approach. Another practitioner referred to the difficulties that individual workers experience in resisting the pressures exerted by large agencies:

> ... once you become a statutory social worker working for a big organisation with all its inadequacies it is very difficult *not* to respond to the organisational pressure (Interview 13, social worker in child protection, emphasis).

The issue of sustaining critical thinking and practice within challenging practice contexts emerged:

> I think within children and family social work anyway people are just so busy and they are not really encouraged to think outside the box ... for new graduates where they are spending maybe two years on a Masters thinking very critically and reflectively and they come into the workplace and it is not really encouraged (Interview 10, social worker in community work context).

This practitioner elaborated:

> It is actually a responsibility of social workers to be engaging in more critical practice. I think we are in quite powerful positions. We are also very skilled workers. We see things from a broad perspective ... so we are really well placed to be doing a lot more of that. But ... who your employer is and what they demand of you can make things difficult.

A practitioner in a neighbourhood youth project (Interview 1) suggested that social work has moved away from the social and is following a business model where the professional focus is on skills and competencies. Buckley (2008) has analysed the impact of the NPM discourse on the Irish child protection system whereby relationship-based practice is replaced by 'business processes' (Buckley, 2008, p. 10) of audit, measurement and defined outcomes. This resonates with the argument that social work has lost its 'critical edge' and has become more concerned with survival in a hostile environment and adherence to dominant discourses such as utilitarianism and economic rationalism (Ife, 2008).

In order to relocate social work practice within a critical social analysis, social workers need the time and opportunity to reflect on their practice. A practitioner in a child protection setting argued passionately that 'You mustn't just do—social work is not about doing. It is about reflecting and evaluating and processing' (Interview 13). It was suggested that social workers need to be constantly aware of the wider context in which they function:

> Social workers have to be grounded in the understanding and the realisation and the connection between poverty, injustice and the people with the problems they are facing ... if they are engaged day after day, year after year, just looking at the symptoms and the problems, they will get burnt out (Interview 3, practice teacher in community drugs project).

This practitioner envisaged a restructuring of his social work team where, instead of one worker undertaking general community development, all social workers would dedicate part of their time to some community development to engage them 'in the wider picture at some level'. This 'outward-looking perspective' (Marston and McDonald, 2012, p. 12) is crucial if social work is to remain relevant and fulfil its commitment to social change in the contemporary context. Sometimes, 'strategic action' can follow collective processes of reflection and dialogue that question 'the motives and outcomes of current arrangements' (Humphries, 2008, p. 73;

see also Askeland and Fook, 2009; Fook, 2012). A practitioner in a statutory agency describes how her agency facilitated a meeting of professionals to discuss the difficulties experienced by the Roma community in an area of a city. The meeting was precipitated by a concern that the needs of the Roma were not being met, despite the existence of a range of services. It was agreed that a community development approach would be used in order to build a relationship with the community. The initial meeting was followed by a series of information-sharing meetings that involved both the Roma and professionals from several disciplines:

> So we set about trying to engage slowly with the Roma community ... it actually worked really well because the primary care social worker was engaged with one family and she slowly spoke to them and they began to engage other families and I think, for me, that was community work .... We have just finished our five information meetings and are looking at what can we do next to begin to engage and empower this community (Interview 10, social worker in a community work context).

Notwithstanding the 'prevailing technocratic stranglehold of social work' (Houston *et al.*, 2005, p. 36), 'opportunities do exist for professional social workers to engage, in their thinking and in their practice, creatively, critically and constructively within the space available to them' (Houston *et al.*, 2005, p. 37). The research reveals that social workers can and do make space for discursive enquiry that may challenge both established practices and dominant discourses. In the next section, we will explore these ideas further using the idea of 'creative activism' to illustrate how practitioners create opportunities to engage in critical practice in different settings.

The potential and practice of creative activism in social work

Practitioners' accounts of critical practice resonate with the literature on new and emerging forms of activism. While social change remains the primary focus (Martin *et al.*, 2007), the forms that civic and political activism take have evolved over time. Citizens of post-industrial society now participate in 'multiple contemporary channels of civic engagement, mobilisation and expression' (Norris, 2003, p. 17) that mirror the shifting and uncertain nature of 'liquid modernity' (Bauman, 2007). Contemporary activism is characterised by actions that may be subtle, situation-specific, small-scale and spontaneous or opportunistic rather than necessarily obtrusive, sustained or extensive (Martin *et al.*, 2007; DeWan, 2010; see also Healy, 2000; Mayo, 2005; Stepney and Popple, 2008). Though broad, this conceptualisation of activism is distinguished by a creativity that is both responsive and adaptable to diverse and shifting situations:

> Sometimes, opportunities are not always going to be there, sometimes you just have to use the chances when they arise and take a chance and practice critically. In critical practice you have to wait ... for the opportunity ... maybe the opportunity arises at some stage to be a bit more creative and maybe use alliances (Interview 1, social worker in neighbourhood youth project).

Some of the activism that practitioners are engaged in is connected to the socio-economic crisis which has had an adverse impact on local community development activity (Lloyd, 2010), much of which is Irish state-funded:

> ... a whole community infrastructure is being dismantled and I think a huge challenge is trying to somehow respond to the dismantling of that programme (community development) because ultimately it is the people who are most disadvantaged ... people who are living in poverty, will become further on the periphery. It is a huge, just a huge challenge to try to respond to that. Then again, we have to. We can't sit on the fence (Interview 11, social worker in community work context).

A practitioner in a community work context referred to the 'relentless campaign' (Interview 5) in which she and her co-workers are engaged to highlight the effects of cutbacks on the community and voluntary sector. These cutbacks affect communities which are already 'pushed to society's margins' (Mertens, 2009, p. 48) and, in turn, have implications for the social work profession which engages with these communities.

It is not uncommon for activists to use a mix of 'insider' and 'outsider' approaches in seeking to influence their own and external agencies (Baker *et al.*, 2004; Mayo, 2005; DeWan, 2010). These approaches are illustrated in practitioners' accounts of working in different settings. For example, a practitioner who works in a neighbourhood youth project described how unsuccessful attempts by his agency to negotiate with a government department on a school issue led to plans to picket the department, before an eventual meeting was proffered. Other social workers portrayed a type of activism that is less obtrusive and more nuanced. A practitioner in a large statutory agency described how she and her colleagues continuously attempt to engage the decision makers in the agency in a dialogue on the impact of their policy and decisions on communities and service users. While painstaking in nature, this approach sometimes yields a 'pay-off'. Another who works in the same agency discussed activism 'behind the scenes' in response to cutbacks in youth services:

> We have been quite limited in what we can do in terms of social action or campaigning compared to maybe other areas ... youth services have had huge cuts to their funding across the country really and I would definitely have been supporting one of the youth services ... to attend their own public day of action. We would (be) behind the scenes trying to encourage people to be involved and would attend campaigns where appropriate but there is definitely a bit of an issue there about working for the State when the issues are against the State (Interview 10, social worker in community work context).

A practitioner in a large voluntary agency discussed working 'within the system' to promote change:

> I would say we do but we just do it differently ... we are doing it very quietly and as politically as we can and trying to bring people on board (Interview 8, social worker in disability services).

The experiences of these social workers underline the flexibility of contemporary activism, which offers 'creative alternatives for activists and organizations suddenly struck by cuts in their state funding and forced to find new ways to make their voices heard' (DeWan, 2010, p. 530). Accounts of social worker activism reveal a variety of approaches, including public advocacy and engagement with the state (Mendes, 2007), recognition of and engagement with service users' experiences of oppression and discrimination (Ferguson and Woodward, 2009; Marston and McDonald, 2012), low-level 'resistance' and more overtly challenging behaviours (Carey and Foster, 2011; Fook, 2012). These accounts also highlight the challenges posed by practice contexts where managerialism is the dominant discourse, particularly the 'management-dominated, highly regulated statutory sector of social work' (Mantle and Backwith, 2010, p. 2384; see also Collins, 2009; Shevellar, 2011). In such contexts, collective action offers a means of effectively pursuing issues while protecting individuals from a backlash (Ferguson and Woodward, 2009). Practitioners describe the benefits of collective action:

> I believe that critical practice should lead to some kind of collective action. The challenge for social workers is to really analyse why it is that I am doing what I am doing ... if the analysis is ... a social analysis, it really determines the intervention and it will determine, I think, social workers building those alliances, building the networks, building solidarity and really constructing a piece of social work that has social justice as its basis (Interview 11, social worker in community work context).

> I think being affiliated to wider organisations keeps us in touch with where we are coming from, our ethos and our values as well and part of a wider network which can act as a support really (Interview 15, social worker in a family resource centre).

This is consistent with the idea of activism as a collective activity that emanates from the everyday experience of individuals who connect with others to seek to 'alter power relations within existing social networks' (Martin *et al.*, 2007, p. 80; see also Crossley and Ibrahim, 2012). It resonates with the concept of 'a more humble' (Marston and McDonald, 2012, p. 14) political agency whereby the everyday interactions between workers and citizens can become sites for meaningful social change.

The accounts of some practitioners illuminate another facet of creative activism. Due to personal commitments, their involvement may be sporadic or intermittent rather than sustained:

> ... my energy has gone into family in looking after some elderly relatives. That would be more where my commitment has been around rather than

issues of social justice that I would have been involved in for many years (Interview 7, social worker in community work context).

This practitioner is describing her engagement in 'episodic' activism (Weller, 2010), whereby involvement is transitory rather than consistent and based on an individual's capacity to devote time to a cause. Individualism and 'conflicting life-choices' (Gane, 2001, p. 269) in the post-modern era can lead to constant tension between personal and professional demands and fighting the cause (Collins, 2009). Episodic activism enables practitioners to seize opportunities when they arise, but does not require constant commitment.

Implications for social work education

The research findings are currently being used to enhance the connections between community development ideas and social work practice on a community work module (twelve hours) taught over the first and second years of the MSW. Research, teaching and learning, and practice are constituent elements of a reciprocal process. Researching practice enriches teaching and learning, thereby building social work students' knowledge and awareness of the complexities of practice situations (Jones, 2012). A 'spirit of enquiry' (Taylor and Rafferty, 2003) is modelled through exposing students to the research process and facilitating their interaction with and critical analysis of different approaches and ideas (Brew, 1999). Professional or practice knowledge offers students practitioner perspectives in relating theory and practice. This process is practice-centred, 'tacit', organic, holistic and inductive in its approach to problems or situations (Nixon and Murr, 2006, p. 807).

On the community work module, students are encouraged to critically reflect on the theoretical ideas, principles and values that underpin social work and community work and develop knowledge and skills for collective approaches to practice. Most students will not undertake a community placement over the course of their training (Barry, 2011); therefore, the audio material from the interviews with practitioners is used to engage them with the community discourse. Small group work and focused questions are used as a mechanism for processes of reflection, discussion, analysis, eliciting feedback, professional socialisation and peer learning. In this way, students interact with the material, explore and discuss the values inherent in the practice examples and reflect on the theories embedded in the myriad of actions taken by practitioners in their work. This stimulates the learning process by building on students' previous knowledge, challenging pre-existing assumptions and beliefs and inviting students to construct new knowledge and ideas about working within a community discourse. It also exposes students to critical perspectives and practice and to the transformational possibilities inherent in collective approaches. The module is assessed through a community work practice analysis whereby students begin to integrate community work ideas into their practice on placement irrespective of the placement context. Students indicate that this enables them to think creatively and critically within diverse practice settings (Lynch and Forde, 2006). Recognition of the value of researching practice is an important aspect of the overall student learning experience.

Conclusion

This paper refers to 'challenging times' and the current socio-economic circumstances in which social work is practised in the Republic of Ireland. Social workers engage with the most vulnerable members of communities and face a range of highly complex social issues. Their positioning reinforces the need for a critical perspective that places the emphasis on social justice, community empowerment and human rights (Ife, 2008). This research reveals that, despite conflicting pressures in their agencies and in their personal lives, social workers are using value-based, collective approaches that encompass social work knowledge and skills of relationship building, collaboration, networking and mobilisation (Dixon and Hoatson, 1999; Barron and Taylor, 2010). Drawing on ideas about contemporary activism in the literature, the paper has developed the concept of 'creative activism' to encapsulate the different forms of collective action that social workers undertake. Without moving outside their regular conceptual and practice frameworks, social workers are seeking innovative ways to sustain critical thinking and practice in their work with individuals, groups and communities. Engaging social work students with these ideas opens up possibilities for an enriched practice based upon core social work values and a broader structural analysis of the issues and problems facing individuals, families and communities in challenging times.

Acknowledgements

The authors would like to acknowledge the support of NAIRTL, the National Academy for Integration of Research, Teaching and Learning, which funded the empirical research on which the article is based.

References

Askeland, G. A. and Fook, J. (2009) 'Critical reflection in social work', *European Journal of Social Work*, **12**(3), pp. 287–92.

Baker, J., Lynch, K., Cantillon, S. and Walsh, J. (2004) *Equality: From Theory to Action*, Basingtoke, Palgrave Macmillan.

Barron, C. and Taylor, B. J. (2010) 'The rights tools for the right job: Social work students learning community development', *Social Work Education*, **29**(4), pp. 372–85.

Barry, A. (2011) 'Social work students' attitudes towards community placements: An exploratory study', Master of Social Work thesis submitted to School of Applied Social Studies, University College Cork, 19 April.

Bauman, Z. (2007) *Liquid Times: Living in an Age of Uncertainty*, Cambridge, Polity Press.

Brew, A. (1999) 'Research and teaching: Changing relationships in a changing context', *Studies in Higher Education*, **24**(3), pp. 291–301.

Buckley, H. (2008) 'Heading for collision? Managerialism, social science, and the Irish child protection system', in K. Burns and D. Lynch (eds), *Child Protection and Welfare Social Work: Contemporary Themes and Practice Perspectives*, Dublin, A.&A. Farmar.

Cameron, D. (2009) 'The Big Society', Hugo Young Memorial Lecture, London, 10 November.

Carey, M. and Foster, V. (2011) 'Introducing "deviant" social work: Contextualising the limits of radical social work whilst understanding (fragmented) resistance within the social work labour process', *British Journal of Social Work*, **41**(3), pp. 576–93.

Charmaz, K. and Henwood, K. L. (2008) 'Grounded theory', in C. Willig and W. Stainton-Rogers (eds), *Handbook of Qualitative Research in Psychology*, London, Sage.

Collins, S. (2009) 'Some critical perspectives on social work and collectives', *British Journal of Social Work*, **39**, pp. 334–52.

Crossley, N. and Ibrahim, J. (2012) 'Critical mass, social networks and collective action: Exploring student political worlds', *Sociology* Advance Access published March 15, 2012, 10.1177/0038038511425560.

DeWan, J. (2010) 'The practice of politics: Feminism, activism and social change in Ireland', in J. Hogan, P. F. Donnelly and B. K. O'Rourke (eds), *Irish Business and Society: Governing, Participating and Transforming in the 21st Century*, Dublin, Gill and Macmillan.

Dixon, J. and Hoatson, L. (1999) 'Retreat from within: Social work's faltering commitment to community work', *Australian Social Work*, **52**(2), pp. 3–9.

Dominelli, L. (2010) *Social Work in a Globalizing World*, Cambridge, Polity Press.

Ellison, N. (2011) 'The Conservative Party and the "Big Society"', in C. Holden, M. Kilkey and G. Ramia (eds), *Social Policy Review 23: Analysis and Debate in Social Policy, 2011*, Bristol, The Policy Press, pp. 45–62.

Featherstone, B., Broadhurst, K. and Holt, K. (2012) 'Thinking systematically—thinking politically: Building strong partnerships with children and families in the context of rising inequality', *British Journal of Social Work*, **42**, pp. 618–33.

Federation for Community Development Learning (2009) *A Summary of the 2009 Community Development National Occupational Standards*, Sheffield, Federation for Community Development Learning.

Ferguson, I. and Woodward, R. (2009) *Radical Social Work in Practice: Making a Difference*, Bristol, Policy Press.

Flick, U. (2009) *An Introduction to Qualitative Research*, 4th edn, London, Sage.

Fook, J. (2012) *Social Work: A Critical Approach to Practice*, 2nd edn, London, Sage.

Gane, N. (2001) 'Zigmunt Bauman—liquid modernity and beyond', *Acta Sociologica*, **44**(3), pp. 267–75.

Gilchrist, A. and Taylor, M. (2011) *The Short Guide to Community Development*, Bristol, Policy Press.

Gray, M. and Webb, S. (2009) 'Critical social work', in M. Gray and S. Webb (eds), *Social Work Theories and Methods*, London, Sage Publications.

Gray, M., Stepney, P. and Webb, S. A. (2012) 'Critical social work', in P. Stepney and D. Ford (eds), *Social Work Models, Methods and Theories: A Framework for Practice*, 2nd edn, Lyme Regis, Russell House Publishing.

Harlow, E., Berg, E., Barry, J. and Chandler, J. (2012) 'Neoliberalism, managerialism and the reconfiguring of social work in Sweden and the United Kingdom', Organization *Advance Access published June 25, 2012, 10.177/1350508412448222.*

Harrison, D. (2009) 'Social work's evolution in the United Kingdom: A study of community care and social control', *Families in Society*, **90**(3), pp. 336–42.

Healy, K. (2000) *Social Work Practices: Contemporary Perspectives on Change*, London, Sage Publications.

Healy, K. (2005) *Social Work Theories in Context*, Basingstoke, Palgrave Macmillan.

Healy, K. (2012) *Social Work Methods and Skills*, Basingstoke, Palgrave Macmillan.

Heenan, D. (2004) 'Learning lessons from the past or re-visiting old mistakes: Social work and community development in Northern Ireland', *British Journal of Social Work*, **34**(6), pp. 793–809.

Houston, S., Skehill, C., Pinkerton, J. and Campbell, J. (2005) 'Prying open the space for social work in the new millenium: Four theoretical perspectives on transformative practice', *Social Work and Social Sciences Review*, **12**(1), pp. 35–52.

Humphries, B. (2008) *Social Work Research for Social Justice*, Basingstoke, Palgrave Macmillan.

Ife, J. (1998) *Rethinking Social Work: Towards Critical Practice*, South Melbourne, Longman.

Ife, J. (2008) 'Comment on John Solas: "What are we fighting for?"', *Australian Social Work*, **61**(2), pp. 137–40.

Ingamells, A., Lathouras, A., Wiseman, R., Westoby, P. and Caniglia, F. (2010) *Community Development Practice: Stories, Method and Meaning*, Melbourne, Common Ground Publishing Pty Ltd.

International Federation of Social Workers (2000) *Definition of Social Work*, available online at *www.ifsw.org/f38000138.html.*

Jones, M. (2012) 'Research minded practice in social work', in P. Stepney and D. Ford (eds), *Social Work Models, Methods and Theories: A Framework for Practice*, 2nd edn, Dorset, Russell House Publishing.

Kenny, S. (2011) *Developing Communities for the Future*, 4th edn, South Melbourne, Cengage Learning Australia.

Kirby, P. and Murphy, M. P. (2011) *Towards A Second Republic: Irish Politics after the Celtic Tiger*, London, Pluto Press.

Ledwith, M. (2005) *Community Development: A Critical Approach*, Bristol, Policy Press.

Ledwith, M. and Springett, J. (2010) *Participatory Practice: Community-Based Action for Transformative Change*, Bristol, Policy Press.

Lister, R. (2011) 'The age of responsibility: Social policy and citizenship in the 21st century', in C. Holden, M. Kilkey and G. Ramia (eds), *Social Policy Review 23: Analysis and Debate in Social Policy, 2011*, Bristol, The Policy Press.

Lloyd, A. (2010) 'The will of the state and the resilience of the community sector in a time of crisis: Obliteration, compliance or an opportunity for renewal?', *Working for Change: The Irish Journal of Community Work*, **2**, pp. 44–63.

Lloyd-Hughes, J. (2010) 'Relevance and redundancy: The contribution and discarding of community development projects in Tallaght', *Working for Change: The Irish Journal of Community Work*, **2**, pp. 102–8.

Lymbery, M. (2012) 'Social work and personalisation', *British Journal of Social Work*, **42**(4), pp. 783–92.

Lynch, D. and Forde, C. (2006) 'Social work within a community discourse: Challenges for teaching', *Social Work Education*, **25**(8), pp. 851–62.

Mantle, G. and Backwith, D. (2010) 'Poverty and social work', *British Journal of Social Work*, **40**(8), pp. 2380–97.

Marston, G. and McDonald, C. (2012) 'Getting beyond "heroic agency" in conceptualising social workers as policy actors in the twenty-first century', *British Journal of Social Work*, **42**(6), pp. 1022–38.

Martin, D. G., Hanson, S. and Fontaine, D. (2007) 'What counts as activism? The role of individuals in creating change', *Women's Studies Quarterly*, **35(3/4)**, pp. 78–94.

Mayo, M. (2005) *Global Citizens: Social Movements and the Challenge of Globalization*, London, Zed Books.

Mendes, P. (2007) 'Social workers and social activism in Victoria, Australia', *Journal of Progressive Human Services*, **18**(1), pp. 25–44.

Mendes, P. (2008) 'Integrating social work and community—development practice in Victoria, Australia', *Asia Pacific Journal of Social Work and Development*, **18**(1), pp. 14–25.

Mertens, D. M. (2009) *Transformative Research and Evaluation*, New York, The Guildford Press.

Munro, E. (2011) *The Munro Review of Child Protection: Final Report: A Child-Centred System*, London, Department of Education.

National Social Work Qualifications Board (2006) *Social Work Posts in Ireland*, Report No. 3, Dublin, NSWQB.

Nixon, S. and Murr, A. (2006) 'Practice learning and the development of professional practice', *Social Work Education*, **25**(8), pp. 798–811.

Norris, P. (2003) 'Young people and political activism: From the politics of loyalty to the politics of choice?', Keynote to the Council of Europe Symposium on Young People and Activism, Strasbourg, 27–28 November.

O'Brien, C. (2012) 'Social work and the media in Ireland: A journalist's perspective', in D. Lynch and K. Burns (eds), *Children's Right and Child Protection: Critical Times, Critical Issues*, Manchester, Manchester University Press.

Parton, N. (2011) 'The Munro Review of child protection: An appraisal', *Children and Society*, **26**(2), pp. 150–62.

Powell, F. and Geoghegan, M. (2007) 'Active citizenship, civil society and the "enabling" state: Political myth or democratic reality?', *Administration*, **55**(3), pp. 31–50.

Ryan, S. (2009) *Commission to Inquire into Child Abuse Report (Volumes I–V)*, Dublin, Stationery Office.

Sarantakos, S. (2005) *Social Research*, 3rd edn, Basingstoke, Palgrave Macmillan.

Shevellar, L. (2011) '"We have to go back to stories": Causal layered analysis and the community development gateaux', *Community Development*, **42**(1), pp. 3–15.

Skehill, C. (1999) *The Nature of Social Work in Ireland: A Historical Perspective*, Credigion, Edwin Mellen Press.

Stepney, P. (2006) 'Mission impossible? Critical practice in social work', *British Journal of Social Work*, **36**(8), pp. 1289–307.

Stepney, P. and Ford, D. (2012) 'Introduction to the second edition', in P. Stepney and D. Ford (eds), *Social Work Models, Methods and Theories: A Framework for Practice*, 2nd edn, Dorset, Russell House Publishing.

Stepney, P. and Popple, K. (2008) *Social Work and the Community: A Critical Context for Practice*, Basingstoke, Palgrave Macmillan.

Szreter, S. and Ishkanian, A. (2011) 'Introduction: What is Big Society? Contemporary social policy in a historical and comparative perspective', in Ishkanian, A. and Szreter, S. (eds), *The Big Society Debate: A New Agenda for Social Policy*, Cheltenham, Edward Elgar Publishing Ltd.

Taylor, I. and Rafferty, J. (2003) 'Integrating research and teaching in social work: Building a strong partnership', *Social Work Education*, **22**(6), pp. 589–602.

Teater, B. and Baldwin, M. (2012) *Social Work in the Community: Making a Difference*, Bristol, Policy Press.

Weller, G. (2010) 'Civil society in Ireland: Antecedents, identity and challenges', in J. Hogan, P. F. Donnelly and B. K. O'Rourke (eds), *Irish Business and Society: Governing, Participating and Transforming in the 21st Century*, Dublin, Gill and Macmillan.

Strengthening the Link: Social Work with Immigrants and Refugees and International Social Work

Lynne M. Healy

SUMMARY. Through exploration of definitional issues and current migration realities, this article discusses ways in which emphasis on the international dimensions of social work with immigrants and refugees offers opportunities to improve practice and to enhance the relevance of international social work to the profession. The international character of present day migration is illustrated through discussion of the transnational family and the economic and other relationships that tie immigrants to their countries of origin. The paper concludes with recommendations for increased cross-national professional collaboration. *[Article copies available for a fee from The Haworth Document Delivery Service: 1-800-HAWORTH. E-mail address: <docdelivery@haworthpress.com> Website: <http://www.HaworthPress.com> © 2004 by The Haworth Press, Inc. All rights reserved.]*

KEYWORDS. International social work, transnationals, immigrants, immigration, remittances

---

Lynne M. Healy, PhD, is Director, Center for International Social Work Studies, and Professor, School of Social Work, University of Connecticut.

[Haworth co-indexing entry note]: "Strengthening the Link: Social Work with Immigrants and Refugees and International Social Work." Healy, Lynne M. Co-published simultaneously in *Journal of Immigrant & Refugee Services* (The Haworth Social Work Practice Press, an imprint of The Haworth Press) Vol. 2, No. 1/2, 2004, pp. 49-67; and: *Immigrants and Social Work: Thinking Beyond the Borders of the United States* (ed: Diane Drachman, and Ana Paulino) The Haworth Social Work Practice Press, an imprint of The Haworth Press, Inc., 2001, pp. 49-67. Single or multiple copies of this article are available for a fee from The Haworth Document Delivery Service [1-800-HAWORTH, 9:00 a.m. - 5:00 p.m. (EST). E-mail address: docdelivery@haworthpress.com].

http://www.haworthpress.com/web/JIRS

Digital Object Identifier: 10.1300/J191v02n01_04

From its earliest conceptualizations, international social work has been intertwined with issues of migration and social work with immigrant and refugee populations. This paper will explore the commonalities, linkages and definitional tensions between the fields of social work with immigrants and refugees and international social work. Both historical and contemporary definitions and issues will be explored. I will argue that emphasis on the international dimensions of social work with immigrants and refugees offers opportunities to improve practice with these groups while enhancing the relevance of international social work to the social work profession.

Definitional issues will be addressed in detail, beginning with an examination of the history of the concept of international social work and its links to migration issues. To illustrate the international character of present day social work migration practice, the paper will discuss the growth in the phenomenon of the permanently transnational family; transnationalism will be further illustrated through a discussion of remittances–the economic transfers made to family members abroad–and a brief consideration of the global context of immigration policy. The paper will close with a recommendation for increased cross-national professional collaboration between sending and receiving countries to improve migration practice in the context of an uncertain future.

DEFINITIONS OF INTERNATIONAL SOCIAL WORK

Definitions in Historical Perspective

The international character of practice with immigrants was recognized early in the history of social work. In a call for more social service involvement in migration research, a committee chaired by Edith Abbott reported: "It (the field of human migration) includes large questions of public policy, involving issues of national prosperity and human rights . . . It presents problems that reach beyond the frontiers of any one nation, and many of its research problems are of international importance and demand international co-operation for their solution" (Human Migration as a Field of Research, 1927, p. 258). The need for knowledge and skill in international casework to serve migrants was discussed at the First International Conference of Social Work, held in Paris in 1928. The presenter drew attention to the "lack of understanding of the international aspects of these problems" (deBacourt, 1929, p. 426). A few years later, it was described in an article in the 3rd edition of the

U.S. *Social Work Yearbook*: "international social casework problems arise in public and private welfare agencies because of the migration of individuals and families to and from the United States" (Warren, 1935, p. 214). Beginning in the next volume of the *Yearbook* in 1937, international casework was subsumed under the definition of international social work as one of three types of activity making up this field of practice: international social casework, international conferences on social work, and international efforts to address problems in the fields of health, labor and protection of women and children (Warren, 1937), a definition later expanded to include other types of international assistance (Warren, 1939).

Recognition of the complexities of problems faced by immigrant families and the concomitant need for broad international knowledge on the part of practitioners were evident in these early articles, as the following example illustrates: The family problems presented are associated with or grow out of the experience of migration, often many years later. All members of a family rarely migrate together. The father or husband generally precedes the other members of the family. Families are thus separated for temporary or longer periods of time. Restrictive immigration and naturalization laws and the act of migration itself interrupt the natural rhythm of family life. Civil and social rights and the benefits of social institutions are unavailable for migrant families during the period of alienage until citizenship in the country of immigration is secured by all members of the family. Deficiencies in civil status thus combine with the handicaps of foreignness and the environmental and personal hazards of family life to present problems for international social case work service (Warren, 1941, p. 271).Warren continues on to discuss the need for information about the cultural backgrounds of the countries from which migrants originate in order to provide adequate services in child welfare, hospitals, the criminal justice system, and other institutions. Thus, in the early part of the 20th century, social work experts recognized the important international dimensions of practice with immigrants and refugees including differences in national cultures, human rights, family separation across borders, immigration laws and foreign policies. Furthermore, knowledge in these areas was recognized as important for social workers in mainstream practice in child welfare, health care, and criminal justice, not just for immigration specialists.

The need for international knowledge in service to refugee and migrant families became even more evident during World War II as large numbers of persons were displaced. In her article on international social work, Larned explained: "Local case workers were baffled because these situations had roots in two or more countries and were complicated not only by distance and separation of families, but also by differences in cultural backgrounds and attitudes of the individuals concerned, differences in national laws affecting family relationships and citizenship, and differences in the concepts of social care" (1945, p. 191).

Throughout the 1920s, 1930s and 1940s, then, social work recognized the special knowledge and practice demands of work with international migrants and often conceptualized this practice as a component of international social work. While a detailed account of shifts in conceptualization of international social work is not warranted here, in brief, changes were evident beginning in the 1950s. A study undertaken in the mid-1950s by a working committee of the Council on Social Work Education stands out. After reviewing multiple definitions of the term international social work including those that addressed work with refugees and immigrants, the Committee broke away from the Warren and Larned definitions and opted for a very narrow definition of international social work focusing on work for intergovernmental or international agencies (Stein, 1957). In the words of the Committee report: "It was the consensus of our sub-committee that the term 'international social work' should properly be confined to programs of social work of international scope, such as those carried on by intergovernmental agencies, chiefly those of the U.N.; governmental; or nongovernmental agencies with international programs" (Stein, 1957, p. 3). This was followed in the 1970s and 1980s by relative isolationism within the profession in North America before a resurgence of interest in internationalism in the 1990s (Healy, 1995; Healy, 1999).

While many factors have contributed to the resurgence of interest in international social work, it is likely that the expansion of international migration and the growth of the foreign born population in the U.S. and many other countries are particularly significant. In the United States, for example, the 1930 census revealed that 11.3% of the population was foreign born and that the foreign born together with their children comprised almost one-third of the total population (Warren, 1935). After several decades of steep decline, the foreign born proportion of the population has again grown to 10.4% as of 2000, close to the 11.3% level of 1930. The growth of immigrant and refugee populations has had a worldwide impact. Guest workers from Southern Europe and North Africa have become long term residents in Northern Europe at the same time that refugee populations have increased, turning previously homogenous countries such as Denmark and Sweden into multicultural ones.

Imported laborers work in many of the Gulf States and in countries such as Cote d'Ivoire that hosts as many as 2 million workers from neighboring Burkina Faso (U.S. Department of State, 2001). Developing countries, too, experience the impact of refugee flows; while refugee resettlement programs in Europe and North America draw considerable attention, most of the world's refugees flee to neighboring countries. In 1996, for example, there were almost 2 million refugees from tiny Rwanda in the neighboring countries of Zaire (now Congo), Burundi, Tanzania and Uganda (UNDP, 1996); the recent flow of Afghan refugees to Pakistan is actually a continuation of a long-term refugee problem in the area. Thus, at the beginning of the 21st century, many if not most countries of the world are faced with significant international populations within their borders. Shifts in the size and diversity of foreign born populations may well shape the conceptualization of both international social work and social work with immigrants and refugees.

Contemporary Definitional Issues

Contemporary dictionary definition of the term "international" supports a link to service to refugees and immigrants. According to the *Random House Webster's College Dictionary* (1995), international can refer to any of the following: "between or among two or more nations, . . . of or pertaining to two or more nations or their citizens, . . . pertaining to the relations between nations, . . . having members or activities in several nations, . . . transcending national boundaries or viewpoints" (p. 704). Work with immigrants clearly pertains to the citizens of two or more nations, and the field of immigration practice and policy indeed transcends national boundaries.

Building on this, a recent action-focused definition of international social work, identified the first of four components of the field as "social work competence in internationally related aspects of domestic social work practice and professional advocacy" (Healy, 2001, p. 7). While there are other aspects of internationally related domestic practice, it is the international movement of people that has changed social agency caseloads and affected social work practice in many countries, especially the United States. Therefore work with international migrant populations is the most important component of internationally related domestic practice.

Some contemporary writers disagree with the inclusion of work with international populations under the international social work umbrella.

Nagy and Falk (2000) suggest that although "some definitions of international social work appear to include social work practice with immigrants, refugees or ethnic minorities, in the social worker's own country" (p. 53) this type of practice should "be distinguished from social work across national borders" (p. 53). They argue that the emphasis in practice with refugees and immigrants should be on inter-cultural or multicultural practice, rather than on international social work. This author agrees that the multicultural perspective has dominated recent social work practice with immigrants and refugees in the U.S., but to its detriment. The result has been diminished application of relevant international knowledge and understanding to provision of services to immigrants and refugees and severely limited capacity to engage in successful policy advocacy on migration issues.

Two important elements differentiate social work with immigrants and refugees from multicultural work with domestic minority groups. The first and most critical is the migration experience. As clearly described by Drachman (1992), effective social work with immigrants and refugees requires knowledge of their country of origin experiences, the factors that led to the decision to migrate, their transit experiences, and resettlement. These fall primarily in the arena of international knowledge. Phases of the process are governed by a complex set of national and international laws on refugee movements, resettlement, entitlements and immigration, by the foreign policies of the nations involved, and by international policy on human rights.

The second element is the ongoing transnational nature of the migration phenomenon. At the micro level, this is reflected in the transnational family; families of many if not most immigrants are now transnational families in that members and relationships span borders throughout the family life cycle. A recent obituary in the Hartford *Courant* illustrates a not unusual case: the deceased was born in rural Jamaica and had lived in the U.S. in both Connecticut and Florida. He left 5 siblings, two in England, one in the U.S., and two in Jamaica. His seven children reside in Canada, the U.S. and Jamaica (April 26, 2001). One can imagine the life of this family and the frequent exchange of communications, money and people across the borders of four countries. In these exchanges, the family would have been touched by laws and economic policies of multiple countries and perhaps, of international organizations. Social workers involved with transnational families face many knowledge demands beyond those of cross-cultural or multicultural social work. Transnationalism also has significant effects at the macro level of national economic development policy and foreign affairs. Understanding the transnational relationships that affect and are affected by migration equips social work to improve practice and to engage in appropriate policy advocacy. These points will be elaborated below.

THE TRANSNATIONAL FAMILY: THE NEW FACE OF INTERNATIONAL MIGRATION

Family Relationships

Increasingly, immigrants are part of families that remain transnational. In some, family members are separated for long periods of time or even permanently by international migration. Others may live simultaneously in two countries, traveling back and forth between employment and family, without or without legal sanction. Still others, long resettled, plan to return some day to their country of origin, and prepare for another round of leaving, transit and resettlement–perhaps creating new family separations in the process.

In each of these situations, family members maintain relationships through communications, exchange of money and goods across borders, and sometimes, visitation and plans for additional family members to immigrate or emigrate. Issues of custody, divorce, support and child visitation are more complicated when parties live in different countries, creating special challenges for social workers. There is a specialized agency, International Social Service, that provides intercountry casework services for cross-national permanency planning, custody evaluations, counseling on inter-country marriages and divorces, tracing of separated family members, child support, and inter-country adoption in 75 countries (see www.iss-ssi.org for more information). However, it serves a relatively small percent of intercountry cases. Most are left to social workers in local immigrant and refugee service agencies and to mainstream social workers in child welfare services, schools, hospitals, and mental health agencies; these workers usually lack specialized training in intercountry work and may fail to recognize the international dimensions of their clients' problems.

More common than intercountry custody, divorce and visitation are the issues raised by family reunification following long periods of separation for social workers in receiving countries while social workers in sending countries deal with the impact of long separations on children. A common pattern of immigration is for a parent to immigrate first, leaving minor children in the care of spouse, grandparents, or others in the home country. Those left behind are sent for once the parent is financially secure and immigration regulations have been satisfied. By then, the period of separation may have stretched to three to five years or even more. Meanwhile, social workers in the sending countries must deal with children who feel abandoned, who are sometimes left in unsatisfactory care situations, and who may lose their motivation for school and other activities as they wait for what they believe will be imminent emigration. In the receiving countries, social workers encounter children and parents who struggle to build relationships after years of separation and often, very little personal communication, while the newly arrived cope with their new environment. That reunification often happens in the early teen years further complicates family adjustment.

Crawford-Brown and Rattray (2001) described a difficult set of cases which they labeled "barrel children." It is common for immigrants from the Caribbean to send home goods to family members, commonly shipping them in barrels. Some of these goods go to the children left behind, usually with relatives. Crawford-Brown, however, documented that some teenage children are left on their own by emigrating parents; the parents send barrels of goods for the children to sell to support themselves. The negative side of the story is of course that children are sometimes physically and emotionally abandoned through immigration, with parents retaining only the role of financial support. Financial support of children and other relatives is, on the other hand, a dominant factor in the transnational phenomenon of migration, as will be addressed in detail below. The issue of remittances has been selected as an example to demonstrate the international dimension of migration at the micro and macro levels, and its impact on social work.

Remittances: Transnational Family Economics

The transnational character of immigration and its impact at family and national levels is clearly demonstrated by remittances–money sent back to family members in the home country by migrants abroad. As described in a recent report by the Inter-American Development Bank, "as the scale of migration has increased in recent years and the growth of remittances has accelerated dramatically, the social and economic impact of this phenomenon now transcends family relationships and is drawing national and international attention" (2001, p. 4). The report estimates that immigrants in North America sent $20 billion dollars to their home countries in Latin America and the Caribbean alone in 2000 (IADB, 2001, p. 6). This represents the accumulation of millions of individual transactions, with the typical migrant sending home about $250 at a time, eight to ten times a year (IADB, p. 6). The reader is reminded that these figures only address the Western hemisphere; globally, the total flow of remittances was estimated at over $71 billion in 1990, a figure that has undoubtedly grown since then (Meyers, 1998).

At the macro level, it is now recognized that remittances are essential to the receiving economies. In Jamaica, the value of remittances is second only to tourism as a source of foreign exchange (PIOJ,1999) and is 35 times more than the amount of foreign aid received (IADB, 2001). Thus, many Jamaicans look to their relatives abroad to help make ends meet; the money received and spent undoubtedly does more to aid the local economy than foreign aid. The significant economic impact is not limited to Jamaica. In five other countries in the region, remittances account for 10% or more of the Gross Domestic Product (GDP): Haiti, Nicaragua, El Salvador, the Dominican Republic and Ecuador (IADB, p. 6). So important are the impacts of these individual efforts combined that they are recognized parts of some countries' foreign policy efforts. One scholar notes that in a recent visit to the U.S. by the President of El Salvador, he requested an increased number of work permits for Salvadoran immigrants to enter or remain in the U.S. in order to help rebuild El Salvador after several natural disasters as "the increased earnings that legally authorized workers could remit would far outweigh the likely foreign aid that would be forthcoming" (Martin, 2001, p. 4). As a final example, Mexico, with an estimated eight million native born Mexicans now residing in the U.S., is the single largest recipient of remittances in Latin America, receiving almost $7 billion in 1999, almost equaling the amount earned from tourism (IADB, 2001).

Emigration clearly has some negative effects on developing countries as it is often the skilled workers who are most likely to leave ("Emigration: Outward Bound," 2002). Understanding the role of remittances clarifies why sending countries may have an interest in maintaining high levels of emigration nonetheless. Emigration is an outlet for areas with high unemployment and limited income-generating possibilities; the remittances received from those who leave represent a significant force in their home country economies, aiding family survival at the micro level, providing at least consumer-level economic stimulus, and assisting with balance of payments at the macro level. A recent study of coping strategies of minimum wage workers in Jamaica showed that "the main support for all groups came from relatives and friends living overseas" (Henry-Lee, Chevannes, Clarke and Ricketts, 2000, p. 26);

47% of domestic helpers, 78% of free zone workers, and 64% of security guards received money from relatives or friends who live abroad.

While remittances tend to subside after one or two generations of immigrants, the new realities of global interdependence and increased transnationalism strengthen the ties of immigrants to their home communities and may lengthen the period of remittances. Martin notes that the increase in transnationalism is due in part to "the transportation and communications revolution that makes it easier to move and keep contact with one's home community"; "migrants can now live at one and the same time in two different countries" by maintaining constant contact, visits, and sending resources home (2001, p. 2).

The practice of remittances obviously has a significant impact on immigrant families in their new country of residence. Social workers need to be aware of this often hidden financial obligation assumed by immigrant families. Both the policy and personal impacts remain under-studied. Martin points out that while remittances obviously benefit poor families in developing countries, "it means that the poorest residents of the U.S. and other wealthy countries are bearing the brunt of assisting people in developing countries. Latin American migrants tend to have low incomes, often living in poverty, yet they remit billions of dollars to their home countries" (2001, p. 5). Client immigrant families may make decisions that puzzle their social worker–for example, not pursuing advanced training or working multiple jobs, seemingly failing to fulfill some family responsibilities such as spending time with their children. During the resettlement phase of work with refugees, their sense of obligation to send remittances to their home country conflicts with the priority on rapid self-sufficiency in resettlement policy, posing a dilemma for social work. A resettlement worker recounted a case in which a man from the Northern Sudan, being resettled in South Dakota, was sending money home to his wife in Sudan, although he did not have enough to pay his bills or even buy adequate food for himself. In keeping with agency and indeed national policy, the social worker repeatedly told him not to send money home until he was fully self-sufficient. Unless the social worker has knowledge of the international picture of immigration, he or she is likely to have an incomplete understanding of family responsibilities as viewed by the immigrant–and indeed, by his or her country of origin. Thus, the international perspective that transcends national boundaries and points of view is important.

IMMIGRATION POLICY: TRANSCENDING NATIONAL BOUNDARIES

Immigration policy is inherently international policy, emanating from broad agreements of international law and refined by each nation's foreign policy imperatives. Social workers' ability to help immigrants and refugees is aided or, more often, constrained by these official global and foreign policies. Understanding of immigration and refugee policy is necessary to properly advise clients on procedures and entitlements and to allow social workers to advocate for more humane and family-oriented immigration policies in their own country and globally.

At the global level, the right to emigrate–to leave one's country–is viewed as an important human right. Article 13 of the Universal Declaration of Human Rights states: "Everyone has the right to leave any country, including his own, and to return to his country" (1948). However, no corresponding right to enter or immigrate is recognized in international law. Other than the protections for officially recognized refugees, this policy mismatch leaves those who wish to emigrate in an insecure position. Refugee policy, too, begins with the internationally recognized definition of a refugee and official recognition of status by the United Nations High Commission on Refugees. Individual country decisions to grant refugee status are governed at least as much by foreign policy as by humanitarian concerns.

The inherent unfairness of immigration policies is troubling to many social workers and others. Indeed, Isbister wrote that in various ways, immigration policy is "inherently immoral" (1996, p. 229). The recent deportation provisions in U.S. Immigration law provide an example of policy of questionable morality and significant international impact. The 1996 Illegal Immigration Reform and Immigrant Responsibility Act and the Anti-Terrorism and Effective Death Penalty Act contained draconian deportation provisions that have had significant national and international impact at both family and societal levels. These acts: increased the number of deportable offenses to include family violence offenses and some fairly minor crimes by reclassifying them retroactively as felonies; called for deportation for offenses committed 20 or more years ago, even if when committed the offense would not have qualified as a felony; and completely eliminated the appeals process (Ward, 1999). Furthermore, those deported are permanently barred from the United States. Deportations have soared since the laws went into effect (Rich, 2000).

In countries of origin that have received increased numbers of deportees since 1996, these have been of two types. Migrants convicted of serious drug and violent offenses were deported home often without warning to officials, unleashing a wave of crime in their home countries (Maxwell, 1990; Guyana Online, 2001). When governments protested, their protests were largely ignored. The U.S. government recently halted issuing visas for citizens of Guyana to retaliate against the Guyana government for refusing to accept criminal deportees, demonstrating again that immigration policy is critical bi-national foreign policy (Guyana Online, 2001). The other type of deportees are those who have committed minor offenses, perhaps years ago when they were young; these deportees may have emigrated at an early age and have few current ties in their home country and therefore no means of support. "Because most of them have lived almost all their adult lives in North America and are more the products of those societies than they are of Guyana, they are in a very real sense strangers in the land of their birth" (Guyana Online, 2001). Obviously, remittances from those deported cease, affecting their families as well. Thus, countries with very limited resources for law enforcement and high rates of unemployment and poverty are forced or pressured to accept back criminal emigres and others with no prospects for jobs or income.

The domestic impact in the U.S. has also been severe. Marital partners have been separated by sudden deportation, and parents have been separated from their U.S. citizen children, sometimes leaving families with no means of support and children without parental supervision (Hedges, 2001). As the law calls for no appeal and permanent ban from reentering the U.S., the separation is permanent unless the children move to their parent's country of origin. Both the personal and fiscal impact of these policies has been locally and internationally harmful.

Social work responsibilities in this arena begin with adequate knowledge of immigration policy in order to avoid doing harm. In some cases, well-meaning social workers advised clients to seek citizenship to remain eligible for the entitlements that were cut off for legal immigrants in another of the 1996 policies. Unfortunately, it was during citizenship application processes that many of the deportees were "uncovered" as prior offenders. Secondly, the professional needs knowledge of the global interactions of immigration policy in order to formulate sound campaigns for reform, both nationally and cross-nationally. These obligations are recognized in the NASW policy statement on Immigrants and Refugees that reads, in part: "Social workers must continue to advocate for family reunification and sanctuary from persecution and insist that due process and fundamental human rights be upheld for immigrants and refugees. The profession must promote greater education and awareness at all levels of the dynamics of U.S. and other countries' foreign policies on immigration and refugee resettlement" (NASW, 2000, p. 176).

PROSPECTS FOR THE FUTURE

International Collaboration in Immigrant Work

Conceptualizing work with immigrants and refugees as international social work and accepting the need for international knowledge can lead to more than an understanding of the transnational family and the global policy context. It may also open up new avenues for intervention. There is considerable untapped potential for international collaboration in social work. Cross-national social work collaboration to smooth the immigration and resettlement processes would be an excellent place to begin such efforts. This is especially true in those areas which receive steady influx of immigrants from particular countries. Working together, social workers in the sending and receiving countries could develop interventions to assist in the leaving and resettlement processes. The process could begin with information sharing about the needs and problems experienced on both sides of the immigration journey. Information about schools, expectations, and other living conditions in the destination areas could be sent to social workers in the countries where children wait to join their parents. One social worker proposed making a video-tape showing school and typical home life, with brief interviews of immigrant children. Social workers in source countries would use such a tape in groups for "children in waiting." Social workers in immigrant-receiving areas might use their knowledge of immigration patterns and children's needs coupled with insights gained through communication with colleagues in the sending country to reach out to immigrants and offer pre-reunification counseling or information sessions to advise parents on the need to stay in personal and emotional contact with their children and to prepare them to cope with the usually unanticipated stresses of reunification (Crawford-Brown and Rattrey, 2001).

Cross-national communication between social workers on a continuing basis could provide cross-cultural consultation to assist social workers in serving immigrant families and meeting the special needs of the transnational family. Finally, such collaborations can be of particular benefit in resolving those cases requiring inter-country casework, such as custody issues, child placement in cases of parental death, deportation, or other causes; preparation for return migration of elders, and other cases involving bi-national legal/social service matters.

The ease of email communications and the possibilities offered by video and web-based technologies for information exchange, outreach and education should not be underestimated.

Post-September 11 Trends in International Aspects of Migration

The aftermath of the terrorist attacks on the U.S. mainland in September, 2001 make long term projections about immigration and about professional and societal openness to emphasis on its international dimensions difficult, not only in the U.S. but in many other countries. Some of the changes anticipated will affect social work practice with immigrants and refugees; most will certainly increase the need for international understanding. Early indications are that many countries are slowing the issuing of visas and exploring ways to protect their borders from terrorists, actions that may impede normal immigration and complicate the lives of members of transnational families (Keep America's Gates Open, 2001; Government of Canada, 2001). These changes are likely to mean slower reunifications and restrictions on visitation of family members who remain separated. Deportations may also increase, with Middle Eastern immigrants a special target. In the U.S., several areas of immigration policy relief have been shelved, most notably the proposal to regularize some undocumented immigrants from Mexico and others to provide relief from deportation provisions of the 1996 laws (Brownstein, 2001; Pena, 2001).

A retreat to isolationism, however, does not look likely. Instead, the events heightened awareness of the need for international knowledge and understanding. Most writers also believe that any downturn in immigration rates will be temporary. The pressures creating high emigration from source countries continue to be strong. In fact, the economic fallout from the September 11 events have increased the push factors for immigration through their negative impact on the economies of developing countries. According to the World Bank, "ripples from the September 11 attacks will be felt across all the world's regions, particularly in countries dependent on tourism, remittances from populations living overseas, and foreign investment" ("Poverty to Rise . . ." 2001, p. 2). The travel and tourism industry has been particularly hit hard; thus in Jamaica, for example, where pre-September 11th unemployment rate was

16% (Thomas, 2001) unemployment in the tourist sector and businesses that supply the tourist sector is soaring as reservations are cancelled. In St. Lucia, the drop in tourist reservations for winter 2002 was so severe that the Club Med resort decided not to open for the season (Ballve, 2002). Overall, the World Bank reported that 65% of vacations booked for the Caribbean had been cancelled as of October 1, 2001. The impact on these economies that rely on tourism as their chief source of revenue has been devastating. The World Bank further estimated that as a result of the terrorist attacks, 10 million more people in developing countries could be pushed below the poverty line of $1 per day ("Poverty to Rise" 2001). Coupled with possible reductions in remittances that have cushioned the effects of poor local economic opportunities, pressures for emigration are high ("Latin American migrants in the United States sending less money home," 2001). Thus, understood in its global context, the aftermath of September 11 terrorist attacks has created both increased pressures for high immigration as economic opportunities diminish in countries of origin and increased resistance to the admittance of immigrants in many countries of destination. The long term impact may well be increases in immigration by those economically dislocated by these events–possibly through extra-legal channels. In an earlier document, the government of Jamaica explained: "Given that the pressures for emigration are high in Jamaica, especially since our labour force continues to increase, undocumented or irregular migration is expected to continue" (Planning Institute of Jamaica, 1995, p. 44).

CONCLUSION: IS SOCIAL WORK WITH IMMIGRANTS AND REFUGEES INTERNATIONAL SOCIAL WORK?

In conclusion, a return to the original question of the paper is in order. First, it may be useful to remember the insights of our professional "ancestors" who recognized the links between local and global events and the human rights and civil liberties elements of migration that are so relevant today. But, regardless of the historical links between migration practice and international social work, contemporary social work should renew the emphasis only if there is clear benefit to one or both knowledge areas. For international social work, work with immigrants and refugee populations provides the clearest and most concrete example of the necessity and applicability of international knowledge to social work. It makes the importance of international knowledge understandable in any society affected by international migration–a near universal phenomenon at the beginning of the 21st century. In countries with high levels of immigration or emigration, this inclusion also extends to all social workers the imperative for international knowledge. Rather than an esoteric specialty of a few, international knowledge is essential for competent social work in a country where one in ten inhabitants is an immigrant. The transnational family makes this as essential in countries with high rates of emigration. Furthermore, inclusion of practice with immigrants within international social work demonstrates the links between domestic and global issues, lending support to the argument that there is no such thing as purely domestic/local social work in the 21st century. Thus, development of the field of international social work is strengthened through linking it to practice with immigrants and refugees.

The benefits to the field of social work with immigrants and refugees may be more compelling and hopefully have been addressed in the preceding pages. Inclusion of international knowledge in practice with immigrants and refugees should improve practice by equipping social workers to understand the pre-migration, migration and resettlement phases of their clients' journeys (Drachman,1992) and preparing them to work with the ongoing transnational family issues faced by their clients. Only through knowledge of the international dimensions of immigration can social workers address the policy issues of work with migrants, including the impacts on sending countries. Finally, recognition of the international nature of immigration work may unleash the largely unexplored potential of cross-national collegial work to improve service to migrant populations.

Therefore, as stated by NASW, "social workers must give consideration to the global dynamic of immigration" (2000, p. 175). In recognizing the important linkages between international social work and social work with immigrants and refugees, both areas of social work will be strengthened.

REFERENCES

Ballve, M. (2002). Hotels Empty, Workers Idle. *Hartford Courant.* January 5, pp. E1, E8.

Brownstein, R. (2001). Green light, red light: Is the push to liberalize immigration policy a casualty of the surprise terrorist attacks on September 11? *The American Prospect.* 12:20, pp. 28- (obtained full text through InfoTrac).

Crawford-Brown, C.P.J. and Rattray, J.M. (2001). "Parent Child Relationships in Caribbean Families" in N. Boyd Webb (ed.) *Culturally Diverse Parent-Child and Family Relationships*. New York: Columbia University Press, pp. 107-32.

Debacourt, F. (1929). The need for international case work for migrants. in *Proceedings of the First International Conference of Social Work 1928*. Volume 2, Paris, International Conference of Social Work, pp. 416-432.

Drachman, D. (1992). A stage-of-migration framework for service to immigrant populations. *Social Work*. 37:1, 68-72.

"Emigration: Outward Bound" (2002). *The Economist*, Vol. 364, Number 8292 (September 26-October 4, 2002), pp. 24-26.

Government of Canada. (2001). Strengthened immigration measures to counter terrorism. News release, October 12, 2001. www.cic.gc.ca/english/press/01/0119-pre.html Accessed Jan. 4, 2002.

Guyana Online. (2001), Meeting public concerns over the deportee influx. 11/21/01. <www.guyanaonline.net/c-news/index> Accessed January 16, 2002.

Healy, L. (2001). *International Social Work: Professional Action in an Interdependent World*. New York: Oxford University Press.

Healy, L. (1999). International social work curriculum in historical perspective. in C.S. Ramanathan and R.J. Link, *All Our Futures: Principles and Resources for Social Work Practice in a Global Era*. Belmont, CA: Brooks/Cole, pp. 14-29.

Healy, L. (1995). Comparative and international overview. in T.D. Watts, D. Elliott, and N.S. Mayadas (Eds). *International handbook on social work education*. Westport, CT: Greenwood Press, pp. 421-439.

Hedges, C. (2001). Spousal deportation, Family ruin as breadwinners are exiled. *The New York Times*. January 10.

Henry-Lee, A., Chevannes, B., Clarke, M., and Ricketts, S. (2000). An assessment of the standard of living and coping strategies of workers in selected occupations who earn a minimum wage. Kingston, Jamaica: Policy Development Unit, Planning Institute of Jamaica.

Human migration as a field of research. (1927). *Social Service Review*. 1:2, 258-269.

Inter-American Development Bank (2001), Remittances to Latin America and the Caribbean: Comparative Statistics. Multilateral Investment Fund (May). accessed from www.iadb.org Accessed January 3, 2002.

International Social Service. (2002). Intercountry casework. <www.iss-ssi.org>. Accessed January 14, 2002.

Isbister, J. (1996). *The Immigration Debate: Remaking America*. West Hartford, CT: Kumarian Press.

Keep America's gates open, just watch them better. (2001). *Business Week*. Nov. 19, 13758. p. 72EU8. Obtained full text through InfoTrac OneFile.

Larned, R. (1945). International social work. in R.H. Kurz, ed., *Social Work Yearbook 1945*. New York: Russell Sage Foundation, 188-194.

Latin American migrants in the United States sending less money home in wake of September 11 attacks (2001). Press Release, December 17, 2001, Inter-American Development Bank. <www.iadb.org/exr/PRENSA/2001/cp23601E.htm>. Accessed January 8, 2002.

Martin, S.F. (2001). Remittance Flows and Impact. Paper prepared for the Remittances as a Development Tool Regional Conference, Inter-American Development Bank. Institute for the Study of International Migration, Georgetown University. www. iadb.org Accessed January 3, 2002.

Maxwell, J.A. (1990). Development of social welfare services and the field of social work in Jamaica. Paper presented at the Caribbean Conference for Social Workers, Paramaribo, Surinam.

Meyers, D.W. (1998). Migrant remittances to Latin America: Reviewing the literature. Working Paper: Inter-American Dialogue and the Tomas Rivera Policy Institute. May, 1998. Available at: www.iadialog.org/meyers.html Accessed January 7, 2002.

Nagy, G. and Falk, D. (2000). Dilemmas in international and cross-cultural social work education. *International Social Work*. 43:1, 49-60.

National Association of Social Workers (2000). Immigrants and refugees. in *Social Work Speaks*. Washington, D.C.: NASW Press, pp. 170-177.

Obituary. (2001) *The Hartford Courant*. Thursday, April 26, p. B6.

Pena, M. (2001). Immigration policy another victim of terrorist attacks. Agencia Efe S.A., Spain, September 17. Accessed through Comtext news (www.comtexnews. com) via InfoTrac.

Planning Institute of Jamaica (PIOJ). (1999). *Economic and Social Survey Jamaica 1998*. Kingston, Jamaica: author.

Planning Institute of Jamaica (PIOJ). (1995). *National Plan of Action on Population and Development Jamaica 1995-2015*. Kingston, Jamaica: Population Unit, PIOJ.

"Poverty to rise in wake of terrorist attacks in US." (2001, Oct. 1). *DevNews: The World Bank's Daily Webzine*. Washington, D.C.: World Bank. www.worldbank. org/developmentnew/stories/html/100101a.htm Accessed January 14, 2002.

Random House Webster's College Dictionary. (1995). New York: Random House.

Rich, E. (2000). Deportations soar under rigid law. *The Hartford Courant*. Vol. CLXII, No. 282. Sunday, October 8, pp. A1, A8, A9.

Stein, H. (1957). An international perspective in the social work curriculum. Paper presented at the Annual Meeting of the Council on Social Work Education, Los Angeles, CA, January, 1957.

Thomas, D. (2001). Jamaica: Economic Situation and Prospects. www.iadb.org/regions/ re3/sep/ja-sep Accessed January 15, 2002.

United Nations (1948). Universal declaration of human rights. New York: U.N. Department of Public Information or www.unhchr.org.ch/

United Nations Development Program (1996). *Human Development Report 1996*. New York: Oxford University Press.

United States Department of State. (2001). Background Note: Cote d'Ivoire. Bureau of African Affairs, November, 2001. *www.state.gov/p/af/ci/iv/* Accessed October 16, 2002.

Ward, C.A. (1999). Consequences of United State Immigration Policy: A Caribbean Perspective. Washington, D.C.: National Coalition on Caribbean Affairs.

Warren, G.L. (1935). International social casework. in F.S. Hall, ed. *Social Work Yearbook 1935*. New York: Russell Sage Foundation, 214-216.

Warren, G.L. (1937) International social work. in R.H. Kurz, ed. *Social Work Yearbook 1937*. New York: Russell Sage Foundation, 224-227.

Warren, G.L. (1939). International social work. in R.H. Kurz, ed. *Social Work Yearbook 1939*. New York: Russell Sage Foundation, 192-196.
Warren, G.L. (1941). International social work. in R.H. Kurz, ed. *Social Work Yearbook 1941*. New York: Russell Sage Foundation, 270-276.

FOR FURTHER READING AND RESEARCH

Drachman, D. (1992), A stage of migration framework for service to immigrant populations. *Social Work* 37:1, 68-72.
Healy, L. (2001). *International Social Work: Professional Action in an Interdependent World*. New York: Oxford University Press. Chapter 1: International Social Work: Why Is It Important and What Is It? and Chapter 9: International/Domestic Practice Interface.
Human migration as a field of research. (1927). *Social Service Review* 1:2, 258-269.
Immigrants and Refugees. (2000). *Social Work Speaks*. Compilation of NASW Policy Statements, Washington, DC: NASW Press.
International Policy on Migration; International Policy on Refugees; International Policy on Displaced Persons. *Policy Papers*. Berne, Switzerland: International Federation of Social Workers. (available at www.ifsw.org).

Resources on Social/Economic Conditions in Other Countries

Human Development Report. Annual. New York: United Nations Development Program (www.undp.org). Paper copy published by Oxford University Press, New York.
State of the World's Refugees. Annual. Geneva: United Nations High Commission on Refugees. (www.unhcr.ch) Paper copy published by Oxford University Press, New York.
World Development Report Annual. Washington, DC: The World Bank. (www.worldbank.org).

Useful Websites on International Populations and on Remittances

Institute for the Study of International Migration, Georgetown University: <www.georgetown.edu/sfs/programs/isim/>
Inter-American Development Bank: <www.iadb.org>
Inter-American Dialogue: <www.iadialog.org>
International Social Service: <www.iss-ssi.org>
United Nations High Commission on Refugees: <www.unhcr.ch>

British Journal of Social Work (2004) **34**, 93–107
DOI: 10.1093/bjsw/bch007

An Unacceptable Role for Social Work: Implementing Immigration Policy

Beth Humphries

Beth Humphries is reader in social work at Lancaster University. Recent publications have been mainly in the area of social work and immigration controls. Her current research is a study of refugees' experiences of seeking work in the north-west of England.

Correspondence to Dr Beth Humphries, Department of Applied Social Science, Lancaster University, Cartmel College, Lancaster, LA1 4YL. E-mail: *b.humphries@lancaster.ac.uk*

Summary

Social work has always had a role in policing the boundaries of welfare, and under New Labour there has been a decisive shift to an increasingly narrow and negative practice. This article takes social work's involvement in internal immigration controls as an example of the profession's complicity in implementing social policies that are degrading and inhuman. It argues that social work has adopted a reactionary and uncritical view of policy, and asks whether there might be a more progressive future for the profession.

Introduction

Social work has only slowly come to accept that an involvement with people subject to immigration controls is its business, because as a profession that deals with the most vulnerable people in society, it is now faced with some of the most oppressed people on the planet as its clients. Not only has it become 'involved' with immigrants and asylum seekers, increasingly it has been drawn into a role of constriction and punishment in its work with such groups. There is no clearer example of the transformation of social work from a concern with welfare to a position of authoritarianism than in this field, paralleling a more general change in the direction of the profession towards a culture of blame and enforcement. This is not to suggest that at some idyllic time in the past, social work was concerned only with caring for and/or liberating 'the oppressed'. Social work has always had a contradictory and ambivalent relationship with those who use state services. It *is* to argue that the balance has shifted decisively towards control, restriction, surveillance and ultimately exclusion. In other words, social work has been engaged in the moralistic aspects of New Labour policy rather than those concerned with attempts to 'empower' (Jordan, 2001). This article uses the field of immigration controls to illustrate this state of affairs and asks whether this negative development is an inevitable future for the profession.

Social work and social policy, a reactionary relationship

First it is necessary to set social work practice in the wider context of recent British social policy. There are at least two related problematic areas in the complex relationship between social work and social policy. The first is that although the government insists on evidence-based practice in all aspects of health, education and welfare delivery, it often ignores the evidence and bases decisions about policy on *ideological* rather than rational concerns. I have given examples of this elsewhere (Humphries, forthcoming *a*), and in particular have pointed up the glaring contradictions between policy and legislation on immigration controls on the one hand, and the available evidence on the other. The second and related problem is that social work is in danger of adopting an uncritical position in relation to this incoherence amongst evidence, policy and practice. The evidence-based practice movement is leading social work research away from initiating policy developments towards one of 'evaluating, monitoring and legitimating them', with an emphasis on exploring the 'effectiveness, efficiency and economy of policy' (Beresford and Evans, 1999, p. 672). As a result a profoundly conservative practice has emerged. Alongside this, the practice of social work is increasingly perceived by government as narrowly concerned with regulation and risk. Butler and Drakeford (2001, p. 7) describe social work's willingness to collaborate with 'a particular form of social authoritarianism', which has robbed it of its radical and transformatory potential. The training curriculum (pursued in the new three year degree structure) for social workers reflects this agenda, with its emphasis on competence, instrumentalism, managerialism and a minimal role for knowledge from the social sciences. One would expect social workers to rebel against this attempt to isolate social work from an understanding of and a critical view of social policy, and indeed many have left the profession because practice no longer converges satisfactorily with their motives for entering the profession. For many who stay in the job, the evidence is that they are stressed, bullied and degraded (Jones, 2001). For yet others, the belief that they are conducting 'anti-oppressive practice' allows them to continue to feel they are acting in humanitarian and helpful ways.

It is in the area of anti-oppressive practice that the rhetoric of government policy and the values to which social work aspires, coincide. Ideas about choice, citizenship, autonomy, community, social inclusion are central to the New Labour programme (Blair, 1998), and perhaps also persuade social workers that the work they do leads to social justice ends. Yet at the same time the government pursues neo-liberal economic and morally repressive policies that systematically degrade public services and punish and exclude those regarded as having been 'given a chance' but having 'failed'. Social workers are amongst other public sector workers required to implement the systems of surveillance that operate such policies. Because they are imbued with an individualistic and unpoliticized view of 'values' concerned with being non-discriminatory, anti-racist and anti-oppressive, they can persuade themselves that 'anti-oppressive' means what they say it means. In the words of a famous author: 'they learn to associate topsy-turveydom with wellbeing; in fact they're only truly happy when they're standing on their heads' (Huxley, 1932, p. 14).

A consideration of the connection among social work, welfare entitlement and immigration controls illustrates the ideological basis of policy, and the ways social work has been drawn into implementing racist policy initiatives, whilst still maintaining its unreflective, self-deceiving, 'anti-oppressive' belief systems. That is the focus of this article.

Although social work involvement is primarily in the area of *internal* controls, one of my complaints about current practice is that it takes place without any understanding of the context within which controls have developed. Were social workers to appreciate the shocking truth, they would find it more difficult to use individualistic models of AOP (anti-oppressive practice) and ARP (anti-racist practice) to justify current practice. In particular, I will argue that immigration controls are inherently racist, and no amount of 'acting in anti-discriminatory ways' will remedy that basic truth. I also hold that the example of state social work's relationship to immigration controls typifies its relationship to social policy generally, in that on the whole it adopts a role of subservience in implementing policies that have exposed the most vulnerable UK populations to:

> poverty, insecurity, housing and environmental distress and all their social consequences. Instead of being a part of a continuing strategy for preventing these social evils . . . public sector social work became the front line response to social polarisation, exclusion, deprivation and all the forms of deviance that were intensified by these changes (Jordan, 2001, p. 539).

In an attempt to address this problem of a lack of understanding, what follows is designed to stimulate an appreciation of the wider policy context, and to identify the ideological basis on which a legitimation of both external and internal controls depends. The implications for social work then follow. This is why I start with a brief history of controls and their intrinsic link with entitlement to welfare.

External immigration controls

It is important to appreciate that immigration controls consist of both external and internal controls. External controls concern restrictions on entry to a country, and are concerned particularly with the policing of borders. There are many types of immigration that are rarely viewed as problematic. For example, the Treaty of Rome guarantees free movement of European Union nationals to seek work and residence in any other member state. While internal borders have been dismantled, there have been increasing efforts towards joint enforcement of external borders and attempts at 'harmonization' of immigration policies, creating a 'Fortress Europe' (Gordon, 1989). The current list of countries whose nationals require a visa to enter European states includes virtually all Third World (poor) countries (Hayter, 2000). It is illegal for airlines and other 'carriers' to allow passengers to travel with false or no documents, and freight searching takes place regularly along the European coast.

Britain has always been a country of emigration and immigration, and control on people's movement into Britain was not introduced until the early twentieth century (though the Poor Laws always regulated internal movement). Then and consistently since, the dominating themes were: (i) a construction of would-be immigrants as inherently problematic—'outsiders', 'aliens', a 'danger' and a 'plague'; and (ii) the burden they would impose on the public purse and particularly the welfare state. These inter-related themes of 'nation', 'cost' and 'welfare' have been central to every piece of legislation since 1905, when the Aliens Act set up barriers to the entry of Jews fleeing pogroms in Eastern Europe. A third factor that has been (almost) continuous in influencing legislation is the demands of the British economy. I say *almost* continuous, because there are examples of legislation that can only be described as designed exclusively to prevent the entry to the UK of people who are not of white western European stock (Cohen, 2003). I return to this point below.

The racism inherent in the 1905 Aliens Act focused on the character of the people seeking asylum. In an age of Social Darwinism there was a preoccupation with the 'health of the nation' and controls on reproduction amongst the unfit, as well as the barring of undesirable aliens—those to be rejected—included the diseased, the insane and the criminal (Cohen, 1996). Prominent social reformers believed that 'non-Britons' came low in the pecking-order of 'races'. Jews were regarded as the chief threat of alien dilution of English blood: 'the real enemy, the invader from the East, the ruffian, the oriental parasite' (cited in Hayes, 2002, p. 37). The discourses about 'race' and nation were established, to be drawn on to justify subsequent exclusionary measures.

After the 1939/45 war, immigration was encouraged to fill labour shortages and many came from the Caribbean and the Asian sub-continent to take up work. As the economy began to contract in the 1960s and 1970s, debates about the 'problem' of immigration re-emerged, focused on the presence of black British citizens from the Commonwealth. Images about their link with disease, crime and the cost to the nation were replayed, culminating in the 1962 Commonwealth Immigrants Act, followed by the 1968 Commonwealth Immigrants Act, the 1971 Immigration Act and the 1981 British Nationality Act. The 1971 Act introduced the concept of 'patriality', which set the parameters of any claim to British nationality. It is this legislation that belies the argument that immigration controls are exclusively market-driven. It went on the statute books at the same time as there was underemployment in hospitals, catering and transport. This phenomenon is repeated in the contemporary policy context, where in 2002 draconian measures to keep 'foreigners' out have been introduced at the same time as there is a shortage of labour. Cohen describes two manifestations of racism at work here, economic and social (Cohen, 2003), thus exposing the ideological motivations inspiring the legislation. Moreover, it is important to reflect on the modern character of racism, for although the assumptions underpinning it do not change, its manifestations do. We have come to regard racism as the systemic and institutionalized construction of inferiority and oppressive treatment of black people (from Africa, the Caribbean and Asia), but there have been other manifestations (against Jews and Irish people for example). A contemporary expression of racism is also against people of Eastern European and Middle-Eastern origin, many of whom are Muslims. Its fluid and adaptive nature needs to be appreciated if we are to recognize and confront its contemporary faces.

The 1981 legislation removed the automatic right to citizenship through birth in the UK and linked citizenship to right of entry. Five categories of British nationality were created, only one of which allowed free access to the country. Henceforth full British nationality could be claimed only by those with a parent or grandparent born in Britain, a provision that effectively excluded people from the Asian subcontinent, Africa and the Caribbean. A myth that has underpinned immigration legislation from the start, of the British nation comprising a distinct race of people of common origin and descent, white and European, was again written into the 1981 Act. As a result, for example, white South Africans and Zimbabweans could gain entry, but not black citizens of these countries. By 1971 primary immigration from the New Commonwealth had largely come to an end, except for some family reunion. Immigration for settlement has been systematically restricted and migrant workers are recruited to match labour requirements.

It is in this sense that immigration policies are inherently racist. Underpinning them are notions of nationalism and chauvinism. All immigration laws depend on the distinction between 'native' and 'foreigner', 'citizen' and 'alien', 'us' and 'them', and therefore 'legal' and 'illegal' (Anderson, 1983; Anthias and Yuval-Davis, 1989; Miles, 1993). The setting up of boundaries involves the management of identities and cultures in inclusionary and exclusionary ways. Thus the 'national character' is projected as homogeneous, invoking images of shared culture and customs, shared values and religion, shared origins and destiny, and crucially, shared *blood* (Humphries, 2002*a*). As Goldberg comments, 'group formation seems destined as eternal, fated as unchanging and unchangeable' (1993, p. 80). From a position inside this myth the foreigner, the outsider, the Other can be constructed as a 'seething mass of refuse and filth' (Garrard, 1971, p. 51), and with it the need for protection by closing off the borders.

The evidence base of social policy initiatives on immigration controls

What can justify these policies? Since New Labour is concerned to base its policies on 'the available evidence' it is important to establish the grounds on which immigration policy is legitimated. This is particularly important for practitioners who require reassurance that the policies they are asked to implement are informed by appropriate and well-grounded studies. So what is the evidence that has required such stern measures?

It has become a commonsense belief, reinforced by government ministers, that controls are necessary for the following reasons: to control numbers of people coming to this overcrowded little island; to preserve the jobs, wealth and welfare of the country against the perceived threat of economic migrants; to allay fears about an increase in racial tension and to ensure good race relations within Britain. Elsewhere I have examined these reasons in detail (Humphries, forthcoming *b*). Here I deal briefly with the available research.

According to Government statistics, the total population of Great Britain is just over 57 million, of which the estimated foreign population (those without citizenship) as a proportion of the total resident population is 3.6 per cent. Non-white ethnic minorities comprise 7 per cent—just over 3 million (Office for National Statistics, 2003). Since the end of primary immigration the main reasons for coming to Britain are to join family members or to fill job vacancies. However it is the *numbers* of asylum seekers coming to the UK that is the focus of a moral panic. The movement of people across the world is directly related to civil war and instability in particular countries. There is now a steadily increasing number of asylum seekers reaching our shores every year. Between 1990 and 1997 the number of applications averaged around 32,000, varying between extremes of 22,000 and 45,000. In the four years between 1997 and 2001, the level of applications rose to 80,000 in 2000 and fell to 71,000 in 2001 (ICAR, 2003). Of 85,865 applications received in 2002, 34 per cent were granted asylum or Exceptional Leave to Remain (ELR—abolished from April 2003), and 66 per cent were refused. On average, during 2001 and 2002 only 15 per cent of applications were successful (Home Office, 2003).

The figures, of course, have to be treated with caution. For example, although the figures show an increase of applications to Britain between 1987 and the late 1990s, they are misleading, as the UNHCR, who produce the statistical overview, changed its method of calculation during this period to include dependents. In addition, a factor often omitted in the debates is related to people *leaving* Britain. Sutcliffe (1998, cited in Hayter, 2000) commented that the demographic effect of immigration and emigration as a whole appears to be almost insignificant. This of course makes its political significance all the more striking.

The argument that immigrants and asylum seekers take jobs from natives, is not supported by the facts. There is a shortage of skilled and unskilled labour in the UK, so much so that the Government has pursued initiatives to seek workers from abroad (Roche, 2000). The 2002 NIA Act has the twin purposes of facilitating the entry of certain migrants as workers, and of controlling even further those who come seeking asylum (Home Office, 2002). This policy is of course contradictory. People are excluded from the UK on the grounds that they are likely to be 'economic migrants'. Indeed this has become a term of abuse. The same justification is given, as expedient, to legitimate the recruitment of foreign workers. Moreover, many asylum seekers already in the UK have the skills and the qualifications needed to fill the jobs where there is a shortage of labour, yet they are excluded from work. Even when they are granted refugee status and entitled to work, somewhere between 75 per cent and 90 per cent are unemployed or underemployed (Ahipeaud, 1998; African Educational Trust, 1998). In research carried out in north-west England, the researchers met dozens of people longing to work, to be independent, to give back to society what they felt they had gained since coming to this country. They are unable to find work and are wondering why. Refugee professionals such as doctors, teachers, nurse/midwives, lawyers are looking for jobs as cleaners, care workers or factory workers because of official restrictions or refusal of employers to give them a job in an appropriate field (Humphries and Khan, forthcoming). Yet it is in these professions that shortages exist. One wonders whether the government really has an interest in 'joined up policy' or whether the urge not to be seen to accommodate refugees in any way at all, is a more dominant factor. Beyond people with skills and motivation to make their contribution to society, there are others whose plight is heartbreaking. There are young men who have been refugees in this country for a number of years and speak English, as they went to school here. They have been on New Deal programmes, yet they hang around community centres unable to get a job, without qualifications and without hope. They are rejected by older people in their own communities and their depression is palpable. What is the future for them? There are women with children in desperate need of free childcare to allow them to even begin to think about looking for work. Some are isolated and confined, and unable to get out to practise their English by speaking to local people. Their depression too is palpable.

The rationale for immigration controls that concerns 'good race relations' is also spurious. The evidence that exists in any substance is of discrimination against immigrants and asylum seekers in jobs, education, health and public life (Home Office, 1998, 2002; Humphries and Khan, forthcoming; Modood, 1997). It is irresponsible for the government to claim that improving race relations depends on controlling numbers of people entering Britain. The 'numbers game' is more a product of hysteria than it is of the evidence. The evidence is that violence is more likely to be perpetuated against refugees and asylum seekers, than it is to be perpetuated *by* them.

The grounds on which immigration controls are justified are very fragile indeed. The available research is often misleading and inconclusive, and despite rhetoric about the importance of sound, scientific evidence, policy and legislation often ignore what evidence there is. Policies are as likely as not to be inspired by *ideological* rather than *rational* concerns. Welfare professionals and others who implement policy have a duty to understand their origins and to have a critical understanding of their implications for people subjected to them. In the case of immigration and asylum, the effects of social policy on those towards whom the UK has an obligation to offer succour and support, is in many situations nothing short of grim. I explore the specifics of this below.

Immigration controls and welfare

Earlier I described the legislation relating to external controls. However, there is more to the process of tightening controls than closing borders. The 1990s brought a number of major changes, concerned mainly with *internal* controls. It is not so much the entry of dependents or of migrant workers that provokes heated controversy. Instead, the focus in the last twenty years has turned to the 'problem' of asylum seekers, and since 1993 we have seen increasingly repressive and punitive measures introduced to discourage groups affected from coming to Britain. If they are allowed to enter, they are channelled into an inferior and inhumane 'welfare' system. Asylum seekers flee conditions of war, torture, rape, murder and state-organized oppression. They often have to leave behind family, documents, proof of qualifications and all other possessions, yet the concern of the British government (and other European governments) and the media is not with the terrors that have driven them from their countries of origin, but with images of them as 'scroungers' and 'economic migrants'. Their flight to survive is regarded as a crime and as a threat to the nation.

Internal immigration controls involves, at its most basic level, identity checks by employers and officials, and has increasingly come to mean the restriction of access to welfare provision on the grounds of immigration status. As noted earlier, the link between immigration controls and welfare has been a feature of immigration control since 1905. An 'undesirable alien' was defined as 'someone who cannot show that he (sic) has in his possession or is in a position to obtain the means of supporting himself and his dependents' or who 'owing to any disease or infirmity appears likely to become a charge on the rates or otherwise a detriment to the public' (quoted in Cohen, 1987, p. 21). The current climate of cut-backs in the welfare state, and the preoccupation with limiting public expenditure, the pursuit of efficiency, economy and effectiveness, and the intrinsic superiority of the market in the provision and delivery of welfare (Spicker, 1995), facilitates the construction of the refugee as burdensome, needy and costly. Controls consistently place at their centre the need to access welfare as grounds for refusal.

The 1993 Asylum and Immigration Appeals Act and the 1996 Asylum and Immigration Act accelerated the process of removing from the welfare state those subject to immigration control, both asylum seekers and others. In 1993 asylum seekers were denied homeless persons accommodation if they could stay anywhere 'however temporary', such as a church floor. With the 1996 Act, housing legislation was introduced to remove rights to homeless accommodation from *all* persons subject to immigration control. It also linked virtually all non-compulsory benefits including child benefit, to immigration status. Asylum seekers remained eligible only for income support, housing and council tax benefit, and then only if the asylum claim was lodged on entering the UK (Cohen, 2003). The particularly controversial 1999 Immigration and Asylum Act, which introduced the National Asylum Support Service (NASS), was explicitly intended by the government to minimize incentives to 'economic migration'. This act removed the right of asylum seekers to claim either state benefits or support from local authorities under the National Assistance Act 1948, or the Children Act 1989. Instead it created a parallel but separate system of support for destitute asylum seekers, administered by NASS. The level of the weekly allowance paid by NASS is set below the poverty level at 70 per cent income support equivalent. Asylum seekers are also dispersed into property about which they have no choice and which may be a long way from family and community. If they remove themselves from such properties they forfeit the 'help' offered by NASS. Under this legislation all people subject to immigration control are denied council housing and a range of non-contributory benefits. These benefits comprise the core means-tested benefits of last resort (income support, income-based job seekers' allowance, housing benefit, council tax benefit, a social fund payment) as well as family and disability benefits (child benefit, working families' tax credit, attendance allowance for disabled people, severe disablement allowance, invalid care allowance, disabled person's tax credit, disability living allowance). Those asylum seekers who are denied NASS support and have other problems beyond destitution may seek social work help from asylum seekers teams based in local authorities.

Cohen (2003) describes the NASS scheme and the dispersal system as the creation of a modern poor law, based on coercion, without choices or protection against eviction. He also draws attention to the surveillance aspects of the scheme where absence has to be reported, and where the local police are given detailed information on asylum seekers dispersed to their area. Research carried out by Refugee Council and Oxfam (2002) examined the level of welfare support to asylum seekers and found it set so low, and the system set up to administer payments so badly designed and poorly run that asylum seekers are forced to live at a level of poverty unacceptable in a civilized society. The study's survey of refugee support organizations was 'deeply disturbing', with reports of clients facing hunger, unable to buy clothes, feed children or maintain good health.

The support asylum seekers receive does not equate to that received by other UK residents claiming income support, and with it a range of benefits and emergency payments, for example premiums for families with children, disabled people and older people, costs towards funerals and winter fuel, and welfare foods such as milk tokens and vitamins. Asylum seekers are not permitted to claim any of these additional benefits.

Social work

On the face of it these are all conditions that require social work intervention, and one would expect social workers and other state officials to protest at the level of subsistence—lower than that of their poorest clients—imposed on people who have already endured the traumas forcing them to leave their country of origin, and the stress of finding their way to and dealing with living in a new country. There is very little evidence of this having happened. Social workers have been drawn in increasingly as part of the surveillance process. During 1996 the government conducted an 'efficiency scrutiny' on the enforcement of immigration law. It sought partnership between the Home Office and the health, education and welfare services in the checking of documentation and general policing of provision. The 2002 NIA Act drew the entire state machinery into this process. Local authorities are now under a duty to furnish, at the request of the Home Office, information on any resident in their area suspected of unlawful presence in the UK. Indeed the requirement goes further than this. Local authorities are obliged, *without* any request from the Home Office, to report on their own initiative any failed asylum seeker or anyone they consider to be here unlawfully and who tries to claim community care provision. This inevitably commits social services departments to be both inquisitors of immigration status and reporters of that status to the Home Office (Cohen, 2003). Banks, employers, the Inland Revenue and a range of other social institutions have also been drawn into acting on behalf of the Home Office in the implementation of these policies.

What is most worrying within this culture of suspicion is the response of social workers to being drawn into practices that are blatantly at odds with principles held by the profession. Although social work has been largely removed from asylum seekers and others subject to immigration controls, they still have contact with people removed from the NASS system facing destitution. Indeed, they can be drawn in to help evict failed asylum seekers from NASS properties. Research that has been done suggests that social workers or their unions have protested little about the new expectations imposed on them to monitor immigration policy. In interviews with social workers, Düvell and Jordan (2000) found that teams were operating well below the standards seen as acceptable for UK citizens. Their study illustrated the fact that social workers 'will volunteer to do the "dirty work" of social policy, even when this involves intentional and systematic deprivation by official agencies, of the means of dignified existence' (p. 140). Jordan concluded that the work of these teams prefigured other aspects of New Labour policy developments in what he calls 'enforcement counselling' (Jordan, 2000, p. 142), which offers no options and gives officials complete power over applicants. A study of unaccompanied asylum seeking children in Greater Manchester found workers with little experience or expertise whose attempts to help did a disservice to the children involved, and worryingly, who regarded the duty to check immigration status as another bureaucratic irritation rather than a major ethical dilemma (Humphries and Mynott, 2001). Other research in the mental health field found teams unwilling to acknowledge their duty towards asylum seekers because they said they did not have the resources to deal with post traumatic stress disorder (Humphries, forthcoming *b*). With regard to children and families, the commitment to promote 'the family' is a major feature of UK social policy. Jones's (2002) research found that this appears not to apply to families that do not comply with the nuclear ideal, and that immigration controls lead to the disruption of family life, the prevention of the upbringing of children in families, and forcible separation of children from parents, with damaging effects on children (p. 100). She found social services departments, voluntary agencies and government bodies responsible for children's welfare, to be complicit in the creation of disadvantage and discrimination against families involved in immigration proceedings. In the area of community care, there is evidence that local authorities are likely to interpret immigration eligibility criteria in the narrowest possible way, resulting in cruel and harsh judgements against those seeking help. Criticism from a Court of Appeal judge of Leicester City Council, included the comment that they had applied 'an inflexible approach to a welfare scheme of last resort' and suggested that they had no business with the applicant's immigration status, 'it should be for the Home Office to decide . . . rather than for local authorities . . . to starve immigrants out of the country by withholding last resort assistance' (cited in Humphries, 2002*b*).

In the summer of 2003, the House of Commons Home Affairs Committee produced a report on asylum removals (House of Commons, 2003), which had taken evidence from a range of organizations, including social services departments. In written evidence a number of local authorities gave their views. Sheffield City Council said: 'The process of removals needs to be open and in order for it to be effective, there needs to be close liaison between local authority asylum teams, private accommodation providers and immigration officials' (Appendix 35). Oxfordshire Social Services Department's contribution criticized 'economic migrants' for 'exploiting the system' and complained that the Home Secretary does not have 'realistic objectives' for 'speedy removals' (Appendix 29).

The evidence so far suggests that social workers and social services have a clear vision of what is required of them by social policy on immigration controls, even to the extent of active cooperation with the removal and deportation of people in the most grim circumstances. They have not resisted the gate-keeping and inhumane role thrust upon them. It is no wonder they are despised and feared by the people they purport to help. We can safely regard the rhetoric about anti-oppressive and anti-racist practice as harmless delusion.

Conclusion

I have tried to convey a number of things in this article. The first is built on the author's belief that external immigration controls are at root unfair and discriminatory against specific groups of people (see also Humphries, 2002*a*). They are also unnecessary and ineffective, since as Hayter (2000) shows, they do not work, in spite of the paraphernalia of repressive measures set up to support them. They are racist in that they are based on irrational beliefs about the undesirability of mixing cultures, and that cultural homogeneity should be preserved. On these grounds they should be opposed vigorously.

Moreover, and especially germane for social workers and other health and welfare professionals, internal controls come close to contravening Human Rights legislation (indeed Section 55 of the 2002 NIA Act was judged to have done exactly that). They have turned people subject to controls into objects of contempt and have legitimized violence against them. Government policy, committed to social inclusion, has created a category of people who are outside the social welfare system, dispersed into impoverished areas, and excluded from decent and appropriate employment. They are required to carry 'smart cards' and have their fingerprints taken. The 2002 NIA Act will create further exclusion through induction centres for asylum seekers (detained for up to six months), accommodation centres (virtual open prisons in isolated areas), removal centres (closed prisons for those awaiting deportation). Those allowed to enter the country will have to pass a stringent language test, show they have 'sufficient knowledge' about life in the UK, swear an oath of allegiance to the queen and pledge loyalty to the country's democratic values. A cloud of official suspicion surrounds them, and they are regarded as more likely to be terrorists or criminals than desperate people fleeing persecution. As I write, the latest government 'leak' is of secret Balkan camps where asylum seekers will be 'processed offshore', that is outside European borders and out of our sight (*Observer*, 15 June 2003).

A response to this last (final?) solution may be that at least the problem will go away, and that social workers and others will have the dilemmas removed from them. It is most unlikely to go away. As history shows, people will find other, perhaps more dangerous ways, of coming to countries where they think they will find refuge.

Meanwhile, many social workers will recognize the image of themselves as 'enforcers', as being used for purposes that are 'narrow and negative, concerned with rationing and risk assessment' (Jordan, 2001, p. 527), of which their contribution in immigration controls is just one manifestation. State social work is being used as an instrument of control of those who have already been excluded from the benefits on offer in New Labour's culture of achievement.

What does social work need to do? First, it needs to stop pretending that what it calls 'anti-oppressive practice' is anything but a gloss to help it feel better about what it is required to do, a gloss that is reinforced by a raft of books and articles that are superficial and void of a political context for practice. It needs to inform itself of theories of power that go beyond individualistic models, and to struggle with the challenges that come from engaging with debates within the social sciences. It needs to grasp the implications of research that is not simply measuring 'what works' but that asks critical questions about the motives behind and the ideologies that inform social policies. It needs to begin to act collectively and in solidarity with those affected and impoverished by reactionary policies, rather than in fragmented, commercialized and exploited situations. There is evidence that the New Labour strategy of 'tough love' is not working. It certainly does not work in the area of immigration and asylum, where the 'love' element is non-existent. Surely it is time for social workers to find that combination of genuine caring for people in big trouble, with the informed anger and rage to galvanize them into action against manifest injustice.

Accepted: June 2003

References

African Educational Trust (1998) *Refugee Education, Training and Development in Inner London: A Base Line Study*, Central London, Focus.

Ahipeaud, M. J. (1998) *Employment Training for Refugees in London: A Survey Analysis*, London, Pan London Refugee and Training Network.

Anderson, B. (1983) *Imagined Communities*, London, Verso.

Anthias, F. and Yuval-Davis, N. (1989) *Woman-Nation-State*, London, Macmillan.

Beresford, P. and Evans, C. (1999) 'Research note: research and empowerment', *British Journal of Social Work*, **29** (5), pp. 671–7.

Blair, T. (1998) *The Third Way: New Politics for the New Century*, Fabian Pamphlet 588, London, The Fabian Society.

Butler, I. and Drakeford, M. (2001) 'Which Blair Project? Communitarianism, social authoritarianism and social work', *Journal of Social Work*, **1** (1), pp. 7–20.

Cohen, S. (1987) *It's the Same Old Story: Immigration Controls against Jewish, Black and Asian People, with Special Reference to Manchester*, Manchester City Council.

Cohen, S. (1996) 'Anti-Semitism, immigration control and the welfare state', in Taylor, D. (ed.), *Critical Social Policy: a Reader*, London, Sage.

Cohen, S. (2003) *No One is Illegal*, Stoke-on-Trent, Trentham Books.

Düvell, F. and Jordan, B. (2000) *'How Low Can You Go?' Dilemmas of Social Work with Asylum Seekers in London*, Exeter, Department of Social Work, Exeter University.

Garrard, J. A. (1971) *The English and Immigration: A Comparative Study of the Jewish Influx, 1880–1910*, London, Oxford University Press.

Goldberg, D. T. (1993) *Racist Culture*, Oxford, Blackwell.

Gordon, P. (1989) *Fortress Europe? The Meaning of 1992*, London, Runnymede Trust.

Hayes, D. (2002) 'From aliens to asylum seekers: a history of immigration controls and welfare in Britain', in Cohen, S., Humphries, B. and Mynott, E. (eds), *From Immigration Controls to Welfare Controls*, London, Routledge, pp. 30–46.

Hayter, T. (2000) *Open Borders: The Case against Immigration Controls*, London, Pluto.

Home Office (1998) *Fairer, Faster and Firmer: A Modern Approach to Immigration and Asylum*, London, Home Office.

Home Office (2002) *Secure Borders, Safe Haven: Integration with Diversity in Modern Britain*, London, Home Office.

Home Office (2003) *Asylum Statistics*, London, Home Office, Immigration and Nationality Directorate.

House of Commons (2003) *The House of Commons Home Affairs Committee Report on Asylum Removals*, London, House of Commons.

Humphries, B. (2002*a*) 'From welfare to authoritarianism: The role of social work in immigration controls', in Cohen, S., Humphries, B. and Mynott, E. (eds), *From Immigration Controls to Welfare Controls*, London, Routledge, pp. 126–40.

Humphries, B (2002*b*) 'Fair immigration controls—or none at all?' in Cohen, S., Humphries, B. and Mynott, E. (eds), *From Immigration Controls to Welfare Controls*, London, Routledge, pp. 203–19.

Humphries, B. (forthcoming *a*) 'Taking sides: Social work research as a political and moral activity', in Lovelock, R., Ballard, J. and Lyons, K., *Reflective Social Work*, London, Routledge.

Humphries, B. (forthcoming *b*) 'Refugees, asylum seekers, welfare and social work', in Hayes, D. and Humphries, B. (eds), *Social Work and Immigration Controls*, London, JKP.

Humphries, B. and Khan, F. (forthcoming) *Refugees and Employment: a Research Report*, Manchester, Refugee Action.

Humphries, B. and Mynott, E. (2001) *Living Your Life Across Boundaries: Young Separated Refugees in Greater Manchester*, Manchester, Save the Children.

Huxley, A. (1932) *Brave New World*, London, Flamingo.

ICAR (2003) *ICAR Statistics Paper 1: Statistics about Asylum Seekers in the UK*, London, The Information Centre about Asylum and Refugees in the UK.

Jones, A. (2002) 'Family life and the pursuit of immigration controls', in Cohen, S., Humphries, B. and Mynott, E. (eds), *From Immigration Controls to Welfare Controls*, London, Routledge, pp. 83–105.

Jones, C. (2001) 'Voices from the front line: state social workers and New Labour', *British Journal of Social Work*, **31** (4), pp. 547–62.

Jordan, B. (2000) *Social Work and the Third Way: Tough Love as Social Policy*, London, Sage.

Jordan, B. (2001) 'Tough Love: social work, social exclusion and the Third Way', *British Journal of Social Work*, **31** (4), pp. 527–46.

Miles, R. (1993) *Racism after Race Relations*, London, Routledge.

Modood, T. (1997) *British Asian Self-Employment: The Interaction of Culture and Economics*, London, Policy Studies Institute.

Office for National Statistics (2003) *Living in Britain*, London, UK Government, available at http://www.statistics.gov.uk/lib/viewerChart305.html.

Refugee Council and Oxfam (2002) *Poverty and Asylum in the UK*, London, Oxfam and Refugee Council.

Roche, B. (2000) 'Migration in a global economy', Speech to Institute for Public Policy Research Conference, 8 September.

Spicker, P. (1995) *Social Policy: Themes and Approaches*, London, Prentice-Hall.

Sutcliffe, B. (1998) *Nacido in otra parte: un ensayo sobre la migratión internaçional, el desarollo y la equidad*, Bilbao, Hegoa.

6

Critical Anti-Racism Praxis: The Concept of Whiteness Implicated

June Ying Yee

The anti-racism perspective began in the 1970s as a critical response to existing understandings about how to deal with difference and diversity in Britain Anti-racism can be deemed critical because of its theoretical roots in the orthodox Marxist tradition (Cox, 1948) and neo-Marxist tradition (Miles, 1989). In these earlier theoretical works, Marxism is negatively viewed as "composed of a unified set of dogmas" (Rex & Mason, 1986, p.85). These metanarratives provided an overly economic deterministic viewpoint; that is, the domination and exploitation of racial minority groups were seen to serve the profit motives of a dominant group in capitalist societies. Yet, in the field of social work practice, many social workers noted that forms of domination enacted upon racial minority clientele did not necessarily serve the conscious motives of an elite group. Rather, explanations were sought to account for the unintended exclusionary practices found within agency structures and practices. Consequently, more sophisticated variants of Marxism have critically accounted for the instances of non-class sites of domination. In particular Louis Althusser's (1971) work shows the overdetermination of social processes in both class and non-class sites of domination. Such an interpretation allows for the creation of a subject capable of resistance and, consequently, extends the discussion beyond a simple class analyses interpretation. Likewise, Antonio Gramsci (1971) examines the ways in which the dominant group in power produces and reproduces its relations of power through ideology in the form of hegemony, an important mechanism of class reproduction.

To better understand the dominant group, a theoretical understanding of the concept of whiteness is required. As commented by Dei (2000, p.31), often in social service agencies "antiracist workers may recognize and discuss systemic racism and yet fail to see themselves as implicated in the structures that perpetuate and reproduce racism" Whiteness as "institutionalised privilege" that perpetuates a "system of dominance" can only be unravelled once the concept of whiteness is critically deconstructed. Racism occurs through the process of false consciousness and is "rooted in commonsensical thought and the material and non-material human condition" (ibid., p.16). The material condition referring to the "socially created structures" (ibid , p 45) that maintains racism and the non-material human condition referring to the knowledge production created about ethno-racial minority people enables their subjugation to the power and privilege of a system of whiteness.

In everyday life, anti-racism began as a social movement that aimed to expose the deep-rooted ideologies that historically (and currently) determined people's attitudinal and institutional responses to those who do not conform to the dominant and/or majority group. Unfortunately, academic writers and social work practitioners who work in the area of anti-racism have been confronted with many barriers and difficulties in trying to carry out this fundamental principle. In the interest of trying to implement the theoretical underpinnings of an anti-racism approach, many academic writers and social work practitioners unintentionally collude with the dominant power structures by perpetuating the general "white" denial of racism.

The dominant and/or majority group refers to the people who hold the most power to shape the collective norms and values of a given society. In Canada, the ideology of the dominant and/or majority group can be seen to manifest concretely in people's social location, which cuts across axioms of race and gender and, in this context, the historical and current power of "White, Anglo-Saxon, Protestant males" (Henry et al., 2000, p.407). Ultimately, those from the dominant and/or majority group are able to tap into strategies of whiteness as a way to maintain their legitimacy and power without anyone questioning them. Therefore, a key component of anti-racism work is to understand how strategies of whiteness work. Whiteness is a key ingredient in holding together the current racist structural formations evident in social service organizations. Anti-racism work cannot be deemed critical if academic writers and social work practitioners fail to provide a theoretical and historical understanding of the social and cultural processes by which people's identities become subject to a system of domination and subordination.

The main purpose of this chapter, then, is to provide a clearer articulation of what is meant by critical anti-racism praxis. This requires a thorough theoretical understanding of the concepts of whiteness and racism. An interrogation of the unspoken central barriers to the effective implementation of a critical anti-racism praxis is discussed, and the work of academic writers and social work practitioners who claim to be engaging in critical anti-racism praxis work is questioned. People cannot speak about racism until they name whiteness for the purpose of dismantling its hidden basis of power relations. To begin, this chapter introduces the concept of whiteness followed by a discussion of the definition and meaning of an anti-racism approach. The anti-racism approach relies on a historical understanding of how people of colour have become racialized, especially in relation to the dominant and/or majority group.

Ostensibly, this paper examines two areas that show the ways in which racism and whiteness work together to create systems of domination and subordination. First, a history of how race is a social construct that works in tandem with the power of whiteness to create a particular set of social relations is discussed. And second, a critique of the commonly accepted ways of addressing culturally diverse populations is explored for the purpose of highlighting how racism does, indeed, operate as a primary structure of oppression This system of domination, also known as whiteness, maintains power by everyone's inability to seriously challenge, notice or even question how the status quo works, and only by making everyone aware of its invisibility can these processes of domination be dismantled. Even if one recognizes the power differentials that rest in this system of domination, problems of marginalization, domination and oppression make people collude or abet in the maintenance of the status quo. After all, those in the dominant and/or majority group positions know how to maintain a synergy with subordinate groups as their own preservation rests on a remarkable capacity to repackage themselves according to particular historical and social circumstances. The final outcome is that many academic writers and social work practitioners face barriers and obstacles in capturing the racist formations in institutional structures and practices.

What Is Whiteness?

Whiteness can be defined as a complex social process that perpetuates and maintains the dominant and/or majority group's power within social service organizations and is the primary mechanism that prevents anti-racist workers from changing today's societal and institutional arrangements. According to Gabriel (1998, p 13), whiteness operates through three mechanisms· (1) exnomination, (2) naturalization, and (3) universalization. Exnomination refers to how the language we use in everyday life is taken for granted as representing a particular understanding about white people. For example, the ethnicity of white people is hardly named, while all ethnic minority people are racialized as the "other." Naturalization points to how white people are normatively positioned as the referential norm without ever having to define themselves And finally, universalization is how white people are able to frame an understanding of the world from their socio-political and historical vantage point without being questioned

Historically, in North America, anti-racism work began with a focus on "awareness training" and "consciousness-raising" strategies for those who were white in order that the problem of racism could be discussed (Katz & Ivey, 1977; Katz, 1978; Hartigan, 2000). This is not a surprise given that these approaches, which were deemed as a part of anti-racism work, emerged from a racist historical past that keeps intact structurally based racist formations. For example, many do not acknowledge the problematic tensions and contradictions in proclaiming the implementation of cultural competency, multiculturalism and ethnic sensitivity, to name a few, as a useful part of anti-racism work. In fact, from a historical perspective, these approaches were not developed by ethno-racial minority groups themselves but primarily by white practitioners who struggled with gaining cultural awareness, sensitivity and understanding in work with culturally diverse clientele (Yee & Dumbrill, 2003). These approaches, which have dominated and informed the social work knowledge base for some time, run contrary to an anti-racism perspective and, moreover, are heavily steeped in strategies of whiteness.

Anti-Racism in Social Work Practice

Fundamentally, anti-racism practice emphasizes the importance of focusing on the structural aspects of inequality, rather than seeing the problem as simply the cultural prejudice and ignorance of social work practitioners. Often social work educators have argued that the dominant and/or majority group's lack of cultural contact with and cultural knowledge about racial minority groups promotes the problem of racism.

The knowledge base, which informs the concept of anti-racism, stems from a particular theoretical understanding about the concept of race, and raises important implications on how social work practitioners are expected to carry out critical anti-racism praxis work. First, the proactive dismantling of current institutional practices requires these exclusionary acts to be identified, named and problematized if the inclusion of a multiplicity of perspectives can be even considered Second, a critical understanding on how people's identity becomes socially located within systems becomes significant. And third, racism works by making everyone believe that people can be biologically and culturally defined If people focus attention on the culture of racial minority groups, then those in positions of power in the dominant and/or majority group can successfully distract social work practitioners from tackling the systemic aspect of prejudicial outcomes For example, equipping service providers with cultural knowledge about various ethnic groups does little to address the ways in which people perpetuate and reinforce the power base of the dominant and/or majority group More often the resource, support and service needs of minority groups fails to be prioritized as a doable action within social service agencies because of various minority's group's lack of power in decision-making processes. Instead, much emphasis is placed on educating the ignorant knowledge base of social work practitioners in order to familiarize them with cultural difference.

Today, practitioners and educators in the social work field have adopted a variant of anti-racism practice commonly known as anti-oppressive practice. Anti-oppressive practice "embodies a person-centred philosophy; an egalitarian value system; [and] a methodology focussing on both process and outcome" (Dominelli, 1996, p.3). Little difference exists between the two approaches other than the way the anti-racism approach makes explicit the importance of a theoretical understanding of race as a primary structure of oppression that is rooted in colonialism, capitalism and patriarchy Often, now, the rhetoric of anti-oppressive practice presents a politically correct code word that has become a method of practice that assumes equality, equity and social justice. In Canadian social work practice, the use of the terms "oppression," "systemic barriers" and "sites of advantage and disadvantage" make many assume that anti-oppressive work is occurring with very little critique (Sullivan, Steinhouse, & Gelfand, 2000, Alaggia & Marziali, 2003; Lacroix, 2003; Tsang & George,

1998). In these approaches, these authors fail to articulate a clearly defined theoretical framework from which such analyses emerge, and more problematically, these approaches have become co-opted into mainstream practices that reinforce the current status quo of focusing on the "other" as opposed to truly challenging the power of the dominant and/or majority group.

One could question whether these practices are truly anti-oppressive given the need to theoretically discuss and flesh out the foundational assumptions upon which each form of intervention is based. Versions of anti-oppressive practice present as progressive and critical work but in no way discuss the means by which minority groups can be empowered to dismantle the primary structures of oppression such as colonialism, patriarchy, heterosexism and ableism. This can be evidenced by many social service agencies' unwillingness to change the current philosophy, which drives the values of the organization and, in the final outcome, justifies their current exclusionary practices.

Henceforth, providing theoretical linkages between the concept of the dominant culture to the study of whiteness analytically moves the discussion from a simplistic generalization of privileged white men to a contemporary understanding of racism that takes into account the ways in which identity, culture and difference work to further perpetuate systemic forms of racism in social service agency practices. Too often, in the Canadian literature, much emphasis rests on minority cultures as opposed to the complex ways that racism works to shape the power base of the dominant culture through a theoretical and conceptual process called "whiteness." In fact, Ruth Frankenberg (1993), bell hooks (1990), Toni Morrison (1992) and Mab Segrest (1994a, 1994b) "were among the first to argue that an important element of the anti-racist agenda is the need to map the terrain of whiteness" (Moon & Flores, 2000, p 99). Yet, many academic writers and social work practitioners tend to speak only generically of white privilege without making visible the processes and strategies by which whiteness operates within social service agencies. One cannot speak about whiteness until one has a firm understanding of how race is a social construction in modern Western culture. Without this background historical knowledge, exclusionary practices cannot be identified and so-called neutral practices will continue to further the power of the dominant and/or majority group

An Historical Understanding of Racism as a Primary Structure of Oppression

In everyday social work practice, workers aim to provide services that are culturally appropriate and relevant to various ethno-racial minority communities. In doing so, the culture and ethnicity of various communities often become synonymously equated with the concept of race. Race is a socially constructed category often used to "classify humankind according to common ancestry and is reliant on differentiation by such physical characteristics as colour of skin, hair texture, stature, and facial characteristics" (Henry et al , 2000, p 409). Such a definition does not capture the complexity and changing meaning of race that has problematically labelled ethno-racial minority communities in negative ways. Similarly, many people hold the view that culture and ethnicity are objective attributes of people and, in turn, create generalizations about whole communities based simply on culture and ethnicity. Yet, people do not recognize that culture is a dynamic entity constantly in flux and in process according to time, environment and interaction with others. When people are examining the culture of a particular person, they are noting that the person presents a worldview that is different from their own social location, including age, ability, sexual orientation and gender identity. Finding ways to accept different worldviews in relation to one's own self-identity is different from gaining knowledge about cultural characteristics that, regrettably, freezes the fluidity of different worldviews. Social workers need to gain an awareness of their own cultures in order to see the power they hold in making some worldviews valid while making others invalid within agency practices.

Oddly, social work practitioners may readily see the problems involved in racializing particular ethnic communities and, at the same time, have no difficulty in focusing on the culture of ethno-racial minority people. Yet, we know that, in everyday life and in social work practice, race still carries meaning within "political and popular discourse" (Mason, 2000, p 8), and often times creates generalizations and stereotypes about groups of people based on "common sense" (Gramsci, 1971) ideas. When people are held accountable for their generalizations by pointing out to them the instances when their group classifications or categorizations do not work, they will try to diminish or minimize awareness of the connection between race and behaviour by stating that they see no difference at all. Likewise, in cultural competency work, social workers see no difficulty in attributing culture to customs and behaviours (Herberg, 1993). This acceptance of fixing culture to people's identity fails to recognize the ideological power of how the "the culture of whiteness" is Eurocentricly valued as the *only* culture. For instance, why is it that academic writers and social work practitioners choose to use the expression "cultural difference" when speaking about racial minority communities? Perhaps the use of the term "difference" is a relational concept to the referential norm of sameness or rather whiteness. It is, thus, important to recognize that culture, race and ethnicity do indeed structure our political, social and economic relationships in liberal democratic societies.

Understanding the culture of various ethno-racial minority communities is inextricably linked to notions of biology and race; that is, the emphasis on various cultures and ethnicities by social workers reflects the current social relations of power that exist in Western society. For example, the term "ethnicity" can be defined as how people would self-identify themselves in terms of their cultural heritage, practices and values as part of a common group In Canada the term "ethnic" by itself can mean "the less dominant or less powerful cultural identit[y]" (Thomas, 1987, p 5). The failure to notice white people as having an ethnicity signifies the power differentials experienced between dominant and subordinate groups and, moreover, suggests one of the ways in which whiteness operates to maintain these particular set of social relations. Whiteness has power by remaining unnamed and unmarked in contrast to the racial "other," who is classified, ordered and defined into cultural and ethnic categories.

As mentioned earlier, what we know as social work practice today emerged from a racist historical past. Race, as a modern concept, developed between the end of the eighteenth and middle of the nineteenth centuries, which was a time of global expansion of European societies. In this time of conquest and glory for European society, racial minority communities struggled against these imperial and colonial powers (Mason, 2000). According to Henry et al (2000, p 406), colonialism refers to "a process by which a foreign power dominates and exploits an indigenous group by appropriating its land and extracting the wealth from it while using the group as cheap labour." Significantly, Europeans expanded their "economic, military, political, cultural hegemony in much of Asia, Africa and the Americas" (ibid). Furthermore, Mason (2000) notes that the expansion and growth of European influence coincided with the development and rise of science. Not surprisingly, then, the modern definition of race emerged from the purview of science's tendency to classify and order the social world; that is, the development of a hierarchical typology that would account for and explain the reasons why the biological human differences existed. In the broader social context, modern day examples of these typologies include social Darwinism and the use of race by Adolf Hitler to justify the Holocaust in World War II. Current understandings about race, therefore, cannot be separated from a historical past that has been shaped and plagued by racist thought, ideology and practices

Similarly, the field of sociology has taken up the concept of race as an area of study and inquiry and has greatly influenced government and policy-makers in knowing how to respond to the harmonious living together of racially different groups of people. One could argue that sociology has been predominated with strategies of whiteness, that is, carried the hidden prejudicial values and biases of society in general. The operation of whiteness did not require intention and relied upon unintentional systemic forms of discrimination in order to have influence and power An understanding of the ethnic "other" from a white person's standpoint meant that policies and practices developed met the needs of the white people as opposed to the marginalized groups themselves.

In North America, Robert Park, an American sociologist and anthropologist, studied the concept of race in the 1920s as a field of social scientific inquiry and greatly influenced the sociological discourse on race in North America His analysis created the sociology of race relations, which determined the development of the assimilation and pluralism approaches that are still in effect to this day The assimilation approach encourages people from different ethnic backgrounds to conform to the dominant and/or majority group's norms and values, while the pluralism approach works to help people to maintain their ethnic identity, which is seen, for example, in the policy of multiculturalism. The anti-racism perspective, however, critically notes how the race relations approach did not take into consideration the problem of power differentials between dominant and subordinate groups and ignored the problem of racial oppression.

It was not until the 1960s, and due to the influence of social movements such as the civil rights marches in the United States, that a shift in conceptual understandings about the source of racial tension occurred and resulted in the need for sociologists to examine the social, economic and political inequalities that existed between various groups of people. Most notably, the 1967 book *Black Power: The Politics of Liberation in America* by Stokely Carmichael and Charles V. Hamilton provides revelatory insight on the distinction between individual racism and systemic racism. The authors examine how institutions and policies can be influenced by common sense understandings about race. Common sense understandings about race reflected not only the prejudicial values of the time, but also showed how the power of whiteness has historically shaped understandings about the ethnic "other."

Recognizing how the definition and meaning of race has changed over time demonstrates the problematic nature of discussing the concept of race. Therefore, race scholars are apt to use the term with both qualification and caution. Robert Miles (1989), quite correctly, has effectively critiqued the use of the concept of race as an analytical category. Miles centrally argues that race has been created for its ideological effect of masking the economic relations of migrant labourers in the capitalist mode of production. Specifically, he points out that race does not exist as a social or biological category and to grant legitimacy to the concept only helps further mystify people's social relations. Instead, Miles suggests that race exists as an ideological effect of social relationships that have become racialized. Consequently, people's cognizance of the real set of social relations never comes to the fore because processes of racialization are full of myth and illusion and, therefore, are hidden from conscious awareness. Yet, to discount the concept of race as an analytical category altogether can result in the paradoxical effect of what is known as race evasion; that is, to deny the racism exists. For example, in Canadian public discourse, those who oppose recognizing issues of race as a societal problem argue that a focus on race perpetuates and maintains racism. A recent illustration can be seen in the Reform Party's multiculturalism critic Deepak Obhrai's view that Census data collection on race is "divisive and potentially exploitative of visible minorities" (Mitchell, 1998).

Unfortunately, the concept of racism remains a relatively contentious area of inquiry. According to Mason (2000, p.9) the study of racism is either "restricted to the realm of ideas and ideologies" (Banton, 1970; Miles, 1989), which in effect means that there can be no such thing as racist practice in social structures or institutions or, for others, racism means "attitudes, beliefs and ideologies and social actions and structures" (Anthias, 1990, 1992; Carmichael & Hamilton, 1967). Consequently, some writers (Miles, 1989; Mason, 2000) in keeping with the definition of race as ideas or ideologies have arguably contested the empirical study of the concept of racism in our structures and institutions. If one begins with the premise that racism stems from ideas, then one assumes the circular argument that racism causes racism

The difficulty in knowing what constitutes racism, therefore, requires specifying the conditions and theoretical grounds of what may constitute racism in general and, in turn, determining the remedy. Social work practice interventions such as cultural competency and ethnic sensitivity have been viewed as part of anti-oppression work and anti-racism work. Yet, as discussed earlier, methods of practice must also be informed at a theoretical level in order to understand their purposes and outcomes. Aside from the practical applications shown in the cultural competency and ethnic sensitivity models, several assumptions made in these approaches must be examined in relation to the theoretical assumptions of anti-racism work.

It is commonly known that cultural competency and ethnic sensitivity models work well on the "how to" deal with the individual level of prejudice and discrimination shown by social worker practitioners towards ethno-racial minority people (Herberg, 1993; Lum, 1999; Lynch & Hanson, 1998) The purpose of these approaches is to focus on tackling the workers' ignorance and lack of cultural knowledge about the ethnic "other." In doing so, however, the emphasis is placed on "method and efficiency" (Kincheloe and McLaren, 2000, p.282) as opposed to truly achieving substantive, accessible and equitable services for ethno-racial minority clientele since they require structural changes in the organization. These approaches cannot do so because, as noted by Alkimat (Birrell, 1989, p 216), "prejudice and discrimination are static and descriptive concepts that obscure the ideological power of racism and only provide the lowest level of theory." Subsequently, one could argue that producing cultural knowledge about various ethno-racial minority groups reduces people's behaviour, customs and traditions, and attitudes to static and descriptive information, similar to the many cultural artifacts viewed in a museum of civilization.

One of the strategies in dismantling whiteness requires the racialization of white people; that is, recognizing how people from the dominant culture hold an ethnic identity as well. Otherwise, those who come from a social location of whiteness remain invisible and unmarked Likewise, neutral practices represent a particular ideology just as much as when people label racism as ideological. Therefore, documenting and tackling the way racism operates, beyond overt prejudice and discrimination, requires an explicit examination of the cultural and social processes by which everyday innocent actions and measures covertly do produce unintentional forms of exclusion and discrimination towards ethno-racial minority people According to Brown (1985, p.678) and similar to Essed (1991), racism is "given materiality-through-practice in articulation with and by interpellation through the dominant mode of understanding, i e, the meritocratic/individualistic ideological base of the exchange relationship." The dominant mode of understanding presents as fair and neutral, but most people fail to recognize the ideology from which these practices operate. Cultural explanations may occur among service providers to account for why ethno-racial minority clientele are unable to fully benefit from the services of mainstream agencies. For example, clients seeking employment may need to consult with their extended family about the appropriateness of choosing a certain field within which to work. The worker in the agency may receive cultural sensitivity training in recognizing the cultural differences, but at the same time fail to structurally accommodate these differences because the agency practices reflect the culture of whiteness. Few would dare to racialize the culture of whiteness as most see these practices as fair, neutral and non-ideological. Thus, although overt racism may not take place, the unintentional forms of systemic racism persists.

Therefore, to understand racism as a primary structure of oppression, the meaning and significance of race must extend beyond merely a descriptive variable As noted by Alkimat (Birrell, 1989, p.216),

> [W]hile concepts of prejudice and discrimination are helpful on an analytical level of theory because they are so easily operationalized and quantified, racism is the more appropriate theoretical description of the problem precisely because it captures the qualitative character of the oppression

Due to the power of the dominant and/or majority group, the strategies of whiteness must be examined at an ideological level in order to examine the contradictions between the surface appearances of fairness and equality and the below-surface reality of how discriminatory actions occur in everyday practices. Underlying much of current social work practice are racist ideologies or rather strategies of whiteness that work to legitimate the hidden power of the dominant and/or majority group, which helps maintain the status quo. Therefore, moving beyond superficial cosmetic changes requires a documentation of the mechanism and processes by which practices of racism are produced and reproduced and also noting the rationalizations provided by those in power to not make the required changes.

Although more than one axiom of a site of oppression occurs at a time, there nonetheless exists a process that enables social service providers to rely upon a structure of oppression to enforce the subordination of various groups of people, including gay and lesbian, transgendered and transsexuals, the disabled and the poor. Such processes exist because service providers may not be so readily consciously aware of the effects of their actions and, when confronted, often evade or resist the naming of their own practices. This is how whiteness operates Therefore, the work of critical anti-racism praxis is to "expose the contradictions of world appearances accepted by the dominant culture as natural and inviolable" (Kincheloe and McLaren, 2000, p.292). The difficulty, however, is that dominant and subordinate groups often collude with each other in maintaining and reproducing these primary structures of oppression; that is, systems of race, class and gender oppression. Consequently, racializing the practices of white people for the purpose of revealing how strategies of whiteness operate is an important first step in dismantling the primary structure of oppression known as racism.

Problems in Current Diversity Strategies

More recent works on anti-racism and anti-oppressive practice typically make reference to the problem of white privilege and dominance, without naming whiteness, in preventing racial minority clientele from receiving culturally appropriate service delivery within social service agencies (Williams, 2001; Barnoff, 2001; Bishop, 1994) In the Canadian context, most understand white privilege and dominance to mean those who come from the dominant and/or majority group However, one of the difficulties in focusing on white privilege and dominance is that this interpretation presents "ideology as a monolithic unidirectional entity that was imposed on individuals by a secret cohort of ruling-class czars" (Kincheloe & McLaren, 2000, p 284). This point of view fails, at both theoretical and conceptual levels, to show how such a group can effectively maintain privilege and power. Perhaps examining how the dominant and/or majority group uses strategies of whiteness to create systems of dominance can better illustrate the productive and reproductive functions of power and control. Frankenberg (1993, p.1) defines three central components that constitute whiteness: (1) "whiteness is a location of structural advantage of race privilege; (2) it is a 'standpoint,' a place from which white people look at ourselves, at others, and at society; and (3) 'whiteness' refers to a set of cultural practices that are usually unmarked and unnamed." A good example to illustrate strategies of whiteness in operation is to trace general trends in the cultural diversity literature in the last few decades.

Much of the literature in cultural diversity (Este, 1999) grew in response to the changing demographics of the North American population, especially in the area of racial and cultural diversity As a result, human service professionals have had to develop models that specifically focused on the cultural and racial needs of diverse populations as the more traditional models of counselling did not work well with those who did not come from the dominant culture, and more importantly, social workers did not feel comfortable in working with cultures different from their own Often social workers came from the dominant and/or majority group and had little experience and knowledge in working with difference. In the larger socio-political context, and up to the 1980s, much of the social work literature about ethno-racial minority communities carried many of the prejudicial values of the times In fact, Tsang & George (1998, p.74) point out that, from the 1960s to the early 1980s, ethno-racial minority communities were largely viewed from the superior position of the dominant and/or majority group as reflected in some literature and reviewed by Casas (1985):

> The inferiority or the pathological model (Padilla, 1981), the deviant model (Rubington & Weinberg, 1971), the disorganizational model (Moynihan, 1965), the culturally deficient model (Padilla, 1981) and the genetically deficient model (Hernstein, 1971)

The psychologization and pathologization of culturally diverse communities reflected the prejudicial biases of the time, which was inherently steeped and imbued with racist understandings about difference. Clearly, the dominant and/or majority group's ability to shape, define and determine the knowledge base about minority cultures documents not only their power to speak on behalf of those who are marginalized in society, but also how society itself normalizes the inferior position of minority cultures. These social processes that take place, without people being consciously aware, are known as whiteness.

During the 1970s and 1980s, some shifts in the cultural diversity literature began as the visibility of ethno-racial minority communities took more of a foothold within North American society. For example, in the 1970s the colour-blind approach, which focuses on the denial of difference, looked to ways of having the culture of ethno-racial minority people recognized as much as the dominant culture by advocating for the practice of multiculturalism. Multiculturalism encouraged racial minority groups to maintain their culture and, in effect, assumes that all cultures are equal. However, this approach effectively denies the occurrence of racism and stands above issues of inequality.

Whiteness operates by making sure that the dominant culture never defines itself while defining all the so-called "different" cultures of society or rather ethnic minority communities as owning a culture. The failure to recognize cultures other than whiteness creates inequality because within the structures and process of social institutions there lies a multiplicity of needs in terms of access to resources, power and services. But also, too, the earlier use of the term "difference" can be deemed problematic because ethnic minority groups are unfairly set in comparison to the dominant culture So in our use in language of the word "difference," we are reinforcing at an unconscious level the unequal position of racial minority cultural groups.

The discourse of multiculturalism in the 1980s, which recognizes the plurality of cultures, created the demand for practitioners to seek knowledge about the cultural characteristics of clients An example of such literature is the book by Monica McGoldrick entitled *Ethnicity and Family Therapy*, which provides a dictionary-type understanding about various ethnic cultures such as Jewish, Chinese and Italian people. Many social work practitioners wanted to acquire cultural information about ethno-racial minority groups in order to feel comfortable in working with difference. This attitude prevailed within a broader socio-political context where ethno-racial minority people were stereotypically deemed as the "other," that is, as foreign and exotic to the dominant cultural norm. Moreover, many of these practices and norms reflected the norms and values of the dominant and/or majority group and, therefore, failed to respond to the "different" cultural and linguistic needs of various ethno-racial minority communities. Social work practitioners did not need to know the culture they came from, but focused more on knowing the culture of their clients. Often, when asked about working with cultural difference, social workers would comment that they would like a brochure or book that would inform them about "different" cultural practices.

Sociological understandings about race continue to this day to affect the social work practice literature and perpetuate a static understanding of culture where much sensitivity and empathy about the cultural adjustment of racial minorities is emphasized while discussion of racism and systemic barriers remains hidden. By the late 1990s, the social work literature on ethnic-sensitive social work practice figured prominently in the mainstream discourse in working with culturally diverse populations (Lynch & Hanson, 1998; McAdoo, 1993). For instance, Devore & Schlesinger (1999, p.3) discuss the ethnic experience as "a source of cohesion, identity and strength; at the same time; it is a source of strain, discord and strife. Some of the strain is related to the struggle to adapt to the possibilities as well as to the stressful expectations of the new society." The ethnic experience assumes to focus on newcomers to the country. Certainly, one cannot discount the cultural adjustment issues of newcomers to the country. However, the responsibility of the host country to provide resources, services and supports in that adjustment process rests less on the part of newcomers and more on the ability of agencies to accommodate to these so-called "differential" needs. This kind of approach also negates the point that native-born racial minorities still experience systemic and structural barriers in receiving full access and opportunities in social service agencies.

Finally, the stereotyping of cultures is commonly found in social work practice work. For example, Fong & Furoto (2001, p.5) point out that the worker must culturally understand that the "Chinese traditionally value achievement and education." Therefore, if the worker, hopefully, understands these values of achievement, then he or she can better plan the service This kind of cultural understanding puts people from a Chinese ethnicity into a pre-defined, frozen cultural identity. That is, if a person who is Chinese does not fit this cultural stereotype, does that make the person less Chinese in relation to the referential norm of whiteness? In other words, have these writers, who typically believe in culture as "different" from that of the cultural norm, socially constructed what is considered typical and normal for people of Chinese descent? Although Tsang & George (1998, p 75) argue that these models of cross-cultural practice "show less prejudice and increased awareness of the meaning and significance of cultural and ethnic differences," the titles of the models show the referential norm of whiteness playing in the background as a comparison to what is considered normal. Other similar models known in the social work field include "the culturally different model, the multicultural model, and the culturally pluralistic or culturally diverse model" (ibid).

Conclusion

More recently, it should be noted that critical anti-racism work has come under attack from scholars who are sympathetic to the politics of the New Conservative Right (Dei, 1999) In fact, the "intellectual dismissal of race-centric politics" (Dei, 1999, p.396) has manifested through fears of McCarthyism and accusations of "political correctness" where people, especially white people, interpreted the practice of anti-racism as forced confessions to acts of racism This has caused critics to "question the validity, usefulness and relevance of race-centric knowledge and practice" (ibid). Such criticisms reinforce a kind of historical amnesia to the history and context of racial domination, which, in turn, helps to reinforce strategies of whiteness. This is not surprising given the power of whiteness is to find ways to re-centre its Eurocentric knowledge base as the *only* knowledge. Prior to the development and implementation of the anti-racism perspective, Humphries (1997, p.293) makes the observation that Gilroy (2002) warned about the "end of anti-racism" by stating the

> (i) uncertainty and confusion around the meaning of racism; (ii) the conception of "race" as a fringe question; (iii) the fragmentation of antiracism into culture and identity; (iv) the isolation of "race" from other political antagonisms, particular class and gender; and (v) the dominance of an instrumentalist curriculum in professional education.

Throughout this chapter, I have discussed the ways in which racism has been conceptually and analytically understood and some of the barriers to its study. But, more significantly, recognizing how various social work practice approaches do focus very much on culture and identity, as opposed to how people are circumscribed into a set of social relations of domination and subordination, brings to light the question of whether models such as cultural competency can be considered to be a part of anti-racism work. By focusing on the method of practice, that is, the "how to," and without a strong theoretical and conceptual understanding of racism that is placed in the context of one's own social location, there is a tendency to view working with cultural "difference" as nothing but mere task- and competency-based work that safely renders intact the primary structures of oppression. Cultural competency work can be seen as part of an instrumentalist curriculum and, therefore, these practices contribute to what Gilroy (2002) calls the "end of anti-racism."

Hence, one of the ways to resolve this dilemma is to be mindful of the need to show how any theoretical understandings of racism can be meaningfully applied to practice. This is why Dei (1996, p 253) argues that, to carry out effective anti-racism work, the person must be both an excellent "theorist and practitioner for social change." Otherwise, without a theoretical understanding of race and racism, anti-racism does become prey to a battle over language and representation rather than "analyzing racialized relations within broader sociological theory which takes into account of the interplay of political, economic and ideological and historical forces" (Macey & Moxen, 1996, p.301). In addition, the value and importance of locating particular individual experiences to the wider social problem of oppression enables one to move beyond the ways in which knowledge is created about the ethnic "other," which results in "difference" and inequality to the actual lived, material conditions that people experience.

Certainly, examining how the concept of race is a socio-political construct, or rather more than a ideological construction that has structural expressions within social service agencies, means that anti-racism activists should focus on the processural nature of knowledge. Dei (1996) and Calliste (1996) have argued that racism creates "race." Therefore, racism must be recognized as a process because structures and ideologies do not exist outside the everyday practices through which they are created and confirmed. Critical anti-racism work cannot be effectively carried out if there is no praxis involved. Harvey (1990, p.22) defines praxis as "practical reflective activity" and is "what changes the world." Moreover, praxis can only be carried out when there is a

> critique of the knowledge we have. Knowledge changes not simply as a result of reflection but as a result of activity too Knowledge changes as a result of praxis .. For critical social research this means that an analysis of oppressive social structures is in itself a political act. (Harvey, 1990, p 23)

Henceforth, critical anti-racism praxis can only change the social work knowledge base if catalytic validity is accomplished in transformative social change work. This involves questioning and critiquing how people come to know what they know, why people no longer question what is taken for granted as valid knowledge and when the outcomes of social work practice work will cause everyone to want to transform the structures of oppression.

References

Alaggia, R & Marziali, E. (2003) Social work practice with Canadians of Italian background Applying cultural concepts in bicultural and intergenerational issues in clinical practice. In Alean Al-Krenwai and John R. Graham (Eds), *Multicultural social work in Canada Working with diverse ethno-racial communities* (pp 150-173). Don Mills· Oxford University Press

Alkalimat, A I (1972). The ideology of Black social science. In J Ladner (Ed), *The death of white sociology* (pp. 173-189). New York: Random House.

Althusser, L. (1971). *Essays on ideology*. London. Verso.

Anthias, F. (1990) Race and class revisited—conceptualizing race and racisms *Sociological Review, 38*(1), 19-42.

Anthias, F. (1992). Connecting "race" and ethnic phenomena. *Sociology, 26*(3), 421-438.

Banton, M (1970). The concept of racism In Sami Zubaida (Ed), *Race and racialism* (pp 17-34), London: Tavistock.

Barnoff, L. (2001) Moving beyond words, Integrating anti-oppression practice into feminist service organizations *Canadian Social Work Review Journal, 18*(1), 67-86

Birrell, S. (1989) Racial relations theories and sport suggestions for a more critical analysis *Sociology of Sport Journal, 6*(3), 212-227.

Bishop, A. (1994) *Becoming an ally· Breaking the cycle of oppression*. Halifax: Fernwood Publishing

Brown, K.M (1985) Turning a blind eye· Racial oppression and the consequences of white "non-racism" *Sociological Review, 33*(4), 670-690

Calliste, A (1996). Antiracism organizing and resistance in nursing· African Canadian women. *The Canadian Review of Sociology and Anthropology, 33*(3), 361-390

Carmichael, S , & Hamilton, C.V (1967) *Black power : The politics of liberation in America* New York Random House

Casas, M J. (1985). A reflection on the status of racial/ethnic minority research *The Counseling Psychologist, 13*(4), 581-598

Cox, O C. (1948) *Caste, class and race*. New York: Doubleday.

Dei, G.S.J. (1996). Critical perspectives in antiracism. *Canadian Review of Sociology and Anthropology, 33*(3), 247-267.

Dei, G S.J. (1999) Knowledge and politics of social change: The implication of anti-racism *British Journal of Sociology of Education, 20*(3), 394-409.

Dei, G S. J. (2000). Towards an anti-racism discursive framework. In *Power, Knowledge and anti-racism Education* (pp.23-40) Halifax: Fernwood Publishing

Dei, G.S.J., & Calliste, A. (Eds.) (2000) Mapping the terrain: Power, knowledge and anti-racism education. In *Power, knowledge and anti-racism education* (pp 11-22). Halifax: Fernwood Publishing

Devore, W., & Schlesinger, E G. (1999) *Ethnic-sensitive social work practice* (5th ed.). Toronto: Allyn and Bacon.

Dominelli, L. (1996). De-professionalizing social work: Anti-oppressive practice, competencies and postmodernism. *British Journal of Social Work, 26*(2), 153-175.

Essed, P. (1991). *Understanding everyday racism: An interdisciplinary theory*. London: Sage Publications, Inc.

Este, D. (1999). *Professional social service delivery in a multicultural world*. Toronto: Canadian Scholars Press.

Fong, R., & and Furoto, S B C L. (Eds.). (2001). *Culturally competent practice: Skills, intervention and evaluations*. Toronto Allyn and Bacon.

Frankenberg, R. (1993). *White women, race matters: The social construction of whiteness*. London. Routledge

Gabriel, J. (1998). *Whitewash: Racialized politics and the media* London: Routledge.

Gilroy, P (2002). The end of antiracism. In P Essed & D.T. Goldberg (Eds.), *Race critical theories* (pp 249-264). Oxford. Blackwell Publishers, Ltd.

Goodman, P.S (1997) Conference seeks to clear up what it means to be white; Berkeley talks draw high turnout. *The Washington Post* (p A16).

Gramsci, A (1971) *Prison notebooks* New York: International Publishers

Hartigan, J (2000). Object lessons in whiteness: Antiracism and the study of white folks. *Identities: Global Studies in Culture and Power, 7*(3), 373-406.

Harvey, L. (1990) *Critical social research* London: Unwin Hyman

Henry, F, Tator, C., Mattis, W., & Rees, T. (2000). *The colour of democracy: Racism in Canadian society* (2nd ed) Toronto: Harcourt Brace Canada.

Herberg, D C. (1993). *Frameworks for cultural and racial diversity*. Toronto: Canadian Scholars Press

Hernstein, R (1971). I Q *Atlantic Monthly, 228*(3), 43-64.

hooks, b (1990). *Yearning: Race, gender, and cultural politics*. Boston: South End.

Humphries, B (1997). The dismantling of anti-discrimination in British social work. A view from social work education. *International Social Work (40)* 289-301.

Katz, J (1978). *White awareness: Handbook for anti-racism training*. USA: University of Oklahoma Press.

Katz, J., & Ivey, A. (1977) Whiteness awareness: The frontier of racism awareness training *The Personnel and Guidance Journal, 55*(8), 485-489.

Kincheloe, J L., & McLaren, P.L. (2000). Rethinking critical theory and qualitative research. In N. Denzin & Y.S Lincoln (Eds), *Handbook of qualitative research methods* (pp 257-313). Thousand Oaks: Sage Publications

Lacroix, M (2003) Culturally appropriate knowledge and skills required for effective multicultural practice with individuals, families and small groups. In A. Al-Krenwai & J R. Graham

(Eds.), *Multicultural social work in Canada: Working with diverse ethno-racial communities* (pp 23-46). Don Mills, Oxford University Press

Lum, D (1999) *Culturally competent practice A framework for growth & action*. Pacific Grove, CA. Brooks/Cole.

Lynch, E., & Hanson, M. (1998) *Developing cross-cultural competence: A Guide for working with young children and their families* (2nd ed.). Baltimore, MD: Brooks.

Macey, M., & Moxon, E. (1996) An examination of anti-racist and anti-oppressive theory and practice in social work education *British Journal of Social Work, 26*(3), 297-314

Mason, D (2000). *Race and ethnicity in modern Britain* (2nd ed.). Oxford: Oxford University Press

McAdoo, H. (Ed). (1993). *Family ethnicity: Strength in diversity*. Newbury Park, CA: Sage Publications

McGoldrick, M (1982) *Ethnicity and family therapy* New York. Guilford Press.

Miles, R (1989). *Racism* London Routledge

Mitchell, Alanna (1998). Face of big cities changing: visible minorities are nearly one-third of Toronto, *The Globe and Mail*, February 18, p Al

Moon, D. and Flores, L.A. (2000). Antiracism and the abolition of whiteness: Rhetorical strategies of domination among "race traitors." *Communication Studies, 51*(2) (summer). 97-115.

Morrison, T. (1992) *Playing in the dark: Whiteness and the literary imagination*. New York: Vintage Books

Moynihan, D P (1965). *The Negro family: The case for national action* Washington, D C.: U.S. Department of Labor, Office of Policy, Planning and Research

Padilla, A.M (1981). Competent communities: A critical analysis of theories and public policy. In O A Barbarin, P R. Good, O M. Pharr, & J A. Siskind (Eds.), *Institutional racism and community competence* (pp. 20-29). Rockville, MD U S. Department of Health and Human Services

Rex, J., & Mason, D (1986) *Theories of race and ethnic relations* Cambridge, Cambridge University Press.

Rubington, E., & Weinberg, M S. (1971) *The study of social problems* New York, Oxford University Press

Segrest, M (1994a). *Memoir of a race traitor* Boston South End

Segrest, M (1994b). When We Don't Get Race, It Kills Us *Race Traitor: Treason to Whiteness is Loyalty to Humanity, 3*, 23-32

Sullivan, N E, Steinhouse, K, & Gelfand, B (2000). *Challenges for social work students Skills, knowledge and values for personal and social change* Toronto: Canadian Scholars Press.

Thomas, B (1987) *Multiculturalism at work: A guide to organizational change* Toronto YWCA

Tsang, A K T., & George, U (1998). Towards an integrated framework for cross-cultural social work practice *Canadian Social Work Review 15*(1), 73-93

Williams, C. (2001). Confronting the racism in research on race and mental health services. *Canadian Social Work Review, 18*(2), 231-248

Yee, J Y, & Dumbrill, G C. (2003). Whiteout Looking for race in Canadian social work practice. In A Al-Krenawi & J R. Graham (Eds). *Multicultural social work in Canada Working with diverse ethno-racial communities* (pp 98-121) Don Mills Oxford University Press

SALVADORIAN WOMEN SPEAK

Coping in Canada with Past Trauma and Loss

Mirna E. Carranza

Abstract: In this study, ten women from El Salvador shared their experiences of coping with the trauma and loss related to the intense civil war in their country of origin. All of these women were of middle age and had come to Canada as refugees between 1980 and 1989. A qualitative approach and grounded theory methodologies were used to explore the complexities of each participant's account. Findings demonstrate that strategies used by these women to cope with their experiences of trauma and loss were often at odds with North American conceptualizations of trauma and recovery, an important consideration for social work practitioners working with refugees.

Abrégé : Dans le cadre de cette étude, dix femmes du Salvador font part de la façon dont elles ont composé avec les événements traumatisants et les pertes liés à l'intense guerre civile qui a sévi dans leur pays d'origine. Toutes ces femmes étaient d'âge moyen et avaient trouvé refuge au Canada entre 1980 et 1989. Une approche qualitative et les méthodologies de la théorie à base empirique ont été utilisées pour étudier les complexités du récit de chaque participante. Les résultats démontrent que les stratégies qu'emploient ces femmes pour composer avec leur vécu de ces événements et pertes allaient souvent à contre-courant des idées que l'on se fait en Amérique du Nord des événements traumatisants et du retour à la normale, un facteur important à considérer pour les praticiens du service social qui travaillent avec les réfugiés.

THE SETTLEMENT process of refugees is strongly, and usually negatively, influenced by the socio-political and historical context of their country of origin (Ostrow, 2002). For the most part, refugees are forced into flight (Martin-Baro, 1996) and have experienced multiple losses, such as the loss of a significant other, the loss of home, and even the

Mirna Carranza is assistant professor in the School of Social Work at McMaster University.
The author would like to thank the journal's anonymous reviewers for their helpful comments.

Canadian Social Work Review, Volume 25, Number 1 (2008) / Revue canadienne de service social, volume 25, numéro 1 (2008)
Printed in Canada / Imprimé au Canada

loss of their sense of self (Kusnir, 2005). For many refugees, such losses occur in the context of extreme trauma, producing feelings of grief mixed with intense memories of the traumatic event (Jacobs, 1999). Practitioners working with refuges need to be sensitive to how the socio-political and cultural context in which loss and trauma occur shapes not only the expression of trauma, but also an individual's coping strategies and capacity for resiliency.

Such a context is illustrated by the findings of a study undertaken with middle-aged Salvadorian women coping with their experiences of trauma and loss related to the war in El Salvador as they settled in Canada. As women in their middle years, many had husbands, children, and in some cases grandchildren who were also affected by or lost in the war. The participants in this study had to contend with the psychological wounds related to trauma and loss both before and after their migration. Most of the women stated that they had been able to find ways to cope with their experiences. Four primary strategies were used by the majority of the women: calling on positive memories; spirituality and religious beliefs; *no pensar*, or not thinking about it; and self-validation and resisting medication. Importantly, these strategies challenge the ways in which trauma and coping have been conceptualized in North America. A liberationist framework that gives voice to the voiceless and brings forth subjugated knowledge (Martin-Baro, 1996) provides space for alternative, more culturally and gender sensitive interventions with survivors of trauma.

Trauma, memory, and coping

Trauma

The experience of intense trauma related to psychological warfare, persecution, and torture is common among immigrants from Central America (Aron, 1988). Rothschild (2000) defines trauma as "a psychological experience, even when the traumatic event causes no bodily harm" (p. 5). The effects of trauma on the body and the mind are well documented (Boyd-Webb, 2004; Levine & Kline, 2007); Post Traumatic Stress Disorder (PTSD) was first included as a diagnosis in the third edition of the *Diagnosis and Statistical Manual of Mental Health Disorders* of the American Psychiatric Association (DSM-III) in 1980. Herman (1997) describes trauma as "an affliction of the powerless. At the moment of trauma the victims are rendered helpless by an overwhelming force. Traumatic events devastate the ordinary systems of care that give people a sense of control, connection and meaning" (p. 33). According to Herman (1992), trauma has an insidious effect on all aspects of the person's psychological functioning, creating feelings of terror, despair, guilt, and shame and eroding the victim's self-worth and self-esteem, sometimes to the point of dehumanization (p. 51).

Although the effects of trauma would seem to share similarities across groups, the expression and subjective experience of trauma may vary by socio-political and cultural context. Moane (1999) contends that social and political context is central in shaping the psychological development of individuals. If this assertion is extended to trauma, then, arguably, experiences of trauma must also be understood in the context of their occurrence. In the context of the civil war in El Salvador, for example, Martin-Baro (1996) maintains that symptoms related to PTSD exhibited by Salvadorian refugees (including hyper-vigilance, mistrust, and paranoid behaviours) are not signs of persecution delirium born of anxiety, but rather the most realistic response to the social situation in which they lived before migration; these psychological reactions become essential for their survival.

Scholars studying the settlement process of refugees argue that, despite their adaptive function in certain contexts, Salvadorians and other refugee groups fleeing war have more difficulties during their settlement process than other immigrant groups due to their history of trauma (Pottie, Brown & Dunns, 2005; Suarez-Orozco, 1989). Behaviours that may have been adaptive in the context of war may result in a divided community and lack of trust among members of the refugee group in their new home. Recognizing whether such expressions of trauma become maladaptive in the settlement country is an important task for the practitioner working with communities and individuals affected by trauma.

Memory and loss

The multiple losses experienced by refugees may hold emotional, social, practical, or spiritual significance (Falicov, 2002). The experience of loss may, in turn, lead to feelings of overwhelming grief (Van der Veer, 1992). Grief is considered a normal reaction to loss (Corr, Nabe & Corr, 2000), especially in the context of the death of a significant other. In recent years, there has been a growing acceptance that other types of losses may result in emotional reactions similar to those associated with death (Boyd-Webb, 2004). Jacobs (1999) argues that, when the loss occurs in a traumatic manner (as is often the case for refugees), the normal responses of grief and yearning are mixed with frightening memories of the traumatic event, which may interfere with the normal bereavement process. Such traumatic grief creates an intense response in the individual characterized by intrusive memories and distressing preoccupation with the traumatic event, which may come to dominate the person's life. For individuals who have experienced trauma, memory and history occupy a central role in their attempt to understand the symbolic and lived experiences of violence (Riaño-Alcalá, 2002). In such cases, individuals may use the purposeful reminiscence of positive memories in an attempt to overcome negative ones (Bryant, Smart & King, 2005).

According to Rothschild (2000), memory is understood as the process by which the human brain records, stores, and recalls information received from the internal and external environments. Schacter (1996) proposes that information that has greater significance or a higher emotional charge (positive or negative) is more likely to be stored than weaker information. Refugees may be able to draw on their strong positive memories to make sense of their traumatic experience and to resist negative memories. For refugees, longing for a lost homeland or loved one may be more than an aspect of the grieving process; instead, it may be a purposeful act of reminiscence on positive memories that helps them reconstruct their lives.

No Pensar: Not thinking about it

It has been argued that, to understand the current lives of Latin American people, we must consider their historical experiences of oppression (for example, the legacy of war and colonialism) (Comaz-Diaz, Lykes & Alarcón, 1998). As this relates to Salvadorians, failure to understand how trauma is shaped by historical context may lead practitioners to misinterpret certain coping mechanisms. The use of *no pensar* (not thinking about it) is one such mechanism.

No pensar is commonly used by Salvadorians as a means of coping with adversity. On the surface, *no pensar* may appear to practitioners as avoidance. Unlike avoidance behaviours, however, *no pensar* begins with the confrontation of the traumatic event, which is often acknowledged through a small ritual that validates its significance. Acknowledgement is followed by a rapid cognitive shift, which entails putting the experience out of one's mind and carrying on without reacting to it. In other words, one reaches a point where the choice is made to carry on with life as if the traumatic experience had not happened. This coping mechanism stems from Salvadorians' socio-political context of historical oppression in which trying not to dwell on traumatic events has become a well-established means of survival (Carranza, 2007). It is a way of managing life's challenges that has been passed from generation to generation through oral traditions (de Gutierrez, 1993).

The women in this study claimed that calling on positive memories, faith, and *no pensar* are key to their survival and to living with trauma in their settlement country. Many drew on these coping strategies while simultaneously resisting their doctors' attempts to treat their symptoms of trauma (such as crying) using (presumably psychotropic) medications. In doing so, they validated their right to grieve given the intensity of their experiences. Understanding how the socio-political context of their country of origin shaped their experiences and resistance to North American conceptualizations of trauma is critical for practitioners trying to assist them in rebuilding their lives and establishing a sense of community in Canada.

Methodology

The findings presented here are part of a larger qualitative study that focused more generally on the acculturation experiences of Salvadorian women residing in Southwestern Ontario. A qualitative approach was chosen to explore the complexities of the participants' contexts and to develop an in-depth analysis of their lived experiences (Marshall & Rossman, 1995).

I undertook this research from the perspective of an "insider"; I am a member of the Salvadorian community. As is typical of an insider researcher, my attunement to the issues enhanced my understanding of the struggle of the study participants. It enabled me to locate the participants' realities within a structural context foreign to their own. Typically, too, it raised boundary and interpretive challenges of which I was mindful throughout the study (Moffatt, George, Lee & McGrath, 2005).

Sample

Ten women were interviewed, ranging in age from their forties to their mid-fifties. Middle-aged women were chosen because the literature on immigration tends to group women of all ages together without considering issues related to the life course. Because of their age, many of the women in this study were wives and mothers; some were grandmothers, and several had adult siblings who had their own children.

At the time of the interviews, most of the participants were living with their sponsoring relatives. All the participants had entered Canada as refugees and, at the time of the study, had lived here for between five and eight years. Their marital status varied: six widows, two single mothers, and two married.

Data collection

As part of recruitment, several meetings were held with faith leaders and other non-religious community leaders to explain the study and answer questions. Copies of the research proposal were provided when requested, in English and Spanish. This served to alleviate the community leaders' concerns about the confidentiality and legitimacy of the research.

The women were interviewed using a semi-structured interview guide, which covered the areas of experience of war, immigration path, and experiences of settlement in Canada. Interviews lasted approximately two hours, were conducted in Spanish, and, with participants' permission, were audio-taped. All interviews were then transcribed.

All participants were interviewed twice. The purpose of the initial interview was to establish rapport since the content of the interview was sensitive and potentially painful. The purpose of the follow-up interviews was twofold: to check data by repeating certain questions; and to ask additional questions that arose from my initial reading of the transcribed first interview (Lincoln & Guba, 1985).

Grounded theory, in which the development of theory is rooted in the data, informed my approach to data analysis (Charmaz, 2005). Grounded theory supports the use of a "bottom up" analytical strategy, which involves the "discovery" of emergent themes (Strauss & Corbin, 1994). Ely (1991) defines a theme as a statement of meaning that either runs through all, or most, of the related data or carries heavy emotional and factual impact. The theme analysis provided a focused picture of the commonalties among the participants.

Participants' context of exit

All of the women in this study fled El Salvador between 1980 and 1989. The context of their departure was a brutal civil war, which began in 1980 and lasted over a decade (Uncles, 1994). During the course of the war, thousands of civilians lost their lives, and the massacre of entire villages was a common practice (Amaya, Danner & Henriquez-Cosalvi, 2006). The Salvadorian Army let loose a wave of death squads as a way of bringing an end to the alleged communist leadership of the popular movements. Members of the military persecuted and tortured members of the church, of universities, and even of political groups that were calling for more democratic reforms (Ascoli, 2007).

Between 1980 and 1982 alone, almost 70,000 non-combatant civilians were assassinated by government death squads or killed by military attacks on villages alleged to be sympathetic to revolutionary groups. An additional 7,000 "disappeared," and more than one million people fled the country (Golden, 1991). For those who left, the horror of the war would continue to affect them in their new homes (Weingarten, 2004).

Participants' social context in Canada

At the time of this study, the women were living in the Region of Waterloo. Although multi-ethnic, the city where this research was carried out does not have the degree of diversity found in larger urban centres. The Spanish-speaking community is relatively small compared with those of metropolitan centres in Canada (Toronto, Montreal, and Vancouver) where the majority of immigrants and refugees from Latin America have settled. In such a city, there may be less acceptance of racial/ethnic diversity and less understanding of the experiences of refugees from developing countries. The majority of city residents are from White, European backgrounds, and their relatives entered Canada as immigrant families. The very different migration experiences of the majority groups, compared with the experiences of Salvadorian refugees, may mean that the participants in this study, in addition to being relatively isolated, found little external support or understanding with respect to their trauma and losses.

Living with trauma and loss

Calling on positive memories

Many of the women interviewed talked about the importance of keeping their positive memories alive, noting that these memories often entailed the small details of their daily round of life before the war. They perceived that these memories were their only connection to the community they had lost. Ana's comment highlights what the women said about this coping mechanism and its ability to overcome memories of loss:

> You'll think that I'm crazy, but I'm going to tell you anyways. Sometimes, I imagine being where we used to live, and I see myself walking around the neighbourhood from beginning to end. I visit each and all the corners of my neighbourhood. I visit all the people and the places that [laughter] you're thinking that this is not possible, but it is true. I do this in my mind when I get depressed.... I go through my mental images. I visit the places that I and my family used to go to. I have these memorized. For example, I see the *Telegrafo* [a building in the downtown of the city of San Salvador that is near a market], and can see and even hear the women selling stuff and yelling out to the other merchants *el cafee, el cafeee!!!* I visit the *Basilica de Guadalupe* [church of the virgin of Guadalupe]. I like to see all that and keep it fresh in my mind. So when I feel sad or depressed over what I left behind, I remember all that. I lived there my whole childhood and my youth, practically my whole life.... The only thing left from my past are my memories. They give me energy to go on here.

Glenda similarly commented on how she called on positive memories to contend with the loss of her homeland, in this case memories of an earlier time with her family:

> My father would take us all there. We would each ride a horse. We would ride together, but the little ones were put together on one horse. My father was afraid of them falling so he tied them up on the horse. We would ride together for hours and hours in the mountains. It was so beautiful. There is not nature here. The forest is gone. I am always behind four walls in this apartment. All I see when I go out is buildings and traffic. I guess remembering all that helps me to know that there are other worlds out there, where the air is pure. When I think about those places in my country I close my eyes and breath the air I can smell the scent of the mountains in my lungs. You'll think that I am crazy but I feel like my lungs are cleaner when I do that.

Salvadorians come from a society that values the oral tradtion (de Gutierrez, 1993). In societies with a strong oral tradition, "the process of memorization is learned right along [with] the process of language itself" (Burgos, 1999, p. 86). Such an emphasis on memories arguably takes on a renewed meaning in the context of El Salvador's civil war. In this context, positive memories provide a spiritual connection to a time that was not tainted with memories of war, trauma, and migration. The memories shared by women in this study were of a time when they felt a sense of belonging as they recounted the minutiae of their everyday experiences. In such a context, the simplest of memories, such as going to the market, take on profound meaning. Their ability to call on their positive memories to cope with life in their settlement country denotes their sense of agency and their mastery over grief. Keeping these positive, even idealized or romanticized, memories alive allows them to stop their grief from overshadowing the emotional nourishing they received from their loved ones in El Salvador. Importantly, the women's accounts of their use of this coping mechanism also demonstrate their sense of isolation as they worry that others will perceive them as "crazy" for calling on their positive memories in such a way. For the women in this study who survived the violence of El Salvador, coping and memory are intrinsically linked.

Increased faith

Most of the women talked about the importance of their religious beliefs to their ability to cope. Many women reported that they pray and read the Bible more often than they did when they lived in El Salvador. They spoke about how their renewed faith in God has helped them move on from their losses. For example, Beatriz, who suffered multiple losses in the war, told us:

> I don't get sad over my house and my disappeared brother anymore as I used to [because] I've found comfort in the words of God. My faith has gotten stronger here. I think that my belief in God has comforted me in the darkest moments. When I get sad or depressed. God helps me. I pray a lot ... here at home. He helps me go on with life here.

Lucy also described how her belief in God helps her resist the trauma of the war: "My strength is my God. I don't know where I'd be if it wasn't for him. He gives me strength in the darkest moments of my life. He is the light that guides me out of those painful memories."

It appears that the women's religious beliefs and spirituality are a source of their resilience from which they draw the strength to go on in spite of the suffering in their lives. Noteworthy is the fact that these women's faith increased after migration. They take refuge in their faith, which allows them to cope after their multiple losses.

"No Pensar"

Some women talked about *no pensar*, a coping mechanism common among Salvadorian people. Key to understanding *no pensar* is an appreciation of the significance of its ritualistic nature. Rather than simply blocking out traumatic loss, *no pensar* involves an acknowledgement of that loss, an acceptance of it as a matter of unalterable fact, and then a cognitive shift (however temporary) that allows these women to go on with their daily lives. Lorena, whose husband disappeared, told me:

> I think about what they did to my husband a lot. He was a good man ... he did not deserve to die like that. I light a candle for him and then I try not to think about that, [especially] when I am not able to cook or do the laundry because of the painful memories. It helps me because I am able to go on with my everyday life and responsibilities. Like I cannot be crying all the time in front of my kids or grandkids. I find that it is better not to think about the things that I can't change; like I can't change the past. So I might as well put it aside like if it did not happen.

For Lorena, the ritual of lighting a candle when painful memories arise allows her to put these memories aside and accept them for a time. In this way, she is able to function in her daily life and not become debilitated by her traumatic experiences.

I asked another woman, whose brothers were mutilated and put on wood stakes for public display, "How do you cope with what happened to your four brothers?" She stated:

> *Pues yo lo que hago es encomendarlos al Señor porque yo se que ellos handan penando, pero yo no puedo hacer nada por ellos entonces yo despues trato de* [Whenever I think of them I ask God to take care of them because I know they are not in peace and then I try to] not think about them. For me it is part of life you know. Yeah, I lived through a war and saw many horrible things; so what? Yeah, the memories are there but as I said, I just don't think about it. I try to go on with life like if those [horrible] things did not happen.

This woman, too, used the ritualistic aspect of *no pensar* to go on with life, in this case by calling on her faith to acknowledge her painful memories of her four brothers. Failure to recognize the process of ritual, acceptance, and the cognitive shift involved in *no pensar* could lead to the assumption that these women were unable to face what had happened to them. On the contrary, the women's use of *no pensar* is a strategy rooted in their history of oppression and resistance, brought across geographical borders into their settlement country. For this group of women, *no pensar* is used as a way of resisting their traumatic memories and grief and going on with life in Canada. This strategy may be essential for their survival; that is, it allows them to fulfil their household responsibilities and to develop positive relationships with family members. Moreover, they conceptualize loss and trauma as a fact of their lives and do not allow themselves to become engulfed by their negative memories. This standpoint denotes not only the central place of their historical cultural origins in their attempts to move on, but also a sense of control over their memories.

Self-validation and resistance to medication

A few women talked about deliberately resisting Western treatments for depression and Post Traumatic Stress Disorder as a way to cope with traumatic experiences and grief. In talking about their rejection of (presumably psychotropic) medications prescribed by their doctors, the women gave evidence that they simultaneously practised self-validation of their emotions and behaviours. Glenda was one of these:

> My doctor told one of my kids that I had something like *estrés the Guerra* [PTSD] or something like that. Something that had to do with the war, I think.... My doctor gave me some pills to help me with the crying, I think. But I stopped taking them [laughter]. My kids got mad at me ... I got thinking, "I lost my husband. I never found my brother. I lost my house. I left my friends, my *comadre*. Don't I have the right to be sad and to cry once in a while?" On top of all these, I am in a place that I don't like. It's too cold. I am even trying to learn English. Yeah, I feel tired and I cry, but I think, "Don't I have the right to rest my body and my mind and to feel sad after everything that I lived through?" I wouldn't be human if I didn't. I told my kids all this so they would stop bringing me to the doctor thinking that I needed a pill to make me happy.

Rosa similarly resisted medication, while asserting her right to express sadness: "My doctor gave me some pills to make me happy but I never bought them. I still have the note [prescription] someplace. I don't even remember where. I figure I am getting old. I am deteriorating as we speak [laughter]. So what if I cry once in a while!... It is not the end of the world...."

For these women, grief may be a testimony and a vital expression of their love toward those they lost. To take away their sadness may be perceived as disrespectful; an injustice that invalidates what they lost during the war. They considered the outward expression of grief as their hard-earned right, even if it means taking a stance against their own children and Western medicine. Instead of experiencing their grief as debilitating or overwhelming, these women were able to validate their own experiences and expressions of traumatic loss when others were unable to do so. That these women found humour in their resistance to medication speaks to the power of their resilience.

Taken together, the coping strategies employed by the women in this study point to the importance of memory and history in their process of recovery. Specifically, the use of these strategies allows the women to gain a sense of control, albeit in some cases only temporarily, over their traumatic experiences and memories and allows them to make sense of the violence they endured prior to coming to Canada.

Discussion

These findings contribute to our understanding of the impact of war-related trauma and loss and the various coping strategies that may be used to live with trauma. They challenge practitioners to understand that we cannot consider all things equal when working with people who have experienced trauma. The participants in this study all lived through a brutal civil war that left them with multiple losses and, in many cases, with extremely painful memories. These women called on coping mechanisms rooted in the socio-political context of El Salvador, and of Latin America more broadly, in an effort to live with and integrate trauma and loss into their every day lives without becoming engulfed by negative memories.

The women in this study appeared to have a strong sense of agency. They did not view themselves as passive recipients of what was to come and instead were actively using coping mechanisms that allowed them to go on with life in their new country. Many provided themselves with self-validation while resisting Western attempts to stifle their grief, or called on their positive memories or their faith as a way to manage their negative memories. Other women called on *no pensar* as a means of compartmentalizing their memories, a strategy that, perhaps because it involves a process of acceptance, appears to be an adaptive coping mechanism.

Overall, the coping mechanisms used by the women in this study reflect their resilience and the centrality of memory and history in experiences and expressions of trauma. Interventions with refugees need to encompass the fact that the people we serve exist in interaction with their past, present, and future. Thus the findings of this study are congruent with Riaño-Alcalá's (2002) argument, that memory and history take an essential place in people's attempts to figure out the symbolic and lived experience of violence.

The concepts discussed above could be applicable to other refugee groups who, like the participants in this study, bring to their settlement country a history of trauma and loss. Such groups may also make sense of their past traumatic experiences and losses in a manner not fully understood by service providers using Western models. In saying this, I do not propose a divorce from these models, but rather that their exclusive use may lead to misinterpretation of coping mechanisms rooted in a particular socio-political and cultural context.

Social workers and other clinicians working with people who have experienced multiple losses and trauma need to explore and validate the diverse ways in which people make sense of these experiences. Clinicians should explore alternative ways of healing that lead to mutual understanding and to an affirmation of the experiences that refugee people bring with them. It is important that clinicians not try to remove people's pain, but instead validate and accept it while attempting to understand the conceptualization of trauma and resilience from the perspective of service seekers.

For refugees, history and memories of violence are not only personal; they are also collective. Yet, for the most part, the participants in this study found themselves isolated from each other as they dealt with aspects related to their past traumatic experiences. Social workers may need to consider interventions aiming at the collective healing of an entire community. Changes at the collective level may facilitate individual and interpersonal changes. This can only be done by working in solidarity with community stakeholders who, in turn, would inform the process of change.

REFERENCES

Amaya, R., M. Danner & C. Henríquez-Cosalvi (2006). *Luciérnagas en El Mozote* (6th ed.). San Salvador: El Museo de la Palabra y la Imagen.

American Psychiatric Association (1980). *Diagnostic and Statistical Manual of Mental Health Disorders* (3rd ed.). Washington, DC: American Psychiatric Association.

Aron, A. (1988). *Flight, Exile, and Return: Mental Health and the Refugee*. San Francisco: Committee for Health Rights in Central America.

Ascoli, J. F. (2007). *Tiempo de Guerra y tiempo de paz: Organización y lucha de las comunidades del nor-oriente del Chalatenango (1974-1994)*. San Salvador: Equipo Maíz.

Boyd-Webb, N. (2004). *Mass Trauma and Violence: Helping Families and Children Cope*. New York: The Guilford Press.

Burgos, E. (1999). "*Testimonio* and Transmission." *Latin American Perspectives* 26, no. 6, 86-88.

Bryant, F. B., C. M. Smart & S. P. King (2005). "Using the Past to Enhance the Present: Boosting Happiness through Positive Reminiscing." *Journal of Happiness Studies* 6, no. 3, 227-260.

Carranza, M. E. (2007). "Salvadorian Mothers and their Daughters Navigating the Hazards of Acculturation in the Canadian Context." Doctoral dissertation, University of Guelph.

Charmaz, K. (2005). "Grounded Theory in the 21st Century: Applications for Advancing Social Justice Studies." In N. Denzin & Y. S. Lincoln, eds., *The Handbook of Qualitative Research* (3rd ed.) (pp. 507-536). Thousand Oaks, CA: Sage.

Comaz-Diaz, L., M. B. Lykes & R. D. Alarcón (1998). "Ethnic Conflict and the Psychology of Liberation in Guatemala, Peru, and Puerto Rico." *American Psychologist* 53, no. 7, 778-792.

Corr, C. A., C. M. Nabe & C. M. Corr (2000). *Death and Dying, Life and Living* (3rd ed.). Belmont, CA: Wadsworth.

Ely, M. (1991). *Doing Qualitative Research: Circles within Circles*. New York: The Falmer Press.

Falicov, C. (2002). "Ambiguous Loss: Risk and Resilience in Latino Immigrant Families." In M. M. Suarez-Orozco & M. Páez, eds., *Latino: Re-making America* (pp. 274-287). Berkeley, CA: University of California Press.

Golden, R. (1991). *The Hour of the Poor, the Hour of Women: Salvadoran Women Speak*. New York: Crossroad Publishing Company.

de Gutierrez, G. A. (1993). *Tradición oral de El Salvador*. San Salvador: Dirección General de Impresos Generales.

Herman, J. L. (1992). *Trauma and Recovery*. New York: Basic Books.

Herman, J. L. (1997). *Trauma and Recovery: The Aftermath of Violence from Domestic Abuse to Political Terror*. New York: Basic Books.

Jacobs, S. C. (1999). *Traumatic Grief: Diagnosis, Treatment, and Prevention*. New York: Brunner/Mazel.

Levine, P .A., & M. Kline (2007). *Trauma through a Child's Eyes: Awakening the Ordinary Miracle of Healing, Infancy through Adolescence*. Berkeley, CA: North Atlantic Books.

Lincoln, I. S., & E. G. Guba (1985). *Naturalistic Inquiry*. Newbury Park, CA: Sage.

Kusnir, D. (2005). "Salvadoran Families." In M. McGoldrick, J. Giordano & J. K. Pearce, eds., *Ethnicity and Family Therapy* (pp. 256-265). New York: The Guilford Press.

Marshall, C., & G. Rossman (1995). *Designing Qualitative Research* (2nd ed.). Thousand Oaks, CA: Sage.

Martin-Baro, I. (1996). *Writings for a Liberation Psychology*. Cambridge, MA: Harvard University Press.

Moane, G. (1999). *Gender and Colonialism: A Psychological Analysis of Oppression and Liberation*. New York: St. Martin's Press.

Moffatt, K., U. George, B. Lee & S. McGrath (2005). "Community Practice and Researchers as Reflective Learners." *British Journal of Social Work* 35, no. 1, 89-104.

Ostrow, L. A. (2002). "Parents' Participation: Salvadorian and Guatemalan Immigrants' Involvement in their Children's Schools." *Dissertation Abstracts International, A: The Humanities and Social Sciences* 62, no. 12, 4355-A.

Pottie, K., J. B. Brown & S. Dunns (2005). "The Resettlement of Central American Men in Canada: From Emotional Distress to Successful Integration." *Refuge* 22, no. 2, 101-111.

Riaño-Alcalá, P. (2002). "Memory, Representations and Narratives: Rethinking Violence in Colombia." *Journal of Latin American Anthropology* 7, no. 1, 222-225.

Rothschild, B. (2000). *The Body Remembers: The Psychophysiology of Trauma and Trauma Treatment*. New York: W. W. Norton Company.

Schacter. D. (1996). *Searching for Memory*. New York: Basic Books.

Strauss, A., & J. Corbin (1994). "Grounded Theory Methodology: An Overview." In N. K. Denzin & Y. S. Lincoln, eds., *Handbook of Qualitative Research* (pp. 273-285). Thousand Oaks, CA: Sage.

Suarez-Orozco, M. (1989). *Central American Refugees and U.S. High Schools*. Stanford, CA: Stanford University Press.

Uncles, M. L. (1994). "Redefining Democracy in El Salvador: New Spaces and New Practices for the 1990s." In S. Jonas & E. J. McCaughan, eds., *Latin America Faces the Twenty-first Century: Reconstructing a Social Justice Agenda* (pp. 142-157). San Francisco: Westview Press.

van der Veer, G. (1992). *Counselling and Therapy with Refugees: Psychological Problems of Victims of War, Torture and Repression*. New York: John Wiley & Sons.

Weingarten, K., (2004). "Witnessing the Effects of Political Violence in Families: Mechanisms of Intergenerational Transmission and Clinical Interventions." *Journal of Marital and Family Therapy* 30, no. 1, 45-60.

FOUR

Validation Principles and Strategies

DBT defines validation as empathy plus the communication that the client's perspective is valid in some way. With empathy, you accurately understand the world from the client's perspective. With validation, you actively communicate that the client's perspective makes sense. To validate you must have empathy so you understand the other person's unique, nuanced perspective. But validation further requires that you seek out and confirm that a response is valid. You substantiate how the client's emotion, thought, or action is completely understandable because it is relevant, meaningful, justifiable, correct, or effective. Were the client to ask, "Can this be true?" empathy would be understanding the "this" and validation would be communicating "yes." Validation is the second set of core strategies in DBT. Validation comes from the client-centered tradition (Linehan, 1997b; see also the excellent book *Empathy Reconsidered* [Bohart & Greenberg, 1997]).

It's tempting to view the change strategies in the last chapter as the main engine of therapy, the most important part of the help you offer, as if behavior therapy were a crowbar that needs a counterweight of validation to pry the client toward change. But these views are wrong-headed and simplistic. They miss the powerful change that validation, *in itself*, produces. These views also mislead the therapist into thinking that validation is so naturally part of who we are as therapists that no particular training or practice is required to provide it. In fact, active, disciplined, precise validation is required to motivate emotion regulation and thereby create conditions for other change. When clients come from a history of pervasive invalidation and are currently emotionally vulnerable, providing validation is a lot harder than you'd think.

UNDERSTANDING INVALIDATION'S ROLE IN EMOTION DYSREGULATION

Case Example: Mia

Mia came to therapy to get help with problems at work, but things had gone too far to save her job. When she was subsequently fired, her therapist suspended her usual therapy fee, agreeing that Mia could carry a balance to be paid when she was again employed. Now, Mia is interviewing for a new job. She comes to session and tells the therapist about an interview with a company she'd be thrilled to work for—but the interviewer was impossibly rude and asked her several leading questions to "make her complain about her former employer." The therapist asks what she thinks are innocuous questions to assess the situation and to learn what Mia wants to do next but she does not validate that the interviewer was impossibly rude. Mia repeats the interviewer's questions with a dramatic, cross-examining voice tone, and goes on to say she has already drafted the "thank you for the interview" email, listing each inappropriate thing he said. The therapist thinks Mia is misinterpreting normative ambiguity and voice tone as the therapist has seen happen in therapy. She wants to help Mia tolerate these unavoidable aspects of interviewing. So she says, "Well, I can see that the tone of voice might have been difficult but the questions themselves are common to any job interview." Mia flames into fury. "If you want me to pay the balance I owe you, I will, just say so!" "Whoa!" says the therapist, in a very gentle tone, "No, you are misreading me, I know this interview was super important to you" and then the therapist, anxious to avoid further antagonizing Mia, yet irritated herself, slips into a slightly sing-song voice tone as she tries to mask her own emotional reaction. "Listen, neither the interviewer nor I are trying to trick you . . . but I know these kinds of situations are really confusing for you." Mia experiences this as condescending and humiliating but what flashes across her face is scorn. The therapist is quiet for a moment, trying to regroup and get her bearings in the conversation, which then prompts Mia's wave of panic as she tearfully anticipates the therapist abandoning her and failing to get the help she needs.

For the therapist, validation and even empathy can be difficult in this situation. If we saw the bubble over the therapist's head it might say: "I've believed in you enough to let you owe me money and you attack my motivations?! I've been working my butt off for you." The thought bubble might also say, "If she sends that email, she's heading into a suicidal crisis . . . let me out of here." But Mia has good reason to suspect others' intentions. Repeated lies, public humiliations, and emotional coercion were the norm in her family, grinding her to a suspiciousness verging on paranoia. She is understandably sensitive and likely to misread situations as setups where she will be tricked and harmed. Knowing Mia's history and sensitivity, the therapist gently offers careful feedback, but even sensitive phrasing feels like stomping and torturing to Mia. When treading through such old, overused patterns to clarify misperceptions, the opportunity for therapist missteps is high.

Mia's responses, however, are not just misperceptions that make sense in light of past invalidation; they occur because she is being invalidated, *now*, by her therapist, in this *current* interaction. The therapist's first move is to check whether Mia is misreading the situation, that is, to find what is mistaken or invalid about Mia's responses. This triggers for Mia a rush of responses that could be expressed as, "No one believes me, no one will protect me, I have to protect myself or things like this will keep happening." The emotional quality of her communication intensifies. As the therapist persists, tense and walking-on-eggshells about Mia's emotionality, Mia feels the therapist keeps missing her message about how disturbing this interviewer was. She begins to wonder *why* the therapist doesn't get it, reading correctly that the therapist is tense, but then mistakenly guessing the tension is because the therapist needs her to take the job in order to pay the outstanding therapy bill. When the therapist comments that "these kinds of situations are confusing for you," she again implies that Mia is misreading the situation. To Mia this feels like a humiliating pronouncement. When the therapist gently reminds Mia that she knows how important the job is to Mia, it triggers a dialectical shift to self-invalidation and intense self-contempt: "I'm so stupid, I overreact to everything. Everyone else can keep a job what's wrong with me?!" The look of scorn the therapist saw on Mia's face was self-directed. Then amid all of this, Mia feels the therapist withdraw. The therapist *needs* to withdraw, and does so in order to regulate herself so she can help Mia. The therapist's withdrawal when Mia needs her, however, further amplifies Mia's distress: if she is really as out of control as she feels, then why doesn't the therapist help? Can't she see how bad things are? Mia feels trapped in a nightmare as nothing she does works and the safety of at least having her therapist on her side slips away. As emotional intensity escalates, so does the probability of extreme behavior. The risk is high that the session will go downhill and Mia will leave in worse shape than she came in. This is a typical scenario and can be incredibly demoralizing to both therapists and clients.

The Normative Effects of Invalidation

In the heat of the interaction, it would be hard for any therapist to see what is valid and normative about Mia's increasingly emotional communication and especially difficult to see that it is the therapist's own responses that make things worse. When Mia's initial emotion fires and is followed by the therapist's invalidation (questioning Mia's "read" of the situation), Mia's experience and expression of emotion escalates. *As it would for each of us.* It is a normal psychological process for invalidation to produce increased arousal and the sense of being out of control (Shenk & Fruzzetti, 2011). We have all had a time when we found ourselves more intensely experiencing and expressing emotion after someone doubted our read of a situation. If we are doubted long enough and thoroughly enough about something with high stakes, our emotional experience and expression become extremely intense. We fail to process new information and make intense efforts to regain control. This is *normative.* In the vignette, the therapist fails to reckon with the *normative* response that her invalidation of Mia will produce: emotional arousal.

In the face of such invalidation, depending on our learning history and temperament, we may habitually escalate our emotional expression or we may make automatic or intentional efforts to downregulate our emotion. When emotion is intense but not overwhelming we might interrupt ourselves, blunt, postpone, numb, mask, avoid, withdraw, or selectively focus our attention. We may react to our own responses with scorn, fear, or shame (i.e., have secondary emotions). Those of us with better emotion regulation skills might have very intense emotional experiences but we have the ability to modulate our expression to fit the social circumstance. For instance, Mia's therapist deliberately shifts to a more relaxed body posture and slows her breathing as she notices the beginning of her own dysregulation.

When the stakes are high (as in Mia's example above) and others fail to respond to our emotional communication, we can each be pushed to the point of dysregulation, where we literally or metaphorically have screamed, "You don't understand!" Obviously, not all of us resort to intentional self-injury to solve the problem of dysregulation, but the basic psychological processes are the same for client and therapist. Invalidation sets

off heightened emotion, narrowing our perception, thinking, and action urges, focusing us to deal with the threat. The only thing that matters is getting our message across.

For our clients, dysregulated experience and expression may become a habitual, lightning-fast response that in turn rapidly triggers tangled interpersonal patterns. The process may happen so quickly and in such unexpected contexts that as therapists we miss this transition from a cue (e.g., our inadvertent invalidation) to intense emotion. We suddenly find our client in an inexplicably dysregulated state. Everything becomes complicated. Therapy feels like a field of landmines, for both parties.

What is difficult to tolerate, for client and therapist, is that invalidation is necessary—the therapist *must* communicate what is ineffective and does not make sense about Mia's responding. Without the therapist's corrective feedback (e.g., about how to best interpret and respond to an interviewer's behavior), Mia will continue to lose job after job; uncorrected, her misinterpretation of the therapist's motives will corrode her trust in the therapist. Her emotion *is* too strong, both normatively and also practically: it will derail work the two must do to prevent her from precipitously emailing the interviewer. It is not viable to drop the topic. Nor does it help to agree with what's invalid (e.g., "The interviewer sounds like a total jerk, it's outrageous that someone would speak to you that way!"). The therapist must invalidate (or at least avoid validating) emotional responses when they are out of proportion or based on mistaken interpretations.

Helping clients change often requires actively and repeatedly invalidating responses that are incompatible with achieving the client's long-term goals. Yet it is normative for repeated invalidation to produce emotional arousal and eventually dysregulation that interferes with learning and flexible responding. When clients are exquisitely sensitive, how can we best promote change and new learning?

Using validation as you might throw an angry dog a bone won't work in these situations. (Just remember the last time you mouthed a "yes, dear, that must've been hard when I did that" to a loved one who was furious with you.) What's needed is more complex. The therapist must simultaneously align with the client's goals and remain open to what's valid about the client's response, without reinforcing dysfunctional behavior, without evoking such emotional reactivity that the therapeutic task is derailed, and without dropping a focus on needed change. For example, with Mia, the therapist needs to stay open to the possibility that the interviewer's tone was indeed nasty; she might need to validate the extreme emotional experience (the anger fires up so intensely because Mia may be blocked from an incredibly important goal) without validating problematic emotional expression (retaliating by sending the email is not in her best interest).

THE EFFECTS OF ACCURATE, PRECISE VALIDATION

Validation in itself reduces physiological arousal. In other words, validation directly down-regulates emotion (Shenk & Fruzzetti, 2011). Validation in itself also cues adaptive responding that regulates emotion. When you validate, accurately, with precision, you not only reduce arousal but also trigger competing responses. Strongly worded and emotionally evocative validation prompts new, more adaptive emotions to fire, which by definition means that the client's whole system reorganizes. Just as a great writer's word choice evokes emotion, so can the therapist's.

Let's say this way of thinking had guided the therapist when Mia relayed how incredibly rude the interviewer was. The therapist might instead have said, genuinely and with intensity, "How frustrating!! You were so looking forward to this interview, you must be *so* disappointed." How would Mia respond?

MIA: I am! And I'm furious! I had researched everything about the company; I talked for hours with a friend about how to handle the gaps in my work history. Then this jerk ruins it all!

THERAPIST: Oh, Mia, I'm so sorry. I know you put in so much effort to prepare, and were really looking forward to it.

MIA: Yes . . . (*Tears come to her eyes as she realizes how much she had riding on this interview.*) I'm just not going to get chances like these, this is a once-in-a-lifetime thing.

THERAPIST: Yes, this is such a unique opportunity. . . .

MIA: (*Tears welling.*)

THERAPIST: It really hurts . . . um hmm.

The therapist slows down her pacing to promote Mia's full expression of the primary adaptive emotion of disappointment. Mia, crying, takes a deeper breath, and sighs. The therapist also takes a deep breath and sighs, taking the moment to appreciate how hard Mia has been working toward this interview and the extent of emotion she herself would feel if a perfect opportunity were taken away. From this fuller appreciation, she begins to frame change interventions that can be sensitive to the hair-trigger of Mia's emotions, or of anyone's emotions with such a huge potential threat on the scene.

The therapist might then continue:

THERAPIST: You know, right now I feel like there's been an explosion and all the alarms are going off and you're right in the middle of it. Even while you're feeling devastated and crying, you also have your guns drawn ready to shoot the first thing that moves. Am I reading you right? The threat here is so big, you're on full alert, full attack mode?

MIA: (*Nods.*) Exactly! (*Raises her fingers as if pointing guns at the therapist.*)

THERAPIST: Exactly. And I want to say, "Don't shoot my head off! I'm friendly!" (*Puts her hands up.*) Before I say another word, I want to say: "Listen, don't shoot—OK?" (*Turns earnest and intense.*) I know how bad you want this, how hard you worked, how much this means, OK? . . . (*Pauses, holding Mia's gaze.*)

MIA: (*Cries but also smiles and relaxes a little.*)

THERAPIST: Can I put my hands down? Before we go on the warpath, I have an idea . . . OK? You with me?

When the therapist validates, he or she can do so in ways that trigger and reinforce adaptive alternative responses in the very situation where they have been absent yet so needed. At a given moment, multiple emotions may be firing, some at full strength, some weaker. When the therapist directs the client's attention and triggers an adaptive emotion with a validating comment then, by definition, the client's perception, sensing, remembering, and action urges of that emotion also are cued. In other words, validation can cue the full coherent response that comprises the adaptive emotion. By doing so, more flexible, adaptive responding may become immediately possible. In the revised vignette above, validation is guided by the intent to both downregulate arousal and cue adaptive emotions. In combination, they make a productive conversation possible with Mia in an emotional but not dysregulated state.

Precise validation can be incredibly powerful, yet incredibly difficult to do when most needed. Therefore in this chapter I'll break things down. First, I'll describe in general what to validate when people are prone to emotion dysregulation. Then, I'll give you four guidelines for using validation strategies: (1) search for the valid; (2) "know thy client"; (3) validate the valid and invalidate the invalid; and (4) validate at the highest possible level. Then with these shared basic concepts in mind, we'll look at how to use validation to strengthen emotion regulation, concluding with an extended clinical example to show how validation and change strategies are combined.

WHAT TO VALIDATE

When a Client Is Emotionally Dysregulated

In nearly all situations and with nearly all clients, you can assume it will be welcome if you validate that the client's problems are important (*problem importance*), that a task is difficult (*task difficulty*), that *emotional pain* or a *sense of being out of control* is justifiable, and that there is *wisdom in the client's ultimate goals*, even if not in the particular means he or she is currently using.

It is essential to validate clients' *location perspective*, that is, their views about where they are, their current views about life problems, and beliefs about how changes can or should be made. Unless the client believes that the therapist truly understands the dilemma (e.g., exactly how painful, difficult to change, or important a problem is) he or she will not trust that the therapist's solutions are appropriate or adequate. Collaboration will be limited and so too the therapist's ability to help the client change.

Say you are away at a conference and you get an emergency page. You phone the number and an emergency room nurse answers and tells you someone you love dearly has been terribly hurt and you must sign the release before needed medical attention can take place. You begin to get directions to the hospital. The nurse tells you to "go to the highway and then head south until you come to . . . " But you tuned her out as soon as she said "south"—you think the conference location is such that you actually need to catch the freeway and head *north*. You try to communicate this. She says, "Oh, no, just catch it south and then . . . " You have a rising sense of panic; she isn't listening! She doesn't know where you are. She *must* understand where you are before she can help you get where you need to go. You intensify your emotional expression—the stakes are tremendous.

It is often like this for our clients. They have a sense of where they are; we then begin to provide directions that feel as if we don't know where they are. We persist. It is infuriating and terrifying for our clients. It matters who has the client's correct location and where that location is relative to where the client wants to go. If that emergency room nurse is right, she needs to win the argument—she will have to calm you by clearly showing you she knows exactly where you are. But if you are right, the nurse must be open to your influence. Often a rift in collaboration comes from exactly this type of disagreement about the client's location relative to their goals, thus it is essential to validate and get consensus on location.

When a Client's Response Is Both Valid and Invalid at the Same Time

You will often need to communicate how the same response is simultaneously valid *and* invalid. The response of self-hatred may be relevant and justifiable (valid), yet at the same time ineffective (invalid) because it is incompatible with the balanced problem solving required to keep oneself from doing the hateful behavior again. Or, for example, say you've forgotten some fact that's important to a client without being aware you have

done so. As the conversation continues, the client becomes overly cheery and stops saying anything of substance about the topic. When you wonder aloud about the change in mood and depth of the conversation, the client airily dismisses your concern. The client's response may be valid in terms of past learning history (e.g., if her cultural background prohibits drawing attention to another's failings or directly expressing irritation about them) or current circumstances (if your tone is even slightly defensive or accusatory and it's logical to infer you won't be open to the feedback). But simultaneously, her response is invalid if it fails to prompt you to correct your behavior when you need the fact to help her.

When It's Hard to See Anything Valid

When it is hard to see what's valid about a response, first look for how it might be relevant and meaningful to the context. In the context of psychotherapy, curiosity about whether my therapist has kids is relevant if I am assessing if she will understand my struggles as a parent (chitchat about the Mariners' new shortstop is not). Sometimes therapists are trained to be suspicious of such curiosity. To validate means to attend to how such questions are relevant, not pathological. Second, see if the response is well grounded or justifiable in some way. Look for the *facts, logical inference, or generally accepted authority* that makes the response sensible. It is logical for a client to infer that I am irritated with him if I greet him less warmly in the waiting area after he has left me a phone message full of personal attacks and criticism. Third, search for how a response is *an effective means* to obtain some immediate end. Even patently invalid behavior may be valid in terms of being immediately effective. Cutting one's arms in response to overwhelming emotional distress makes sense, given that it often produces relief from unbearable emotions: it is an effective emotion regulation strategy. Of course, a response can be valid in more than one way. When a client says she hates herself, hatred is both relevant and justifiable if the person violated her own important values (e.g., had deliberately harmed another person out of anger). Ultimately, every response is valid in terms of historically making sense—all factors needed for the behavior to develop have occurred: therefore, how could the behavior be other than it is?

Other Validation Targets

In any given situation, you can validate emotional, behavioral, or cognitive responses as well as the client's ultimate ability to attain goals. For adaptive emotion regulation, one must experience and express primary emotions. Validation is required to develop this ability. Therefore, read the client's emotions, directly validate primary emotions (e.g., "feeling sad makes sense"), and encourage emotional expression. Observe and label clients' emotions (e.g., "Your eyes look teary; I wonder if you feel sad right now"). This helps to teach client these skills.

To validate behavioral responses, observe and label behaviors. For example, observe when demands are self-imposed; standards for acceptable behavior are unrealistic; and guilt, self-berating, or other punishment strategies are used (identify the "should"). Counter the "should" (i.e., communicate that all behavior is understandable in principle). Accept the "should" (i.e., respond to the client's behavior nonjudgmentally and discover whether there is truth to the "should" when phrased as "should in order to").

To validate cognitive responses, elicit and reflect thoughts and assumptions, find the "kernel of truth" in the client's cognitions, acknowledge the client's intuitive ability to know what is wise or correct (wise mind), and respect the client's values.

To validate the person's ability to attain desired goals, assume the best, encourage, focus on strengths, contradict/modulate external criticism, and be realistic in assessment of capabilities. (I've always liked Linehan's [1993a] use of "cheerleading" for this type of validation. Whether your team is up by 14 or losing badly in the last minutes, on a muddy field—your response as a cheerleader is the same. Right there on the sideline until the whistle blows, there on the bus home, there at the next practice.)

The above guidelines on what to validate are summarized in Table 4.1. Now, with these concepts in mind, let's break the complex use of validation strategies into four component steps.

TABLE 4.1. What to Validate

- The client's primary emotional responses and expressions
- The client's behaviors: observe and label
- The client's cognitions: reflect his or her thoughts, assumptions, and values
- The client's ability to attain his or her ultimate goals

When a client is dysregulated, validate:
- The problem's importance
- The task's difficulty
- The client's emotional pain
- The client's reasons for feeling out of control
- Wisdom in the client's ultimate goals (if not the means selected)
- The client's location perspective

When it's hard to see what to validate, validate:
- Past learning history
- Whatever is justifiable in terms of facts, logical inferences, or accepted authority
- Whatever is an appropriate or effective means to an end

HOW TO VALIDATE

Search for the Valid

Actively search for what is valid, and assume that there always is *something* valid. You don't make the client's response valid. You *find* what is valid. "The therapist observes, experiences and affirms but does not create validity. That which is valid pre-exists the therapeutic action" (Linehan, 1997b, p. 356).

Know Thy Client (and the Psychopathology and Normal Psychology Literatures)

Be aware of what is valid and invalid for the specific client. This is where a thorough grounding in psychological science to understand what is normative and how psychopathology develops and is maintained becomes a true asset for therapists. Remember your case formulation, especially, the emotion sequences that are habitual for this client—what are likely primary emotions and secondary emotions for this particular client? Constantly be aware of the client's current emotional arousal and how it affects the ability to process new information, then balance change and validation accordingly.

Validate the Valid; Invalidate the Invalid

Be precise about what you are validating. For example, Bettina is thinking of moving in with the archetypal Bad Boy she met this weekend after he charmed her at the dance club (the fourth Bad Boy in the last 3 months). She asks that all of today's session focus on how to hang on to this relationship. As has happened before, Bettina cancelled plans with friends and blew off important obligations in case the new boy called, and she had no energy to further her job search. From past experience, this situation is a looming disaster in Bettina's parents' view. What is invalid may jump out at you and you may come to ignore or trivialize her feelings of love and the intense desire she has to make this relationship work. But dismissiveness invalidates both the valid and invalid aspects of the request.

Instead, validate the valid (perhaps identify the wisdom of the ultimate goal of romantic love or of the specific qualities she is attracted by) while invalidating the invalid (e.g., by insisting that the session agenda include an adequate plan to proactively address the life crises). To invalidate the invalid, be descriptive and nonjudgmental, articulating how the response does not make sense or does not work. For example, Bettina's therapist might say:

"I agree—one of our most important goals is helping you have intense loving relationships that really work for you, and one aspect of that is that when a new love starts you lose all motivation to work on things that give you self-respect. This increases self-hatred; then you feel more needy and put incredible pressure on the lover to make you feel good about yourself. If we're not smart about our session time today, things could go downhill in a hurry."

When you can genuinely, with empathy, describe both what is valid and what is invalid, you don't need to walk on eggshells. You can go "where angels fear to tread," freed up to tell it like it is without alienating your client.

Validate at the Highest Possible Level; Actions Speak Louder Than Words

Linehan (1997b) distinguishes six levels of validation (described below); Level 6 is the highest. At each level, do not rely solely on explicit verbal validation: nonverbal expressions are both required and often more powerful. In other words, if you were trapped at a 4th-floor window of a burning building, and a firefighter showed interest, accurately reflected your distress, and genuinely communicated how it made sense, it would still be insufficient! What you need is for him to grab your arm and get you to safety. Functional validation—responding to the client's experience as valid, and therefore compelling—is essential. Verbal validation alone, when functional validation is required, is an error often made by therapists.

Level 1: Listen with Complete Awareness, Be Awake

Listen and observe in an unbiased manner, and communicate that the client's responses are valid by listening without prejudging. So, for example, the therapist hears Bettina's request to talk about a love interest as if it were completely new, without construing it solely in terms of a pathological recurrent pattern.

Level 2: Accurately Reflect the Client's Communication

Communicate understanding by repeating or rephrasing, using words close to the client's own without added interpretation. Remain nonjudgmental, that is, not focused on improvement or encouragement or evaluating effectiveness or merit, but instead on the simple "is-ness." "This is how it is for you right now."

Level 3: Articulate Nonverbalized Emotions, Thoughts, or Behavior Patterns

Perceptively understand what is not stated but meant without the client having to explain things. Clients with a pervasive history of invalidation are so sensitized that often they disclose a tiny bit but feel they have told you everything; or so habitually mask or control expression that you need to intuit the rest from small signals. Greenberg (2002) reprinted a quote from Truax and Carkhuff (1967) that captures what is aspired to in these first three levels of validation. The validating therapist:

> (U)nerringly responds to the client's full range of feelings in their exact intensity. Without hesitation, the therapist recognizes each emotional nuance and communicates an understanding of every deepest feeling. The therapist is completely attuned to the client's shifting emotional content, senses each of the client's feelings, and reflects them in words and voice. With sensitive accuracy, the therapist expands the client's hints into full-scale (though tentative) elaboration of feeling or experience. (Greenberg, 2002, p. 78)

Level 4: Describe How the Client's Behavior Makes Sense in Terms of Past Learning History or Biology

Identify the probable factors that caused the client's response. For example, to a client who constantly seeks reassurance that therapy "is going okay," the therapist might validate by saying, "given the unpredictability of your parents, it makes sense to have the feeling of waiting for the other shoe to drop and seek reassurance."

Level 5: Actively Search for the Ways That the Client's Behavior Makes Sense in the Current Circumstances, and Communicate This

Find the ways a response is currently valid, whenever possible, and remember not to rely only on verbal validation. For example, say you were walking to a movie theater with a friend who'd been raped in an alley, and you proposed that you take a shortcut through an alley so that you wouldn't be late for the movie and your friend said she did not want to because she was afraid. Saying, "Of course you're afraid, you were raped in an alley, how insensitive of me" would be a Level 4 validation. Saying, "Of course you are afraid, alleys are dangerous, let's walk around" would be a Level 5 validation. When you can find a Level 5 validation (and search like a fiend for it), use it rather than a Level 4. Especially here, remember that *you* may in fact be the source of current invalidation. So, for example, with the client seeking reassurance, the therapist might search for ways that he or she is communicating ambivalence or in some other way cuing the client's anxious response, so that seeking reassurance is sensible. Validating in terms of the past (unpredictable parents) when in fact there are aspects in the current situation (therapist ambivalence) prompting the response is experienced as extremely invalidating. ("Yes, yes. I know you are angry with me, but could we discuss how this reminds you also of your family of origin?") Level 5 is like saying, "This response is *not* completely screwed up; here is how it makes sense *now* in the current context." Level 5 is the antithesis of pathologizing. Instead of emphasizing what's wrong, you find what is effective, adaptive and relevant about the response in the current circumstance.

Level 6: Be Radically Genuine

Act in a manner that communicates respect for the client as a person and an equal, rather than as "client" or "disorder." Play to the person's strengths rather than to fragility, in a manner comparable to how you'd offer help to a treasured colleague or loved one. This is clear-eyed and unflinching—you are what you are and I can handle it and you can handle it. The therapist validates the individual rather than any particular response or behavioral pattern. Kelly Wilson (Wilson & Dufrene, 2009) has talked about this same quality as treating our clients as sunsets, rather than math problems. Rogers and Truax (1967) have described this radically genuine stance:

> He is without front or façade, openly being the feelings and attitudes which at the moment are flowing in him. It involves the element of self-awareness, meaning that the feelings the therapist is experiencing are available to his awareness, and also that he is able to live these feelings, to be them in the relationship, and able to communicate them if appropriate. It means that he comes into a direct personal encounter with his client, meeting him on a person-to-person basis. It means he is being himself, not denying himself. (p. 101)

While empathy and functional validation should remain high throughout therapy, the active verbal validation to provide corrective feedback or to balance pathologizing should be faded from an initially high level early in therapy to normative levels late in therapy. For example, Bettina's parents were highly critical and tended toward the most pathologizing explanation of Bettina's behavior. Early in therapy, the therapist actively offered counterpoints of how Bettina's behavior also was valid. Later in therapy, the therapist expected Bettina to self-validate as well as critique her own behavior in a balanced manner, seeing what is effective and ineffective.

HOW TO USE VALIDATION TO STRENGTHEN EMOTION REGULATION

Effective emotion regulation requires blending the ability to experience and express emotion (accept emotion) and the ability to actively regulate emotion (change emotion). Les Greenberg writes about this as "emotional wisdom," knowing when to be changed by emotion and when to change emotion (2002, p. xvi).

Prerequisite to either accepting or changing emotion is the ability to identify and label the emotion and make sense of the information the emotion provides. When people have experienced both a lack of validation and pervasive invalidation, they often have significant deficits here (e.g., Ebner-Priemer et al., 2008). Learning to correctly discriminate and label emotions and needs requires caregivers to appropriately attend to those emotions and needs. For example, a 25-year-old client had been raised by a single mother who had been overwhelmed by her own struggles and so self-focused that she never asked questions or noticed much about her daughter (the client). Once the therapist noticed the client's lips looked dry and said, "You look thirsty, would you like some water?" The client had never noticed the sensation of dry lips before nor labeled the internal sensation as "thirsty" (in fact she seldom drank, even with meals).

By using validation strategies, you teach your client to recognize and use his or her experience of emotion (e.g., "Yes, what you are feeling is healthy sadness, it reflects grieving for this important thing you lost" or "Yes, that fear is organizing you to escape this situation that is potentially harmful for you"). This reestablishes the innate, wise-mind, adaptive use of one's own emotional responses to identify what works and is effective. With Mia, for example, validation helps her learn to use anger and its intensity as a signal to identify what need or goal is thwarted and then to choose whether to retaliate (go with the action urge of anger) or to check the facts about the threat and find ways around it to reach her goal or meet her need. Validation strategies can also be used as an informal exposure procedure to strengthen abilities to experience and accept emotion, as well as be used to change emotion by cuing adaptive emotion.

Using Validation as an Informal Exposure Procedure: Accepting Primary Emotions

As discussed in Chapters 1 and 2, the biosocial theory argues that our clients learned that expressing valid needs, emotions, thoughts, or other natural and genuine primary responses brings invalidation. Because these inclinations and responses have been pervasively invalidated, the person learns to avoid his own genuine, primary behavior. In pervasively invalidating environments, fear conditioning takes place so that we not only avoid the feared object (invalidation) but also avoid any experience of the private events (thoughts, sensations, emotions, etc.) which might lead anywhere near invalidation. We become extremely sensitized to all cues that have to do with invalidation *and* we become phobic of our own valid, natural responses. Letting ourselves respond naturally is often as evocative as if you dropped a spider in a spider phobic's lap. Our own primary emotions—those valid first flashes of response—are rapidly followed by escape, that is, a secondary response that ends or modulates the primary response. The avoidance may be subtle. For example, we sense a slight inattention in our therapist as we speak and so we change what we were going to say to a less risky self-disclosure. We feel irritated with our partner without awareness of the more vulnerable first flash of sadness or shame that we rapidly escaped. Escape and avoidance may also be more obvious such as through dissociating in session, or intentional self-injury.

These conditioned emotional reactions and avoidance patterns may come up when you validate or invalidate clients' responses. Consequently, principles of exposure therapy can guide your work. As in more formal use of exposure and response prevention, you identify what specifically cues the difficult emotion(s) and what behaviors function as escape. Then you gradually shape increased emotional experience and expression with cue exposure and response prevention. Over time, with such informal exposures, the client learns to experience and express valid responses with less disruption and less avoidance. It's easiest to see the nuance of this with a clinical example.

One day in session with you, as your client tells you something important about his week, there's an abrupt shift in affect and he looks ashamed. Within a few sentences he is making extreme statements about how he is making no progress, he is a burden to you; he is not using your time well. He looks spacey, and ends with an irritated, "What are we even working on in here?"

The first five times this happened, you went right along with the stated question. Maybe you had an unclear hypothesis about what was going on, a vague sense that he was ashamed. You tried to reduce shame by saying that change is normally often a slow, difficult process. You replied, "Would it be helpful to go back over our goals together and how today's session relates to that?" Now, in this sixth re-run, you realize this scenario plays over and over. Your attempts at reassurance and validation of progress seem to have no effect.

Today, guided by ideas about fear conditioning and exposure therapy, your first move would be to assess what happened that led to the shift, hypothesizing that perhaps a routinized escape pattern has fired. Perhaps shame is a secondary response to a more primary emotion. You

ask, "Did something just happen? We were talking about *X*, then I said *Y*, and then somewhere you had a big spike in hopeless statements. Can we go back? When I said *Y*, how did that affect you?" You go microsecond to microsecond to track his experience, using chain analysis to identify the controlling variables of the in-session emotion dysregulation. You learn he began the session glad to see you. The shift was cued when you misunderstood something important he had said.

The first primary flash of emotion was his hurt at being misunderstood. He then instantly judged himself for feeling hurt—he felt ashamed and humiliated to be longing for your understanding. This spiraled into a virulent stream of self-invalidation (the thought "you're an f'ing baby, a bottomless pit") with the theme that he was being immature and overreactive. Then his anger flared up at the therapist as a primary response to not getting an important need met and at himself as an escape response from these painful, vulnerable emotions. Then he got spacey, irritated that he couldn't focus and irritated with you as nothing therapeutic was happening. You hypothesize that the cue of you misunderstanding him set off a cascade of secondary responses which functioned as escape from the discomfort of *primary emotions* of *longing* (to be understood) and *hurt* (by you misreading him).

It can be hard to sort out what is primary and what is secondary. Greenberg (2002) writes that primary emotions have the quality of shifting in response to the moment's circumstances, feeling fresh or new, feeling whole, deep, and "good" even if not happy. This is in contrast to secondary emotions. When secondary emotions fire, they often obscure or feel diffuse, and the person feels upset, hopeless, confused, or inhibited, and has low energy and is whiney.

With informal exposure then, you would want to re-present the cue. For instance, you might say, "So, when I misunderstood you . . . " When clients are prone to dysregulation, you titrate the presence of the cue to match their tolerance, gradually increasing the intensity of the cue. For example, to gradually intensify the cue for an arachnophobe, starting with pictures of spiders, then moving to having a small spider moving across the room, to eventually handling a tarantula. You are not doing flooding or implosion therapy. To encourage contact and increase tolerance with different private experiences, you provide gentle direction to focus internally—you can instruct the client in the skills of mindfulness of current emotion and of observing and describing emotion. The chain analysis, too, is emotion-focused: you help him put emotions into words, especially encouraging the differentiation and elaboration of primary emotions.

In the above example, the therapist might begin with nearly verbatim paraphrasing of the client and then gently add more intense emotional descriptions of the client's experience as they proceed: "So even though part of you judges your reactions and says it shouldn't bother you, at the same time it *did* bother you. It hurt a little . . . and to me that makes sense, I need and want understanding at moments like that, too" (*Level 5 validation*). A bit further along the therapist validated the emotional need more intensely, still titrating the cue by indirectly validating with a metaphor. "To me emotional needs are like needing water—if I'm crossing the desert and come across a cup of water, it is a big deal. Deprivation naturally makes everything more intense."

The next task in informal exposure is to block avoidance behavior. You help the client experience the primary emotion without escape or other maladaptive coping. The idea is to prevent avoidance responses but to do so in a way that enhances the person's sense of control over the situation and himself. Therefore, before blocking avoidance behaviors, you may explicitly discuss the benefits and drawbacks of avoiding and disrupting primary emotional experience or expression to micro-orient to the rationale to help the client clearly see the benefit of collaborating on the therapy task. As in more formal exposure protocols, you also may ask clients to describe or enact all the ways they avoid (i.e., interrupt or inhibit themselves) when they don't want to feel or express primary emotions or other valid responses. While the ways to avoid emotional experience are myriad, keep your eye out for two common ones that function as escape behaviors. These end contact with emotional experience and thereby disrupt adaptive emotion and other valid behavior: (1) secondary emotions and (2) self-invalidation. Returning to the example above, when you comment that the client felt hurt, you bring him into contact with hurt and disappointment, which gently blocks avoidance. When he then says, "Yeah, but it's silly to feel sad, it was such a small thing" you'd say, "Right, it isn't a huge thing, and yet still it was important to you so you feel a little hurt. I feel hurt, too, when someone misunderstands me on something important." You gently block efforts to escape through habitual self-invalidation, re-present the cue, and validate the primary emotion. Over many such informal exposure interactions, the client increases his tolerance for the painful emotion and engages in less maladaptive avoidance. We can either stay with this until he fully experiences and explores his primary experience of hurt and any action urge that eventually arises from that. Or, if the client has great difficulty experiencing or expressing emotion, even a momentary increase in staying with the experience or expression might best shape approximations toward more regulated emotion.

The final component of informal exposure is to help the client respond differently to primary emotions and other genuine responses. Opposite action is the DBT skill designed to help clients do this. Linehan (1993b) has written about this as literally doing exactly the opposite of the action

tendency of the targeted emotion. For example, the action tendency of fear is to freeze or flee. To do the opposite would be to approach. The action urge of shame is to hide and the opposite action would be, for example, to speak openly with upright posture about the "transgression." In the context of using validation as informal exposure, the idea is to stay with, rather than escape, primary emotional experience, and may be even to deliberately lean into the experience instead of pulling away.

However, validation can be incredibly evocative and difficult. Your validating comment about a previously avoided primary emotion or response may increase fear to such an extent that it becomes disruptive and disorganizing. For some clients, validation is actually more difficult to bear than invalidation. Some clients fear that experiencing emotion itself will be traumatic, and they have *in fact experienced* emotions that have overwhelmed them to the point where they have lost control, sometimes in debilitating ways. For example, after a difficult session, a client can't get out of bed for three days. When people have this secondary target of emotion vulnerability, it creates a complex, hard-to-convey blend of shame, despair, desperation, resignation, exhaustion, and an isolating, terrifying certainty that no one can help. For these clients, the trauma associated with emotional experience itself may best be treated by *changing* emotion or skillfully modulating it. Instead of leaning into or deepening emotional experience, the client needs to learn how to move away from emotional experience, but to do so in ways that are not harmful, that accentuate his sense of control, and that diminish the sense of isolation with the experience. One way to help clients develop this ability to change emotion is to use validation to cue adaptive emotion.

Using Validation to Cue Adaptive Emotion: Changing Emotion

Emotions evolved to help us rapidly adapt. Our emotional system constantly registers and rapidly interprets our context, reorganizing and mobilizing us so that our behavior, inclinations, and orientations are constantly shifting to locate and adapt us to our continually changing context. Kelly Wilson's teaching story about the rabbit and the rabbit hole illustrates this process (Wilson & DuFrene, 2008). As a bunny sits on the grassy meadow, he has a full repertoire of behaviors that are possible, some stronger than others. In that sunny, safe context, the bunny eats, looks around, scratches, grooms, lays down. There is a fluid, shifting nature to this responding. But if there is a rustle in the bushes from a predator, those bunnies whose behavioral repertoire narrows to a single response—bolt for the rabbit hole—have considerable survival advantage. In that context, behaviors of stopping for a last scratch or bite to eat become (literally) extinct. Emotionally sensitive bunnies that bolted as soon as they registered the other bunnies' fear also had survival advantage. Emotions work like that according to Greenberg (2002), and emotion theorists like Fridja (1986), Izard (1991); and Tomkins (1963, 1983). We are wired for certain cues to generate complex full-body responses that include rapid assessment of the environment and one's relationship to it, as well as motivation of action and communication to others.

When you validate (or invalidate), you often cue emotion. You can deliberately use this to your client's advantage. When emotion fires it disrupts ongoing activity and organizes the person for the next situation. Using validation to cue adaptive emotion helps activate the entire skillful repertoire associated with the adaptive emotion. In other words, cuing adaptive emotion can rapidly reorganize the client for more adaptive behavior, as shown earlier with Mia. Mia is just like the bunny. She enters the therapy session after the difficult job interview, and she has a whole repertoire of things she can do in session, some more at strength and likely to dominate the moment, others less likely, but all possible and in a meaningful way, *present*, even though not manifest. The therapist's comment to Mia, "That must have been so disappointing!" directs the client's attention and evokes an intensified experience of sadness and disappointment; other disappointing elements of the situation come to mind, followed by tears. When you cue an emotion you cue the *whole* response system that is that emotion. This is as true for adaptive emotions as it is for problematic ones. If you keep this in mind, you can deliberately choose to validate adaptive primary emotions that are present and genuine for the client in a troubling context.

To cue the adaptive emotion, scan for the primary adaptive emotions that are present but in the background of the client's most obvious emotion. This is like being in the forest in a raging windstorm and deliberately listening for the waterfall. Note what the client says yet search for what is also present but less dominant in the person's experience. For example, if someone cuts me off on the freeway, the strongest sensation I feel is anger. But I also feel surprised, disappointed that people drive like that, scared, and humbled as I also at times drive poorly, and so on. If you made a validating comment about any one of these aspects, it would bring me into contact with that part of my experience and likely increase my flexibility: I will not only feel and act angry, but I will also be influenced by whatever else you bring to my attention.

Validating to cue adaptive emotion can't be done as a bait and switch. In other words, if you try to get me off a problematic response by validating something else, it communicates that my primary response is invalid. The trick when scanning for adaptive emotions is to think dialectically, seeing the "truth" in all responses by articulating what is valid about each

emotional response. This differentiates the emotions, helping the client have a clearer sense of the action urge and information from his or her emotions. For example, Greenberg (2002) refers to the whining complaint of "why me?" as "the voice of protest" and says this can be thought of as a fused or undifferentiated blend of anger and sadness. Validating to differentiate sadness (e.g., "you are of course terribly disappointed") and irritation (e.g., "what a frustrating situation!") can resolve the experience into a changed emotional and self-organization where the action urge of one emotion becomes more predominant and leads naturally to action.

Cuing adaptive emotion requires the therapist to believe that primary emotion is adaptive and will usefully organize the client. The therapist must resist the temptation to rescue the client from experiencing sadness or despair. Primary emotions are like "a spotlight that turns on to show us what [problem] needs cognition" (Greenberg, 2002). When there is clarity about emotion, its action tendency is naturally harnessed to problem solving.

Emotion "processing" literally takes time. Like potatoes steaming it can't be rushed. But it can be helped. You are looking to strike the right balance between conveying compassion, support, and providing direction. Confirm and focus on what is experienced while offering explicit instructions about how to proceed and new emotional problem-solving strategies. Offer process directions much as you would offer instructions to a new climber on a steep, technically difficult rock face. You can see the next hold, she can't. Tell her where the hold is; instruct her how to shift her weight to her left leg because she's going to have to lunge to reach the hold. You can see the path she needs to take to avoid an impossible reach. There's no use telling her about three holds forward—you provide the instruction as she needs it.

Further, if the climber is panicked, you must somehow reach through the dysregulated state to get her attention. Sometimes the client is so caught in the isolating, dreadful secondary target of emotion vulnerability that he or she fundamentally loses contact with your warmth and support or even at times your presence. Just as the therapist with Mia did in the earlier example, you may need to make certain the client can actually experience your warmth and connection so that you cue enough adaptive emotion to enable collaboration and new learning.

Therefore, when you use validation to cue adaptive emotion, you sometimes travel the high road—strengthening the person's responses in a context where they have been needed but absent, helping to modulate and transform the emotion. When you validate a difficult emotion that's been avoided, it increases contact and acceptance of emotional experience and expression. It may be exactly this shifting from one state to another, bringing disjunctive states together, that is key to transforming maladaptive emotions (Greenberg, 2002). In DBT, you strengthen *both* the ability to effectively change emotion and the ability to accept experience of emotion.

These validation strategies are illustrated in detail in the clinical example that follows. You'll see how the client's attempts to regulate the primary emotion of sadness drives problematic behaviors such as self-invalidation. You'll see different levels of validation, different targets of validation, and the use of validation as informal exposure and a way to cue adaptive emotion.

CASE EXAMPLE: LARA

LARA: I'm hurt and I'm angry and I don't feel like crying about Neal, you know? I'll look like shit, I'll feel worse, you know? So, I don't feel like crying. (*Avoids sadness.*)

THERAPIST: Do you feel worse when you cry? (*Assesses how avoiding sadness may make sense.*)

LARA: No, I just want to be in control, I don't want to be all out of control with everything.

THERAPIST: When you cry, you are out of control? (*Gently challenges the client's perspective that expressing sadness equates to being out of control—the therapist gently invalidates what she views as a maladaptive response.*)

LARA: I'm going to look like shit. I go to work, I look like shit right now. I just want to move on. (*The client responds to the therapist's challenging by intensifying her statement that avoiding expressing sadness is needed.*)

THERAPIST: Do you think you look like shit right now? (*Again challenges the client's view that expressing sadness is problematic and to be avoided.*)

LARA: Yeah, I do. I'm tired, I'm not getting any sleep. It's one o'clock, two o'clock, I have to get up at 7 in the morning. You know? Plus I have to take Neal's stuff back.

THERAPIST: Do you *have* to do that before work? (*Implies this will not be effective for client.*)

LARA: I'm going to do it. (*Voice rises in anger. She feels invalidated—not only that, she was invalidated.*)

THERAPIST: Lara . . . (*Attempts to block escalation by gaining Lara's attention.*)

LARA: I'm going to do it.

THERAPIST: Lara, that's fine if you're going to do it. (*Explicit validation.*) (*Gently.*) I want to help you get through this day. If you want that help, I can give you that help. (*Offers in a tone suggestive of helping the client make genuine choice, not in punitive manner.*) And, what I also want to help you do is not shut off important emotions prematurely because then they keep coming back. (*Orients and cues alternative adaptive emotion of sadness.*)

LARA: (*Cries.*) I've got the wrong makeup on today and it's going to streak all over my face. Why these emotions now, why do I feel like crying? (*Shifts to self-invalidation, a bit of avoidance.*)

THERAPIST: I can think of a lot of reasons you'd feel like crying right now. It seems like a pretty normal response to what's going on, Lara. (*Level 5 validation which sustains contact with cue, sadness, which is usually avoided.*) You've had a lot of sadness and a lot of pain around this, and a lot of hurt. Because you do care about him. (*Again facilitates experience of sadness by validating it.*)

LARA: It's too bad if I care about him. (*Self-invalidation, secondary reaction of anger at self, functions as maladaptive self-regulation of sadness.*)

THERAPIST: OK, hang on. Hang on with me, OK? OK, hang on. (*Blocks escape.*) And what's going on is you're doing it right now—those feelings feel really overwhelming, that sadness, and that feeling of "I don't want to be doing this. I don't want to be out of control." So, your brain flashes to anger. And you feel a little more in control and a little less overwhelmed maybe, with the anger. (*Validates the effectiveness of current thoughts and emotions.*) And so, one way is to try to just stick with the sadness with me for a little while. Then I'll help you put it away in this session and you can go out and do what you need to do, return his stuff, and feel some mastery from doing that. (*Orients.*)

LARA: How can you feel well enough to go to work when you're tired and everything?

THERAPIST: Well you're not going to feel well, but . . .

LARA: I'm going to lose my job. (*For this client, hopelessness is a frequent secondary reaction and functions as avoidance.*)

THERAPIST: That's a hopeless thought, right there. (*Labels to help get distance from the thought and block avoidance.*)

LARA: Well, I will because I am not functioning well. I didn't function Sunday on my job.

THERAPIST: OK, what happened? (*Because the client has had significant problems at work, the therapist has second therapy task here of assessing whether there's a crisis brewing and thus needs to shift the priority of what gets done this session.*)

LARA: I just felt really insecure. I felt hurt, and just like I couldn't get my brain to function or anything.

THERAPIST: OK, now those are three very different things—feeling insecure, not getting your brain to function, and not doing well on the job.

LARA: I didn't feel any sense of self-esteem, the way I used to feel. I don't feel that anymore.

THERAPIST: OK, but do you have any evidence that you didn't actually do well on the job? Or were you just feeling . . .

LARA: The person I worked with was a drag. . . . No, I know my boss loves me, but I can't function!

THERAPIST: OK. (*Decides no crisis is brewing so shifts back to task of experiencing and expressing sadness without attendant avoidance.*) That's what I want to help you with because I think if you spend a little bit of time with the sadness, that would help you regulate it so you are not overwhelmed. (*Reorients to the task of informal exposure to facilitate emotion regulation.*) See what happens is, you get close to it and then you run away from it—you never have a chance to get past it.

LARA: I'm crying now, aren't I?

THERAPIST: You are crying now. (*Gently.*) So you're feeling a lot of hurt.

LARA: Yeah.

THERAPIST: Yeah. Tell me about that. (*Level 1 validation functions to re-present the cue to extend informal exposure.*)

LARA: Well, the hurt is a realization that the man is really sick and I cannot be with him. I will not be with him.

THERAPIST: And how do you feel when you think about not being with him? (*Gentle pressure to keep focusing on sadness.*)

LARA: I feel sad, but at the same time I feel a sense of relief, too.

THERAPIST: Do you? You feel both?

LARA: Yes.

THERAPIST: And what else comes up when you think about not being with him? (*Continues gentle pressure to keep focusing on sadness.*)

LARA: Loneliness.

THERAPIST: Yeah.

LARA: I'm not worth anything as a woman.

THERAPIST: Yeah.

LARA: You know?

THERAPIST: Yeah, let's stick with that a moment. (*Senses that loneliness is important primary emotion, likely adaptive, and directs attention to this.*)

LARA: Which is not true. I know, I know I can get better than him.

THERAPIST: um hmm. So, this is the sort of thing that you do to try to keep those feelings under control . . . to tell yourself you know it'll get better. (*Highlights secondary response of cognitive counterevidence.*) And you know what you're saying is not true, so OK.

LARA: I'm being real careful not to turn the anger on myself, which is part of what happens with women who stay with men who are bad for them.

THERAPIST: So let's stick with the loneliness, OK—not with the other, there's no one really. (*Again re-presents cue for loneliness.*)

LARA: I've got friends. (*Avoids.*)

THERAPIST: OK, so we're talking about men. (*Again re-presents cue for loneliness.*)

LARA: I've been asked out on dates. I was asked out the next night. (*Avoids.*)

THERAPIST: OK now.

LARA: That's not a problem, but I don't want to date anybody right now.

THERAPIST: OK, what I'm doing is trying to . . . (*Blocks avoidance and now orients to increase Lara's collaboration and insight into the pattern.*)

LARA: But you're going to look at it differently.

THERAPIST: Yeah, it seems like the thought of loneliness is so scary that you've got to say "but I've got dates. . . . " It's difficult to just stick to the fact that maybe you'll be alone. Maybe you'll feel lonely.

LARA: Yeah, but I won't forever.

THERAPIST: You may not. But do you follow what I'm saying? I'm trying to . . .

LARA: . . . get me to accept the fact that I feel lonely.

THERAPIST: And the reason for that is . . . I think that's a very scary thing for you.

LARA: Yeah.

THERAPIST: And it starts triggering all these thoughts and all these behaviors, like calling Neal. The whole thing with fear is we need to confront what we're afraid of to get over that fear. So, sometimes it is real good to tell yourself it's not going to last, it's going to change. But right now I want you not to do that. I want you to just experience being alone and being lonely and whatever comes up with that. To know that you can experience that and move on without having to run from it.

LARA: OK.

THERAPIST: OK, so right now Neal is out of your life. (*Resumes presenting cue of loneliness and encouraging experience.*)

LARA: Yes.

THERAPIST: There's not anyone else. Even if you've got people calling you, there's not anyone that really knows you, really cares about you yet, and there may not be . . .

LARA: Well, there's Mario.

THERAPIST: Yeah, he's married.

LARA: Yeah, he's only a friend.

THERAPIST: Yeah, only a friend—so that's different. (*Again the therapist views loneliness as a key emotion, so, she re-presents the cues associated with loneliness to help better differentiate the emotions.*)

LARA: Even though I feel like that, it's not really . . .

THERAPIST: So, what's coming up when you think about lonely is a lot of statements about . . .

LARA: My worth.

THERAPIST: So, what's the feeling associated with that?

LARA: Another failed relationship.

THERAPIST: "Another failed relationship," "I can't . . . " what? (*Attempts to further assess what's most painful and avoided.*)

LARA: Well, I shouldn't think those thoughts. (*Self-invalidates.*)

THERAPIST: But, wait a minute. You *should* think those thoughts right now, OK, because those are the thoughts that come into your head (*Level 5 validation.*) So, you keep trying to . . . is this what you normally do? You say, "I shouldn't think those thoughts, and . . . (*Begins to highlight the way these secondary reactions function as avoidance.*)

LARA: Well, if I think despairing thoughts, I'm going to feel despairing . . .

THERAPIST: Right.

LARA: I don't want to think that. It'll pull me down. (*Wants to avoid despair, a primary maladaptive emotion for her that is extremely difficult and a link to intentional self-injury and suicidal behavior. In other words, "know thy client."*)

THERAPIST: Right, I think what we're doing is going to help that.

LARA: Why?

THERAPIST: Because we're exposing you to the feelings that come up with

these thoughts. The feelings keep coming back, because you say things like "I shouldn't think that way," but the problem is you *are* thinking that way. So the solution is not to say "I shouldn't think that way." I mean, you don't want to think hopeless thoughts and dwell and dwell. But you get these emotions that come up as a result of loss, not just from the thoughts, and then you think thoughts to cope with that. (*Level 5 validation orients.*)

LARA: Like "I shouldn't feel this way."

THERAPIST: Right.

LARA: I shouldn't feel a sense of loss.

THERAPIST: Right. So, I want to stay with one thought that's really big for you, which is "I'm not worth anything." What's the feeling that comes up with that thought? (*Again returns to gentle focus on emotional experience.*)

LARA: Shame.

THERAPIST: Shame. Can you feel that now, while we're talking?

LARA: Yeah, shameful and guilty.

THERAPIST: OK, let's stay focused on your feelings. We know he triggers a lot of those feelings. We know it's a given.

LARA: I'm just so used to feeling ashamed and I berate myself, judge myself. Like I called him the other day, and then I think, that totally undermines my credibility. If it's as bad as I say it is why am I calling him. That's crazy. I'm exaggerating the whole thing.

THERAPIST: OK, so wait, that's what happens right? It's happening right now. You felt lonely and called him, then you judge yourself. How could you do something different right there? Let's just take that: you shouldn't have called Neal.

LARA: I could say, "So I called Neal. It's not the end of the world. I made a mistake." I've read that rational-emotive therapy.

THERAPIST: And it seems like you have been practicing that some. When I was trying to get you to stay with an emotion you were coming back with thoughts to kind of change that emotion. So it seems like that's a skill you have. What you want to be careful with, though, is to use it wisely. Don't try to cut off your emotion really quickly all the time. Unless you need to cut it off right away—like you need to go to work, for example. Is there a way that you don't have to invalidate it? Like what you said right there: "OK, I called him. I made a mistake." I might not say . . .

LARA: You don't have to be upset about it (*self-invalidation*).

THERAPIST: But you *do* feel upset. See, that's what you have to be really careful about with changing your thoughts. You don't want to invalidate your feelings in the process. So, maybe instead, could we try this— (*Notes time left in session, knows the client's experiencing and expression in this session were very high for her and now wants to help the client more actively regulate in preparation for winding down the session.*) Could it be that you feel the upset, the guilt? Yes? You don't want to invalidate a single one. You may soothe yourself a little bit by saying, "OK, I feel guilty about this, I feel a lot of emotions, that's OK, that is totally normal, hard but normal. I can move through this, feel what I feel, and take good care of myself." Let's start to look at how you can observe and describe emotions today, OK, and then do self-soothing and self-validation. Let's get a plan of how to get through today without having to push away and escape the emotion, OK? (*Offers skills that will replace self-invalidation and foster emotional experience while moderating intensity of emotion.*)

In this example, the therapist uses validation strategies to strengthen the client's ability to regulate emotion. The dialogue begins with the client hurt and angry. Using validation as informal exposure, the therapist helps the client to experience and express the primary emotion of first sadness and then loneliness and blocks the client's habitual use of self-invalidation to manage overwhelming emotion. There are also change strategies (as described in Chapter 3) woven throughout this dialogue such as micro-orienting. The therapist also shifts gears briefly to assess whether a higher-priority target (job difficulties) might need to be addressed but decides that treating this link of accepting difficult emotions and helping the client practice this in session will best ward off crises that come from the client's more habitual ways of escaping painful emotions.

In general, when a client is dysregulated, I validate problem importance, task difficulty, emotional pain, the sense of being out of control, the wisdom in the client's ultimate goals, and in particular the client's location perspective. Remember to search for the valid; "know thy client"; validate the valid, and invalidate the invalid; and validate at the highest possible level, based on Linehan's levels of validation.

Precise validation with people who are exquisitely sensitive to invalidation can be difficult, and therefore is among the most essential abilities to cultivate as a DBT therapist. In DBT, you balance acceptance-oriented validation strategies and change oriented strategies to match the client's

actual vulnerabilities as you benevolently demand needed change. Developing a stance of holding seemingly contradictory elements in mind at the same time is the focus of the next chapter on Dialectics. Dialectics helps the therapist cultivate the capacity of unwavering centeredness needed to bear the intense pain our clients experience and to bear, too, the knowledge that we sometimes inadvertently or unavoidably add to the pain, even as we help the client change to alleviate suffering.

Relationship-based practice and reflective practice: holistic approaches to contemporary child care social work

Gillian Ruch
Division of Social Work, University of Southampton, Southampton, UK

Correspondence:
Gillian Ruch,
Division of Social Work,
University of Southampton,
Highfield,
Southampton SO17 1BJ,
UK
E-mail: g.m.ruch@soton.ac.uk

Keywords: psycho-social model, reflective practice, relationship-based practice, uncertainty, uniqueness

Accepted for publication: December 2004

ABSTRACT

The renewed interest in relationship-based practice can be understood in the child care social work context as a response to the call to re-focus practice in this field. Relationship-based practice challenges the prevailing trends which emphasize reductionist understandings of human behaviour and narrowly conceived bureaucratic responses to complex problems. In so doing practitioners engaged in relationship-based practice need to be able to cope with the uniqueness of each individual's circumstances and the diverse knowledge sources required to make sense of complex, unpredictable problems. This paper argues that if relationship-based practice is to become an established and effective approach to practice, practitioners need to develop their reflective capabilities. An outline of contemporary understandings of relationship-based and reflective practice is offered and findings from doctoral research drawn on to identify how reflective practice complements relationship-based practice. The product of this complementary relationship is enhanced understandings across four aspects of practice: the client, the professional self, the organizational context and the knowledges informing practice. The paper concludes by acknowledging the inextricably interconnected nature of relationship-based and reflective practice and emphasizes the importance of practitioners being afforded opportunities to practise in relational and reflective ways.

INTRODUCTION

It is almost 10 years since the publication in Britain of *Messages from Research* (Department of Health 1995). Over the past decade, in response to the findings of this research, child care social work in Britain has been struggling to 're-focus' itself towards more preventative and family support-orientated practice. A corollary of this shift in emphasis has been the growing interest in contemporary understandings of relationship-based practice (Howe 1998a; Schofield 1998; Chamberlyne & Sudbery 2001; Sudbery 2002; Trevithick 2003).

In this paper I am interested in exploring the connections between relationship-based practice and another emergent component of contemporary practice – reflective practice. Relationships and reflection are not new phenomena within social work practice and are integral and interrelated components of established psycho-dynamic approaches to social work practice (Ferard & Hunnybun 1962; Hollis 1964; Mattinson 1975). Despite the overlaps between the relationship-based and reflective components of practice, they have developed conceptually in isolation from each other. Drawing on findings from doctoral research (Ruch 2004) this paper suggests that for the potential of relationship-based practice to be fully realized practitioners need to develop their reflective capabilities. In order for relationship-based practice to develop and flourish, the uncertainty and anxiety associated with the emotionally charged subject matter that social work comprises must be effectively addressed. Reflective practice, which recognizes both the diverse sources of knowledge informing practice and the unique, unpredictable nature of social work practice, offers a way of effectively containing the challenges of contemporary child care social work in Britain and enhancing the potential for relationship-based practice. The potential for relationship-based and reflective practice is not, however, restricted to the child care social work context. Whilst the research from which this paper draws was located in child care settings, its findings and the argument underpinning this paper have broader applicability to all social work contexts.

The paper begins by outlining the historical backdrop to relationship-based practice and the characteristics of a contemporary model of practice. With this framework in mind the paper moves on to explore understandings of reflective practice and four shared implications of relationship-based and reflective practice: enhanced understandings of the client, the personal and professional self, the social and organizational contexts of practice and the diverse knowledges informing practice. The paper concludes by suggesting that the effectiveness of contemporary child care social work is heavily contingent on practitioners who have the ability to practise in relationship-based and reflective ways and on the existence of organizational contexts which are willing and able to support these forms of practice.

RECENT TRENDS IN CHILD CARE SOCIAL WORK

Social work in Britain has been in a crisis for several years but the explanations as to why it has reached its current 'crisis' remain disputed. Despite the different approaches that have been adopted to social work practice, progress has not produced the changes, which are required for the efficacy of social work practice to be significantly improved, as illustrated by the findings of the Victoria Climbié Inquiry and other similar reports (Department of Health 2003; Reder & Duncan 2003). Some academics (Howe 1994; Parton 1994) conceptualize the prevailing trends towards managerialism and risk-averse practice from a post-modern theoretical perspective and consider them to be a reaction to the social conditions of uncertainty and fragmentation associated with the emergence of post-modernity. Others understand the shifts to be the result of the extensive and pervasive influence of neo-liberal political ideology (Smith & White 1997). Two key characteristics of, and challenges for, practice, however, can be identified which are common to all the different practice approaches adopted in recent years: firstly, conceptualizations of the individual which are reductionist and privilege rational understandings of human behaviour; and secondly, bureaucratic responses to the uncertainty, complexity, risk and anxiety which are inherent in social work practice.

The conceptualization of the individual

The impact on child care social work practice of the dominant socio-political contexts in which it is located has resulted in altered perceptions of clients. These perceptions reduce clients to straightforward, rational beings and dismiss understandings of individuals, which acknowledge the irrational and emotional aspects of human behaviour. The complexity, risk and uncertainty inherent in child care social work has been bypassed by the re-conceptualization of clients from 'individuals with difficulties' to 'service users' (Adams 1998; Parton 1998b; Munro 2000). Alongside these restrictive and reductionist understandings of human behaviour has been a shift in understanding of human behaviour as complex and unique to each individual to one which engages only superficially with the presenting problem and does not explore its roots (Howe 1994; Howe & Hinings 1995; Parton 1998a). As a consequence of these developments the practitioner–service user relationship emphasizes legal and administrative requirements and tasks and outcomes (Howe 1997), as opposed to the professional relationship and emotional aspects of an individual's circumstances.

Procedures, uncertainty and anxiety

The second significant characteristic of contemporary child care social work is the domination of practice by procedures and bureaucracy. As the Social Services Inspectorate (1997) recognized, good procedural foundations are the 'bedrock' of effective child care practice. Paradoxically, whilst procedures are necessary, the domination of practice by procedural and managerialist responses is a significant factor in the current crisis in child care social work. It is precisely because of the complexity of human behaviour, the unique, unpredictable nature of social work activities and the professional anxiety these phenomena provoke that the bureaucratic and procedural responses to the 'change agenda' in child care social work have burgeoned (Blaug 1995; Department of Health 1995, 2001; Social Services Inspectorate 1997; Spratt & Houston 1999). Procedures in themselves, however, are insufficient to meet the challenges and demands of contemporary child care social work (Cooper *et al.* 2003).

One explanation for the emergence of procedurally dominated practice lies in its role as a defence against the anxiety inherent in emotionally charged professional practice (Menzies-Lyth 1988). According to Stevenson (1999), the enforcement of systems of accountability and control is a predictable organizational response to heightened anxiety. By adopting procedural responses to child care social work practice it is possible to ignore its unpredictability and complexity. The danger lies in them being inappropriate for an individual's circumstances and becoming

> ... a substitute for human contact and exploration, denying the necessity for professional judgement in assessing high risk situations. (Hughes & Pengelly 1997, p. 140)

This paradoxical situation raises fundamental questions about why, instead of procedurally driven practice, relationship-based and reflective approaches are not considered to be viable responses to the anxiety-provoking nature of social work and what it is that stops such responses being adopted. A partial answer to this question can be identified when the nature of relationship-based and reflective approaches to practice and their implications for practitioners are examined.

CONTEMPORARY UNDERSTANDINGS OF RELATIONSHIP-BASED PRACTICE

For models of child care social work practice to be able to offer an effective means of addressing the contemporary challenges facing practitioners they must acknowledge and respond to the complexities of the people and the practice with which they engage. Relationship-based practice is an emergent approach to social work practice, which responds to the shortcomings of the existing approaches to social work practice and understandings of human behaviour (Howe 1998a; Schofield 1998; Chamberlyne & Sudbery 2001; Sudbery 2002; Trevithick 2003). The potential of this approach lies in its ability to transform the current obstacles to effective practice into building blocks for a more responsive and realistic model of practice. Relationship-based practice explores not only the 'how and what' but also the 'why' of practice and is compatible with understandings of social work practice, which recognize the interpretative nature of social work activity, the importance of reflective responses to unique and unpredictable situations and the holistic nature of human behaviour. A holistic understanding involves practitioners engaging with both the rational and emotional or irrational aspects of a client's behaviour (and the practitioner's behaviour, as I argue below) and recognizes that when considered 'holistically' individuals are complex, multifaceted and 'more than the sum of their parts' (Oxford English Dictionary).

All social work is conducted through the medium of relationship, whether the relationship is short, medium or long term and whether, as is the case in more therapeutically orientated social work contexts, the relationship is the primary means of intervention, i.e. 'the end in itself' or it is utilized as a means to an end (Network of Psycho-Social Policy and Practice 2002). Given that all social work interventions involve an interpersonal dimension, to a greater or lesser extent, it could be argued that all social work practice is by definition relationship based. This perspective, however, denies the specific characteristics of relationship-based practice. Definitions of relationship-based practice are hard to come by but, as Trevithick (2003) recognizes, it is closely related to and builds on psycho-social approaches to practice and the psychodynamically informed casework tradition (Hollis 1964). The central premise of the psycho-social model and the model of relationship-based practice informing this paper is the emphasis placed on the professional relationship as the medium through which the practitioner can engage with the complexity of an individual's internal and external worlds and intervene. The practitioner–client relationship is recognized to be an important source of information for the practitioner to understand how best to help, and simultaneously this relationship is the means by which any help or intervention is offered. Further defining characteristics are the focus on the inseparable nature of the internal and external worlds of individuals and the importance of integrated – psycho-social – as opposed to polarized responses to social problems (Brearley 1991; Chamberlyne & Sudbery 2001).

Relationship-based practice involves practitioners developing and sustaining supportive professional relationships in unique and challenging situations (Howe 1998a) and requires practitioners to re-evaluate their styles of practice and sources of professional knowledge in a social work context of complexity and uncertainty (Lishman 1998; Parton 1999). Interest in relationship-based practice is not, however, unequivocal, and reflects the division between practitioners who find addressing the internal and external worlds of clients through the application of psycho-dynamic concepts helpful for understanding complex, social situations and those who do not (Stevenson 1991; Yelloly & Henkel 1995). In order to understand the ambivalence towards relationship-based practice that exists within the social work profession it is necessary to understand its historical context and the perspectives of its critics. This context provides the backdrop for a contemporary relationship-based model of practice.

THE HISTORICAL CONTEXT OF PSYCHO-SOCIAL MODELS OF SOCIAL WORK PRACTICE

The origins of relationship-based practice can be traced back to the emergence of psycho-analytic theory and practice in the 1920s and 1930s, which underpinned the casework practices of the Children's Departments in Britain in the 1950s. The 1960s saw the psycho-social model (Hollis 1964) widely adopted as the most appropriate adaptation of psycho-analytic theory and principles for social work. This model focused attention on the diagnosis and treatment of the individual's difficulties and emphasized the internal and external worlds of the client. The relationship between the practitioner and the client was seen as central to the potential effectiveness of this approach (Biestek 1961; Ferard & Hunnybun 1962; Butrym 1976). Over a period of approximately 20 years the psycho-social approach became well established in social work practice. During the late 1960s, however, its influence began to wane as aspects of the approach were subjected to criticism (Brewer & Lait 1980; Munro 1996; Howe 1998a,b; Cooper *et al.* 2003). Critics challenged the roots of the psycho-social model in Freudian psycho-analytic theory, and its manifestation in the therapeutic alliance with its patriarchal, western, class-biased, pathologizing, expert-orientated outlook, which was deemed to be incompatible with statutory social work contexts (Nathan 1993; Payne 1997). Furthermore, the emergence of behavioural psychology as a dominant and influential theoretical framework for social work challenged the psycho-dynamic approach. Behavioural psychology with its short-term, outcome focus and apparent ability to prove its effectiveness (Payne 1997; Cosis-Brown 1998; Howe 1998b; Munro 2000) was perceived to be more responsive to the demands for certainty and absolutes associated with the prevailing political, practical and philosophical climate (Howe 1994; Parton 1994, 1998b; Smith & White 1997; Cooper 2002). At the same time another challenge came from the ascendancy of political and structural approaches to practice. Anti-oppressive practice challenged, in particular, the power relations inherent in psycho-social approaches to practice. The result of these combined factors was the fall from favour of the psycho-social model.

For the re-emergence of psycho-social understandings of social work practice to be credible and acceptable a clear explanation of the differences between the earlier models of practice and the model currently being advocated is required. Of particular importance is the capacity of the new model to embrace the more recently established anti-oppressive and empowerment dimensions of social work practice. A further obstacle to the widespread adoption of contemporary relationship-based models of practice relates to the shift it requires practitioners to make from procedural and legalistic responses to ones based on uniqueness, uncertainty and relationship. For many practitioners such a shift requires them to confront unfamiliar aspects of practice. Widespread acceptance of relationship-based practice therefore requires sensitive handling, realistic timescales and the existence of support structures to sustain it.

THE CHARACTERISTICS OF A CONTEMPORARY RELATIONSHIP-BASED MODEL OF PRACTICE

In spite of the criticisms of the earlier models of relationship-based practice, new approaches are now slowly emerging (Howe 1997, 1998b; Schofield 1998). Historically the centrality and significance of the client–practitioner relationship has altered according to the dominant socio-political ideology (Yelloly & Henkel 1995; Adams 1998; Howe 1998a). Irrespective of the political slant on practice, however, social work practice by its very nature has to acknowledge the inner and outer worlds of the individual and balance the individual and the structural components of experience (Preston-Shoot & Agass 1990; Brearley 1991; Payne 1997). The relationship-based model's emphasis on an integrated understanding of the individual–structural causes of social distress and dysfunction has been welcomed, and allayed concerns about the onus on practitioners if individualized understandings of the origins of social problems were a dominant feature of revised models of relationship-based practice.

The underlying and all-pervasive feature of relationship-based practice is the acknowledgement and management of anxiety (practitioners and clients), as it recognizes this to be the primitive emotional response to distressing and uncertain situations (Salzberger-Wittenberger 1976; Woodhouse & Pengelly 1991; Trowell 1995; Howe 1998a). Positive early relationships and attachments generate feelings of security and trust. Inconsistent, hostile and negative experiences generate anxiety and mistrust (Howe 1995). According to Howe (1998b), relationship-based practice, informed by attachment theory and social understandings of the 'self', has the potential to contain anxiety for clients by enabling them to feel in control of their emotional, mental and social states. Howe believes relationship-based practice can help clients enhance their sense of well-being and reduce their anxiety and its associated behaviours, which are often what bring individuals to the attention of social agents. From the practitioners' perspective such approaches enable them to engage in more comprehensive assessments and accurate interventions with individuals and families (Howe 1998b). Schofield (1998) acknowledges the importance of the practitioner's ability to hold together the cognitive, emotional and practical aspects of a client's life as it provides a sense of security and therefore reduces anxiety. Schofield also identifies the importance of the social work profession becoming clearer about the nature of the client–practitioner relationship in light of the move away from contractual to relationship-based understandings of practice. For Schofield the social work relationship needs to be reclaimed as a vital resource in an increasingly resource-led, resource-deficient environment, and the theoretical approach she promotes places equal value on the practical tasks and emotional/psychological aspects of practice and considers them to be inseparable.

Further contributions to the development of a model of relationship-based practice have been provided by Sudbery (2002) and Turney & Tanner (2001). Turney & Tanner (2001) respond to the criticisms of psycho-social models of practice, which accused practitioners of abusing their power and pathologizing clients, by emphasizing the importance of incorporating understandings of power and difference, under the auspices of theories of anti-oppressive practice. To this end relationship-based approaches to practice seek to be participatory and empowering, acknowledging the expertise of the client as well as the practitioner (Horwath & Morrison 1991; Turney & Tanner 2001). The integration of ideas from the anti-oppressive and empowerment approaches to practice with psychodynamically derived ideas makes an important contribution to the development of a mature and integrated model of relationship-based practice.

REFLECTIVE PRACTICE – RE-CONCEPTUALIZING THE PRACTITIONER IN SOCIAL WORK PRACTICE

The re-conceptualizing of the individual in social work practice to embrace holistic understandings of his/her functioning involves practitioners confronting the complexity, ambiguity and uncertainty that characterizes human behaviour and people's lives and therefore, by implication, the professional social work relationship (Parton 1998a). Whilst challenging, the risks inherent in engaging in relationship-based practice appear to be worth taking if it leads to the well-being of children and their families being more sensitively and accurately understood and effectively responded to. Such a shift in practice perspective, however, generates further challenges for practitioners. If clients are recognized as emotional as well as rational beings, by implication practitioners must be too. Re-conceptualizing the practitioner means acknowledging his/her emotional responses and the emotional impact of practice on him/her. If this can be realized, one of the key obstacles to the effective implementation of relationship-based practice can be overcome. The anxieties, which arise from uncertain and risky situations, need containing not only for clients but for practitioners as well. Reflective practice (Schon 1983; Payne 1998), which has been embraced within social work over the past decade and acknowledges the uncertainty and risk inherent in social work practice, has the potential to respond to the needs of practitioners arising from the adoption of relationship-based approaches to practice. Reflective practice is a key determinant in the successful and effective application of relationship-based practice.

CONTEMPORARY UNDERSTANDINGS OF REFLECTIVE PRACTICE

Reflective practice has emerged in recent years in the professional social work arena in response to the failure of orthodox, technical–rational understandings of knowledge to provide an effective framework for practice (Yelloly & Henkel 1995; Gould 1996). As identified above, the desperate attempts to cling on to certainty and eliminate risk through the application of increasingly proceduralized responses to the challenges of practice have proved fruitless. Considerable literature exists in the fields of nursing and teaching which explores understandings of reflection and the reflection process, but definitions of reflective practice and accounts of reflective practice in social work contexts are more elusive. Reflective practice is generally associated with social constructivist, hermeneutic understandings of knowledge (Schon 1983; Gould 1996; Rolfe *et al.* 2001) and strives to identify knowledge for practice that is derived not only from sources external to the practice arena but also from within practice. Reflective practice acknowledges the relevance of diverse sources of knowledge – practice wisdom, intuition, tacit knowledge and artistry as well as theory and research – for understanding of human behaviour. In adopting an inclusive epistemological stance, reflective practice challenges the supremacy and superiority that, up until recently, has been afforded to technical–rational sources of knowledge (Schon 1983; Goldstein 1990; Peile 1993; Gould 1996; Rolfe 1998). Furthermore, by engaging with a diverse range of knowledges, practitioners develop a holistic understanding of clients and consequently develop into reflectively, rather than technically, competent professionals. Reflective practice enables practitioners to theorize their practice by drawing on knowledge embedded in practice (Palmer 1994; Fisher 1997) and to practise theoretically by making connections between espoused theory and practice (Gould 1996).

Given its social constructivist and hermeneutic epistemological roots, an exploration of the nature of reflective practice is inherently complex and multifaceted. The combination of the internalized nature and unique features of reflective practice and the complex process of externalizing these internal features makes it a difficult concept to understand, define, conceptualize and operationalize (Fitzgerald 1994; Clarke *et al.* 1996; Ixer 1999, 2000; Moon 1999). One of the recurrent features in the literature on reflective practice is the confusion about what precisely it embraces and its inherently ambiguous nature, which defies simple definition (Copeland *et al.* 1993; Eraut 1994; van Manen 1995; Morrison 1997; Ixer 1999, 2000). One way of understanding reflective practice is to conceptualize it as the concrete application of reflective processes in professional contexts. From this perspective it is then possible to examine how the different types of reflection identified in the literature are manifested in practice. Part of the difficulty of defining reflective practice can be attributed to its dual function as it both generates knowledge through the reflective process and is the vehicle by which it is applied in practice. When understood in this way it is possible to see how reflective practice, like relationship-based practice, is a complex concept which involves engaging in practice at a content and process level.

In order to explore how practitioners understand reflective practice, doctoral research was undertaken which explored how child care practitioners understood and operationalized reflective practice. Findings from this research (Ruch 2004) suggested that the types of reflection identified in the literature – technical, practice, critical and process (van Manen 1977; Clift *et al.* 1990; Bengtsson 1995; Hatton & Smith 1995; Ruch 2000) – can be re-categorized into two main groupings – technical and holistic reflective practice. The type of reflective practice practitioners identified with was the type of practice they engaged in. The research, which was conducted over a period of a year and involved ethnographic observation of and interviews with practitioners and managers located in two family support teams in different local authorities, discovered that in comparison with technically reflective practitioners, holistically reflective practitioners adopted more 'relationship-based' and 'risk-taking' approaches to their practice.

Holistic reflective practice

The overriding characteristic of holistically reflective practitioners was their integrated, multilayered understanding of knowledge which embraced all four types of reflective practice identified in the literature – technical–rational, practical, critical and process. Holistic reflective practice is informed by the technical–rational sources of knowledge but this knowledge source is enhanced by practical, critical and process sources of knowledge, i.e. experiential knowledge drawn from personal and professional contexts. In embracing the multifaceted nature of knowing, holistic practitioners engage in practice that, as with the definition of holistic understandings of human behaviour, is more than the sum of the parts. Holistically reflective practitioners demonstrate their ability to conceptualize practical–moral knowledges and integrate them with technical–rational perspectives. A recurrent feature of holistically reflective practitioners is their integration of these personal, propositional and process knowledges and their ability to constantly exercise professional curiosity and ask the question 'why?' in relation to their practice. The interplay between technical–rational and practical–moral sources of knowledge is considered crucial by holistically reflective practitioners as it ensures that the potential of the different knowledge sources is maximized:

GR: Are there other sources of information or knowledge? [other than the systemic family therapy theoretical model already mentioned]
Practitioner One: Well, the family and the meeting with the people involved informs it in a way and they say what the problem is they want to work with me on, then I might then think what I've seen of them, what they present me with, what do I think would be helpful so in a way you cannot separate out the two. And the clues they give. And I think it's also a bit about me and my style; no matter how helpful I think a model might be, if I didn't feel comfortable with the model I wouldn't be able to work with it so there is something about myself in all of that. I wouldn't be happy if the model was manipulative in any sort of way. So I think there are three things – the family, myself and the theoretical model all coming together. (Interview)

Two specific characteristics of holistically reflective practitioners which were identified as important were the relationship-based and risk-tolerant nature of their practice.

Relationship-based aspects of holistic reflective practice

As the above example illustrates, a defining characteristic of holistic practice is its ability to embrace the relational complexity of practice. Knowledge is understood to be not only holistic but also dynamic and specific to each situation. As a consequence holistically reflective practitioners engage with practice from a position of each encounter being unique, unpredictable and requiring negotiation through the professional relationship. The distinctive quality of holistically reflective practitioners is the attention they pay to the processes operating in practice as well as to its content:

Practitioner One: I think the first is to think systemically about a piece of work, try not to get caught up in the content of the referral but to think. The next component I think is to really listen to what the family is saying. We get some families here who are sent, they are not customers, they are visitors so to really listen to why they have been sent and to try and make sense with them about that, to try and get some, to see if you can form an alliance you can work with. Because if they are coming because they are sent and you're doing it because you have to do it then I'm not quite sure how far ultimately that work will go. So it's like taking a step back and talking to the family about what they understand about what it is a person has referred them for, where can you find an agreement somewhere along the line and if you can't then you have to step back and think why then has someone else got that worry. It might be that it is someone else's worry and it's not really a worry. (Interview)

In order to be able to establish realistic objectives and to effectively respond to and survive the emotionally charged nature of the work, holistically reflective practitioners recognize the place of informed self-awareness – awareness of their personal and professional experiences, beliefs and values – and open communication with clients and others, both in relation to what the practitioners' personal and professional experiences bring to the work and how the work impacts on them:

Practitioner Two: . . . you are opening yourself to criticizing what you are doing. You are not going in with an arrogance that whatever I do is right. You're really questioning what you have done and why you have done it and what you haven't done and why you haven't approached that subject for whatever reason or you're frightened of the response. Stepping back and really trying to look on the situation and amending it or patting yourself on the back . . . (Interview)

In the case of this practitioner she had taken to recording, alongside her case notes, her affective responses when engaged with clients and was able to draw on this knowledge to inform her future interventions. In another case a practitioner acknowledged the emotional impact of working with a mother who was considering placing her child for adoption. For this practitioner considerable attention was paid to the emotional processes she and the mother experienced and how they informed the professional relationship and interventions.

All of the holistically reflective practitioners were committed to working in reflective and relationship-based ways but recognized this was a demanding way of working. In order to work in a relationship-based holistically reflective way, practitioners recognized the importance of relationship-based, reflective support mechanisms. Collaborative and communicative ways of working – informal and formal discussions with colleagues, co-working and regular consultation sessions (in addition to supervision) – were all identified by the practitioners as vital sources of support, which enabled them to maintain their holistically reflective stance.

In marked contrast to holistically reflective practitioners, practitioners who hold a predominantly technically reflective orientation tend to be more practically inclined and focus on 'what' they did and 'how' with a view to doing it 'better' next time. What they, unlike the holistically reflective practitioners, tend not to address is the question 'why', i.e. why something did or did not occur. As a consequence of their orientation these practitioners exhibit more restrictive and prescriptive responses to practice situations and find it more difficult to establish responsive, relationship-based approaches.

Risk-taking aspects of holistic reflective practice

A second distinctive feature of holistically reflective practitioners is their capacity, in risk-averse organizational contexts, to engage with risk. For such practitioners risk-taking behaviour is understood to involve practitioners adopting creative and innovative strategies with clients, which, by implication in relation to child protection cases, involves re-defining notions of risk. These definitions of risk are broader, less defensive and less procedurally restrictive. The open, creative and 'risky' responses of holistically reflective practitioners are connected to their relationship-based perspective and their ability to tolerate uncertainty and 'not knowing'. For these practitioners practice involves grappling with uncertainty and complexity and depends on a relationship-based approach to reach an agreed understanding of acceptable risk. The heart of their practice lies in the relationships between family members and between individuals, families and practitioners.

An example arising from the research was an assessment undertaken to determine the risks for a young person of rehabilitating into the family the perpetrator of the abuse. The Area Team's initial response to the case had involved devising increasingly rigorous contracts in an attempt to eliminate any possible risk, which the family experienced as having imposed on them. In contrast the Family Centre practitioners engaged with the family in an inclusive and collaborative manner to reach a negotiated and agreed recommendation, which was presented to the child protection conference. The refusal to accept simplistic or prescriptive, technical solutions to the problem or to collude with polarized 'right–wrong' perspectives on their work enabled the practitioners to adopt risk-tolerant, relationship-based responses, which were informed but realistic about the existence of risk.

THE CONTRIBUTION OF HOLISTIC REFLECTIVE PRACTICE TO THE DEVELOPMENT OF RELATIONSHIP-BASED PRACTICE

The potential of holistic reflective practice to contribute to the development of relationship-based practice arises from the compatibility between the perspectives and practices of practitioners engaged in holistic reflective practice and the key features of relationship-based practice. The relationship between reflective and relationship-based practice, however, is complex. From the research findings, reflective practice and relationship-based practice can be understood to be interdependent components of each other. Holistically reflective practitioners, as a consequence of their perspective, engage in relationship-based work and conversely relationship-based approaches promote practitioners who are holistically reflective. Alternatively, and more expansively, reflective practice could be considered as occupying a 'meta' position (Cooper, pers. comm., 2004), overarching relationship-based and other approaches to practice. For the purposes of this paper the former conceptualization is adhered to. Four common features of reflective and relationship-based practice, which contribute to their complex interdependence, are explored below.

Relationship-based and reflective understandings of the client

One of the main reasons for the emergence of relationship-based approaches to social work practice has been the recognition that technical–rational knowledge offers only a partial insight into and explanation of the complexity of human behaviour (Howe & Hinings 1995; Howe 1997). In a similar vein, reflective practice challenges reductionist understandings of human behaviour and the inefficacy of existing defensive and proceduralized attempts to tackle the demands of practice. The strength and value of holistic reflective practice lies in the importance it places on the unique, complex, unpredictable and irrational nature of human behaviour. This emphasis is clearly compatible with relationship-based responses to the uncertainties and ambiguities of contemporary practice situations (Agass 1992; Howe 1997, 1998b; Parton 1998b; Schofield 1998; Sudbery 2002; Ruch 2004).

In the midst of the wealth of legislative and procedural guidelines and the expectations placed on practitioners to ascertain clients' perceptions and participation, the need for practitioners to 'make sense' of clients' circumstances and to 'hold the child in mind' has never been greater (Pietroni 1995; Trowell 1995; Brandon *et al.* 1998; Department of Health 2003). The openness to alternative inter-subjective and dynamic ways of 'knowing' that holistic reflective practice encourages increases the capacity of practitioners to respond sensitively and in empowering and emancipatory ways to the specific and unique needs of each client (Horwath & Morrison 1991; Blaug 1995; Turney & Tanner 2001). As a consequence, holistic reflective practice promotes practice that is fundamentally relational, dynamic and situated, a form of practice which is recognized as important in the literature for the development of relationship-based practice (Woodhouse & Pengelly 1991). Furthermore, by contextualizing the client(s) and ensuring that both the individual and structural aspects of each client's circumstances are equally addressed, holistically reflective practice responds to concerns about relationship-based practice being too individualistic in orientation.

Relationship-based and reflective understandings of the role of the 'self'

As has already been acknowledged, the attention paid by the emerging models of relationship-based practice to the re-conceptualization of the nature of human behaviour has implications not only for how clients are perceived by practitioners but also for how practitioners understand themselves in their professional role (Ash 1992, 1995; Lishman 1998; Ward 1998a). Holistic reflective practice enables practitioners to engage with the complexities of the self in professional practice and avoid the temptation (and risk) of resorting to a 'safe' reductionist position. The potential of reflective practice to contribute to the development of relationship-based practice is twofold: firstly it attends to subjective sources of knowledge; secondly, it embraces the professional use of self, which involves practitioners gaining an understanding of themselves and of the relevance of this knowledge for their practice. Through reflective practice, practitioners can hold the inner and outer worlds of not only their clients but also themselves, in a healthy and informative tension (Yelloly & Henkel 1995). Central to holistic reflective practice and to relationship-based practice is the place of 'self' – both the personal self and the professional self (Ash 1992; Sudbery & Bradley 1996; Lishman 1998). By developing their self-awareness practitioners can appropriately disentangle (and utilize) the interpersonal dynamics of their practice and ensure the best interests of the client are promoted.

Given the content of social work practice, its potential to distress and disturb practitioners who are engaged in sustained professional relationships with clients is considerable. The consequences of denying, avoiding or repressing anxiety are widely recognized as being manifest in low staff morale, stress-related sickness, depression and burnout (Morrison 1990; Agass 1992; Preston-Shoot 1996; Sudbery & Bradley 1996). By developing self-understanding and reflective responses the likelihood of being able to sustain relationship-based practice is increased. For all the holistically reflective practitioners considerable importance was attached to the communicative and collaborative team practices, referred to earlier, which encouraged respectful and supportive collegial relationships and enabled them to develop their professional identity and competence:

> Practitioner Three: ... so many personalities within the team, we have a wide skill base and personality base and that is in itself such an advantage to have. Someone will say 'Have you thought of it this way, have you done that, just take a deep breath, now what has gone on and I can understand your frustration and why you are so concerned but have you thought about ... ', and that is sort of loose supervision within the team and that is good because they are looking at it, you are amongst this chaos, this stuck process and they say have you thought about what process you are going through and it is like reflective stuff ... (Interview)

Interestingly, several practitioners also commented on how these collegial relationships had an important influence on the type of relationships they established with clients.

Relationship-based and reflective understandings of the social and organizational context of practice

One of the criticisms of earlier models of relationship-based practice was their marginalizing of the social dimensions of clients' lives. More recent models recognize the structural aspects to be of importance when deciding on appropriate interventions (Schofield 1998). A parallel trend can be identified in relation to practitioners where a narrow focus on the professional self can detract from attending to the organizational context in which this 'self' is located. Reflective practice encourages practitioners to view their practice in a broad context, and critical reflection in particular challenges the 'constitutive interests' influencing practice (Clift *et al.* 1990; Hatton & Smith 1995, p. 35).

The significance of the societal contexts in which clients are located and the organizational contexts in which practitioners are situated cannot be underestimated (Boud & Knights 1996; Boud & Walker 1998; Taylor 1999), nor can the epistemology around which organizations are structured (Connelly & Clandinin 1992). Practitioners find themselves at the confluence of the individual stresses percolating upwards from clients and the organizational stresses permeating down (Brown & Bourne 1996). The turbulent nature of the welfare sector with its constantly shifting organizational structures and trends towards integrated multi-professional service provision generates considerable anxiety for those it affects – both practitioners and clients (Preston-Shoot & Braye 1991; Moon 1999; Huntingdon 2000). An increasingly task-orientated, pressurized decision-making environment exacerbates this anxiety. Reflective practice as a means of 'making sense' of organizational and professional behaviours is particularly pertinent in the current political climate.

The work of Menzies-Lyth (1988) on social structures as defences against anxiety highlighted the extent to which uncontained anxiety can result in organizational systems which may, in the process of seeking to contain uncertainty and anxiety, create social structures which prevent the task being fulfilled as effectively as it could be (Sudbery & Bradley 1996). A more recent model of individual and organizational responses to work-generated anxiety is Morrison's (1990) adaptation of the Accommodation Syndrome originally developed by Summit (1983) in response to practitioners' experiences of working with sexual abuse. In Morrison's adaptation the five stages of accommodation – secrecy, helplessness, entrapment and accommodation, delayed disclosure and retraction – are all seen as relevant to staff and organizations which are unable to process the emotional impact of the work. What the model highlights is the interrelated nature of individual and institutional anxiety. In light of this the scope for practitioners to reflect on how organizations are responding to anxiety-provoking situations is vital if they are to keep the welfare of the client paramount (Hughes & Pengelly 1997; Ward 1998a).

Observational evidence from the research demonstrated how team and allocation meetings were used to facilitate thoughtful, holistically reflective discussions, which included consideration of different theoretical perspectives and evidence-based approaches alongside responses grounded in practice wisdom and intuition. Such forums considered both the individual needs and social context of the particular case under discussion and inter-agency and organizational dynamics. As a consequence practitioners were better equipped to engage with families with a more informed and realistic understanding of the client's circumstances and their own professional position.

The most common defences to anxiety-provoking practice are the de-personalizing of the practitioner–client relationship through procedurally dominated practice (Preston-Shoot & Braye 1991; Hughes & Pengelly 1997; Ward 1998b) and the restrictive definition of the primary task frequently evidenced in ineffective or fraught inter-agency collaboration (Woodhouse & Pengelly 1991; Hughes & Pengelly 1997). The importance for the development of relationship-based practice of the open-minded, reflective responses to organizational issues associated with holistic reflective practice is reinforced by the increasingly multidisciplinary context of practice, which is evolving within a culture of mistrust and poor communication (Cooper *et al.* 2003; Department of Health 2003). Such contexts require social work practitioners to work in the best interests of clients not only through relationships with them but also through positive relationships with the other professionals working with their clients. Reflective practice allows practitioners to remain thoughtful, flexible and critical of rigid defence mechanisms, which are characteristic of organizations unable to face the emotional implications and unconscious aspects of the work. In adopting a reflective stance, practitioners are aware of the containing aspects of the organization that need to exist for relationship-based practice to be sustained.

Relationship-based and reflective understandings of the knowledges informing practice

The integrated and conceptualized approach to reflective practice associated with holistically reflective practitioners ensures that such practitioners embrace and respond to the complexity of human nature recognized by relationship-based practice and the uncertainty, ambiguity and risk inherent in such practice (Howe 1994, 1997; Howe & Hinings 1995). As a consequence of their outlook, the risk of holistically reflective practitioners resorting, in the face of social and political pressures, to reductionist understandings of human behaviour and to restrictive, bureaucratic approaches to practice is significantly reduced. The challenge that faces practitioners, however, is to hold the diverse sources of knowledge informing their practice in a creative tension. To this end practitioners need help in developing what Bower (2003) refers to as an internal professional structure. In Bower's model, practice is informed by technical–rational and practical–moral knowledges, which are integrated in practice by practitioners adopting the third position –

the reflective position – which allows them to conceptualize the different sources of knowledge and to draw on these knowledges to inform their relationship-based practice.

CONCLUDING THOUGHTS

This paper suggests that relationship-based practice has the potential to respond to some of the existing shortcomings of practice. However, to facilitate the development of relationship-based approaches, which embrace a holistic understanding of clients, of practitioners and of the nature and contexts of social work practice, there is a need for practitioners to be afforded the time and space to respond thoughtfully – reflectively – to the unique, complex, and dynamic situations they encounter. By facilitating and promoting reflective practice, relationship-based practice will emerge; by engaging in relationship-based encounters with clients practitioners' reflective capabilities will out of necessity develop. This interdependence is crucial and central to effective practice. It is imperative that the organizational contexts for child care social work attend to this interdependence and begin to identify and provide the conditions in which it can flourish.

ACKNOWLEDGEMENTS

I gratefully thank Jackie Powell for supervising my research, my colleague Chris Warren-Adamson for his helpful comments on an earlier draft version, and the assessors whose comments contributed to the honing of this final version.

REFERENCES

Adams, R. (1998) Social work processes. In: *Social Work Themes, Issues and Critical Debates* (eds R. Adams, L. Dominelli & M. Payne), pp. 253–272. Macmillan, Basingstoke.

Agass, D. (1992) On the wrong track: reflections on a failed encounter. *Journal of Social Work Practice*, **16**, 7–17.

Ash, E. (1992) The personal–professional interface in learning: towards reflective education. *Journal of Interprofessional Care*, **6**, 61–71.

Ash, E. (1995) Taking account of feelings. In: *Good Practice in Supervision* (ed. J. Pritchard), pp. 20–30. Jessica Kingsley, London.

Bengtsson, J. (1995) What is reflection? On reflection in the teaching profession and teacher education. *Teacher and Teaching: Theory and Practice*, **1**, 23–32.

Biestek, F. (1961) *The Casework Relationship*. Allen Unwin, London.

Blaug, R. (1995) Distortion of the face-to-face: communication, reason and social work practice. *British Journal of Social Work*, **25**, 424–439.

Boud, D. & Knights, S. (1996) Course design for reflective practice. In: *Reflective Learning for Social Work* (eds N. Gould & I. Taylor), pp. 23–34. Arena, Aldershot.

Boud, D. & Walker, D. (1998) Promoting reflection on professional courses: The challenge of context. *Studies in Higher Education*, **23**, 191–206.

Bower, M. (2003) Broken and twisted. *Journal of Social Work Practice*, **17**, 143–153.

Brandon, M., Schofield, G. & Trinder, L. (1998) *Social Work with Children*. Macmillan, Basingstoke.

Brearley, J. (1991) A psychodynamic approach to social work. In: *A Handbook of Theory for Practice Teachers in Social Work* (ed. J. Lishman), pp. 48–63. Jessica Kingsley, London.

Brewer, C. & Lait, J. (1980) *Can Social Work Survive?* Temple Smith, London.

Brown, A. & Bourne, L. (1996) *The Social Work Supervisor*. Open University Press, Buckingham.

Butrym, Z. (1976) *The Nature of Social Work*. Macmillan, London.

Chamberlyne, P. & Sudbery, J. (2001) Editorial. *Journal of Social Work Practice*, **15**, 125–129.

Clarke, B., James, C. & Kelly, J. (1996) Reflective practice: reviewing the issues and refocussing the debate. *International Journal of Nursing Studies*, **33**, 171–180.

Clift, R., Houston, J. & Pugagh, M. (1990) *Encouraging Reflective Practice in Education*. Teachers College Press, London.

Connelly, M. & Clandinin, J. (1992) An interview with Donald Schon. *Orbit: Ideas About Teaching and Learning*, **23**, 2–5.

Cooper, A. (2002) Keeping our heads: preserving therapeutic values in a time of change. *Journal of Social Work Practice*, **16**, 7–14.

Cooper, A., Hetherington, R. & Katz, I. (2003) *The Risk Factor: Making the Child Protection System Work for Children*. Demos, London.

Copeland, W.D., Birmingham, C., De la Cruz, E. & Lewin, B. (1993) The reflective practitioner in teaching: towards a research agenda. *Teaching and Learning*, **9**, 347–359.

Cosis-Brown, H. (1998) Counselling. In: *Social Work Themes, Issues and Critical Debates* (eds R. Adams, L. Dominelli & M. Payne), pp. 138–148. Macmillan, Basingstoke.

Department of Health (1995) *Child Protection: Messages from Research*. HMSO, London.

Department of Health (2001) *The Children Act Now: Messages from Research*. HMSO, London.

Department of Health (2003) *The Victoria Climbié Inquiry. Report of An Inquiry*. HMSO, London.

Eraut, M. (1994) *Developing Professional Knowledge and Competence*. Falmer, London.

Ferard, M.L. & Hunnybun, N. (1962) *The Caseworker's Use of Relationship*. Tavistock, London.

Fisher, T. (1997) Learning about child protection. *Social Work Education*, **16**, 93–111.

Fitzgerald, M. (1994) Theories of reflection for learning. In:

Reflective Practice in Nursing (eds A. Palmer, S. Burns & C. Bulman), pp. 63–84. Blackwell Scientific Publications, Oxford.

Goldstein, H. (1990) The knowledge base of social work practice: theory, wisdom, analogue or art? *Families in Society: The Journal of Contemporary Human Services*, January, 32–43.

Gould, N. (1996) Introduction: social work education and the crisis of the professions. In: *Reflective Learning for Social Work* (eds N. Gould & I. Taylor), pp. 1–10. Arena, Aldershot.

Hatton, N. & Smith, D. (1995) Reflection in teacher education: towards definition and implementation. *Teacher and Teaching*, **11**, 33–49.

Hollis, F. (1964) *A Psycho-Social Therapy*. Random House, New York.

Horwath, J. & Morrison, T. (1991) *Effective Staff Training in Social Care: From Theory to Practice*. Routledge, London.

Howe, D. (1994) Modernity, postmodernity and social work. *British Journal of Social Work*, **25**, 513–532.

Howe, D. (1995) *Attachment Theory for Social Work Practice*. Macmillan, London.

Howe, D. (1997) Psychosocial and relationship-based theories for child and family social work: politics, philosophy, psychology and welfare practice. *Child and Family Social Work*, **2**, 162–169.

Howe, D. (1998a) Relationship-based thinking and practice in social work. *Journal of Social Work Practice*, **12**, 45–56.

Howe, D. (1998b) Psychosocial work. In: *Social Work Themes, Issues and Critical Debates* (eds R. Adams, L. Dominelli & M. Payne), pp. 173–183. Macmillan, Basingstoke.

Howe, D. & Hinings, D. (1995) Reason and emotion in social work practice: managing relationships with difficult clients. *Journal of Social Work Practice*, **9**, 5–14.

Hughes, L. & Pengelly, P. (1997) *Staff Supervision in a Turbulent Environment: Managing Process and Task in Frontline Services*. Jessica Kingsley, London.

Huntingdon, A. (2000) Children and families social work: visions of the future. In: *Reclaiming Social Work: The Southport Papers Volume Two* (eds J. Harris, L. Froggett & I. Paylor), pp. 113–128. Venture Press, Birmingham.

Ixer, G. (1999) There's no such thing as reflection. *British Journal of Social Work*, **29**, 513–527.

Ixer, G. (2000) Assumptions about reflective practice. In: *Reclaiming Social Work: The Southport Papers Volume One* (eds J. Harris, L. Froggett & I. Paylor), pp. 79–87. Venture Press, Birmingham.

Lishman, J. (1998) Personal and professional development. In: *Social Work Themes, Issues and Critical Debates* (eds R. Adams, L. Dominelli & M. Payne), pp. 89–102. Macmillan, Basingstoke.

van Manen, J. (1977) Linking ways of knowing and ways of being. *Curriculum Enquiry*, **6**, 205–208.

van Manen, J. (1995) On the epistemology of reflective practice. *Teacher and Teaching: Theory and Practice*, **1**, 33–50.

Mattinson, J. (1975) *The Reflective Process in Social Work Supervision*. Tavistock Institute of Marital Studies, London.

Menzies-Lyth, I. (1988) *Containing Anxiety in Institutions: Selected Essays Volume One*. Free Association Books, London.

Moon, J. (1999) *Reflection in Learning and Professional Development: Theory and Practice*. Kogan Page, London.

Morrison, T. (1990) The emotional effects of child protection work on the worker. *Practice*, **4**, 253–271.

Morrison, T. (1997) Learning, training and change in child protection work: towards reflective organisations. *Social Work Education*, **16**, 20–43.

Munro, E. (1996) Avoidable and unavoidable mistakes in child protection work. *British Journal of Social Work*, **26**, 793–808.

Munro, E. (2000) Defending professional social work practice. In: *Reclaiming Social Work: The Southport Papers Volume One* (eds J. Harris, L. Froggett & I. Paylor), pp. 1–10. Venture Press, Birmingham.

Nathan, J. (1993) The battered social worker: a psychodynamic contribution to practice, supervision and policy. *Journal of Social Work Practice*, **7**, 73–80.

Network of Psycho-Social Policy and Practice (2002) *Network of Psycho-Social Policy and Practice: Draft Mission Statement*. Tavistock Clinic, London.

Palmer, A. (1994) Introduction. In: *Reflective Practice in Nursing* (eds A. Palmer, S. Burns & C. Bulman), pp. 1–9. Blackwell Scientific Publications, Oxford.

Parton, N. (1994) Problematics of government, (post)modernity and social work. *British Journal of Social Work*, **24**, 9–32.

Parton, N. (1998a) Risk, advanced liberalism and child welfare: the need to rediscover uncertainty and ambiguity. *British Journal of Social Work*, **28**, 5–27.

Parton, N. (1998b) *Child Protection and Family Support: Possible Future Directions for Social Work*. 18th Annual Lecture. Department of Social Work Studies, University of Southampton, Southampton.

Parton, N. (1999) *Some Thoughts on the Relationship between Theory and Practice in and for Social Work*. ESRC Seminar Series on Theorising Social Work Research, Seminar 1: What Kinds of Knowledge?

Payne, M. (1997) *Modern Social Work Theory*. Macmillan, London.

Payne, M. (1998) Social work theories and reflective practice. In: *Social Work Themes, Issues and Critical Debates* (eds R. Adams, L. Dominelli & M. Payne), pp. 117–137. Macmillan, Basingstoke.

Peile, C. (1993) Determinism versus creativity. *Social Work*, **38**, 127–134.

Pietroni, M. (1995) The nature and aims of professional education. In: *Learning and Teaching in Social Work: Towards Reflective Practice* (eds M. Yelloly & M. Henkel), pp. 34–50. Jessica Kingsley, London.

Preston-Shoot, M. (1996) On retaining a reflective space: making sense of interactions in work and work groups. *Journal of Social Work Practice*, **10**, 9–23.

Preston-Shoot, M. & Agass, D. (1990) *Making Sense of Social Work*. Macmillan, Basingstoke.

Preston-Shoot, M. & Braye, S. (1991) Managing the personal experience of work. *Practice*, **5**, 13–33.

Reder, P. & Duncan, S. (2003) Making the most of the Victoria Climbié Inquiry. *Child Abuse Review*, **13**, 95–114.

Rolfe, G. (1998) *Expanding Nursing Knowledge: Understanding and Researching Your Own Practice*. Butterworth-Heinemann, Oxford.

Rolfe, G., Freshwater, D. & Jasper, M. (2001) *Critical Reflection for Nursing and the Helping Professions: A User's Guide*. Palgrave, Basingstoke.

Ruch, G. (2000) Self in social work: towards an integrated model of learning. *Journal of Social Work Practice*, **14**, 99–112.

Ruch, G. (2004) *Reflective practice in contemporary child care social work*. Unpublished PhD thesis, University of Southampton, Southampton.

Salzberger-Wittenberger, I. (1976) *Psycho-Analytic Insight and Relationships: A Kleinian Approach*. Routledge Kegan Paul, London.

Schofield, G. (1998) Inner and outer worlds: a psychosocial framework for child and family social work. *Child and Family Social Work*, **3**, 57–67.

Schon, D. (1983) *The Reflective Practitioner*. Basic Books, New York.

Smith, C. & White, S. (1997) Parton, Howe and postmodernity: a critical comment on mistaken identity. *British Journal of Social Work*, **27**, 275–295.

Social Services Inspectorate (1997) *Evaluating Child Protection Services: Findings and Issues*. HMSO, London.

Spratt, T. & Houston, S. (1999) Developing critical social work in theory and practice: child protection and communicative reasoning. *Child and Family Social Work*, **4**, 315–324.

Stevenson, O. (1991) Foreword. In: *Anxiety and the Dynamics of Collaboration* (eds D. Woodhouse & P. Pengelly), pp. v–vi. Aberdeen University Press, Aberdeen.

Stevenson, O. (1999) Social work with children and families. In: *Child Welfare in the United Kingdom* (ed. O. Stevenson), pp. 79–100. Blackwell Science, Oxford.

Sudbery, J. (2002) Key features of therapeutic social work: the use of relationship. *Journal of Social Work Practice*, **16**, 149–161.

Sudbery, J. & Bradley, J. (1996) Supervision in organisations providing therapeutic care. *Journal of Social Work Practice*, **10**, 51–62.

Summit, R. (1983) The child sexual abuse accommodation syndrome. *Child Abuse and Neglect*, **7**, 177–193.

Taylor, I. (1999) Critical commentary: social work education. *British Journal of Social Work*, **29**, 175–180.

Trevithick, P. (2003) Effective relationship-based practice: a theoretical exploration. *Journal of Social Work Practice*, **17**, 163–176.

Trowell, J. (1995) Key psychoanalytic concepts. In: *The Emotional Needs of Young Children and Their Families: Using Psychoanalytic Ideas in the Community* (eds J. Trowell & M. Bower), pp. 12–21. Routledge, London.

Turney, D. & Tanner, K. (2001) Working with neglected children and their families. *Journal of Social Work Practice*, **15**, 193–120.

Ward, A. (1998a) The difficulty of helping. In: *Intuition Is Not Enough: Matching Learning with Practice in Therapeutic Child Care* (eds A. Ward & L. McMahon), pp. 55–63. Routledge, London.

Ward, A. (1998b) On reflection. In: *Intuition Is Not Enough: Matching Learning with Practice in Therapeutic Child Care* (eds A. Ward & L. McMahon), pp. 217–224. Routledge, London.

Woodhouse, D. & Pengelly, P. (1991) *Anxiety and the Dynamics of Collaboration*. Aberdeen University Press, Aberdeen.

Yelloly, M. & Henkel, M. (eds) (1995) Introduction. In: *Learning and Teaching in Social Work: Towards Reflective Practice* (eds M. Yelloly & M. Henkel), pp. 1–11. Jessica Kingsley, London.

Article

Health
17(1) 37–56

DOI: 10.1177/1363459312447253
hea.sagepub.com
SAGE

Working around a contested diagnosis: Borderline personality disorder in adolescence

Kristy Koehne and Bridget Hamilton
The University of Melbourne, Australia

Natisha Sands
Deakin University, Australia

Cathy Humphreys
The University of Melbourne, Australia

Abstract

This discourse analytic study sits at the intersection of everyday communications with young people in mental health settings and the enduring sociological critique of diagnoses in psychiatry. The diagnosis of borderline personality disorder (BPD) is both contested and stigmatized, in mental health and general health settings. Its legitimacy is further contested within the specialist adolescent mental health setting. In this setting, clinicians face a quandary regarding the application of adult diagnostic criteria to an adolescent population, aged less than 18 years. This article presents an analysis of interviews undertaken with Child and Adolescent Mental Health Services (CAMHS) clinicians in two publicly funded Australian services, about their use of the BPD diagnosis. In contrast with notions of primacy of diagnosis or of transparency in communications, doctors, nurses and allied health clinicians resisted and subverted a diagnosis of BPD in their work with adolescents. We delineate specific social and discursive strategies that clinicians displayed and reflected on, including: team rules which discouraged diagnostic disclosure; the lexical strategy of hedging when using the diagnosis; the prohibition and utility of informal 'borderline talk' among clinicians; and reframing the diagnosis with young people. For clinicians, these strategies legitimated their scepticism and enabled them to work with diagnostic uncertainty, in a population identified as vulnerable. For

Corresponding author:
Bridget Hamilton, The University of Melbourne, Walter Boas Building, Monash Road, Carlton, Victoria, 3101, Australia
Email: bh@unimelb.edu.au

adolescent identities, these strategies served to forestall a BPD trajectory, allowing room for troubled adolescents to move and grow. These findings illuminate how the contest surrounding this diagnosis in principle is expressed in everyday clinical practice.

Keywords
adolescent, borderline personality disorder, disclosure, discourse analysis, subjectivity

Introduction

The field of psychiatric diagnosis is a fertile one for sociological critique (Whooley, 2010). Critique is deep and longstanding, challenging the premise for psychiatric nosology overall and questioning the utility of specific diagnoses (Parker et al., 1995). The diagnosis of borderline personality disorder (BPD) is among the most vexed. In an era where medical consultations are expected to include frank communication of diagnoses, psychiatric diagnoses remain stigmatized and communication is often problematic (Gallagher et al., 2010).

This article is concerned with an analysis of 23 clinicians' talk at interview about the diagnosis of BPD in adolescent mental health contexts, and derives from a PhD thesis by the first author. Through semi-structured interviews with nurses, doctors and allied health clinicians, we investigated the ways these clinicians understood and made use of diagnoses, in the everyday settings of publicly funded adolescent mental health services. In this article, we detail the major set of findings about the ways clinicians understood and worked with the diagnosis of BPD in adolescence.

This study was motivated initially by curiosity and some frustration regarding the tendency for mental health clinicians in inpatient adolescent mental health services to use BPD as a descriptor in discussions among clinicians, while withholding talk about BPD with their adolescent clients. This observation was based on the experience of the researchers as clinicians in a limited array of teams. However, to us the practice of talk behind the scenes and of non-disclosure with clients seemed entrenched and taken-for-granted. Our common-sense perspective was to favour the ethical stance that when a diagnosis is made, it should be shared. Still there were simultaneous concerns about the diagnosis, its stigma and its utility.

Research questions that drove this study include:

- Do mental health clinicians share diagnostic information about BPD with their adolescent clients, and if so how?
- What are the factors that guide clinical practice in the decision to disclose or to withhold a diagnosis of emerging BPD to adolescents?

While these questions guided the design of clinician interviews, the question at the core of this article is simply: how do CAMHS clinicians talk about BPD? Questions of 'how' direct the focus of analysis towards the structure of language, seeking to examine: 'How certain things came to be said or done, and what has enabled and/or constrained what can be spoken or written in a particular context' (Cheek, 2004: 1147).

Background

Personality disorders occupy a precarious diagnostic position, subject to challenge both broadly as a psychiatric diagnosis and also *within* psychiatry, consigned to Axis II and so excluded from categorization as a major mental disorder in the Diagnostic and Statistical Manual (DSM) (American Psychiatric Association, 1980, 2000).

Psychiatry continues to be troubled by diagnoses that lack reliability, validity, clear aetiology and the ability to predict treatment responsiveness (Pilgrim, 2001), arguably enduring a marginal status within the medical profession (Kirk and Kutchins, 1992; Manning, 2000). By continuing to strive for those diagnostic goals of general medicine, psychiatry seeks 'predictive power in a situation where certainty is low' (Cooksey and Brown, 1998: 533). Certainty is low for important reasons. For instance, psychiatric diagnoses rely upon an interpretive approach, heavily depending upon patient communications of *symptoms* rather than the measurement of somatic changes, or *signs* (Pilgrim, 2007). Diagnosis based upon interpretation engenders ambiguity, which is at odds with a firm categorical system. Furthermore, the interpretation of human conduct may be considered analogous to judgement, thus subjecting psychiatric diagnosis to the criticism that it comprises value judgements made against criteria of normality (Faust and Miner, 1986; Spitzer, 1981).

The BPD diagnosis in particular has been the subject of considerable debate. It has been touted a 'hot subfield' of research, generating more research than all other personality disorder diagnoses combined (Boschen and Warner, 2009: 139). Being diagnosed with a personality disorder renders one a 'contested patient', where medical jurisdiction is blurred (Pilgrim, 2001: 254). Theorists critique BPD as a construction that pathologizes deviation from a coherent, unified self or rationality (Shaw and Proctor, 2005; Wirth-Cauchon, 2001). For example, Wirth-Cauchon (2001) argues that psychiatric discourse (i.e. BPD) positions women who cross the borders of 'normal femininity' as *other*, while neglecting social causes of distress.

Conjecture surrounding the utility of the BPD diagnosis intensifies in an adolescent population. Diagnostic criteria in the current iterations of the DSM IV-TR are not age specific (APA, 2000), prompting debate about the appropriateness of applying adult criteria during the fluid developmental period of adolescence (Bleiberg, 1994).

A review of empirical investigations indicates reasonable consensus around the adolescent BPD construct (Chanen et al., 2009; Gunderson, 2009; Miller et al., 2008a; Paris, 2008; Silk, 2008), however it is common for diagnostic advocacy to be paired with caution. For example, longitudinal researchers call for modification of the DSM to specify that adolescent personality disorder *may not* persist into adulthood (Cohen et al., 2005; Silk, 2008), with apprehension raised regarding the heterogenic nature and weak predictive validity of BPD in adolescence (Becker and Grilo, 2006). Or, alongside a push for early intervention there is concurrent concern for the unknown impact of stigma, the potential for refusal of health services and for iatrogenic harm resulting from the increased utilization of personality disorder diagnoses in adolescence (Chanen and McCutcheon, 2008). Despite research on diagnostic idiosyncrasies of validity and predictive ability, the question of *how the diagnosis is used* and *whether it is disclosed* in everyday practice is not addressed.

Researchers and ethicists agree in principle that disclosure of diagnosis is a feature of good practice (Buckman, 1996) and in line with patient expectations (Benbassat et al., 1998). Yet clinical practice regarding the communication of diagnoses of mental illness remains ambiguous. A diagnosis of mental illness is likely to be more contentious and dependent upon professional judgement, thus impacting upon communication to clients (Gallagher et al., 2010). Research on the disclosure of BPD in adults is scant, but indicates a reluctance to communicate this diagnosis (Hersh, 2008; Lequesne and Hersh, 2004; McDonald-Scott et al., 1992). While the extent of disclosure to an adolescent population is unknown, it is likely that practice is impacted significantly by the contested nature of this diagnosis.

Currently, BPD is defined by a pervasive pattern of instability of interpersonal relationships, self-image and affects, and marked impulsivity that begins by early adulthood and is present in a variety of contexts (APA, 2000). While the DSM permits the use of the BPD diagnosis in adolescence (if symptoms have been present for 12 months) the definition remains vague (Miller et al., 2008) and the evidence base for treatment options is minimal (National Institute for Health and Clinical Excellence (NICE), 2009).

In response to ambiguities, and in light of the clinical need to respond to these young people, some researchers champion the pathway of making a provisional diagnosis with adolescent patients. Specialty adolescent mental health services in Australia offer a treatment model to adolescents with sub-syndromal BPD (i.e. meeting three or more of nine criteria) thus advocating for early identification and treatment (Chanen et al., 2009). While these clinicians support the frank communication of a BPD diagnosis among clinicians, they remain silent on the issue of disclosure to the adolescent client.

Theoretical tools

We detail here the theoretical framing of this discourse analysis, including the way we conceptualize texts and practices.

Discourse analysis

The discourse analysis in this research is framed by post-structuralism. Post-structuralism enables a critical examination of language, and locates power as constituted through language (Fairclough, 1989; Fox, 1993). This theoretical stance draws from broader postmodern philosophies which challenge modernist notions of truth, rationality, the individual and social structure (Fox, 1993). We apply postmodern philosophy to challenge the diagnostic construct of borderline personality disorder and to consider those subject positions created by this diagnosis (i.e. clinician and adolescent client).

Methods of discourse analysis encompass diverse theoretical influences and approaches to data. Discourse analysis as applied here relies upon the pivotal work of Foucault (1972), via his studies of discourse, medicine and governmentality. In particular we take up his commitment to rethink that which is taken for granted, considered unproblematic or apolitical. In doing so, we consider the conditions (expressed in everyday practice and language) that support what is taken for granted (Gastaldo and Holmes, 1999) in adolescent mental health care, the diagnostic system and the place of BPD in both. Our research therefore aims to surface different spaces for manoeuvre and resistance (Parker, 1990).

We use Fairclough to pin down discourse and to structure the discourse analysis. Defining discourse as the socially determined use of language (Fairclough, 1989), he provides a valuable adjunct to Foucault, through his attention to socio-linguistics (Rudge, 1998). Data were subsequently analysed at three levels: the text; discursive practice; and social practice. These levels will be outlined in brief, with influential theorists identified at each level.

Textual analysis

Transcripts generated from individual clinician interviews, field notes and author reflections formed the basis for textual analysis, with interview transcripts constituting the bulk of discussion in this article. Analysis at this level incorporates an examination of metaphor, lexical choice and modality; textual features identified as pertinent within Fairclough's (1992) critical discourse analysis. Lexical choice for example, refers to the way in which speakers select descriptive terms to fit with the institutional setting, or their role within it (Drew and Heritage, 1992). Modality denotes the extent to which a person commits themselves or conversely distances themselves from a statement (Fairclough, 1992), as delineated in the discussion on 'Hedges'.

Discursive practice

Analysis of discursive practice is akin to an interpretative, micro-sociological examination which focuses on one dimension or moment of social practice (Phillips and Jorgensen, 2002). Scrutiny at this level provides an insight into how people create and follow a set of shared 'common-sense' rules in everyday practices (Fairclough, 1992; Phillips and Jorgensen, 2002). Aspects from the work of Goffman (1959) are drawn upon to examine the notion of teamwork and clinician subjectivities. We use Goffman's theatrical sensibility to illustrate vividly the constructed nature of interactions between clinicians and clients.

Goffman (1959: 104) analysed roles played in a performance across a range of domains including 'the team' which he defined as 'a set of individuals whose intimate co-operation is required, if a given projected definition of the situation is to be maintained'. The way in which BPD is defined by teams provides insight into the minutiae of daily interactions (Handler, 2009) and points to those localized networks of power operating within institutions (Foucault, 1984).

Analysis of disciplinary roles, practice settings and the shaping of a case is extended by Barrett's (1996) examination of the work of a psychiatric team and the diagnosis of schizophrenia. As in Barrett's research, our study of disciplinary idiosyncrasies turns the objectifying gaze of the 'psy-complex' back on itself (Parker et al., 1995).

Social practice

Attending to social practice takes the discourse analysis to the macro-sociological level, where connections between language, power and ideology are surfaced (Fairclough, 1989). At this level, Foucault's work provides the predominant theoretical guide with his ideas taken up using the analogy of a 'toolbox' (Humphreys, 1990: 317). The tools used in this article include: an examination of enunciative modalities and use of semantics in the medical gaze; and diagnosis and discipline between clinicians.

Foucault's (1972: 50) theorizing of 'enunciative modalities' prompted questions of the data such as 'Who is speaking? Who, among the totality of speaking individuals is accorded the right to use this sort of language? Who is qualified to do so?' Such inquiry provided fertile ground for analysis of clinicians' talk. We asked both 'Who can speak?' and 'From where can they speak?' (Rose, 1996: 174). We viewed clinicians' language use as an exercise of power. As described by Linnet (2004: 11), 'language is not what it describes, it is something else. But it can reveal, point at, or evoke, and make us sharply aware of reality – or it can soften, smooth over, and mislead.' Previous sociological studies have considered the way clinicians work around those DSM diagnoses which engender ambivalence (Whooley, 2010). In drawing together these three dimensions of analysis, we pinpoint particular lexical strategies and modes of performance used by clinicians, as they take up the contested discourse of BPD.

Analysis is also shaped by Foucault's (1989: xiii) notion of the clinical gaze, occurring when 'a millennial gaze paused over men's sufferings', thus revealing that manifest and secret space. Clinical perception is made concrete through the use of language and description. This article examines the gaze in operation between clinicians and adolescents and among clinicians, producing situated subjects. Accordingly, we redirect the gaze, 'not at the mad but at the culture, institutions, and language which make madness matter so much' (Parker et al., 1995: 14).

Research design

Participants

Clinicians were recruited and interviewed in two public mental health service sites in the city of Melbourne, Australia. These teams provided specialist services to adolescents who lived within a defined catchment area and were under 18 years of age. Adolescents were referred to the specialist mental health services from a variety of sources: family physicians; schools; hospital emergency departments; family members; government child protection agencies and so on.

Upon gaining ethical approval, each team was visited to introduce the research and all clinicians were invited to participate. Fifteen clinicians were interviewed from site one, comprised of four community teams and a community day programme. Eight clinicians were interviewed from site two; an adolescent acute inpatient unit in another metropolitan region. Participants came from disciplines including nursing, social work, psychiatry, occupational therapy, psychology and general medicine.

Ethics

The study was designed and conducted in line with the Australian NHMRC guidelines for the ethical conduct of research (National Health and Medical Research Council, 2007). Approval to recruit staff and adolescents was granted by the Human Research

Ethics Committees at the two healthcare institutions. In order to maintain confidentiality, potentially identifiable words including names, services and occasionally elements of medical history were replaced in the transcripts with a brief description (i.e. Case manager). Pseudonyms were allocated for each participant.

Analysis of interview data

An individual, semi-structured interview was audio-taped with the permission of each participant at their place of work. Analysis commenced during initial reading of the interview transcripts, with the first author building a set of theme files. The term 'theme' was applied broadly at this first stage to include objects, subjects and discourses, in keeping with the theoretical lens. Passages were sampled for their distinctive use of language, when they showed *how* clinicians talked about BPD (as an object) and also when they pointed to those rules or team practices which underpinned each stance.

Transcripts were examined several times, with essentially three different approaches to reading and listening. When reviewing the transcripts for the first time, themes were noted. Then transcripts were examined in more detail for recurring, dominant and deviant themes (Potter, 2004; Silverman, 2006). At the third level of scrutiny, transcripts were re-visited to look for themes which were not immediately striking, but perhaps provided a more subtle response to the research questions. This returning to the transcripts was done with the deliberate intention of challenging the researchers' expectations of the research outcomes.

Findings

This analysis begins with a structural examination of the sites where the research was undertaken, including a discussion of some of the disciplinary roles, team norms and nuances within each site. After providing an overview of the institutional influences upon talking about BPD in adolescence, we then consider how this talk was structured.

Conducting diagnosis in context: community versus inpatient settings

Across both sites, the only consistent features of disciplinary roles in relation to diagnosis applied to psychiatry. Psychiatrists were overwhelmingly positioned by clinicians and also positioned themselves as the head of the team or hierarchy. This rank derived from the status of psychiatry as a specialty within the medical profession, and those statutory powers held by psychiatrists to prescribe medication or invoke elements of mental health legislation (Barrett, 1996). The ascribed power to diagnose accords with Barrett's observation that power is linked to the capacity to define a psychiatric case.

At site one (community-based service), all clinicians with the exception of the day programme team leader were expected to make diagnoses, regardless of disciplinary background. The direct involvement of the psychiatrist was not considered essential in every diagnostic formulation, however the psychiatrist's hierarchical position was confirmed as the person with whom to consult, if needing diagnostic clarification or when facing a 'diagnostic dilemma' (Interview, Ryan). Psychiatrists also provided the 'sign off' (Interview, Ruth) on diagnoses made within their teams.

Disciplinary demarcation between psychology, nursing, social work and occupational therapy was subtle at site one. The community setting and CAMHS membership at this site proved more indicative of roles and responsibilities than individual disciplines. The only 'jostling for space' (Parker et al., 1995: 50) was noted with external agencies, or the neighbouring adolescent inpatient unit, rather than among team members.

Site two (inpatient unit) provided a notable contrast, with the lone psychiatrist considered by all clinicians, including other medical staff, to hold responsibility for making diagnoses within the unit. Here, disciplinary identities were clearly evident, with nursing and medical roles adhering more closely to stereotypes, in terms of diagnostic practice. Of potential significance was the absence of social work, occupational therapy and psychology professionals on the unit at the time of conducting interviews; this represented a rare period in the unit's staffing history.

At site two, the way in which care was provided also differed, with nurses 'on the floor' (Interview, Holly) providing a constant care that contrasted with the intermittent care of community mental health services. Thus, 'the status of psychiatric nursing, the distinctiveness of its practice, and the uniqueness of its perspective on the case, were defined in terms of *proximity* to the patient' (Barrett, 1996: 53, emphasis in original). Proximity had direct consequences for diagnostic talk, with Amy finding that this closeness rendered some diagnostic conversations inappropriate and outside of her nursing role:

Interviewer: Is it harder being in an inpatient setting than say if you were in the community?

Amy: I think so because the staff have so many roles on the unit, they're not just nurses, they're counsellors, they're parents, they're friends, they're siblings, they cover so many ... obviously not friends with them but you know, cover so many different roles in order to keep the kids safe, contained and try and provide some kind of therapy, that sometimes maybe it's not appropriate for nursing staff on the unit to be doing that kind of stuff I think. It would be better as a community case manager or something like that where your role is more clearly defined. (Interview, Amy; 325–333)

Overall, one could quickly surmise the disciplinary background of those clinicians interviewed at site two, through their comments on proximity and diagnostic responsibility. While psychiatric nurses dominated the unit in terms of numbers, they still jostled for diagnostic space and role credibility. This site-specific idiosyncrasy proved central to diagnostic deliberations about BPD.

Not disclosing diagnosis: holding the team line

Within teams, participants established an agreed 'definition of the situation' and team members displayed a tacit set of rules regarding the disclosure of BPD. The working consensus privileged the claims of particular participants, rather than representing unanimity on an issue (Goffman, 1959).

At site two, the consultant psychiatrist was considered to have the greatest stake in decision making and disclosing the BPD diagnosis. This was clearly articulated by Holly:

Interviewer: So if your Consultant Psychiatrist is primarily responsible for making diagnoses and it sounds like his practice is tending not to talk to the young person about it, does that filter down to other staff or would there be some staff here who you think do have those kind of conversations?

Holly: You don't tend to because you know that it is, it is not what the Consultant has diagnosed, so if he's not formally diagnosing it you don't like to follow up and you don't want to, you don't want to step on his toes ... I know certain people on the team have broached, you know, saying you know it looks like you've got kind of emerging borderline personality traits ... and that's not giving them a diagnosis but that's giving them some idea of kind of the behaviours that they're exhibiting ... and I think that's good but I think you just have to very careful when you work in a team to keep it very cohesive and that's not treading on other people's toes, especially the ones that are dealing with the risk factors and are making the diagnosis and being respectful towards them. (Interview, Holly; 314–332)

The preference of the psychiatrist *not* to make and disclose this diagnosis was consistently noted by nurses and medical staff on the inpatient unit. References to the danger of mis-diagnosing and over-diagnosing were audible from most team members. While Holly also identified occasions when she felt the young person *should* have been notified of this diagnosis, she adhered to the team line, bound by the need to maintain cohesion and respect those discourses of risk and responsibility.

Unsurprisingly, team lines were less rigid at site one, as the differences in setting influenced team dynamics. Here, clinicians functioned at several levels: as solo practitioners; within their local teams; and also as members of the larger multi-team organization of CAMHS. Clinicians at this site were permitted to speak about diagnoses including BPD among clinicians *and* with clients. Team lines were less directive and tended more towards organizational ideologies. For example, team leaders hoped, expected and believed that their team members were 'cautious and considered' (Interview, Robyn) and 'as thorough and thoughtful as possible' (Interview, Angela) in making and talking about a BPD diagnosis. Team members aligned with these expectations, frequently positioning themselves as careful, or 'very, very, very careful' when using borderline terminology (Interview, Laura).

While team expectations regarding BPD appeared less prescriptive at site one, there were still examples whereby clinicians conformed to institutional expectations. For example, despite objecting to the BPD label, Robyn remained loyal to the DSM terminology endorsed by CAMHS:

> I've got to say I'm not a fan of the label BPD. I actually tend to think in my head, either a complex post-traumatic stress disorder symptom[at]ology, but the language I know that I need to, we kind of need to use is BPD. (Interview, Robyn; 91–94)

A further example of tension between team expectations and professional identity occurred when discussing the overall role of psychiatric diagnoses. It was widely acknowledged by participants that CAMHS policy demanded that a diagnosis be reached for every client, for routine service reporting purposes. However this requirement posed a dilemma for some clinicians:

> I know diagnosis is very important, it's a short-hand way of describing a set of presenting symptoms, it's often a way of offering funding and linking up funding for, yeah, funding for treatment. I can see the relevance in a physical setting and I can see the relevance in a, in a mental health setting. But I just, my whole philosophy on human beings is that they're always moving forward and changing which kind of doesn't fit with the categories and the diagnostic things. (Interview, Eve; 113–118)

In order to manage this tension, Eve adhered to diagnostic formulation, but voiced scepticism to her clients:

> And if you, you're sat in front of a young person, who says 'do I have OCD, am I going to be like this for the rest of my life?' And you're talking to a 13 year old, I feel it's ethical to say these are diagnoses that are not necessarily based on research solely, they're based on the opinions of American psychiatrists, they came about because they needed a way to apportion insurance funding often. (Interview, Eve; 580–589)

Eve's 'performance' falls into a grey area, not adequately accounted for by Goffman in his analysis of team roles. However, in Foucauldian terms, Eve challenges the truth status of the DSM and views the young person's identity as contested territory.

In short, participants fell into line with diagnosis as a practice, but sometimes challenged the authority of the diagnosis, positioning themselves as apart from and critical of the discourse. At other times participants made use of diagnosis, while drawing upon qualifying language to establish a sceptical position towards the diagnosis.

Hedges

As noted earlier, the use of language is pivotal in constructing the clinical culture. Semantic strategies such as 'hedges' are words or phrases used to modify the degree of membership within a statement (Brown and Levinson, 1987), allowing clinicians to either commit or distance themselves from a statement (Fairclough, 1992). Clinicians overwhelmingly advocated for the use of hedges such as 'emerging' and 'traits' to respectively preface or follow the term 'borderline personality disorder'. Lakoff (1973: 471) suggests that hedges are words 'whose job is to make things fuzzier or less fuzzy'. The use of hedges in adolescent applications of the BPD diagnosis served to make things fuzzier, as a way of softening (Interview, Ruth) or cushioning (Interview, Robyn) the diagnosis. Yet, they were also relied upon in an attempt to define a grey zone, or as a way of giving the benefit of the doubt (Interview, Simon).

The term 'traits' worked to offset the permanency otherwise associated with a personality disorder diagnosis. Scott, for example described his rationale for employing hedges:

> Interviewer: Do you see a difference in the terminology between saying say this person has BPD and this person has BPD *traits* or *emerging* BPD?

Scott: [*sigh*] *I* think it's better to have traits, I think you know, the sake of splitting hairs but I think it's actually, it's a lot more beneficial for an adolescent just to have traits or it may be emerging than to have a full blown I have it and that's it.

Interviewer: Yep, why?

Scott: It's too final because it can, emerging and, and traits means it's just, you have some of these areas that potentially could change and I think that's a much nicer, I, you know, I think adolescent psychiatry is all about hope, you have to have the hope and if you don't provide hope, if you say something's it and final that's it, you know. (Interview, Scott; 154–166, emphases in original)

For Holly, hedges allowed her to continue to talk about and describe BPD. Within her account, Holly also makes reference to an external and prohibiting authority, though the identity of this authority remained nebulous:

Interviewer: Do you think that terminology like emerging or traits is useful?

Holly: I think it is 'cos, it's, it's good to be able to identify because you can't, because they don't like to give a diagnosis, but if you, if we weren't able to say that these are emerging traits and things like that you couldn't pinpoint them, then it's very hard to, to work with what's going on. (Interview, Holly; 57–61)

Owen was the only clinician who objected to the use of hedges describing them as 'just a bit cowardly, I think it's just hiding behind the fact that you can't give a diagnosis 'til they're 18, isn't it?' (Interview, Owen; 206–208)

While we anticipated that hedges would be commonly used to buttress the BPD diagnosis, the ubiquity of this practice was surprising. Identifying the origins and proliferation of this practice proved challenging, as this modified vocabulary for adolescents seems to have occurred in isolation from the DSM, which defines the BPD diagnosis. One may surmise that a customized CAMHS vocabulary emerged in clinical practice as a resistance to the generic criteria of BPD, which clearly delineates between normal and abnormal, and may be considered a poor fit for the developing adolescent. The use of hedges indicates a functional demand for descriptors regarding this diagnosis in adolescence, yet a reluctance to embrace categorically the personality disorder vocabulary and its implications. Another strategy in language will now be examined; the role of borderline talk in clinical practice.

Borderline talk

Returning to Foucault's enunciative modalities, site two provided a glaring example of who was accorded the right to speak freely about BPD. The consultant psychiatrist was authorized to name BPD at any time and in any environment, both among clinicians, and to clients and families. Team members however, were restricted in their enunciative forums. Overall, clinicians in this sample tended *not* to talk to clients about BPD. This restricted their audience to other clinicians. Using Goffman's (1959) terminology, nursing staff were limited to discussing BPD backstage, rather than front stage.

Backstage talk about BPD was described as common by interview participants at site two, with Amy describing a typical example:

> Well I guess during handover or even just within the office environment, if people were just, if young people were displaying behaviours that someone thought was that kind of personality disorder traits then it might be discussed, and I guess if it's talked about enough people start to get the idea even if the person hasn't got the diagnosis that they, they label them anyway to a degree. (Interview, Amy; 149–153)

Nurses showed that talk about BPD may be received differently, depending upon the backstage region. Thus there were *degrees* of backstage, whereby nursing handovers, for example, represented a setting where it was relatively safe to use borderline descriptors, despite individual staff preferences. But during backstage discussions attended by the consultant psychiatrist (i.e. team handovers, office discussions, etc.) the informal mention of borderline traits became risky:

> Interviewer: Do the terms get used much verbally if not always documented?
> Holly: Yeah I think they get used verbally more than they get documented.
> Interviewer: Can you give me an example?
> Holly: Just when there's, there's situations on the unit where their behaviours are, are a bit more destructive or out of control. I know staff here will mention that they, they seem to have emerging traits and you'll say that to the Consultant and, and the Consultant's very quick to turn around and say well you need to tell me exactly what they are because I don't want them being labelled. So I s'pose, and I think that's, it's important too that he does do that, that we're not just giving out a label for, for behaviours that can just be adolescent, behaviours, so … (Interview, Holly; 108–120)

Lester (2009: 285, emphases in original) coined the phrase 'borderline talk' to describe the

> mode of everyday discourse among clinicians that ascribes BPD as shorthand to clusters of behavioural and interpersonal concerns. … It can be *explanatory*, accounting for a client's behaviour … It can be *cautionary*, as a way of preparing another clinician for an encounter … It can also become a way for therapists to communicate to each other their *personal struggles* or even burn out.

Participant accounts within this research support Lester's hypotheses. For example, when asked whether borderline talk was useful, Holly (and others) identified a *cautionary* usefulness:

> It is 'cos sometimes you can be caught out and when they can be staff splitting and manipulating and things like that, and it just keeps you on your toes, it makes you more aware that, that this

> is what the young person has been kind of known to do and, yeah, it just, it does, it does make you more aware. (Interview, Holly; 185–188)

At site one, borderline talk was mentioned, with Catherine reporting the practice of people talking 'about it professionally, oh with other professionals sorry, but actually not with the young person' (Interview, Catherine; 241–242). In alliance with site two, Alex described an *explanatory* use of borderline talk in the community setting:

> Ah we've got to be able communicate these ideas somehow. And ah, ah you know I, once again I think as long as we understand you know, as long as language is used in a way that ah the best interests of the client you know are kept to the fore, then I think it is productive. But when it's used to close doors and you know to, to shut out and to ah to discount, ah that's when it's negative. (Interview, Alex; 495–499)

However, generally there was cohesion around the application of borderline terminology within CAMHS and 'borderline talk' served fewer functions than on the inpatient unit.

Borderline talk was never acclaimed as entirely positive, with all clinicians also describing disadvantages to its use. Patrick, a community psychiatrist (from site one), described this predicament as a 'two edged sword', seeing utility in the borderline concept, but also the potential for it to be used in a 'scathing way'.

Furthermore, while Dana (a psychiatry trainee at site two) described a prescriptive function to borderline talk, she also saw this as reductionist and negative:

> Often the, the conversation comes up in terms of admissions, so if we've got a transfer of a patient who we've had before who has marked borderline traits for example, I think there's an assumption that their admission is going to be difficult, that the milieu of the ward is going to change, and that they won't necessarily remain as an inpatient for a long time. So I think that it's, it's a way of describing some of the difficult patients without having to actually go through specific issues so there's a lot of assumptions that are made and so forth, but it's always said in quite a negative way. (Interview, Dana; 446–452)

Owen, Scott and Michael, three of the senior nursing and medical staff at site two, primarily objected to borderline talk because of the potential to stigmatize the client among staff. Owen suggested that it was used by people who were not qualified to make diagnoses, and sometimes to 'opt out' of working with these young people. As nurse manager, Scott felt that borderline descriptors prevented people from going beyond the diagnosis, to what the person was really about. His suggestion that it often came from nurses who were in a 'bad place', aligned with Lester's (2009) function of communicating *personal struggles*. The psychiatrist, Michael was 'not in favour of' the practice of borderline talk and believed it was often used in a dismissive way. Regardless of this stance by three of the most senior staff on the unit, all acknowledged a well-entrenched pattern of borderline talk among clinicians. While Michael retained sole authority to diagnose BPD formally and speak uncensored in both front- and backstage, nursing staff resisted this psychiatric dominance, through their continued employment of borderline talk.

The persistence of borderline talk may reflect nursing's reliance on the oral culture of knowledge transmission. In handover for example, nurses draw upon stereotypical identities to provide their colleagues with a 'sense of the lie of the land' (Parker and Wiltshire, 1995: 148). Such formulations are necessarily brief and not always erudite (Hamilton and Manias, 2009). While medical and some nursing staff objected to the imprecision of stereotypical 'borderline' constructions, the functionality of borderline talk remained powerful, as a tool to explain, caution, communicate personal struggles and inform treatment decisions.

Thus, the territory surrounding borderline talk was contested, with disciplinary techniques traversing both staff groups. Through their clinical gaze and subsequent determinations of treatment and length of stays, clinicians used borderline talk to regulate adolescent inpatients. Running counter to these techniques was the exercise of the psychiatrist's powerful gaze upon staff, in an attempt to clamp down on the use of borderline talk. Michael also sought to introduce a screening tool, to ensure more accurate use of the borderline diagnosis. Against the authority of Michael's position, 'borderline talk' may be more appropriately termed a tenacious discourse.

'How' to talk to adolescents – reframing BPD

The BPD label provided a clear example of psychiatric terminology which achieves a very low level of precision in its attempts to describe moods and mental states (Linnet, 2004). Clinicians struggled with the semantics of BPD, especially when talking with adolescents. Its inherent ambiguity was considered problematic by several clinicians. Simon suggested:

> I think it's hard for people to know what borderline means. I mean I've certainly had patients ask me what does it mean that I'm borderline? Ah, and you sort of explain it but, it ... doesn't sort of make sense to people, in the way that, say depression does, that's sort of a more understandable sort of diagnosis. (Interview, Simon; 248–253)

As a result of dissatisfaction with the BPD label, clinicians sought to 'fashion and tailor' (Interview, Simon), 're-frame' (Interview, Margot) or 'steer away from' (Interview, Robyn) the words borderline personality disorder. Robyn used sensory metaphors to describe her position, preferring to describe diagnosis and 'flesh it out, as opposed to always just going bamo, this is it' (383–384). Robyn noted the importance of giving people time to 'digest' their diagnoses and felt that BPD was a '*whack* of a diagnosis to give someone, particularly as they *hit* the adult system' (121–122, *emphases added*).

Preferring to offer a behavioural or symptom descriptor was a strong rhetoric throughout clinician interviews. Natasha spoke of her tendency *not* to name the BPD diagnosis, instead 'naming the behaviour, the consequences, the interpersonal relationships, the, kind of the symptoms of, without giving it the label' (Interview, Natasha; 505–506).

Clinicians were consistently wary of naming diagnoses, of adopting a vocabulary that authorized 'comparison, generalization and establishment within a totality' (Foucault, 1989: 139). Natasha worried about the permanent connotations of a personality disorder label:

> I don't know, but it feels a bit like there's nothing for them to work towards, there's nothing for the therapy to work towards if it's given a label that feels permanent. If it's given a descriptor

> about behaviour and interactions, there's something more fluid about that, we can change your behaviour, we can work on our interactions, but our personality is kind of stuck. (Interview, Natasha; 519–523)

At site two, the nurse manager Scott reiterated those rules governing disclosure of BPD:

> What we do is, what we *would* do is identify issues and patterns of behaviour and feed back to a young person but we don't neccess- we don't put it in diagnostic terms, and I don't actually think in adolescents having diagnostic terms is often that useful for certain disorders. I think it's better to look at the problems. What's causing your problem? Look at the strengths and weaknesses of a kid and then look at that. (Interview, Scott; 47–51, emphasis in original)

This position aligns with behavioural therapy, which originated through the need to treat those disorders not considered amenable to physical or pharmacological treatment, or those people 'not sick' within psychiatry's domain (Rose, 1989). When defined in behaviourist terms, personality disorders are problems of behaviour and able to be re-shaped. Accordingly, clinicians in this study saw adolescent personalities as 'malleable' (Interviews, Ryan, Laura, Margot), 'still forming' (*Interview,* Margot), 'developing' (*Interview,* Laura), 'maturing' (*Interview,* Holly) and 'in a state of flux' (*Interview,* Michael). The opportunity to re-shape personality and watch for improvement was also considered as a hallmark of adolescence, linked closely to the expression of clinical optimism and hopefulness:

> And that's the biggest difference I see in CAMHS versus adult, that's why I work in CAMHS because I know things can change, I've experienced that, I've been a part of the change, and I know it can, and young people do evolve, they develop, they grow up, they mature, thank God! (Interview, Angela; 382–386)

Overall, clinicians consistently re-shaped BPD when talking to adolescents, finessing language to accord with their own preferences and to match the perceived needs of their adolescent clients. Resistance to disclose the BPD diagnosis stemmed from both dissatisfaction with this label and also a desire to retain hopefulness, which was better served by lay definitions of problems.

Discussion

The study shows how the category of BPD exists as an object of psychopathology within a complex group of social and power relations. The differences in roles across sites highlighted the power of the setting to determine clinician roles, team functioning and ways of interacting with adolescents. For nurses in an inpatient unit, the setting framed their roles in relation to diagnoses, organizing them to observe and report diagnostic features 'up the line' to the psychiatrist. Prohibitions to diagnose and restrictions on talking about the BPD diagnosis were striking and consistent. The setting also dictated the way in which nurses engaged with adolescents. Their roles were multifaceted; arising from their proximity to adolescents over time and space and the concomitant responsibility they carried to manage safety and behaviour.

Practice in the inpatient unit was consistent with Barrett's (1996: 48) description of a psychiatric hospital, where, 'although other professions had an informal warrant to advance diagnostic opinions when talking with their colleagues, only psychiatry was licensed to make formal diagnostic statements of illness that could be entered into the official case record'. In part, this distinction proved to be a significant point of difference between the sites, with such power differentials much more visible at site two. Furthermore, the informal warrant to make diagnostic statements manifested at site two in the form of borderline talk, as detailed. In addition to providing a summary of the utility of borderline talk, this discussion also considers the way in which the identity work done by clinicians impacted upon adolescent identities – allowing both agents room to move.

The utility of the BPD diagnosis among clinicians

The findings indicate how little scope there was for frank use of the diagnosis of BPD in the adolescent clinical setting. With BPD in particular, clinicians tended to talk to clients in terms of symptoms, problems and behaviours rather than use diagnostic speak. By focusing upon *anything but* diagnosis, in both clinical formulations and communications, clinicians often preferred an approach which 'remained at the level of the problem itself' (Rose, 1989: 234).

Rhodes (1991) described the status of diagnosis in an acute psychiatric unit as contradictory; central *and* peripheral, key to defining psychiatric patients, yet often valued more for strategic rather than medical purposes. Rhodes (1991: 95, emphasis in original) watched medical students 'learn that diagnosis was true, useful *and* tentative, even meaningless'. These observations accord closely with the findings of this research. At both sites, clinicians in this project did not always herald diagnosis as true, however they did identify dichotomies of diagnosis; as necessary and unnecessary, helpful and unhelpful, contributing to and detracting from their ability to know a young person. Overall, diagnosis was imperfect and fallible, and therefore clinicians were judicious in their use of diagnoses.

The imprint of clinician identity work upon adolescent identities

Clinicians and adolescents were linked together in a disciplinary space, where both parties were active in looking over and *being* looked over (Dreyfus and Rabinow, 1982). Clinicians looked over each other in the diverse disciplinary spaces of inpatient units, in team meetings and handovers. Their gaze was astutely focused on attitudes and language use in the highly charged realm of BPD. Clinicians powerfully disciplined each other, in their silences and in their oblique use of language associated with the diagnosis of BPD.

Clinicians found room to adopt positions of *scepticism* around the meaning and utility of the BPD diagnosis, a positioning identified by Whooley (2010) as common also among a sample of US psychiatrists working with a range of DSM diagnoses. At site two, clinicians primarily positioned themselves as *not authorized* to use the BPD diagnosis, thus making space for reservations. At both sites, clinicians resisted the permanent connotations of personality disorder diagnoses. While clinicians could not avoid interacting with the issue of diagnosis as they appraised adolescents in their care, their gripe was with the limits of the BPD diagnostic nosology itself. In our analysis, and in line with the DSM IV-TR (APA, 2000), personality *traits* in Axis II diagnoses were taken to infer permanency in contrast with those episodic *states* in Axis I diagnoses. However, used by clinicians in everyday practice, the term 'traits' functioned as a hedge. It denoted only partial achievement of diagnostic criteria and the incomplete fulfilment of a BPD identity, thus assembling an identity which could be discredited over time. So the notions of traits and of emerging diagnosis acted as qualifiers in speech, disrupting or postponing claims to diagnostic permanency. The unanimous preference for hedges preserved the clinicians' own sceptical identities as well as producing room for adolescents to move.

Transitional identities: allowing room for adolescents to move

In the course of this analysis, it became evident that when clinicians made decisions not to talk to adolescents about emerging BPD, it was rarely as a result of disregarding the adolescent position. In fact, clinicians were often positioned 'between a rock and a hard place' and their decisions overwhelmingly reflected their need to work with fallible diagnostic categories.

As indicated in the findings, clinicians predominantly sought to resist any vocabulary which positioned adolescents within a totality. Instead, behavioural descriptors were relied upon for their ability to emphasize temporality. Behaviour can be thought of as fleeting, occurring in time and space, as a phenomenon that could pass and be left behind. Description of phenomena as 'behaviour' links to both lay and normal psychology perspectives of problems of adolescence, denoting temporary aberrations, with the potential to be outgrown or discarded.

The course of BPD resembled a pathway or trajectory within clinician accounts. The act of closure on a diagnosis of BPD was loaded with prognostic meanings which did not hold true, alongside their understandings of the adolescents in their care. By resisting foreclosure on a BPD diagnosis, clinicians could allow troubled adolescents who met *some* criteria to defy the BPD trajectory with which they were familiar.

Conclusion

We began this article by noting the frustration experienced in clinical settings, where the BPD diagnosis was routinely not disclosed to adolescents. Through the process of undertaking interviews, it became clear that a black and white stance (i.e. either for or against disclosure) would nullify the research. In fact, the complexity, contradiction and flaws inherent in this diagnostic category essentially drove the practices identified in this research. The findings richly illustrate clinicians negotiating diagnostic talk in a situation of uncertainty and with vulnerable populations. Discursive strategies to work around the diagnosis operated at the level of individual practitioners, clinicians grouped by discipline and whole teams in particular settings. These can be seen as robust and everyday expressions of the enduring contest surrounding psychiatric diagnoses in general and BPD more than most.

References

American Psychiatric Association (APA) (1980) *Diagnostic and Statistical Manual of Mental Disorders*. Washington, DC: APA.

American Psychiatric Association (APA) (2000) *Diagnostic and Statistical Manual of Mental Disorders*. Text revision. Washington, DC: APA.

Barrett R (1996) *The Psychiatric Team and the Social Definition of Schizophrenia*. Cambridge: Cambridge University Press.

Becker DF and Grilo CM (2006) Validation studies of the borderline personality disorder construct in adolescents: Implications for theory and practice. *Adolescent Psychiatry* 29: 217–235.

Benbassat J, Pilpel D and Tidhar M (1998) Patients' preferences for participation in clinical decision making: A review of published surveys. *Behavioral Medicine* 24(2): 81–88.

Bleiberg E (1994) Borderline disorders in children and adolescents: The concept, the diagnosis, and the controversies. *Bulletin of the Menninger Clinic* 58(2): 169–196.

Boschen M and Warner J (2009) Publication trends in individual DSM personality disorder: 1971–2015. *Australian Psychologist* 44(2): 136–142.

Brown P and Levinson S (1987) *Politeness: Some Universals in Language Usage*. Cambridge: Cambridge University Press.

Buckman R (1996) Talking to patients about cancer: No excuse now for not doing it. *British Medical Journal* 313(7059): 699–700.

Chanen AM and McCutcheon L (2008) Complex case: Personality disorder in adolescence; the diagnosis that dare not speak its name. *Personality and Mental Health* 2: 35–41.

Chanen AM, McCutcheon LK, Germano D, Nistico H, Jackson HJ and McGorry PD (2009) The HYPE Clinic: An early intervention service for borderline personality disorder. *Journal of Psychiatric Practice* 15(3): 163–172.

Cheek J (2004) At the margins? Discourse analysis and qualitative research. *Qualitative Health Research* 14(8): 1140–1150.

Cohen P, Crawford TN, Johnson JG and Kasen S (2005) The children in the community study of developmental course of personality disorder. *Journal of Personality Disorders* 19(5): 466–486.

Cooksey EC and Brown P (1998) Spinning on its axes: DSM and the social construction of psychiatric diagnosis. *International Journal of Health Services* 28(3): 525–554.

Drew P and Heritage J (1992) *Talk at Work: Interaction in Institutional Settings*. Cambridge: Cambridge University Press.

Dreyfus H and Rabinow P (1982) *Michel Foucault: Beyond Structuralism and Hermeneutics with an Afterword by Michel Foucault*. Brighton: The Harvester Press.

Fairclough N (1989) *Language and Power*. Essex: Longman Group UK.

Fairclough N (1992) *Discourse and Social Change*. Oxford: Polity Press.

Faust D and Miner RA (1986) The empiricist and his new clothes: DSM-III in perspective. *American Journal of Psychiatry* 143(8): 962–967.

Foucault M (1972) *The Archaeology of Knowledge*. London: Tavistock.

Foucault M (1984) Politics and ethics: An interview. In: Rabinow P (ed.) *The Foucault Reader*. London: Penguin Books, pp. 373–380.

Foucault M (1989) *The Birth of the Clinic*. London: Routledge.

Fox N (1993) Discourse, organisation and the surgical ward round. *Sociology of Health and Illness* 15(1): 16–42.

Gallagher A, Arber A, Chaplin R and Quirk A (2010) Service users' experience of receiving bad news about their mental health. *Journal of Mental Health* 19(1): 34–42.

Gastaldo D and Holmes D (1999) Foucault and nursing: A history of the present. *Nursing Inquiry* 6(4): 231–240.

Goffman E (1959) *The Presentation of Self in Everyday Life*. Middlesex: Penguin Books.
Gunderson JG (2009) Borderline personality disorder: Ontogeny of a diagnosis. *American Journal of Psychiatry* 166(5): 530–539.
Hamilton B and Manias E (2009) Foucault's concept of 'local knowledges' for researching nursing practice. *Aporia* 1(3): 7–17.
Handler R (2009) Erving Goffman and the gestural dynamics of modern selfhood. *Past and Present* Suppl. 4: 280–300.
Hersh R (2008) Confronting myths and stereotypes about borderline personality disorder. *Social Work in Mental Health* 6(1/2): 13–32.
Humphreys C (1990) *Disclosure of Child Sexual Assault: Mothers in Crisis*. Sydney: University of New South Wales, School of Social Work.
Kirk S and Kutchins H (1992) *The Selling of DSM: The Rhetoric of Science in Psychiatry*. New York: Aldine De Gruyter.
Lakoff G (1973) Hedges: A study in meaning criteria and the logic of fuzzy concepts. *Journal of Philosophical Logic* 2: 458–508.
Lequesne ER and Hersh RG (2004) Disclosure of a diagnosis of borderline personality disorder. *Journal of Psychiatric Practice* 10(3): 170–176.
Lester R (2009) Brokering authenticity: Borderline personality disorder and the ethics of care in an American eating disorder clinic. *Current Anthropology* 50(3): 281–302.
Linnet P (2004) A matter of semantics. *Asylum* 12(2): 10–14.
Manning N (2000) Psychiatric diagnosis under conditions of uncertainty: Personality disorder, science and professional legitimacy. *Sociology of Health and Illness* 22(5): 621–639.
McDonald-Scott P, Machizawa S and Satoh H (1992) Diagnostic disclosure: A tale in two cultures. *Psychological Medicine* 22(1): 147–157.
Miller AL, Muehlenkamp JJ and Jacobson CM (2008a) Fact or fiction: Diagnosing borderline personality disorder in adolescents. *Clinical Psychology Review* 28(6): 969–981.
Miller AL, Neft D and Golombeck N (2008) Borderline personality disorder and adolescence. *Social Work in Mental Health* 6(1–2): 85–98.
National Health and Medical Research Council, Australian Vice-Chancellors' Committee & Australian Research Council (2007) *National Statement on Ethical Conduct in Human Research*. Canberra, ACT: National Health and Medical Research Council, Australian Vice-Chancellors' Committee & Australian Research Council.
National Institute for Health and Clinical Excellence (NICE) (2009) *Borderline Personality Disorder: Treatment and Management*. NICE clinical guideline 78. London: NICE.
Paris J (2008) Commentary: Personality disorder in adolescence: The diagnosis that dare not speak its name. *Personality and Mental Health* 2: 42–43.
Parker I (1990) Discourse: Definitions and contradictions. *Philosophical Psychology* 3(2/3): 189–204.
Parker I, Georgaca E, Harper D, McLaughlin T and Stowell-Smith M (1995) *Deconstructing Psychopathology*. London: SAGE.
Parker J and Wiltshire J (1995) The handover: Three modes of nursing practice knowledge. In: Parker J (ed.) *A Body of Work: Collected Writings on Nursing*. London: Nursing Praxis International.
Phillips L and Jorgensen M (2002) *Discourse Analysis: As Theory and Method*. London: SAGE.
Pilgrim D (2001) Disordered personalities and disordered concepts. *Journal of Mental Health* 10(3): 253–265.
Pilgrim D (2007) The survival of psychiatric diagnosis. *Social Science and Medicine* 65(3): 536–547.
Potter J (2004) Discourse analysis as a way of analysing naturally occurring talk. In: Silverman D (ed.) *Qualitative Research: Theory, Method and Practice*. London: SAGE, pp. 200–221.

Rhodes L (1991) *Emptying Beds: The Work of an Emergency Psychiatric Unit.* Berkeley, CA: University of California Press.
Rose N (1989) *Governing the Soul: Technologies of Human Subjectivity.* London: Routledge.
Rose N (1996) *Inventing our Selves: Psychology, Power and Personhood.* Cambridge: Cambridge University Press.
Rudge T (1998) Skin as cover: The discursive effects of 'covering' metaphors on wound care practices. *Nursing Inquiry* 5(4): 228–237.
Shaw C and Proctor G (2005) Women at the margins: A critique of the diagnosis of borderline personality disorder. *Feminism and Psychology* 15: 483–490.
Silk K (2008) Commentary: Personality disorder in adolescence: The diagnosis that dare not speak its name. *Personality and Mental Health* 2: 46–48.
Silverman D (2006) *Interpreting Qualitative Data: Methods for Analyzing Talk, Text and Interaction.* London: SAGE.
Spitzer RL (1981) The diagnostic status of homosexuality in DSM-III: A reformulation of the issues. *American Journal of Psychiatry* 138(2): 210–215.
Whooley O (2010) Diagnostic ambivalence: Psychiatric workarounds and the *Diagnostic and Statistical Manual of Mental Disorders. Sociology of Health and Illness* 32(3): 452–469.
Wirth-Cauchon J (2001) *Women and Borderline Personality Disorder.* New Brunswick: Rutgers University Press.

Author biographies

Kristy Koehne RPN, BN(Hons), PhD specialises in Child and Adolescent Mental Health in research and clinical practice. In addition to her PhD examination of borderline personality disorder discourse in adolescence, research interests include self-harm, suicidality and the early intervention construct in psychiatry.

Bridget Hamilton RN, BN(Hons), PhD is Senior Lecturer at the Department of Nursing, The University of Melbourne. She is connected to clinical practice as a Clinical Nurse Consultant at St.Vincent's Mental Health, Melbourne. Her research centres on post-structural analyses of everyday practices in healthcare. She is interested in law and coercion, and in amplifying diverse voices in health care settings.

Natisha Sands (PhD) is Associate Professor at the School of Nursing and Midwifery, Deakin University. She investigates mental health triage clinical practice, mental health care in the emergency department and clinical risk assessment. She is committed to developing evidence-based frameworks and education programs to support clinicians in improving the quality and consistency of triage and practice.

Cathy Humphreys BSW, PhD is Professor of Social Work in the Department of Social Work, The University of Melbourne. Her research interests lie in the areas of domestic violence and child abuse including the impact on mental health and child development.

Children and Youth Services Review 32 (2010) 1683–1689

ELSEVIER

Contents lists available at ScienceDirect

Children and Youth Services Review

journal homepage: www.elsevier.com/locate/childyouth

Voices from the periphery: Prospects and challenges for the homeless youth service sector

Kiaras Gharabaghi *, Carol Stuart [1]

School of Child & Youth Care, Ryerson University, 350 Victoria Street, Toronto, ON, Canada M5B 2K3

ARTICLE INFO

Article history:
Received 10 April 2010
Received in revised form 19 July 2010
Accepted 22 July 2010
Available online 27 July 2010

Keywords:
Homeless youth
Shelter services
Child and youth care practice
System collaboration
Mental health
Informal service provision

ABSTRACT

As a result of its focus on transitionally-aged youth (16–24), the homeless youth service sector finds itself on the periphery of both the children's service sectors, represented by children's mental health, child welfare, education and youth justice, and the adult service sectors that seek to address the varying needs of adults for social assistance and mental health services. Based on an extensive literature review and a series of interviews with service providers, stakeholders and youth within this sector, in the Central East Service Region of the Ontario Ministry of Children and Youth Services, the authors synthesize core themes and issues that help to situate the current prospects and challenges facing this sector. Feedback from informants positioned the concept of "relationship" as a central feature of both service provision and service use on the part of youth. The Central East Region is a mixed urban, suburban and semi-rural region situated in close proximity to Canada's largest urban centre, Toronto. With a population of nearly 2 million, the Region is often perceived as diverse, encompassing a series of highly affluent commuter communities, relatively isolated rural and small town communities and urban working class communities. While social issues such as homelessness and poverty have long been recognized in urban communities, they have only recently been acknowledged as community concerns in the geographically large suburban areas of this region.

1. Introduction

Services for homeless youth in most Ontario communities exist at the margins of much larger, institutionalized service sectors for children, youth and families (Karabanow, 2004; Youth Shelter Interagency Network, 2007). Given its focus on transitionally-aged youth (16–24), the sector finds itself on the periphery of both the children's service sectors, represented by children's mental health, child welfare, education and youth justice, and the adult service sectors that seek to address the varying issues of adults in need of assistance. As a result of its peripheral position in relation to these more established service sectors, the homeless youth service sector is constantly seeking its place in a continuum of services characterized by major gaps and limitations (Kidd & Davidson, 2006; Kurtz, Jarvis, & Kurtz, 1991). Service providers within this sector have had to develop innovative and highly creative approaches to navigating a system of funding opportunities and related service expectations in order to continue to meet the ever-increasing needs and challenges faced by homeless youth in the community (City of Toronto, 2008; Durham Region, 2007; Karabanow, 2004). Services for homeless youth in rural or semi-rural areas face added challenges related to geographic isolation, social stigma and community expectations (Cloke, Johnsen, & May, 2007; Elias, 2009; Skott-Myhre, 2008).

In this paper, we give voice to the service providers and the youth they engage with in order to articulate the prospects and challenges facing this particular component of an otherwise formalized and institutional service system. In our discussions with a wide range of stakeholders in the homeless youth service sector, we were impressed by the centrality of the concept of "relationship" to virtually every aspect of this system's dynamics. Executive leadership as well as youth themselves...front line staff as well as academic observers...all agreed that the informality of the sector is both its strength and its impediment; the latter because the sector lacks the resources and clinical skills to address the frequent and often intense mental health concerns of homeless youth, and the former because youth themselves are engaged not so much by the quality of service structures, but by the prospects of on-going relationships with particular agencies, programs and professionals. In our discussion of the voices of the homeless youth service sector, we will, therefore, emphasize the relationship context of service provision and youth engagement.

2. Youth homelessness in Central East Region

A snapshot of youth homelessness in Central East Region, and the services currently in place to address this challenge, will help to provide a background for the voices of the various stakeholders. The region, situated north of Toronto, stretches from Richmond Hill north

* Corresponding author. Tel.: +1 416 979 5000x4813; fax: +1 416 598 5940.
E-mail addresses: k.gharabaghi@ryerson.ca (K. Gharabaghi), cstuart@ryerson.ca (C. Stuart).
[1] Tel.: +1 416 979 5000x6203; fax: +1 416 598 5940.

0190-7409/$ – see front matter © 2010 Elsevier Ltd. All rights reserved.
doi:10.1016/j.childyouth.2010.07.011

to Haliburton and east to Peterborough, and is one of nine regions for the provincial ministry responsible for all services to children, youth and families, except education. The long-standing perception that most areas within this region are affluent, with primarily suburban lifestyles, has resulted in the marginalization of social issues and concerns within the public political agenda and narrative. Much of the service system to address youth homelessness in this region is relatively new, and outside of the working class communities in the eastern part of the region, homeless youth themselves have been largely invisible (Pathways, York Region, 2007/08).

The region is home to an extensive network of formal, institutionalized services for children, youth and families, including five children's aid societies, Canada's largest children's mental health centre and a network of mental health services available through hospitals and community agencies. A large number of private sector residential and community-based services are also present, typically working closely with the children's aid societies for the purpose of providing services to children and youth in care.

A number of recent regional studies have pointed to increases in youth homelessness, broadly defined (Durham Region, 2007; Simcoe County Alliance to End Homelessness, 2006; York Region Alliance to End Homelessness, in press; York Region Homelessness Task Force, 2002). Within this region, youth homelessness includes youth living on the streets and in shelters, and also those with no stable housing who "couch surf" or inhabit unsecure or unsuitable residences in the private housing market. Similarly to other regions in Ontario and throughout Canada, the population of homeless youth includes those transitioning or aging out of other sectors, notably children's mental health and child welfare, as well as those finding themselves without secure housing after leaving or being rejected by family at age 16 or older. In some cases, youth find themselves homeless after being discharged from youth justice facilities with no plan for housing (Haggart, 2007). The prevalence of mental health concerns, while not the subject of targeted measurement, is said to be very high, as are personal histories of trauma, abuse, family conflict, poverty and newcomer status (Van Daalen-Smith & Lamont, 2006).

The service system in place to provide intervention and support to homeless youth consists of a somewhat fragmented collection of service providers who offer emergency shelter and transitional and semi-independent residential group care services, as well as outreach services, drop-in centres and mobile crisis support. The funding for these services is highly differentiated, with some of the residential facilities receiving transfer payment funds from the regional Ministry office, and other services receiving municipal funding, as well as private donations, to maintain programs.

3. Methodology

The research for this paper was undertaken in partnership with the Central East Region office of the Ontario Ministry of Children and Youth Services (MCYS). As part of a review of their residential mental health services, the office was interested in better understanding the mental health needs and related issues specific to the population of homeless and hard-to-house youth in the region. A wide range of informants and stakeholders were consulted, including the executive leadership of MCYS-funded agencies serving homeless youth, regional experts and peripheral stakeholders within the homelessness system in Ontario and beyond, and the youth themselves. The emphasis in this study was to listen to the multiple perspectives of service providers, stakeholders and youth in order to identify their core themes and issues. To that end, a series of interviews and focus groups was conducted across the region using a snowball sampling technique; participants who could speak to service sector concerns, as well as to the experience of using services within this sector, were recruited.

Interviews were initiated with the executive leaders (3) of services funded by Central East MCYS to provide housing for homeless youth (under the mental health funding envelope). These leaders referred the researchers to other stakeholders (4) who provided similar services or were considered to have expertise in homelessness issues in the region or in the Greater Toronto area. In the course of the research, the researchers learned of additional service providers familiar with the population, and these providers were also invited to participate in an interview. Six invitations were extended to direct service providers running municipally-funded shelters, youth recreation programs and a mental health support group. One interview was completed, and additional information was received by email. Frontline and specialized staff members were also present at some of the interviews with the executive leaders.

Youth participants were recruited using posters providing a brief project description, along with the group interview dates and contact information, which were distributed by staff in the (MCYS-funded) youth shelters. Youth over the age of 18 were invited to contact the researchers directly, or to show up at a group meeting at a local drop-in program. Each youth who agreed to attend a focus group or be interviewed individually received a cash payment of $25. Three focus groups took place, with six participants in Newmarket, nine in Richmond Hill, and six in Oshawa, along with one individual interview, representing a total of 22 youth.

All interviews and focus groups were audiotaped with participant consent. The tapes were reviewed independently by each investigator, and themes were distilled from the data. A collective review of the themes identified commonalities, as well as themes unique to each group. All the research protocols employed in this study were reviewed and approved by Ryerson University's Research Ethics Board.

4. Findings

Although there was considerable overlap between the voices of service providers, external stakeholders and the youth themselves, we are presenting these voices separately in order to highlight the specific concerns and challenges identified by each of these subgroups. In addition to the previously mentioned focus on relationships, a notable feature of all the interviews and focus groups was the degree to which the participants identified as being on the periphery of broader social service systems in the region and beyond. The language used to frame this marginalization most commonly included references to "formal" and "informal" sectors. The former seem to include agencies and services areas that are associated with stable government funding as well as relatively large bureaucratic organizations (eg: children's aid societies, hospitals), while the latter include smaller, not-for-profit or private organizations that are characterized by unstable funding and the need for fundraising; limited regulatory oversight; and frequently small or single person management teams (e.g. shelters, drop-in programs, neighbourhood centres).

4.1. Service provider voices

Several core themes emerged from the discussions with service providers; however, the most central concern was funding. While virtually all the service providers indicated that current funding was adequate for basic on-going operations, all lamented the associated limitations in service provision. First and foremost, service providers were concerned about the staffing levels in the shelters. In the residential shelter programs for homeless youth, staffing ratios were typically very low in spite of significant needs. Shelters operated with a staff/youth ratio of 1:7 in the evenings only. As a result, adequate levels of safe supervision and care were not always available to youth with notable mental health concerns. Since service providers were concerned about the safety of these youth, as well as the safety of the other youth and staff in the program, the low staffing levels resulted in the exclusion of youth with significant mental health issues from such services,. Service providers were also concerned about the lack of meaningful access to mental health services, and even where such access was possible, the resulting appointments, and related travel costs and time, required extra staffing for transportation and follow-up.

Inadequate staffing levels also impacted transitions for youth. All of the residential service providers indicated insufficient resources to prepare and support youth as they transitioned from residential services to independent housing situations. The consequence was a significant relapse – financial collapse and loss of housing – as well as involvement with the criminal justice system, drug use and abuse and mental health episodes in which self-harm or even suicide were significant risks: "We have one transition worker and at least one hundred youth in need of her support! She has to take care of transitions into the program, out of the program as well as keeping in touch with the youth who have been out there for a while and are finding things more difficult that they thought. How can this possibly do justice to the young people?"

In spite of concerns about staffing levels, service providers took considerable initiative to ensure that youth had access to and were involved in essential services wherever possible. All of the residential service providers were actively engaged in advocacy, on behalf of "their" youth, with other service providers representing other systems, including housing, health care, adult mental health systems, and where applicable, with the children's mental health, education and child welfare systems. In many instances, staff from these service providers participated in case conferences where appropriate, and were actively involved in the development and monitoring of care plans and goals for the youth. Indeed, a major strength of these residential service providers is their ability to connect the youth with outside resources and monitor how they are experiencing those services, as well as advocating on their behalf where necessary.

Aside from the issue of funding, service providers highlighted the need for informality and pragmatism in developing rules and regulations related to service delivery. Virtually all of the service providers emphasized the unique nature of the needs of homeless and street-involved youth, and suggested that programs and services that are helpful to them must be easily accessible, tolerant of repeated failure to achieve goals and focused on longer-term engagement. To this end, both the residential service providers and the drop-in services devoted much of their work to providing for the basic needs of the youth (food and shelter), and connecting with them with a view to developing longer-term relationships. Staff recognized that many youth would not be able to make an immediate connection or follow through on expectations, but generally thought that providing logistical and practical supports would create effective long-term relationships.

Service providers within the homeless youth sector saw themselves on the periphery of social service systems within their community. In their experience, homeless and street-involved youth experience a great deal of social stigmatization, which also reflects on the service providers. While all of the service providers who participated in this study regularly made an effort to maintain connections and positive relationships in their neighbourhoods and local communities, they also had to perpetually make the case for services and supports for homeless youth, and "hustle" funding for their programs and service.

In their experiences of interaction and attempted collaboration with the formal service sector, service providers described instances of meaningful collaboration and partnership as well as instances of failed collaboration and communication difficulties. Moreover, the service providers lamented the formalities, such as extensive intake processes and appointment-based meetings, so that youth were not always able to follow through on. In general, service providers reported relatively low motivation on the part of youth to engage with formal services long-term. They indicated that the most commonly used formal services are those that can respond during crises, such as hospitals in particular, something that was also indicated by the youth themselves (see below).

On the other hand, all of the service providers also highlighted partnerships with formal service providers that were of great value and that had proven sustainable. In differentiating such partnerships from other collaborative initiatives, time and time again service providers described the importance of inter-professional relationships with specific individuals within the formal service sector. One area in which such partnerships were particularly valuable was in relation to assessments for youth experiencing mental health concerns. While there were significant issues related to managing the implications of assessments and collaborating on developing appropriate service responses, at least the assessment function itself resulted in enhanced access to other types of services within the formal sector. Such partnerships, while valuable were nevertheless scarce, much to the dismay of the service providers.

Many of the informal sector service providers sought to develop their own specialized services, including counseling, employment-related and housing services, instead of partnering with others in the formal service sector. In several cases, community partnerships proved unsustainable for a variety of reasons, resulting in a service provider trying to duplicate services already available but difficult to access in the community.

While the majority of services available through the informal sector are intended for youth ages 16 and up, the vast majority of youth using these services are 18 years of age and older. Service providers within the informal sector noted repeatedly the difficulties associated with providing services to the 15–17 year age group. They pointed to a system gap, whereby youth in this age group are too old for the formal children's mental health system and too young for the informal homelessness system and adult mental health services. One outcome of this gap is that youth often find themselves experiencing very difficult situations that lead to long-term system involvement, including trauma related to street life, substance use and addictions; in the case of girls, they are vulnerable to sexual abuse and exploitation, as well as teenage pregnancy.

In response to these issues, service providers suggested that there was a need for a greater emphasis on early intervention initiatives by both sectors, as well as for the formal and informal sector service providers to work together on identifying and intervening with children and youth at risk of homelessness. However, they were not able to provide a great deal of detail on what such collaboration or early intervention might look like.

4.2. Voices from stakeholders

Stakeholders in the homelessness sector, both inside and outside of the Central East Region, echoed many of the issues and themes cited by the service providers themselves. In addition, however, these stakeholders raised several other themes and highlighted the urgency of developing new approaches to responding to homeless youth.

Stakeholders indicated much more emphatically than the service providers that the day-to-day experiences of working with homeless youth frequently felt like "an imposition from the formal systems onto the informal ones". They had many anecdotes related to youth transitioning from formal mental health services to the homelessness system, instances such as youth being dropped off at homeless shelters, without a plan or even medications after spending weeks in in-patient psychiatric hospital wards or jail. Another area of criticism was the lack of collaborative efforts related to ensuring that youth with mental health issues had access to appropriate services and care. It was also very clear that in the view of stakeholders, the "typical" homeless youth shelters, with an average staffing ratio of 1:15 (in the Toronto area), were not appropriate placements for youth with serious mental health issues. Furthermore, when such placements were made without any inter-system communication or consultation, the ethical foundations of the system were questioned.

Stakeholders believed that a great deal of the perceived dysfunction related to the transition from formal to informal systems was associated with a lack of understanding of the specific issues and struggles of homeless youth on the part of the formal system. Both the personal and the community resources available to homeless youth were thought to be over-estimated by the formal systems, and this was reflected in the perceived assumption that there was a high level of stability and predictability in the lives of the youth.

Stakeholders provided a range of suggestions related to resolving the gaps between the formal and informal systems. In one case, considerable pessimism was expressed along with a lack of confidence that the formal systems could change their approaches sufficiently to become useful to homeless and street-involved youth. Therefore, the most meaningful strategy was thought to be that the informal system should develop its own services similar to the services offered by the formal systems but taking into account the specific needs of homeless youth. The "One Stop Shop" concept that underlies much of this thinking was frequently referenced. On the other hand, some stakeholders were critical of this perspective, arguing that informal services are not well suited to offering clinical interventions, in part because these service providers would not be able to attract qualified staff given lower funding levels. These stakeholders advocated for more concrete approaches to collaboration, including the sharing of staffing and knowledge resources between formal and informal systems. As a very specific strategy, proponents of this approach suggested that formal service providers could allocate limited staff time for clinical positions to be transferred to the informal sector. This would result in a greater appreciation of the needs of homeless youth by having these staff share their experiences back in their primary work place in the formal sector. Conversely, it was suggested that the informal sector could assist the formal sector with training and developing cultural competency with respect to homeless, street-involved and under-housed youth and families that would assist the formal sector to improve its own services and to develop more meaningful outreach capacities.

Stakeholders in the youth homelessness system also agreed with service providers that housing represents the most urgent and acute need of homeless youth, and that a national housing strategy should therefore take precedent over all other types of services. The efficacy of treatment within either system was thought to be significantly compromised, particularly for youth with mental health issues, when they had no stable and safe place to live. Stakeholders expressed grave concern over the ever-increasing visibility of substance use and addictions, and associated concurrent disorders.

Stakeholders emphasized the urgent need for early intervention strategies specifically targeting younger homeless youth, ages 16 to 18. From their perspective, mental health issues were less complex and less entrenched within this age group, and therefore it would still be possible to influence the experiences of these youth positively. They emphasized the need for access to a greater range of services that take into account the developmental and cultural specificity of this group, including services that were able to connect with youth and their families. Stakeholders also noted the potential of peer mentorship programs as a way of reaching youth who would not on their own access services in the formal system. Particularly with respect to mental health services, peer mentorship was thought to have the potential to help youth overcome their hesitations to engage with formal sector service providers, as well as to ensure greater follow through with multi-step access procedures.

4.3. Voices from youth

There were twenty-two youth that participated from three communities; six of them were female, the rest were male. Four of them were parents themselves (three young men and one young woman), who were actively parenting or trying to. As described in other surveys on this population (Evenson, 2009; The McCreary Centre Society, 2001, 2002; Public Health Agency of Canada, 2006, 2007; Streetkids International, 2008), the overwhelming majority had experienced multiple placements in foster care and group care, both child protection and residential mental health services. Almost all of them identified family "problems" from an early age. About half had finished high school, and had aspirations for post-secondary education, if they could find the funding to support this direction. Four of the group members had immigrated with some of their families to Canada.

The youth voices were much less focused on service design and the need for clinical competence within the system, and much more focused on practical solutions to everyday problems. Overall, the youth emphasized the importance of meaningful connections with service providers and individual staff members, as well as their desire for stability and safety on an every day basis. Of particular note were three themes discussed by the youth: housing, addictions and self-determination.

4.3.1. Housing

Having access to clean and safe housing in their own community was the number one concern before youth could consider any other health issues. Not all of the youth who participated in the focus groups were living in shelters. Indeed, shelters were often seen as accommodations of last resort. Some youth shelters were generally thought of as safe, though not preferred since they were crowded and you had to live with unknown peers. However, adult shelters were thought to be very unsafe.

> "I've been clean for two months. Staying at the shelter is tough, there's a lot of drugs there."

If possible, youth preferred to stay with the parents of friends or supportive friends, or to sleep in cars or alleyways, rather than going to a shelter. Employment or collecting social assistance was a prerequisite for finding clean, safe accommodation, and staying in a shelter worked against getting employment, while social assistance did not provide sufficient funding for clean accommodation.

> "When they give you housing, they give you a "shithole", it's infested with bugs ... maybe you are going to rent a room, or it's falling apart... [subsidized housing] is full of bugs, cockroaches or bedbugs and you have to deal with that... it's horrible... I gave up my housing."

Solving the housing dilemma required having someone to live with, and often the only person(s) that the young person had to live with was someone else who was homeless or facing difficult conditions of their own. Family members were either not appropriate (due to previous abuse or mental illness), or not available as a support system until the youth could show some long-standing evidence of having changed their life. In order to be healthy and move forward with their lives, they felt that they needed to leave their "Street" friends, but at the same time these friends were the only support system available. Staying with the current support system meant risking relapse to substance abuse or criminal activity.

> "Just because you have that little room or that bachelor apartment, doesn't necessarily mean that you are out of the street; you are still "streets"; you might have somewhere to go back to, but it's not necessarily a safe place, or a clean place that you can maintain and get yourself on your feet to go to school. You're only a heartbeat away from... just because you have 4 walls around you doesn't mean that you are housed. When it comes to maintaining it or making something of it; you're still homeless; you're still not out of the clear."

Youth stated clearly that housing in their home community, and more housing for youth having difficulty, was essential, but that the members of local communities resisted having subsidized or inexpensive housing in their community. The youth also described a need for practical support for employment, and were generally unaware of how to engage in effective job searches given today's economic climate. Youth described mentoring each other to understand the system, particularly in regard to accessing social assistance, being able to get ID and health cards, and finding the appropriate funding for the things that they needed, including ongoing medical care and medication. When service providers such as Ontario Works (social assistance) social workers and addictions counselors came to the centre, it was not only convenient, but the youth were more likely to get the practical help that they needed.

4.3.2. Addictions

Substance use, substance abuse and addiction were part of the ongoing struggle that youth engaged in to deal with the stresses of life, including diagnosed mental illness, family violence, parental mental illness and poverty. Many of the youth recounted depression and turning to drugs at an early age, generally 12 to 13, as well as the ongoing use of substances throughout their lifetime. They knew of no resources to deal with addictions or substance abuse prior to the age of 18, and indeed indicated that they might not have been ready at that time but felt it was important to deal with.

> "You can try and lead someone, but ultimately at that age they are going to do what they do. Offering them non-judgmental resources that they can go back to. They have to go through the system, they have to go to jail, and when they've had enough and they see-Listen-I CAN DIE then they've had enough and pretty much that's when.... And now I can stand up for myself, I can say NO, I know where you're going and that path leads THERE and I'm not going THERE."

> "A good worker has to have that patience, you'll have your bad days, but a good worker will just take it as an understanding of your person...getting better takes time... you learn a little bit each time"

Use of substances, mixing substances or overdosing often resulted in hospital stays for youth or their friends, and typically young people were responsible for taking their peers to a secure setting to detoxify or to deal with suicidal threats (almost invariably a hospital emergency room). Waiting lists to get into programs are long and the motivation to change may have left the person by the time they get access to the service. For those over the age of 18, a range of adult-serving institutions was available to them to deal with their addictions. Most of the clients in these settings were over 40 and, in the eyes of the youth, were chronic users whom they did not want to resemble; in some cases, youth spoke very positively about the safety and acceptance they encountered at some adult-based addictions (detox) services.

4.3.3. Self-determination

Most of the youth were very clear that the source of their problems was family. Parents had struggled with unemployment, addictions, violence, and mental illness, and rarely were the interventions effective or practical if they were present. By the time they reached the age of 15 or 16, they were on their own and determined to make it, or they were close to exhausting the child welfare and children's mental health residential programs, having already been to most of them.

Helping relationships that made a difference were characterized by youth as ones that existed over a long period of time (3 to 5 years), and allowed them to move in and out of the relationship. Youth came to the person when they were ready to make some personal changes, and felt accepted and cared about by the person. They could return, after a period of addiction, depression, and/or homelessness, and be accepted and begin trying again to move their lives forward. The young people that we spoke to felt privileged to have found someone that could do this for them. In general, it was rare to find a counselor who was this accepting and would be available to them when they were ready. Most of the time, they were focused on practical day-to-day realities, like finding a place to sleep and food. Only when these were achieved could they return to a safe accepting relationship that would help them work on personal issues and enhance their mental health.

Young people also provided assistance to each other, mentoring new youth on the street to understand how to get ID, how to access social assistance, where they were safe, how to find a place to sleep; they watched out for them as they got deeper and deeper into addictions or criminal activity, trying to ensure that they didn't make a fatal error and getting them to hospital when necessary. They recognized that when you are a teenager, you don't really care and don't necessarily want to be helped, but you still need someone to watch out for you — that was the role of the older peers.

> "When you are on the street, you're swimmin' with a bunch of fishes and whatever they're doin', you're doin',..cause they're makin' sure that you eat and stuff. When you are off, you're housed, but you're alone, it's still not normal."

Basically, if their friends go for help, young people will follow them and go for help too, when they are at that younger age. There are also more people willing to help, even when help is not necessarily desired.

> "When you are 14, everybody wants to help you. Friends take you in; group homes;"

> "When you were younger it didn't matter, you didn't care. It kind of dawns on you when you are 18 or 19, and you realize you have nowhere else to go and you get depressed, into alcohol or drugs, or go to jail. You choose your path, you know...."

Youth felt that voluntary commission for substance use or for mental illness was essential to successful treatment. Getting in for treatment required a commitment on the part of the young person, and they had to do the work while they were there. Once the work was done, support for transitioning out was essential. The residential treatment centre was safe. Everyone accepted the young person, and there were no temptations or risks to deal with. Once they returned to the community, young people had no money, no place to live and plenty of temptation. Youth felt that they needed a lot of practical support, immediately following treatment. A social worker or support person might be assigned, but without family or a home to return to, they needed plenty of hands-on guidance in order to get a job, find a safe place to live and maintain an addiction-free lifestyle and/or mental health. While jail time did not necessarily include treatment, the transition back to the community had even fewer supports in place and the same risks.

5. Discussion

While those interviewed did not use the term themselves, it is reasonable to characterize their self-perception as "informal services" that stand in the shadow of "formal services" delivered by larger and better funded institutions such as children's mental health centres, hospitals and child welfare agencies. The "informal sector" associated with itself a culture which values pragmatism and grass-roots initiatives more so than clinical sophistication and organizational prestige.

Services for homeless youth who exhibit mental health concerns in Central East Region are clearly caught in a duality of children's services that appears structurally entrenched. On the one hand, children's services are well funded and resourced, and generally include clinically sophisticated approaches to working with children and youth. On the other hand, those systems are not always successful in stabilizing and strengthening the life circumstances of youth, and very little support is extended to those youth once they age out at 16, or are excluded from service because of lack of family involvement or criminal behavior. Instead, these youth now find themselves seeking assistance from the homeless youth service providers, who are not nearly as well resourced to manage their issues, the same issues that the children's services were unable to manage. Moreover, the children's service sector provides very little in terms of transitional supports; once a client has moved on, the services by and large end (Bucher & Coward, 2008; Yonge Street Mission, 2009).

It is within this framework of service exclusion and limitations that service providers within the homeless youth service sector seek to establish themselves as meaningful places and spaces for homeless youth. Through the discussions with executive leaders within this sector, it has become clear that the basis of service provision is relationship. What is particularly noteworthy, however, is that this service sector extends the concept of relationship to every level of day-to-day activity, including worker–client and worker–system interactions, and even the development of systems and approaches to securing resources and funding.

In the absence of clinical resources, the homeless youth service system bases its everyday activities on the provision of logistical support that can have immediate, tangible impacts for youth. The assistance provided in relation to food, housing, employment and personal support and nurturing create the foundation for a longer-term relational engagement between service providers and homeless youth. Whether it is through the drop-in program or a residential service, service providers are finding their connections with youth strengthened and deeply embedded in their everyday interactions. Youth themselves express their appreciation for these day-to-day services and supports; they are very clear that, in spite of inadequate facilities especially in the context of long term housing, they feel supported and cared for by the temporary housing solutions provided by the sector.

The youth themselves were very much committed to the idea of self-determination, and they overwhelmingly endorsed the concept of "readiness for change"; from their perspective, no clinical intervention or service is likely to advance their readiness to make changes and seek out sustainable growth and development. Ultimately, they seek relational engagements with a wide range of individuals, including peers and child and youth care staff, in order to manage the often lengthy time period during which they experience significant ups and downs in their everyday life experiences. To the extent that these experiences might feature moments of crisis, youth are much more open to using established and institutional services such as hospital emergency rooms, rather than targeted services such as community mental health programs where they could develop ongoing counseling relationships. Instead, they prefer the existing supportive relationships of their peers and/or the service providers in the homeless sector.

Most of the youth we spoke to were able to articulate clear goals for their future, and they had clear ideas about how to achieve these goals. Most, however, did not believe themselves to be ready to commit to a sustainable and disciplined life style that might get them closer to achieving their goals. For most, an on-going engagement in the homeless youth service sector was inevitable for a few more years.

The idea of relationship does not, however, end with the youth-staff relationships that clearly provide the foundation for the everyday interactions within this sector. Although some services were not available through their own sector, staff and leaders did not rely on formalized collaborations with agencies in other sectors to provide support to their clients. Instead, they focused on the development of professional relationships with individuals in those other sectors who might be able to open doors for their youth. Gaining access to the established and clinically-based services in both the children's and adult service sector was most likely when the referring person from the homeless youth service sector had specific professional contacts with an individual in the more formal service sector. Staff in the informal sector value these contacts a great deal, and work hard to nurture such relationships on behalf of the youth they serve.

Finally, even in the context of resource acquisition and government funding schemes, service providers within the homeless youth service sector fostered individualized professional relationships with other professionals from funding agencies and government departments. Executive leaders were very clear that their attempts to follow official processes and procedures in order to compete with the formal sector for funding and resources were not likely to yield positive results. Ultimately, virtually all initiatives within this sector begin with an activation of already existing relationships between the service provider and specific professionals from the funding government department.

6. From the periphery into the core

While the voices of the homeless youth service sector captured for this study clearly expressed some frustration with the formal systems and the lack of services provided for young people who are not eligible to access the formal system, neither were the parties of this sector interested in or engaged in creating systemic change. Youth themselves expressed clear preferences for the grass roots informality represented by the homeless youth serving agencies and their staff, while the service providers expressed hesitation to invest time and energy in more structured and formalized collaborations with the formal sector. Ultimately, homeless youth are a difficult social group for which to design publicly-funded services. They are neither children nor adults, and their transient status and high levels of mobility exile them to the periphery.

On the other hand, in spite of the clear presence of significant resilience and strength amongst these youth (Bender, Thomson, McManus, Lantry, & Flynn, 2007; Griffin, 2008; Karabanow, 2003), there are some less promising trends that require our attention. While many youth will eventually discover their readiness for change (Karabanow, 2008), many others will fall victim to addictions and accumulate more trauma and victimization than they will be able to recover (Baron, 2008; Baron, Forde, & Kennedy, 2001; Werb, Kerr, Li, Montaner, & Wood, 2008; Stewart et al., 2004). Self-determination as a driving force for change must be responded to quickly, and the formal systems are unable to do so. The interventions currently available through the homeless youth service sector are strong, meaningful and logistically highly relevant, but they do not always address the underlying causes or contributors to homelessness and high risk life-styles (Whitbeck, Hoyt, & Bao, 2000). It is therefore essential for informal services to find ways of connecting with their formal counterparts in both the children and adult service sectors (Nichols, 2008), in order to support the expressed desire of these youth for self-determination.

In order for the periphery to gain access to the core, without having to relinquish its organizational commitment to the everyday interactions with youth based on logistical considerations and a desire for longer-term relational engagements, a more coordinated strategy for system-to-system relationships is needed. This would be facilitated by funding to support active collaboration between sectors and systems, based on an understanding that homeless youth are not a social group to be left to its own devices on the periphery. Rather, children and adult services share some level of responsibility to engage with the periphery. Until this happens, it is our belief that the voices of service providers and youth must be heard. With this article, we endeavour to bring the voices from the periphery to the forefront.

Acknowledgements

The authors wish to acknowledge funding for this research from the Central East Office of the Ontario Ministry of Children and Youth Services.

References

Baron, S. (2008). Street youth, unemployment, and crime: Is it that simple? Using General Strain Theory to untangle the relationship. *Canadian Journal of Criminology and Criminal Justice, 50*(4), 399–435.

Baron, S., Forde, D., & Kennedy, L. (2001). Rough justice: Street youth and violence. *Journal of Interpersonal Violence, 16*(7), 662–678.

Bender, K., Thompson, S. J., McManus, H., Lantry, J., & Flynn, P. M. (2007). Capacity for survival: Exploring strengths of homeless street youth. *Child and Youth Care Forum, 36*(1), 25–42.

Bucher, C., & Coward, C. E. (2008). Towards a needs-based typology of homeless youth. *Journal of Adolescent Health, 42*(6), 549–554.

City of Toronto (2008). *How Toronto is solving youth homelessness. Shelter, Support and Housing Administration Division.* Retrieved on May 17, 2010 from www.toronto.ca/housing/pdf/youth_homelessness.pdf

Cloke, P., Johnsen, S., & May, J. (2007). The periphery of care: Emergency services for homeless people in rural areas. *Journal of Rural Studies, 23*(4), 387–401.

Durham Region (2007). *The community plan for homelessness in Durham Region: Update 2007–2009.* Retreived from http://www.durham.ca/social.asp?nr=/departments/social/SocialHousing/homeless/homelessinside.htm&setFooter=includes/socialHousingFooter.inc

Elias, B.M. (2009). Without intention: Rural responses to uncovering the hidden aspects of homelessness in Ontario 2000-2007. Doctoral Dissertation. University of Toronto, Department of Adult Education and Counseling Psychology, Toronto, Ontario.

Evenson, J. (2009). *Youth homelessness in Canada: The road to solutions.*Toronto: Raising the Roof/Chez Toit Retrieved from http://www.raisingtheroof.org/RoadtoSolutions_fullrept_english.pdf

Griffin, S. (2008). The spatial environments of street-involved youth: Can the streets be a therapeutic milieu? *Relational Child and Youth Care Practice, 21*(4), 16–27.

Haggart, J.E.V. (2007). "Because you're homeless, you're a bad kid": The criminalization of youth who are homeless in York Region. Masters Thesis, York University, School of Social Work, Toronto, Ontario.

Karabanow, J. (2003). Creating a culture of hope: Lessons from street children agencies in Canada and Guatemala. *International Social Work, 46*(3), 369–386.

Karabanow, J. (2004). Changing faces: The story of two Canadian street youth shelters. *International Journal of Social Welfare, 13*(2), 304–314.

Karabanow, J. (2008). Getting off the street. *American Behavioural Scientist, 51*(6), 772–788.

Kidd, S. A., & Davidson, L. (2006). Youth homelessness: A call for partnerships between research and policy.*Canadian Journal of Public Health* Retrieved from http://journal.cpha.ca/index.php/cjph/article/viewFile/785/785

Kurtz, P. D., Jarvis, S. V., & Kurtz, G. (1991). The problems of homeless youth: Empirical findings and human service issues. *Social Work, 36*, 309–314.

Nichols, N. E. (2008). Gimme shelter! Investigating the social service interface from the standpoint of youth. *Journal of Youth Studies, 11*(6), 685–699.

Pathways York Region (2007/08). Annual report Retrieved from http://www.pathwaysyorkregion.org/assets/pathways/files/annual%20report%20200708%20color.pdf

Public Health Agency of Canada (2007). *Canadian street youth and substance use: Findings from enhanced surveillance of Canadian street youth, 1999-2003.*Ottawa: Author Retrieved from http://dsp-psd.pwgsc.gc.ca/collection_2008/phac-aspc/HP5-23-2007E.pdf

Public Health Agency of Canada (2006). *Street youth in Canada: Findings from enhanced surveillance of Canadian street youth, 1999-2003.*Ottawa: Author Retrieved from: http://www.phac-aspc.gc.ca/std-mts/reports_06/pdf/street_youth_e.pdf

Simcoe County Alliance to End Homelessness (2006). *Community plan to end & prevent homelessness in Simcoe County.*Barrie: Author Available from the author.

Skott-Myhre, H. (2008). Towards a delivery system of services for rural youth: A literature review and case study. *Child and Youth Care Forum, 2*(37), 87–102.

Stewart, A. G., Steiman, M., Cauce, A. M., Cochran, B. N., Whitbeck, L. B., & Hoyt, D. R. (2004). Victimization and posttraumatic stress disorder among homeless adolescents. *Child & Adolescent Psychiatry, 43*(3), 325–331.

Streetkids International (2008). *NGO and private sector partnerships: A framework for success.* Retrieved on May 17, 2010 from www.streetkids.org/assets/pdf/2008/0806_ngo_private_sector_partners.pdf

The McCreary Centre Society (2001). *No place to call home: A profile of street youth in British Columbia.*Burnaby: Author Retrieved from http://www.ihpr.ubc.ca/media/McCreary2001.pdf

The McCreary Centre Society (2002). *Between the cracks: Homeless youth in Vancouver.* Burnaby: Author Retrieved from: http://www.ihpr.ubc.ca/media/McCreary2002.pdf

Van Daalen-Smith, C., & Lamont, R. (2006). *Anybody's couch: Understanding the lives, health and service needs of York region homeless youth.*City of York: York University Retrieved from: http://www.atkinson.yorku.ca/NURS/graduate/pdf/AnybodyCouch.pdf

Werb, D., Kerr, T., Li, K., Montaner, J., & Wood, E. (2008). Risks surrounding drug trade involvement among street-involved youth. *The American Journal of Drug and Alcohol Abuse, 34*(6), 810–820.

Whitbeck, L. B., Hoyt, D. R., & Bao, W. N. (2000). Depressive symptoms and co-occurring depressive symptoms, substance abuse, and conduct problems among runaway and homeless adolescents. *Child Development, 71*(3), 721–732.

York Region Alliance to End Homelessness (unpublished). Get honest: Our youth matter. Proceedings of event held April 22nd, 2009, Aurora, ON. Co-hosted with Street Kids International.

York Region Homelessness Task Force (2002). Seeking a shared strategy for youth: A call to action. *Summary report of the context and proceedings of the York Region Youth Summit, 2001.* Newmarket: Regional Municipality of York.

Yonge Street Mission (2009). Changing patterns for street-involved youth. *A Project of Yonge Street Mission and World Vision Canada* Retreived from www.ysm.ca

Youth Shelter Interagency Network (2007). *System in crisis: An action plan for the future of Toronto's homeless youth.* Retrieved from http://www.toronto.ca/legdocs/mmis/2007/cd/bgrd/backgroundfile-2777.pdf

Disability Studies Quarterly
the first journal in the field of disability studies

The Madwoman in the Academy, or, Revealing the Invisible Straightjacket: Theorizing and Teaching Saneism and Sane Privilege

PhebeAnn M. Wolframe
PhD Candidate
Department of English and Cultural Studies, McMaster University
E-mail: pmwolframe@gmail.com

Keywords:

saneism, mentalism, mad studies, privilege, feminism, intersectionality, pedagogy

Abstract

In this paper, I suggest that one way to bring mad perspectives and discussions about saneism/mentalism—systemic discrimination against people who have been diagnosed as, or are perceived to be "mentally ill"—into higher eduction is to situate them within existing curricula across disciplines. One of the ways curricula can be modified is by adapting existing theoretical frameworks from other interdisciplinary fields to mad issues and contexts. As an example of this adaptation, I turn Peggy McIntosh's article "White Privilege: Unpacking the Invisible Knapsack" (1988), a staple of undergraduate humanities curricula, into a teaching tool for showing not only the ways in which "sane" people—those who have never been psychiatrized or perceived as "mentally ill"—have access to privileges that mad people do not, but also the ways in which saneism/mentalism intersects with other forms of oppression such as racism, sexism, classism, heterosexism and ableism.

My history of involvement in the mental health system dates back to late childhood, when I began to suffer from depression and anxiety and was prescribed anti-depressants by my pediatrician. At the age of 16, I was assigned to a new psychiatrist and given a new "adult" diagnosis. I was treated for this supposed disease—on both an inpatient and outpatient basis, using a cocktail of different drugs—for approximately six years. Although I questioned my diagnosis before I got clear of psychiatry in my early 20's, it was not until I became a graduate student that I first read about the mad movement and finally had words to describe my experiences other than those used by psychiatry. I only wish I had heard about the mad movement earlier, and that I could have, as an undergraduate student in English and Women's Studies, talked about saneism along-side racism, heterosexism, cissexism, 1 ageism, classism and all those other isms. As I recall, our discussion of ableism in Women's Studies courses was brief, and both ableism and saneism 2 —discrimination against those who have been given a psychiatric diagnosis and/or who are perceived to be "mentally ill"—were not something we delved into. Arguably, the way in which psychiatry functions as an oppressive tool, and the systematic oppression of psychiatrized people both inside and outside of the mental health system, are still largely overlooked in academia. As James Overboe notes, "anti-oppression movements may have lessened the medical pathology based on racialization or gender. However, the experience of being psychiatrized continues to be pathologised [within liberal discourse] as a condition requiring a cure" (23). Now a teacher myself, I take every opportunity to educate students about interlocking systems of oppression, and to challenge colleagues and students when they use pathologising discourses to describe not only people who have been psychiatrized, but also those who have been marginalized in other ways. I want to show that "sane" people—those who have never had involvement with psychiatry and who are generally not perceived to be "mentally ill"—are privileged, just like people who are white and heterosexual and cisgender and able-bodied hold privilege. 3 This privilege is what makes it so easy to fall back on saneist language and assumptions.

During my undergraduate education, I learned a language which allowed me to frame gender and other aspects of identity as socially constructed categories. Courses taught from a feminist perspective showed me that my own experiences were important to the way in which I understood the subjects I was learning. I always felt that my own knowledge and identity (as a woman, and as queer) had a place in the classroom; however, feminist and other critical theories, as they were taught to me, did not give me a way to talk about my experiences as a psychiatric patient. A key critical premise of this essay is that it is especially important to introduce saneism to the humanities vocabulary as we move into a more inclusive era, one which recognizes the often racist, ableist, and heterosexist errors of the past. Unfortunately, despite having gained some recognition, those of us on the fringes are often not given spaces within existing institutions—whether they be universities, hospitals or government offices—to theorize our own experiences of oppression. Interdisciplinary programs such as Women's Studies, Queer Studies, Disability Studies, and Indigenous Studies, even when they are well-established in a university, are routinely devalued and constantly face the threat of funding cuts. In a university climate which is increasingly being depoliticized and corporatized, and which is evermore hostile to the arts and humanities, 4 it seems unlikely that there will be a department of Madness Studies any day soon. I still believe, however, that there are ways to bring the mad movement into academia.

I have been bringing the history of the mad movement and the perspectives of mad people into the classroom since I began graduate work, and I have specifically been using the term Mad(ness) Studies to describe my research into mad people's history, literature, culture, and activism. The fact that faculty and colleagues alike in my department and in others have shown interest in and have encouraged my work in Mad Studies has been heartening. Several colleagues have approached me to talk about their own or their loved ones' experiences in the mental health system and their doubts about that system. Many have taken great interest in the ways in which the dominant ideas about sanity and madness might be deconstructed, and have asked me to point them towards resources relating to the history of psychiatry and of psychiatric resistance. 5

It is not only faculty and colleagues, however, who are interested in madness: students are equally engaged. Recently, I led a discussion group for a first-year survey class called Shorter Genres. One of the short stories the class read was American writer Charlotte Perkins Gillman's story "The Yellow Wallpaper" (1892). The story is an autobiographical first-person account of a middle-class white woman's experience of what was then called hysteria. The woman, who is unnamed throughout, has been prescribed the rest cure: an order to remain at home and inactive, mentally and physically. The protagonist resists this "cure," however, continuing to write in secret. As time goes on, the woman's feelings of isolation begin to manifest in a belief that there are women trapped behind the pattern of the wallpaper in her bedroom. Stealthily, she begins to peel the wallpaper off, eventually liberating the wallpaper women, and achieving a feeling of freedom herself. Although some students quickly dismissed the narrator as a "psychotic" person hallucinating people living in her wallpaper, others sympathized with the woman, identifying the way in which the restrictions placed upon her by her husband and by society might account for her seeming insanity. With a minimum of prompting, the students were able to extend this critique of the woman's "hysteria" to ideas about "mental illness" today, which, as they identified, play out all around them, in everything from news to popular culture. In that class, we were doing Mad Studies work, even if we were in a literature class. Those students took to a critique of the medicalization of madness readily, and they were excited about it.

Aside from reading fiction through a mad lens, another way I've found to incorporate mad perspectives and issues into the curriculum is to introduce them into already-existing theoretical frameworks. Peggy McIntosh's article, "White Privilege: Unpacking the Invisible Knapsack" (1988), for example, has become a standby text for explaining privilege, and is staple reading in undergraduate humanities curricula across Canada and the United States. It makes a provocative model for talking about what I have started to refer to as sane privilege. In her article, McIntosh explains how she came up with the metaphor of an "invisible knapsack of privilege." She states:

> Through work to bring materials from Women's Studies into the rest of the curriculum, I have often noticed men's unwillingness to grant that they are over privileged, even though they may grant that women are disadvantaged...
>
> Thinking through unacknowledged male privilege as a phenomenon, I realized that since hierarchies in our society are interlocking, there was most likely a phenomenon of white privilege, which was similarly denied and protected...

> I think whites are carefully taught not to recognize white privilege, as males are taught not to recognize male privilege… I have come to see white privilege as an invisible package of unearned assets which I can count on cashing in each day, but about which I was 'meant' to remain oblivious. White privilege is like an invisible weightless knapsack of special provisions, maps, passports, codebooks, visas, clothes, tools and blank checks. (10)

Following this introduction, McIntosh goes on to list some of these privileges of whiteness in day-to-day life. I initially encountered McIntosh's article in my first year Women's Studies class, and it was a huge eye-opener for me, because for the first time, I saw clearly that not only does racism oppress people of colour on a systemic level, but that I, as a white person, benefit from that oppression, whether I want to or not. Interestingly, although I quickly recognized that: 1) I have certain unearned assets that others do not because I am white and middle-class and able-bodied and cisgender; and 2) that others have privileges I do not because they are men and/or heterosexual, I did *not* recognize for some time the fact that people who had never been labeled mentally ill—as I had been—and who were thus sane by default, had access to privileges that I did not. I was aware of the discrimination I had faced as a "mentally ill" person, but I accepted that oppression. I believed, at the time, that I was sick, and I believed that this sickness caused me to hurt myself and others. Should I not then, I reasoned, be restrained by the straightjacket of unequal treatment?

It was only later when I came to reject the medical model of madness **6** that I questioned my own internalization of an oppression I came to know as saneism. Though I began to think through the idea of saneism at the same time as I got free of psychiatry, in 2005, I only started to recognize sane privilege recently, as I have increasingly gained that privilege myself. When I began graduate school in 2007, I moved away from my home town. Nobody where I currently reside knew that I was, or ever had been, a psychiatric patient. Initially, I was reserved about my history of psychiatrization, because I feared that if I told my colleagues and professors, they wouldn't trust me, or would think me less capable. As Margaret Price argues, "the necessity of passing for survival perpetuates the conventional view of academe as an 'ivory tower'—an immaculate location humming with mental agility and energy, only occasionally threatened (from the outside) by the destructive force of insanity" (7). Even though I now talk quite openly about my psychiatrization, and about mad activism, in the context of both my personal and my academic life—with the aim of challenging this very image of academe as a space where only "sane" minds think, create, learn and teach—I am still perceived to be sane and am treated as though I am sane most of the time; I think this is partly because I have not been a psychiatric patient for a number of years, and never in my current community. It is also partly because people seem to assume that someone doing a PhD, someone who *willingly spends a decade as a university student*, must be sane, or at least not suffering from a "serious and persistent mental illness." Since people have not always treated me as though I am reasonable, trustworthy, safe to be around, and capable of taking care of and making decisions for myself, because they knew I had been diagnosed as, or they perceived me to be mentally ill, I very much notice it now that they do treat me as though I am all of these things most of the time. 7 Now that I am experiencing it, sane privilege has become obvious to me. It is not necessarily so obvious to those who have never lost that privilege, however; therefore, I propose to create a list, similar to the list McIntosh created for white privilege, to explain the invisible advantages granted to people who have never been psychiatrized, or perceived as mad. It is my hope that this list will not only prove to be a useful teaching tool but also that it might prompt educators to reflect on our own assumptions and practices regarding madness.

McIntosh herself encourages the expansion of how we think of privilege in a longer version of her knapsack article. She states: "since race and sex are not the only advantaging systems at work, we need to similarly examine the daily experience of having age advantage, or ethnic advantage, or physical ability, or advantage related to nationality, religion or sexual orientation" ("White Privilege and Male Privilege" 157). Indeed, many of the items on her list apply directly to sane privilege, and others can be adapted. There are also some items that I would add to McIntosh's white privilege list which are more specific to mad people. Below, then, is a list of the daily effects of sane privilege, from the perspective of a mad person, who most of the time has access to that privilege, along with some commentary to explain why some of these effects do not extend to the majority of mad people. This list is not exhaustive, but it does give some sense of what sane privilege looks like. List items marked with a single star (*) are adapted from McIntosh's short paper, "White Privilege, Unpacking the Invisible Knapsack." Items marked with a double star (**) are adapted from McIntosh's longer version of that paper, "White Privilege and Male Privilege: A Personal Account of Coming to See Correspondences Through Work in Women's Studies." For the purposes of this article I use the term mad person to describe anyone who has been given a mental illness label, and/or who is perceived as "mentally ill" or mad. 8

As a person who is presumed to be sane (and particularly if I am a person who has access to other forms of privilege, such as white privilege, able-bodied privilege or cissexual privilege):

I can see other "sane" people (and particularly those who have access to other types of privilege) for the most part positively, on television, in the news and in other media.* The idea that mad people will inevitably do harm to themselves or others is perhaps the most prevalent saneist stereotype out there. Mad people are, for the most part, portrayed as volatile, manipulative and violent and/or as savants, prophets or "mad geniuses" in both the news media and popular culture. 9 As Erick Fabris remarks, "most people believe that madness begets violence; they believe that strange ideas eventually lead to a chain of events: confusion, ambivalence, distress, irritability, aggression, and finally unpredictable violence" (37-8). As Margaret Price furthermore argues, the stereotype of mad people as violent is prevalent in the context of higher education, where "faculty and staff are encouraged to be alert for signs of immediate violence in student writing, in an atmosphere that Benjamin Reiss has called 'quasi-psychiatric surveillance'" (3). The presumed threat of violence is used as a justification for not only the saneist policing of mad people in educational and employment environments, and public spaces, but also for forced incarceration, both physical (hospitalization, criminalization) and chemical (drugs); this fear of violence is unjustified, however, since, as Fabris notes "decades of statistics show that 'madness' and violence are not linked" (45). In other words, mad people are no more violent than anybody else.

I am never asked to speak for "sane" people.* As a mad person, I frequently speak on behalf of mad people, who are devoiced within academic, social service and government institutions. I do not, and cannot, however, represent mad people as a whole. As you will see in this list, we all have different intersections of identity which means that there are great variations in our experiences of being mad, and in the ways we are privileged and disadvantaged. Furthermore, I should not have to be the "token mad person," the only one responsible for identifying and challenging saneist discourse and behaviour. I and other mad people must be allowed to choose *not* to speak about mad identity, mad politics, and/or our personal histories of psychiatrization and madness when we don't feel comfortable doing so. "Sane" folks can use their privilege to call others out on saneism, too.

I can be pretty sure of finding people willing to give me career advice that is based around my abilities and ambitions, rather than their assumptions about my sanity.** When asking professors, counselors and family members for career advice, they have alternated between cautioning me to not set goals that are "unrealistic" for a person who is "mentally ill" and denying my madness ("you're no crazier than anyone else") despite my psychiatric history and my current mad identity. When I was 17, my psychiatrist told me I would probably never be "well" enough to go to university. Psychiatric survivors Anne Wilson and Peter Beresford relate similar stories of being pushed towards "less stressful" occupations, such as employment as a retail clerk, by their psychiatrists (153). Survivor and mad activist Pat Capponi's mental health professionals likewise encouraged her to do something less demanding, such as furniture reupholstering, despite her college education and experience working in a group home (Capponi 77). This condescending style of advice-giving feeds, and is fed by, the stereotype of mad people as incapacitated or unproductive, where productivity is defined as earning money or a degree. On the other hand, however, when mad people do well (or excel) in school, at work, or as activists we may be treated as exceptional for having "overcome mental illness." In such cases, mad people may also be told we are successful only because we received special accommodation, or because people feel sorry for us. When talking to mad people about our ambitions, take what we tell you about our dreams, goals, needs and limitations at face value, rather than making assumptions or projecting stereotypes onto us.

It is unlikely that, as a "sane" person, my employer will ask me about current or past medical information and feel that they can legitimately do so. Mad people's medical histories are often on display in a way that "sane" people's are not. As Overboe notes, "it only takes an initial documented diagnosis of psychiatric problems to affect how others read your past, present [and] future" and the longer you remain in the psychiatric system, the more this history comes to weigh on your life (24-5). Wilson and Beresford similarly point out that "an individual's psychiatric record, once written, constitutes the dominant version of that person and serves to place restrictions... on future life opportunities, understandings, rights and possibilities" (144). The visibility of mad people's medical histories can be particularly weighty in the contexts of employment and education. If you go mad, and it becomes public, you will indefinitely be the subject of gossip, and the recipient of patronizing inquiries of "how *are* you?" Even if you work and learn in a place where people have not witnessed your madness, or your absence due to madness, your supervisor, and possibly your colleagues, may become aware of your history when you ask for accommodation or make use of disability or accessibility services. Like many mad people, I am wary of expressing too much emotion (or not enough, or the wrong kind) at school or at work, lest those around me consider it a symptom. I fear they will either ostracize me as crazy, or encourage (or force) me to get medical "help." Regardless of what you know, or think you know, about someone's psychiatric history, don't make assumptions about what kind of "care," treatment, or intervention they require. If a colleague, student or employee seems distressed, ask them what you can do to support them.

I can choose religious or spiritual beliefs and practices, eating habits, and political affiliations without people wondering if or assuming these choices are symptoms of a disease. While particular religions may be more normalized in certain cultural contexts than in others, most "sane" people are not labeled mentally ill because, for example, they talk to God. For people who have been given a psychiatric diagnosis, however, there is a thin line between such practices being considered religion or being categorized as "delusions." Mad people's political affiliations (for example, choosing to take part in a public protest) 10 and food choices (for example, being a "picky" eater, a vegan etc.) can similarly be framed as symptoms within the context of having been given a psychiatric diagnosis. 11 Mad people differ from one another in politics, spiritual beliefs and cultural backgrounds, and express these aspects of their identities in a variety of ways, just like "sane" people do.

It is less likely that my sexual orientation, my gender identity or performance, my relationship style, or my choice of partners will be considered symptoms of a disease. These aspects of identity may contribute to a person's psychiatrization, however. While homosexuality was removed from the list of psychiatric disorders in the *Diagnostic and Statistical Manual* (*DSM*), in 1986, you can still be psychiatrized if you're distressed or depressed or unsure about your sexual identity. Furthermore, many forms of sexual and gender identity are still listed in the *DSM*. Being transgender is still considered a mental illness, for example (it's called "Gender Dysphoria" in *DSM-IV*). So is being asexual (*DSM-IV* calls it "Sexual Aversion Disorder"). In some cases, a person's sexuality or gender, especially if fluid, can be considered the symptom of a disorder, such as Borderline Personality Disorder, which is characterized by an "unstable self-image" (APA). Being non-monogamous or polyamorous is also sometimes labeled "promiscuity," considered "self-harm," and counted as a symptom. Take mad people's gender and sexual self-identifications at face value. Do not ask whether these aspects of our identities are tied to "mental illness" or assume that they are signs of our "confusion" or "instability."

I can choose to use some recreational drugs, or not to take certain prescription drugs, without these choices being considered symptoms of a

disease. Although this varies by social circle, "sane" people can generally get tipsy at a party, or share a joint with friends, and not be labeled as engaging in high risk behaviour. The same is not true for people who have a psychiatric diagnosis. When mad people use drugs and alcohol, this is generally considered self-medicating at best, or a symptom of either an existing or new disorder (such as alcoholism) at worst. A "sane" person can also choose not to use an elective drug (such as hormonal contraceptives, or pain medication) and to instead use an alternative (barrier contraception, massage therapy) without this decision being medicalized. In contrast to this, a mad person who decides not to take psych drugs is considered "non-compliant," or "lacking insight" into their condition, and their choice is considered further evidence of their disease. "Sane" people, just like mad people, make both good and bad choices about substance use. While it is okay to take the car key away from a mad friend who has had too much to drink at your party, do not assume that their substance use warrants any more policing than that of any of your "sane" friends.

I can criticize the mental health system, corporations, and the government without being called a conspiracy theorist, or having my opinions dismissed as a sign of illness. * When I have spoken out about injustices and corruption in the mental health system, I have often been treated with suspicion, doubt and scorn. For example, I was once called "nasty" and accused of being paranoid when I suggested to an acquaintance (a mental health professional who is aware of my psychiatric history) that the people who write the *DSM* are not primarily interested in consumer welfare, since in many cases, they work for pharmaceutical companies. 12 The act of speaking out against psychiatric oppression, like choosing not to take psychiatric medications, is often framed as a "lack of insight" into, or further evidence of, one's "illness." If someone talks to you about their negative experiences of, their suspicions about, or their research into the workings of the mental health system, corporations, or the government, keep an open mind, even if what they are saying seems "crazy." Whether what they are saying is true or not (and it very well may be!) you risk (re)pathologising that person when you dismiss their critiques.

Being a sane person (and particularly one privileged in other ways) means that I have never had to fear the power of authority figures, particularly those in the medical professions.** As a person who has had traumatizing experiences of health care, I am afraid every single time I go to the doctor. I worry that if my general practitioner, or a doctor in a walk-in clinic or emergency room finds out about my full medical history, that they will force me to undergo psychiatric evaluation and treatment. I am afraid to show too much anxiety, or social awkwardness or eccentricity, lest these be seen as symptoms. Once I accidentally cut my wrist, and had to go to an emergency room in my home town to have it stitched up. Since my patient records there indicated past suicide attempts, I was subjected to a psychiatric evaluation before I was allowed to leave the hospital. As a result of experiences like that one, I am ever wary of interacting with people who have any authority to potentially force me into "treatment." If you are in a position of power, that means you have to work harder to put people who have been hurt by authority figures at ease. Do not ask invasive questions, focus on the issue at hand, and do not call what we say into question simply because we are mad.

I am not made acutely aware that my physical shape, bearing, clothing, hairstyle, manner of speaking and other aspects of my physical and verbal presentation will be taken as a reflection of my madness.**

An untidy appearance or "strange" speech, within the context of psychiatry, are treated as the first signs of mental disorder in psychiatrized or potentially mad people, and are apt to be recorded as evidence in doctors' notes. 13 People who are identified by others as "mentally ill" because of physical characteristics or behaviour—whether it be an "odd" appearance or speech, or bodily movements such as tremors or tics (often side-effects of medication)—are commonly either ignored when they attempt to interact with others, or are asked to leave shopping areas, restaurants, libraries and other public spaces. The proprietor, other patrons, or security personnel in these spaces may fear that mad individuals will shoplift, act violently, or simply make others uncomfortable. Because of the assumptions made about appearance, I am always conscientious about "looking sane" especially when outing myself as mad, so that nobody thinks I'm mad enough to (still) require intervention.

Some mad people, however, have less choice in how they present themselves, and those who cannot "pass" as more-or-less normal are those most likely to face discrimination and erasure. As Cynthia Lewiechi-Wilson argues, the liberal humanist subject is defined by their ability to engage in verbal rhetoric. This emphasis on speech "creates a barrier excluding the severely mentally disabled not only from rhetoricity but also from full citizenship, tied as traditional rhetoric is to the liberal ideology of the public forum, where good men [sic], speaking well, engage in civic debate" (158). In other words, those who cannot, or choose not to assert themselves through speech in ways that are recognizable according to social norms, including some mad people, are all-too-easily dismissed as delusional, sick, stupid, dangerous, and generally not worth listening to. Catherine Prendergast similarly notes in her work on the schizophrenic as a postmodern metaphor that "typically schizophrenics are considered beings with speech, but speech that is generally treated as an index of sanity or insanity, with referentiality only to diagnostic criteria, and without referentiality to the civic world" (60). In other words, the speech of people who have been labeled with certain psychiatric diagnoses is only recognized as a marker of how "sane" they are in any given moment, and not as communication with the world around them. In order to be heard and recognized as citizens, and not just treated as patients, Prendergast suggests that those who have been psychiatrized must speak rhetorically some of the time. She further argues, however, that the very possibility of rhetorical mad speech challenges the stereotype of mad people as incapable of "rational" communication. Lewiechi-Wilson, in a different approach, advocates for the acceptance of assisted communication or "mediated rhetoricity" for mad and other "mentally disabled" people, a suggestion which points to the necessity of broadening our notions of listenable speech. One of the ways we can undermine saneism is by calling ourselves to task for our assumptions about appearance and speech. Additionally, those of us with sane privilege and able-bodied privilege can use that advantage to encourage others to listen to—and consider the perspectives of— individuals whose communications may otherwise go unacknowledged or be dismissed.

I can choose to ignore developments in mad peer-support, advocacy, and activist programs. Regardless of whether I choose to disparage them or learn from them, it is unlikely that I will have to face the consequences of this choice directly.** Mad people risk being remedicalized or criminalized when there aren't alternative and peer-run sources of advocacy, community, and acceptance for them to turn to in a time of crisis. We are directly and immediately affected when ongoing support services such as drop-in centres and patient advocacy boards are de-funded or amalgamated with main-stream mental health services. Since anyone could potentially become mad in the course of their lifetime, I argue that a wider availability of and support for alternatives to psychiatry would benefit everyone. Furthermore, most of us are apt to come into contact with a person experiencing madness of some sort at some point; rather than referring that person to the handiest psychiatric crisis hotline or centre, why not consider also finding out about the peer-run and mad-positive services in your community so that you can support friends, colleagues, students or clients who are looking for alternatives?

If I should need to move, I can be pretty sure of renting or purchasing housing in an area which I can afford and in which I would want to live. My neighbours in such a location will likely be neutral or pleasant to me.* Housing has particularly been a problem for mad people since deinstitutionalization. 14 Psychiatric consumers and survivors often have low incomes or are on social assistance, and live in areas where housing is substandard. Sometimes they are assigned to (underfunded) city-run boarding houses, such as the one Torontonian and mad activist Pat Capponi lived in during the time portrayed in her memoir *Upstairs in the Crazy House* (1992). Areas where mad people live become the object of stigma. Simply being attached to a particular address can result in being treated with suspicion or disdain. Even psychiatric consumers and survivors who can afford to live in non-stigmatized areas may not be welcomed by their "sane" neighbours. Be neighborly to your mad neighbours, and advocate against saneism and gentrification in your community.

I can go home from most meetings of organizations I belong to feeling somewhat tied in, rather than isolated, out-of-place, outnumbered, unheard, held at a distance, or feared.** In her work on happiness, Sara Ahmed argues that certain bodies get "seen as converting bad feeling into good and good feeling into bad" (126). Feminists and people of colour, for example, are often perceived as "killjoys" because they remind others (often through their mere presence) of their role in oppressive structures (127). Ahmed describes this experience through the metaphor of "bad feelings" getting "stuck" to certain types of bodies. Let me suggest that bad feelings often get "stuck" to mad people and people with other forms of visible disAbility (125). Our expressions of feeling (whether this be "bad" feelings, like anxiety, sadness and anger, or "good" feelings, like joy and amusement) are often framed as "crazy" behaviour which unnerves others, making them feel uncomfortable. Our protests against saneist assumptions are also often seen as killing the joy of those who are "only trying to help" (generally by reinforcing psychiatric discourse) or who feel they have legitimate reasons to fear or ostracize mad people. When someone calls us out on saneism or any other type of oppressive speech or action, that means it is time to listen, and reflect on our behaviour, not to get defensive. Remember that even the best ally falters sometimes.

Because I am sane, it is unlikely that someone will question my ability to raise my children, to care for a sick or disAbled friend or relative, or to have a pet. Mad people's parenting capabilities, on the other hand, are routinely questioned, and images of abusive mad parents abound in the media and popular culture. As S.E. Smith notes in *Bitch* magazine online,

> Pop culture tells us a number of dangerous things about parenting and mental illness, *particularly* when it comes to mothering. Parenting, we are told, is simply not possible with mental illness... You are too unstable to be trusted with the tremendous responsibility of childrearing, unless you are willing to abide by very strict rules for the management of your condition. (emphasis original)

As Wilson and Beresford note, it can also be difficult for mad parents to access fertility services, or to become foster or adoptive parents (149). 15 All parents and caregivers, mad or sane, need support. We need to ask parents and caregivers what we can do to help, rather than assuming that mad people are any less capable of, or entitled to, that important work and relationship.

I am unlikely to be forcibly subjected to treatment which, though carried out in the name of my health and well-being, might be considered torture in other contexts. Some current psychiatric treatment methods, such as electroconvulsive therapy (ECT), as well as certain drugs, such as neuroleptics (anti-psychotics), have been used as torture methods for political dissidents, notably in the Soviet Union (Fireside 49). 16 Many people who have no or little experience of the mental health system are surprised when I tell them that ECT is still a commonly used treatment in Canada and the United States, and that it is even prescribed to children and the elderly. Educate yourself about different perspectives on current psychiatric treatment methods. Listen to and believe mad people if and when they chose to share their experiences of these treatments with you.

I am unlikely to be incarcerated without being charged with a crime, given a chance to defend myself, or being allowed to speak with a lawyer or other advocate. Although there are certainly problems and biases within the criminal justice system, there is also some form of due process. Under the current Ontario Mental Health Act, however, anyone can submit evidence to a justice of the peace which shows that a person who has previously been treated for a "mental disorder" is now suffering from this same disorder and cannot make his/her own decisions. 17 If the justice of the peace approves this application, he or she can order the police to take the "mentally disordered" person into custody and deliver them to a psychiatric facility for evaluation. The attending doctor may then certify an involuntary admission or community treatment order (CTO). (A third party can also call police directly, if they believe someone to be a danger to themselves or others.) Through this kind of legislation, which exists not only in Canada, but also in other jurisdictions across the West, mad people can be subject to both police and psychiatric detainment without committing a specific offense, and without being given a chance to defend themselves, or to be defended by another person. If you feel threatened by a mad person, interrogate your own fear before seeking legal, medical or police intervention. Are you, or that person, actually at risk of being harmed? Or are saneist stereotypes playing into your fear? Would you seek outside intervention if that person did not have a psychiatric history? Consider that in most cases, forced treatment poses a greater risk to a mad person than they pose to themselves. Support mad people's choices about their use of psychiatric drugs and services.

When I seek police assistance or medical attention, my history of sanity will not result in me being assaulted, ignored, dismissed, made to wait, or treated as though I am lying, or in receiving diminished quality of care.** People of colour, trans people, the homeless and street-involved, sex workers, criminalized people and mad people are particularly subject to harassment and/or assault at the hands of police. Race, class, gender, sexual orientation, previous medical history (such as HIV+ status or a mental health diagnosis) may also affect quality of care in a hospital. In the case of Jamaican immigrant Esmin Green, for example—who died because of neglect in King's Country Hospital in Brooklyn, New York, while waiting for an involuntary psychiatric evaluation—racism, sexism, classism and saneism were all intertwining factors in the way in which she was perceived and treated both before and after her death. 18

If my day, week or year is going badly, I don't wonder if each negative situation I experienced happened because I am perceived as sane.* For many mad people, however, it may be difficult to discern whether their day, week, or year is going badly because of saneism, or because of a number of interlocking systems of oppression and privilege. Mad people are more likely to be re-medicalized or to come into conflict with the law if they are people of colour, if they are poor, or if they are (or appear to be) queer or transgender. As I have tried to show in many of the examples above, there are many intersections between sane privilege and privilege based on race, gender, sexuality, class and ability.

I want to focus on these links between sane privilege and other types of privilege because I think it is important to note, in the spirit of intersectional feminism, that oppressions work in overlapping ways. I also want to emphasize, however, that the advantages associated with different types of privilege are not the same, even though there are many similarities between them. Being mad or psychiatrized, for one thing, is not as consistently visible as, say, being a person of colour. Generally, people have the same skin colour all the time, whereas many mad people may only be perceived as mad some of the time, and our history of psychiatrization may only be on display in certain contexts; that being said, "sane" people can loose their sane privilege at any point in their lives if they are deemed mentally ill, and people who are already oppressed because of their sex, race, gender, sexuality, age and/or disAbility are more likely to be psychiatrized. For somebody living with multiple intersecting oppressions it may be difficult, if not impossible, to distinguish instances of saneism from other types of discrimination, since saneism is often so closely bound up with other mutually-reinforcing forms of oppression.

You might be wondering, now that you have read this list, why is it important, and how might it be used. This list, like the white privilege list, is important because it shows the way that sane privilege operates, and, as with white people and white privilege and men and male privilege, sane people are taught not to recognize sane privilege. McIntosh notes the ways in which men in the academy deny their privilege in curriculum discussions, justifying the exclusion of women's or feminist materials. She writes: "when the talk turns to giving men *less* cultural room, even the most thoughtful and fair-minded of the men... tend to... fall back on conservative assumptions about... distributions of power, calling on precedent or sociobiology and psychobiology to demonstrate that male domination is natural" ("White Privilege and Male Privilege" 149, emphasis original). In similar fashion, and often in a way that is intertwined with this sexism, I have found that many "sane" people, when addressed with the idea of mad scholarship, fall back on the medical model, justifying exclusion of particular materials or approaches by saying that those who suffer from "mental illness" are just not amenable to inclusion in the same way. The plight of the "mentally ill" is to be pitied, but it is a biological problem that we should leave to doctors and scientists. Alternately, I have been told that mad issues are already being addressed under the rubric of disability awareness, a claim which not only overlooks the specificity of mad culture, identities, and experiences, but also disAbled people who do not subscribe to a medical model of disability, 19 and who, in any case, are still largely ignored in the context of higher education. 20

In her article, McIntosh also cites Elizabeth Minnich's argument that "whites are taught to think of their lives as morally neutral, normative, and average, and also ideal, so that when we work to benefit others, this is seen as work which will allow 'them' to be more like 'us'" (149-50). Similarly, those who have not been psychiatrized—and particularly those have never been called weird or freakish or treated as though they are abnormal in some way—assume that they are sane, morally neutral, and average, and that their "normal" ways of thinking and interacting with the world are envied by people who are mad or "mentally ill." They don't understand why we would want to bring mad perspectives into the classroom, because they see these as diametrically opposed to the rationality espoused by the academy. This discourse of academic rationality and neutrality, I might note, is still heavily dependent on patriarchal and colonialist discourses of both gender and racial otherness. In these discourses, women and people of colour, in addition to people considered to be disabled or mad, are, as a rule, not considered rational, and are thus not worthy of being included in intellectual discussions. 21 Although sane privilege may benefit the "sane," it also disadvantages them. It stops those who experience the world "normally" from learning from mad people's experiences. Showing "sane" people how the lived experiences of mad people differ from their own, and how they might learn from them, is the first step in enlisting them as allies. One of the best ways for "sane" people to become allies of the mad community is for them to come to recognize and challenge the discourses of sane privilege. A list like the one above is a step in helping to do that.

I have yet to fully test out different ways that the concept of sane privilege might be used pedagogically, but one of the methods that I have found effective in getting people to think through how sane privilege operates is to get them to generate a similar list of their own in a seminar focused on the idea of privilege. It helps to have folks read McIntosh's "White Privilege: Unpacking the Invisible Knapsack" ahead of time, or to go over it together as a group, to give everyone a sense of what privilege looks like. Once the audience understands the concept of privilege, they can work in small groups to brainstorm a list of the unearned assets held by those who have sane privilege and/or other forms of privilege. Ideally, this exercise should get them to see that there are both similarities and differences among types of privilege, and that systems of oppression and privilege interlock with one another, often compounding people's experiences of marginalization, discrimination and violence. I tried this exercise for the first time in June 2011 with a group of people who attended a panel I was part of at *PsychOut: A Conference for Organizing Resistance Against Psychiatry*, in New York City. Although I already had the suggestions above (as well as a few more items) written down as a back-up list in case the groups had trouble coming up with examples, I needn't have worried. The audience at this particular conference, which was made up of mostly mad people and our allies, easily brainstormed most of the items I have presented here, as well as others, because they themselves have experienced and/or witnessed saneism.

In the case of a more mixed audience, however, such as a group of undergraduate students, there may be more resistance to the idea of sane privilege, either from non-psychiatrized people who are uncomfortable with the idea of their own privilege, or from psychiatrized people who accept themselves as mentally ill, but who do not see themselves as disadvantaged or even different because of it. Many students also see madness as something private, not something to be "out" about or proud of. I have encountered fierce opposition when talking about the history of the mad movement and alternate perspectives on mental health in classroom spaces, often from students who have a "mentally ill" family member, or who have themselves had (generally positive) experiences of the mental health system. In these cases, I am careful to note that I support people's various self-identifications, their decisions to be "out" as mad or mentally ill or not, and their choice about what kinds of treatments and/or supports they access. I emphasize that my aim is to show that there is more than one perspective outside of the dominant medical model of madness, rather than to debate whether or not that model is correct. I also point out that, even if we were to accept that "mental illness" is an inherent, biological difference, we would still need to undermine the idea that that "the mentally ill" are therefore less deserving of dignity, rights, choices or participation in the public sphere. I stress the importance of challenging the sane/mentally ill binary. As Wilson and Beresford point out "the world does not consist of 'normals' and 'the mentally ill'; it consists of *people*, all of whom may experience mental and emotional distress at some time(s) in their lives" (144, emphasis original). Like Wilson and Beresford, I am interested in critiquing, and in teaching students to think critically about, the ways in which biomedical notions of madness often work to construct psychiatrized people as other. One function of this othering is the creation of hierarchies between "normal" mental health services users—or as Wilson and Beresford put it, the "worried well"—who see counsellors or take anti-depressants, but who are not visibly mad—and the "real crazy people," (who Wilson and Beresford call the "threateningly mad"): those who have been diagnosed with a "serious mental illness," who are visibly mad, strange or different (by choice or not) and/or who have made more extensive use of psychiatric services (also by choice or not) (153). It is important to point out to students that sane privilege and saneism is often reinforced through just such a denial of affinity with mad people of various identifications, on the part of both "sane" individuals and other mental health service users, who may or may not consider themselves mad or mentally ill. 22

In some cases, it may not be practical to do a full class on saneism, or even on privilege more generally, particularly in teaching environments where (as was the case for me when I was a TA) you may have limited control over the course content and/or pedagogical methods. Even when this is the case, however, the ubiquity of madness (whether it's an overt theme, something mentioned offhand, or merely a covert subtext) in course content across disciplines allows points for inserting discussion of saneism and sane privilege into broader conversations about privilege, oppression, self and other, the categorization and regulation of bodies, and discourses of madness. The sane privilege list can be used not only in a targeted exercise focused on making privilege visible, but the specific examples it includes can also help teachers to think through ways in which they might incorporate discussions of saneism into their courses, as I did when discussing *The Yellow Wallpaper* with first year students of literature.

Although I have directed this article mainly towards allies who have not been psychiatrized, and who are generally perceived as "sane," I'd like to close by noting that mad people also need to think through the ways in which various oppressions intersect in saneism. I am continually frustrated when mad people are resistant to recognizing the differences and inequalities among us. While we need to ask mad allies to educate themselves about and to challenge saneism and sane privilege, we also, as mad people, need to continually educate ourselves about, recognize the ways we are implicated in, and speak out against aspects of saneism we might not have experienced first hand. 23 This project of inclusivity and intersectionality also entails acknowledging and actively resisting other forms of oppression which we may not have experienced. Sexism, racism, heterosexism, cissexism, ableism, ageism and classism have an impact not only on many mad people, but many of our allies and potential allies as well.

Deepest thanks go out to S. Brophy, G. Reaume and A. Das for their helpful edits and input into this article. Thank you to those who attended my presentations at PsychOut 2010 in Toronto and PsychOut 2011 in New York City. Your positive response to my presentations, and your feedback, inspired me to merge the two papers into an article. Thanks also to my two DSQ peer reviewers, who provided helpful suggestions for revising this piece.

Works Cited

Ahmed, Sara. "Multiculturalism and the Promise of Happiness." New Formations. 63 (2008): 121-137. Web.

—. *On Being Included: Racism and Diversity in Institutional Life*. Durham: Duke University Press, 2012. Print.

American Psychiatric Association. "DSM-5 Development." *DSM-5: The Future of Psychiatric Diagnosis*. 2010. Web. 6 Dec. 2011.

Beresford, Peter and Anne Wilson. "Madness, Distress and Postmodernity." *Disability/Postmodernity*. London: Continuum, 2002. 143-158. Print.

Beresford, P., G. Gifford, and P. Harrison. "What has Disability got to do with Psychiatric Survivors?" *Speaking our Minds: An Anthology of Personal Experiences of Mental Distress and Its Consequences*. ed. Jim Read and Jill Reynolds. Basingstoke: Macmillan 1996. 209-14. Print.

Bergstresser, Sara M. "The Death of Esmin Green: Considering Ongoing Injustice In Psychiatric Institutions." *The International Journal of Feminist Approaches to Bioethics*. 4.1 (2011): 221-30. Web.

Birnbaum, Rebecca. "My Father's Advocacy for a Right to Treatment." *Journal of the American Academy of Psychiatry and the Law*. 38.1 (2010):115-23. Web.

Bousquet, Marc. *How the University Works: Higher Education and the Low Wage Nation*. New York: New York UP, 2008. Print.

Braithwaite, Ann. *Troubling Women's Studies: Pasts, Presents, and Possibilities*. Toronto: Sumach Press, 2004. Print.

Burstow, Bonnie and Don Weitz. *Shrink Resistant: The Struggle against Psychiatry in Canada*. Vancouver, BC: New Star Books, 1988. Print.

Capponi, Pat. *Upstairs in the Crazy House*. Toronto: Viking, 1992. Print.

Chamberlin, Judi. *On Our Own: Patient Controlled Alternatives to the Mental Health System*. New York: Hawthorn Books, 1978. Print.

Cosgrove, Lisa, Sheldon Krimsky, Manisha Vijayaraghavan and Lisa Schneider. "Financial Ties between DSM-IV Panel Members and the Pharmaceutical Industry." *Psychotherapy and Psychosomatics*. 75 (2006): 154-160. Print.

Fabris, Erick. *Tranquil Prisons: Chemical Incarceration Under Community Treatment Orders*. Toronto: U of Toronto P, 2011. Print.

Fireside, Harvey. *Soviet Psychoprisons*. New York: Norton, 1979. Print.

Gilman, Charlotte Perkins. "The Yellow Wallpaper." 1892. *University of Virginia Library Electronic Text Centre*. Web. 6 Dec. 2011.

Kutchins, Herb, and Stuart A. Kirk. *Making Us Crazy: Dsm : the Psychiatric Bible and the Creation of Mental Disorders*. New York: Free Press, 1997. Print.

Lewiecki-Wilson, Cynthia. "Rethinking Rhetoric Through Mental Disabilities." *Rhetoric Review*. 22.2 (2003): 156-67. Web.

Loomba, Ania. *Colonialism/Postcolonialism*. New York: Routledge, 1998. Print.

Mangold, James, dir. *Girl, Interrupted.* Perf. Winona Ryder, Angelina Jolie, Brittany Murphy, Whoopi Goldberg. Columbia Tristar, 2003. DVD.

McIntosh, Peggy. "White Privilege and Male Privilege: A Personal Account of Coming to See Correspondences Through Work in Women's Studies." *Race, Class, and Gender: An Anthology.* ed. Margaret L. Andersen and Patricia Hill Collins. Belmont: Wadsworth Publishing Co, 1992. 70-81. Print.

—. "White Privilege: Unpacking the Invisible Knapsack." *Peace and Freedom.* July/August 1989. 10-12. Print.

McNamera, Julie. "Out of Order: Madness is a Feminist and a Disability Issue." *Encounters with Strangers: Feminism and Disability.* ed. Jenny Morris. London: Women's Press, 1996. Print.

Mindfreedom International. "Psychiatric Survivor Movement History." mindfreedom.org. web. 18 May, 2012.

Morrison, Lydia. *Talking Back to Psychiatry: The Psychiatric Consumer/Survivor/Ex -patient Movement.* New York: Routledge, 2005. Print.

Nabbali, Essya M. "A 'Mad' Critique of the Social Model of Disability." *The International Journal of Diversity in Organizations, Communities and Nations.* 9.4 (2009): 1-12. Print.

Nussbaum, Martha. *Not for Profit: Why Democracy Needs Higher Education.* Princeton: Princeton UP, 2010. Print.

Minkowitz, Tina. "The United Nations Convention on the Rights of Persons with Disabilities and the Right to be Free from Nonconsensual Psychiatric Interventions." *Syracuse Journal of International Law and Commerce.* 34 (2007): 405-28. Web.

Moncrieff, Joanna. "Neoliberalism and Biopsychiatry: A Marriage of Convenience." *Liberatory Psychiatry: Philosophy, Politics, and Mental Health.* Ed. Cohen, Carl I and Sami Timimi. Cambridge, UK: Cambridge UP, 2008. Print. 235-257.

Movement Defence Committee, The. "A Legal Guide for Activists." *movementdefence.org.* 28 Nov. 2011. Web. 6 Dec. 2011.

Ontario, Government of. "Mental Health Act." *Service Ontario E-Laws.* 2010. Web. 7 Dec. 2011.

Overboe, James. "Vitalism: Subjectivity Exceeding Racism, Sexism and (Psychiatric) Ableism." *Wagadu.* 4 (2007). 23-34. Web.

Prendergast, Catherine. "The Unexceptional Schizophrenic: a Post Modern Introduction." *Journal of Literary Disability.* 2.1 (2008): 55-62. Web.

Price, Margaret. *Mad at School: Rhetorics of Mental Disability and Academic Life.* Ann Arbor: U of Michigan P, 2011. Print.

Reading, Bill. *The University in Ruins.* Cambridge: Harvard UP, 1996. Print.

Scull, Andrew. "'Nobody's Fault?': Mental Health Policy in Modern America." *The Insanity of Place/The Place of Insanity: Essays on the History of Psychiatry.* New York: Routledge, 2006. Print.

Serano, Julia. *Whipping Girl: A Transexual Woman on Sexism and the Scapegoating of Femininity.* Emeryville: Seal Press, 2007. Print.

Shimrat, Irit. *Call Me Crazy: Stories from the Mad Movement.* Vancouver: Press Gang Publishers, 1997. Print.

Smith, S.E. "We're All Mad Here: Parenting While Crazy." *bitchmedia: Bitch magazine online.* 7 Sept. 2011. Web. 6 Dec. 2011.

Steinberg, Deborah Lynn. *Bodies in Glass: Genetics, Eugenics, Embryo Ethics.* Manchester: Manchester UP, 1997. Print.

Titchkosky, Tanya. *The Question of Access: Disability, Space, Meaning.* Toronto: University of Toronto Press, 2011. Print.

Wolframe, PhebeAnn. "The Invisible Straightjacket: Theorizing and Teaching Saneism and Sane Privilege." *PsychOut: A Conference for Organizing Resistance Against Psychiatry.* PhD Program in Environmental Psychology, The Graduate Centre, City University New York, New York, NY. 19 June, 2011.

PhebeAnn Wolframe is a psychiatric survivor, a member of the Mad Students Society (Toronto) and a member of the Psychiatric Survivor Archives of Toronto. She is also a PhD Candidate in English and Cultural Studies at McMaster University (Hamilton, Ontario, Canada). Her thesis project examines the ways in which post-WWII Eugenic-Atlantic women's literature works to critique psychiatry as an apparatus of biopolitics and to envision madness both as a way of reading texts, and as a space for building new kinds of community.

Endnotes

1. Cissexism refers to systemic discrimination against transgender (trans) people and others who do not easily fit into a binary system of sex and gender. Although I do not believe the term cissexism had been coined during my undergraduate days, I recall discussing gender discrimination in a fairly broad sense. (This may not be true of all Women's Studies programs). Julia Serano defines cissexism as "the belief that transsexuals' identified genders are inferior to, or less authentic than, those of cisexuals" (33). Cisexual is the opposite of transsexual, while cisgender is the opposite of transgender, but the two are often used interchangeably. Cisgendered means that one's physical sex characteristics (ie. penis) matches up with the gender they were assigned at birth (ie. boy), and with how they currently experience and

perceive their gender identity (ie. man).
Return to Text

2. As Erick Fabris notes, saneism, which "means prejudgement or prejudice against mentally ill people" was coined by Mortin Brinbaum in conversation with Florynce Kennedy (Birnbaum 10). Fabris, however, "uses the term to mean the very constructions of difference as 'madness' and the dividing of bodies into mad and sound" (9). I use the term saneism to mean both discrimination against those who have been given a psychiatric diagnosis (who may or may not be perceived as "mentally ill" in some or all situations), as well as discrimination against people who are perceived to be "mentally ill," delusional, mad etc. (who may or may not have a psychiatric diagnosis, or be psychiatric users/consumers/survivors). It is important to note that another term, mentalism, is used often synonymously with saneism. Mentalism, a term first attributed in print to Judi Chamberlin, refers to discrimination on the basis of intellectual or psychiatric disability (Fabris 29-30, Chamberlin 66).
Return to Text

3. Although some mad people use the term ableism in addition to, or instead of, mentalism/saneism, others prefer not to use the term ableism at all because they do not consider themselves disabled. This devision in terminology is reflective of the complex and often fraught relationship between madness and disability. This tension affects mad and disability activist communities as well as academic (inter)disciplines. For further reading, see Wilson and Beresford 145; Nabbali 4; Price 14; Beresford et al in *Speaking our Minds*, and Judi Johnny's piece in Shimrat's *Call me Crazy*, 38-42.
Return to Text

4. For further discussion of the corporatizing of the university, the purpose of higher education, and place of the humanities in the university, see Bill Reading's *The University in Ruins* (1996), Marc Bousquet's *How the University Works* (2008) and Martha Nussbaum's *Not for Profit* (2010). For work more specific to feminist and equity politics in the university, see Ann Braithwaite et al's *Troubling Women's Studies* (2004) and Sara Ahmed's *On Being Included* (2012).
Return to Text

5. For more on the history of psychiatric resistance and the mad movement, see Burstow and Weitz's *Shrink Resistant* (1988), Irit Shimrat's *Call Me Crazy* (1997), Morrison's *Talking Back to Psychiatry* (2005), Judi Chamberlin's *On Our Own* (1978) and the history links on the Mind Freedom International webpage.
Return to Text

6. The medical model of madness is that which frames mental difference and/or distress as illness. The medical model typically understands mental illness to be primarily based in genetics and other aspects of biology, rather than as a

principally social, cultural and/or spiritual phenomenon.
Return to Text

7. My experiences are only one example of the way in which one can similarly be both privileged and disadvantaged. James Overboe describes a similar struggle with being both. On one hand, he has gained the rights of full citizenship through his access to particular discourses, and to a position as a university professor; on the other hand, his "cerebral palsy and spasms" signal "a (potential) impediment to [his] full participation within a political life," a life of full citizenship that is routinely denied to disabled people (26).
Return to Text

8. People who have had experience of the mental health system, as well as people who perceive themselves to be, or are perceived by others as mentally different, may choose to use a variety of identity labels including, but not limited to: mad, crazy, psychiatric survivor, ex-patient, mentally ill/disabled, psychiatric consumer and neurodiverse. Individuals and communities choose and define these terms in different ways depending on their geographical location(s), generational/historical location(s), personal experiences of mental difference and psychiatrization, intersections with other aspects of identity, politics and activist goals, and desires to reclaim or resist certain labels.
Return to Text

9. Bitch magazine online has a series called "We're All Mad Here," which reviews portrayals of mad people in popular culture. (I cite one of the articles in this series in this list). I am also currently working on a research blog project in which mad people can review depictions of madness and mental health treatment as part of an online reading community. Through this project, I hope to explore the ways in which people's experiences of the mental health system do or do not affect their interpretations of depictions of madness.
Return to Text

10. As The Movement Defence Committee (an autonomous working group of the Law Union of Ontario) notes in in their Legal Guide for Activists, "certain people face increased risk of being targeted by the police because they are a member of a marginalized group, because of their political beliefs, or because of how they look." This includes "people with disabilities, people of colour, visibly queer or trans/intersexed people, psych survivors and people with mental health issues, parents or caregivers, people with criminal records, and those with precarious immigration status" (movementdefence.org, emphasis added).
Return to Text

11. An example of dietary choices being considered a symptom is the case of Leonard Roy Frank, whose parents, in the 1970s, arranged for his psychiatric

commitment when he began observing Orthodox Jewish dietary laws and became a vegetarian (Chamberlin 5). The idea of food-choice-as-symptom continues today: in the upcoming DSM-5, as currently proposed, will include "Avoidant/Restrictive Food Intake Disorder" According to this diagnosis, being a picky eater, or choosing a restrictive diet such as veganism, could be interpreted as a psychiatric disorder in and of itself as long as it is deemed to be significantly impacting a person's life. The diagnostic criteria also notes, however, that "if the eating disturbance occurs in the context of a medical condition or another mental disorder, it is sufficiently severe to warrant independent clinical attention" (APA, K02, emphasis added). Thus if a person already has a psychiatric label, being a "picky eater" can be considered more significant or "severe" than it would in someone without a prior diagnosis. This only adds to the constant monitoring of diet that mad people endure.
Return to Text

12. A study conducted by Lisa Cosgrove et al reveals that 56% of members sitting on the review panel for the Diagnostic and Statistical Manual of Mental Disorders have financial ties with pharmaceutical companies. As Cosgrove et al additionally note: "the connections [between drug companies and panelists] are especially strong in those diagnostic areas where drugs are the first line of treatment for mental disorders" (154). See also Kutchins and Kirk, *Making Us Crazy: DSM — The Psychiatric Bible and the Creation of Mental Disorders.*
Return to Text

13. An untidy appearance is also, I'd argue, a trope of representations of mad people on television, in film and in novels—whether it's Beethoven's mad genius, with his wildly fly-away hair, or Angelina Jolie, kicking and screaming as femme fatale Lisa in the film version of *Girl, Interrupted.*
Return to Text

14. Deinstitutionalization refers to the move from the treatment of the "mentally ill" in hospitals and other types of long-term care institutions to treatment in the community. Deinstitutionalization began in Canada, the United States and Britain following World War II as patient populations boomed (Scull 105). Institutional closures became increasingly frequent in the late 1970s to the 1990s, however, spurred by a neo-liberal agenda of more effective patient management for less expenditure through community treatment orders (CTOs) which allow patients to be treated both voluntarily and involuntarily on an outpatient basis (Moncrieff 237). Deinstitutionalization has been supported by CTO legislation in all three countries: The National Health Service and Community Care Act (1990) and the Mental Health Act (2007) in the UK, and in the US and Canada, policies at the state/provincial level such as Kendra's Law in New York (1999), and the Mental Health Act in Ontario (1990, 2010).
Return to Text

15. See Steinberg 86-7; McNamara 199.
Return to Text

16. Psychiatric survivor and human rights lawyer Tina Minkowitz has also argued successfully to the UN Rapporteur on Torture that forced treatment is a form of torture, and that it infringes on the rights of persons with disabilities (405).
Return to Text

17. For the order to be passed, the person must also be deemed either a danger to themselves or others, or unable to care for themselves (Ontario Mental Health Act 16.1). The person must also have "shown clinical improvement as a result of their [previous] treatment" (16.1.1.b). These measures, are, of course, subjectively determined.
Return to Text

18. For a discussion of Esmin Green's case, see Sara Bergstresser's "The Death of Esmin Green: Considering Ongoing Injustice In Psychiatric Institutions."
Return to Text

19. A medical model of disability defines disability as a physical, biological problem to be solved through medical means. A social model of disability sees non-inclusive infrastructure and social environments as the cause of disability. That is, physical difference is not experienced as a problem in an environment that accommodates that difference.
Return to Text

20. For a further discussion of the disAbility (dis)inclusion within the context of higher education, see Tanya Tichkosky's *The Question of Access* (2011).
Return to Text

21. For an overview of the ties between Anglo-American educational histories, colonialism, and discourses of race, sex and rationality, see Ania Loomba's *Colonialism/Postcolonialism* (1998). See also Margaret Price's chapter "Listening to the Subject of Mental Disability: Intersections of Academic and Medical Discourses" for a discussion of the ways in which notions of rhetoric and reason—which systematically exclude mentally disabled people—are at the foundation of academic discourse.
Return to Text

22. See also Overboe's discussion of the way in which both the general public and psychiatric service users often surveil and report upon one another's behaviour (and are encouraged to do so) as a way to assert their own compliance, normality and/or recovery (25).
Return to Text

23. The mad movement has historically been made up mostly of white, heterosexual, able-bodied people. Though Judi Chamberlin argues in On Our Own (a book foundational to the movement) that peer support needs to take multiple identities and oppressions into account, people with disabilities, members of the queer community and people of colour have often felt excluded from the mad movement (19). That being said, there are mad activists who have been working since the 1980s, but particularly in recent years, to address issues of exclusion in mad communities and to recognize intersectionality (Shimrat 138-141).
    Return to Text

Return to Top of Page

Smith College Studies in Social Work, 81:314–327, 2011

ISSN: 0037-7317 print/1553-0426 online
DOI: 10.1080/00377317.2011.616839

Gender Identity Disorder, the Gender Binary, and Transgender Oppression: Implications for Ethical Social Work

ERIN R. MARKMAN
Hunter College School of Social Work, New York, New York, USA

This article argues that social workers are ethically obligated to serve as allies of transgender and gender-nonconforming communities and, thus, should critically examine the diagnosis of gender identity disorder and the oppression inherent in pathologizing gender nonconformity. Social workers should also consider the oppression inherent in the socially constructed gender binary that is the root of the perceived psychosis in gender nonconformance and should fight against this oppression and, therefore, against that binary. This article proposes several action steps that social workers can take to advocate for the transgender and gender-nonconforming communities.

KEYWORDS transgender, gender identity, oppression, social work, ethics, diagnostic and statistical manual of mental disorders

INTRODUCTION AND THE AUTHOR'S RELATIONSHIP TO THE COMMUNITY

In this article I intend to display that social workers, as ethically obligated allies of transgender and gender-nonconforming individuals, should be aware of and active in the discussion around the inclusion of gender identity disorder in the *Diagnostic and Statistical Manual of Mental Disorders* (4th ed.; *DSM-IV*) (American Psychiatric Association [APA], 1994) and the proposed inclusion of gender incongruence in the *DSM-V* (APA, 2010b). It is the ethical responsibility of social workers to explore and advocate for the

Received 6 February 2011; accepted 2 August 2011.
Address correspondence to Erin R. Markman, 81 8th Avenue, #6, Brooklyn, NY 11215, USA. E-mail. Markman Erin@gmail.com

possibility of eliminating such psychiatric diagnoses in favor of a nonpsychiatric medical diagnosis in the *International Statistical Classification of Diseases and Related Health Problems* (World Health Organization, 2007) that would allow transgender and gender-nonconforming individuals access to health care and medical procedures without labeling their identity as pathological, as does the psychiatric diagnosis. Social workers should also consider the oppression inherent in the socially constructed male/female gender binary and should fight against this oppression, and therefore against that binary (Burdge, 2007). I propose several action steps that social workers can take to advocate for the transgender and gender nonconforming communities.

Those most directly affected by the diagnosis of gender identity disorder (GID)—transgender and gender-nonconforming individuals—are the experts in their own experience. I take guidance from materials generated by community members, and by individuals who seem to me, from their research and practice history, to be respectful, accountable allies. I hope to add to the literature with an ally's eye—listening, learning, and challenging internalized transphobia.

I identify as a cisgender woman—*cisgender* being a relatively newly coined term that derives from the Latin *cis* for "on the same side as"; that is, my gender identity is on the same side as the sex I was assigned at birth. Using the term *cisgender* is a way of distinguishing people who do not identify themselves as transgender without the implications of normalcy and determinism that come from terms like "biological woman" or the power implied in assuming that when one says simply "woman" that one means a nontransgender woman (Stryker, 2008). The gender binary affects all people, as all people have gender identities shaped and constrained by social constructs. It is also important to note that as a white[2] and economically privileged person, who is citing from a largely white body of academic literature, and maintaining a particular focus on the medical establishment, which takes economic resources to access, I do not sufficiently address issues of racism and classism in body of this article. Readers are directed to the final section of Stryker and Whittle's (2006) compilation for several pieces addressing racism in the discourse around transgender identity, as well as to organizations such as the Audre Lorde Project and the Sylvia Rivera Law Project, which are explicit and intentional in highlighting the marginalization of low income individuals and people of color.

AN ETHICAL OBLIGATION

Issues of transgender oppression—in general and as they relate to GID—should be of paramount concern to social workers, not only because social workers are involved with the diagnoses and treatment of individuals, but also because social workers are governed by a set of ethical guidelines that draw attention to transgender oppression. Social workers, as stipulated in the National Association for Social Workers (NASW; 2008) *Code of Ethics*, "should obtain education about and seek to understand the nature of social diversity and oppression with respect to ... gender identity or expression" ("Cultural Competence," para. 3), should not "practice, condone, facilitate, or collaborate with any form of discrimination on the basis of ... gender identity or expression" ("Discrimination," para. 1), and should "act to prevent and eliminate domination of, exploitation of, and discrimination against any person, group, or class on the basis" thereof ("Social and Political Action," para. 4).

Social workers who engage clients' personal lives and the communities in which they live are thus ethically obligated and uniquely situated to become educated about and work to eliminate issues of oppression faced by the transgender and gender-nonconforming communities (Burdge, 2007; Burgess, 2009).

TERMINOLOGY

I will borrow from Zandvliet (2000) to define *gender* "as the sum of a person's non-physical and non-biological characteristics that determine their sense of being male, female or neither or any combination" (p. 181). Gender is an identity that exists separate from the constraints of physical sex characteristics and the dictates of a binary that our society has imposed (Nagoshi & Burzuzy, 2010).

The term *transgender* is a broad category (Elliot, 2001; Meyerowitz, 2002). In this article it will serve (unless being quoted by someone who sees fit to use it otherwise) as a broad umbrella term that includes the behaviors but rejects the pathological implications in the terminology of terms such as transvestism (dressing like a gender other than the one that person was ascribed at birth, for any number of reasons), transsexualism (having the desire to alter physical sex characteristics to change one's gender) (Stryker, 2008), and any other presentation seen as gender-nonconformance by a society that operates with an untenable binary that does not make space for the lived experience of gender. Note that a political use of language occurs above. *Transsexual* is a medical term. Representatives of the transgender community have reclaimed and altered it to read *transexual* as a sign of ownership and affirmation (Davis, 2009; Meyerowitz, 2002). The double *s* is used here because reference is made to a diagnostic category created using potentially oppressive language.

The use of *transgender* is not intended to label any particular individual before that individual has the opportunity to self-identify. The term *transgender* is intended to be mutable and broad and must ultimately be chosen and owned by those to whom it applies. If a gender-nonconforming individual chooses to identify as transgender, then that individual is. If that individual chooses instead to identify as genderqueer, two spirit, queer, aggressive (AG), or anything else, then that is that individual's proper referent. One may use multiple identity terms, and identities may shift over time. I use the phrase *transgender and gender-nonconforming communities* in this article to emphasize that, though the term *transgender* is intended to be inclusive, there is a multiplicity of identities that should not be neglected.

There is a tendency in the literature (see, e.g., Pleak, 2009) to include highly charged and potentially vicious words like "tranny" in the umbrella of transgender without reference to these words' historical and present-day meanings and politics. I do not include such a list, as these terms are defamatory ones reclaimed by certain community members who have the right to use them if they choose. My privilege as an out-group member infuses them with violence. There is no desire to erase these labels and the communities they represent, but the language has little utility here. Davis (2009) has an extensive list of self-ascribed labels from gender-nonconforming communities that can be referenced as necessary.

I view transgender and gender-nonconforming identities as normal and valid. Transgender identity is a point in a constellation of lived gender identities—like my cisgender identity. The socially constructed male/female binary that is strictly imposed in this society simply fails to reflect that.

THE GENDER BINARY

The pervasive concept of male/female binary gender governs our lived experiences. As DeCrescenzo and Mallon (2000) articulated, "[s]trict boundaries have historically regulated gender in Western society, therefore, when one is defined by traditional theories and environmental expectations, no acceptable ways are currently available to achieve full status as a person who identifies as transgender" (p. viii). A binary sex and gender system, with concrete male/female dualities and no fluidity, is simply not a coherent way to make sense of the lived identity experiences that actually exist in the world (Bockting, 2008).

Positing the gender binary as oppressive does not mean that all people who identify as transgender reject that binary. Certainly not all transgender individuals share precisely the same idea of gender and gender fluidity (Nagoshi & Burzuzy, 2010). Nor, as Elliot (2001) stated, is "gender irrelevant or dispensable for transsexuals" just because they were failed by "gender norms" (p. 309). And the truth of sexism that arises from the binary is not to be dismissed by the assertion that gender is a social construction. But the fact that the societal definition of *gender* as binary leaves no space for transgender experience to be considered normal and does not reflect the lived experience of gender within society is problematic and oppressive. The result of the strict enforcement of the binary is that the individual who feels gender nonconforming and thus generates friction against the construct of gender is the one who is pathologized, instead of the critique being focused on the idea of gender in its current pervasive conception as being overly rigid. Too often the locus of the problem is seen as situated within the individual who does not conform to societal expectations, rather than with the societal expectations themselves.

Social workers can actively pursue theoretical modalities that facilitate a challenge of the gender binary. Nagoshi and Burzuzy (2010), for example, advanced a transgender theory that subverts the binary. Spade (2006) applied Foucalt's theories of power to the medical model and the binary. Malpas (2006) identified that a deconstructive theoretical approach to gender allows clinicians to view gender as socially constructed and relationally defined, and to move beyond binary thinking to best serve clients, while still meeting clients wherever they are in their conceptions of gender.

The idea of eradicating, subverting, or progressing beyond binary gender is a contentious and idealistic goal. I hold it as an ultimate desired future. A world in which many genders are recognized as healthy—without the male/female—would be a world in which everyone's gender, no matter how they choose to perform it, and no matter their genitals, would be accepted as part of the human experience.

HISTORICAL FOUNDATIONS OF GENDER IDENTITY DISORDER: A BRIEF HISTORY

Medical and mental health sciences have long been the loci of labeling, classifying, and regulating the lives of transgender and gender-nonconforming people. Some transgender and gender-nonconforming people feel it necessary to have medical intervention (hormone therapy and/or surgeries) to actualize their gender appropriately. In the early and mid-1900s, much of the discourse on issues of gender identity was new to those in the medical profession, and access to surgical options for reconstructing or reconfiguring gender was limited (Meyerowitz, 2002; Stryker, 2008). At the beginning of the 1970s, after an extended period of often-heated debate over issues of gender identity, the medical community began to use the terminology of *gender dysphoria syndrome* (which soon become *gender identity disorder*) as an umbrella term that was then lauded by advocates as a step that liberalized rigid diagnostic categories that stood in the way of gender-modifying operations for transgender and gender-nonconforming individuals (Meyerowitz, 2002).

However progressive these steps, the oppression of transgender and gender-nonconforming individuals and the adamant adherence to a gender binary prevailed. The pursuit of medical treatment by those transgender and gender-nonconforming individuals who felt they needed medical intervention "became entangled with a socially conservative attempt to maintain traditional gender, in which changing sex was grudgingly permitted for the few of those seeking to do so, to the extent that the practice did not trouble the gender binary for the many" (Stryker, 2008, p. 94). There was evident discrimination by the medical establishment against those (among the subset who sought medical intervention) whose desired presentation presented a challenge to the binary, and a preference for those who were more "repressed and depressed" (Meyerowitz, 2002, p.197) and conformed more strictly to gender norms. Perhaps to preserve the viability of their practices in the public eye, and almost certainly because of personal biases, many "doctors rejected candidates who would not conform after surgery to the dominant conventions of gender and sexuality" (Meyerowitz, 2002, p.225). This is the foundational history from which present-day diagnosis and treatment has arisen, a history essential to consider because, though there are reforms, mental health science builds on itself, and the inequities of its legacy influence its present-day iterations (Cosgrove, 2005; Reich, Pinkard, & Davidson, 2008). Despite the activism of transgender and gender-nonconforming individuals and the compassion of some medical and psychiatric professionals, discrimination, oppression, and an unrealistic gender binary have prevailed.

In 1980, the American Psychiatric Association included transsexualism and gender identity disorder of childhood in *DSM-III-R* (APA, 1980; Meyerowitz, 2002). It was not until publication of the *DSM-IV* that the diagnosis GID as applied to adults was codified (APA, 1994).

It is important to note that GID was added to the *DSM* the same year that homosexuality was removed, and some believe it may have been intended as, and is currently in use as, a diagnosis in children that functions to predict and attempt to prevent homosexuality (Lev, 2004; Mallon & DeCrescenzo, 2009). The authors of the *DSM-IV* (APA, 1994) still include language to indicate that "about three-quarters of boys who had a childhood history of Gender Identity Disorder report a homosexual or bisexual orientation, but without concurrent Gender Identity Disorder" (p. 536). There is concern that this information is being used as predictive indicator by those who want to "cure" homosexuality, and the use of the literature by groups like the National Association for Research and Therapy of Homosexuality (NARTH) (York, 2008) that promotes so-called treatment to help people get rid of unwanted homosexuality is a disturbing corroboration of these fears.

GENDER IDENTITY DISORDER: REIFYING THE GENDER BINARY AND ATTRIBUTING THE EFFECTS OF A SOCIETAL PROBLEM TO THE PERCEIVED PATHOLOGY OF AN INDIVIDUAL

The World Professional Association for Transgender Health, formerly known as the Harry Benjamin International Gender Dysphoria Association, has, since 1979 published a set of clinical guidelines for use by medical practitioners treating transgender individuals (World Professional Association for Transgender Health, 2011, para. 1). The Harry Benjamin Standards of Care, as these guidelines are called, are widely utilized by medical professionals when considering treatment of transgender individuals (Bockting, 2008). These standards, and a legacy of professional tradition, dictate that people who wish to have access to medical treatment to modify their gender (hormone therapy, reconstructive surgeries, etc.) must have a diagnosis of GID (Meyer et al., 2001).

As a result of the wide acceptance of these standards, transgender and gender-nonconforming people wishing to access gender-specific medical procedures must pursue the GID diagnosis—which reifies the idea that the dissonance between the gender performance of an individual and the expectations of society are the result of a psychological problem within the individual rather than a societal problem with defining gender.

Currently, to be diagnosed with GID a person must exhibit "[a] strong and persistent cross-gender identification (not merely a desire for any perceived cultural advantages of being the other sex)" and "[p]ersistent discomfort with his or her sex or sense of inappropriateness in the gender role of that sex," and must also experience "clinically significant distress or impairment in social, occupational, or other important areas of functioning," all without having "a physical intersex condition"(APA, 1994, pp. 537–538).[1] The required "persistent discomfort" for adolescents and adults "is manifested by symptoms such as preoccupation with getting rid of primary and secondary sex characteristics . . . or the belief that he or she was born the wrong sex" (APA, 1994, p. 538).

The authors of the *DSM-IV* (APA, 1994) clearly stated that "[n]either deviant behavior (e.g. political, religious, or sexual) *nor conflicts between the individual and society* are mental disorders unless the deviance or conflict is a symptom of a dysfunction in the individual" (p. xxii, italics added). Yet in the GID definition, what is diagnosed as GID is a conflict between the identity of an individual and the views of a society for which, counter to the philosophy of the *DSM-IV*'s authors, the individual is held pathologically responsible.

The diagnosis is mandated social conformity to a structure of gender that is artificial and improperly reflective of actual lived gender experience. DeCrescenzo and Mallon (2000) put it well in their discussion of transgender youth: "[t]he biological and psychological distress of transgender youth are often symptomatic of pressures created from the macro and mezzo social systems surrounding these young people" (p. 8). It is not their identity that is causing these children pain, it is their identity in a culture of oppression, fear, and misinformation.

The impairment in social, occupational, and other areas of life experienced by those diagnosed with GID is indeed problematic, but it is due largely to the fact that those realms of life are often intolerant and hostile to transgender and gender-nonconforming people. Pervasive discrimination and acts of emotional and physical violence are perpetrated against the transgender and gender-nonconforming communities—ranging from demonstrably discriminatory hiring practices at stores (Pearson, 2010), to, tragically often, physical assault and murder (Smith, 2010). The fact that transgender individuals may experience a range of negative psychosocial consequences resultant from those forces is not the fault of some individual pathology. These are problems generated by the society and the failure of the gender binary, not by gender-nonconforming individuals. The distress experienced by transgender and gender variant people is a result of societal ignorance, prejudice, and bigotry, and not of an individual pathology. As Lev (2005) said,

> [i]t is worth noting that in other areas where children are routinely bullied, for example racial or ethnic discrimination and physical or mental disabilities, the focus of intervention has been policy directed toward changing the social conditions that maintain abuse, not changing children to better fit in to oppressive circumstances. (p. 49)

What is needed is not an individual intervention, but a social one.

GENDER LABELS IN THE *DSM-IV*

In addition to the problems inherent in the diagnosis itself, there is also a troubling and persistent misuse of gender labels in the *DSM-IV* (APA, 1994). In the *DSM-IV* (APA, 1994) individuals are consistently referred to by the gender label they were assigned at birth, despite the fact that this is, given they are transgender, likely not the label they would select for themselves. The text refers to "males" who undergo electrolysis and hormone treatment and "cross-dressing" as part of "passing convincingly as the other sex" (p. 533). There is no mention made in the text of the fact that a person who has gone to such lengths to pass as a woman would almost certainly not choose to be identified as "male." Operating under the ethical principle of respect for "the inherent dignity and worth of the person" outlined in the NASW *Code of Ethics* (NASW, 2002) and the APA ethical principle of providing "competent medical care with compassion and respect for human dignity and rights" (APA, 2009, p. 3), it is reasonable to assert that an individual must be referred to by his or her pronoun of choice. That is, if a person tells you he uses the pronoun "he" then that is the proper pronoun to use, regardless of what you know about his genital composition at birth. Improper gender labels and pronoun use can also be seen in the literature. See for example Pleak (2009) who used "he" to refer to a female-identified client in transition. Labeling theory and stigma theory (Yang et al., 2007) point toward the fact that the misuse of pronouns is not only disrespectful, reinforcing of pathology, and confusing, but can likely cause actual psychosocial damage to individuals. Unfortunately the APA, which publishes the *DSM*, has a code of ethics which does not explicitly protect individuals from exclusion, segregation, or demeaning treatment on the basis of gender identity (APA, 2009). Patients are explicitly protected from this type of discrimination based on "ethnic origin, race, sex, creed, age, socioeconomic status, or sexual orientation" (APA, 2009, p. 3). The APA should revise the language of this document.

THE *DSM-V*

The proposed revision in terminology from GID in the *DSM-IV* to gender incongruence (GI) in the *DSM-V*, the authors profess, is an attempt to adopt a "term that better reflects the core of the problem: an incongruence between, on the one hand, what identity one experiences and/or expresses and, on the other hand, how one is expected to live based on one's assigned gender (usually at birth)" (APA, 2010b, 'Rationale' endnote 1). This seems an apt description of the problem at hand: that gender as it is currently defined does not reflect gender as it is actually experienced. However, the substance of the diagnosis remains largely the same as in the *DSM-IV*. The new diagnosis still locates the source of dissonance between the experiences of transgender people and the expectations of society as within the individual and as the result of pathology.

The chair and psychologist in chief of the working group assembled to handle sexual and gender identity disorders for the *DSM-V* is Kenneth Zucker (APA, 2010a) who is a well-established voice in the literature, and a voice that neither affirms transgender and gender-variant identities nor challenges the gender binary (Zucker, 1999). Zucker has defended in print the initial GID diagnoses (Zucker, 1999) despite objections from the community that they were pathologizing a nondisordered state of being. Zucker advocates for so-called restorative therapy in which the intended goal is for a child not to transition (National Public Radio [NPR], 2008). In a 2008 interview on NPR, Zucker was critical of therapeutic practices that support early transitions in children and spoke of children's thoughts about transition as "a 'fantasy solution,' that being the other sex will make them happy." That Zucker is the chair of the group evaluating GI for the *DSM-V* seems illustrative of the fact that little of substance has changed in the organization's approach to transgender identity.

Options, Obligations, and Precedent for Change

The *DSM* is a mutable document. Organized populations of people such as women and the gay community have successfully organized and pressured the psychiatric establishment to revise or remove diagnoses that stigmatized and oppressed them (Lev, 2005; Stryker, 2008). Transgender and gender-nonconforming communities have a long legacy of successful self- advocacy and organizing (Stryker, 2008). The sad fact that the double bind of diagnosis means that transgender individuals must have some kind of diagnosis to access appropriate health care, but don't want one that pathologizes them, is a difficult, but by no means insurmountable burden to successful organizing.

One potential action step is to entirely remove the diagnosis from the *DSM* and to instead rely on an amended version of the diagnosis of transsexualism already present in the *International Statistical Classification of Diseases and Related Health Problems* (World Health Organization, 2007) to demonstrate that transgender individuals who require and desire treatment are entitled to it based on a medical (Axis III) condition (Lev, 2005). The diagnosis in the *ICD* has its own set of problems, but removing the patholigization of a psychiatric diagnosis would be powerful. Any mental health issues that the person might experience can then be recorded as such, without undo reference to gender identity, as Axis I or II diagnosis. Depathologizing the identity and treating any actual mental illnesses as they arise (either as a result of oppression and discrimination, or for other reasons) is a viable, achievable, and justice-oriented action step. But it is only a step. The depatholigization of transgender and gender-nonconforming individuals by removal of diagnoses from the *DSM-V* is not sufficient to address gender binary bias and transphobia in the social work and psychiatric communities. There are many advocacy groups active in the fight against oppression of transgender and gender-nonconforming people. I intend to support and augment, and not to occlude, the voices of those within the community who have successfully, consistently, and persistently organized to advocate for the systemic and societal changes they feel they need and deserve. Groups such as the GLOBE project of Make the Road New York, The Transgender Law and Policy Institute, FTM International, The Intersex Society of North America, The International Foundation for Gender Education, and many more.

Social workers, given their ethical obligation to become allies to the transgender and gender-nonconforming communities, should utilize the feedback processes in place to communicate to the authors and committees of the *DSM-V* regarding transgender oppression. Individuals can register on the *DSM-V* website (www.dsm5.org) to send feedback about proposed diagnostic revisions. In addition to continued attention to the *DSM-V* diagnosis, social workers can take responsibility in their professional roles for advancing the rights of these groups who they are ethically obligated to defend.

Social workers can advocate for immediate change in their agencies in the following areas (in no particular order):

- Encourage education about and dialogue around gender identity within agencies and schools. Sharing literature, community-vetted websites, or inviting transgender sensitivity trainers to an agency can be a valuable way to start a dialogue and promote competent, respectful practice (Forshee, 2007).
- Amend agency intake forms, charts, and other material to reflect a gender continuum. The common practice of requiring staff and clients to check a box for "male" or for "female" reinforces the gender binary and ignores transgender and gender nonconforming identities (Davis, 2009). Leaving a blank space for clients to fill in their own gender is an easy and empowering solution.
- Encourage and institutionalize the practice of asking for preferred gender pronouns, and the use of modeling by practitioners to provide safety and affirmation around this practice ("My name is Erin. My preferred gender pronouns are 'she' and 'her' and I also use 'they'"). This allows people to self-identify and reminds all of us that our pronouns are socially constructed and ascribed. Gender-neutral pronouns like "they" used in the singular, "hir," "sie," and "zhe" can be used by those who do not feel "him" or "her" fit them well.
- Change agency bathrooms as necessary to be gender neutral. Male/female-gendered bathrooms can be a source of discomfort, confusion, and violence for transgender and gender-nonconforming individuals. Creating gender neutral or "all-gender" bathrooms cultivates safety for all people, regardless of their gender identity. If there are concerns in the agency, covering or blocking off the urinals and asking all people to use only stalls is a way to increase comfort. Put a sign on the bathroom door saying why gender neutrality and a safe space are important. Ideally, have one or more multistall all gender bathrooms and one or more single-stall bathrooms with locking doors to ensure that everyone can choose a situation in which they feel safe.
- Revise agency and organizational codes of ethics (including that of the APA) to include gender orientation and identity in all sections about protection against discrimination (DeCrescenzo & Mallon, 2000).
- Enforce social work ethics and challenge the gender binary. Use a deconstructive approach (Malpas, 2006) to view gender as socially constructed, relational, and fluid and as an identity we should examine in ourselves, as clinicians, to best serve our clients. Promote the idea (as articulated by Burdge, 2007) that it is ethically incumbent on social workers to deconstruct and challenge the gender binary.

Simultaneous to the fight for the removal of GID and GI from the *DSM-V*, and the implementation of basic transfriendly policies, there is an overarching and ultimate need for a revision of the idea of gender. As Zandvliet (2000) put it, a concept of "queer" that includes a broad range of genders and sexual orientations paves the way for "a creative validation of ambiguity" (p. 179). Embracing ambiguity in this way would enable social workers and other helping professionals to treat their clients with greater respect and would fulfill their ethical obligation to find and fight oppression. Ultimately, it is ethically incumbent on social workers to deconstruct and challenge the gender binary (Burdge, 2007). The ultimate goal should be a revised concept of gender itself.

NOTES

1. There is much beyond the scope of this article to be said about the historical and modern-day fight of the intersex community. Chase (1998) offers an excellent overview of issues such as the pervasive practice of operating on the genitals of infants to ascribe a socially acceptable gender

2. The lowercase 'w' is used here, as recommended by McIntyre (2008), to challenge historically constructed beliefs about control and power and a legacy of oppression that the uppercase "White" can connote.

REFERENCES

American Psychiatric Association. (1980). *Diagnostic and statistical manual of mental disorders* (3rd ed.). Washington, DC: Author.

American Psychiatric Association. (1994). *Diagnostic and statistical manual of mental disorders* (4th ed.). Washington, DC: Author.

American Psychiatric Association. (2009). The principles of medical ethics: with annotations especially applicable to psychiatry (edition revised). *APA Online.* Retrieved from http://www.psych.org/MainMenu/PsychiatricPractice/Ethics/ResourcesStandards.aspx

American Psychiatric Association. (2010a). APA DSM-V Task Force Member Disclosure Report: Kenneth Zucker. *DSM-5 Development (online).* Retrieved from http://www.dsm5.org/MeetUs/Documents/TaskForce/Zucker Disclosure 1-20-10.pdf

American Psychiatric Association. (2010b). Proposed revision 302.85: Gender identity disorder in adolescents or adults. *DSM-5 Development (online).* Retrieved from http://www.dsm5.org/ProposedRevisions/Pages/proposedrevision.aspx?rid=482

Bockting, W. O. (2008). Psychotherapy and the real-life experience: From gender dichotomy to gender diversity. *Sexologies, 17,* 211–222.

Burdge, B. J. (2007). Bending gender, ending gender: Theoretical foundations for social work practice with the transgender community. *Social Work, 52*(3), 243–250.

Burgess, W. C. (2009). Internal and external stress factors associated with the identity development of transgender and gender variant youth. In G. P. Mallon (Ed.), *Social work practice with transgender and gender variant youth* (2nd ed., pp. 53–64). New York, NY: Routledge.

Chase, C. (1998). Hermaphrodites with attitude: Mapping the emergence of intersex political activism. *GLQ: A Journal of Lesbian and Gay Studies, 4*(2), 189–211.

Cosgrove, L. (2005). When labels mask oppression: Implications for teaching psychiatric taxonomy to mental health counselors. *Journal of Mental Health Counseling*, *27*(4), 283–296.

Davis, C. (2009). Introduction to practice with transgender and gender variant youth. In G. P. Mallon (Ed.), *Social work practice with transgender and gender variant youth* (2nd ed., pp. 1–22). New York, NY: Routledge.

DeCrescenzo, T., & Mallon, G. P. (2000). *Serving transgender youth: the role of child welfare systems; proceedings of a colloquium*. Washington, DC: Child Welfare League of America.

Elliot, P. (2001). A psychoanalytic reading of transsexual embodiment. *Studies in Gender and Sexuality*, *2*(4), 295–325.

Forshee, A. S. (2007). Turning off the gender autopilot: Meeting the human service needs of transgender men. *Human Service Education*, *27*(1), 25–38.

Lev, A. I. (2004). *Transgender emergence: Therapeutic guidelines for working with gender- variant people and their families*. New York, NY: Haworth Clinical Practice Press.

Lev, A. I. (2005). Disordering gender identity: gender identity disorder in the *DSM-IV-TR*. *Journal of Psychology & Human Sexuality*, *17*(3/4), 35–68.

Malpas, J. (2006). From otherness to alliance: Transgender couples in therapy. *Journal of GLBT Family Studies*, *2*(3), 183–206.

Mallon, G. P., & DeCrescenzo, T. (2009). Social work practice with transgender and gender variant children and youth. In G. P. Mallon (Ed.), *Social work practice with transgender and gender variant youth* (2nd ed., pp. 65–86). New York, NY: Routledge.

McIntyre, A. (2008). *Participatory action research*. Thousand Oaks, CA: Sage Publications Inc.

Meyer III, W., Bockting, W., Cohen-Kettins, P., Coleman, E., DiCeglie, D., Devor, H., . . . Weeler, C. C. (2001). The Harry Benjamin International Gender Dysphoria Association's Standards of Care for Gender Identity Disorders, Sixth Version. *Journal of Psychology & Human Sexuality*, *13*(1), 1–30.

Meyerowitz, J. (2002). *How sex changed. A history of transsexuality in the United States*. Cambridge, MA: Harvard University Press.

Nagoshi, J. L., & Burzuzy, S. (2010). Transgender theory: Embodying research and practice. *Affilia*, *25*(4), 431–443.

National Association for Social Workers. (2008). *Code of ethics*. Retrieved from http://www.socialworkers.org/pubs/code/code.asp

National Public Radio. (2008). *Q&A: Therapists on gender identity issues in kids*. Retrieved from http://www.npr.org/templates/story/story.php?storyId=90229789

Pearson, E. (2010)." Transgender people need not apply at J. Crew" says Make the Road New York advocacy group. *New York Daily News Online*. Retrieved from http://www.nydailynews.com/news/2010/03/14/2010-03-14_report_says_j_crew_biased_in_its_hiring.html

Pleak, R. (2009). Formation of transgender identities in adolescence. *Journal of Gay & Lesbian Mental Health*, *13*(4), 282–291.

Reich, S. M., Pinkard, T., & Davidson, H. (2008). Including history in the study of psychological and political power. *Journal of Community Psychology*, *36*(2), 173–186.

Spade, D. (2006). Mutilating gender. In S. Strykers & S. Whittle (Eds.), *The transgender studies reader* (pp. 315–334). New York, NY: Routledge.

Smith, G. A. (2010). *Remembering our dead online*. Retrieved from http://www.gender.org/remember/#

Stryker, S. (2008) *Transgender history*. Berkeley, CA: Seal Press.

Stryker, S., & Whittle, S. (2006). *The transgender studies reader*. New York, NY: Routledge.

World Health Organization. (2007). International Statistical Classification of Diseases and Related Health Problems, 10th revision. *World Health Organization Online*. Retrieved From http://www.who.int/classifications/icd/ICD-10_2nd_ed_volume2.pdf

World Professional Association for Transgender Health. (2011). *Standards of care*. Retrieved from http://www.wpath.org/publications_standards.cfm

Yang, L. H., Kleinman, A., Link, B. G., Phelan, J. C., Lee, S., & Good, B. (2007). Culture and stigma: Adding moral experience to stigma theory. *Social Science & Medicine, 64*, 524–535.

York, F. (2008). How should clinicians deal with GID in children? *National Association for Research and Therapy of Homosexuality Online*. Retrieved from http://www.narth com/docs/gid.html

Zandvliet, T. (2000). Transgender issues in therapy. In C. Neal & D. Davies (Eds.), *Issues in therapy with lesbian, gay, bisexual and transgender clients* (pp. 176–190). Buckingham, UK: Open University Press.

Zucker, K. J. (1999). Letter to the Editor: Gender identity disorder in the DSM-IV. *Journal of Sex & Marital Therapy, 25*(1), 59.

Journal of GLBT Family Studies, 9:273–287, 2013

ISSN: 1550-428X print / 1550-4298 online
DOI: 10.1080/1550428X.2013.781909

De Novo Lesbian Families: Legitimizing the Other Mother

BRENDA HAYMAN
University of Western Sydney, New South Wales, Australia

LESLEY WILKES
University of Western Sydney, New South Wales, Australia and Nepean Blue Mountains Local Health District

DEBRA JACKSON
University of Technology Sydney, New South Wales, Australia

ELIZABETH HALCOMB
University of Western Sydney, New South Wales, Australia

This study aimed to explore the experiences of other mothers in de novo *or planned lesbian-led families in Australia to elaborate on one theme: legitimizing our families. Little is known or understood about how lesbians construct mothering within their families. Even less is understood about the experiences of the often marginalized and invisible other mother; that is, the non-birth mother in lesbian families. Fifteen self-identified lesbian couples participated in semistructured, in-depth interviews (as couples) using a story-sharing approach, undertook journaling, and completed a demographic data collection sheet. To be included in the study, participants had to have planned, conceived, birthed, and be raising their children together. A process of constant comparative analysis was used to analyse the data and generate themes and subthemes.*

Legitimizing our families was described by participants in terms of several subthemes, including the following: the role of the other mother in planning, conception, pregnancy, and birth; symbols of family connection; and negotiating health care. Other mothers participating in the study were acutely aware that people in society generally did not perceive them as genuine parents. This finding was consistent with the concepts of Others and Othering. To this end, other mothers sought to legitimize their role within

Address correspondence to Brenda Hayman, School of Nursing & Midwifery, University of Western Sydney, Locked Bag 1797, Penrith NSW 2751, Australia. E-mail: b.hayman@uws.edu.au

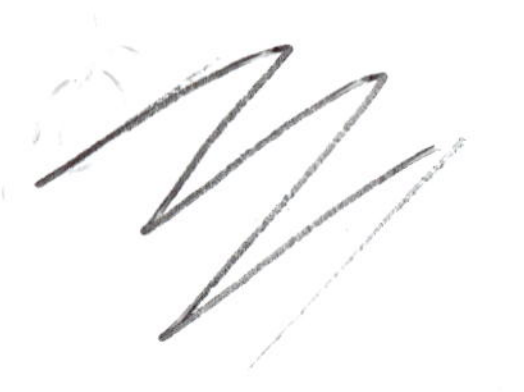

their families by establishing symbols and using ceremonies, names, and other methods of formal recognition to justify their role as an authentic mother and signify legitimate de novo *family connections.*

KEYWORDS *lesbian,* de novo, *lesbian mother, lesbian parenting, other mother*

INTRODUCTION

De novo is a term that was first used by McNair (2004) to describe lesbian-couple families. *De novo* families, and in particular *other* mothers, have encountered invisibility and exclusion and experience fear of homophobia (Lee, Taylor, & Raitt, 2011) because their sexual orientation and family construction were incongruent with social norms and expectations. The term "*other* mother" has been chosen here as there is no universally acceptable alternative term to describe non-birth mothers in *de novo* families. Increasing visibility and acceptance of homosexual orientation has encouraged more gay and lesbian couples to consider parenthood (McManus, Hunter, & Renn, 2006). Subsequently, mothering in the context of a lesbian relationship has also become increasingly prevalent (Goldberg & Perry-Jenkins, 2007). Little is known or understood, however, about how lesbians construct mothering within their families. Even less is understood about the experiences of the often marginalized and invisible *other* mother; that is, the non-birth mother in lesbian families (McNair et al., 2008). *Other* mothers challenge dominant and heteronormative family ideologies that affirm biological relatedness as critical to the establishment of legitimate and genuine families (Ryan & Berkowitz, 2009).

Background

Over the past decade there has been a distinct increase in literature examining the experiences of lesbian mothers (for example, Bergen, Suter, & Daas, 2006; Brown & Perlesz, 2008; Dondorp, De Wert, & Janssens, 2010; Millbank, 2008; Padavic & Butterfield, 2011). This is not surprising, given shifting social attitudes and the growing availability of assistive reproductive technologies that has led to a significant increase in lesbians choosing motherhood (Lee et al., 2011). Much of the literature focuses on homophobia (see, for example, Lindsay et al.,2006), outcomes for children of lesbian mothers (see, for example, McNair, Dempsey, Wise, & Perlesz, 2002, and Bos, van Balen, & van den Boom, 2007), health care (see, for example, Webber, 2010, and Lee et al., 2011), and division of labour (see, for example, Patterson, 1995, Tasker & Golombok, 1998, and Dondorp et al., 2010) in *de novo* families.

Other mothers are positioned as Others—that is, outside what is socially accepted and expected in relation to family construction and in particular mothering—and because of their Other position, are "perceived as different or marginal" (Jackson et al., 2011, p. 103). Marginalization locates the *other* mother outside the normal, or heterosexual, family construct, and relegates her as powerless and vulnerable, essentially excluding her from the position of a legitimate mother in *de novo* families. This concept of "Other" and "Othering" can be used to explore the *other* mothers identified here. While "Other" has been primarily discussed in the literature in relation to gender, more recently, the phenomenon has been used to understand additional marginalized and vulnerable groups—for example, those from minority groups based on race, age and socioeconomic status. It would be reasonable to add sexual orientation to this list of groups who are consigned to the position of "Other." Essentially, "Others" are those who are not ourselves (MacCallum, 2002), and are those who represent difference (Weis, 1995). While it is not the purpose of this paper to problematize the concept of Other and Othering, it is important to recognise the phenomenon in relation to the *other* mothers referred to in this paper as a way of understanding their resistance to social (heterosexual) expectation and simultaneously striving to achieve recognition as a member of the motherhood collective.

Other mothers can be seen as disconcerting the socially accepted and expected binary family structures that consist of one male and one female parent (Padavic & Butterfield, 2011). The unsettling of the binary gender roles by *de novo* families can cause social discomfort, which could lead to attitudes and behaviors that render *other* mothers invisible, vulnerable, and excluded, particularly in social and health care settings (Dalton & Bielby, 2000; Brown & Perlesz, 2008; Markus, Weingarten, Duplessi, & Jones, 2010; Gartrell et al., 1999). The *other* mother is legally disenfranchised and this can lead to her feeling "jealous, devalued, excluded and confused" (Morrow, 2001, p. 64) and socially invisible (Dalton & Bielby, 2000). *Other* mothers have reported exclusion and neglect by health care providers (Stevens, 1995; Dalton & Bielby, 2000) and some *other* mothers have found themselves essentially excluded during health care interactions (Wilton & Kaufmann, 2001).

Millbank (2008) identified the importance of validating the *other* mother in *de novo* families in a societal environment where biological motherhood is privileged over social motherhood (Almack, 2005). A social mother is not a biological mother but a mother because of the relationship she has with a child's biological parent (Bos, van Balen, & van den Boom, 2004; Braeways, Ponjaert, Van Hall, & Golombok, 1997) and particularly because of the mothering relationship she has with the biological children of her partner (Brown & Perlesz, 2007). Ehrensaft (2008) described the balancing act that is sometimes experienced by the *other* mother, who may struggle with the debate of genetic ties versus legitimacy of her role as mother, and adds that "blood ties trump social bonds" (p. 173). *Other* mothers must strive to develop a social mothering relationship with their child in the absence of a biological bond and genuine role models.

While *other* mothers experience a destabilized parental position, they are compelled to justify their motherhood more so than heterosexual fathers are required to justify their fatherhood (Bos, 2004). *Other* mothers may not have had lesbian mother role models from which to construct their social mothering role (Vanfraussen, Ponjaert-Kristoffersen, & Braeways, 2003) and they are required to continually "justify their family structure" (Padavic & Butterfield, 2011, p. 17). As revealed in the literature, the invisibility of the *other* mother is a challenge as she struggles to legitimize her role as an authentic mother in a hetero-centric society.

Research Aim

This article explores one of the four themes generated during a study that examined the experiences of lesbian mothers in Australia. The theme that is the focus of this article pertains specifically to the experiences of the *other* mother in *de novo* families and is titled Legitimizing Our Families. Exploration of the other themes will be published elsewhere, and will include, for example, lesbians accessing health care and the journey to motherhood for lesbian couples.

METHOD

Data were collected in three ways; demographic data sheet, in-depth semistructured couple interviews, and journaling (Hayman, Wilkes, & Jackson, 2012). Interviews were the primary source of data and a story-sharing approach was employed (Hayman, Wilkes, Jackson, & Halcomb, 2012). The interviews were constructed around a framework that has, embedded within it, feminist values such as receptivity, trust, listening, subjectivity, cooperation, collaboration, and connection (Kvale, 1996). During the interviews, participants were asked to describe their mothering stories and were encouraged to share in detail their experiences. A list of questions was developed to guide the interviews; however, the couples tended to share their story chronologically once the interview began. The list was then used primarily at the end of each interview, by the interviewer, to double check that each topic had been sufficiently addressed.

Participants

A convenience sample of 15 self-identified lesbian couples who had planned, conceived, birthed, and were raising their children together was recruited through women's health care services, lesbian publications, and snowballing. Participants were between ages 28 and 58 years (mean age 39.8 years) and 13 couples resided in urban areas. Couples came from New South Wales (N = 9), Victoria (N = 4), South Australia (N = 1), and Canberra (N =

1). Most participants identified as Australian ($N = 11$), with one Italian-Australian, one Dutch, one Filipino, and one Lebanese-Australian. They had been in their relationship for between 3 and 18 years (mean 9.6 years) and had been cohabitating for between 2.5 and 17 years (mean 9.0 years). Collectively the couples had achieved 21 term pregnancies, producing 23 children. The 11 boys and 12 girls included three sets of non-identical twins. The children's ages ranged from 2 months to 10 years (mean age 2.6 years). Each couple's (combined) annual income ranged from $AU23, 000 to $AU400, 000 (mean income $AU118, 000).

Data Collection

Semistructured, in-depth interviews were conducted with participating couples between March 2010 and August 2010. The interviews were either audio-recorded ($N = 13$) or captured as text via an online messaging program (MSN instant messenger) ($N = 2$). Seven interviews were undertaken face-to-face ($N = 7$), with others undertaken via an Internet web camera program (Skype) ($N = 5$), instant messaging ($N = 2$), or via telephone ($N = 1$). The interviews lasted between 45 minutes and 2 hours (mean 81.5 minutes).

At the time of interview the demographic data sheet also was completed by each participant. This sheet collected information about the participant's age, general geographic location, length of time in her current relationship, duration of cohabitation, employment and income, religion/spirituality, and number, ages, and gender of children.

Couples also commenced a diary, or journal entry system, after their joint interview and journaling continued for up to one month subsequently. Journaling has been described as a valid data collection method that can document specific experiences and the associated feelings (Hayman, Wilkes, & Jackson, 2012). Journaling was undertaken online via a popular social networking website (Facebook) where closed and secure pages were generated for individual participants. All but one couple had regular Internet access, so that couple engaged in an e-mail journal with the principal researcher. The frequency of journal entries varied and contributions included text, music, lyrics, photos, and drawings.

Ethical Considerations

All potential participants were provided with an information sheet that detailed the study and a consent form. All participants provided written consent prior to data collection. Ethics approval was gained from the University of Western Sydney Human Ethics Research Committee. Confidentiality has been maintained with the use of pseudonyms.

Data Analysis

Data were analyzed and coded using a process of constant comparative analysis of the interview and journal data to identify themes in the participants' stories (Thorne, 2000). To ensure rigor, a reflexive approach promoted through reflection, journaling, and discussion within the team facilitated the raising of consciousness in relation to the researchers' beliefs, biases, and patterns of thinking and identified how they could influence interpretation of the data. An audit trail was established to provide a clear pathway leading from the data to the themes.

FINDINGS

Role of the *Other* Mother in Planning, Conception, Pregnancy, and Birth

Planning

Prior to conception, most couples held lengthy discussions about who would conceive or, if both women hoped to conceive, which one would attempt pregnancy first. Jane confirmed this, stating: "Children is [sic] always something that I wanted or intended to have. So it was a conversation that we had very early on." Decisions were negotiated based on age, health, and roles within the family. Lilly stated: ". . . the only reason why I thought I'd be the best one is because of my age," and Jenny added, "[her partner] had expressed more of a desire to carry the child. I said I would if she couldn't but I didn't have that strong desire to actually carry the child." Several couples identified as butch-femme dyads, and for those couples it was essentially unthinkable that the self-identified butch woman of the dyad would prefer to be pregnant.

Extensive dialogue also reportedly transpired between the women and their friends, potential sperm donors, and family about ovulation (patterns/cycles), sperm donor options (known or unknown), methods of conception, and pregnancy. These conversations occurred over a period of years for several of the couples, and involved substantial research, primarily via the Internet. Fran stated:

> *We talked a lot in the early stages about the pros and cons of what would it mean to have a child in a same-sex relationship and what that would mean for a child, like would it be a fair thing to do from the child's point of view, how that might impact having two mothers and not the usual nuclear family of a mother and father, so we got literature.*

Most couples also sought out other lesbian mothers to discuss their experiences.

One of the focal points of pre-pregnancy discussion was around what constituted a "suitable" sperm donor. Donor considerations included willingness for health screening, contact/role with prospective children, availability during ovulation, age, ethnicity, physical characteristics, intellect, and family health history. These were all identified as equally important issues when considering a donor. Six couples opted for a donor who had similar physical characteristics to the *other* mother in an attempt to produce a physical likeness between her and the child. Participants expressed that society often (from birth) made judgments about the child based on their physical characteristics. Optimizing the similarity of physical characteristics between the child and the *other* mother was deemed to enhance perceived familial connection and ties. This is also evidence of the couples strategically promoting connectedness and kinship between the child and the *other* mother.

A further consideration around sperm donation was whether to opt for known versus anonymous donation. The main concern in choosing a known sperm donor was that he might be able to lay claim to the child at a later date, could want to influence parenting choices and decisions, or could want a relationship with the child that was unacceptable to the mothers. This concern was juxtaposed with the perceived importance of the child wanting or needing to have knowledge of the sperm donor at some point. Some of the *other* mother participants felt very strongly about not choosing a known donor who could potentially intrude on their parental role; nevertheless most participants ($N = 14$, 82.3%) opted for a known donor. The rationale for choosing a known donor was described by Brooklyn in the following way: "We had to have a known donor for the child's sake. I believe he now has a choice. Just knowing where he really comes from and having that option available if he [their son] wants it." Meanwhile, Ellie stated, "We only wanted a registered donor, so that when the kids turn 18, they are able to contact him."

Conception

De novo families engaged in various strategies to achieve a pregnancy. Participants either used Assistive Reproductive Technology (ART) via fertility clinics ($N = 9$) or Alternate Insemination (AI) at home ($N = 8$). Several couples tried both AI and ART. For those who used ART, the fertility clinic arranged sperm collection and storage, as well as providing pre-conception counseling and information/education sessions, preparation for conception (for example, stimulating ovulation), insemination, as well as follow-up pregnancy testing and support. In contrast, participants described AI as a process where sperm collection and storage was negotiated privately, collected at ovulation time, and used soon after at home to inseminate the woman. For all couples choosing AI, the prospective birth mothers were inseminated by their partners.

The choice of conception method was either based on personal choice or was necessitated because of limitations like health concerns, age, availability of donor sperm, cost, and legal restrictions/reservations. Couples choosing to conceive via AI generally had no known medical (particularly gynecological) conditions that could complicate conception, pregnancy, and/or delivery, were comfortable with a known donor, had access to the donor sperm, or could not afford ART. Two couples articulated that they used AI because ART was cost prohibitive. Whatever method of conception, it was important to both mothers that the *other* mother was involved as much as possible in the process.

The couples choosing ART created a shared experience by attending appointments together. The *other* mothers collectively agreed that this was a special time that they wanted to share. The importance of both women being involved in ART conception was expressed by Kristie, who stated, "We were together, so it was so nice. It felt kind of like a joint thing we were doing" and also by Jessica, who stated, "It was nice to have someone to share it [insemination] with." The shared experience facilitated a sense of involvement for the *other* mother that aimed to fortify her parental role. For most couples, the *other* mother was present during intrauterine insemination (IUI) or embryo transfer. However, some ($N = 2$) *other* mothers were excluded from procedures by clinic staff because they were not male partners. Exclusion was perceived by the *other* mothers to be based on homophobic values. Homophobia experienced by participants is addressed in more detail later.

The role of the *other* mother in the process of AI was determined, by all women, to be an important one in legitimizing the *other* mother's role. In all cases the *other* mothers collected sperm and performed the inseminations. Lyn described her involvement, saying, " . . . I set up the room with candles and. . . with pillows. I did it with a syringe given to us by Jamie's doctor. And then we did the deed and laughed a lot. And then Jamie lied [sic] there for a while with her legs in the air."

Pregnancy

Once a pregnancy was achieved, the *other* mother participants expressed a sense of connectedness with their pregnant partners. Amanda said, "We were close. I think I was supportive. We both went through it together." The *other* mothers watched over their pregnant partner; made sure she ate and drank adequately, was comfortable, and rested sufficiently. The *other* mothers described taking on extra household chores during the pregnancy to reduce workload and stress for the pregnant partner. Eden stated, "I went into looking-after mode, so did a bit more of the cooking and stuff around the house but I certainly didn't mind doing that. I felt it was my contribution being supportive." Both women engaged in the preparation stage prior to the birth. Together they purchased clothing, furniture, and baby equipment.

Birth

It was important to both partners that the *other* mother was present at the birth. All birth mothers gave birth in a hospital. Ten mothers had a vaginal delivery and eight delivered their babies by cesarean section, four of which were elective cesareans. All but two partners were present for the delivery. One *other* mother (Abbie) missed the delivery because her partner went into labour rapidly and delivered much quicker than anticipated. Abbie later said, "We're still really disappointed, and it was seven months ago." Another couple was separated during the delivery because the maternal grandmother (mother of the birth mother, who did not approve of her daughter's same-sex relationship) insisted on being present for the cesarean delivery. The *other* mother in this dyad respectfully but regrettably allowed her partner's mother to be present. Ellie was preparing for her cesarean delivery and had been separated from her partner during her epidural procedure. At this time she expressed anxiety about her partner missing the delivery and wondered if the staff would not try too hard to ensure Phoebe was there because they are "*only* a lesbian couple." She said, "I was a bit anxious in all of that, because there's no dad, do they just go, oh well stuff it." Phoebe expressed that because they were a lesbian couple, the staff might not attribute the same importance to both parents being present during the delivery as they would to a heterosexual couple, in which a "dad" was available.

Participating in the labor and delivery was very important to the *other* mothers as it sought to justify their position as a legitimate parent. In relation to cutting the umbilical cord, Ellie said, "traditionally there is this whole thing that that's what the other parent does, and I was the other parent, so I wanted to do that." Lyn (birth mother) stated that she was "very happy when she saw Jamie there, she was right with me. She was scrubbed up. She was just on the other side of the door when he was getting born." Some participants recounted that sharing in the birth of their child connected them in a new way and deepened their union. The *other* mothers expressed "joy" and "amazement" with the birth of their child. Brooklyn said that when she saw her son for the first time she felt "instant love." Holly said, "He was just beautiful, and perfect and ours."

Symbols of Family Connection

While diverse families are becoming more prevalent and socially acceptable, acknowledgement of the legitimacy of *de novo* families was a challenge that participants expressed repeatedly. Conventional heterosexual-couple families benefit from assumed and socially accepted family connections while *de novo* families have to actively construct and then work to preserve those family connections. This burden is intensified for the *other* mother in *de novo* families, as she is often not seen by society, or even her own family, as a legitimate mother. To facilitate legitimacy, participants established symbols using ceremonies, names, and methods of formal recognition to affirm the *other* mother as an authentic mother and symbolise legitimate *de novo* family connections.

Ceremonies

The lesbian couples were precluded from many formal ceremonies such as engagement and marriage ceremonies that legitimize their relationship. As *de novo* families, the women participated in ceremonies such as naming days for their children and commitment ceremonies in an attempt to symbolize their relationship and family.

Names

Choosing surnames for children and their *other* mothers was another significant strategy that *de novo* families used to justify their authenticity as a family. Most participants ($N = 10$) gave their child(ren) the surname of the *other* mother. Other participants opted for a double-barrelled surname consisting of both mothers' surnames. One couple used the *other* mother's surname as the child's middle name. Choosing names that connected the *other* mother and the child represented a public and tangible connection and commitment to the relationship between the *two*. Phoebe said that it was important for her children to have her partner's surname so that "they're always attached to her in a symbolic way." Four participants had taken on their partner's surname prior to having children and the children were subsequently given the same surname. Beth's family all share the same surname. She stated, "that way she is connected to both of us." Mae (*other* mother) was concerned about how she would create ties to her children. She stated, "I started to feel like I would have no connection with them and like there's nothing of me that's part of them, and I said to her really, the only thing I can think of to give them that's mine, is my surname." So Mae and Lilly's babies were given Mae's surname.

Couples also carefully considered what the child(ren) should call their *other* mother. The name mum or mummy was essentially assigned to the birth mother and there was a desire to not cause confusion. Therefore, names like mama, ma, daddy, first names, and non-English words for mummy/daddy (for example, "tatay," which is Tagalog for daddy and "mutti," which is German for mummy) were used. The choice of the word "daddy," or its alternative in another language, represents conformation to heterosexual ideals and norms. Though potentially problematic because "daddy" is used traditionally to represent a biologically male parent, the use of the word "daddy" in the *de novo* context clearly signifies a parental role that allows differentiation of two female parents. Others chose "mummy/mum" for the birth mother and "mama" for the *other* mother. Debbie and Gemma encouraged their children to use their first names to differentiate each mother. These names gave meaning and value to the *other* mother and also provided differentiation between the two mothers.

Methods of Formal Recognition

In recent years, Australian *de novo* families have benefited from changes to the laws allowing both birth and non-birth mothers' names to appear on the child's birth certificate. In 2008, the Miscellaneous Acts Amendment (Same Sex Relationships) Act 2008 (NSW) was established. The act specified that children born through ART to lesbian couples will have two legally recognized mothers. Given the retrospective nature of the act, participants were also able to have birth certificates amended (for children born prior to 2008) to reflect both mothers as legal parents. This was important to ensure both the birth mother and *other* mother had equal legal parenting rights to their children. Ellie (*other* mother) stated, "symbolically, it [having both mothers' names] was important to me. It is public recognition that I am as much the parent as Phoebe." This could be important if one mother (in particular the birth mother) dies or becomes significantly incapacitated, that the *other* mother is recognized as a mother and the legal guardian of her child(ren). Formal recognition is particularly important also in relation to a non-birth mother's interface with school and health care providers for her child(ren).

Negotiating Health Care

When interacting with health services, participant *other* mothers reported experiencing homophobia and feeling stigmatised. The reality of negative societal attitudes caused participants to think and behave in a self-protective manner. Strategies to avoid homophobia were often a daily consideration. Some *other* mothers experienced homophobia in the form of exclusion and refusal of services. One couple described being refused fertility assistance because they were deemed to be "socially infertile" and did not have a "genuine" fertility problem. Other participants reported being excluded from fertility clinic procedures because they were not male. Another was excluded from the neonatal intensive care unit because she was "not the real mother." The *other* mothers reported finding this frustrating and upsetting. One couple recounted being told they should try another hospital when booking in for antenatal care because the religious ethos of that private hospital did not condone homosexuality.

Heterosexual assumptions about the women's relationships, and identifying their partnerships as mother/daughter, niece/aunty, friends or sisters in health care environments, were considered unacceptable by participants. Jenny and Blair described a situation where hospital staff assumed they were sisters because they had the same surname. Despite regularly correcting the staff, several participants identified that health care providers would persist with calling the *other* mother anything but a partner; much less the child's *other* mother. One couple described being shown around the labour and delivery ward of a hospital where they were planning to have their baby when the midwife asked, "Where's the father?" The women found this question offensive because, again, it assumed heterosexual orientation. Given the assumption of heterosexual orientation, the *other* mother was essentially disqualified and excluded from being a legitimate partner and parent.

Heterosexism ostracizes the *other* mother and reduces her role from that of a mother to the equivalent of someone outside the immediate family. It minimizes her position in the *de novo* family and excludes her from important events that heterosexual couples expect without question. Participants identified that the joy and thrill of the new baby was sometimes obscured by the *other* mother's experience of heterosexism. In all its forms, heterosexism creates barriers to effective health care for *de novo* families.

DISCUSSION

Essentially, *other* mothers participating in the study revealed that they felt a constant need to justify their position as a legitimate parent. Together with their partners, they made decisions around conception, pregnancy, and birth that promoted connectedness and familial ties. In addition, they described experiences—in particular when interfacing with health care services—that sought to dismiss societal judgment that the *other* mother is extraneous to her family and simultaneously resist being relegated to the vulnerable outsider or marginalized Other. *Other* mothers, supported resolutely by their partners, implemented conscious choices to position themselves as a genuine part of their families with legitimate parental ties with their children.

Some of the decisions participants made were done so deliberately with the express purpose of protecting and/or enhancing the parental position of the *other* mother and consequently resisting their positioning as the marginalized Other. Choosing a known or unknown sperm donor, actively seeking out a donor who had similar physical characteristics to the *other* mother, including the *other* mother as much as possible in the planning, conception, pregnancy, and birth of her child, choosing particular names (also identified by Almack, 2005) , engaging in ceremonies, and using methods of formal recognition where available were all decisions made by the couples to fortify the parental position of the *other* mother and were consistent with the findings of Bergen and colleagues (2006). In many ways, these decisions may have taken part in attempting to legitimize their families to the outside world.

Study Limitations

The main limitation of this study is the small sample size. However, the depth of data compensated for the small sample size. This limitation was anticipated by the researchers, and subsequently deliberate and careful decisions were made by the research team about when to cease data collection. Data collection was only considered complete when we were certain that data saturation had been achieved. The retrospective nature of stories means there is possibility the content or context of the story may have changed over time for the storyteller. This limitation is outweighed by the richness of the stories that allow comparison of similarities and differences across a number of participants and provide detailed description of the phenomenon under investigation.

CONCLUSION

The findings of this study have significant implications for health care providers. To achieve acceptable and inclusive health services, two strategies are required: examination of the current heteronormative social environments, and most significantly education for all service providers. Heteronormativity, for example assumed heterosexuality, limits the way health care providers are able to interact with clients and can create barriers between lesbian women and health care providers. Education for health care providers about issues specific to lesbian health care (similar to those identified by McNair et al., 2008) and methods of providing inclusive services would potentially increase the quality of health care received by lesbian women. Raising awareness of the concept of Otherness and how this phenomenon affects the way health care is delivered is another important consideration.

Like Short (2007), we found that most of the *other* mothers participating in the study described feeling anger at having to constantly justify their parental position but had also accepted it as part of their path to parenthood in the current social environment. Participants expressed hope that in the future, society's attitudes would change to become more inclusive and tolerant of diverse family structures.

REFERENCES

Almack, K. (2005). What's in a name? The significance of the choice of surnames given to children born within lesbian-parent families. *Sexualities*, *8*(2), 239–254.

Bergen, K. B., Suter, E. A., & Daas, K. L. (2006). About as solid as a fish net: Symbolic construction of a legitimate parental identity for nonbiological lesbian mothers. *Journal of Family Communication*, *6*(3), 201–220.

Bos, H. (2004). *Parenting in planned lesbian families*. Amsterdam, The Netherlands: University of Amsterdam.

Bos, H., van Balen, F., & van den Boom, D. C. (2004). Experience of parenthood, couple relationship, social support and child rearing goals in planned lesbian mother families. *Journal of Child Psychology and Psychiatry*, *45*, 755–764.

Bos, H. M. W., van Balen, F., & van den Boom, D. C. (2007). Child adjustment and parenting in planned lesbian-parent families. *American Journal of Orthopsychiatry*, *77*(1), 38–48.

Braeways, A., Ponjaert, I., Van Hall, E. V., & Golombok, S. (1997). Donor insemination: Child development and family functioning in lesbian mother families. *Human Reproduction*, *12*, 1349–1359.

Brown, R., & Perlesz, A. (2007). Not the "other" mother: How language constructs lesbian co-parenting relationships. *Journal of GLBT Family Studies*, *3*, 267–308.

Brown, R., & Perlesz, A. (2008). In search of a name for lesbians who mother their non-biological children. *Journal of GLBT Studies*, *4*(4), 453–467.

Dalton, S. E., & Bielby, D. D. (2000). "That's our kind of constellation": Lesbian mothers negotiate institutionalized understandings of gender within the family. *Gender and Society*, *14*(1), 36–61.

Dondorp, W. J., De Wert, G. M., & Janssens, P. M. W. (2010). Shared lesbian motherhood a challenge of established concepts and frameworks. *Human Reproduction*, *25*(4), 812–814.

Ehrensaft, D. (2008). Just Molly and me, and donor makes three: Lesbian motherhood in the age of assisted reproductive technology. *Journal of Lesbian Studies*, *12*(2–3), 161–178.

Gartrell, N., Banks, A., Hamilton, J., Reed, N., Bishop, H., & Rodas, C. (1999). The national lesbian family study: 2. Interviews with mothers of toddlers. *Journal of Orthopsychiatry*, *69*, 362–369.

Goldberg, A. E., & Perry-Jenkins, M. (2007). The division of labor and perceptions of parental roles: Lesbian couples across the transition to parenthood. *Journal of Social and Personal Relationships*, *24*(2), 297–318.

Hayman, B., Wilkes, L., & Jackson, D. (2012). Journaling: Identification of challenges and reflection on strategies. *Nurse Researcher*, *19*(3), 27–31.

Hayman, B., Wilkes, L., Jackson, D., & Halcomb, E. (2012). Exchange and equality during data collection: Relationships through story sharing with lesbian mothers. *Nurse Researcher*, *19*(4), 6–10.

Jackson, D., Hutchinson, M., Everett, B., Mannix, J., Peters, K., Weaver, R., & Salamonson, Y. (2011). Struggling for legitimacy: Nursing students' stories of organisational aggression, resilience and resistance. *Nursing Inquiry*, *18*(2), 102–110.

Kvale, S. (1996). *Interviews: An introduction to qualitative research interviewing*. London, England: Sage.

Lee, E., Taylor, J., & Raitt, F. (2011). "It's not me, it's them": How lesbian women make sense of negative experiences of maternity care: A hermeneutic study. *Journal of Advanced Nursing*, *67*(5), 982–990.

Lindsay, J., Perlesz, A., Brown, R., McNair, R., de Vaus, D., & Pitts, M. (2006). Stigma or respect: Lesbian parented families negotiating school settings. *Sociology, 40*(6), 1059–1077.

MacCallum, E. J. (2002). Othering and psychiatric nursing. *Journal of Psychiatric and Mental Health Nursing, 9*, 87–94.

Markus, E., Weingarten, A., Duplessi, Y., & Jones, J. (2010). Lesbian couples seeking pregnancy with donor insemination. *Journal of Midwifery and Women's Health, 55*(2), 124–132.

McManus, A. J., Hunter, L. P., & Renn, H. (2006). Lesbian experiences and needs during childbirth: Guidance for healthcare providers. *Journal of Obstetric, Gynacologic and Neonatal Nursing, 35*(1), 13–23.

McNair, R. P. (2004). *Outcomes for the children born of ART in a diverse range of families.* (Occasional paper). Melbourne, Australia: Victorian Law Reform Commission.

McNair, R., Brown, R., Perlesz, A., Lindsay, J., De Vaus, D., & Pitts, M. (2008). Lesbian parents negotiating the healthcare system in Australia. *Health Care for Women International, 29*, 91–114.

McNair, R. P., Dempsey, D., Wise, S., & Perlesz, A. (2002). Lesbian parenting: Issues, strengths and challenges. *Family Matters, 63*, 40–49.

Millbank, J. (2008). Unlikely fissures and uneasy resonances: Lesbian co-mothers, surrogate parenthood and fathers' rights. *Feminist Legal Studies, 16*, 141–167.

Morrow, C. (2001). Narrating maternity: Authorizing the "other" mother in lesbian family stories. *Journal of Lesbian Studies, 5*(4), 3–90.

Padavic, I., & Butterfield, J. (2011). Mothers, father and "mathers": Negotiating a lesbian co-parental identity. *Gender and Society, 25*(2), 176–196.

Patterson, C. J. (1995). Families of the lesbian baby boom: Parents' division of labor and children's adjustment. *Developmental Psychology, 31*(1), 115–125.

Ryan, M., & Berkowitz, D. (2009). Constructing gay and lesbian parent families "beyond the closet." *Qualitative Sociology, 32*, 153–172.

Short, L. (2007). Lesbian mothers living well in the context of heterosexism and discrimination: Resources, strategies and legislative change. *Feminism Psychology, 17*, 57–74.

Stevens, P. (1995). Structural and interpersonal impact of heterosexual assumptions on lesbian health care clients. *Nursing Research, 44*, 25–30.

Tasker, F., & Golombok, S. (1998). The role of co-mothers in planned lesbian-led families. *Journal of Lesbian Studies, 2*(4), 49–68.

Thorne, S. (2000). Data analysis in qualitative research. *Evidence Based Nursing, 3*, 68–70. doi: 10.1136/ebn.3.3.68

Vanfraussen, K., Ponjaert-Kristoffersen, I., & Braeways, A. (2003). Family functioning in lesbian families created by donor insemination. *American Journal of Orthopsychiatry, 73*, 78–90.

Webber, S. (2010). Nursing care of families with parents who are lesbian, gay, bisexual or transgender. *Journal of Child and Adolescent Psychiatric Nursing, 23*(1), 11–16.

Weis, L. (1995). Identity formation and the process of "othering": Unravelling sexual threads. *Educational Foundations, 9*(1), 17–33.

Wilton, T., & Kaufmann, T. (2001). Lesbian mothers' experiences of maternity care in the UK. *Midwifery, 17*, 203–211.

Journal of GLBT Family Studies, 9:152–178, 2013

ISSN: 1550-428X print / 1550-4298 online
DOI: 10.1080/1550428X.2013.765262

Meaning Matters: Framing Trans Identity in the Context of Family Relationships

KRISTEN NORWOOD
Saint Louis University, St. Louis, Missouri, USA

Disclosure of trans identities has been shown to bring about change in family relationships, yet little is known about how trans identities function as family stressors. The meanings we make for family stressors determine how we experience them and thus are consequential to our well-being (Boss, 1992) as well as to relational outcomes. In this study, I conducted telephone interviews with 37 family members of someone who is trans-identified. Using qualitative, dialogic analysis, I examined the meanings they assigned to trans identity, the complex processes by which they arrived at those meanings, and how meanings fostered or hindered support for their trans relative or partner. Participants constructed trans identity as a medical condition, a natural nuance of gender identity, or a lifestyle choice in light of their allegiance to their trans-identified family members, the possibility of criticism from outsiders, and their own global meaning systems.

KEYWORDS *trans identity, meaning, family stressor, dialogism, family relationships*

INTRODUCTION

Trans identities are not only significant for trans-identified persons, but also for their families. After disclosure or discovery of trans identity, family members are likely to ask, "What does this mean?," "How did this happen?," and "Why is this happening?" (Zamboni, 2006, p. 175). Whether the bonds of family are tested, broken, or made stronger in response to trans identity

The author wishes to thank the study participants who shared their stories and made this research possible.

Address correspondence to Kristen Norwood, Office of Academic Affairs, Saint Louis University, 3733 West Pine Mall, Xavier Hall Rm 313, St. Louis, MO 63103, USA. E-mail: knorwoo1@slu.edu may hinge on the answers at which family members arrive (McCubbin & McCubbin, 1987). The meanings family members construct for family stressors, particularly those involving social stigma, are important for their emotional well-being and their acceptance of the stigmatized member (Lazarus & Folkman, 1984).

Meaning-making is socially situated; thus family members must draw upon cultural discourses already circulating (Bakhtin, 1979/1986) to make sense of their relative's or partner's identity. Denny (2004) argues there are two competing meanings in U.S. culture surrounding trans identity: a medicalized model, which characterizes it as a disorder, and a cultural model, which characterizes such identities as natural nuances that are considered as illegitimate against socially constructed binaries. Bound up in these discourses are issues of stigma and responsibility, which certainly will figure into family members' meanings and, consequently, relational outcomes.

In this article, I have employed some of Bakhtin's central concepts to understand the complicated endeavor of constructing meaning for trans identity in the family context. Particularly, I draw upon his concept of authoring, which is the act of making meaning for experiences through speech communication (Bakhtin, 1990), as well as three concepts that illustrate the complexity of such authoring: heteroglossia, or the presence of multiple and competing discourses surrounding a given object of meaning (Bakhtin, 1975/1981), addressivity, or the idea that an author must respond to existing and future viewpoints as he or she constructs meaning (Bakhtin, 1979/1986), and, finally, answerability, or the idea that an author is accountable for the meanings he or she constructs (Bakhtin, 1990). Using these concepts to analyze data from family members of trans-identified persons, I argue that the process of constructing meaning for trans identity in the context of family relationships is a complex, dialogic endeavor wherein individuals must contend with competing discourses, multiple audiences, and various kinds of responsibility for the meanings they construct. Ultimately, through this process, family members construct meanings that facilitate or hinder their acceptance and support of the trans-identified relative, partner, or spouse.

LITERATURE REVIEW

There are many gender-variant identities and terms to describe them. In this study I have focused on the meanings assigned to trans identity by family members of those who identify as transsexual, transgender, and gender queer. Therefore I use the terms *trans-identified* and *trans* in an attempt to be inclusive. Research shows that trans identities are experienced as family stressors (Hines, 2006; Zamboni, 2006) or "life events or occurrences of sufficient magnitude to bring about change in the family system" (McCubbin et al., 1980, p. 857). Some have suggested that transitions happen not only for trans persons (if they pursue them), but also for their families, in terms of emotions and relational dynamics (Connolly, 2006).

Zamboni (2006) has said that trans identity "Touches on fundamental aspects of identity with regard to gender and sexuality—and challenges one's notion of these concepts" (p. 175). As he further elaborated:

> Family members do not necessarily know what it means to be transgendered and what implications it has.... Families may be aware of the stigma attached to being transgender and have their own biases toward transgenderism, both of which can drive their emotional responses. (p. 175)

The conclusions family members reach about the nature and cause of trans identity are thoroughly significant because the meanings made for stressors determine their effects (Boss, 1992; Lazarus & Folkman, 1984; Park & Folkman, 1997). Answering the question of why a stressor exists is important because constructing a reasonable explanation helps family members adjust to a situation that may be otherwise overly stressful (Kawanishi, 2005).

Meanings of Family Stressors Involving Stigma

In the case of family stressors that involve social stigma, causal attributions are particularly important (Lazarus & Folkman, 1984). Family members often are more accepting of stigmatizing stressors if they are reasoned to be beyond the individual's control (Altemeyer, 2001; Hewitt & Moore, 2002). For example, families contending with mental illness may make sense of it as caused by family dysfunction, a genetic disorder, or a chemical imbalance. These varied explanations may lessen or exacerbate stigma attached to mental illness, as well as personal feelings of guilt or blaming of others (Kawanishi, 2005). In the case of schizophrenia, Henrichsen and Lieberman (1999) found that for family members, causal attributions played the largest role in the prediction of amount of burden the stressor induced. When family members attributed a relative's condition to moral causes or psychological failings, they had poorer emotional adjustment and were more likely to reject the schizophrenic member. Similar results have emerged in research concerning meanings constructed for the causes of alcoholism (Furnham & Lowick, 1984), attention-deficit/hyperactivity disorder (ADHD) (Collett & Gimple, 2004), HIV/AIDS (Becares & Turner, 2004), and homosexuality (Altemeyer, 2001).

Research on homosexuality is most informative for the present study, as gay and lesbian identities deviate from heteronormative life scripts, which trans identities also transgress. Acceptance and supportive attitudes have been found to correspond to the belief that homosexuality is not a choice, but is beyond the individual's control (Armesto & Weisman, 2001; Hewitt &

Moore, 2002). Although such beliefs may foster positive effects for families with a gay, lesbian, or bisexual member, adopting these beliefs may be easier said than done. Our global meaning systems serve as the foundation for the ways we make sense of events (Park & Folkman, 1997); therefore a particular stressor may be easily worked into existing beliefs (Davis, Nolen-Hoeksema, & Larson, 1998) or may challenge them in a way that makes familial relationships problematic (Willoughby, Doty, & Malik, 2008). For example, parents who are highly religious, or who have strong traditional family values, have been found to reject their gay and lesbian children at times (Newman & Muzzonigro, 1993).

In the case of gay, lesbian, and bi- sexualities, issues of controllability are inscribed through two cultural discourses, one that holds there is a genetic or otherwise inborn cause of homosexuality (aka "the gay gene"; Kuo, 2006) and a competing discourse that holds sexuality is culturally situated, fluid, and emergent—a preference as opposed to an orientation (DeLamater & Hude, 1998). Similarly, there are two predominant, competing cultural discourses surrounding trans identity that likely serve as resources for family members as they construct meanings.

Cultural Discourses Surrounding Trans Identities

Denny (2004) outlines two chief discourses surrounding trans identities in Western cultures, a medical model and a social constructionist model, discourses of *transsexualism* and *transgenderism*, respectively. The former is the longest-enduring and most dominant understanding of trans identity in medical and scholarly communities (Denny, 2004), as well as the general public (Sloop, 2004). The transsexual model has delineated trans people as persons who feel they are "trapped in the wrong body" and seek to transition from one category to the other, often via surgeries and hormone treatments, to relieve the conflict between the mind and body (Denny, 2004, p. 26). The American Psychiatric Association has recognized this as a psychological syndrome, categorizing it as Gender Identity Disorder in the current but soon-to-be-updated *Diagnostic and Statistical Manual of Mental Disorders* (*DSM*-IV; American Psychiatric Association [APA], 1994). Historically, various causes for the disorder have been offered, from explanations of sexual perversion (Wiedeman, 1953), to repressed homosexuality (Socarides, 1969), to differences in the brain (Zhou, Hofman, Gooren, & Swaab, 1995).

In contrast, under the transgender model (2004), trans identities are not considered disordered, but simply a matter of human variability in gender identity. This view holds that trans individuals are not in conflict with themselves, but with cultural binaries (Boswell, 1991). Therefore, some trans persons may not desire to transition to the *opposite* sex category. Roen (2002) has referred to this perspective as one of "both/neither ... a transgender position of refusing to fit within categories of woman and man" (p. 505). She has noted that this discourse is central to transgender politics.

The model of transsexualism has provided a meaning that is somewhat easy for those outside the trans community to grasp because it to some degree fits into the cultural dichotomy of sex (Roen, 2002). Second, the model protects the trans-identified to some extent, characterizing a trans identity as "a medical problem, not a moral problem" (Denny, 2004, p. 28). Similarly, Ellis and Eriksen (2002) have argued, "If transgender people can be shown to be different biologically, then they cannot be blamed for their differences" (p. 291). Finally, medicalization has facilitated the availability of technologies that aid trans-identified persons in transitioning (Denny, 2004). While the transgender model works to de-pathologize trans identities and indict culture, it simultaneously endangers legal protections and treatment options for those who are not comfortable with fluid identities (Denny, 2004).

Certainly, participants will consider such implications for themselves and their family members as they navigate these meaning systems. To understand how meaning is constructed through and in light of competing discourses and in consideration of the self and other(s), I have utilized Bakhtin's dialogism. This perspective has been particularly helpful in understanding the experience of family stressors, since meaning-making is especially salient and dialogic at "sites of rupture, challenge, or change" (Baxter, 2011, p. 153).

BAKHTIN'S DIALOGISM AND THE SOCIAL CONSTRUCTION OF MEANING

Bakhtin was concerned with the workings of the social world, particularly language, communication, and the relationship between self and other (Clark & Holquist, 1984). Central to his work is the argument that meaning-making or authoring is a social, not an individual, phenomenon. As we "shape values into forms" (Clark & Holquist, 1984, p. 10), using language in ways that satisfy our own purposes, we are situated in a context of other people and multiple worldviews. Therefore, meaning-making is a dialogic process characterized by polyphony, addressivity, and answerability.

The process of authoring is polyphonic in that every utterance is embedded in a larger chain of speech communication and cannot help but answer utterances that came before it: "Every utterance must be regarded primarily as a *response* to preceding utterances of the given sphere.... Each utterance refutes, affirms, supplements, and relies on the others, presupposes them to be known, and somehow takes them into account" (Bakhtin, 1979/1986, p. 91). Therefore, speakers must navigate the field of cultural discourses in a given sphere of speech communication as they author their experiences, which will mean acknowledging, endorsing, and rejecting various discourses. How we navigate this field may depend on the force of various discourses.

Some discourses are socially dominant or centripetal (Bakhtin, 1975/1981). However, even dominant discourses are not all-powerful, as they "operate in the midst of heteroglossia" (Bakhtin, 1975/1981, p. 271) and are in concert with "centrifugal, stratifying forces" (p. 272).

Furthermore, every utterance is directed toward another; not only must speakers respond to utterances that came before, they must anticipate utterances that might follow. In fact, Bakhtin (1979/1986) argued that there are three parties involved in meaning-making: the author, the addressee(s), and the "superaddressee." The addressee is the immediate audience or the particular person(s) whose understanding we seek. In addition, though, we have in mind the presence of a more abstracted "superaddressee"

> ... whose absolutely just responsive understanding is presumed.... In various ages and with various understandings of the world, this superaddressee ... assume[s] various ideological expressions (God, absolute truth, the court of human conscience, the people, the court of history, science, and so forth). (Bakhtin, 1979/1986, p. 126)

Therefore, the "superaddressee" "stands above" participants of a dialogue as a source of judgment beyond the immediate other. Addressivity affects the activity of authoring in that "Both the composition and, particularly, the style of the utterance depend on those to whom the utterance is addressed, how the speaker (or writer) senses and imagines his addressees, and the force of their effect on the utterance" (Bakhtin, 1979/1986, p. 95).

Finally, communication is dialogic in that we are accountable to others for the meanings we make. Bakhtin (1990) believed that an ability to respond to the social world is what constitutes a self. Therefore, the self is always connected to others. In this, Bakhtin says: "... The individual must become answerable through and through: all of his constituent moments must not only fit next to each other in the temporal sequence of his life, but must also interpenetrate each other in the unity of guilt and answerability" (Bakhtin, 1990, p. 2).

Here, Bakhtin seems to say that not only is the self responsible for the manner in which it responds to others, but also it is held accountable for some measure of consistency in manner, because our meanings will not be evaluated in isolation, but alongside of and in concert with one another.

All of these forces make the process of meaning-making a struggle. When we author our experiences, we must wrangle with cultural discourses, anticipate responses from others, and consider how we are answerable for what we say. Exploring these factors in family members' sense-making of trans identity can help us to understand not only the substance of the meanings they construct, but also the social forces that complicate their authoring processes. Most significantly, we can begin to understand how meanings of trans identity are connected to familial acceptance and support of trans persons. Toward these aims, I have posed three analytic questions: (1) What meanings do family members construct for trans identity? (2) How do they navigate issues of heteroglossia, addressivity, and answerability as they construct meanings? (3) How does meaning-making facilitate or hinder support for the trans-identified member?

METHODOLOGY

To collect data for this study I conducted 37 telephone interviews, ranging from 36 to 102 minutes in length, with those who considered themselves family of trans-identified persons. The larger study for which interviews were conducted was broader in focus, incorporating the ways family members constructed meanings for sex, gender, and the self in relation to transition. Despite the fact that interviews were not focused on the cause of trans identity, this topic came up in every interview. Therefore, I took this to be important to family members' experiences and worthy of analysis.

Participant Recruitment

The study was approved by the University of Iowa Institutional Review Board before recruitment began. Participants were recruited using several strategies. First, information was posted on two trans support Web sites and on a Web site for academics studying trans issues. Second, I e-mailed trans and significant others, friends, family, and allies (SOFFA) support groups within driving distance, asking if I could either come to a meeting or provide study information via e-mail. Finally, information was circulated on an electronic discussion list for those who study gender and on an electronic discussion list for the gay, lesbian, bisexual, and transgender (GLBT) community at the University of Iowa.

Participant Information

I interviewed 19 mothers, 5 fathers, 4 siblings, and 3 adult children as well as 1 former and 2 current spouses and 3 current partners of trans-identified persons. Nineteen participants' family members were described as female-to-male (F2M) transgender or transsexual, meaning they were born female-bodied and were transitioning or had transitioned to a male sex/gender category. Sixteen were described as male-to-female (M2F) transgender or transsexual, meaning they were born male-bodied and were transitioning or had transitioned to a female sex/gender category. Two participants had relatives/partners who identify as trans or gender queer. These persons were born female-bodied and had made transitional changes, but were not transitioning to a male sex/gender category. Participants lived in more than

15 states, including California, Indiana, Kentucky, Missouri, Massachusetts, New York, Texas, Washington, as well as in Canada. Five participants reported they were male and 32 female. Their ages ranged from 18 to 70, with an average of 45 years. Participants were largely Caucasian, but two identified as Hispanic and one as Asian. The youngest trans person discussed was 6 years old and the oldest was over 60. The majority of trans persons discussed were at least 18, but 5 interviews involved parents of young trans persons (between the ages of 6 and 16).

Data Collection

I began interview discussions by asking participants to tell their stories. I followed this with questions related to emotional responses, relational outcomes, and communication dynamics. It is important to note that participants told their stories to me as the most immediate addressee and, as Bakhtin argued, audience matters. Before telling their stories, many of them asked if I am trans, myself, or if I had a family member who was. I am not and did not have a trans person in my family, and the fact that they were addressing an outsider undoubtedly affected the content and style of participants' stories.

I began preliminary analysis as I gathered data, so that I could recognize when theoretical saturation was reached. I reached this point at interview 28 when additional data did not produce new information or help to refine established themes (Lindlof & Taylor, 2002). However, I continued to conduct interviews to ensure validity of my analysis. When transcribing interviews, I replaced names with the pseudonyms that are used in the presentation of findings.

Data Analysis

To analyze the data, I used a combination of thematic and dialogic analysis, informed by Bakhtin's concepts explicated previously. In the first phase, I used the constant comparative method (Strauss & Corbin, 1998) to identify and refine themes that spoke to the first research question. For example, three of my initial themes regarding meanings of trans identity were labeled *disease*, *birth defect*, and *cannot be helped*. In refining themes, I combined these into one thematic category, a meaning construction that I labeled *biomedical condition*. Once I refined themes into meaning categories, I then focused on the second research question.

While the first research question concerned the products of participants' meaning-making, the second concerned the process of meaning-making, namely: how those meanings were dialogically created. Bakhtin (1975/1981) has said, "Every concrete utterance of a speaking subject serves as a point where centrifugal as well as centripetal forces are brought to bear" making each utterance "... a contradiction-ridden, tension-filled unity of two embattled tendencies" (p. 272) wherein we can witness a dialogic process of centralization/marginalization and of dis/unification.

To explicate this process, I attended to direct and indirect polyphony, or moments when a participant implicated multiple viewpoints (Bakhtin, 1979/1986). I analyzed how the transgender and transsexual discourses as well as other emergent discourses were positioned in relation to one another and the meanings that emerged from this. In addition to prior utterances, I identified the presence of others in family members' meaning constructions, noting the consideration of particular and "superaddressees." In addition to addressivity, I examined participants' talk for awareness of answerability. Specifically, I noted moments when they recognized their responsibility for their meanings, either in anticipating critique or considering meanings of trans identity in relation to their global meaning systems. Finally, I analyzed the data for connections between participants' views of trans identity and relational outcomes. Within interviews, I noted participants' references to how understandings of trans identity inclined or disinclined them or other family members to support the trans-identified member. I also noted implicit patterns of connection among meanings and relational outcomes.

Generalizability is not a goal of qualitative research as it is for quantitative analysis; instead, one measure of validity is the *transferability* of findings (Lincoln & Guba, 1985). It is the responsibility of the qualitative researcher to provide a thick description and interpretation of data so that readers can judge whether findings are relevant to them and/or transferable to other situations. Another means for validation is *dependability*, achieved when others can readily see how a researcher got from one point to another in the analysis (Lincoln & Guba, 1985). To satisfy these criteria, I provide a comprehensive overview of the findings, detailed descriptions of themes, and analyses of exemplars to illustrate my interpretations.

FINDINGS

The Act of Authoring: Making Sense of Trans Identity in the Context of Family

The meanings family members constructed for trans identity were largely similar. The majority drew from the transsexual discourse to construct trans identity as a biomedical condition over which neither the affected individual, nor the family, had control. In the process of constructing this meaning, participants commonly rejected a prior utterance that trans identity is something people choose. The biomedical frame facilitated support among family members, as they reasoned that an ailment is not grounds for rejecting family members.

There were a handful of participants who constructed different meanings. Three centered on the transgender model, constructing trans identity as a variation in gender identity at odds with mainstream society's binaries of sex and gender. Each of these participants was supportive of their loved one. Finally, two participants constructed trans identity as a lifestyle choice rooted not in defiance of cultural dichotomies, but in a misguided desire for attention. Although these participants both maintained relationships with their trans-identified relative, neither accepted the relative's identity. Issues of addressivity and answerability were prominent in participants' meaning-making. They took into account the ways their trans-identified relatives or partners made meanings for their own identities, the ways discourses of trans identity aligned (or didn't) with their larger belief systems, the ways other family and friends might respond to their meanings, and the ways they and trans-identified relatives or partners might be viewed in larger society.

In what follows, I have presented participants' meaning constructions in more detail and then provided analyses of exemplars to give in-depth insight into the complexities of the dialogic process by which they were made. I have integrated into these sections further discussion regarding the unique positions in which family members find themselves and the relational outcomes facilitated by their meaning-making. Finally, I have contextualized their meanings for trans identity in light of other beliefs about difference, morality, and family.

Trans Identity As a Biomedical Condition

Trans identity was predominantly constructed as a biological or medical condition—often in contrast to another meaning, which was not the transgender discourse. Instead, participants showed awareness that some people regard trans identity as a lifestyle choice, not motivated by a political stand, but by a flaw in their moral character. In constructing trans identity as a biomedical condition, participants often defended against this view and the condemnation attached to it.

Roxy, mother of a 19-year-old trans-identified person (F2M), described her child's identity as a condition. In doing so, she shows both awareness of an alternative meaning and answerability for herself and her child, making this a thoroughly dialogic utterance:

> It wasn't our choice. We had this thrust on us just the same way that parents who have an autistic child or a child with cystic fibrosis. You have this situation and society doesn't just accept and accommodate.... And to be perfectly honest, I had feelings of "how will he be accepted in the world and how will I be viewed? Will I be viewed as being an overly permissive parent who lets their kid have this ridiculous fantasy that's born of adolescent self-hatred or whatever?" ... and I really had to look at myself and say, "who are we talking about? This is not about me. This is about my child." (Interview #21)

As a parent of a child who transitioned before he was 18 years old, Roxy recognizes that she is answerable to a superaddressee, *society*, whom she believes views trans identity as a choice. However, Roxy defends against critique, saying trans identity was "thrust upon" the family and comparing it to a psychological condition and a physical disease. Seemingly, she believes that although society is not accommodating to autism or cystic fibrosis, those affected are not blamed, nor are their parents. With this comparison, Roxy has constructed her child's identity as undeserving of condemnation, her identity as a parent as undeserving of censure, and anyone who would level such criticisms as cruel.

Another example comes from Karrie, mother of 18-year-old Toby (F2M), whose talk showed a direct connection between the framing of trans identity and relational outcomes. She supported her child's identity because she saw it as inborn:

> I knew Toby was different. I figured, "I'm gonna have a lesbian daughter." And I was okay with that because I know it's not a choice .... And that is one thing that I think infuriates me more than anything is when people tell me that my son chose to be transgender, because it is not a choice and if it was, who would choose to go through what a transgender person goes through?

Thus, Karrie vehemently rejected the discourse of choice. She discredited it by questioning why anyone would elect to go through the difficulties trans persons face. Karrie went on to explain that while she saw trans identity as an inherent mismatch of mind and body, she did not consider it as a defect but simply as a difference. Nevertheless, due to issues of addressivity and answerability she constructed it as a defect at times:

> For me, while I don't try to recognize one being transgender as a birth defect, sometimes it's an analogy that people can come closest to understanding, that, you know, it does happen in utero, the signals are mixed up or whatever and the baby is born male minded or female minded and you know when they're old enough to tell you who they are.

Later in her interview Karrie lamented how many trans-identified persons struggled in silence before coming out. She attributed this to society's condemnation of trans identity as a perversion:

> Society says "if you are a transgender ... you are a social deviant!" I had a preacher ... tried to lump Toby with rapists and child molesters ... I was about ready to—the mamma bear was coming out! ... I can see it changing now, we're making strides ... awakening the public to what it means, that we do have a transgender society and that it's okay! One of my favorite quotes is "difference isn't wrong, it just is." There's shades

of gray, there's differences everywhere and there's differences in gender. (Interview #20)

Interestingly, Karrie's construction seemed to integrate parts of both the transsexual and transgender discourses. While she believed that there was a biological issue that caused an abnormality, she did not believe this had to be regarded as defective, but simply as different.

Just as it did for Karrie, the locus of control mattered for Amber's husband. Amber, the 39-year-old mother of a young trans child (M2F), explained how at first her husband had held her responsible. She said, " ... he was hell-bent that he was gonna change this kid.... He blamed me. It was my fault. I babied him [the child] too much." Amber then described a reframing process that led to her husband's acceptance of their child:

> He was very prejudiced against people who were gay or lesbian. He just didn't understand why they would make that choice. He couldn't understand why a man would go out to the grocery store with a dress on.... He's like, "What is wrong with these people?" But in all the research that I did, all the articles that I found that talk about this is hard-wired in the brain in utero, all of the sudden there was like a total turnaround. Just like, "Oh, my gosh! This is just like someone who's in a wheelchair! They can't help it! This is just who they are!"

Amber contextualized her husband's reaction within his larger belief system, which included his general contempt for transgressions of heteronormativity. While her husband first constructed trans identity as something that was created and that could be controlled through parenting, Amber endeavored to use scientific research to help him to reframe trans identity as a condition or disability—something that, although stigmatized, can hardly be cause for blame. This reframing did important work for this couple, as it was the basis on which they came to support their child, on which they answered for doing so, and on which they addressed others who did not. In her narrative Amber shifted the moral burden to others by saying, "I just don't have space in my life for people who can't acknowledge the fact that my child has a medical condition and we're doing what we can to treat it" (Interview #18).

Liz, the spouse of a trans-identified person (M2F), also dismissed the idea that one should be ostracized for being trans. She described her family and friends' reaction to her spouse:

> ... a lot of them said, "Oh, you've got to leave him immediately," and I'm like ... It's not gonna work that way. I'm not into abandoning people because they are inconvenient, socially." And when I put it that way, people realized what they were saying.

Liz's family and friends seemed to regard trans identity as something that merited relational dissolution. However, Liz indicated that she did not give a lot of weight to the opinion of these particular addressees, but instead answered to a superaddressee—a higher moral order. In fact, she constructed her friends and family as morally irresponsible. Liz outlined her frame for trans identity as she told me how her spouse's trans identity was explained to her child:

> We just kind of, "Oh, some people this and some people that," type of thing. And as she grew older and could understand ... we explained what was going on with Beth ... in scientific terms. That some people are born between genders or looking like one and being the other and because we explained it as just a natural part of the world, she never felt this jolt. (Interview #36)

Liz's construction was similar to Karrie's in that she saw trans identity as something that someone was born with, as "just the way it is," as a condition that naturally occurred. She taught her child about this sort of difference in the same way she might explain that some people are born with dwarfism.

Violet constructed trans identity as a condition, even though her trans-identified teenager constructed his identity differently:

> Yeah. I'm trying to find another disease—I think it's like MS or something that has about the same incidence ... but I'm trying to come up with something so I can say to people, "Well, you know, my child has a disorder that puts him at greater risk of violent death prior to the age of 25," and I want to say, "It happens to the same amount of people as MS or whatever, and it's called, you know, transgender." ... I present it completely as a condition....

Violet explicitly referenced a need to make outsiders understand, as she drew upon a medical discourse. She also contrasted this with her child's framing of trans identity:

> He's like, "I am who I am, I'm built the way I'm built, it's okay. He didn't have a hatred of his body.... He didn't have that anger that something was wrong. He has this, "I'm a girl in a guy's body—that's what I am." And I've seen a little bit of that as I do my research, that this younger group of transgender is coming up going, "Hey, you call it a disorder, I call it me!" (Interview #29)

One interpretation of the difference in Violet's meaning and her child's could be that as a parent, who was legally responsible for a child under 18 years old, Violet can be seen to bear more answerability for her child's identity than even he did. She could be indicted by others for being responsible for causing him to be trans, or for allowing him to make bad choices. This seemed to be a concern for many parents interviewed. It may be that even if their children did not identify with the transsexual discourse, parents thought that they could better protect their families by constructing trans identity as a medical condition to outsiders.

Michelle, the ex-spouse of a M2F trans person, had struggled to construct meaning for trans identity and also struggled with the moral implications that followed from doing so:

> If you accept the premise that this is a medical condition, like a birth defect or something ... then you say to yourself, "Okay, well gee ... so why can't I accept this?" and then I feel really bad, I feel like I'm this mean horrible person. I think, "Well gee whiz, if he had, I don't know like diabetes or a kidney problem or a heart problem or whatever, I wouldn't reject him because of that!" You know? So, you do feel like: "What's wrong with me? I'm a horrible person because I'm having a hard time accepting this!"(Interview #8)

With the phrase "accept the premise," Michelle apparently recognized that there were multiple discourses available. She argued that if one accepted the medical view, but did not accept the person, there was something wrong with that. Regarding the difference between trans identity and diabetes, she said, "I'm not sure ... my friends say, 'Well, this is completely different!'" Later, she said that she wanted to accept the medical view, but had not been able to do so. This might mean that Michelle felt answerable for consistency in her global meaning system at least in presenting it to me during her interview; if before she had considered trans identity a choice, then to suddenly change her belief might seem disingenuous. Michelle also seemed to feel answerable to her ex, to a moral order, and to her social network. Her struggle demonstrated how complicated the process of authoring an account of trans identity could be for family members.

Trans Identity As an Imprudent Lifestyle Choice

I spoke with two participants who constructed trans identity in the way that the majority of participants had defended against; these two participants saw it as a selfish, and even sinful, choice. These participants, Chuck and Kay, were married and one of their children, Alex, was trans-identified (F2M). Alex was living with them at the time Chuck and Kay were interviewed, so these parents had not dissolved their relationship with him completely. Neither Chuck nor Kay, however, accepted Alex's identity. I have drawn out the following excerpt from Chuck's interview to demonstrate his construction of trans identity as a choice. He said:

> Alex and Mimi were living with a couple that were transgender, so I'm thinking to myself, "Well, Alex being a follower. . . ." Alex was never like that, never, before she moved there. . . . I think Alexandra was talked into this ... her gender therapist ... they're only in it for the money. They don't really give a hell, damn, shit about who the real person is. . . . I think what Alexandra is trying to do, I don't know if she just wants attention, "Oh, how far do I want to go to get attention?" ... I think maybe she got in with the wrong crowd or she didn't think things through for herself ... it's a huge mistake, but ... she's a very stubborn person. When she gets her mind set to something, look out!

Chuck constructed trans identity as a choice in saying that Alex had set his mind on it. He saw it as something his child claimed either to get attention or saw it as something others had influenced him to do, or both. Chuck referred to the perceived "influencers" as greedy gender therapists and "the wrong crowd," using a phrase that conjured up images of drug pushers or vandals. Chuck, however, had not cut ties with his child, but described himself as "dealing with it—not accepting it. There's a difference." When I asked what the difference was, he replied, "Accepting it is me saying, 'this is not my daughter, this is my son.' Dealing with it, 'this is my kid'." Hence, Chuck's construction of trans identity as a choice did not facilitate familial acceptance, but also did not necessarily lead to estrangement.

Chuck showed awareness of answerability, both in terms of society and his own global meaning systems, when we discussed the fact that before Alex came out as trans Alex had identified as lesbian. I asked why Alex's trans identity had been harder to accept than Alex's lesbian identity. Chuck said:

> Because transgender and transsexual is a taboo. It's a very, very difficult taboo. Especially in this country ... for us to sit there and say, "Oh, okay, now you're this, oh well we love you anyway, we're gonna accept you any way you are" there comes times when we look at each other and say, "Well, what the hell did we do wrong now?"

Here, Chuck implies he and his wife would have been wrong to accept their child's trans identity. I responded by asking if he had been comfortable when Alex was lesbian. He said:

> No, no! I'm not, mentally not even comfortable with that! . . . It's lesser of the two evils I guess. . . . I don't like the idea of homosexuality either. It's un-Christian, it's an abomination, it's wrong, you know? (Interview #6)

Thus, Chuck had filed trans identity in the same general place as queer sexuality, but categorized trans identity as one worse in terms of morality and social offensiveness.

Trans Identity As a Natural yet Culturally Transgressive Gender Identity

While most participants constructed trans identity as a disorder, three participants constructed cultural binaries as "disordered" and instead saw trans identities as merely part of a spectrum of gender identity that naturally existed. In a sense, these three participants who centered the transgender discourse took less ownership of the meaning, but seemingly did so out of respect for their relative or partner. One of these participants was a partner of a trans person, one was a sibling, and one a parent. Isabella, the sibling of Jess, voiced more than one discourse as she explained her sibling's identity:

> Um, it was very explicitly, "It is not that I feel like a man trapped in a woman's body," um, it was more, "I feel like I don't fit into traditional gender norms and feel more comfortable operating in a more nuanced space as far as gender goes." ... Jess likes the term "trans" or "gender queer," kind of likes the term "transgender," but doesn't identify as transsexual. (Interview #4)

Isabella's talk clearly outlined both models of trans identity, and positioned the transsexual model as the centripetal view when she reported that her sibling did not "feel like a man trapped in a woman's body," indicating that she thought this was the most common cultural model of trans identity.

Notably, each of the participants who drew from the transgender discourse to construct their meaning absolutely supported their trans-identified relative or partner. And yet, they did not indicate that it was their construction of trans identity that allowed them to be accepting. Presumably, if one perceived nothing wrong with trans identity, then whether or not a person had control over their trans identity was a moot point. Interestingly, these participants also did not defend against possible responses from others that trans identity was a stain on someone's character. One commonality shared by these three participants was that all three were unabashedly socially or politically progressive, highly educated, and seemed to surround themselves with similar others, and this could partially explain why participants did not feel the need to defend against others' responses. For example, in talking about her own identity, Isabella said:

> I play around with the term "heteroqueer." I like men, identify as a female-bodied, female-gendered person, but the majority of folks who are dear to me in my life are in some sort of queer community ... and I'm studying to become a Unitarian, Universal minister.

So, perhaps, for these participants, their global meaning systems and their social circles were amenable to their framings such that they did not feel answerable to critics like other participants did.

The Importance of Global Meaning Systems and the Meaning of Family

While I noted considerations of answerability in the previous sections, the issue of global meaning systems warranted further analysis. In addition to being mentioned by participants as reasons why they themselves were or were not supportive, aspects such as religious beliefs or social and political values were important in framing participants' anticipation of other family members' and outsiders' reactions to disclosure. In their own constructions, participants often focused in on, or gave greatest weight to, one particular part of their global meaning system. In particular, their beliefs about the nature of family relationships were exceedingly important to relational outcomes. The exemplars selected in the following discussion further demonstrate the ways in which global meaning systems were implicated in family experience.

Participants approached the decision of whether and how to disclose to extended family members by anticipating their responses. They based these expectations on what they assumed, or knew, to be the others' global belief systems. Participants implicated demographic characteristics as markers of belief systems that facilitated or hindered family support. Gabbie, the mother of a trans-identified person (F2M), discussed the responses of some family members, explaining their responses with reference to their larger sense-making frameworks.

> I do have a brother who is, I call him and his wife Mr. and Mrs. Catholic ... their religion teaches them that this is an abomination of God ... at one point his lovely wife had wanted him to give to me the phone number of their pastor of their church, in case I feel the need to discuss this with the Catholic Church.... I laughed in his face and I said, "Are you kidding me? You think I give a shit what the Catholic Church thinks about me and my kid? Really, Ted?"(Interview #27)

Gabbie negotiated this situation by explaining to her brother Ted that the answerability he might feel to Catholicism carried no weight for her. Others chose to approach extended family members in a way that limited their ability to respond. Amanda, the mother of a trans-identified young adult (M2F), crafted her disclosure in a way that worked to close down the possibilities for negative reactions from other family members. She explained:

> ... my husband and I talked ... and just felt the best way to tell people was that we were asking for their support. I've always believed ... when you show that you're okay with something ... they're gonna be okay with it and that's pretty much what we saw across the board. You know, "We're fine with this. We're supporting Simone. And we need your

support too." No ifs, ands, buts, no questions, you know, we didn't really give anybody an out. (Interview #10)

Amanda explained how in addressing others she did not ask their opinion and that she also indicated the response she desired from them, thus she limited the dialogic potential of these exchanges. Also, she believed and hoped that her own response to, and framing of, her child's trans identity would serve as the model for others' responses.

Other participants chose to avoid addressing extended family members and the answerability that comes with disclosure. However, there were a good number who reluctantly disclosed and found support where they least expected it. For example, Evelyn, mother of an adult trans person (M2F), explained that religion, social prejudice, and traditional masculinity did not hinder her larger family's support for her child, as she expected it would:

> I have one Evangelical, nutcase sister ... and her son ... they were absolutely lovely! And the nephew, Nala's cousin, this boy who I thought was macho and I really never liked him. I've gotten to like him very much. He's given Nala big hugs.... And then there's ... a hillbilly relative who is anti-black and gay and everything else and he did just fine! ... I was very pleasantly surprised.... I think maybe it's my mother ... even though she belongs to this stupid church, she's always been a very loving person and, really, it is that family overrides every time. Her daughters and son are all perfect and anyone who disagrees with that—that's a nice way to have your mother be. That's all I can guess, that my mom might have had a very important role in influencing some of them. (Interview #15)

This and other exemplars demonstrate that when meaning is constructed for *trans identity* in the context of *family*, the meaning we give to the latter concept may heavily influence the content, or at least the consequences of, the meaning we give to the former.

Many participants explained their willingness to accept trans identity by referencing their own values and beliefs, either about their principled acceptance of difference in general, or about the nature of family relationships. For example, Lilly explained why she and her husband were supportive of their child: "We don't make fun of people, we're not prejudice—really, literally—at all ... it doesn't make a difference to us who people are or where they came from." And, when I asked her what advice she would give to other families, she recommended they ignore responses from outsiders and focus on their family members:

> If they're dealing with children, you're going to get a lot of opinions ... a lot of resistance. You have to keep going until you find help that will be ... accepting of your child, not trying to fix your child ... and any families that are dealing with transgender people in general, even if it's

> not children, just accept people ... and just love them because they're your kids or your family member. If you loved them before, why should that change now? You don't always have to get it .... I don't know if I fully get it, but it doesn't mean that you have to reject that person. Or hurt that family member. (Interview #26)

Most participants echoed this sentiment, implying it would be immoral to end relationships with family members, because we should have allegiance to family over self or others. Edward, father of an adult trans person (F2M), constructed family, and in particular the parent-child relationship, as absolute. Regarding what advice he would give to other parents, he said, "Love your children unconditionally and support them in every way you can. What else can we do? The reality is the reality and if they can't count on their parents' love then what can they count on?"(Interview #13). By posing two rhetorical questions, Edward rejected the idea that sometimes family ties should be broken. He asked, "What else can we do?" suggesting that there was no other option but to love and support family. With the next question he asserted that, if anyone had a duty to someone, then parents had a duty to their children.

Chuck, on the other hand, did not believe that family members were obliged to support one another. In fact, while he acknowledged that this was a dominant discourse on family, he challenged the rationality of it. When I asked Chuck if he had any advice for other families, he said:

> Yeah, stand your ground. If you don't feel comfortable with this, tell them. You don't have to accept it. There's a major misconception in life, "Well, whatever your children do you have to love and understand, respect, bla, bla, bla, and accept it." Would you accept your child as an axe murderer? ... My family doesn't have to deal with it.... If that sounds cold-hearted, I'm sorry!

Chuck, therefore, gave voice to idea that parents have unconditional obligation to children, and then called it a "major misconception in life." And, using the same discursive device as Edward did, Chuck used a rhetorical question to discredit the idea. In his discourse Chuck compared acceptance of a transgender child to accepting a child who was a murderer, implying both children were similarly immoral. In effect, he implied that there were sometimes legitimate reasons to withdraw support from and dissolve relationships with family members. Chuck then anticipated the judgment of others, saying, "If this sounds cold-hearted, I'm sorry!" Chuck did not believe he would be criticized for framing trans identity in this way, but he did anticipate censure for his meaning of family.

DISCUSSION

The way we experience trans identity in families depends wholly on the meanings we assign to such identities as well as to family relationships. As Voloshinov said, "It is not experience that organizes expression, but the other way around—*expression organizes experience*" (1929/1986, p. 85). I set out to understand this process through a dialogic lens in an attempt to capture its complex, social nature. Next, I reflect upon the meanings that were present and absent in the data, their dialogic texture, and the ethics of their construction. Finally, I outline limitations, contributions, and future directions for this research.

Present, Absent, and Unfinalized Meanings

Although there was clearly a dominant discourse in the data, there was also the unmistakable presence of multiple viewpoints. In fact, differentiation from competing views was the mechanism through which meaning was constructed. While the transsexual discourse occupied the centripetal position across the data, participants' talk showed that an opposing view also had a strong presence in U.S. culture—that being trans was a lifestyle choice. Denny (2004) did not account for this third discourse, although in an earlier work she and colleagues had suggested the stigma surrounding trans identities was likely to be greater if it was not considered as a medical issue (Cole, Denny, Eyler, & Samons, 2000).

At first glance, the discourse of choice may have seemed to stem from the transgender discourse, as the latter holds that trans persons should choose not to live within culturally legitimated categories of sex/gender; however, the discourse of choice diverged in both the causal attribution of trans identity and in the valuing of it. Instead of considering trans identities as part of a natural spectrum of gender identities, the discourse of choice considered them to be a matter of arbitrary preference. Furthermore, in the transgender discourse, the choice to live as "both/neither" male or female (Roen, 2002, p. 505) was framed as a personal and/or political stand against gender oppression, while the choice discourse framed being trans as being perverse and selfish.

Although the transsexual discourse was centered by most participants, there was a certain strand of this discourse that was almost totally absent in the data—the construction of trans identity as a mental illness. When participants constructed trans identity as a disorder, they explicitly indicated it was a physical or physiological issue. Nevertheless, participants did sometimes mention psychological conditions, like autism or bipolar disorder, when they compared trans identity to other things. Largely, though, they steered clear of such comparisons and of this construction presumably because the physical and physiological constructions not only served the purpose of deflecting the choice discourse, but also served to protect the trans person and their family from blame. As Kawanishi (2005) showed, among the attributions made for mental illness were genetic defect, chemical imbalance, and family dysfunction. Perhaps, then, family members wanted to distance themselves from the accusation that family dynamics were to blame.

There is an alternative interpretation of this finding, although the two are not mutually exclusive. There may have been movement between discourses or the integration of multiple framings due to the ongoing renegotiation of the meaning of trans identity in larger society. In addition to the occasional conflation of psychological and physiological causes for trans identity, there was evidence that some participants blended both transsexual and transgender discourses together. These instances where divergent meanings were positioned as compatible showed that the cultural discourses surrounding trans identity can be reconciled and/or that they were fluid. We can see evidence of this in cultural artifacts as well as in academic and social movements.

Papoulias (2006) has argued that in recent years scholars have turned to neurobiology for explanations of gender identity (e.g., sexed brains). This scholarly shift might be implicated in laypersons' schemas of gender identity moving away from connections with mental illness. In addition, the trans community has pushed for recognition of multiple kinds of trans identities, arguing that the American Psychiatric Association's (APA) diagnosis of Gender Identity Disorder was not relevant for all who identify as trans. In response, the APA will revise the *DSM*-V to include a diagnosis of Gender Dysphoria instead of Gender Identity Disorder. By framing trans identity as "a temporary mental state rather than an all-encompassing disorder" (Beredjick, 2012, para 4), the *DSM* revision is intended to reduce stigma and be more inclusive. This official change can be seen as both reflecting and producing an evolving construction of trans identity. As the new *DSM* psychiatric meaning of gender dysphoria becomes institutionalized, family members' meaning frames may also change accordingly.

Nevertheless, the official line of the APA will still exist alongside centrifugal meanings that oppose it, interact with it, and may eventually reshape it. According to Bakhtin (1929/1984), meaning cannot be finalized: " . . . the ultimate word of the world and about the world has not yet been spoken, the world is open and free, everything is still in the future and will always remain in the future" (p. 166). Bakhtin viewed the perpetual renegotiation of meaning as paramount to the functioning of society, because it allows for a multitude of voices to be heard and for new meanings (or at least new versions of meanings) to emerge.

The Ethics of Authoring

Not only did Bakhtin idealize dialogue, he also condemned monologue, its exclusionary opposite "characterized by an addressor's failure to adopt the role of addressee: it is neither shaped nor moved by the voices with which it interacts, thereby *creating* for itself a position of authority" (Guilfoyle, 2003, p. 332). For Bakhtin, to fix meaning, objectify the other, or attempt to ignore the demands of answerability, is to act unethically. While the participants in my study firmly asserted some meanings, rejected others, and attempted to preempt some objections, I did not interpret their authoring as monologic. Even if they attempted to quiet certain addressees, they still responded to their presence. To view this as ethical authoring, a more complex consideration of the relationship between self and other may be in order. The fact is there is not only one *other* in relation to one self, but many *others*. And, if the viewpoints of multiple addressees' viewpoints are antagonistic, we may have to decide to whom we should most wholly orient, and for what we are most answerable. In some circumstances, we may feel obligated to approach monologue, silencing some others, in order to defend those to whom we feel more ethically bound. That is, we take into account issues of allegiance along with addressivity and answerability.

Adding Allegiance to Addressivity and Answerability

Family members of trans-identified persons can be seen as occupying a unique position in that they must contend with competing cultural discourses of trans identity while answering to (1) a family member who is, presumably, looking for support, (2) a society that stigmatizes trans identity, (3) social networks that may impose judgment, and (4) their own belief systems that may or may not be amenable to the acceptance of trans identity. While participants may have recognized the presence of each of these social forces, one or two of these may have been especially significant for them while the others may have receded from the center of their consciousness.

Almost all participants showed allegiance to their trans-identified family members over other addressees or sources of answerability. One way they did so was to align their meanings with their trans relative's or partner's meaning. For example, most often, when the trans person privileged a transgender discourse, so did their family members. And, because these participants' global meaning systems were not challenged by this discourse, they referenced larger beliefs only as an explanation for why support came easily for them. Presumably, this is why "society" as a superaddressee was less important for these participants. Finally, because their social networks were described as holding similar belief systems, they were not seen as an apparent threat.

Participants also showed allegiance to trans family members by constructing trans identity as a biomedical condition. In one case, a participant constructed this meaning even though her trans child did not. This may be because as a part of their allegiance to their family members, these participants often took a defensive stance, giving a great deal of attention to addressees who were critical of trans identity. This was not surprising, as many of them were parents whose children were struggling, or had struggled with, their identities at a young age. Because they were responsible for their children's well-being, answerability was central to their experience as parents. If outsiders did not accept the transsexual discourse, or if they believed trans identity was a psychological disorder, outsiders may have assumed that parents caused it to happen. An important factor in allegiance for family members who saw trans identity as a condition was the belief that family bonds should be reinforced rather than reneged when a member faced such a hardship.

However, there was evidence that other aspects of family members' global meaning systems like religious beliefs, or social prejudices, could bring about a renouncement of family obligation. Family members who constructed trans identity as a damnable lifestyle choice showed allegiance to their own global meaning systems more than anything or anyone else. They seemed to feel most answerable to a religious moral code rather than to the institution of family.

Limitations

While the data from the present study have provided a meaningful look at how trans identity is experienced as a family stressor, this study was limited in scope. All participants had maintained relationships with their trans-identified relatives, (ex-) spouses, or partners, which implied tolerance, if not acceptance. I had difficulty finding non-supportive participants because many of the outlets through which I recruited were support groups and Web sites. Plus, individuals who had rejected family members were probably less inclined to share their stories. In addition, the similarity in meanings generated across the participants in my study could have been as a result of the discourse that is commonly circulated within support groups. Finally, with regard to the sample, the significant contingent of participants who were parents of trans children, or of adults who had identified as trans from a young age, likely contributed to the homogeneity of meanings across the participant sample pool.

In addition to sample limitations, no doubt my identity, the topic, and the method of this research might have created limitations. As an outsider researching a stigmatized topic, I may have made participants feel that they had to defend their loved ones by offering more positive stories than they otherwise might have told. Finally, I collected data at only one point in time, which only allowed me a snapshot of participants' meaning-making processes, rather than a more dynamic moving picture, which longitudinal research could more closely approximate.

Contributions

Despite these limitations, the findings have clear theoretical and practical applications. The study has added to the research literature on family stressors by demonstrating that not only does the framing of a family stressor matter in absolute terms to the way family members experience it, but also that the process of constructing meaning was complicated by the presence of cultural stigma, the recognition of multiple audiences (including other family members, friends, and even "society"), and the existence of contradictory systems of meaning surrounding trans identity. More specifically, this study has worked toward an understanding of how trans identity functioned in different ways as a family stressor, pointing to factors that might be "difference makers" for families in terms of framing, coping, and relational outcomes. The analysis also has contributed to dialogic research, demonstrating that the personal meanings given were inherently social, connected to others, and to their cultural and historical context. Furthermore, it has given texture to some of Bakhtin's most central, yet often abstracted concepts, and has built upon his conceptualization of ethics.

The findings also should hold practical relevance for trans-identified persons and their families. If families can understand the importance of framing meaning to experience, perhaps they can then actively engage in reframing processes that may help them reach a desired state. These findings may help trans persons understand family members' unique experiences as well as highlight some of the reasons why families might struggle with support; perhaps family members have been unable to integrate a positive framing of trans identity into their global meaning systems, or perhaps they have been concerned for their own identities, or maybe they have felt responsibility to society or other addressees. Practitioners could use these findings to help families facing trans identity understand how meaning matters to their experiences. Counselors might even consider taking a dialogic approach in order to help families give meaning to their experiences or to reframe their experiences to achieve positive outcomes.

Future Research

A greater number and variety of family members should be included in future research to better understand the multitude of meanings that might be constructed for trans identity and what relational outcomes follow from them. There may be other discourses that family members draw upon, or other meanings that blend established discourses. For example, there could be family members who concede their trans-identified relatives were born that way, but who also believe trans persons can, and should, choose to suppress their differences and live within the sex categories to which they were assigned. In addition, researchers should attempt to capture a more detailed picture of what family systems go through when experiencing this family stressor. We might do this by interviewing family members both separately and together to understand jointly constructed meanings as well as individual ones. It might be fruitful to determine whether and how a trans-identified family member had a significant influence on others' meaning-making or whether and when there was an open divergence of meaning even among supportive family members.

Longitudinal methods especially would be beneficial to this research because meanings are constantly being negotiated. We might find that family members' meanings change in conjunction with changes to the *DSM*, or that the parents of trans kids shift their framing of trans identity as their child grows up, or alternatively that family members re-create the same meanings over time. Eventually, we may be able to map family trajectories from disclosure through adjustment to support or, conversely, from disclosure through conflict to rejection. Finally, we should attempt to identify differences in supportive and non-supportive families, or distressed and non-distressed families facing trans identity. For example, these families may differ on general family communication patterns (Koerner & Fitzpatrick, 2002) or on global meaning orientations (Park & Folkman, 1997). Findings like those from the present study could be very important to the well-being of trans persons and their families. Thus, it is important to understand all that we can about the meanings families construct and their connections to relational outcomes.

REFERENCES

Altemeyer, B. (2001). Changes in attitudes toward homosexuals. *Journal of Homosexuality, 42*, 3–76.

American Psychiatric Association. (1994). *Diagnostic and statistical manual of mental disorders, fourth edition (DSM-IV)*. Washington, DC: American Psychiatric Association.

Armesto, J., & Weisman, A. G. (2001). Parents' reactions to the identity disclosure of a homosexual child. *Family Process, 40*, 145–161.

Bakhtin, M. M. (1981). Discourse in the novel. In M. Holquist (Ed.) (C. Emerson & M. Holquist, Trans.), *The dialogic imagination: Four essays by M. M. Bakhtin* (pp. 259–422). Austin, TX: University of Texas Press. (Original work published 1975)

Bakhtin, M. M. (1984). *Problems of Dostoevsky's poetics* (C. Emerson, Ed. & Trans.). Minneapolis, MN: University of Minnesota Press. (Original work published 1929)

Bakhtin, M. M. (1986). The problem of speech genres. In C. Emerson & M. Holquist (Eds.) (V. W. McGee, Trans.), *Speech genres & other late essays* (pp. 60–102). Austin, TX: University of Texas Press. (Original published in 1979)

Bakhtin, M. M. (1990). *Art and answerability: Early philosophical essays* (M. Holquist & V. Liapunov, Eds.; V. Liapunov, Trans.). Austin, TX: University of Texas Press.

Baxter, L. A. (2011). *Voicing relationships*. Thousand Oaks, CA: Sage.

Becares, L., & Turner, C. (2004). Sex, college major, and attribution of responsibility in empathic responding to persons with HIV infection. *Psychological Reports, 95*, 467–476.

Beredjick, C. (2012, July 23). DSM-V to rename gender identity disorder "gender dysphoria". Retrieved from http://www.advocate.com/politics/transgender/2012/07/23/dsm-replaces-gender-identity-disorder-gender-dysphoria

Boss, P. (1992). Primacy of perception in family stress theory and measurement. *Journal of Family Psychology, 6*, 113–119.

Boswell, H. (1991). The transgender alternative. *Chrysalis Quarterly, 2*, 29–31.

Clark, K., & Holquist, M. (1984). *Mikhail Bakhtin*. Cambridge, MA: Harvard University Press.

Cole, S. S., Denny, D., Eyler, A. E., & Samons, S. L. (2000). Issues of transgender. In L. T. Szuchman & F. Muscarella (Eds.), *Psychological perspectives on human sexuality* (pp. 149–195). New York, NY: John Wiley.

Collett, B. R., & Gimple, G. A. (2004). Maternal and child attributions in ADHD versus non-ADHD populations. *Journal of Attention Disorders, 7*, 187–196.

Connolly, C. M. (2006). A process of change: The intersection of the GLBT individual and his or her family of origin. In J. J. Bigner (Ed.), *An introduction to GLBT family studies* (pp. 5–21). Binghamton, NY: Haworth Press.

Davis, C. G., Nolen-Hoeksema, S., & Larson, J. (1998). Making sense of loss and benefiting from the experience: Two construals of meaning. *Journal of Personality and Social Psychology, 75*, 561–574.

DeLamater, J. D., & Hude, J. S. (1998). Essentialism vs. social constructionism in the study of human sexuality. *Journal of Sex Research, 35*, 10–18.

Denny, D. (2004). Changing models of transsexualism. *Journal of Gay & Lesbian Psychotherapy, 1/2*, 25–40.

Ellis, K. M., & Eriksen, K. (2002). Transsexual and transgenderist experiences and treatment options. *The Family Journal: Counseling and Therapy for Couples and Families, 3*, 289–299.

Furnham, A., & Lowick, V. (1984). Lay theories of the causes of alcoholism. *British Journal of Medical Psychology, 57*, 319–332.

Guilfoyle, M. (2003). Dialogue and power: A critical analysis of power in dialogical therapy. *Family Process, 42*, 331–343.

Henrichsen, G. A., & Lieberman, J. A. (1999). Family attributions and coping in the prediction of emotional adjustment in family members of patients with first-episode schizophrenia. *ActaPsychiatricaScandinavica, 100*, 359–366.

Hewitt, E. C., & Moore, L. D. (2002). The role of lay theories of the etiologies of homosexuality in attitudes towards lesbians and gay men. *Journal of Lesbian Studies, 6*, 59–72.

Hines, S. (2006). Intimate transitions: Transgender practices of partnering and parenting. *Sociology, 2*, 353–371.

Kawanishi, Y. (2005). The process of causal attribution and interpretation of the mental illness by the patients' family members in the United States and Japan. *International Journal of Mental Health, 33*(4), 19–34.

Koerner, A. F., & Fitzpatrick, M. A. (2002). Understanding family communication patterns and family functioning: The roles of conversation orientation and conformity orientation. *Communication Yearbook, 26*, 37–68.
Kuo, J. S. (2006). Coming out to the future: The gay gene debate and the heteronormative discourse. *Concentric: Literary and Cultural Studies, 32*(2), 183–204.
Lazarus, R. S., & Folkman, S. (1984). Cognitive theories of stress and the issue of circularity. In M. Appley & R. Trambull (Eds.), *Dynamics of stress: Physiological, psychological, and social perspectives* (pp. 63–80). New York, NY: Plenum.
Lincoln, Y. S., & Guba, E. G. (1985). *Naturalistic inquiry.* Beverly Hills, CA: Sage.
Lindlof, T. R., & Taylor, B. C. (2002). *Qualitative communication research methods* (2nd ed.). Thousand Oaks, CA: Sage.
McCubbin, H. I., Joy, C.B., Cauble, A.E., Comeau, J.K., Patterson, J.M., & Needle, R. H. (1980). Family stress and coping: A decade review. *Journal of Marriage and Family, 42*, 855–871.
McCubbin, H. I., & McCubbin, M. A. (1987). Family stress theory and assessment: The Double ABCX model of family adjustments and adaptation. In H. I. McCubbin & J. I. Thompson (Eds.), *Family assessment inventories for research and practice* (pp. 3–34). Madison, WI: University of Wisconsin.
Newman, B. S., & Muzzonigro, P. G. (1993). The effects of traditional family values on the coming out process of gay male adolescents. *Adolescence, 28*, 213–226.
Park, C. L., & Folkman, S. (1997). Meaning in the context of stress and coping. *Review of General Psychology, 1*, 115–144.
Papoulias, C. (2006). Transgender. *Theory Culture Society, 23*, 231–233.
Roen, K. (2002). "Either/or" and "both/neither": Discursive tensions in transgender politics. *Signs, 2*, 501–522.
Sloop, J. M. (2004). *Disciplining gender: Rhetorics of sex identity in contemporary U.S. culture.* Amherst, MA: University of Massachusetts Press.
Socarides, C. W. (1969). The desire for sexual transformation: A psychiatric evaluation of transsexualism. *American Journal of Psychiatry, 125*, 1419–1425.
Strauss, A., & Corbin, J. (1998). *Basics of qualitative research: Techniques and procedures for developing grounded theory (2*nd *ed.).* Thousand Oaks, CA: Sage.
Voloshinov, V. N. (1986). *Marxism and the philosophy of language* (L. Matejka & I. R. Titunik, Trans.). Cambridge, MA: Harvard University Press. (Original work published 1929)
Wiedman, G. H. (1953). Letter to the editor. *Journal of American Medical Association, 152*, 1167.
Willoughby, B. L. B., Doty, N. D., & Malik, N. M. (2008). Parental reactions to their child's sexual orientation disclosure: A family stress perspective. *Parenting: Science and Practice, 8*, 70–91.
Zamboni, B. D. (2006). Therapeutic considerations in working with the family, friends, and partners of transgendered individuals. *The Family Journal, 14*, 174–179.
Zhou, J. N., Hofman, M. A., Gooren, L. J., & Swaab, D. F. (1995). A sex difference in the human brain and its relation to transsexuality. *Nature, 378*, 68–70.

Article

International Social Work
55(2) 155–167

DOI: 10.1177/0020872811425807
isw.sagepub.com
SAGE

Promoting diversity or confirming hegemony? In search of new insights for social work

Kerry Brydon
Monash University, Australia

Abstract

All human societies have constructed indigenous strategies for responding to human need. While there are calls for social work to embrace diversity, there remains dissatisfaction with the hegemonic spread of Western social work. Analysis reveals different cultural orientations in a number of contexts and suggests that the Western context is indigenous defined by values and characteristics that are inconsistent with the other cultural orientations. This reality not only gives rise to serious questions regarding the applicability of Western social work to other cultural orientations, but also points to the need to develop new skills, values and theories for social work.

Keywords

difference, diversity, indigenous practices, insights, Western context

Introduction

Any discussion concerning the nature of international social work embraces a fundamental question as to whether the discussion is relevant outside the realm of academic debate. The reality is that most practitioners in all contexts remain primarily concerned with the demands and challenges of their day-to-day work. However, there is a compelling argument that practitioners do

Corresponding author: Kerry Brydon, Monash University, PO Box 197, Caulfield East 3145, Australia.
Email: kerry.brydon@monash.edu

need to pay attention to the nature of international social work. There is increasing evidence that under a framework of globalization, problems that originate in one context increasingly have to be addressed by practitioners in another context.

A clear issue, upon reflection, that pervaded my practice was that cross-cultural sensitivity urged me to be sympathetic towards, and sensitive to, other culture viewpoints or ways of knowing. There was not, however, any fundamental challenge to re-consider my own ways of knowing and to critically reflect on these and consider the extent to which they have to be modified. Nor was there a primary challenge to the theories, models and skills of social work theory and questions about a need for new social work theory.

This was to change a few years ago when I left the field and became involved in the delivery of a cross-national social work education programme offered by an Australian University in Singapore. In particular, my curiosity was piqued by the debates concerning Western hegemony and professional imperialism in both practice and social work education (Askeland and Payne, 2006; Gray and Fook, 2004); the tensions between universalism and indigenization (Gray, 2005); and the extent to which core social work values can be held to be true in a wide range of diverse contexts (Sewpaul, 2005).

This discussion will begin by offering an overview of the literature and then by the findings of an analysis, developed from a literature review, of the different ways in which it is possible to view the world. The conclusions will emphasize the need for those in the Western paradigm to challenge their own thinking and to come to an understanding of the extent to which Western thought is 'merely' an indigenized form of knowledge and thought. It is only by (re)constructing Western knowledge in this light that it will become possible to move from Western hegemony towards the embrace of diversity.

An overview of the debates

There is consistency among commentators that throughout history, human societies have constructed particular, or indigenous, ways of responding to human need and ensuring that particular social structures are adhered to in order to main social order (Payne, 2005; Rwomire and Radithlhokwa, 1996), thus opening a way to understanding that there are many ways of responding to need. As well, religion has played a significant part in the formulation of response to social need in many contexts (Payne, 2005; Tsang and Yan, 2001). In part, social work emerged in the Western context as a consequence of the secularization of the welfare role of organized religion (Payne, 2005).

Social work emerged in the Western context as a response to the problems of that time as they related to the consequences of social problems that arose in response to industrialization and urbanization, as well as in response to concerns about social unrest that arose from these processes and the need to maintain social order (Lorenz, 2008). At the time that social work emerged, as in the current Western context, the culture was not homogenous but displayed particular power constellations and dynamics among divergent social groups. This set the scene for social work to develop along the lines of the care/control dichotomy. Specifically, the functions of social work initially, and later social work education, were tied to the cultural, social, economic and political realities of the context (Cheung and Liu, 2004; Gray, 2005), in this instance to the United States and Western Europe. From an international perspective, this means that social work can be constructed as a product of the Western world (Tsang and Yan, 2001), although some argue that social work has always been international in nature (Brown et al., 2005; Healy, 2001; Hegar, 2008; McDonald, 2006).

The definition of international social work remains both contested and elusive. One definition talks about action and the capacity for action at the international level by social workers (Healy, 2001). Some commonalities in social work across the globe appear to include assuming a wide range of responsibilities and largely being concerned with problems of poverty, child and family welfare concerns and questions of social exclusion (Healy, 2001).

It has been argued that international social work has been constructed to reflect globalized Western traditions held to be universally relevant (Haug, 2005). This view of globalized (Western) traditions as being universally applicable is not necessarily held by others. Social work services, as defined by Western standards, are only available to a minority of the world's people (Tsang and Yan, 2001). Further, access to the discourse on international social work is dependent on the ability to speak with the conceptual and linguistic capacity of those in the West who construct the conversation (Haug, 2005). This author goes on to express concern about power balances that undermine the capacity to achieve mutual exchange and dialogue, and argues that the paradigm from which international social work discourse has been constructed represents a localized tradition that has been presented as a universal knowledge system that is universally applicable. What is important here is that there is no evidence that the Western paradigm is either universal, including in the so-called Western context, or that it has relevance in a range of contexts.

An analysis of different world views

The analysis is based on a review of literature that was undertaken in order to gain insight into the characteristic features of differing perspectives about how particular cultural orientations construct their understanding of the world.

This literature review was a component of a larger literature review concerning international social work. The literature review commenced in 2006 and is ongoing.

A particular challenge in undertaking this analysis is that the different paradigms do not fall into neat, homogenous groups. Neither does a dominant characteristic of one culture mean that a similar theme does not exist in another culture. Culture concerns the sum total of ways of living developed by a group of human beings to meet biological, psychological, social and spiritual needs. It refers to elements such as values, norms, beliefs, attitudes, folk ways, behaviour styles and traditions that are linked together to form an integrated whole that functions as a group (Lee and Greene, 1999).

The indigenization of social work refers to a process of relating the social work and social work education function to the cultural, political and social realities of a particular country (Cheung and Liu, 2004; Gray, 2005; Gray and Fook, 2004). Indigenous is a contested term raising issues about who has the right to call themselves indigenous as well as complex political issues concerning land rights and appropriate responses to social problems. The *Macquarie Concise Dictionary* (1998) defines indigenous to mean originating in and characterizing a particular region or country; inherent in and natural to (p. 573). In the social work context there is argument that the term infers concern with the developing world (Marais and Marais, 2007). These authors further argue that without the incorporation of indigenous beliefs into social work's core values it will not be possible to identify a unified worldview of social work.

Calls for indigenization are based on discontent with the dominant paradigm. This calls for the articulation of local traditions and thought in order to enable these to be adapted to Western social work models, while at the same time using local thought to challenge and refine methods and models from the Western school (Ferguson, 2005). What is suggested is that the relationship between social work theories and indigenous traditions ought not to be constructed as linear but as multi-directional (Ferguson, 2005).

What is important is that processes of indigenization are managed within a conceptual framework that carefully considers the merits of indigenized knowledge and structures, as well as the merits of existing knowledge and approaches, with a view to blending both paradigms into the local setting. It is important to avoid the pitfalls of assuming all that is indigenous is inherently what is required, just as all that is introduced is inherently undesired (Huang and Zhang, 2008). This returns to the notion of multi-directional flows of knowledge as previously suggested (Ferguson, 2005), demanding that there is careful review of both local and imported knowledge with a view to determining how to blend the two sources of knowledge for local application.

To review the context of multi-directional flows of knowledge and information it is necessary to consider some of the different perspectives that exist concerning the structure of society and welfare provision. In the Western tradition there is separation of Church and State as the fundamental way in which freedom of religion can be achieved (Yousif, 2000), but in other contexts there is a concern to ensure that there is an emphasis on spiritual frameworks as the fundamental way in which social relationships are organized. For example, Islam concerns itself with God's relationship with his people and is used as the means of ordering social relations, social and political institutions and issues of economic prosperity (Saeed, 2006). Spirituality forms the cornerstone of African views and holds that all elements of the universe are connected since they are dependent on each other (Graham, 2000), while the Hindu approach emphasizes interdependence, community and divinity (Hodge, 2004).

One further way of distinguishing social order is to consider the nature of individual and collective approaches. In contexts such as Islam, Asian contexts, African contexts and Indian contexts, emphasis is placed on loyalty to the group (Dwairy, 2006); the interests of society generally assume precedence over individual interests (Yousif, 2000); human beings care viewed as a collective meaning that what happens to the individual happens to the group (Graham, 2000); and core values may be expressed in terms of harmony with the land, omnipresent spirituality and interconnectivity between people and their environment (Briskman, 2007). While there may be concern that individual needs are overlooked due to the focus on the group in these societies, in the Western context there is an expectation that individuals can provide for themselves (Payne, 2005), and once that the State assumed responsibility for its citizens individuals were no longer dependent on their families (Dwairy, 2006).

The broad individualist/collectivist divide has implications for the affording of rights. The separation of Church and State assumes that the individual is autonomous and able to make judgements that that are not pre-determined by faith (Scott, 2007). The Islamic context takes a position that human rights are inviolable and every individual is a sacred entity, while also holding that the individual must behave with a sense of social responsibility (Ahmad, 2000). In other contexts, such as the Hindu tradition, there is a concept of duty owed to individuals and institutions such as the duty of a son to his father and a wife to her husband (Hodge, 2004). In the African tradition there are challenges for the provision of individual rights as the experience of colonization, in many instances, led to dispossession, oppression and marginalization that gave rise to structural disadvantage across a number of domains including economic, health and education (Yiman, 1990), meaning that there are problems not easily addressed by the provision of individual rights.

As started previously, all societies have developed ways of responding to human need and many responses involve charitable giving. While some would argue that these traditions of charity and benevolence have less concern with taking care of the poor and more concern with bargaining with the Gods (Chan and Chui, 2002), other traditional forms of helping emphasize solidarity, mutuality, collective responsibility, spirituality and community-based personhood (Graham, 2000).

Discussion

Social work has been defined as 'a profession that promotes social change, problem solving in human relationships and the empowerment and liberation of people. Principles of human rights and social justice are fundamental to social work' (International Federation of Social Workers, 2000). Powell and Geoghegan (2005) describe civil society as the space between the state and the market. Civil society can be linked to social work activities that seek to construct clients as citizens, not customers, and that seek to empower clients through strategies of inclusion (Powell and Geoghegan, 2005).

Contemporary debates concerning social work cannot ignore consideration of internationalization and globalization. This refers to relations between states (*Macquarie Concise Dictionary*, 1998). It leaves the nation-state as the essential unit and is generally characterized by bi-lateral relations. It presumes a product developed in one nation-state will have currency in another. This has particular relevance for social work as the definition infers that social work developed in one context will be relevant in another, a position clearly debated in social work. Globalization is multi-dimensional term that is usually defined from an economic perspective. It describes the ways in which previously separate societies come into increased contact with each other (Lyons, 1999). At the heart of globalization, as understood in the currently dominant neo-liberal tradition, is a concern with profits and decision-making according to market forces (Dominelli, 2010).

Western social work is indigenous in so far that it originated in and characterizes a specific location. Practitioner values and approaches are shaped by their personal, religious and other values; local and international Codes of Ethics; the nature of local social problems and needs; local models of response whether these be remedial, developmental, individualized or community focused; the nature of local laws and institutional structures; and the historical context including experiences of colonization. Different cultural contexts have different cultural norms, but they also have different traditions of helping along with different expectations of being helped.

To accept and incorporate other worldviews into one's frame of reference is difficult. It is necessary to move beyond 'sensitivity' to the cultural views of others. This relates to an introductory comment concerning my own efforts to grapple with the question of the extent to which social work values can be held to be universal. A central challenge is in seeking to identify those aspects of social work that are universal and those which can be accepted as indigenous, including indigenous to the Western world. There may be defining characteristics of social work that hold true in most contexts and there may be defining features of social work that only hold true in a specific context. For example, social work, universally, has concern for those in society who are marginalized, but the ways in which society and social work respond to need varies according to contextual factors including time, history, place and stage of development.

According to Gray (2005), universal social work is about issues and problems that arise across national boundaries and the identification of commonalities in theory and practice. Many of the debates in contemporary social work, however, claim to embrace diversity but remain vested in Western hegemony concerned with both the concepts and language that define the discourse about international social work. By contrast, emphasis needs to rest on the identification of commonalities while also embracing difference. One way to achieve this is to posit Western social work in an indigenous form of practice and to consider ways in which it can relate to other indigenous paradigms of practice, a position so eloquently put by Haug (2005). Another way to achieve this is through taking the time to explore the contours of both how social problems are defined in other contexts at the same time as exploring the rationale that underpins the selection of a particular approach to social problems.

Cross-cultural awareness tends to imply that the primary challenge (for Western social workers) is to gain insight, and therefore a better understanding, about other cultures. As culture is held to affect all spheres of an individual's life it is, therefore, not possible to construct a culture-free form of social work (Lee and Greene, 1999). Lee and Greene (1999) also urge social workers to gain cultural sensitivity into the views, experiences and expectations of their clients. This is a valid position, but it neglects the challenge to social workers to gain insight into their own culture and to appreciate the extent to which their culture offers but a single lens through which to view the world. This position has the potential to reinforce notions of Western hegemony by reinforcing the dominance of Western culture and ideas as meaning that the need is to understand the exotic other but not to shift one's own views.

It becomes evident that there are two primary issues to be considered. Each paradigm of cultural perspective has evolved over a very long period of time. How then, is it possible for the Western position to claim it is has reached a somehow superior level of evolution? The other primary issue is that the Western paradigm, when placed into the global context, is something of a minority.

These themes, however, exist at the macro-level and there are more pertinent questions to be considered through more micro analysis; these have clear implications for the nature of both social work theory and practice, while social work has been defined as a profession concerned with human rights and social justice as fundamental to social work (International Federation of Social Workers, 2000).

It is also evident that the separation of Church and State, a fundamental principle of Western society through which religion is relegated to the private realm, is out-of-step with all other traditions where religion/spirituality is inherently intertwined with day-to-day life. This has significant implications for secular theories of social work and the need to seek ways to connect the secular and the spiritual in order to offer meaning through intervention with a wide range of people.

In Western social work, the social worker is generally constructed in terms of maintaining a certain professional distance from their client, ensuring that they do not cross what are constructed as professional boundaries and enabling the client to identify their own solutions to their own problems. This position does not appear to accommodate clients who, from their cultural perspective, look to the social worker as an expert able to offer solutions (Ejaz, 1989; Lee, 2004). More significantly, the position does not accommodate a view that holds subjectivity to be an illusion and holds that both the social worker and the client can gain from the encounter (Schiele, 1997). These issues go to the heart of the way in which the professional relationship is constructed and have implications for both basic helping skills, particularly concerning the ways in which the professional role might be articulated, as well as the ways in which interventions will be constructed.

With its commitment to individual autonomy, however compromised and complex this might be (Green and McDermott, 2010), there are serious implications for a number of social work's more closely held values. More importantly, if the individual constructs themselves as existing as part of a wider network of family and community to an extent that individual preferences are subordinated to group needs, there arise important questions about how social workers might harness the will and energy of the group to help bring about desired change. Clearly, the traditional 1:1 casework relationship would seem limited in such context, suggesting that group and community approaches might be more effective. Regardless of the method of intervention, there arise significant challenges to notions of (individual) client self-determination and to notions of confidentiality.

Such questions do not sit easily with the social work tradition that has embraced confidentiality and self-determination as core skills and characteristics shaping social work. Notwithstanding the fact that these values originated in the Western context, they have been incorporated into social work practice in other contexts.

Clearly, there are many urgent and complex tasks confronting social work in a bid to develop a body of theory, skills and values that afford all cultural paradigms equal status and respect. One way to construct this could be to position our understanding of social work as involving information flow between social work and a number of different cultural paradigms. These different cultural paradigms have the capacity to relate both to each other and to social work, suggesting that the interplay of forces is more important than differences between the paradigms.

Social work is influenced, shaped and defined by a number of factors, including the specific practice context within which social work is being delivered. The strength of such a conceptual framework is that it both avoids the competitiveness of paradigms and affords all paradigms equal importance in shaping the practice of social work in the individual context and cultural tradition. A further conceptual strength is that this allows for the development of social work both in context and over time. The key question is not concerned with how we position ourselves in relation to each other, but rather what we can learn from each other.

Typically, social work enters new territory through a transmission stage but is followed by indigenization as there is reaction to various aspects of the model transmitted, followed by authentification as there is reorganization to suit local circumstances (Cheung and Liu, 2004). New models and new understandings emerge, capable of being transmitted back to the original source.

An underpinning view is that no cultural tradition is absolute. Hence, when considering the defining characteristics of collectivist traditions, it would appear these are not absolute. While the well-being of the family may be an important, if not primary, consideration, it does not mean that the needs of the individual are not also taken into consideration. The individualist tradition of the West, in similar vein, is not absolute and the presumption of individual rights does not preclude consideration of the needs and rights of the family or community.

Returning to the theme of collectivist versus individualist society, it is important to emphasize that these concepts are not exclusive but rather should be understood to exist on a continuum. While for the individual there may be a dominance of the values, as defined by their social context, this is not to imply that, for example, there is an absence of collectivist traits in a primarily individualist society. Within this framework, what each of us determines to be right or wrong, good or bad, is largely determined by the dominant values of the culture, the normative expectations that underlie individual and social conduct (Laungani, 2004). In any culture there are four dominant themes, each of these being inter-related and able to be represented as in Figure 1.

Figure 1 suggests that culture is constructed through a number of paradigms, each of which experiences some inherent tensions. The issue here is that there

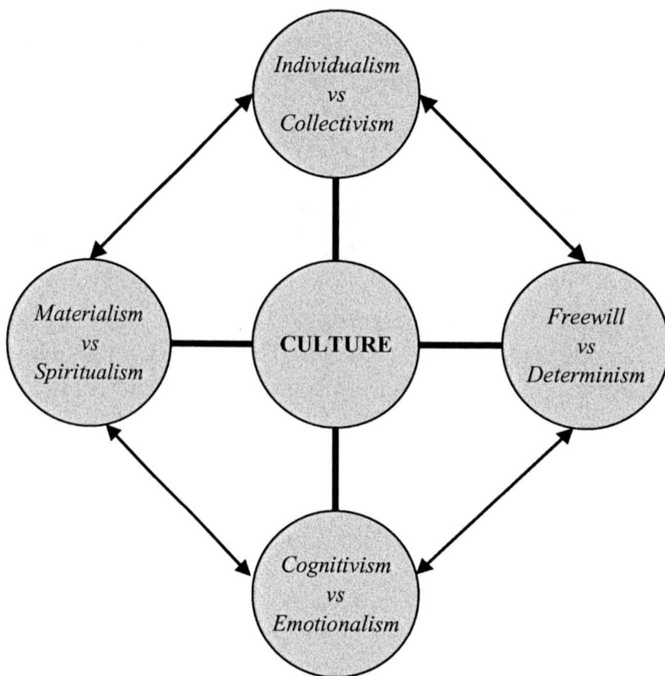

Figure 1. A framework for cultural relativity

is need to explore the cultural worldview based on the determinants of social conduct. This is much more than undergoing cross-cultural training that tends to veer towards racism and 'political correctness' (Laungani, 2004; Marais and Marais, 2007), rather than to seek a deeper analysis that explores the implications of culture for the individual and how they view the world. Implicit in this position is the need for social work, and social workers, to consider the impact of their own values and cultural tradition on their behaviour while simultaneously undertaking a similar analysis with respect to their client(s).

A particular strength of this approach is that the values are not presented as absolutes but as two sides to the same coin. Specifically, for example, there will be the positioning of individuals on a scale between materialism and spirituality with there being differences in emphases according to culture, context time and individual preferences.

Conclusions

One difficulty with ascribing traditions to a collective of countries is, of course, that countries conforming to that tradition are by no means homogeneous. All countries achieve their own individual solutions and within a country there is further heterogeneity. Nevertheless, there are clear strands of common approach emergent from the analysis.

The foregoing analysis demonstrates that many of the cultural orientations of the West contradict all other cultural orientations. This ought to be sufficient basis to begin first, reviewing and second, developing more culturally appropriate skills and theories for social work. Calls for cultural sensitivity are a starting point but not an end point unless Western social workers are prepared to critique their own cultural orientations and move towards different ways of knowing and experiencing the world.

A pertinent question, therefore, is the extent to which the Western context is prepared to forgo its hegemony and to challenge its own understanding of social work and its inherent values, skills and theories. There is a significant set of challenges that become apparent in terms of moving the debate away from macro-concepts towards the more micro focus on the development of new theories, skills, values and understanding for social work in its global context.

Funding

This research received no specific grant from any funding agency in the public, commercial, or not-for-profit sectors.

Acknowledgement

The anonymous reviewer of this article applied a rigorous critique that both stimulated and challenged my thinking. The time spent by the reviewer is deeply appreciated.

References

Ahmad, K. (2000) 'Islam and Democracy: Some Conceptual and Contemporary Dimensions', *The Muslim World* 90(1/ 2): 1–21.

Askeland, G. and M. Payne (2006) 'Social Work Education's Cultural Hegemony', *International Social Work* 49(6): 731–43.

Briskman, L. (2007) *Social Work with Indigenous Communities*. Sydney: The Federation Press.

Brown, T., K. Brydon, B. Tan, L. Ng, S. Han and P. Woo (2005) 'Harmonising the Local and the International in Social Work Education and Practice'. Presentation to the 18th Asian Pacific Social Work Conference, Seoul.

Chan, C. and E. Chui (2002) 'Making Hong Kong a Better Place: The Contribution of Social Workers to Innovation', in D. Shek, L. Chow, A. Fai and J. Lee (eds) *Advances in Social Welfare in Hong Kong*, pp. 59–80. Hong Kong: The Chinese University Press.

Cheung, M. and M. Liu (2004) 'The Self-concept of Chinese Women and the Indigenization of Social Work in China', *International Social Work* 47(1): 109–27.

Dominelli, L. (2010) 'Globalization, Contemporary Challenges and Social Work Practice', *International Social Work* 53(5): 599–612.

Dwairy, M. (2006) *Counselling and Psychotherapy with Arabs and Muslims: A Culturally Sensitive Approach*. New York: Teachers College Press.

Ejaz, F. (1989) 'The Nature of Casework Practice in India: A Study of Social Workers' Perceptions in Bombay', *International Social Work* 32(1): 25–38.

Ferguson, K. (2005) 'Beyond Indigenization and Reconcepitalization: Towards a Global, Multidirectional Model of Technology Transfer', *International Social Work* 48(5): 519–35.

Graham, M. (2000) 'Honouring Social Work Principles – Exploring the Connections between Anti-racist Social Work and African-centred Worldviews', *Social Work Education* 19(5): 423–36.

Gray, M. (2005) 'Dilemmas of International Social Work: Paradoxical Processes of Indigenisation, Universalism and Imperialism', *International Journal of Social Welfare* 14: 231–8.

Gray, M. and J. Fook (2004) 'The Quest for a Universal Social Work: Some Issues and Implications', *Social Work Education* 23(5): 625–44.

Green, D. and F. McDermott (2010) 'Social Work from Inside and between Complex Systems: Perspectives on Person-in-environment for Today's Social Work', *British Journal of Social Work* 40(8): 2414–30.

Haug, E. (2005) 'Critical Reflections on the Emerging Discourse of International Social Work', *International Social Work* 48(2): 126–35.

Healy, L. (2001) *International Social work: Professional Action in an Interdependent World*. New York: Oxford University Press.

Hegar, R. (2008) 'Transatlantic Transfers in Social Work: Contributions of Three Pioneers', *British Journal of Social Work* 38: 716–33.

Hodge, D. (2004) 'Working with Hindu Clients on a Spiritually Sensitive Manner', *Social Work* 49(1): 27–38.

Huang, Y. and X. Zhang (2008) 'A Reflection on the Indigenization Discourse in Social Work', *International Social Work* 51(5): 611–22.

International Federation of Social Workers (2000) *Definition of Social Work*. Geneva: International Federation of Social Workers. Available online at: www.ifsw.org (accessed 16 February 2006).

Laungani, P. (2004) *Asian Perspectives in Counselling and Psychotherapy*. Hove: Brunner-Routledge.

Lee, E. (2004) 'The Ways of Being a Social Worker: Implications for Confucianism to Social Work Education and Clinical Practice', *Smith College Studies in Social Work* 74(2): 393–408.

Lee, M. and G. Greene (1999) 'A Social Constructivist Framework for Integrating Cross-cultural Issues in Teaching Clinical Social Work', *Journal of Social Work Education* 35(1): 21–37.

Lorenz, W. (2008) 'Paradigms and Politics: Understanding Methods Paradigms in an Historical Context', *British Journal of Social Work* 28: 625–44.

Lyons, K. (1999) *International Social Work: Themes and Perspectives*. Aldershot: Ashgate.

McDonald, C. (2006) *Challenging Social Work: The Context of Practice*. Basingstoke: Palgrave Macmillan.

Macquarie Concise Dictionary (1998) 3rd edn. Sydney: Macquarie University Press.
Marais, L. and L. Marais (2007) 'Walking between Two Worlds: An Exploration of the Interface between Indigenous and First-world Industrialized Culture', *International Social Work* 50(6): 809–20.
Payne, M. (2005) *The Origins of Social Work: Continuity and Change*. Basingstoke: Palgrave Macmillan.
Powell, F. and M. Geoghegan (2005) 'Reclaiming Civil Society: The Future of Global Social Work?', *European Journal of Social Work* 8(2): 129–44.
Rwomire, A. and L. Radithlhokwa (1996) 'Social Work in Africa: Issues and Challenges', *Journal of Social Development in Africa* 11(2): 5–19.
Saeed, A. (2006) *Islamic Thought: An Introduction*. Abingdon: Routledge.
Schiele, J. (1997) 'The Contour and Meaning of Africentric Social Work', *Journal of Black Studies* 27(6): 800–19.
Scott, R. (2007) 'Contextual Citizenship in Modern Islamic Thought', *Islam and Christian–Muslim Relations* 18(1): 1–18.
Sewpaul, V. (2005) 'Global Standards: Promise and Pitfalls for Re-inscribing Social Work in Civil Society', *International Journal of Social Welfare* 14: 210–17.
Tsang, A. and M. Yan (2001) 'Chinese Corpus, Western Application: The Chinese Strategy of Engagement with Western Social Work Discourse', *International Social Work* 44(4): 433–54.
Yiman, A. (1990) *Social Development in Africa 1950–1985*. Aldershot: Avebury.
Yousif, A. (2000) 'Islam, Minorities and Religious Freedom: A Challenge to Modern Theory of Pluralism', *Journal of Muslim Minority Affairs* 20(1): 29–41.

Author biography

Kerry Brydon is a lecturer and Singapore Program Coordinator, Social Work at Monash University.

Hearing the stories of Australian Aboriginal and Torres Strait Islander social workers: challenging and educating the system

Bindi Bennett and Joanna Zubrzycki

Hearing the stories of Australian Aboriginal and Torres Strait Islander social workers highlights the powerful influence that cultural identity has on their practice. Their identity is continuously negotiated alongside a professional social work identity that is dominated by Western discourse. The tensions that these social workers experience in their practice is revealed in the findings of a qualitative research project conducted by an Indigenous and a non-Indigenous practitioner and researcher. The researchers spoke to Aboriginal and Torres Strait Islander social workers engaged in diverse areas of practice across Australia. Their stories reveal a complex range of cultural and professional challenges. These include the difficulties encountered when working with their own kinship networks and the need to constantly negotiate personal and professional boundaries. The paper concludes with some thoughts about how the practice of Indigenous social workers can provide valuable lessons for Australian social work.

Keywords
boundaries, Indigenous, social work.

Introduction

Aboriginal and Torres Strait Islander social workers juggle multiple identities and practice within a framework that is informed by the history of the oppression of Aboriginal Australians and the daily realities of disadvantage experienced by their own families and communities. The purpose of this article is to present the findings of a collaborative research project undertaken with a group of six Aboriginal and Torres Strait Islander social workers over an 18-month period (2000–2001). The aims of the research were to identify how this group of social work practitioners:

1 Reconcile their Indigenous identity with their professional social work roles
2 Balance their cultural knowledge and practices alongside a professional social

Bindi Bennett is a counsellor with Centacare, Canberra. Formerly she lectured at Charles Sturt University. She has also had practice experience in Child and Adolescent Mental Health.
Email: bindi_bennett@hotmail.com,
Joanna Zubrzycki is a lecturer at the School of Social Work, Australian Catholic University and a PhD student at Curtin University, Western Australia.
Email: J.Zubrzycki@signadou.acu.edu.au

work discourse that reflects the dominant culture

3 Construct their professional and personal boundaries

This paper also documents the process of developing a collaborative research partnership between an Indigenous and a non-Indigenous social worker.

The experiences of Australian Aboriginal and Torres Strait Islander social workers

There has been scant research about the roles that Indigenous social workers play in their communities or in the broader social work context. A review of the professional literature indicates a strong emphasis on the documentation of Indigenous disadvantage including the involvement of social workers and welfare authorities in the historical oppression of Aboriginal and Torres Strait Islander communities (Reynolds 2000; Gilbert 2001). Welfare professionals are encouraged to address this disadvantage arising from our history and aim for cultural competence in their practice (Weaver 1999; Bessarab 2000).

The work of indigenous practitioners is primarily documented in research that explores the experiences of Aboriginal health workers (Soong 1983; Folds 1985). These workers are often regarded as cultural brokers, people who mediate between two cultures and who subsequently experience the tensions of being caught between conflicting professional and cultural expectations (Soong 1983). This juggling of professional and cultural identities and obligations resonates strongly with our research participants.

Highlighting similar tensions, '*Murri way!*' (Lynn *et al.* 1998), research conducted in North Queensland, identifies unique features of Aboriginal and Torres Strait Islander welfare and social work practices. The study documents the issues that welfare practitioners experience in relation to obligation, boundaries and professional development. Our research is a continuation of their work, focusing more specifically on the practice of Indigenous social workers.

The research journey

Joanna's story

I was the initial researcher posing the following question: how do Australian social workers construct their personal and professional boundaries? I was interested in exploring the influence of a worker's cultural heritage and gender on their practice. One of the motivating factors for conducting this research was that as a social worker from a Polish–Australian background, my cultural identity strongly influences how I practice and teach social work. The larger research project (part of my Doctoral research) involves interviewing social workers from non-English speaking, Anglo and Indigenous backgrounds. I was particularly keen to include Aboriginal and Torres Strait Islander practitioners in the study as they are often working with some of the most marginalised people in Australia and hence the pressures arising from this area of practice are complex and warrant exploration and documentation. The research process began in 2000 with a pilot interview with an Aboriginal social worker, Bindi. Bindi's response to the interview facilitated her role changing from participant to co-researcher and shifted the initial focus of the research to a collaborative exploration of Indigenous social work.

Bindi's voice

I was interested in the research because it involved Aboriginal practice. For the first time I was given permission to talk about what I really did on a day to day level. When I read the transcript of my interview I rang Joanna to ask her '*Did I really say all that? Do I really do all that?* It was a lifting of the secret of how I work. I wanted to be part of this journey of discovering what it is to be an Aboriginal social worker.

An evolving methodology

A qualitative methodology was chosen to allow new knowledge and theory to develop from the data (Alston & Bowles 1998). This methodology is identified by a number of Indigenous (Lynn et al. 1998) and non-Indigenous researchers (Nelson & Allison 2000) as culturally appropriate because '*it facilitates the emergence of the personal experiences and perspectives of the Indigenous participants as data rather than the researcher predetermining the issues*' (p. 29).

The second aspect of the methodology recognised Bindi's role as co-researcher. This involved undertaking the research as a collaborative inquiry (also referred to as action research). Gibbs (2001) identifies research that embraces collaboration between the researcher and the participants as having the potential to achieve shared decision making and analysis of the data and greater accountability towards the participants and their communities. Importantly the research recognises the participants as owners or co-owners of the information. Forming collaborative research partnerships with Indigenous people signals a '*message to participants that they are viewed as knowledgeable potential partners, as keepers or guardians of treasured cultural and personal information and as worthy advisers*' (p. 30).

The research literature also documents the dangers of exploitation and co-opting that can occur when a non-Indigenous researcher conducts research with Indigenous people and maintains ownership and control (Lynn *et al.* 1998). It is important to ensure that an Indigenous co-worker is involved in research projects conducted by non-Indigenous people (Ivanitz 1999).

A snowball sampling method was chosen to identify possible participants (Yegidis *et al.* 1999; p.184). An initial group of Aboriginal and Torres Strait Islander social workers were invited to participate in the research and they were then asked to identify others who might be interested in being interviewed. Joanna adopted a semi-structured technique while individually interviewing participants. Transcripts of the taped interviews were sent to participants and they were encouraged to change any aspect of the data.

As the project changed and Bindi became a joint researcher, Joanna informed the other participants and they were also invited to become co-researchers. They were happy about Bindi's participation but due to their own commitments they chose to remain in contact and offer encouragement rather than become co-researchers. At the completion of the interviews Bindi and Joanna jointly conducted a thematic analyses of the data using techniques of grounded theory (Lynn *et al.* 1998). A copy of this paper was sent to the participants for comment before a final draft was prepared. As joint owners of the knowledge, the participants have already used the research to share and discuss ideas and issues among other Indigenous people.

Six stories of Aboriginal and Torres Strait Islander social work practice

We have chosen to present a number of themes that highlight key features of Indigenous social work practice. Pseudonyms have been adopted where requested by the participants. We will begin by locating these workers in their context.

The six Aboriginal and Torres Strait Islander social workers come from Queensland, New South Wales, Northern Territory, Australian Capital Territory and Western Australia. They have been qualified as social workers for 2–6 years. Their practice experiences are varied and include; child protection, family support, income support, child and adolescent mental health, juvenile justice, social policy, research and teaching. The participants work in both Indigenous specific and mainstream positions. They are aged between 20 and 40. Two men and four women were interviewed. The workers regard the research as a unique opportunity to talk about the complexity of their practice. They often feel unheard and misunderstood by the non-Indigenous social work community.

Growing up in Aboriginal and Torres Strait Islander communities and being a social work student

Some of the issues that participants confronted in their childhood included; high levels of incarceration of young people, high levels of school drop out, racism, family violence and ongoing experiences of loss and grief caused by the frequent death of peers and family members. This leads to a significant lack of positive adult role models.

While all participants shared these stories there was also recognition of the diversity of cultural practices and issues in Aboriginal and Torres Strait Islander communities. Bayliss (1995) reinforces the recognition of cultural pluralism as a key aspect of developing effective cross-cultural practice. Importantly the participants experiences engendered a commitment to somehow '*give back to their community*'(All).

'I've always had contact with social workers all through my life. Right from the time of being a young child and having experienced removal, through to being an adult and being married with small children and one of my children being sick and dealing with social workers at that level. So it's always been a part of my life. Being

unhappy with quite a bit of the contact that I've had with social workers, I actually thought that I wanted to change the way that social workers interact with Indigenous people and parents of sick children. I thought one of the ways of doing that was to go and become a social worker myself'. (Sue)

However, the process of committing themselves to studying social work also meant that they were joining a profession that was (and some would argue still is) involved in the oppression of Indigenous people (Human Rights & Equal Opportunity Commission 1997). Some participants spoke of their communities wary and suspicious responses about their decision to study social work, while others felt supported and encouraged.

'Social workers do have quite a bad name within the Aboriginal community and mainly around the removal of children. But the Indigenous community has also tried to get Indigenous people to become social workers. Once you're in the system, people get very frightened of you because now you have this white education and you are a social worker and so you are a potential threat to the removal of people's children from them. The community also gets worried about people going off and getting educated that they may lose that person from their community or that they somehow change' (Sue)

The experiences of being an Indigenous social work student reveals a mix of determination to get through the course, isolation and alienation in terms of their perspectives and values, coupled with high expectations from their lecturers that they understood all things Aboriginal. One participant shared her story of alienation when she attended a lecture on Indigenous issues delivered by a non-Indigenous 'expert'.

'She was talking about what Indigenous people say and do. It did not make sense to me. I did not recognise any of the information that I was hearing. This is defining who I am but yet I don't recognise it so does that mean that I am a lie or that my whole life is a lie?' (Jess)

Some of the participants felt overwhelmed by the content of the subjects, especially those relating to Indigenous stories and culture.

'The women they are talking about are my Mum. They are talking about my life here and I used to get really angry. I got really angry learning about Aboriginal history as well. It taught me a lot about my mother, my family, my past' (Clinton)

Most of the participants noted that the support of other Indigenous students and friends as well as access to University based Indigenous resource centres were vital in helping them get through their degrees (Bin-Sallik 2000).

The challenge of maintaining boundaries

The participants recalled that the teaching of personal and professional boundaries was unrealistic and failed to prepare them for working with Aboriginal and Torres Strait Islander communities. The dominant professional discourse insists on the maintenance of separateness between the personal and professional self, for example not developing friendships with clients or adopting a professional role with family members (AASW 2000). The experience of our participants is that these identities coexist and converge as a result of kinship ties, obligation and the realities of living and working in small communities.

Kinship ties

Due to the history of Indigenous Australia, Aboriginal people are often related to each other, if not directly then through links between families, for example by marriage. The social worker often finds themselves working with people with whom they have many complex ties. Compounding this is the fact that workers are usually isolated in a service in terms of qualifications and numbers, for example the only Indigenous mental health worker in the area (Bindi, Alf, Clinton) and this means that referral on is not applicable.

Obligation

Indigenous cultural identity encompasses an obligation to share resources and care for each other. This means that the worker/client relationship becomes influenced and informed by the importance of doing whatever is needed to help the client/family. Thus the helping relationship may be long-term and at times unpredictable.

'I just found this whole boundary thing very confusing. What are you supposed to do when you've got someone ringing you at 2 am? You know this has happened there is a crisis, they have been locked up, can you come and help me? What can you do? Well you can't just say no, because that is what happens and that would happen even if you were not a social worker. The whole professional thing is very blurry' (Alf)

Our research highlights that the cultural commitments of Indigenous social workers permeates all practice experiences. The participants acknowledge that it is important to learn about how to maintain ethical and professional practice within their communities, however, further research needs to be conducted as to how to balance professional and cultural demands.

The use of self in practice

Our findings suggest that Indigenous social workers embrace the self as a key element of their practice. Their personal experiences create a powerful link with the Indigenous and non-Indigenous people that they work with. This is supported by Lynn *et al.'s* (1998) research which identified that; '*considered and deliberate use was made by the workers of their own experience and problems and their way of dealing with them*' (p. 35).

One of the most important aspects of the use of self occurs during the introduction process. The participants spoke of the need, when working with other Indigenous people, to introduce not only their professional role, but also their cultural identity. This involves identifying birthplace and kinship ties, which remain a lifelong reference point. Due to the kinship system, workers often find themselves related to their clients and this needs to be established at the moment of introduction. This is both a professional and cultural responsibility and requires the establishment of culturally respectful communication and the need to clarify issues such as confidentiality especially in small communities (Lynn *et al.* 1998).

The introduction process can also involve sharing personal stories and experiences. The participants spoke about using self-disclosure, carefully recognising that it is often necessary to share their stories in order to enhance working relationships and establish credibility.

'People would always ask where are you from, where have you been and how did you get here? Often elder Aboriginal people will ask me what experiences have you got in this situation? Have you been depressed or anxious? How long have you been in this community? What is your story? So I think I don't really want to commit to this, but I have to' (Bindi)

The nature of Aboriginal and Torres Strait Islander social work practice

Acknowledging the influence of the kinship system also means engaging with the family as opposed to being individually focused. For example, it is important to get family permission to talk to and work with others as they may have a more appropriate intervention strategy than the worker and also have established more trust with the individual.

'So when you work with Aboriginal people you've got to expect that you're working with the family and not working with an individual, and you've got to respect that often the answers are within that family' (Jess and Sue).

Lynn *et al.*'s (1998) research reinforces these aspects of Indigenous social work intervention. '*Use of family as a resource and as part of the helping strategy was almost always the first option to be explored by the helper (p. 35).*' Kinship ties can sometimes preclude the worker from engaging with the individual or family. For example when dealing with family violence issues, some Indigenous workers may be seen by the client as too closely aligned with the community, potentially compromising confidentiality (Bennett 1997).

Another aspect of Indigenous social work is the influence that gender and age has on practice and relationships within the community. The community is regarded as the focal point for negotiating appropriate gender relations. It is generally not appropriate for workers to practice with people of a different age and gender. These differences can highlight gaps in power, status, authority and knowledge. All of the participants gave examples of working jointly with community members to restore age and gender balance. Workers also needed to be sensitive when working with the elders of the community.

'The community is the reference point, they're the point at which everyone determines what's going to happen and how through consultation. It is through them that a range of understandings about gender and age issues within different communities from rural to urban perspectives comes into play' (Julwul).

Supervision

The participants regard their supervisory relationships (usually with non-Indigenous senior workers) as complex and often inadequate. Workers are rarely given credibility for their cultural knowledge and social work supervisors generally do not understand key cultural aspects of social work practice. These included '*koori time*', home visits, the importance of maintaining a strong community identity and the reality that Aboriginal and Torres Strait Islander people often attend without appointments (All). Supervisors also may not have specific cultural knowledge to share with their workers and this leaves the Indigenous workers educating their supervisors on historical events, the importance of sharing personal experiences as well as other aspects of culturally sensitive practice.

I get really good non-Indigenous social work supervision. It is really structured, you do this with depression, you do that with anxiety and I get very poor cultural supervision. I spend most of the time trying to explain why I am working in this way (Bindi).

There are also gender issues in supervision with male Indigenous social workers unable to talk to female supervisors about men's issues and vice versa (Alf, Sue and Bindi).

Agency issues

The workers who are employed in Aboriginal and Torres Strait Islander specific positions feel restricted in their capacity to practice in their communities (Julwul, Alf & Clinton). Agency staff often lack a clear understanding of how 'best practice' and 'Indigenous practice' can coexist and as a consequence do not support workers to employ Indigenous practices, leaving the community alienated from the system. Workers feel compromised when they are required to encourage Indigenous people to use a service that is oppressive and alienating. For example, agency policies that enforce appointment schedules and do not support home visits, thus restricting the capacity of Indigenous workers to implement community based models of therapy (Alf, Clinton, Bindi). It is also suggested by some of the Indigenous social workers that they have to work harder in order to be recognised as a professional (Alf, Clinton, Julwul & Jess).

'Organisations want people there who are Indigenous and make a big 'who ha' about employing Indigenous people. But they don't make any room for people to be Indigenous. So what they really want is employees who just happen to be Indigenous rather than Indigenous employees' (Jess).

Our collective vision

Our research highlights the need to critically reflect on some of the dominant cultural assumptions implicit in contemporary Australian social work education and practice. Fundamentally Australian social work has historically developed as a 'white' profession hence our practice standards reflect the assumptions and realities of the dominant culture. This research challenges these assimilationist principles. The Aboriginal and Torres Strait Islander social workers clearly articulate a different practice reality in which their cultural, personal and professional identities converge. These workers are also expressing the need to be acknowledged and supported by the professional community.

There are some important issues that need to be considered:

- The social work profession should critically reflect on its professional culture. This research highlights aspects of social work knowledge and practice which are alienating to Aboriginal and Torres Strait Islander practitioners and communities, and can be regarded as oppressive in their application to Indigenous realities. To address this, Indigenous practice needs to be positioned as core social work knowledge and accepted as transferable across cultures and not marginalised. For example the teaching of issues such as the use of self needs to encompass the realities of worker's cultural obligations.
- All social workers need to develop networks with Indigenous communities and acknowledge, respect, listen, follow and consult. The recognition of individuals' knowledge, life stories and skills should be central to our practice, making collaboration and joint learning possible.
- Social workers need to support and acknowledge Aboriginal and Torres Strait Islander practitioners and recognise that these workers will not always have all of the answers about Indigenous issues.
- Social workers, and in particular supervisors, who are working with Indigenous workers need ongoing education around Indigenous issues. There also needs to be recognition that cultural supervision can exist alongside professional supervision.
- It is important that organisations begin to understand diversity within Indigenous communities, such as the difference between urban and rural cultures. Engaging with Aboriginal and Torres Strait Islander people is a lifelong learning endeavour for both Indigenous and non-Indigenous social workers.

Conclusion

'To some extent social work does recognise that Indigenous people are different, but it only seems to be able to do it on a very limited level. So yeah, people are different, but then we work at getting them to still fit into the mould, rather than go yeah people are different and we have to change the mould' (Julwul).

Acknowledgements

The authors would like to acknowledge and thank the research participants and their communities. The authors would also like to express their appreciation for the ongoing encouragement and support of Professor Jim Ife and Emeritus Professor Maev O'Collins.

References

ALSTON M & BOWLES W (1998), *Research for Social Workers.* Allen & Unwin, Sydney.

AUSTRALIAN ASSOCIATION OF SOCIAL WORKERS (2000), *Code of Ethics.* AASW, Canberra.

BAYLISS S (1995), Towards developing a multicultural service model for working in remote Cape York communities and the Torres Strait Islands. In: Camilleri P and Allen-Kelly K (eds), *Welfare and Diversity of Practice in North Queensland.* James Cook University Press, Townsville.

BENNETT B (1997), Domestic Violence. *Aboriginal and Islander Health Worker Journal,* 21 (July/August), 11–13.

BESSARAB D (2000), Working with Aboriginal Families: A Cultural Approach. In: Weeks W and Quinn M (eds), *Issues Facing Australian Families: Human Services Respond*, 3rd edn. Pearson Education, Sydney.

BIN-SALLIK MA (2000), *Aboriginal Women by Degrees*. University of Queensland Press, St Lucia.

FOLDS R (1985), Constraints on the Role of Aboriginal Health and Education Workers as Community Developers. *Australian Journal of Social Issues*, 20 (3), 228–233.

GIBBS A (2001), Social Work and empowerment-based research: Possibilities, process and question. *Australian Social Work*, 54 (1), 29–40.

GILBERT S (2001), Social Work with Indigenous Australians. In: Alston M and McKinnon J (eds), *Social Work: Fields of Practice*. Oxford University Press, Melbourne.

HUMAN RIGHTS and EQUAL OPPORTUNITY COMMISSION (1997), *Guide to the Findings and recommendations of the National Inquiry into the separation of Aboriginal and Torres Strait Islander children from their families*. Australian Government Publishing Service, Canberra.

IVANITZ M (1999), Culture, ethics and participatory methodology in cross-cultural research. *Australian Aboriginal Studies*, 2, 46–58.

LYNN R, THORPE R, MILES D, CUTTS C, BUTCHER A & FORD L (1998), *'Murri Way!' – Aborigines and Torres Strait Islanders Reconstruct Social Welfare Practice*. Report on Aboriginal and Torres Strait Islander helping styles in Social Welfare Practice in North Queensland. James Cook University, Townsville.

NELSON A & ALLISON H (2000), Values of urban Aboriginal parents: Food before thought. *Australian Occupational Therapy Journal*, 47, 28–40.

REYNOLDS H (2000), Indigenous social welfare: From low priority to recognition and reconciliation. In: McMahon A, Thompson J & Williams C (eds), *Understanding the Welfare State: Key Documents and Themes*. Tertiary Press, Victoria.

SOONG FS (1983), The role of Aboriginal Health Workers as cultural brokers: Some findings and their implications. *Australian Journal of Social Issues*, 18 (4), 268–273.

WEAVER H (1999), Indigenous People and the Social Work Profession: Defining Culturally Competent Services. *Social Work*, 44, 203–211.

YEGIDIS B, WEINBECH R & MORRISON-RODRIGUEZ B (1999), *Research Methods for Social Workers*. Allyn and Bacon, Boston.

Article accepted for publication August 2002

15

Aboriginal Approaches to Counselling

ROD McCORMICK

It is an exciting time to write a chapter on Aboriginal counselling approaches, as this ancient yet new profession is experiencing a period of rapid growth and development. To be clear, the profession of counselling is ancient because Aboriginal people have sought out guidance and "counselling" from expert helpers in their communities and on their lands for a long, long time. The counselling field is also new and emerging because resourceful healers and counsellors have recently started combining mainstream psychological approaches and traditional healing approaches in a complementary fashion, thereby creating new and increasingly effective ways to help others. Some clients will always prefer the traditional approaches to healing and will seek out traditional healers, whereas others will opt for treatment via mainstream psychological therapies. Aboriginal people seeking help now have a third option: to see a therapist/healer who is able to use and combine aspects of both teachings in a complementary way.

In this chapter I will describe a few of these innovative approaches and in doing so provide a brief overview of Aboriginal counselling. The chapter will first examine aspects of Aboriginal worldviews that are relevant to counselling, such as balance, connectedness, spirituality, nature, ceremony, and culture. An overview of mainstream and traditional approaches that facilitate healing for Aboriginal people will then be provided as a background to what happens when it is possible to combine the best of both. Research results describing the general theme of facilitation of healing will be described. Following that, examples of Aboriginal counselling and healing approaches will be provided for a broad range of counselling concerns, including counselling victims of physical and sexual abuse, career and vocational counselling, suicide prevention, and substance-abuse counselling. It should be noted that much of the information in this chapter is presented in the form of results from research performed by the author and other specialists in the field of Aboriginal counselling. This reliance on research findings is not accidental but represents a personal and professional bias of the author that practice must be based on sound research. Note that I use the term "Aboriginal" but sometimes refer to "First Nations" or "indigenous" peoples; in such cases, I am referring to the same peoples. As noted elsewhere in this volume, there is great diversity among Aboriginal peoples, and although it is therefore improper to generalize, there are also great similarities between Aboriginal peoples. Thus I use some generalizations to distinguish between Aboriginal and non-Aboriginal cultures.

Aboriginal Worldviews

Counselling and psychotherapy cannot take place without communication, and we cannot communicate with someone unless we have a shared language and worldview (Torrey 1986). To communicate with and provide counselling services to Aboriginal people, providers must understand the traditional worldview of Aboriginal people. Worldview inevitably affects our belief systems, decision making, assumptions, and modes of problem solving (Ibrahim 1984). LaFromboise, Trimble, and Mohatt summarize this concept clearly when they state: "Knowledge of and respect for an Aboriginal worldview and value system – which varies according to the client's tribe, level of acculturation, and other personal characteristics – is fundamental not only for creating the trusting counsellor-client relationship vital to the helping process but also for defining the counselling style or approach most appropriate for each client" (1990, 629).

Balance

The Aboriginal medicine wheel is perhaps the best representation of an Aboriginal worldview related to healing. The medicine wheel describes the separate dimensions of the self – mental, physical, emotional, and spiritual – as equal and as parts of a larger whole. The medicine wheel represents the balance that exists between all things. Traditional Aboriginal healing incorporates the physical, social, psychological, and spiritual being. It is difficult to isolate any one aspect (Primeaux 1977). It is thought that people become ill when they live in an unbalanced way (Medicine Eagle 1989). Balance, then, is essential for the Aboriginal person because the world itself is seen as a balance of transcendental forces, human beings, and the natural environment (Hammerschlag 1988). Counsellors must therefore realize that Aboriginal clients expect their counsellor to address their problems in a holistic way that incorporates the mental, physical, emotional, and spiritual dimensions of experience. It is also very important that the counsellor be balanced and centred when working with Aboriginal clients (Hart 2002).

Connectedness

The individual's connection to the world outside the self plays a significant role in Aboriginal healing. This theme of interconnectedness is prevalent throughout most Aboriginal

cultures and has been aptly described as a series of relationships, starting with the family, that reaches further and further out so that it encompasses the universe (Epes-Brown 1989). Traditional Aboriginal therapeutic approaches, unlike many Western approaches, usually involve more than just the therapist and client. Relatives and community members are often asked to be part of the healing process. Healing is often in the form of a community-sanctioned and community-run cleansing ceremony that involves the whole community (Ross 1992; Torrey 1986). For problems that arise within the Aboriginal community, it is thought that the best place to develop and initiate programs to deal with such problems is in the community itself (Nelson and McCoy 1992). Even in the case of individual problems, connections with family, community, and the larger environment often hold the keys to understanding the problems and facilitating healing. The one-on-one interaction characteristic of many Western counselling approaches is isolated outside the context of the community and family; therefore, it must be questioned as a valid means of dealing with Aboriginal client problems (Dauphinais, Dauphinais, and Rowe 1981).

Spirituality

For Aboriginal people, spirit plays as large a role in sickness and wellness as do the functioning of mind and body (Hammerschlag 1988). For many Aboriginal people, spirit means being connected with all of creation. Many different Aboriginal healing ceremonies and healing programs stress the need for reconnection with one's spirituality in order to heal. In the vision quest ceremony, for example, the Aboriginal person makes contact with his or her spiritual identity (Hodgson and Kothare 1990). Although the vision quest ceremony itself varied from nation to nation, there were many aspects common to all. The following description of the vision quest therefore attempts to be generic:

> About the time of puberty a boy was encouraged to go into the forest or the hills for several days at a time, fast during the day, and dream at night. To stay out for four days at a time was highly desirable. The fast was either a complete one or one with very little water and almost no food. The intent was to clear the mind so that they would be able to see the vision. Embarking on the Vision Quest, the youth would first enter a sweat lodge and go through a body purification. Then clutching sage grass in his hand, he would climb to an elevated site, either on a hilltop or in a perch in a tree, high above the world. There the youth would pray and fast waiting on the Great Spirit. Eventually, he would make contact and commune with his spirit, symbolic of his spiritual identity. Through this vision he would come to terms with his innermost self and accept his strengths and weaknesses. (Hodgson and Kothare 1990, 112)

Regardless of the ceremonies or practices used to connect with, strengthen, or cleanse the spirit, there exists a close association between illness and the spirit for most indigenous people around the world (Torrey 1986).

Nature

Nature, in the sense of the natural world outside cities and human habitations, is an important source of healing for many Aboriginal people, whereas mainstream psychological theory and practice reinforce the separation of healing practices from nature. This often leads to people disregarding nature as a means of healing. For many Aboriginal people there is a spiritual connection that exists between nature and humans because humans are seen as part of nature. All of creation is seen as being equal and part of the whole and is therefore equal in the eyes of the Creator. Connection to nature – which may be experienced by going out on the land and engaging in traditional land-based activities – often helps Aboriginal people who are seeking help to feel part of something much larger as well as to feel less lonely, stronger, more grounded, and more secure. The following comment by a young woman from a West Coast tribe who worked with the author illustrates one of the principles of connection with nature: "Learning to open up my heart to nature helped. The Elders have a name for that in my language – '*kan dalfta*.' This means heart opened up. When I opened up my heart to the beauty and peace of nature, it made me feel good. Problems aren't that great that you can't solve them once you have reached that level where you can go with the flow of nature."

Ceremony

Ritual and ceremony are tried and true ways for many Aboriginal people to give expression to personal experience while at the same time connecting with others in their community (Hammerschlag 1993). Ceremonies such as the spirit dances, the sweat lodge, and the pipe ceremonies are tools to maintain and deepen the individual's sense of connectedness to all things (Ross 1992). Although there has not been empirical research conducted on the efficacy of traditional healing ceremonies such as those mentioned, anecdotal evidence exists within the literature to attest to their effectiveness in healing (Hammerschlag 1988; Jilek 1982; Torrey 1986).

Tradition/Culture

One of the major roles of therapy and healing for traditional Aboriginal people is to reaffirm cultural values (LaFromboise et al. 1990). In a study examining Aboriginal drug and

alcohol counselling in British Columbia, a suggested culturally sensitive counselling framework for Aboriginal people included the theme of importance of personal and cultural identity (Anderson 1993). In a study conducted to determine the characteristics of recovery of personal meaning for Aboriginal people, one of the major themes or characteristics that emerged was that individuals valued knowledge of traditional Aboriginal culture (More 1985). Another characteristic of personal recovery in that same study was that the Aboriginal language was maintained or relearned. It is not surprising that the teaching of traditional culture has been found to be a successful way to facilitate healing in Aboriginal people. In one Aboriginal community, it was possible to reduce dramatically the teen suicide rate by having tribal Elders teach traditional culture to the teens in a group setting (Neligh 1990). By providing Aboriginal people with culture through stories and shared cultural activities, Elders were able to provide community members with guidance, direction, and self-understanding (Halfe 1993). This incorporation of self, or identity, with traditional ideology also provides Aboriginal people with strength for coping in the mainstream environment (Axelson 1985). This movement toward reconnecting with cultural beliefs, tradition, and ceremony as a way to overcome problems has been referred to as "retraditionalization" (LaFromboise et al. 1990).

What Facilitates Healing for Aboriginal People?

The major part of the literature that examines healing for Aboriginal people tends to be based on opinion and conjecture, not on research. In the field of counselling, the literature often provides advice to counsellors so that they can be more effective with Aboriginal clients, but it does not provide empirical evidence to support such advice. Several researchers (Dauphinais et al. 1981; Wohl 1989) refer to the lack of empirical studies that examine the effectiveness of specific counselling approaches with Aboriginal people. Having noted the lack of research in this field, this chapter will briefly examine some of the research and writing that does exist in an effort to identify effective counselling strategies and the key factors that facilitate healing for Aboriginal people.

Effective Mainstream Counselling Approaches with Aboriginal Clients

Western, or mainstream, healing approaches have been only partially successful in assisting Aboriginal people with their healing (LaFromboise et al. 1990; Sue and Sue 1990). There are several reasons for this. First, mental health programs and interventions that have been designed from a mainstream biomedical perspective do not recognize or meet the health needs of Aboriginal people, for they ignore the cultural, historical, and sociopolitical context (Smye and Mussell 2001). The traditions, values, and health belief systems of Aboriginal people are poorly understood by mental health providers and often not respected or even considered (Smye and Mussell 2001). Aboriginal clients have sometimes complained that mainstream therapy tries to shape their behaviour in a way that conflicts with Aboriginal lifestyle orientations and preferences (LaFromboise et al. 1990). Aboriginal clients may also fear that the mainstream therapist may try to change their cultural values and thereby alienate them from their own people and traditions (LaFromboise et al. 1990). In a discussion paper for the Royal Commission on Aboriginal Peoples entitled "The development of Aboriginal counselling," Peavy (1993) identifies several faulty assumptions and negative consequences that arise when mainstream counselling practices are imposed on Aboriginal people. These include cultural misconceptions of what is normal; an emphasis on individualism; fragmentation of the mental, physical, emotional, and spiritual dimensions of the person; neglect of Aboriginal history; and neglect of the client's social-support system. Nevertheless, and despite widespread difficulties in access, many Aboriginal people have turned to psychotherapy and counselling, although it may take considerable time and experience in talking with a therapist before they can begin to establish an effective working relationship with that therapist (Wing and Crow 1995). In one of the only reviews of the use of mainstream therapies with Aboriginal clients, LaFromboise and colleagues (1990) found that social-learning therapy and behavioural therapy had the most to offer Aboriginal people. Social-learning theory has strengths in terms of its use with Aboriginal clients, as it extensively uses role modelling (LaFromboise et al. 1990). Behavioural therapy can be effective because of its action-oriented focus on the present rather than the past. Both behavioural and social-learning therapies may be misused, however, when the therapist adopts a narrow or inappropriate focus that does not represent the client's goals (LaFromboise et al. 1990). Behaviour therapy, with its focus on behaviour rather than on feelings, is compatible with Aboriginal culture as long as counsellors help their clients to assess the possible consequences of making behavioural change. Cognitive therapy can also be popular, as its cognitive focus may downplay the expression of feelings. Each form of therapy is based on tacit models of the person and associated cultural values (Kirmayer 2007). Although the dominant theories of counselling emphasize individualism, for many Aboriginal peoples, relational notions of the self that connect the person to others (sociocentric), to the natural world, and to the spirit world are important. The danger is that without adequate understanding and respect for Aboriginal cultural values, the therapist may mistakenly try to change core cultural values of their Aboriginal clients.

In addition to individual approaches to therapy, some group approaches have seen successfully used with Aboriginal people. The attraction of group approaches to therapy is that they are similar to Aboriginal healing approaches such as the sweat lodge (Garrett and Osborne 1995). Family-systems therapy may be especially appropriate because of the importance many Aboriginal people place on the extended family. Indeed, the field of family therapy itself has been influenced by Aboriginal perspectives, notably in the development of family-network therapy (France, McCormick, and Rodriguez 2004; Speck

and Attneave 1973). The danger here again, however, is that the values of mainstream counselling, such as individuation, self-actualization, independence, and self-expression, may not be embraced by many Aboriginal clients.

The Role of the Family and Community in Counselling Aboriginal People

A key factor in healing for Aboriginal people is the process of dealing with problems with the assistance of others rather than by oneself. Assistance can be obtained from friends, the family, and the community as well as in the context of group counselling or on a social basis. According to traditional Aboriginal views, a person's psychological welfare must be considered in the context of the community (Trimble and Hayes 1984). Similarly, therapy for Aboriginal people should encourage the client to transcend him or herself by conceptualizing the self as being embedded in and expressive of community (Katz and Rolde 1981). Traditional healing methods often prove effective because they include the participation of family and community members, which increases the social support of the individual (Renfrey 1992). In a study with a Washington Tribe, Guilmet and Whited (1987) also found that the extended family was essential to most Aboriginal clients in terms of emotional support.

Should Western and Traditional Approaches to Healing be Combined?

In one review of successful healing strategies utilized by 50 Aboriginal people in British Columbia, it was found that the successful programs stressed traditional values, spirituality, and activities that enhanced self-esteem (McCormick 1995). Although most successful Aboriginal healing programs have been run using Aboriginal values and approaches, it is recommended by some that they could be enhanced by a fusion with mainstream psychological techniques (Anderson 1993). In an article considering the vision quest ceremony from an attachment-theory perspective, McCormick (1997) demonstrates how this traditional Aboriginal ceremony and a well-known mainstream psychological theory provide very similar teachings. According to attachment theory, a therapist must attempt to provide a secure base in order to help the client to reconstruct his or her faulty childhood parental attachment in a positive way. A traditional healing approach aims to foster reattachment not to a therapist but to the Great Spirit as manifested in nature (i.e., to the individual's spirituality). The reattachment process could be in the form of a vision quest ceremony in which the child or adult could attach him or herself to "Father Sky" or "Mother Earth" as metaphors of a spiritual bonding with nature and all of creation.

Integration is often not the easiest or best solution, however, as there exists a power differential between Western medicine and traditional healing. Western medicine has the power of the government, the law, and the medical system behind it and is therefore likely simply to overwhelm and assimilate traditional medicine in any attempt at integration. A more balanced and appropriate form of partnership may be a complementary one in which both systems collaborate, working side by side.

Facilitation of Healing

A study was conducted in the field of counselling psychology by McCormick (1995) to examine what facilitates healing for Aboriginal people. By asking Aboriginal people what actually worked for them in their own healing journeys, it was possible to obtain important information from the "real experts." The participants in this study were Aboriginal people ranging in age from the early twenties to the early fifties. The mean age was 35. Geographically, the 50 participants came from approximately 40 different communities in British Columbia. The location of these communities ranged from the interior of the province to the west coast of Vancouver Island and from as far north as Fort Nelson to as far south as the Musqueam reserve in Vancouver. Fifteen of the participants were male and 35 were female. Four of the participants originally came from another province but had been living in British Columbia for at least 5 years. Nineteen of the participants were university students, while 31 were employed in a wide variety of occupations such as housewife, administrator, secretary, and labourer. Through interviews with the 50 participants, 437 critical incidents or healing events were obtained that described what facilitated healing for the participants. The 437 events were placed into 14 categories that were found to be reasonably reliable. These categories are participation in ceremony, expression of emotion, learning from a role model, establishing a connection with nature, exercise, involvement in challenging activities, establishing a social connection, gaining an understanding of the problem, establishing a spiritual connection, obtaining help/support from others, self-care, setting goals, anchoring self in tradition, and helping others. These categories were then organized into 4 divisions that reflect the path of healing: separating from an unhealthy life, obtaining social support and resources, experiencing a healthy life, and living a healthy life.

This initial analysis of the healing path was not intended to represent a fixed sequence of steps or stages, as it is theorized that individuals may follow different paths and sequences. It is interesting to note, however, that these tentative stages parallel the three stages of ritual identified by van Gennep (1960). Based on an extensive analysis of ceremonies and the content and order of the activities associated with these ceremonies, van Gennep was able to discern three phases of transition: separation, transition, and incorporation. Separation involves detachment from the present life or way of being. Transition requires the dying of the old life and the birth of a new one. Incorporation means that the individual is incorporated or reincorporated into the community in his or her new state, role, and way of being.

A preliminary examination of the healing outcomes for Aboriginal people in the study found five main outcomes: empowerment, cleansing, balance, discipline, and belonging. Distinct themes in Aboriginal healing were also developed as a result of analyzing narrative accounts of participants. These themes are as follows: a broad spectrum of healing resources are available to Aboriginal people; Aboriginal people have a different way of seeing the world, which has to be understood before effective counselling services can be provided; Aboriginal people expect that whatever is healing should help them to attain and/or maintain balance; self-transcendence followed by connectedness is a common route to healing for Aboriginal people; and Aboriginal people act as agents for their own healing. Similar healing themes and goals are described by Michael Hart (2002) in his account of social-work practice based on Cree values. According to Hart, the goal of attaining *mino-pimatisiwin* (the good life) involves a lifelong healing journey in which one grows toward centredness, which includes balance, harmony, connection, and wholeness.

Counselling Victims of Physical and Sexual Abuse

Aboriginal peoples in Canada are currently engaged in mediation, negotiation, and legal battles with the Canadian government and Canadian churches for reparation to all those Aboriginal children (now adults) who were physically and sexually abused in the residential schools. For approximately 120 years, Aboriginal children in Canada were forced to attend church- and government-operated residential schools. The Government of Canada and the Assembly of First Nations have only recently agreed to a settlement whereby all who attended these schools will receive a cash payment for their suffering. Many of the children who attended these schools experienced physical and sexual abuse by the nuns and priests. It is thought that many of the mental health problems plaguing Aboriginal peoples today can also be traced to that legacy of abuse (Royal Commission on Aboriginal Peoples 1996).

A few years ago, the author was fortunate to supervise a study for the Association of BC First Nations Treatment Programs (2002) that examined the successful healing journeys of two groups: approximately 100 residential school survivors who were victims of physical and sexual abuse and those affected on an intergenerational level. The results of this study confirm and extend the research concerning the facilitation of healing for Aboriginal people. Previous scholars have stressed a number of factors that they believe have facilitated healing for Aboriginal survivors of physical and sexual abuse. These factors were empirically supported in this research, which confirmed the following categories: participation in ceremony, traditional healer/medicine person, cleansing, cultural connection, changing thinking, identifying and expressing emotions, therapist/counsellor, shared experiences, forgiveness, Elders, role model/mentor, group psychotherapy, connection with nature, spiritual connection, treatment/healing centres, support groups, seeing intergenerational patterns, self-acceptance, workshops/programs, family support, personal identity, peer support, helping others, community connection, apologized to, and self-care. This research went beyond these 23 previously identified categories by providing evidence for the importance of additional categories of facilitating factors: self-knowledge, sobriety, humour, Aboriginal identity, dreams and visions, training, accepting responsibility, bodywork, learning, family role, self-expression, telling your story, and knowledge of residential school history. All of these categories represent potential ways to facilitate healing for Aboriginal survivors of physical and sexual abuse.

Career and Vocational Counselling

Another area that has seen considerable development for the Aboriginal population is career and vocational counselling. The failure of mainstream models of career counselling for Aboriginal clients has led to efforts to develop more culturally appropriate models (Dolan 1995; Herring 1990). As stated by Ahia, "whenever alien psychologies are applied to different cultures without modification or contextualization – the result is professional discouragement and stagnation" (1984, 340). Currently, there are very few career-counselling models for Aboriginal people and a general lack of research on Aboriginal career development (Herring 1990). Most contemporary career-development models are based on generalizations taken from white, middle-class, male populations (Axelson 1993; Osipow and Littlejohn 1995); and it is the generally held opinion that these approaches reflect Western cultural values. Counselling services provided to Aboriginal people in the past have been based on adherence to these contemporary approaches despite a mismatch between mainstream career-development models and an Aboriginal worldview (McCormick and Amundson 1997). For example, research has shown that in career counselling with Aboriginal clients, it is culturally appropriate and desirable for clients' family and community members to have input into clients' career decisions (McCormick and France 1995; McCormick and Amundson 1997). Family and community members can help clients to identify their interests, aptitudes, needs, values, and temperament.

The Aboriginal Career-Life Planning Model, developed by McCormick and Amundson (1997), was designed to respect an Aboriginal worldview and its values. Aboriginal culture does not emphasize a philosophy of individualism but reflects a collective orientation. Lee (1984) found that compared to their non-Aboriginal counterparts, Aboriginal students' career choices were more influenced by parents. By involving family and community members in the career-counselling process for young people, the Aboriginal Career-Life Planning Model focuses on individual potential in the context of family and community roles and responsibilities. *Guiding circles*, an Aboriginal workbook for career self-exploration developed by McCormick, Amundson, and Poehnell (2002), continues with the tradition of involving family and community input in a process of client self-exploration. At present, it is the most widely used career-exploration tool for Aboriginal people.[1]

Counselling Suicidal Youth

Another crucial area that is demanding attention from counsellors and other providers and researchers of mental health services concerns how best to help Aboriginal youth who are suicidal. A preliminary study conducted by McCormick and Arvay (forthcoming), points to some of the factors that can help suicidal youth. Further research such as this study needs to be conducted on a national level in order to inform counselling practitioners and other mental health providers about how best to assist Aboriginal people who are suicidal. In this study, the critical-incident technique was also utilized, as it was important to hear from the real experts: Aboriginal people who had successfully recovered from being suicidal. Through interviews with 25 participants, 280 critical incidents were elicited that facilitated healing and recovery for Aboriginal youth who were suicidal. The 280 critical incidents were then grouped into 22 categories. Listed in order from most significant to least significant, the categories that facilitated healing and recovery for Aboriginal youth were: self-esteem/self-acceptance, obtaining help from others, changing thinking, connection with culture/tradition, expressing emotions/cleansing, spiritual connection, responsibility to others, future goals/hope, learning from others/role models, participation in ceremonies, connection to nature, guiding visions/dreams, understanding the problem, helping others, keeping occupied, recognizing/identifying emotions, exercise/sports, shutting down emotions, humour/perspective, learning problem-solving/communication skills, removing self from bad environment, and eliminating drugs and alcohol.

Substance-Abuse Counselling

One of the best-known applications of Aboriginal approaches to counselling is in the field of substance-abuse treatment for Aboriginal people. For over a quarter-century, Aboriginal people have been developing culturally appropriate ways to help clients who suffer from addictions. Attempts made by mainstream health-service providers to assist Aboriginal people in recovering from alcohol and substance abuse have led to only minimal success (Wing and Crow 1995). Ross (1992) argues that assistance measures taken by the majority culture to assist Aboriginal people have been, and continue to be, misguided and counterproductive. For various reasons, Aboriginal people tend not to use the services provided by the majority culture, and of those who do, approximately half drop out after the first session (Sue and Sue 1990). Differences in value orientations between Aboriginal people and mainstream health-service providers may lead to different beliefs concerning the causes and solutions of mental health problems (Darou 1987; McCormick 1996; Trimble 1981; Wohl 1989). An obstacle to utilization of mainstream services by Aboriginal people concerns differences in help-seeking behaviour. Wing and Crow (1995) describe two common cultural barriers to obtaining help. One obstacle is that for traditional Aboriginal people, it can be very shameful and embarrassing to admit to having problems of drug and alcohol abuse. This embarrassment is aggravated by common stereotypes in Canadian society that portray Aboriginal people as prone to alcohol and substance abuse and related problems (see Samson, Chapter 5; Culhane, Chapter 7; Tait, Chapter 9). This stigma and embarrassment can prevent individuals from seeking help. A second common barrier reflects the distinction between family and community members and outsiders. It may take Aboriginal people considerable time with a therapist before they can begin to establish an effective working relationship. Trust and intimacy are not things that are freely shared with strangers. This may be especially true with non-Aboriginal therapists because the history of colonialism, misunderstanding, and oppressive relationships may influence the development of the therapeutic relationship. These examples illustrate some of the reasons why alcohol-treatment programs based on the medical model favoured by many mainstream service providers often fail in their efforts with Aboriginal people.

Aboriginal Conceptualization of Substance Abuse

The Aboriginal conceptualization of alcohol abuse and its treatment encompasses more than the biological and psychological explanations emphasized by mainstream medicine. To understand Aboriginal traditions in the treatment of substance abuse, health professionals must also have an understanding of the spiritual component of substance abuse. Duran and Duran put this as follows: "Traditional Native people have a way to describe alcohol and the conceptualization of alcohol that differs from non-Natives. Alcohol is perceived as a spiritual entity that has been destructive of Native American ways of life. The alcohol 'spirits' continually wage war within the spiritual arena and it is in the spiritual arena that the struggle continues" (1995, 139).

For Aboriginal people, spirituality can be described in terms of "getting beyond the self." It is only through getting beyond the self that humans are able to connect with the rest of creation. Creation is described in terms of family, community, culture, the natural world, and the spiritual world. Traditional cultural values provide Aboriginal people with teachings on how to attain and maintain connection with creation. Many of the mental health problems experienced by Aboriginal people can be attributed to a disconnection from their culture. Inducing this disconnection was a "deliberate" strategy utilized by various churches and the Government of Canada in an attempt to assimilate Aboriginal people into Euro-Western culture. For many Aboriginal people, consumption of alcohol has been their attempt to deal with the state of powerlessness and hopelessness that has arisen due to the devastation of traditional cultural values. Research has demonstrated that cultural breakdown is strongly linked with alcohol abuse (Duran and Duran 1995; York 1990). The degeneration of traditional culture experienced by Aboriginal people has led to the taking of desperate measures. From this perspective, "alcohol use and even

suicide may be functional behavioral adaptations within a hostile and hopeless social environment" (Duran and Duran 1995, 193).

An Existential Conceptualization

Many Aboriginal Elders and healers believe that reconnection to culture, community, and spirituality is healing for Aboriginal people. This belief makes perfect sense when one realizes that, for many individuals and communities, it was disconnection from these sources of meaning and support that made Aboriginal people unhealthy in the first place. A Euro-Western theory of psychotherapy that approximates this way of thinking is logotherapy (Frankl 1962). As an existential-humanistic approach, logotherapy is based on the claim that the primary motivation for people is to obtain meaning in their lives. According to the theory, meaning can be obtained through sources such as spirituality, work, significant relationships with others, and contributing to one's community. Values are described as collective sources of meaning (Fabry 1968). Values are the activities that provide meaning to families, communities, and whole cultures. A collectively oriented culture, such as Aboriginal culture, is more likely to provide sources of meaning to its members through family, community, and cultural values than is an individually oriented culture. To be disconnected from those values is to be disconnected from potential sources of meaning. In an individually oriented society such as mainstream Canada or the United States, meaning tends to be derived from individual activities and generally not from collective sources. This is because the individual is less likely to be influenced by family, community, or cultural values. Due to the increasing trend toward individualism, the extended family, the church, and the state no longer have the influence on North American people that they once enjoyed (Fabry 1968). Individuals must seek out meaning on their own. Failure to find meaning can result in existential anxiety. According to logotherapy, existential anxiety can be dealt with constructively if it is used as a means to motivate and enable people to take actions that will connect them to those activities that provide them with meaning.

Unfortunately, not everyone deals with anxiety in a constructive way. Existential anxiety can cause some people to feel sad and hopeless. Alcohol use is one of the ways that people seek to replace this sad and anxious feeling with an artificial state of happiness. For Aboriginal people, this alternative became all too easy when faced with the abundance of alcohol provided by the early traders and others who wanted to take their land. The artificial "spirit" found in alcohol has been used as a poor substitute for the real "spirit" possessed by Aboriginal people who are connected to their culture and to creation. In research on effective health care practices for treating alcohol abuse among the Muscogee (Creek) Indians of the south-eastern United States, Wing and Crow (1995) found that traditional Aboriginal people believe that alcoholism is caused by a lack of spirituality. Hammerschlag (1993) writes of the effects of disconnection from spirit, culture, and creation in his book *Theft of the spirit*. Although he initially describes the effects that this "theft" has had on Aboriginal people, Hammerschlag suggests that other cultures, including Euro-American culture, have also experienced the effects of a loss of spirit. Aboriginal people of Canada are perhaps more aware of the effects of disconnection from cultural values because their loss has been the result of a transparent, relatively recent, and purposeful attempt at assimilation. The devastating effects of these attempts at cultural genocide have revealed to Aboriginal people the strong link between cultural dislocation and sickness. Alcohol abuse has simply been one symptom of this sickness. The path to wellness has also been revealed to Aboriginal people in this same link. Quite simply, this path is reconnection to one's "spirit" and "culture" and to one's inherent sources of meaning. Connection to traditional Aboriginal culture and values means that a person must become connected to extended family, community, the natural world, and the spirit world – in essence, to all of creation.

Strategies That Work

Although information on the prevalence of alcohol abuse among Aboriginal people and the various attempts at treatment can be readily found in the research literature, what is much less evident are studies of successful substance-abuse treatment strategies used by Aboriginal people. Aboriginal people have a rich heritage of healing strategies in dealing with substance abuse. For Aboriginal people, the most effective solution is based on cultural and spiritual survival and renewal (Maracle 1993). For example, cultural and spiritual revival has been the strategy used by the Aboriginal community of Alkali Lake, located in central British Columbia. This community employed traditional Aboriginal healers to help its members revive traditional dances, ceremonies, and spiritual practices. Community members were introduced to cultural activities such as Pow-Wow dancing, sweet-grass and sweat-lodge ceremonies, and drumming. The treatment strategy used by the people of Alkali Lake has been copied by other Aboriginal treatment programs, such as those at Poundmaker Lodge and Round Lake. The guiding philosophy of these treatment programs has been: "Culture is treatment, and all healing is spiritual" (York 1990). The outcomes of programs using this philosophy/strategy have been very promising (Guillory, Willie, and Duran 1988).

Community and Family Ownership

Counselling interventions in Aboriginal communities can complement the political movement toward self-determination by encouraging local initiatives in substance-abuse treatment and intervention. Considerable commitments have been made by many Aboriginal communities toward the treatment and prevention of substance abuse. This community

involvement is essential if strategies are to work (Edwards and Edwards 1988). The community must acknowledge that a substance-abuse problem exists and must be committed to and involved in addressing the problem. The substance abuser's family also plays an important role in effective treatment and prevention. For Aboriginal people, the extended family is important in determining positive and negative behaviours (Trotter and Rolf 1997). In response to the devastating impact of alcohol on their community, leaders in Alkali Lake mobilized their community toward a goal of sobriety (Johnson and Johnson 1993). Based on a historical study of the interventions used in this program between 1972 and 1993 as well as on the data gathered in a research study, Johnson and Johnson (1993) found that the family was described by community members as the second most effective intervention after spiritual support. When participants were asked, "What significant event or thing caused you to commit to be sober?" almost half (48%) of the respondents identified family as the cause. It can be argued that the extended family is still the central institution in Aboriginal cultures, even for urban dwellers. Inside the family, norms of sharing and mutual support traditionally provided a safety net for every individual. These norms were severely disrupted by assimilationist policies such as residential schools and the forcible removal of Aboriginal children from their families through foster placement and adoption. Testimony given to the Royal Commission on Aboriginal Peoples (1996) continuously stressed the importance of family in Aboriginal society. Many Aboriginal people told the commission that the future they wish for is impossible unless the bonds of the family that give individuals and communities their stability are reclaimed and strengthened. Graveline refers to this reclamation or revival as "spiritual resistance which flourishes through treasuring our children and honouring the visions and words of our ancestors" (1998, 45).

Many types of connection have been stressed in this discussion of substance-abuse counselling, including connection to meaning, family, spirituality, and identity. One connection that cannot be emphasized enough is the connection to culture. The understanding of this connection is the reason why Round Lake Treatment Centre in British Columbia uses the motto "Culture is treatment" on all of its correspondence. It is essential that both researchers and practitioners recognize this connection and incorporate culture into the field of Aboriginal substance-abuse treatment. Because substance abuse conflicts with traditional Aboriginal cultural beliefs about courage, humility, generosity, and family honour, cultural wholeness can serve as both a preventative and a curative agent in substance-abuse treatment.

Aboriginal people are currently developing strategies to deal with the pain of cultural dislocation and the resultant problem of substance abuse. These strategies utilize the community and family to provide culturally appropriate alternatives to the abuse of alcohol and drugs. Traditional cultural values, ceremonies, and healing techniques have been known to provide substance abusers with the knowledge and skills to attain and maintain a meaningful connection with creation. It is to these values and teachings that Aboriginal people are now turning in an effort to let the "good spirits" guide them.

Conclusion

In this chapter I have attempted to provide a brief overview of the basic values and perspectives of Aboriginal counselling while describing some of the innovative approaches being developed by Aboriginal counsellors and mental health professionals. Respect for Aboriginal worldviews is essential if counselling is to establish the therapeutic relationship and to engage cultural resources for healing. Concepts of balance, connectedness, spirituality, nature, ceremony, and culture are all important aspects of healing for Aboriginal people. Uniquely Aboriginal perspectives on counselling and healing are being developed in several areas, including counselling for victims of physical and sexual abuse, career and vocational counselling, suicide prevention, and substance-abuse counselling. The future will undoubtedly bring important new efforts to integrate Aboriginal and mainstream counselling perspectives as well as new modes of collaboration between the different helping and healing traditions. Emerging research in this field is addressing some of the gaps in the literature. There is a need for empirical research to validate the effectiveness of different counselling and healing approaches. Research is also needed to explore the link between the level of individual psychological problems and the larger issues of politics and identity. Finally, work is needed on ways to understand the differences and to promote collaboration between traditional and mainstream helping professionals.

Note

1 The workbook is currently marketed and distributed by the Aboriginal Human Resources Development Council of Canada (AHRDCC).

References

Ahia, C.E. 1984. Cross-cultural counseling concerns. *The Personnel and Guidance Journal* 62: 339-41.

Anderson, B.M. 1993. Aboriginal counselling and healing processes. MA thesis, University of British Columbia.

Association of BC First Nations Treatment Programs. 2002. *Report on therapeutic safety in healing: Facilitation of healing for Aboriginal school survivors*. Vernon, BC: Association of BC First Nations Treatment Programs.

Axelson, J. 1985. *Counseling and development in a multicultural society.* Monterey, CA: Brooks Cole.

–. 1993. *Counseling and development in a multicultural society.* 2nd ed. Pacific Grove, CA: Brooks Cole.

Darou, W.G. 1987. Counselling the northern Native. *Canadian Journal of Counselling* 21 (1): 33-41.

Dauphinais, P., L. Dauphinais, and W. Rowe. 1981. Effect of race and communication style on Indian perceptions of counselor effectiveness. *Counselor Education and Supervision* 21 (1): 72-80.

Dolan, C.A. 1995. A study of the mismatch between Native students' counselling needs and available services. *Canadian Journal of Counselling* 29 (3): 234-43.

Duran, E., and B. Duran. 1995. *Native American postcolonial psychology.* New York: SUNY Press.

Edwards, E.D., and M.E. Edwards. 1988. Alcoholism prevention/treatment and Native American youth: A community approach. *Journal of Drug Issues* 18 (1): 103-14.

Epes-Brown, J. 1989. Becoming part of it. In D.M. Dooling and P. Jordan-Smith, eds., *I became part of it: Sacred dimensions in Native American life*, 9-20. San Francisco, CA: Harper.

Fabry, J.B. 1968. *The pursuit of meaning*. Boston, MA: Beacon Press.

France, M.H., R. McCormick, and M. Rodriguez. 2004. Issues in counselling for the First Nations community. In M.H. France, M. Rodriguez, and G. Hett, eds., *Diversity, culture, and counselling*, 59-75. Calgary: Detselig.

Frankl, V. 1962. *Man's search for meaning: An introduction to logotherapy*. Boston, MA: Beacon Press.

Garrett, M.W., and W.L. Osborne. 1995. The Native American sweat lodge as a metaphor for group work. *The Journal for Specialists in Group Work* 20 (1): 33-39.

Graveline, F.J. 1998. *Circle works: Transforming Eurocentric consciousness*. Halifax, NS: Fernwood.

Guillory, B.M., E. Willie, and E.F. Duran. 1988. Analysis of a community organizing case study: Alkali Lake. *Journal of Rural Community Psychology* 9 (1): 27-36.

Guilmet, G.M., and D.L. Whited. 1987. Cultural lessons for clinical mental health practice: The Puyallup tribal community. *American Indian and Alaskan Native Mental Health Research* 1 (2): 1-141.

Halfe, L. 1993. Native healing. *Cognica* 26 (1): 21-27.

Hammerschlag, C.A. 1988. *The dancing healers: A doctor's journey of healing with Native Americans.* San Francisco, CA: Harper and Rowe.

–. 1993. *The theft of the spirit: A journey to spiritual healing with Native Americans.* New York: Simon and Schuster.

Hart, M.A. 2002. *Seeking mino-pimatisiwin: An Aboriginal approach to helping*. Halifax, NS: Fernwood.

Herring, R.D. 1990. Attacking career myths among Native Americans: Implications for counseling. *School Counselor* 38 (1): 13-18.

Hodgson, J., and J. Kothare. 1990 *Native spirituality and the church in Canada*. Toronto, ON: Anglican Book Centre.

Ibrahim, F.A. 1984. Cross-cultural counseling and psychotherapy: An existential psychological perspective. *International Journal for the Advancement of Counseling* 7: 159-69.

Jilek, W. 1982. *Indian healing: Shamanic ceremonialism in the Pacific Northwest today*. Surrey, BC: Hancock House.

Johnson, J., and F. Johnson. 1993. Community development sobriety and after-care at Alkali Lake Band. In *The path to healing: Report of the National Round Table on Aboriginal Health and Social Issues*, 227-30. Ottawa, ON: Royal Commission on Aboriginal Peoples.

Katz, R., and E. Rolde. 1981. Community alternatives to psychotherapy. *Psychotherapy, Theory, Research and Practice* 18: 365-74.

Kirmayer, L.J. 2007. Psychotherapy and the cultural concept of the person. *Transcultural Psychiatry* 44 (2): 232-57.

LaFromboise, T., J. Trimble, and G. Mohatt. 1990. Counseling intervention and American Indian tradition: An integrative approach. *The Counseling Psychologist* 18 (4): 628-54.

Lee, C. 1984. Predicting the career choice attitudes of rural black, white, and American Indian high school students. *Vocational Guidance Quarterly* 32: 177-84.

Maracle, B. 1993. *Crazy water: Native voices on addiction and recovery.* Toronto, ON: Penguin.

McCormick, R.M. 1995. The facilitation of healing for the First Nations people of British Columbia. *Canadian Journal of Native Education* 21 (2): 251-319.

–. 1996. Culturally appropriate means and ends of counselling as described by the First Nations people of British Columbia. *International Journal for the Advancement of Counselling* 18 (3): 163-72.

–. 1997. An integration of healing wisdom: The vision quest ceremony from an attachment theory perspective. *Guidance and Counselling* 12 (2): 18-22.

–, and M.H. France. 1995. Counselling First Nations students on career issues: Implications for the school counsellor. *Journal of Guidance and Counselling* 10: 27-31.

–, and N.E. Amundson. 1997. A career/life planning model for First Nations people. *Journal of Employment Counselling* 34: 171-79.

–, N.E. Amundson, and G. Poehnell. 2002. *Guiding circles: An Aboriginal guide to self-discovery*. Saskatoon, SK: Aboriginal Human Resources Development Council of Canada.

–, and M. Arvay. Forthcoming. The facilitation of healing for Candian Aboriginal youth who are suicidal.

Medicine Eagle, B. 1989. The circle of healing. In R. Carlson and J. Brugh, eds., *Healers on healing*, 58-62. New York: J.P. Tarcher/Putnam.

More, J.M. 1985. Cultural foundations of personal meaning: Their loss and recovery. MA thesis, University of British Columbia.

Neligh, G. 1990. Mental health programs for American Indians: Their logic, structure and function. *American Indian and Alaskan Native Mental Health Research* 3 (3): 1-280.

Nelson, S.H., and G.F. McCoy. 1992. An overview of mental health services for American Indians and Alaskan Natives in the 1990s. *Hospital and Community Psychiatry* 43 (3): 257-61.

Osipow, S.H., and E.M. Littlejohn. 1995. Toward a multicultural theory of career development: Prospects and dilemmas. In F.T. Leong, ed., *Career development and vocational behavior of racial and ethnic minorities*, 251-61. Mahwah, NJ: Lawrence Erlbaum Associates.

Peavy, R.V. 1993. Development of Aboriginal counselling. Brief submitted to the Royal Commission for Aboriginal Peoples.

Primeaux, M.H. 1977. American Indian health care practices: A cross-cultural perspective. *Nursing Clinics of North America* 12 (1): 55-65.

Renfrey, G.S. 1992. Cognitive behaviour therapy and the Native American client. *Behaviour Therapy* 23 (3): 321-40.

Ross, R. 1992. *Dancing with a ghost: Exploring Indian reality*. Markham, ON: Octopus.

Royal Commission on Aboriginal Peoples. 1996. *People to people, Nation to nation: Highlights from the report of the Royal Commission on Aboriginal Peoples*. Ottawa, ON: Canadian Ministry of Supply and Services.

Smye, V., and B. Mussell. 2001. Aboriginal mental health: What works best. Unpublished discussion paper.

Speck, R.V., and C.L. Attneave. 1973. *Family networks: Retribalization and healing*. New York: Pantheon.

Sue, D.W., and D. Sue. 1990. *Counselling the culturally different: Theory and practice*. 2nd ed. Toronto, ON: John Wiley and Sons.

Torrey, E.F. 1986. *Witchdoctors and psychiatrists: The common roots of psychotherapy and its future*. New York: Harper Row.

Trimble, J.E. 1981. Value differentials and their importance in counseling American Indians. In P. Pederson, J. Draguns, W. Lonner, and J.E. Trimble, eds., *Counseling across cultures*, 3rd ed., 177-204. Honolulu, HI: University of Hawaii Press.

–, and S. Hayes. 1984. Mental health intervention in the psychosocial contexts of American Indian communities. In W. O'Conner and B. Lubin, eds., *Ecological approaches to clinical and community psychology*, 293-321. New York: Wiley.

Trotter, R.T., and J.E. Rolf. 1997. Cultural models of inhalant use among Navajo youth. *Drugs and Society* 10 (2): 39-59.

van Gennep, A. 1960. *The rites of passage*. Chicago, IL: University of Chicago Press.

Wing, D.M., and S.S. Crow. 1995. An ethnonursing study of Muscogee (Creek) Indians and effective health care practices for treating alcohol abuse. *Family and Community Health* 18 (2): 52-64.

Wohl, J. 1989. Cross-cultural psychotherapy. In P.B. Pederson, J.G. Draguns, W.J. Lonner, and J.E. Trimble, eds., *Counseling across cultures*, 3rd ed., 177-204. Honolulu, HI: University of Hawaii Press.

York, G. 1990. *The dispossessed: Life and death in Native Canada*. London, ON: Vintage.

Service Users' Knowledges and Social Work Theory: Conflict or Collaboration?

Peter Beresford

Peter Beresford is Professor of Social Policy, Brunel University, a worker with Open Services Project, a long-term user of mental health services and active in the psychiatric system survivors' movement. E-mail: peter.beresford@brunel.ac.uk

Summary

So far, service users have not been systematically involved in social work theorizing. However, disabled people's movements, mental health service users/survivors and other service users have developed their own knowledges based on direct experience and they have generated their own conceptual frameworks and bodies of theory. There are fundamental problems in social work seeking to interpret service user knowledges. Their development and interpretation require the direct involvement of service users and their organizations in social work theorizing. There are strong practical, philosophical and political arguments for involving the knowledges and theories of service users and their organizations in the process of social work theory-building. This paper considers an inclusive approach to social work theorizing. While highlighting the importance of service users and their organizations being effectively included in social work theorizing, it also argues the need for them to have support and opportunities to develop their own prior and separate discussions about theory, including social work theory.

> Nothing about us without us
> The disabled people's movement

This discussion is concerned with two concurrent developments; the increasing significance of service users'[1] movements in public, political, policy and professional

[1] The term 'service users' is used in this discussion to describe people who receive or are eligible to receive social work and social care services. This embraces people included in a wide range of categories, including mental health service users/survivors, people living with HIV/AIDS, children and young people in state 'care' or who are fostered or adopted, disabled people, older people, people with learning difficulties, people with addictions to alcohol and proscribed drugs, etc. People may receive social work and social care services voluntarily or involuntarily. The term 'service users' is problematic, because it conceives of people primarily in terms of their use of services, which may well not be how they would define themselves. However, there is no other umbrella term which can helpfully be used to include all these overlapping groups. For example, some may include themselves as and be included as disabled, but others would not. Therefore the term 'service user' is used as a shorthand to describe the subjects of social work and social care, without seeking to impose any other meanings or interpretations upon it or them.

debates and the concern in social work to take forward debate on its theorizing. My aim, as someone with a joint interest and affiliation as a service user and researcher, is to connect these two developments, examining their relations and beginning to explore ways of understanding and improving their links for the future.

The seminar series that provided the starting point for this discussion, reflects the broader history of social work theorizing. It started from the position of trying to challenge the wider response to social work as an area of research and theory-building. As the application for support to the ESRC for the seminar series stated, it sought:

> To put social work 'on the map' as a research-based discipline . . . for it to be recognized by the ESRC as a discipline in its own right, by debating the specific contribution it could make to social science research activity. Though many social work researchers are involved in ESRC-funded work, social work itself is invisible because applications are required always to cite Discipline Codes that do not include it.

Social Work Discussion of Theory

As this suggests, social work has long seemed to need theory more than theory has apparently needed or wanted social work. Conventionally, social work commentators clearly see its theoretical underpinnings as important. As Joan Orme observed in 1998, in a standard text for social work students and novice practitioners:

> Social work needs to articulate, celebrate and broadcast the theoretical frameworks that inform, structure and facilitate its operation (Coulshed and Orme, 1998, p. 3).

At the same time non-social workers seem frequently to despise social work's raiding of the social science cookbook for handy theoretical recipes. (Jones, 1996, p. 203). The concern to strengthen what might be called social work's theoretical credibility appears to be linked to its professional and intellectual vulnerability, insecurity and low status. There is an understandable defensiveness about many social work discussions of theory. Social work is a practical hands-on activity that has never commanded much official respect. It is a profession predominantly made up of women, which has made determined efforts to include within its ranks black and minority ethnic groups and which operates in some of the most contentious areas of state intervention. As such it is perhaps to be expected that it would come in for regular ideological, political and media attack, particularly given its refusal to accept the 'handmaiden' status imposed upon some comparable human service roles.

Social work discussions about theory have tended to be reactive. There has been a concern to highlight the theoretical credentials of social work. Theory in relation to social work has tended to be presented in terms of legitimation, as if the more social work could demonstrate its theoretical connections, the more credibility would be attached to it.

Theories in social work are still often set out as a list of different approaches, including, for example, person-centred counselling, family therapy, task-centred work, cognitive-behavioural therapy, networking, group work, psychoanalytical theory, anti-discriminatory/oppressive practice and feminist theory. (Davies, 1997) or alternatively, crisis intervention, the psycho-social approach, behavioural social work, working with families, etc. (Coulshed and Orme, 1998). The lists vary, but generally what they have in common is that the approaches and associated theories do not originate from and are not specific to social work. Social work has also raised more critical questions about its own theorizing, for instance:

- acknowledging that there is no agreement about the nature or meaning of social work theory;
- recognizing its own limited role in theory-building;
- questioning the idea of foundational theory;
- appreciating that theorizing is a political and social process;
- recognizing a distinction between postmodernist views of 'theory' and alternatively, modernist, positivist or 'hard science' views of social work 'theory' (Payne, 1997, p. 27).

All this however has to some extent further confused the meaning of theory in social work. In one sense at least social work is inevitably based on theory. There is an inextricable link between social work and theory—or at least between social work and unevidenced hypotheses—whether these are technical, social or psychological theories or hypotheses. This is true however much adverse criticism is levelled against social work for being atheoretical. Implicitly if not explicitly, it has developed and been undertaken on the basis of certain assumptions and expectations about what it is, what it does, what it is for, what its effects are and what it can achieve. This is true for social work, just like any other human activity.

While postmodern discussion of social work theory has helped connect it with broader contemporary theoretical discussions and highlighted the social production of theory, it hasn't resulted in a radical reassessment of the role of service users in social work theory-building. But now that social work theory is under particular scrutiny, this urgently needs to be reviewed, particularly given the new significance given to the involvement of 'service users' and the emergence of service users' own organizations and movements. A number of interrelated strands need to be reviewed.

The Emphasis on 'User Involvement'

From the late 1980s discussion if not action on social work and social care has been transformed by the emergence of the idea of 'user involvement'. It has become one of the guiding formal principles of social services. Requirements for user involvement are built into both childcare and community care government guidance and legislation. This has found expression in a massive increase in market research and consultation initiatives in social work and social care (Beresford and Croft, 1993). The consumerist commitment of Conservative administrations to user involvement, or at least a variant of it, is now embedded in New Labour's 'third way' (Giddens, 1998). This is reflected in an interest in new forms of political process and local democracy and 'best value' in local government policies and services. User involvement has become established as a formal component at levels of both collective policy and individual practice. It is embodied as a measure in both official audit and learning 'competencies'.

The Emergence of Service Users and their Organizations

While the 1990's emphasis on user involvement can be seen as an expression of changes in political ideology and new 'mixed economy' approaches to public and welfare services, alongside it there has run a distinct but interrelated development: the emergence of movements of service users. At its most basic, this development represents a strong collective reaction from people included in social care categories to their negative experiences of welfarist and professional responses to them. It is also related to a number of other broader social and political changes over the same period (Croft and Beresford, 1996). The disabled people's movement is perhaps the most strongly established and visible of these movements, with the most well worked-out philosophy (Oliver and Barnes, 1998; Shakespeare, 1999; Barnes *et al.*, 1999), but this should not divert attention from other movements, for example, of psychiatric system survivors, people with learning difficulties, people living with HIV/AIDS, etc. (Beresford, 1999). What distinguishes these movements is that they have been determinedly:

- based on self-identification: for example, as movements of disabled people, mental health service users/psychiatric system survivors or older people;
- self-organized and self-run: organized around local, national and international groups and organizations based on their own identities, which they themselves control, developing their own ways of working, philosophies and objectives;
- committed to both parliamentary and direct action: the latter reflected, for example, in the activities of the disabled people's movement's Direct Action Network (DAN) and psychiatric system survivors' Reclaim Bedlam and Mad Pride campaigns.

These characteristics significantly distinguish such movements from traditional challenges to state social policy and associated social and economic inequalities, reflected still, for example, in anti-poverty and unemployment campaigning. This has come predominantly from organizations and agencies which have not been controlled by the people directly affected by the problem, but which have ostensibly campaigned and advocated on their behalf. This is not to say that the latter have not struggled and sought to be at the heart of such opposition.

Service Users' Knowledges and Theories

There have always been service users' knowledges—from the earliest days of secular and religious charity and the beginnings of state intervention and the old Poor Law.

What is different now is that there are both formal expressions of interest in and commitments to such knowledges and service users and their organizations have the capacity to place, indeed sometimes to force, such knowledges on to political, professional, academic and policy-making agendas. One key quality distinguishes such knowledges from all others involved in social care and social policy provision. They alone are based on *direct* experience of such policy and provision from the *receiving end.* Service users' knowledges grow out of their personal and collective experience of policy, practice and services. They also explicitly emphasize this. They are not based solely on an intellectual, occupational or political concern. As in all identity based groupings and movements, they are experientially based. Thus the introduction of service users' knowledges into the discussion, analysis and development of social work and social care brings into the arena a crucially different relationship between experience and knowledge and between direct experience and social work and social care discourses. As we shall see, the importance of this cannot be overstated. It has fundamental implications for social work analysis and theorizing.

Service users' knowledges are developing and being shared in a range of formal and informal settings; through the contact that service users have with each other both within and outside the service system; in self-advocacy and user groups; at meetings and in campaigns. There is of course an enormous body of unrecorded and hidden users' knowledge in the form of user wisdom, advice and learning. More recently though such knowledges have increasingly been recorded in the form of service users' accounts, testimonies, critiques and discussions (Read and Reynolds, 1996; Beresford *et al.*, 1997; Campbell and Oliver, 1996). These are to be found in users' newsletters, journals and other publications. There is a tendency for these to be devalued in dominant professional discourses as 'grey literature', as if they did not have the same authority as commercially produced materials, but service users and their organizations have also begun to be included in specialist professional publications and mainstream print and broadcast media. In addition, they are now producing their own histories (Campbell and Oliver, 1996; Campbell, 1996).

Just as service users' knowledge is inextricable from their experience, so is their theorizing, and theory-building has played an important part in the movements of service users. Perhaps the most important single expression of this is the social model of disability developed by the disabled people's movement.

This is a sea change theory. It represents one of the most important theoretical developments in modern social policy, if not the most important, as well as being important in public policy and political thought more broadly. As yet it has not generally been seen as such in mainstream debates (Abberley, 1998; Barnes, 1998). It provides an effective challenge to hundreds of years of individual interpretations of disability and more than a century of the dominance of medicalized individual interpretations. It has made a fundamental impact on the consciousness of many thousands if not millions of disabled people worldwide. It has also impacted significantly on politics, policy and culture in the UK, mainland Europe and North America, even though efforts have been made in policy and practice to subvert it.

Coupled with the idea of independent living, it has provided both a philosophical basis for the disabled people's movement and a touchstone for living for individual disabled people (Morris, 1993). It has made the crucial coupling between people's human and civil status by reframing disability in terms of rights, anti-discrimination and equal opportunities.

While, for example, psychiatric system survivors have not yet developed an equivalent theoretical basis for their movement, although this is now in progress, theory building, at both micro and macro levels is also an inherent part of this movement, challenging, for example, dominant medicalized categorizations and 'treatments'; reinterpreting the experience, perceptions and behaviour of survivors and reconceiving psychiatrically structured and individualized 'problems' like eating distress and self-harm to make sense of their social relations and role as solutions to personal and social problems (for example, Pembroke, 1994*a*, 1994*b*).

Service Users and Research

Another expression of service users' theory building and knowledge generation is their involvement in research. This takes two forms; first their development of their own research methodologies and findings and second their involvement in mainstream research. The disabled people's movement has pioneered the development of emancipatory research. Mike Oliver, the disability activist and academic, characterizes this as:

> an alternative, emancipatory approach in order to make disability research both more relevant to the lives of disabled people and more influential in improving their material circumstances. The two key fundamentals on which such an approach must be based are empowerment and reciprocity. These fundamentals can be built in by encouraging self-reflection and a deeper understanding of the research situation by the research subjects themselves as well as enabling researchers to identify with their research subjects (Oliver, 1996, p. 141).

The starting point for many service users' view of research is as part of a structure of discrimination and oppression; an activity which is both intrusive and disempowering in its own right and which serves the damaging and oppressive purposes of a service system over which they can exert little or no influence or control. Oliver argues for a different social process for the production of research (Oliver, 1996). There is now a large and growing body of research and evaluation undertaken by service users and their organizations. This includes both qualitative and quantitative research and it is being undertaken by a wide range of service users, including disabled and older people, people with learning difficulties and psychiatric system survivors (Barnes and Mercer, 1997). Service user organizations are also now commissioning research. The British Council of Disabled People has its own Disability Research Unit at the University of Leeds. Organizations like the Sainsbury Centre for Mental Health and Mental Health Foundation have also established strategic initiatives to support user research. My own Centre at Brunel University, the Centre for Citizen Participation, is committed to undertaking and developing user led and user controlled research.

The development of their own research by the disabled people's and service user movements has been coupled with their increasing demands for changed social relations in mainstream research, with a more active and equal role for research participants. This has led to an increasing interest in the degree of *control* that service users have in research (Evans and Fisher, 1999). Thus alongside participatory and emancipatory paradigms, discussion has developed about user-led and user-controlled research. This discussion focuses on the degree of user involvement and control in all key aspects of research including:

- the origination of research;
- who gains the benefits of research;
- the accountability of the research;
- who undertakes the research;
- research funding;
- research design and process;
- dissemination of research findings;
- action following from research.

Service users have set out a range of degrees of involvement in research from none to control over it (Beresford and Evans, 1999). Initiatives from service user organizations have also been coupled with increasing interest from funders in the involvement of service users in research. This ranges from the interest of the ESRC in the involvement of research users, including 'end users' in research that it funds, to the commitment of independent funders like the Joseph Rowntree Foundation to service users' involvement as a principle of support. User involvement in research ranges from none, through the kind of democratically negotiated and agreed partnership between non-disabled researcher and disabled people's organization which was the basis for Mark Priestley's exploration of community care and the politics of the disabled people's movement, (Priestley, 1999) to user controlled initiatives like the evaluation of the Wiltshire Independent Living Support Service or the Citizens' Commission on the Future of the Welfare State. (Wiltshire and Swindon User Network, 1996; Beresford and Turner, 1997).

Service Users and Social Work Theorizing

There has traditionally been a tendency in social policy to marginalize and invalidate service users' viewpoints and knowledges (Beresford, 1997; Croft and Beresford, 1998). The knowledge of disabled people has been dismissed on the basis of their perceived incapacity; that of survivors because of the assumed unreliability and irrationality of their perceptions and understandings and those of people with learning difficulties on the basis of their perceived intellectual deficiencies. Discrimination on grounds of ageism, disablism and mentalism have all been at work. It is important to reiterate that these knowledges have always existed. The point is that it is only recently that service users have been able to mount an effective challenge to dominant discourses. Social work and social care are probably at the leading edge in involving the perspectives of service users. They are certainly more advanced than some other related academic disciplines or areas of professional activity. There is, however, still far to go. The involvement of the knowledges of service users in social work analysis and theory building is still at an early stage. This has yet to develop in a systematic, structured and coherent way. In this it reflects other areas of social work and social care activity, like professional education and practice, where there have been numerous individual and local initiatives to involve service users, but as yet this has not resulted in a coherent or strategic approach to policy or practice. As far as the present author knows, the ESRC seminar series: Theorising Social Work, marks the first occasion on which this issue has been explicitly addressed in social work discussions.

Social Work Theory and Knowledge

While academic discussions have begun to consider the issue of social work knowledge, they have so far generally failed to connect this with service users, their organizations and activities. Social work's commentators point to a shift in focus in recent years 'from the substantive areas of social work theory towards a greater interest in the very process by which knowledge is developed' (Peile and McCouat, 1997, p. 343). Theoretical discussions have shown an increasing interest in conceptualizing the role and nature of knowledge in social work, concerns about unbridled 'relativism' in theory building and a desire to develop general social work theories (see also, for example, White, 1997; Sheppard, 1998). The relation between such theory about theory and 'practice' as yet seems to be tenuous. So far social work practitioners, that is to say people whose time is currently and centrally spent in direct contact with service users, have played a minimal part in such epistemological discussions. The *Social Work 2000* initiative convened by the National Institute for Social Work and Brunel University and supported by the Central Council for Education and Training in Social Work to support social work practitioners to take forward their own discussions about the intellectual and policy future of social work grew out of concern about this marginalization of practitioners' knowledges and experience.

In their discussion of the future of theory and knowledge development in social work, Peile and McCouat, argue that:

> We need to get on with the collective job of exploring a creative way forward which allows and preserves social work's capacity, on the one hand, to understand a variety of voices and to critique dominating voices (relativism), and, on the other hand, to be able to respond in a clear, enthusiastic, imaginative way to unlock the potential of the people with whom social workers work, particularly those who have been the most constrained and limited (Peile and McCouat, 1997, p. 357).

But neither they nor any other of the discussants concerned with reviewing social work knowledge prior to this publication, have either included the views of service users in their inquiry, or involved service users and their organizations in the process.

Even if they were to address service users' perspectives, the issue would still be problematic. Many service users, including this writer, would argue that such theorizing cannot accurately reflect service user perspectives, because it remains part of a dominant discourse which has traditionally defined and continues to define service users in ways which they see as oppressive. If knowledge is not taken as given, then what we are actually seeing here are different and competing knowledge claims; those of social work theoreticians and those of social work service users and their organizations. Academic knowledge claims have no greater validity than service user ones, although the common presumption is that they do have (Harding, 1993; Bar On, 1993). Social work theory building needs to take account of service users' own discussions about knowledge and their own theory building.

Service Users and Theory

What might we expect the relationship between professional social work and service user theorizing to be? We can expect it to be different. We know that social work was traditionally reliant on dominant individualized medical models of both disability and madness and distress. The two strands of theory building; professional and user, have been different in philosophy, process, focus and objectives. While, for example, service users have deliberately sought to be participatory in their understanding of and approach to intellectual work, social work has much more closely reflected broader academic and professional processes. The coming of 'disability studies' and the emergence of discrete disability movement academics and of 'user researchers' reflects a developing division of labour in intellectual activity within service user movements, but the process of developing knowledge and ideas is still one which self-consciously seeks both to draw in a wide range of service users and activists and to be accountable back to them. Also as Jane Campbell, the disability activist has said of the disabled people's movement:

> The movement is multi-faccted. There is direct action campaigning on the street. There is letter writing and political work in parliament. There is intellectual work and arts. The movement involves all of these and people cross over. People who write the books are also on the picket line. This has given us a much fuller representation because we have a much more holistic approach and understanding (Beresford and Campbell, 1994, p. 321).

Theory building is also not only a written process. As we might expect of movements that highlight speaking for yourself, grassroots involvement and collective action, it also develops through people coming together formally and informally, as part of meetings and the democratic and political process of organizations and groups. While social work theorizing has been concerned with advancing the intellectual basis of its practice, policy, teaching and research, the theory building of service user movements has been most directly and explicitly linked with action and making change.

Relating Service Users and Social Work Theorizing

None of this means that social work and service users' approaches to theory and its development are necessarily incompatible or antagonistic. This is particularly so given social work's longstanding professional commitment to social approaches and self-determination. But it does mean that seeking to connect the two will require some understanding of their different histories, cultures and power relations and that these need to be acknowledged and negotiated if the two are to be brought closer together.

This raises the question of what the relation should be between social work theorizing and service users and their knowledges. Traditionally in social work as in other social policy areas, the social work profession tended to be the arbiter and interpreter of such knowledge, at theoretical as well as practice levels. In social work, a distinct area of research developed which came to be called 'client studies', pioneered by the book *The Client Speaks* (Mayer and Timms, 1970).

Thus while we might expect service user's knowledges to be included in social work theorizing routinely to at least some degree, with the development of service users' own powerful and democratically constituted organizations and movements, the longstanding role of social work academics and practitioners as interpreters and mediators of service users' knowledges and perspectives can no longer go unquestioned. Instead the matter of involving service users and their organizations themselves is raised. Thus the issue for social work theorizing is not just of including the knowledges of service users. Instead it becomes one of including service users themselves. This involvement must also be more than seeking their responses to social work's own intellectual agendas, priorities and concerns if it is to avoid tokenization and incorporation. It means including their:

- *perspectives;*
- *knowledges;*
- *analyses*—including their interpretations, meanings, hypotheses and theories.

Why though should service users be involved in social work theorizing? At least three key arguments can be identified. These are:

1 practical and methods-based;
2 philosophical and methodological;
3 political.

1 Practical and Methods-Based

Including service users in social work theorizing makes it possible to include their insights, understandings and experience and helps fill a key gap that would otherwise be left. Their first hand knowledge and experience offer a unique basis for developing theory as they do policy and practice. Debate about social work theory can only be better informed if those directly affected are part of it. Their involvement makes it possible for the debate to identify, reflect and advance their needs, concerns and interests more accurately and closely and can enable more relevant and participatory research and analysis. It accords with both traditional social science concerns to address all sources of data and the commitment of postmodernist approaches to multiple perspectives and interpretations.

2 Philosophical and Methodological

The exclusion of service users from social work theorizing undermines them both. Including service users is part of the broader issue of addressing rather than reinforcing their restricted rights and citizenship. It signifies respect for them; an acknowledgement that they have something to offer, that their contribution is important, worthwhile and valued, and shows recognition of their expertise in their own experience and beyond. It challenges their objectification and has a symbolic as well as a practical significance. Service users and their organizations see themselves as having a right to be involved in discussion and action that affect them. Their exclusion is incompatible with values associated with both social work and social inclusion.

Historically, as already indicated, the knowledge base of social work has been derived from social research conducted using traditional methods of inquiry which claim to be 'objective', 'neutral' and 'value free' and to produce knowledge which is independent of the persons carrying out the research. There has also recently been a renewal of interest in 'scientific' research with the importation to social work and social care from medical research of narrowly interpreted 'evidence based' research, which prioritizes random control trials and other traditional quantitative research techniques (for example, MacDonald, 1999).

Feminist researchers have, for more than two decades, argued that the independence and objectivity of conventional social research is illusory, for example, failing adequately to represent the experiences of women (Stanley and Wise, 1993). In her discussion of *standpoint theory* Sandra Harding highlights the socially situated nature of (all) knowledge claims and the implications this has for generating critical questions about received belief (Harding, 1993, pp. 54–55). Standpoint theory would hold that service users who are on the receiving end of social work theory and practice which directly relates to them are likely to be better placed to generate critical questions and knowledge claims about them than outside academics or practitioners.

3 Political

Social work theory-building that includes service users and their organizations is increasingly likely to be seen as having more credibility and authority than that which does not. It is likely to have more political weight in several senses. The service user movements now arguably carry more clout with politicians and policy makers than professional and academic social work and social care discourses. The disabled people's movement, for example, is now a significant intellectual and political force in policy making. Service users' organizations are unlikely to lend their support to a process of theorizing from which they are excluded or marginalized. Service users' involvement provides the basis for stronger and more effective action following from theorizing. Social policy and social work discussions and campaigns which have not involved their subjects have tended to have limited success. The lesson of recent politics is that popular discussions and campaigns are the ones which seem to make the most impact. We can see expressions of this new participatory politics and analysis in campaigns for disabled people's rights, the environment and against road building and GM food as well as in the black people's, gay men and lesbians' movements. Such broad-based campaigns and their successes stand in contrast with narrowly based welfare and anti-poverty intellectualizing and campaigning.

Ways Forward

As social work makes concerted efforts to take forward its theorizing, it is also faced with the challenge and opportunity of involving service users and their organizations systematically in the process. It is difficult to see how such a process of theorizing can be effective, inclusive or justified otherwise.

The first requirement is for there to be full and equal access to theoretical discussion for service users and organizations. This relates to addressing:

- the support needs of people with physical, intellectual and sensory impairments, people who communicate differently and people experiencing distress;
- the categorization of individuals and groups included in social care categories in terms of 'deserving' and 'undeserving' and conventional reluctance to include the latter;
- the dismissal of service users and their organizations as 'unrepresentative', particularly when their views conflict with the status quo (Beresford and Campbell, 1994).

To set in train an inclusive process of theory development means working towards equality between service users and other actors in discussion and action in three main areas. These are:

1 equality of respect;
2 equality of validity of contributions;
3 equality of ownership and control of the debate and of knowledge.

Equality of Respect

The same respect should be attached to users of services as to other participants, without any imposition of stigma or assumption of their incapacity or inferiority, challenging rather than reinforcing dominant discriminations.

Equality of Validity of Contributions

Contributions to theory building from people associated with service use must be accorded the same validity as others. Assumptions about objective, neutral and value free social science cannot be sustained. Recognition should be given to the validity of the subjective knowledges, analyses and perspectives of people included in social care categories.

Equality of Ownership and Control of the Debate and of Knowledge

More than a few token users must be included in the process and they should have equal ownership of it. There needs to be a shift in power, in the control of knowledge and what counts as knowledge, with service users having more say in both.

Key requirements for working for inclusive debate include:

- support for people to take part in discussion about social work theory. This includes information, practical support, support for people to increase their confidence and self-esteem, development costs, personal assistance, etc. (Croft and Beresford, 1993, pp. 51–3);
- support for equal opportunities, to ensure that everyone can take part on equal terms regardless of age, 'race', gender, sexuality, disability, distress or class;
- open debate which includes service users on equal terms.

The involvement of service users in social work theorizing needs to be seen as an opportunity for, not an obligation imposed upon them. Some service users and their organizations may not be interested in being involved and not see it as worthwhile or productive. Others are likely to be suspicious, expecting from previous experience that attempts will be made either to co-opt or ignore them. Service users and their organizations have limited resources and other priorities, not least maintaining and taking forward their own discussions and objectives.

This highlights the importance not only of supporting the involvement of service users in social work's own process of theory building, but also supporting service users' own debates about social work theory. In this way individuals and organizations who wish to can be helped to get together, explore and develop their own ideas, agendas and discussion on their own, in safety and confidence, prior to, as well as in addition to taking part in social work's own discussions. This will help make it possible to relate their own theoretical discussions to those of social work. It will also further limit the risk of service users being incorporated in professionally initiated, directed and dominated theory development.

Accepted: March 2000

References

Abberley, P. (1998) 'The spectre at the feast: Disabled people and social theory', in Shakespeare, T. (ed.), *The Disability Reader: Social Science Perspectives*, London, Cassell, pp. 79–93.

Barnes, C. (1998) 'The social model of disability: A sociological phenomenon ignored by sociologists?', in Shakespeare, T. (ed.), *The Disability Reader: Social Science Perspectives*, London, Cassell, pp. 65–78.

Barnes, C and Mercer, G. (eds.) (1997) *Doing Disability Research*, Leeds, The Disability Press.

Barnes, C., Mercer, G., Shakespeare, T. (1999) *Exploring Disability: A Sociological Introduction*, Cambridge, Polity Press.

Bar On, B. A. (1993) 'Marginality and epistemic privilege', in Alcoff, L. and Potter, E. (eds.), *Feminist Epistemologies*, London, Routledge.

Beresford, P. (1997) 'The last social division?: Revisiting the relationship between social policy, its producers and consumers', in May, M., Brunsdon, E., Craig, G., (eds.), *Social Policy Review 9*, London, Social Policy Association, pp. 203–26.

Beresford, P. (1999) 'Making participation possible: Movements of disabled people and psychiatric survivors', in Jordan, T. and Lent, A., *Storming The Millennium*, Lawrence and Wishart, London, pp. 35–50.

Beresford, P and Campbell, J. (1994) 'Disabled people, service users, user involvement and representation', *Disability and Society* **9**(3), pp. 315–25.

Beresford, P. and Croft, S. (1993) *Citizen Involvement: A Practical Guide for Change*, Basingstoke, Macmillan.

Beresford, P. and Evans, C. (1999) 'Research and empowerment', *British Journal of Social Work* **29**, pp. 671–7.

Beresford, P. and Turner, M. (1997) *It's Our Welfare, Report of the Citizens' Commission on the Future of the Welfare State*, London, National Institute for Social Work.

Beresford, P., Stalker, K. and Wilson, A. (1997) *Speaking For Ourselves: A Bibliography*, London, Open Services Project in association with the Social Work Research Centre, University of Stirling.

Campbell, P. (1996) 'The history of the user movement in the United Kingdom', in Heller, T., Reynolds, J., Gomm, R., Muston, R. and Pattison, S. (eds.), *Mental Health Matters*, Basingstoke, Macmillan.

Campbell, J. and Oliver, M. (1996) *Disability Politics: Understanding our Past, Changing Our Future*, Basingstoke, Macmillan.

Coulshed, V. and Orme, J. (1998) *Social Work Practice: An Introduction*, 3rd edn, Basingstoke, Macmillan.

Croft, S. and Beresford, P. (1993) *Getting Involved: A Practical Manual for Change*, London, Open Services Project/Joseph Rowntree Foundation.

Croft, S. and Beresford, P. (1996) 'The politics of participation', in Taylor, D. (ed.), *Critical Social Policy: A Reader*, London, Sage, pp. 175–98.

Croft, S. and Beresford, P. (1998) 'Postmodernity and the future of welfare: Whose critiques, whose social policy?' in Carter, J. (ed.), *Postmodernity and the Fragmentation of Welfare*, London, Routledge, pp. 103–20.

Davies, M. (ed.) (1997) *The Blackwell Companion to Social Work*, Oxford, Blackwell.

Evans C and Fisher M, (1999) 'Collaborative evaluation with service users: Moving towards user controlled research', in Shaw, I. and Lishman, J. (eds.), *Evaluation and Social Work Practice*, London, Sage.

Giddens, A. (1998) *The Third Way: The Renewal of Social Democracy*, Cambridge, Polity Press.

Harding, S. (1993) 'Rethinking standpoint epistemology: What is "strong objectivity?"', in Alcoff, L. and Potter, E. (eds.), *Feminist Epistemologies*, London, Routledge.

Jones, C. (1996) 'Anti-intellectualism and the peculiarities of British social work education', in Parton, N. (ed.), *Social Theory, Social Change and Social Work*, London, Routledge.

MacDonald, G. (1999) 'Evidence-based social care: Wheels off the runway?', *Public Money & Management*, January–March, pp. 25–32.

Mayer, J. E. and Timms, N. (1970) *The Client Speaks: Working Class Impressions of Casework*, London, Routledge and Kegan Paul.

Morris, J. (1993) *Independent Lives: Community Care and Disabled People*, Basingstoke, Macmillan.

Oliver, M. (1996) *Understanding Disability: From Theory to Practice*, Basingstoke, Macmillan.

Oliver, M. and Barnes, C. (1998) *Disabled People and Society: From Exclusion to Inclusion*, London, Longman.

Payne, M. (1997) *Modern Social Work Theory*, 2nd edn, Basingstoke, Macmillan.

Peile, C. and McCouat, M. (1997) 'The rise of relativism: The future of theory and knowledge development in social work', *British Journal of Social Work* **27**, pp. 343–60.

Pembroke, L. R. (ed.) (1994*a*) *Eating Distress: Perspectives From Personal Experience*, London, Survivors Speak Out.

Pembroke, L. R. (ed.) (1994*b*) *Self Harm: Perspectives from Personal Experience*, London, Survivors Speak Out.

Priestley, M. (1999) *Disability Politics and Community Care*, London, Jessica Kingsley Publishers.

Read, J. and Reynolds, J. (eds.) (1996) *Speaking Our Minds: An Anthology*, Basingstoke, Macmillan.

Shakespeare, T. (ed.) (1999) *The Disability Reader: Social Science Perspectives*, London, Cassell.

Sheppard, M. (1998) 'Practice Validity, Reflexivity And Knowledge For Social Work', *British Journal of Social Work* **28**, pp. 763–81.

Stanley, L. and Wise, S. (1993) *Breaking Out Again: Feminist Ontology and Epistemology*, London, Routledge.

White, S. (1997) 'Beyond retroduction?: Hermeneutics, reflexivity and social work practice', *British Journal of Social Work* **27**, pp. 739–53.

Wiltshire and Swindon Users Network (1996) *I Am In Control*, Devizes, Wiltshire and Swindon Users Network.

Social Work 4D06 A

378162

Custom Publishing

Everything in one book.

The Campus Store and Media Production Services are proud partners in the production of this custom publication. All material is printed with copyright permission.

This custom publication is non-returnable